YEARS OF EXPANSION
BRITAIN 1815-1914

Edited by Michael Scott-Baumann

Clive Beh ... Byrne, Davi ... er

Hodder & Stoughton

A MEMBER OF THE HODDER HEADLINE GROUP

ACKNOWLEDGEMENTS

The authors would like to thank Dr Boyd Hilton, Dr J P Parry and Professor Paul Smith for having read, and advised on, parts of this book. We are also grateful to Professor Francis Fish for compiling the index and to David Lea and Clare Weaver for their editorial support.

The publishers would like to thank the following for permission to reproduce copyright illustrations in this volume:

The House of Commons 1833, Sir George Hayter, By Courtesy of the National Portrait Gallery, London-cover; The British Library p81, p461; Punch Publications p107; By permission of the Warden and Fellows of Keble College, Oxford p215; Tate Gallery p216, p218, p219, p220 (both); Delaware Art Museum, Samuel and Mary R. Bancroft Memorial p217; Ford Madox Brown, *Work*, © Manchester City Art Galleries p221; National Trust Photographic Library p222; Merthyr Tydfil Borough Council p451.

The publishers would also like to thank the following for permission to reproduce copyright material for this volume:

Cambridge University Press for the table from BR Mitchell & P Deane, *An Abstract of British Historical Statistics* (1962.

Every effort has been made to trace and acknowledge ownership of copyright. The publishers will be glad to make suitable arrangements with any copyright holders whom it has not been possible to contact.

British Library Cataloguing in Publication Data

Scott-Baumann, Michael
Years of Expansion:Britain, 1815–1914
I. Title
941.081

ISBN 0 340 55510–6

First published 1995
Impression number 10 9 8 7 6 5 4
Year 1999 1998 1997

Typeset by Wearset, Boldon, Tyne and Wear
Printed in Great Britain for Hodder & Stoughton Educational, a division of Hodder Headline Plc, 338 Euston Road, London NW1 3BH by Redwood Books, Trowbridge, Wiltshire.

CONTENTS

List of Illustrations

List of Maps

PREFACE: HOW TO USE THIS BOOK

1 A NEW TEXTBOOK

AN INCREASING number of A Level students are embarking on the study of nineteenth-century British history. Topic books abound but there are few, if any, appropriate textbooks. This book meets that need. At its core is the explanatory narrative, informed by recent historical scholarship and made accessible by experienced A Level practitioners. But it is more than a textbook: it is also a workbook, with a rich variety of exercises, piloted with Sixth Formers, which are intended both for class use and for self study.

The book contains guidance on essay-writing and the study of sources, both primary and secondary. It has cartoons and colour plates of contemporary paintings, with questions accompanying them, as well as numerous documentary extracts. It invites the student to engage in individual research tasks and to participate in problem-solving exercises which develop essential historical skills.

The historical scope of the book is outlined in the first section of chapter 1.

2 DOCUMENTS

Throughout the book, short documentary extracts are incorporated into the body of the text. They form an important part of the narrative especially where they, or the student's answers to the questions that follow, provide some of the facts or interpretations essential to an understanding of a central issue.

3 BIBLIOGRAPHIES

At the end of every chapter are suggestions for further reading. The books chosen are those which are thought to be most accessible to Sixth

Formers and likely to be available in libraries. Brief comments are also made on the scope of the books listed and on how each might be used. The bibliography at the end of chapter 1 suggests books which cover all or a large part of the century.

4 Discussion points and essay questions

The *discussion points* are aimed to test understanding of the main issues outlined in the chapter. They can be used to stimulate class debate and also to guide note-making. The *essay questions* are similar to those which have appeared in the English (and Welsh) Board A Level papers in recent years.

5 Exercises

Each chapter, apart from the introductory one, contains one or more exercises. The *essay-writing exercises* introduce you to the different types of A Level question and suggest how to address them. They provide guidance on how to plan and build up an answer and they invite you to exercise your essay-writing skills in answering a wide variety of questions.

The *documentary exercises* require you to analyse and compare different sources and thus to engage in historical debate on one or more of the chapter's central themes. These exercises often present you with contrasting historical interpretations so that the reader is confronted with the challenges and problems of the practising historian.

There are also exercises in role-playing, mostly based on primary sources, in the analysis of election results and other statistics, and there are suggestions for pursuing particular lines of historical enquiry.

6 Time lines

At the end of the book (*page 492*) is a table indicating the names of the key figures in government. This is preceded by four double-page time lines (*pages 484–91*) which highlight the main events and developments referred to in the text.

I

INTRODUCTION

1 A CENTURY OF EXPANSION

TODAY we all live in a rapidly changing society. Whereas 30 years ago there were no computers in our classrooms, today we take them for granted. In another 20 years every pupil will no doubt have his or her own note-book computer at school. We all expect change; it is commonplace. However, in 1815, most of Britain looked very much as it had done for hundreds of years previously. There were extensive areas of mountain and forest, while much of the rest was divided into fields enclosed by hedges, fences and ditches in what was the most cultivated land in Europe. Most people lived in small villages and worked on the land. Agriculture was by far the biggest source of employment. The country was sparsely populated: there were only 13 million people (a mere half million of them in Wales and one and a half million in Scotland) and only three cities had populations of more than 100 000.

Most people lived in simple stone cottages but in Leicestershire, the writer William Cobbett found

> miserable sheds . . . hovels made of mud and straw; bits of glass, or of old off-cast windows, without frame or hinge frequently, but merely stuck in the mud wall.

Few roads were anything more than dirt tracks. In fact, few people ever travelled far from where they were born. Few went to school and only a minority had the vote.

By 1914, when the First World War broke out, all this had changed. The population had more than trebled and Britain had become a highly industrialised nation. In fact, even by 1850, Britain was already producing and exporting more iron than all other countries put together.

The years from 1815 to 1914 were to be a century of dramatic change and unparalleled expansion. Not only was the population to rise from 13 million to 42 million (including 2½ million in Wales and 4½ million in Scotland) but Gross National Product (GNP), which is the value of wealth created annually, was to rise from £203 million to over £2000 million. New cities sprouted up and, by 1914, there were over 40 towns or cities with populations of more than 100 000.

Whereas in 1815, most Britons earned their living by working on farms, by 1914 most worked in factories and workshops and lived in the towns and cities. These were now linked by a railway network which had reduced the travelling time from Edinburgh to London to less than eight hours. (In 1815, it had taken several days by stage-coach.) A huge industrial working class had developed. This workforce was largely literate: by 1914, all children were sent to school and most men (although no women) became voters at 21. Politics had been transformed from the pastime of the landowners to something recognisably similar to the business it is today. Furthermore, there had been a huge increase in the role of government. (For instance, education and public health, in which the state had played no part in 1815, were major governmental responsibilities by 1914.) The three main political parties of today had emerged by 1914 – the Conservatives, the Liberals and the Labour Party. MPs from middle-class backgrounds outnumbered those from the aristocracy and the first working-class man had entered Parliament.

This process of change and expansion did not take place without strain and stress. The rise in population led to the growth of a society that threatened to burst apart at the seams. Trying to prevent this happening occupied the energies of nearly every government in the nineteenth century; time and again crises were overcome by stitching together political alliances and by hurrying through social and political reforms. In this way the fabric of society was kept intact.

It is the purpose of this book to identify and analyse all these and many other developments. For instance, parliamentary reform which was carried out in 1832, 1867 and 1884, is examined in chapters II and XI, while Government measures of social, economic and administrative reform are discussed in chapter III. Although British policy toward Ireland is dealt with in several chapters (for example, in chapters V, VIII and IX), mainly because of its dramatic effect on party politics, the place of Ireland in nineteenth-century Britain is examined from an Irish perspective in chapter X. This chapter also contains a final section which concludes with the partition of Ireland and the creation of the Province of Northern Ireland in 1921. The development of modern party politics and of the increasing role of government is traced in several chapters, while an analysis of why and how successive British governments strove to maintain and extend British influence in Europe, in the Eastern Mediterranean and Africa, and in India and the Far East, is to be found in chapters VI and XII.

The final chapter in the book examines developments in Britain in the years leading up to the First World War. They illustrate just how near Britain was to tearing itself apart in those years, as it had been in 1815, and how much the role of government had increased, with education and insurance against unemployment, sickness and old age now added to the traditional governmental responsibilities of defence and the maintenance of law and order.

A novel feature of this book is the chapter on 'Victorian Values' which, coming in the middle of the book, provides a link between the Britain of the 1830s and 1840s – with its crises over Reform of Parliament and Chartism – and the Britain of the later part of the century. It explores the sometimes contradictory attitudes and values, fears and hopes of mid-Victorian society and, above all, of the growing middle class. These values are shown in their paintings (some of which are reproduced between pages 215 and 222) and their writings, in their attitudes toward women and the working class, toward prostitution and pubs. The chapter also analyses the development of popular culture and the 'new model' unions as a way of understanding the values of the mid-century period.

2 THE INDUSTRIAL REVOLUTION

First, it is necessary to look more closely at what Britain was actually like in 1815. The preceding paragraphs might lead you to believe that economy and society were more or less static in 1815 and that change was to come only *after* that date. In reality, Britain in 1815 was already undergoing major structural changes. Compared to today's changes, they may seem less dramatic. Certainly they were taking place more gradually but they were, nevertheless, of fundamental importance because they were transforming the very way people lived and worked. Central to these revolutionary changes were new developments in technology. For instance, instead of relying solely on muscle power, more and more workshops, factories, mills and mines were using water power, or even steam power. There were still, it is true, far more handloom weavers producing woollen and cotton cloth than there were factory workers. Similarly, there was a continuing expansion in the number of small workshops producing manufactured goods in cities like Birmingham and London (the capital was by far the biggest and fastest expanding city in Britain).

However, the most advanced factories and mills were now being built on the coal fields so that they could employ steam-driven machinery to produce cloth, to pump water out of coal mines and to provide the blast for iron-producing furnaces. William Cobbett, who travelled thousands of miles round Britain on horseback, wrote:

> All the way along from Leeds to Sheffield it is coal and iron, and iron and coal. It was dark before we reached Sheffield; so

> that we saw the iron furnaces in all the horrible splendour of their everlasting blaze. Nothing can be conceived more grand or more terrific than the yellow waves of fire that incessantly issue from the top of these furnaces . . .

The installation of large, heavy and expensive machinery led to the growth of factories employing not just ten or twenty, but hundreds of workers. Housing for these workers was built alongside the factories so that large new towns grew up. These were densely populated and polluted, with foul-smelling air and blackened buildings. In the 1830s, Sheffield was described as 'poisoned in its own excrement'.

The development of factories and towns on the coal fields of the North of England, the Midlands, South Wales and the Scottish Lowlands were, in 1815, comparatively recent developments. They were made possible only by the availability of cheap labour. The latter was itself made possible only by the sustained rise in population which had been taking place since the mid-eighteenth century and by the improvements in agriculture which enabled more and more urban workers to rely on a regular supply of cheap, plentiful food. Such demographic changes (the rise in population and the growth of a specifically urban populace), the increased productivity of agriculture, the technological developments in the coal, iron and textile industries and the improved transport provided by the canals, together constituted what historians have since come to call the Industrial Revolution.

3 THE POLITICAL STRUCTURE

Although, in 1815, Britons continued to live and work in the same way as they had for generations, the country was, as we have seen, undergoing sweeping economic and social changes. Yet the political structure, built up in the eighteenth century by and for landowners, remained largely unchanged.

At the very top of this structure was the Crown. In 1815, George III was on the throne. He had been king since 1760 but he was increasingly ill; amongst other symptoms, he had been found talking to trees at Windsor and, in 1811, he had been declared unfit to govern. His eldest son, George, became Prince Regent (and later king, in 1820, when his father died). The Prince Regent, for his part, was too lazy or incompetent to take anything more than a superficial interest in government and politics so that the government of the country continued to be left more and more to the king's ministers. Furthermore, the number of posts and pensions which the king could offer to members of Parliament and their families, and thus influence the way they voted, had been reduced in recent years in order to save money.

The king could still appoint and dismiss a Prime Minister and he could also insist on having a say in the appointment of other ministers. However, the monarch had to take account of the wishes of Parliament if he was to influence their policies and get them to agree to the taxes without which his government could not operate. Thus, if a parliamentary leader had a large body of support in the House of Commons, the king was usually obliged to make him Prime Minister. That person, in 1815, was Lord Liverpool. He had already been Prime Minister for three years, and the Prince Regent relied very heavily on Liverpool and his Cabinet ministers to control Parliament and govern the land.

The main responsibilities of the State, or central government, were defence, the control of trade (especially through customs and excise duties) and the supervision of law and order. (The government was not, for instance, expected to provide schools and hospitals as it is today.) It was *local* government which most affected people in the early nineteenth century. Here, as at Westminister, it was the landowning classes who predominated, for Britain was largely governed by a few thousand landowning families who, between them, owned more than half the agricultural land (and this was at a time when land was still the greatest source of wealth and most people were still employed on the land). Generation after generation inherited the land and, with it, the wide-ranging power and influence which they had wielded for hundreds of years.

The landowning aristocracy assumed their right to supremacy to be natural. Their status was hereditary (the right to a seat in the House of Lords, for example, was passed on from generation to generation) and their central power base was the House of Lords. The House of Commons was largely filled with their dependants; nearly half of the 658 MPs owed their seats to peers and, of those, many were related to the aristocracy. The landed classes held the highest positions in the Church, the armed services, the judiciary and the civil service. They also ruled the countryside and it is at the administration of the localities that we must now look in more detail.

At the top of local society was the Lord-Lieutenant of the county who was usually the biggest landowner. He was the king's representative in the county and he reported back to the central government in London. Under him were the magistrates or Justices of the Peace (JPs). These were the men who bore the brunt of the governing of Britain. They had the major responsibility for preserving peace and for preventing crime and disorder in an age when there was no professional police force. They were appointed by a Royal Commission (as they are today), usually on the recommendation of the Lord-Lieutenant, and were mostly landowners. About a quarter were clergy of the Church of England. JPs were unpaid and untrained. As men of property (they were often the biggest employers in a locality) they possessed considerable status while their role as JPs brought them added power and influence. They had the authority to arrest, fine and imprison people for minor offences and to recommend trial by a higher court for major offences. They also saw to the upkeep of roads and bridges and were responsible for prisons and the care of the poor. In what was a highly deferential society in which many people would be dependent, as their tenants or hired labourers, on the landowning JPs, great respect was paid to the magistrates. If, however, they proved unable to deal with local disorder, they could call out the yeomanry, a mounted volunteer force which, like the JPs, was unpaid and consisted largely of men of property. In the case of a major disturbance, and there were many in the years after 1815 (*see pages 13–18*), the central government could be asked to send in troops to restore order.

4 Britain in 1815

In 1815, Britain was a society under strain. The most obvious reason for this was the population explosion. (In the decade from 1810 to 1820 the population rose faster than in any decade before or since.) The twin processes of industrialisation and urbanisation also contributed. For instance, many handloom weavers and other skilled craftsmen feared that they would be thrown out of work by the increasing use of machines in the new factories. Coming on top of these developments, and making the strain even greater, was post-war depression.

With the defeat of the French under Napoleon at the Battle of Waterloo in 1815, Britain emerged from the longest war (1793–1815) in which she had been engaged since the fifteenth century. She was now established as the greatest of the Great Powers. She had the largest navy, the biggest share of the world's trade and the most developed industry, while London was the biggest city and the financial capital of the world. However, the war was also the costliest in Britain's history and the country emerged with a vastly increased National Debt of £861 million and an unprecedentedly high tax burden, much of which fell on those sections of society which were least able to pay. Furthermore, the boosts which government contracts had given to the textile industry (for uniforms) and the iron and armaments industries (for weapons) during the war were suddenly withdrawn and this led to increased unemployment. The demobilisation of hundreds of thousands of soldiers and sailors with no pension or any other kind of government support increased the extent of the hardship. If there was a bad harvest and bread prices rose (and the average price of wheat was higher at this time than at any other time in the nineteenth century), millions faced the prospect of great hunger, if not starvation.

'Distress', as contemporaries called it, was undoubtedly related to the growth of working-class unrest in the period after 1815 but, as chapters II and IV show, this was a complex relationship. The government, however, reacted to such unrest and, in particular, to demands from the working classes for a voice in Parliament, with great alarm and fear. They remembered from their youth hearing about the overthrow of the monarchy and of the ruling classes in the French Revolution. This period of popular agitation, and the government's response to it, is the subject of the next chapter.

5 Bibliography

While this book is aimed specifically at A Level and Higher Grade students, there are a number of textbooks written primarily for university students. Most cover only a part of the period 1815–1914. For the 50 years up to 1865, the following are worth consulting by the student who wishes to read further: – E J Evans *The Forging of the Modern State 1783–1870* (Longman, 1983); A Briggs *The Age of Improvement 1787–1867* (Longman, 1959) is a little dated but marvellously perceptive; N Gash *Aristocracy and People, Britain 1815–1865* (Edward Arnold, 1979) is demanding, but expert and sophisticated.

For the period 1865 to 1914, E J Feuchtwanger *Democracy and Empire, Britain 1865–1914* (Edward Arnold, 1985) and R Shannon *The Crisis of Imperialism 1865–1915* (Paladin, 1976) are both valuable. M Bentley *Politics Without Democracy 1815–1914* (Fontana, 1984) examines the 'high politics' of the whole period and has some brilliant insights, while N McCord *British History 1815–1906* (Oxford University Press, 1991) also covers nearly all of the period.

For an economic and social perspective, F M L Thompson *The Rise of Respectable Society – A Social History of Victorian Britain 1830–1900* (Fontana, 1988) and J F C Harrison *Late Victorian Britain 1875–1901* (Fontana, 1990) are good, wide-ranging, general surveys.

II

THE GOVERNMENT AND THE PEOPLE. POPULAR PROTEST AND GOVERNMENT RESPONSE 1815–32

1 INTRODUCTION: FROM THE 'LABOURING POOR' TO THE 'WORKING CLASS'?

THE period 1815 to 1832 saw the appearance of a series of mass-based political protest movements. These were supported by an active press and drew together a large number of adherents through a rich variety of political organisations. Undoubtedly, the most spectacular expressions of this growing radicalism were the many mass meetings held throughout this period, often consisting of tens of thousands of people, at which Parliament was called upon to reform itself into a more democratic body. Within a few years of the end of the Napoleonic Wars a loosely defined political programme had begun to emerge, which successive movements made their own. Among the many changes in the political system that were called for were, that all men over the age of 21 should have the vote (universal manhood suffrage), that there should be a shorter time between parliaments (to increase the number of elections) and that voting should become a private matter by means of the secret ballot (to ensure that working people could vote without interference from their employers or landlords). Added together these measures represented a very different version of the way the relationship between the government and the people should operate from that which existed at the time. This public debate about how the country should be run, would continue throughout the nineteenth century, and it will be traced in subsequent chapters via the Chartist movement (chapter IV), the creation of a mass electorate (chapter XI) and the emergence of the Labour Party (chapter XIII). In the years from 1815 to 1832 we can see both the origins of popular radicalism and its apparent success in 1832, when what is often known as, the 'Great Reform Act' was passed. This significantly changed the structure of the electorate but the alleged 'greatness' of the measure escaped the thousands of working people who had campaigned for reform in these years. For them, the Reform Act of 1832 was a huge disappointment and a spur to further reform activity.

It is the involvement of large numbers of working people in these developments that is the main source of discussion and speculation among historians. Some historians share the view of many contemporaries that mass participation in radical politics was largely the result of hunger, initially induced by the end of the wars and subsequently exacerbated by the fluctuations of an immature industrial economy. This notion of 'hunger politics' is, however, contested by others who point to a fundamental shift in outlook on the part of the working community in these years and relate this to the wider changes associated with the Industrial Revolution. In particular, Edward Thompson in his book *The Making of the English Working Class* (1963), has argued that the period from 1780–1832 saw the conversion of the highly fragmented 'labouring poor' into a far more coherent and unified 'working-class'. Within this hypothesis the role of the post-war period was central to the creation of a new kind of social formation; a class with a common experience of economic change and a shared position on radical politics.

In this chapter we will explore the radical movements of these years and the response to them of the governments of the day. In particular we will concentrate on two significant sub-periods, 1815–20 and 1830–32, when the call for political change was intense and the social order appeared to contemporaries to be threatened. In the process of exploring the experience of these years, the wider issues of historical interpretation raised by the growing participation of working people in politics will provide a central focus for our analysis. But first we must turn to the structure of politics at the start of the period and the arguments that were marshalled at the time both for and against the unreformed system.

2 'OLD CORRUPTION': THE UNREFORMED PARLIAMENTARY SYSTEM

British government revolved around the monarch, the House of Lords, and the House of Commons. The House of Commons controlled finances, although the monarch and the Lords possessed the right to reject (veto) legislation introduced by the Lower House. As the centrepiece of the system, the Commons drew its authority from its elected status. British government, therefore was focused on a body, the

Commons, which saw itself as representative of the nation as a whole. Yet just how representative of the people of the United Kingdom was the House of Commons before 1832?

After 1800 and the Act of Union, which abolished the Irish Parliament and transferred the Irish representation to Westminster, there were 658 Members of Parliament sitting in the Commons. The English MPs made up well over three-quarters of this number. Four of these members represented the universities of Oxford and Cambridge. The rest of the English members came from two types of constituencies, the counties and the Parliamentary boroughs. The size of the electorate in each of these constituencies varied greatly as did the nature of the voting qualification (franchise). In the English counties, responsible for electing a total of 82 MPs, the vote was held by individuals owning freehold land to the value of 40 shillings (£2). This franchise dated from 1430 and the changing value of money from that time meant that most county electorates were large. They varied from Rutland with 800 voters to Yorkshire with a massive 23 000 electors.

The Parliamentary boroughs were mostly towns which had been granted the right to elect MPs at some time, often in the distant past. These were numerically the most significant of all constituencies since they accounted for 403 of the total MPs in the House of Commons. In the boroughs the franchise varied widely and was often of antique origin. For example, in the 'scot and lot' boroughs the franchise was held by any man who paid the poor rates. Here the electorate was often numerous; for example the borough of Westminster had 10 000 voters. Yet 24 of these boroughs had less than 600 voters, the most extreme case being Gatton in Surrey. This consisted of only six houses, the owner of which was free to nominate two MPs. In the burgage boroughs the vote was held by virtue of ownership of particular pieces of land and none of the 35 constituencies in this category possessed more than 300 electors. In fact, Old Sarum in Wiltshire possessed no voters at all. In this case, whoever owned the piece of land, which the radical journalist William Cobbett referred to as the 'Accursed Hill', also nominated two MPs. In Dunwich, a freeman borough in Suffolk, few of the 30 men, qualified to vote by virtue of their status as freemen of the borough, actually lived in the constituency. One could hardly blame them, most of Dunwich having long since disappeared under the North Sea as a result of coastal erosion.

The problem of Parliamentary representation might be summarised as follows. Most MPs in the House of Commons were elected by the English boroughs. Over half of these boroughs had less than 600 electors and the majority were located in the south of the country. Although in the early nineteenth century most of the population still lived in this area, it became increasingly clear that the existing representation reflected the economic structure of an earlier age. The large towns of the Midlands and North, which grew from the mid-eighteenth century as a result of industrialisation, were often unrepresented except by their county members. Put alongside the lack of MPs representing towns such as Manchester, Birmingham and Leeds, the smallness of most borough electorates was increasingly difficult to justify.

There was also widespread concern at the apparent corruption of the electoral procedure and this was most marked in the constituencies with small electorates. In the absence of a secret ballot, voters were, it was argued, open to bribery and intimidation. Tenants might vote for their landlord's choice of candidate to curry favour or to escape eviction. Others simply sold their vote to the highest bidder. Seats were also marketable commodities and were bought and sold openly. In boroughs with small electorates the process of controlling elections was easiest and these were termed 'pocket boroughs', 'nomination boroughs' or 'rotten boroughs'. In 1827 one authority estimated that 276 seats were held by direct nomination and many more were the subject of influence. Ownership of a borough was highly prized. It affirmed social status, and possibly material rewards in the form of government positions, sinecures or pensions, for the owner and his dependents. Involvement in politics was expensive and, it was felt, becoming more so as time went on. The 'rotten borough' of Gatton, for example, changed hands for the last time in 1830 for £180 000.

The point has often been made by historians that voters in the unreformed system seem to have had a very different attitude to politics from that which operates in a modern democratic system. The unreformed system was not, it has often been argued, a system of active voters, voting for the person and party which they felt would best govern the country. Rather this was an electorate that could be manipulated, cajoled and purchased. But this common interpretation of the pre-reform electorate has been robustly challenged by Frank O'Gorman in a detailed study of the electoral history of the period 1734 to 1832, *Voters, Patrons and Parties* (1989). The unreformed system has, he argues, been misunderstood by modern historians applying their contemporary perspectives. In charting the growth of a mass electorate in the nineteenth and twentieth centuries, historians demonised, to the point of distortion, the unreformed system by which it had been preceded.

O'Gorman draws our attention to the high level of activity that surrounded elections in the eighteenth and early nineteenth centuries. Although set in a national context, general elections were an expression of the nature of local authority. Through them, local elites attempted to maintain their position within the community, by securing the election of the members of their choice. Nevertheless, in order to do this they had to secure the support of local interests, as represented by the electorate. O'Gorman puts it bluntly, 'The attitudes and behaviour of the voters themselves do not permit us to conclude that they were mindless fodder for venal agents.' Elections also often involved the active participation of non-electors, who expressed their views through public meetings and rituals. Far from being the token gestures or excuses for exessive indulgence as they are often portrayed, elections were a serious business in the unreformed system. Whilst voters were open to persuasion, elections were not closed affairs whose outcomes were foregone conclusions. Rather voters saw themselves as exercising a high degree of independent choice. From this point of view, the electoral system may be seen to have contributed significantly to the acknowledged stability of Hanoverian Britain.

O'Gorman's work is helpful in a number of ways. Above all, it reminds us that in order to judge the unreformed system we have to appreciate the way it worked at the time. Clearly, by 1832 many voices were being raised against the old system. The structure of the nation's wealthy elite was changing and the effective exclusion of many industrial areas cast serious doubt on the ability of the system to represent the new middle class. It was also becoming clear that working people in these areas wanted a formal voice in politics. Nevertheless, O'Gorman's work helps us to understand the difficulties of changing a system that had always fulfilled an important role in establishing and maintaining the *status quo*.

Certainly, for many at the time the best argument in favour of the existing system was that it appeared to have worked well for generations. In 1790, the respected Whig statesman, Edmund Burke, expressed his opposition to the democratic forces associated with the recent developments in France. His *Reflections on the Revolution in France,* was effectively a defence of the *ancien regime* in a British context. For him Parliament was a representative body: a point that he made as follows;

> We know that the British House of Commons, without shutting its doors to any merit in any class, is by the sure operation of adequate causes, filled with everything illustrious in rank, in descent, in hereditary and in aquired opulence, in cultivated talents, in military, civil, naval, and politic distinction that the country can afford.

Contemporaries like Burke argued that the system had withstood the test of time, and that it worked, performing an important stabilising function at both a national and a local level. Government, it was argued, should represent, not numbers of population, as we should expect, but rather the significant *interests* in the nation, such as Land, the City of London, the Universities, the corporate towns, and the Church. If these interest groups were represented at Westminster then, the argument ran, the nation was represented. For most people, of course, this would give only a *virtual representation* of their interests rather than a direct representation. Most importantly, the rich would represent the poor. Very few among the wealthy disputed this definition of representative government. However, after 1815, it was being increasingly recognised that industrialisation had created a *new* interest group in the form of the industrial middle class. Without quite a sizeable reform of the system this interest group would remain effectively excluded from the political system. It is important to note that when reform did come, in 1832, it was designed to rectify this problem and not to remodel the system on fundamentally different principles.

3 The Growth of Popular Radicalism 1790–1820

The period from 1815 to 1820 also saw the origins and growth of popular radicalism, which drew its support from the working community. This was based on a very different analysis of politics. Far from arguing that the existing system needed only to be extended to include the interests of the new industrial elite in the large towns, this critique recommended far reaching change. This was because it made radically different assumptions about the nature of representative government. The arguments were perhaps most effectively made by Thomas Paine in his book *The Rights of Man* (1791). This was published to counter Burke's earlier defence of the system. Drawing on personal experience of both the American and French Revolutions, Paine argued that the corruption of the British Parliamentary system lay in its failure to represent 'the people' in any direct sense. He claimed that, while most of the country was crippled by high levels of taxation, the small minority who controlled politics lived off the proceeds of taxation. This state of affairs was perpetuated by the restriction of the right to vote to a small section of the population. The vote, he argued, was a 'natural right', to which every man was entitled and which had been taken away at some point in the past. If this right was restored it would lead to the regaining of other important freedoms. Among these were the freedoms of expression, assembly, conscience and equality before the law. Paine argued his case in terms of men only. It fell to another writer in the same tradition, Mary Wollstonecraft, to point out in her book *A Vindication of the Rights of Woman* (1792), that if there really were 'natural rights' then women were also entitled to exercise them.

Paine's book was said to have sold 200 000 copies by 1793. The government, recognising its subversive nature (particularly in the light of revolutionary events in France), declared it to be illegal. This act of censorship only served to substantiate Paine's points about the loss of fundamental freedoms, and this increased the book's popularity. At the heart of Paine's argument was the notion that ordinary people were entitled to participate in national politics.

During the war with France the governments of the day succeeded in restricting the radical supporters of Paine's views to small, isolated, groups in centres like Manchester, London, Norwich, Sheffield and Birmingham. This changed with the end of the war in 1815. British industry had grown during the wars. An economic system well placed for expansion now found itself with an increased demand for its primary industries; textiles, metalware, shipbuilding, and mining. Capital investment increased and employers re-organised their enterprises to increase productivity. This often meant the introduction of machinery, or the dilution of skilled workers with less skilled, perhaps child, workers. This re-organisation to meet increased demand caused resentment among the workforce and the Combination Acts were often unable to prevent the development of illegal trade societies. In Lancashire and Yorkshire, in the years 1811–13 working men destroyed the new machines being introduced into the textile industries. In Nottinghamshire, in the same years, stocking weavers who agreed to work for employers at lower than trade society prices were attacked. The self-styled 'Luddites', in these areas, claimed to be following the orders of the mythical leader General Ned Ludd, but their actions were not co-ordinated by any one leader. Rather, these outbreaks reflected a fairly widespread concern that industrialisation was damaging the way of life of well-established working communities. The Luddites were suppressed by military intervention and the declaration, in 1812, that machine smashing was a capital offence. In 1813, 16 Yorkshire Luddites were executed for attacks on factories and the murder of an employer.

The Peace of Vienna, which marked the end of the war with France in 1815, ushered in a period of recession. As government contracts for uniforms and armaments fell off, so the demand for textiles and for coal and iron dropped. As troops were demobilised so the cost of poor relief rose dramatically. The labouring population found itself underemployed. Parliament, consisting largely of landowners, passed the Corn Laws of 1815 prohibiting the importation of foreign corn until home grown corn reached the price of 80 shillings (£4) per quarter. This was intended to ensure that the price of corn remained high, and therefore landowners' profits and rents remained high. It had the effect of raising the cost of a loaf of bread. Increasing numbers of working people found themselves dependent upon parish relief for the basic necessities of life.

The immediate post-war years also saw a growth of Painite political radicalism as the working community increasingly regarded its economic position in political terms. Often the lead was taken by 'gentlemen reformers', members of the upper class who, unlike most of their social equals, accepted the need for a really extensive Parliamentary reform. For example, John Cartwright established the Hampden Club in London in 1812, to agitate for what was called a 'general suffrage'. Cartwright was a landed gentleman from Lincolnshire who, after a period in the Navy, became a major in the Nottinghamshire militia. His political writings from the 1770s onwards, expressed the view that manhood suffrage and other rights had been guaranteed under a Saxon constitution and had been lost at the time of the Norman conquest in 1066. The London Hampden Club never attracted the 'respectable' support he had hoped for; most members of his own class still feared a re-enactment of the French Revolution on British soil. Nevertheless, the idea was taken up enthusiastically in the provinces. Over the next few years Hampden clubs were set up by working people in towns and villages in the industrial areas of Lancashire, the Midlands, and Yorkshire. They were open to any man able to pay a penny a week subscription, this money being devoted to the publication of pamphlets and broadsheets supporting a programme which included universal suffrage, annual parliaments and the abolition of the Corn Laws.

In November and December 1816 Henry Hunt held three large public meetings in Spa-Fields, London, calling upon Parliament to introduce universal manhood suffrage and extensive Parliamentary reform. Hunt, the son of a Wiltshire farmer, was the leading radical of his day and a good example of a new breed of radical politician, the platform orator. Hunt, more than any other radical, popularised the large-scale, open-air, public meeting as a strategy for expressing the strength of radical opinion. The intention behind such meetings was to exercise the right to petition Parliament for a redress of grievances. But at the second of the Spa-Fields meetings a part of the crowd rioted. The following January the Prince Regent, whose profligate expenditure made him the object of popular resentment, was mobbed while returning from the opening of Parliament and the window of his coach was smashed. Lord Liverpool's Tory administration, fearful of the development of the Hampden clubs in the provinces, used these two incidents to introduce repressive legislation, which became known as the 'Gagging Acts'. *Habeas Corpus*, under which an arrested person was to be charged within 24 hours or be released, was suspended for four months, thus allowing arrest and imprisonment on suspicion only, and restrictions on public meetings were extended.

This did little to discourage the growth of radical organisation. The parliamentary session of 1817 saw the submission of nearly 700 petitions for reform, from localities throughout the country, as part of a national campaign organised by Sir Francis Burdett. A gentleman reformer, Burdett was a Leicestershire landowner who married into the wealthy Coutts banking family. He was in France from 1790 to 1793 and witnessed the French Revolution at first hand. As MP for Westminster, he led the small group of members who supported the cause of radical reform in Parliament. The 1817 campaign demonstrated the strength of support in the country as a whole. In March 1817 a group of Lancashire weavers set out to march to London to present their petition personally, intending to hold meetings along the way and to draw in numbers for a tumultuous entry to the capital. This was the 'March of the Blanketeers', so called because each man carried only a blanket and provisions for the journey. Fearing the implications of even an unarmed march on London, the government ordered the arrest of the leaders and the marchers were turned back.

As the radical movement gathered strength it built itself around peaceful and constitutional strategies, though there were those among the radicals who advocated the more direct methods of confrontation and revolution. The government's repressive legislation in 1817 drove the movement underground and increased the fear of a violent uprising. In order to counteract this, the Home Office employed an *agent provocateur*, a spy code-named 'Oliver', to travel through the country and to make contact with radical groups. He was to pretend to be planning exactly the rebellion which the government feared and in this way draw local activists into the open. This resulted in the tragedy of the 'Pentridge Uprising'. On the night of 9 June 1817, (the date Oliver had set for his 'uprising') 200–300 armed men set out from the remote weaving village of Pentridge in Derbyshire, intent on taking Nottingham, as agreed with Oliver. In the process a local farmer was killed and the would-be rebels were easily rounded-up. The trial and subsequent execution of the three leaders, including Jeremiah Brandreth who had organised the affair, exposed details of the government's policy of ensnarement and this led to a public outcry. The last words on the scaffold of William Turner, a stonemason and one of the rebels, were 'This is the work of the Government and Oliver'.

Despite the repressive measures of Liverpool's government, the movement for reform grew, particularly in the industrial districts. In August 1819, Hunt called a meeting in St. Peter's Fields, Manchester. Estimates of the numbers involved varied enormously, but somewhere between 50 000–200 000 people from the towns and villages throughout Lancashire marched to the meeting. The arrangements described by the handloom weaver Samuel Bamford for the march from his Lancashire village of Middleton seem to have been typical of the conduct of proceedings.

> First we selected twelve of the most comely and decent looking youths, who we placed in two rows of six each, with each a branch of laurel held presented in his hand as a token of amity and peace,–then followed the men of several districts in fives–then the band of music, an excellent one,–then the colours; a blue one of silk, with inscriptions in golden letters, 'UNITY IS STRENGTH.' 'LIBERTY AND FRATERNITY.' A green one of silk, with golden letters, 'PARLIAMENTS ANNUAL.' 'SUFFRAGE UNIVERSAL.'; and betwixt them on a staff, a handsome cap of crimson velvet... Every hundred men had a leader who was distinguished by a spring of laurel in his hat;

others, similarly distinguished, were appointed over these, and the whole were to obey the directions of a principal conductor, who took his place at the head of the column, with a bugleman to sound his orders.

1 *What does Bamford's account tell us about the radical movement in the area at the time?*
2 *Why were such elaborate arrangements made for the march to the meeting?*
3 *What was the significance of the banners carried by the Middleton party?*

In the event the meeting was broken up by the Manchester Yeomanry, attempting to arrest Hunt, under orders from the magistrates. The Yeomanry was a volunteer cavalry force drawn from the Manchester middle class, mostly businessmen, and shopkeepers. Their inexperience in dealing with large crowds, as well as their resentment at the nature of the meeting, showed as they panicked and began cutting at the crowd with their sabres. In the ensuing melee 11 members of the crowd were killed and over 400 were injured in what swiftly became known as the 'Peterloo Massacre'. The reformers protested that the presence of small children at the meeting testified to its peaceful intent. The Home Secretary, Lord Sidmouth, praised the magistrates for what he called their 'prompt, decisive and efficient measures for the preservation of public tranquility.' As a result the public outcry that followed was directed as much at the government as it was at the Manchester authorities.

There is some speculation among historians as to whether this should be seen as a premeditated attack or simply a piece of policing which got out of hand as a result of the inexperience of local officials. There is no doubt, however, that the telling and re-telling of the story of the 'Peterloo Massacre' did much to popularise the radical cause, providing as it did a clear-cut example that government at local and national level did not represent the interests of the 'people'. In his biography of Henry Hunt, *Orator Hunt* (1985), John Belchem argues that the radicals failed to capitalise on this moment, largely because the leadership were so committed to legal strategies and refused to contemplate the use of force.

His view is that the reformers demonstrated a 'debilitating obsession with legitimacy.' This highlights an important point about the radical tradition as it emerged in these years. In the main, the popular movement for radical reform of Parliament utilised constitutional strategies for achieving its aim: the mass demonstration of public support, the press, the petition to Parliament, and the public defence in open court when accused. These strategies were all inherited by the Chartists and a number of historians would agree with Belchem's point that this provided a fatal weakness for the movement. Alternatively, of course, we should recognise that the British army was strong, battle-tested and loyal. The Chartist leader Feargus O'Connor was later to warn constantly against armed opposition for the simple reason that a citizen army would not succeed against such a trained force.

In the event, it was Liverpool's government that took the initiative by passing what were known as the Six Acts. These suppressed the popular movement by restricting public meetings, tightening the definition of seditious libel (to restrict what radical papers could publish about the government), increasing the tax on newspapers (to hit the working-class readership of radical journals) and extending the right to enter and search private premises. Successful prosecutions of radicals increased dramatically, in both London and the provinces. This broke up the reform organisation, whilst an improvement in trade, in the early 1820s, eroded popular support for the cause. The arrest and execution, in 1820, of Arthur Thistlewood and his three collaborators for their part in the desperate 'Cato Street Conspiracy' which plotted to kill the members of the Cabinet, marks the end of this period of agitation. We may now consider its significance.

4 RE-CONSIDERING THE POPULAR MOVEMENT 1815–20

A *Lessons for the radicals*

In the years that followed this period of agitation, the chief magistrate of Manchester kept, in his study, a Cap of Liberty (a hat worn by the French revolutionaries and adopted by the British radicals) which he had taken at 'Peterloo'. For him, and many others of his class, the reformers' claim to universal manhood suffrage; vote by ballot, annual Parliaments and the disenfranchisement of rotten boroughs, represented a challenge to authority of the sort that had taken place in France.

As far as the reformers were concerned the popular movement had, by 1820, gained a political programme and also a taste of firm opposition from a determined government. It was the vulnerability of the movement to repression that was the great lesson of the 1815–20 period. 'Oliver' and 'Peterloo' made subsequent movements, like Chartism, fear a direct attack by the State. Although the post-war movement had attracted its share of gentleman-reformers, such as Cartwright and Burdett, its strength lay in the support of artisans and other workers in the towns and villages of the industrial districts. The new middle class took little part in the campaign, fearing the implications for law and order, and failing to share the radicals' enthusiasm for votes for the propertyless. The ease with which Liverpool's government contained the campaign also emphasised the fact that a popular movement would always be vulnerable to repression unless it could muster the support of the wealthy. Having learned this lesson the hard way, the radicals endeavoured, during the Reform Bill campaign that followed, to maintain a good working alliance with the middle class supporters of the Bill.

The period also established the *platform* (the public open-air meeting) and the radical newspaper *press* as the twin pillars of radical strategy. These were be central to the way the Chartists made their case in the 1830s and 1840s and both media posed problems for the government. As was shown by Liverpool's repressive legislation in 1817 and 1819, mass meetings could easily be portrayed as a threat to law and order and banned (though as 'Peterloo' demonstrated they were not so easy to disperse once assembled). Similarly, radical journalists could be prosecuted for seditious libel and (as in the Six Acts of 1819) newspapers could be taxed out of the reach of working people. Yet, the reformers' case hinged around the assertion that the corrupt nature of government was demonstrated by its infringment of the rights of the 'free-born Englishman', notably freedom of assembly and freedom of expression. For this reason, the kind of repression engaged in by the Liverpool government could only ever achieve short-term success since it made the reformers' point so well that it was bound to encourage the very movements it sought to destroy.

Public meetings were built around the right to petition Parliament for the redress of wrongs. They also provided an opportunity to demonstrate the extent of popular support for reform and its highly organised nature. The radical press grew in these years despite the Liverpool government's concerted attempts to prosecute the people who wrote and distributed the many newspapers, periodicals and pamphlets which appeared in London and the regions. Through this medium radical ideas were shared, news was conveyed from one region to another and the feeling was fostered that a movement existed rather than a series of local initiatives. Many of the weekly newspapers adopted names to instil fear into the authorities, like *The Black Dwarf, The Republican, The Medusa, The Cap of Liberty*, or *The Gorgon*. Probably, the most important of the radical journalists (a point he never tired of making himself) was William Cobbett. *Cobbett's Political Register* appeared, more or less continuously, from 1802 until his death in 1835. His direct and irreverent style made him a great favourite with working people and in 1817 the poet Southey, after touring the country, warned the Prime Minister that the *Register* was 'read aloud in every alehouse'.

B *Hunger and politics: interpreting popular radicalism*

The extent of working-class involvement in the radical movement from 1815 onwards is a matter of great controversy among historians. Disagreement is focused upon how much to read into their involvement; was this the product of real political commitment or is it explicable in other ways? Certainly, before the last decade of the eighteenth century it is difficult to see any great involvement in radical politics by the labouring poor. The most common form of protest was the food riot, which was a swift and direct way of making feelings known to the authorities. Indeed, as we have seen, where the populace of the towns had expressed a political view before 1815 it was generally directed against those who supported the cause of Parliamentary reform. So, where did the crowds come from to fill St. Peter's Field in August 1819? How did Cobbett manage to find a huge readership for his *Political Register* from such unpromising material?

We may identify two main ways of interpreting the growth of popular radicalism. Since these are used, to a greater or lesser degree, to explain all subsequent popular movements, such as the Reform Bill agitation and Chartism, it may be useful to identify them now. First, there is the view that these movements were primarily responses to the economic situation of the moment. The war was followed by a trade depression and this made working people inclined to accept the arguments of the radical leaders. It is indisputable that this, and all subsequent mass-based movements took place during times of hunger (notably the Reform Bill agitation of 1830–2 and the periods of Chartism's greatest strength 1838–9, 1842 and 1848). The historian, W W Rostow, has demonstrated this by means of a 'social tension chart' by which he is able to correlate closely the development of protest movements and the high price of bread. As we will see when we look at the Chartist movement, (*see pages 108 to 112*) one explanation of the massive support for political reform in the 1830s and 1840s is that it reflects the prevalence of 'breakfastless tables and fireless grates' in working-class homes in these years.

Behind this approach to the popular reform movement lies a particular view of the capabilities of the labouring poor which stresses its lack of formal education and also its regional fragmentation. For a really cohesive popular movement to have existed, the argument goes, it would have had to unite, within a national identity, groups of people whose loyalties and vision went no further than their locality and their trade. The repeated failure of popular radical initiatives to achieve universal manhood suffrage and the other aims that were set, can be seen to reinforce the point that working people did not form a unified block of public opinion that any government felt it had to recognise. As Norman McCord puts it in his book *British History 1815–1906* (Oxford, 1991),

> In a society in which farm labourers and domestic servants provided the largest elements among the workers, in which many workers lived in small, locally oriented communities, in which many workers worked long hours for low wages, and in which communications and the level of literacy were still

> limited, there was not much in the way of promising material for class conflict on a broad scale.

This kind of approach was seriously contested by the Marxist historian Edward Thompson in his book *The Making of the English Working Class* (1963). In this he argues that in the period from 1780–1832 the 'labouring poor' became the 'working class'. At exactly the moment when the economic changes of the Industrial Revolution were having their maximum effect, the political ideas of the French Revolution, through which the experience of economic change might be interpreted, became available. Combined with the repressive actions of the wartime and post-war governments this created a 'common experience' for working people which enabled them to empathise with one another despite the regional or trade variations in their daily lives. The labouring poor had become politicised, that is to say, the radical movements which first emerged in 1815–20 and which culminated in Chartism 20 years later, were a deeply-felt expression of the way the working class now saw the world. Thompson dismisses, as 'the enormous condecension of posterity', the view that working people were incapable of understanding political debate, or that this is signalled in the failure of radical initiatives. To accept Burke's contemporary view of the labouring poor as the 'swinish multitude' is to underestimate seriously the extent to which the communities which made up the 'industrial districts' were based on traditions of mutual support and self-education. The extent of the readership of the radical press, for example, suggests a higher level of literacy within the working community than is sometimes recognised. As the textile manufacturer Richard Cobden put it, 'the operatives living so much together, and generally having families, there is usually one in the family who can write.' The ability to read is likely to have been even more common.

In good times the working class focused attention on trade union protest, since this was more effective when the demand for labour was high. In bad times the pendulum swung back to mass-based political activity as the best suited to those circumstances. Hunger was a particularly good political educator; a political system which cannot ensure the necessities of life for its workforce advertises itself as the object of reform. The result of the twin experiences of social change and repression, Thompson argues, brought into being an articulate and politically active working class. As he puts it;

> In the period between 1780 and 1832 most English working people came to feel an identity of interests as between themselves and as against their rulers and employers.

As a Marxist historian, Thompson focuses on class conflict. He sees the most significant historical moments as being those points of conflict between working people, acting as a cohesive class, and their rulers, also acting as a cohesive class. Liberal historians, however, tend to stress the points of mutual agreement between social groups as being the really important moments in any historical period. From historians with this point of view, the feeling is that Thompson has overstated the potential for independent action as a cohesive class by a fragmented workforce. At the heart of the controversy lies the issue of what the labouring poor were really capable of: was working-class support for political reform simply an instinctive reaction to hunger and despair or was it a reasoned response?

As we shall see in subsequent chapters, these alternative explanations for the strength of the radical movement remain unresolved. But for Thompson, it was the next phase of popular protest which provided the significant moment in the 'making' of the working class. The Reform Bill agitation of 1830–2 saw a government threatened, for the first and only time, with an alliance of middle-class and working-class radicals. But the Act of 1832 left the working community isolated in its political exclusion, thus giving political expression to their 'common experience' of social and economic change.

5 The Reform Bill Campaign

a *Political changes 1820–30*

Lord Liverpool, who was Prime Minister from 1812 until his death in 1827, remained implacably opposed to any radical reform of Parliament despite the extensive post-war popular movement. He did accept, however, that the growing middle class, and the changing economic basis of the country, would have to be recognised. The notion of 'Liberal Toryism' is sometimes applied to the government in the years after 1822 while the period before is generally seen as a different, reactionary, phase of the administration. In fact, Liverpool saw these two approaches as being closely related. To maintain aristocratic control, in the face of change, he had to maintain law and order, by containing working-class discontent, and placate the growing industrial interest in a way that fell short of Parliamentary reform. In 1819 the government took the decision to return the currency to the gold standard which, although unpopular at the time, provided the sound currency needed for a trade revival in the early 1820s. This revival was reinforced by a growing commitment to free trade. Under William Huskisson, President of the Board of Trade, tariffs were reduced on a wide range of goods and the old protective Navigation Laws were relaxed to permit the colonies to trade with foreign countries. Liverpool even signalled his willingness to make some minor modification to the Corn Laws by introducing a sliding scale, although this did not take effect until 1828.

Despite the beneficial effect of 'Liberal Toryism' upon trade in the 1820s, the issue of Parliamentary reform would not go away. In 1823, an Irish barrister named Daniel O'Connell formed the Catholic Association, in Ireland, to campaign for the right of Roman Catholics to enter Parliament (*see pages 303–4*). A trade depression from 1827 revived middle-class demands to be represented in government by men of their own class. The death of Liverpool from a stroke in 1827 seemed to open up the possibility of change. Nevertheless, attempts to use private members' bills to disenfranchise the 'rotten boroughs' of Penryn and East Retford, and transfer their seats to Manchester and Birmingham, failed. Clearly, the time had come for a more general measure that the government would sponsor and the House of Commons would support, and this point was increasingly accepted across the country. One notable exeption to this feeling was the Duke of Wellington, who became Prime Minister in 1828 following very brief periods in that office by George Canning and Viscount Goderich. In 1828 the Test and Corporations Acts were repealed, thus lifting the restrictions on Nonconformists entering Parliament. This was followed by a protracted, and for the Tories, damaging battle over Roman Catholic emancipation. Backed by the Catholic Association, O'Connell was elected MP for County Clare in Ireland in 1828, directly challenging the law debarring Roman Catholics. Such was the intensity of the agitation that, fearing civil war, Wellington's government reluctantly supported emancipation, which was achieved in 1829. (*This is discussed further in chapters V and X.*)

The issue of Catholic emancipation put the Tory party under considerable internal stress. Yet the pressure was building for a further reform, to adjust the franchise to recognise formally the industrial and commercial interest. This was further than Wellington was prepared to take his party and he resigned in November 1830. The Whigs, in opposition almost continuously since 1784, saw their chance to seize and retain power. Under the leadership of Earl Grey they formed a government and introduced a Reform Bill. This planned to redistribute the representation from a number of rotten boroughs to new industrial districts and, at the same time, introduce a uniform £10 householder franchise in all boroughs. By this, men who owned a house rated at the value of £10 a year would be able to vote. Grey was a wealthy landowner who, unlike Wellington, understood how widespread the call for reform had become. But there was a good deal of opposition from the Commons and Grey's first bill passed its second reading, in March 1831, by only one vote. Following this, Grey persuaded the king to dissolve Parliament so he might seek support from the country in a general election. The Whigs were re-elected, on a reform platform, by a large majority of over 130 seats.

Grey took this as a mandate to re-introduce reform and a second Reform Bill passed through the Commons in July 1831. Yet it is worth bearing in mind that, however revolutionary and threatening the Whigs' proposals were seen to be amongst the landed classes, Grey had no wish to change the *status quo*. He wanted to use what was really a rather limited reform to reinforce the system rather than to change it fundamentally. Above all, the working-class voter was to be excluded. As Grey assured the House of Lords in November 1832, 'there is no one more decided against annual parliaments, universal suffrage, and vote by ballot, than I am. My object is not to favour, but to put an end to such hopes.'

B *The campaign in the country*

Outside Parliament, agitation for reform focused on the figure of Thomas Attwood, a Birmingham banker whose family fortune had been made in the Midlands iron trade. He had already gained some attention as a currency reformer who believed that the decision to return to the gold standard had been damaging for commerce. Attwood argued that domestic demand could be stimulated by inflating the economy with paper money. By political inclination Attwood was a Tory, and he had taken no part in the post-war reform movement since he was deeply opposed to universal suffrage. However, Attwood attracted the support of men of his own class when he argued that the economy would continue to be unstable while the new industrial middle class was excluded from government.

Attwood, and many others who shared his views, were inspired by the success of the Catholic Association in extracting emancipation from Wellington's government by the use of popular pressure. Though he remained fearful of the consequences of harnessing mass support, O'Connell's success certainly stressed the potential of a mass-based movement. In 1830 Attwood formed the Birmingham Political Union (BPU) and modelled it closely on O'Connell's organisation. Attwood's objective was a political union in which a middle-class leadership and a working-class rank and file would be bound together by a common objective. The problem with Parliament, he now argued, was the absence of men representing productive capital, that is men active in the world of commerce and industry (in fact, men like Attwood!). He stressed the common interests of employers and employees who he saw as making up a single 'productive' class. As he said:

> The interests of masters and men are, in fact, one. If the masters flourish the men flourish with them; and if the masters suffer difficulties their difficulties must shortly affect the workmen in three-fold degree.

Attwood's view was really only a variation of 'virtual representation'; the worker would be represented by his employer because their interests were supposedly similar. It was not always a convincing argument. After all, if the economic interests of the two groups were so close how does one explain the growth of so much aggressive trade unionism in this period? It is also important to note that Attwood's argument was very different from the Painite position that most of the BPU's working-class membership supported. For Attwood, universal suffrage was not necessary. Given the common interests of employers and employees, in that both stood to gain if industry flourished, the needs of the labouring population would be fully catered for by the election of employers to Parliament. This approach was also enshrined in the structure of the BPU, whose central Political Council consisted entirely of middle-class men. As Attwood put it: 'Who would ever think ... of sending even a disciplined army into the field without officers?'.

Despite this heavily qualified commitment to democracy on the part of its founder, the BPU was enormously popular and it attracted extensive working-class support. Its outdoor meetings, at which Attwood was a regular and favourite speaker, frequently drew audiences of 50 000–100 000 people. Similar political unions were established in towns throughout the country, most significantly the Northern Political Union in Newcastle and, in London, the National Political Union. The latter was organised by Francis Place, a tailor who had been active in the earlier period of radicalism and who now accepted the need to work with, in his words, men of 'money and influence'. These political unions now backed the Whig reform bill. Yet, given the far wider objectives of the earlier period of radicalism, why was there now so much support for the comparatively limited Whig proposal and for a reform organisation that was self-consciously elitist in structure?

In fact, the earlier programme had not been forgotten. Throughout the Reform Bill campaign it was advocated by the London based National Union of the Working Classes, formed in 1831. This organisation never attracted mass-support but, with its radical programme and its network of branches throughout the country, it was an influential forerunner of Chartism. Through the medium of its illegal but very popular newspaper the *Poor Man's Guardian*, the NUWC expressed distrust for the Bill and its middle-class advocates, particularly Attwood. Yet, taken as a whole, working people do seem to have given the Bill their genuine support. This partly reflected a belief that its enactment would be the initial step towards full democracy. This was certainly not in the minds of the men who framed the Bill. They sought the minimum adjustment necessary to retain the *status quo*. But, at this stage, gradual reform still seemed a viable way forward. After all, the earlier movement, with its wider programme, had failed. The lessons of 1815–20 had been learned, and the advantages of lining-up behind men of wealth were recognised within the working community. As Bronterre O'Brien, editor of the *Poor Man's Guardian*, said of the Bill, 'with all its faults we are willing to accept it as an instalment or part payment of the debt of right due to us.'

For their part, Attwood and his supporters recognised that the greater the numbers behind the political unions, the more they could claim to represent 'the people' with all the authority that this suggested. This point was made constantly through 1831 and 1832 by means of a large number of public meetings calling upon Parliament to accept the Bill. The House of Commons seems to have been influenced by this pressure. Here the opposition to the Bill was fragmented anyway. Robert Peel, who led the Tories in the Commons, certainly opposed the bill as being too far reaching a measure but he also rejected the traditional Toryism of the die-hard Ultra-Tories who would consider no reform at all. Peel did not accept that the unreformed system was as exclusive as its critics suggested. His own father had been a textile manufacturer who had entered Parliament by purchasing a seat. But he did accept that the system was now discredited and needed its worst excesses removed to restore public confidence in government. Tory disunity in the Commons was to prove crucial to the Bill's eventual success. The House of Lords, where Wellington was the main Tory influence, was a different matter. Made up largely of the county aristocracy, it was less aware of, or concerned about, the agitation centred on the large towns and industrial districts. The Bill was passed in the Commons in September 1831, but was rejected by the Lords in October.

The rejection gave rise to extensive rioting in Nottingham, Derby and Bristol which had to be suppressed by troops. In November 1831 the BPU announced its intention to put itself on a military footing. This was immediately declared illegal by Royal Proclamation and the plan was dropped, but Attwood had made his point. A revised Bill, with a slightly more restrictive franchise, was now introduced. This was passed in the Commons the following March, but it was widely feared that the Lords would reject it when they debated it in May 1832. The Cabinet demanded that the king, William IV, create new peers to ensure the bill's passage in the Upper House. When he refused Grey resigned. It was now expected that the king would appoint Wellington as Prime Minister and that he, in turn, would order the arrest of the leading reformers.

On 11 May 1832 representatives of the BPU and other political unions met Francis Place in London to discuss their possible response to such moves. According to Place, they considered a run on the banks, under the slogan 'To defeat the Duke go for gold!', non-payment of taxes, and a plan of armed resistance. The days that followed were particularly tense, with Attwood clearly contemplating a fight with the Duke of Wellington. At a rally in Birmingham he told an audience of around 200 000 people:

> I would rather die than see the great Bill of reform rejected or

> mutilated . . . I see that you are all of one mind on the subject. Answer me then, had you not all rather die than live the slaves of the boroughmongers? (All! All!)

This notion of a resort to force if necessary was part of the heroic image that Attwood created for himself as a platform orator. It was clearly what his, mostly working-class, audience wanted to hear, as a popular ballad of the moment testifies:

> So join your hands with Attwood boys,
> Unto his wish comply,
> He says he'll set the nation free
> Or he will nobly die.

In the event, the Commons voted to support Grey's outgoing ministry, Wellington recognised that he could not form a government that could be viable in the Commons, and the king agreed to the creation of new peers. This proved to be unnecessary: under threat, the Lords capitulated and passed the Bill which then became law in June.

6 RIDING THE TIGER: THE THREAT OF REVOLUTION IN THE REFORM BILL CAMPAIGN

How close did Britain come to a revolution during the Reform Bill campaign? Historians are divided. E P Thompson claims that 'Britain was within an ace of revolution' and he identifies the autumn of 1831 with the riots that followed the Lords' rejection, and the 'Days of May' 1832, as the potentially revolutionary moments. It may be, of course, that Thompson's political perspective as a Marxist historian leads him to overstate the existence of revolutionary situations generally in this period. But most historians would agree that autumn 1831 and May 1832 are the critical moments to be examined. Eric Evans, in his book *The Forging of the Modern State* (1983), accepts Francis Place's account of the drawing-up of a plan of resistance in May 1832, but adds 'whether Place and his co-adjutors had any intention of bringing it into effect is a matter of doubt. Certainly, a revolution led by Francis Place would have been an incongruous phenomenon.' Joseph Hamburger, in his book *James Mill and the Art of Revolution* (1963) claims that the middle-class reformers were engaged in an elaborate form of bluff. They played up the extent of their national support and exaggerated its violent potential, in order to force the Bill through a reluctant Parliament. There never was a real threat of revolution; 'The professional reformer like the public relations man', claims Hamburger, 'dealt in images.' Others have argued that the heroic stand of figures such as Attwood became part of the folklore of the radical tradition and their actions became exaggerated in the re-telling. It could also be said that the major factor influencing Wellington to stand down in May 1832 was the vote in the House of Commons and not the pressure of the popular movement.

Yet, as both government and reformers alike were aware, the popular movement always carried with it the threat of a violent confrontation with the authorities. This had been the case in 1815–20 and, from this experience, working-class reformers knew what to expect from an anti-reform Tory government of the sort that Wellington might have formed in May 1832. Far from massaging images and manipulating figures of attendance, as Hamburger claims, the middle-class leaders of the campaign were 'riding the tiger' in relation to the working-class rank and file. As we have seen, the working community possessed by this time a tradition of political activity and also a programme of reform far more radical than that envisaged by men like Place and Attwood. The crucial problem for the middle-class radicals was not the creation of false images to frighten the government, but rather retaining the leadership of a mass-based movement and directing it towards a moderate reform of Parliament. Riding the tiger is an exhilarating activity, but the rider is never totally in charge since the tiger has a mind of its own. Also, it is arguable that Wellington's apparent discounting of popular pressure in reaching his decision to stand down made the situation more revolutionary in nature rather than less. It was precisely Wellington's unawareness of public feeling that would have made him a dangerous man as Prime Minister.

This is not to deny that bluff figured somewhere in the reformers' calculations. Attwood frequently referred to, what he called, the tactics of 'wholesome terror' whereby the peaceful process of petitioning Parliament was backed by the rhetoric of violent language. An example of this, from May 1832, was cited earlier. Such oratory was designed to have its impact not only upon the audience, but also upon those in authority. There had been another revolution in France in 1830, and memories of the post-war radical movement were still fresh. Certainly, when the BPU published its plan to arm in November 1831, the king wrote to Wellington that he feared a revolutionary intent on the Union's part. Nevertheless, we should remember that this was primarily a peaceful movement to petition Parliament in support of a limited reform measure (however radical it might look to the Ultra-Tories) which had the sponsorship of the government of the day and had already been accepted by the Commons.

Any revolutionary threat came not from the conscious intent of the reformers, but from the circumstances of the moment, and these were, in many ways, beyond their control. Above all, this was the only time in British history when the working class and the middle class were firmly united in an extra-Parliamentary campaign for political reform. This had not been the case in the post-war period and it would not be so in Chartism. By May 1832 the movement included a broad social spectrum. Support ranged from wealthy industrialists, professionals and merchants, who simply sought an adjustment to allow the urban interest into the political system via a restricted property franchise, right through to the labouring poor who saw the Bill as the first step towards full citizenship. The wealth of an excluded middle class, backed by the numerical strength of an excluded working class, united behind the slogan 'The Bill, the whole Bill, and nothing but the Bill!', faced the intransigence of the House of Lords led by a man who had announced, when Prime Minister in 1830, that in his view the political system needed no reform of any kind.

Had Wellington become Prime Minister in May 1832 and moved against the reformers it is difficult to see how bloodshed would have been avoided. The riots of 1831 had given some idea of what a Lords' rejection might trigger. In April 1832, in the run-up to the debate in the Upper House, the *Poor Man's Guardian*, published a guide to street fighting by an Italian political refugee named Macerone. His *Defensive Instructions for the People* included, among other things, detailed instructions on the construction of home-made pikes and how they might be employed against troops to maximum advantage. Thus, revolution was more likely to be precipitated by an injudicious act by Wellington, had he become Prime Minister in May 1832, than by the conscious intent of reformers like Attwood and Place. This situation never occurred but the expectation of such events is clear if one looks back to May 1832. A London lawyer, Matthew Davenport-Hill wrote to the Whig reformer Lord Brougham in October 1831:

> I have been two days in Birmingham and have taken some pains to ascertain the feelings of the people. Peace will however be preserved I have no doubt, if a speedy prospect can be held out of passing the Bill. I have also been through the West of England and South Wales and the result of my observations is that nothing but a speedy reform can avert revolution.

During the 'Days of May' Matthew received a letter from his brother, Frederick Hill, who was a schoolmaster living in the family home town of Birmingham. Frederick's letter seems to capture the uncertainty of this historical moment:

> The middle classes are, I think, rapidly prepared as a whole to refuse the payment of taxes. The general expectation is that the Duke will instantly resort to violent measures. An arrest of all the members of the [BPU Political] Council is looked upon as a probable measure. I much fear that the people will not be able to restrain themselves in this case.

1. *What is meant by the term 'the people' in these extracts?*
2. *What grounds were there, by May 1832, for Frederick's view that 'the people will not be able to restrain themselves'?*

7 The Reform Act and its Significance

The intransigence of the House of Lords converted the Reform Act into a heroic measure, an image which it could scarcely have sustained on its own merits. Its passing did little to dismantle the system which Burke defended so fiercely in 1790, since it accepted the principle that the franchise should be based on the ownership of property. Fifty-five boroughs with less than 1000 inhabitants were disenfranchised and lost both MPs, whilst 33 boroughts with less than 2000 inhabitants lost one of their MPs. This released 143 seats for re-distribution and these were mostly assigned to the industrial towns. Five new seats were given to Ireland, eight to Scotland and four to Wales. In the boroughs the older franchises were replaced by the £10 householder franchise. By this provision all male residents, whose houses were valued for the purposes of levying rates, at £10 a year or over were given the vote. This was actually more restrictive than it sounds. In England and Wales one man in every five now had the vote, in Scotland one man in eight, and in Ireland one man in twenty. In Birmingham, for example, some 4000 men were entitled to vote in the newly created borough from a total population of around 144 000. In the years to come the majority of MPs continued to come from landed backgrounds.

The basis of the political system had not been changed. The new House of Commons, elected in 1832, looked very much like the old institution and acted in very familiar ways. But the urban middle class had been admitted to political life and their presence would be felt increasingly over the coming decades. This was really all that most middle-class reformers had wished to achieve; a recognition of the new middle-class 'interest' within a stable system built upon the defence of property. Some, like Attwood, had expected a sudden change in the way the country was run, to favour the 'men of productive capital'. Elected MP for Birmingham in the reformed Parliament he made no secret of his disappointment. He told a meeting only a year after the passing of the Act, 'My friends I have been grieviously deceived. Almost on the first day of the session I discovered this . . . '. A visitor to Birmingham at about this time reported the rather more explicit sentiment 'Damn Earl Grey's bloody head off' scrawled on the walls of the town.

For working people there was only disappointment. The 'reforming Whigs' were, after all, a party of traditional landowners. This point had been signalled by their firm suppression of the 'Swing' agricultural disturbances in 1830 (*see page 71*). The actions of the reformed Parliament, particularly the passing of the Poor Law Amendment Act (*see page 53*), and the Whigs' attack on trade unions in 1834 (*see page 75*), left working-class radicals in no doubt that the Act had not, in fact, been passed as a 'first instalment' of a wider reform of the system. The Reform Act left a legacy of bitterness, and working-class euphoria at its passing did not last long. This sense of betrayal took working-class reformers back to their earlier political programme and this was now expressed in Chartism. Despite this, the Reform Bill campaign became the model which all subsequent popular movements attempted to emulate. The combination of massive public meetings, good publicity through an active press, and the use of constitutional arguments backed by 'wholesome terror' would all be characteristics of Chartism.

8 Bibliography

C Behagg *Politics and Production in the Early Nineteenth Century* (Routledge, 1990). The author's study of class relations in Birmingham provides a local study of the themes of the chapter you have just read. Chapter four ('Riding the Tiger') deals with popular radicalism 1815–32.

J Belchem *Orator Hunt* (Oxford University Press). This overview of Hunt's role in the popular radical movement provides a detailed insight into the importance of the 'mass-platform' in the period 1815–20.

M Brock *The Great Reform Act* (Hutchinson, 1973). This is perhaps the best detailed study of the passing of the Reform Act. The author matches events in Parliament with the growth of the popular movement to provide a good blend of 'high politics' and 'history from below'.

J R Dinwiddy *From Luddism to the Great Reform Act* (Blackwell, 1986). This Historical Association pamphlet provides detail on, and insight into, a range of popular movements in the period.

R J Morris *Class and Class Consciousness in the Industrial Revolution 1780–1850* (Methuen, 1979). A good discussion of the issues surrounding the interpretation of popular movements.

E P Thompson *The Making of the English Working Class* (Pelican, 1968). This is a central text for any analysis of the period under discussion. It is a very long book which will reward detailed study; but a good sense of the argument presented will be derived from the Preface (not to be missed under any circumstances) followed by chapters 4, 6, 8, 10, 15 and 16.

9 Discussion Points and Exercises

A

1 What were the problems with the unreformed House of Commons?

2 What was the motivation behind reform initiatives in the period 1815–20?

3 Why did these initiatives fail?
4 Why was there a fresh reform initiative in the late 1820s?
5 Compare the popular movement of 1815–20 with that of 1830–2.
6 How close did the country come to a revolution in 1830–2?
7 What changes to the political system did the Reform Act make?

B *Essay questions*

1 What part was played by economic depression in stimulating radical politics in the period 1815–20?
2 What pressures brought about a reform of Parliament in 1832?
3 Why were its opponents unable to prevent the passing of the Reform Act in 1832?
4 Assess the impact of popular agitation on the British political system in the period 1815–32.
5 Why was the cause of Parliamentary reform so unsuccessful in the years up to 1830?
6 How close did Britain come to a revolution in the reform crisis of 1831–2?

C *Exercise – comparing historical interpretations*

Re-read section 3 of the chapter and then consider carefully these two, very different, interpretations of the Pentridge Uprising of 1817 (*see page 16*).

(a) Writing within a liberal political tradition the historian R J White summed-up the objectives of Brandreth, the leader of the rebels, in the following way:

> He possessed one fixed idea: that the government must be overthrown and the poor men of England vindicated in the form of better victuals and brighter living. He talked not of ballot-boxes but of rum, guineas, bands of music and pleasure parties on the Trent. But first, always first, came the task of overthrowing the Government. It was his fierce obsession with this immediate task that gave him his hold over his associates, the children – like himself – of the rough, often brutal, always passionate world of the poor. That world, with its recent memories of the Jacobite armies, the gallows, the press-gang and the prize ring, was passing away. Brandreth knew no other, and he carried its traditions of violence, in word and deed, into the political arena of the Regency.
>
> R J White *Waterloo to Peterloo* (1957)

(b) This might be contrasted with Thompson's view of the events.

> We may see the Pentridge rising as one of the first attempts in history to mount a wholly proletarian insurrection,

> without any middle-class support. The objectives of this revolutionary movement cannot perhaps be better characterised than in the words of the Belper street song 'The Levolution is begun . . .' The attempt throws light on the extreme isolation into which the northern and Midlands workers had been forced during the Wars, and it is a transitional moment between Luddism and the 'populist' radicalism of 1818–20 and 1830–32. Even without Oliver's patent provocations, some kind of insurrection would probably have been attempted, and perhaps with a greater measure of success.

E P Thompson *The Making of the English Working Class* (1963).

1 What does White mean, or imply, by the phrase 'the passionate world of the poor'?
2 What does Thompson mean, or imply, by the phrase 'a wholly proletarian insurrection'?
3 What contrasting images of the Pentridge rebels come across from each of these extracts?
4 Why might Thompson object to the way White portrays the rebels?

D *Parliamentary reform: contemporary views.*
This may be carried out as an individual exercise, or with the assistance of two colleagues (each person representing a particular social group's viewpoint), or as a wider discussion between three groups (each group discussing their 'case' and then arguing it in a plenary session).

1 How might the aristocracy have justified their dominance of government in the period before 1832?
2 What was the case for the franchise being extended to the middle class?
3 What was the case for the vote being extended to the working class?

10 ESSAY WRITING – THE THREAT OF REVOLUTION IN 1832?

(i) Consider essay 6 on page 32 in the light of what you have read. You will need to assess carefully the evidence of a revolutionary situation, always bearing in mind one indisputable historical fact; that a revolution did not take place. It is equally certain, however, that contemporaries did not have the benefit of hindsight and it is helpful to our understanding to speculate on how the situation looked at the time. It might be useful to define first what is meant by the term 'revolution'; a good dictionary will help here.

(ii) Once you have this straight in your head, you may begin the weighing of the evidence. Begin by simply listing your thoughts under two appropriate headings, perhaps as follows;

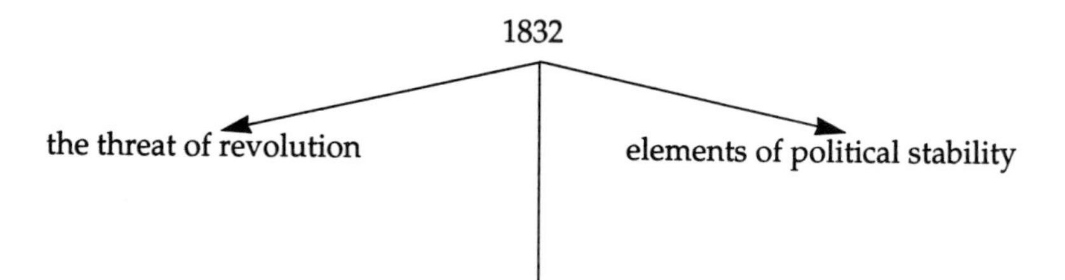

(iii) You should not forget the historiographical element in a question of this sort, since it is emphatically interpretive in its nature. Frankly, nobody knows for certain how close revolution was, so it will be useful to identify alternative ways in which historians have analysed the situation.

(iv) Also, you must recognise the importance of chronology in any history essay. Here, you are asked to make a judgement on 1832 but it is perfectly legitimate to widen the chronological scope, to take in the build-up to 1832 or even the earlier period of radicalism, *as long as you are relating earlier events to the year in question*. After each paragraph ask yourself the question 'How does the information I have given in this paragraph help the reader to understand 1832?'.

(v) Finally, one pitfall to avoid: you must not leave the reader in doubt as to your view. It is easy, in undertaking a listing exercise such as suggested above, to conclude that there is much evidence on both sides and so you cannot make a judgement; or that, since learned historians clearly disagree on the subject, who are you to say one way or the other? Historical analysis is about reaching conclusions that are, ultimately, a matter of opinion and interpretation. In writing this essay you are a historian and you must have an opinion and one which you can justify by taking the reader through the evidence. So, build-up your courage, look at your lists of evidence, and offer the reader a clear and reasoned viewpoint!

11 Documentary Exercises – The Nature of the Reform Bill

Read carefully the following statements from contemporaries on the nature of the Reform Bill, and answer the questions that follow.

> 1 When Sir Robert Peel charged them [the Whig ministers]: with going to make a democratical House of Commons . . . they said 'No, we are going to keep the power out of the hands of the

rabble' .... Their policy ... was to get one million of the middle classes, the little shopkeepers and those people, to join the higher classes, in order to raise the yeomanry corps and keep up standing armies, and thus unite together to keep their hands still in the pockets of the seven millions.

Speech by Henry Hunt at Manchester, April 1831.

2 It is clear *we* GAIN nothing by it; but it is said that these middle men, whom this measure admits into a share of the legislature, will be more inclined to hear our appeal for justice, and will return a majority favourable to it: think it not; – why already – before even they have gained their own admittance – do they not shut the doors of Parliament against you? for will they *tolerate* our *mention* of 'Universal Suffrage' etc? ... – do they not plainly tell you, even when they solicit your 'sweet voices' to swell *their own* cry for *their own* reform, – do they not plainly tell you that they like not *universal suffrage*? – do they not scout the very mention of equality? – and is not 'property', which you have not, the very pivot on which all their thoughts and wishes turn?

Poor Man's Guardian, 24 September 1831

3 Every argument, sir, which would induce me to oppose universal suffrage, induces me to support this measure which is now before us. I oppose universal suffrage because I think it would produce a destructive revolution ... I support this measure because I am sure that it is now our best security against a revolution ... I support this measure as a measure of reform; but I support it still more as a measure of conservation.

Speech by Thomas Babington Macaulay in the House of Commons, 2 July 1831.

4 to prepare: the outline of a measure ... large enough to satisfy public opinion and to afford sure ground of resistance to further innovation, yet so based on property, and on existing franchises and territorial divisions, as to run no risk of overthrowing the existing form of government.

Sir James Graham (writing in 1851) recalling the instructions given by the Cabinet to a committee of four (of whom he was one), appointed to draft the Reform Bill in January 1831.

1 *explain the meaning, in the context of these documents, of the following:*

a *'a democratical House of Commons' (Hunt)*

b *'is not 'property' ... the very pivot on which all their thoughts and wishes turn?' (Poor Man's Guardian)*

c *'a measure of conservation' (Macaulay)*

d *'resistance to further innovation' (Graham)*

2 *How justified were the reservations expressed in extracts 1 and 2?*

3 *Why did working people support the campaign for the Reform Bill despite the reservations expressed in extracts 1 and 2?*

4 *Why might the Bill have been considered 'our best security against revolution' (Macaulay)?*

III

THE 'CONDITION OF ENGLAND QUESTION': REFORM AND THE STATE 1830–50

—

1 INTRODUCTION

IN THE 20 years between 1830 and 1850 Parliament passed legislation to deal with a number of issues that were considered to be social problems. These included poverty, public health, local government, factory conditions, and law and order. This thrust towards social reform was accompanied by a widespread debate about what was termed the 'Condition of England Question'. The political thinker Thomas Carlyle focused attention on this area in his emotive pamphlet *Chartism*, published in 1839. In this he drew attention to the potential threat to society of what he called 'delirious Chartism' and expressed the view that 'the condition of the working classes is a rather ominous matter at present.' As he put it:

> What means this bitter discontent of the working classes? Whence comes it, whither goes it? Above all, at what price, on what terms will it probably consent to depart from us and die into rest? These are questions.

Like many of his contemporaries, Carlyle was concerned at the problems created by the social and economic changes that had recently taken place. Industrialisation, and particularly the rapid growth of towns, highlighted the problems that required intervention. Very few of these were new problems; poverty, crime, and disease, for example, were hardly nineteenth-century creations. Nevertheless, the industrial revolution placed these, often age-old, problems into a new context. It was one thing for poverty, disease and crime to occur in a pre-industrial society, where the population was small, labour mobility was restricted and the relationship between rich and poor was on the basis of personal knowledge. In these conditions stability and order could be maintained through face-to-face relationships. It was quite another thing to deal with these same problems in an industrial society, with a large and often highly mobile labour force gathered together in large towns and industrial districts where the different classes were geographically dispersed over a large area.

The way social problems are identified and dealt with in any society will provide a good reflection of the ideas and beliefs upon which that society is based. This chapter is devoted to an exploration of the broad context of state intervention in this period, relating the measures that were taken to the underlying values of the world's first industrial society.

The main social and administrative legislation between 1832 and 1850 may be listed as follows;

1833	Factory Act (Althorp's Act)
	Abolition of Slavery in British colonies
1834	Poor Law Amendment Act
1835	Municipal Corporations Act
	Prisons Act
1837	Civil Registration and Marriages Acts
1839	County Police Act
1842	Mines and Collieries Act
1844	Factory Act (Graham's Act)
1847	Factory Act (Ten Hours Act)
	Poor Law Act
1848	Public Health Act
1850	Factory Act

For the most part, this legislation dealt with issues related, in one way or another, to an expansion of population and the growth of towns. There was undoubtedly an increased awareness that industrial society had generated social problems that had to be dealt with, and that this would involve an interventionist role for the state and local authorities. The Factory Acts of these years attempted to control working conditions in textile mills and mines for child workers and women workers; the Poor Law Amendment Act aimed to transform completely the basis on which poverty was relieved and this was extended by the 1847 legislation. The Public Health Act of 1848 tried to improve the unhealthy sanitary condition of urban areas. The Municipal Corporations Act allowed for the creation of elected town councils to address all these issues at a local level. Urban police forces were one of the first fruits of this development and in 1839 country areas were encouraged to develop similar police forces through the County Police

Act. The creation of police forces was complemented by an overhaul of the prison system, begun with the Prisons Act of 1835. The Registration Acts of 1837 made it compulsory to record details of births, deaths and marriages. This would begin the task of accumulating the social statistics on which future legislation might be based.

2 SOCIAL REFORM AND THE HISTORIANS

Many historians have argued that this increased awareness of the problems of an industrialising society reflected a growth of humanitarianism, from which the Welfare State emerged after the Second World War. Proof of the growing spirit of humanitarian feeling is often seen in the abolition of slavery in British colonies in 1833 and the growing tolerance towards religious dissent. Oliver MacDonagh argues that the reforms of these years represented a 'revolution in government'. In his book, *Early Victorian Government* (1977), he explains: 'By a relatively early stage in the nineteenth century, humanitarian sentiment prevailed in public attitudes, whatever private conduct or personal motivation may have been'. MacDonagh's model for the development of governmental responsibility hinges upon the exposure of 'social evils' (perhaps by a report, a social novel or a campaigning newspaper) and the notion that the 'climate of opinion' responded by declaring the problem to have reached 'intolerable' proportions. Legislation would therefore follow on from the awakening of a humanitarian public opinion. David Roberts takes a similar approach in his book, which is significantly titled *The Victorian Origins of the British Welfare State* (1960). Here he identifies the close correlation between concern over the 'condition of England' and the ensuing legislation;

> They had only to describe the chaotic administration of the Poor Law, the exploitation of children, the disgraceful state of prisons, the increasing crime, the unhealthiness of the slums, and the profound ignorance of the working classes to convince of the need for reform.

By contrast, other historians, far from identifying a revolution in government, have seen these years as part of a period of *'laissez-faire'* ('leave alone') in public policy. By this policy, it is argued, governments consciously *restricted* their interventionist role in all areas in order to encourage a free market economy. This view originated with the Liberal historian A V Dicey, writing in 1905, who emphasised his own contemporary period (that is, post-1875) as the time when most welfare legislation originated. He saw the first 75 years of the nineteenth century as a period when free market capitalism was relatively unchecked by the hand of the State. This view of an early nineteenth century, in which economic expansion dominated at the expense of state intervention, has more recently been taken up by historians on the left, who stress the oppressive nature of the new society for the working class. Eric Hobsbawm has argued that 'by the middle of the nineteenth century government policy in Britain came as near *laissez-faire* as has ever been practicable in a modern state' (*Industry and Empire* 1968).

So, there are two models of interpretation operating here. One argues the progressive increase in protection afforded to the individual by government intervention, and that this was brought about by a wide variety of contributory factors, of which popular humanitarianism was one of the most important. The other model highlights the way industrialisation exposed those who were vulnerable, in a way that remained relatively unchecked by state intervention and that this policy was inspired by free market economics. Confusing though this extreme polarisation of views may at first appear, the existing debate can help us to frame our central question; upon what basis did the state intervene in matters of social reform in the years 1830 to 1850?

The first point to make is that neither of these models is particularly satisfactory. On the one hand, there was simply too much interventionist legislation passed for this to be seen as a period of pure *laissez-faire.* On the other hand, it is perhaps too easy for us to stress the importance of humanitarian public opinion. It may be comforting for us to think that our ancestors always did the right thing, and that modern welfarism was pioneered from a very early stage in industrial society, but the issues involved here are a good deal more complex than this would suggest. For example, whilst the abolition of slavery in 1833 was undoubtedly a major achievement it should be remembered that it was British merchants who had transported and sold 2.8 million slaves between 1701 and 1807, and that abolition was passed only in the face of a good deal of opposition from the pro-slavery lobby. Similarly, the Public Health Act of 1848 was clearly a response to the publication of a number of reports in the 1840s which revealed appalling conditions and high death rates in the urban areas. Yet the Act was not a success, being widely evaded by the local authorities in the areas in which it was applied. Were there, therefore, not one but two 'public opinions' at work at this time; one operating at the national level and responding in a humanitarian way by creating the 1848 Act, and the other operating at a local level to ensure that the Act never worked in the way its framers intended? The notion of a predominantly humanitarian public opinion responding responsibly to 'intolerable' evils raises more questions than it answers. It also ignores the fact that most social reforms were the work of small groups of dedicated individuals, lobbying parliament via a variety of agencies, and fighting against a good deal of opposition from their contemporaries.

It is also important to appreciate that the early Victorians saw these problems through their own set of social values. That is to say, they did not necessarily see these problems as subsequent societies (including our own) would come to see them. Take, as an example, the following statement made by the man who was perhaps the leading reformer of the day, Edwin Chadwick, in relation to the shocking living conditions in the towns which were identified by his famous Sanitary Inquiry of 1842 (upon which the 1848 Public Health Act was largely based):

> the noxious physical agencies depress the health and bodily condition of the population, and act as obstacles to education and to culture; that in abridging the duration of the adult life of the working classes they check the growth of productive skill, and abridge the amount of social experience and steady moral habits in the community: that they substitute for a population that accumulates and preserves instruction and is steadily progressive, a population that is young, inexperienced, ignorant, credulous, irritable, passionate, and dangerous...
>
> (*Report on the Sanitary Condition of the Labouring Population*, 1842).

1. *Why might poor living conditions be seen as 'obstacles to education'?*
2. *How were poor living conditions operating to 'check the growth of productive skill', and why might this be considered a problem?*
3. *How might poor living conditions create a population that was 'irritable, passionate, and dangerous' and why would this be considered a problem?*
4. *Why, in Chadwick's opinion, should the government do something about public health?*
5. *What reforms might be recommended on the basis of this analysis?*

In order to understand the Public Health Act, and the associated legislation passed to deal with the 'problem' of the urban areas, we need to understand the problem through Chadwick's eyes. For him, in common with most middle-class observers, the 'Condition of England' question was a moral issue, an economic issue and an issue of public order, all of which might be addressed by the creation of efficient government intervention. Some of this response may be covered by the term 'humanitarian' but much of it cannot be explained in this way, since the term is not broad enough to cover the range of considerations which moved contemporaries.

If we are to place social reform in its creative contemporary context we need to identify and explore three sets of ideas that contributed to the framework of values through which the reformers operated; free market economics, Utilitarianism, and Evangelicalism.

3 FREE MARKET ECONOMICS AND THE ROLE OF GOVERNMENT

As it entered the industrial age the British economy was encumbered by a range of legal restrictions inherited from earlier times. For example, tariffs made trade a complicated business with import and export duties hindering the free flow of goods. The export of machinery was largely prohibited until 1825. The Corn Laws of 1815 were a late addition to the list of restrictive tariffs that regulated British trade. Besides this, the relationship between employers and employees was also controlled by a variety of agencies. For instance, in the eighteenth century, magistrates had often set the level of wages in their area to ensure the welfare of the the labouring poor. Under the Statute of Artificers, passed in the reign of Elizabeth I, the number of apprentices that an employer could take on might be restricted, and this remained in force until 1813.

Traditionally, the marketing of foodstuffs was also restricted by a body of custom and law. The movement of grain from one area to another was seen as legitimate only if local needs had first been met. Private deals between farmers and corn merchants, which did not take place publicly in the local market place, were illegal. This legislative framework reflected a paternalistic society in which the gulf between the rich and the poor was justified by the recognition that the possession of wealth entailed certain obligations towards the poor.

With the onset of industrialisation it was increasingly argued that such paternalistic provision would restrict economic growth and that, for instance, the able bodied poor should be encouraged to move about the country in search of work. Adam Smith argued in his influential book, *The Wealth of Nations* (1776), that the economy should be allowed to flourish without hindrance from government interference. Individuals should be left to follow what they perceived as their own best interests and by doing so the common good would be furthered by a flourishing economy. As he put it 'It is not from the benevolence of the butcher, the brewer, or the baker, that we expect our dinner but from their regard for their own interest.' Above all, the contractual relationship between employer and employee should be above government interference. If it was made by two free agents in the open market each side would ensure that their own best interest was served in the arrangement. For example, when an employer and an employee negotiated their individual wage contract, both would try to obtain whatever was best for them. The level of wages that was agreed between them would be determined by market forces, for example, the skill that the worker could offer, the amount of competing labour available to the employer, the profit level of the employer's business, or the demand for the goods that were to be produced. That governments should try to intervene in this relationship, by setting levels of wages, or conditions of employment was, in Smith's words, 'as impertinent as it is oppressive'.

This was a market-based analysis of the way a society should work and it was essentially optimistic in its tone. Smith, and the free market economists who followed him in the nineteenth century, believed that contractual freedom between individuals would create a harmonious society as the economy developed to provide full employment, high profits and good wages. In other words, the interests of employers and employees were fundamentally the same, since both stood to gain from a sound economy. Much later, Karl Marx would devote himself to refuting this view of economic individualism. He argued in his work, *Capital* (1867), that, far from being characterised by a harmony of interests, such systems contained inherent conflicts. Individualism, he argued, depended upon employers exploiting workers: wages could only go up at the expense of profits and the worker did not make a contract with an employer on the basis of equality. The idea of labour as a free agent in a harmonious market place was a myth.

Nevertheless, the idea that the economy would grow, with individuals interacting in an harmonious way, as long as the State did not interfere, gained extensive credence in the nineteenth century. It was widely accepted that, in the main, individuals should be free to dispose of their property as they saw fit. This deep-rooted commitment to individualism also provides the key to understanding the pronounced objection that was invariably expressed towards increases in government taxes or local rates. Of course, both were regarded with suspicion simply because they cost the taxpayer and ratepayer more. But increased costs of this sort also flew in the face of free market economics. Taxes and rates reduced the stock of an individual's personal capital and forced him or her to dispose of it in a way determined by somebody other than the individual. This could be seen as an infringement of the very economic freedom that Smith saw as central to the whole free market system. This was always a powerful argument against extending the activities of either central or local government, beyond a bare minimum, since this would invariably increase the burden on the tax and rate payers.

Individualism, however, raised two related difficulties. First, it was all very well to allow individuals to dispose of their property as they saw fit, but what if they conceived of their own 'best interests' as lying, for example, in the building of slums, or in the gross exploitation of groups unable to defend themselves, or in the operation of brothels? Under these circumstances the interests of the individual and the wider society might be at odds. Secondly, the concern with levels of tax from central government and rates from local government might reduce the ability of both these bodies to deal with the problems that confronted the whole of society, like crime, disease, or the need for education. Was it always the case that the market would provide for these sorts of areas and, if it did not, would the antipathy to high taxes and rates severely restrict the ability of society to deal with its problems?

The difficulty here lay in the need to reconcile free market economics with the role of central and local government agencies. To put this another way, what bounds should be put on the individual in the interests of the common good and efficient government? In the early nineteenth century the answer was provided by Jeremy Bentham and the philosophy of Utilitarianism.

4 UTILITARIANISM: JEREMY BENTHAM AND THE SCIENCE OF GOVERNMENT

Many of the reforms of this period are associated, directly or indirectly, with the ideas of the political thinker, Jeremy Bentham (1748–1832). The clearest examples of this are the Factory Acts (1833 and 1844), the Poor Law Amendment Act (1834), the County Police Act (1839), the Mines and Collieries Act (1842) and the Public Health Act (1848). Whilst none of these reforms was purely Benthamite in its nature, each piece of legislation reflects the influence of the body of ideas with which he is associated and a group of reformers who supported his point of view. In many cases this influence was promoted by the direct involvement of Edwin Chadwick, Bentham's one time secretary, in forming and framing the legislation.

Bentham accepted the concept of economic freedom associated with a free market economy, and which we have explored through the work of Smith. Like Smith, he saw individualism as the key to economic growth. The state should not intervene in the economy, other than by freeing it of restrictive regulations, since public and private wealth would expand most rapidly in a situation where individuals were left to pursue what they perceived as being in their own best interests. Nevertheless, Bentham accepted that there were a number of occasions where government intervention would be necessary. He recognised, for example, that the state would need to act to provide security for its citizens. The law should protect individuals and their property since, without such protection, individuals could not really be free to pursue their own interests.

The provision of such security would, of necessity, involve legislation that might broadly be termed social reform. Bentham, for example, extended the concept of security to cover the issue of what he referred to as 'subsistence'. However much the economy flourished there would always be those who could not work (the 'indigent poor') and they would need to be provided for in some way, although they should never be confused with those who *could* work but who chose not to. Individuals would also have to be protected against accidents or epidemics by good public health and safety regulation. As Bentham put it,

'Without law there is no security'. State intervention should always, Bentham argued, be subject to what was called the 'principle of utility'. According to this, governments would only intervene to promote the 'greatest happiness of the greatest number'. The phrase is far from self-explanatory and really makes sense only if we relate it to Bentham's overall analysis (after all, most governments, of whatever complexion, claim to operate for the greatest happiness of the greatest number of their subjects). The intention behind government intervention, as far as Bentham was concerned, was to provide sufficient protection to allow the individual to enjoy economic freedom and so promote his or her own happiness. The principle of utility recognised that some individuals would have to be coerced in order to secure the interests of the wider public. That is, in some instances individuals would not be left to pursue what they saw as their own best interests since this threatened the happiness of the wider society. The intervention to coerce these individuals would be in the form of legislation. But how could the state be certain that its intervention would not trespass on the much cherished economic freedom of the majority?

Bentham answered this question by identifying a series of tests against which legislation could be measured.

(i) rule and exception–it should be recognised that as a rule the state would not intervene; exceptionally it might have to do so. Bentham's view of the state role was minimalist, it would intervene only in exceptional cases. This notion of 'rule and exception' was determined by the desire not to infringe on the right of the individual to promote his or her own happiness and welfare. This point was widely accepted throughout the nineteenth century and is one reason why social legislation was so patchy in its nature–it invariably aimed to deal with an acknowledged problem by a minimum of intervention.

(ii) empirical analysis–in order to establish what this minimum of state provision should be, legislation would need to be preceded by a thorough investigation of the problem. Legislation should reflect an understanding of the problem. Again, this point was broadly accepted and it became standard procedure to investigate issues prior to legislation by means of either a Select Committee of the House of Commons or the House of Lords or a Royal Commission. The Victorians were great empiricists, believing that scientific investigation would reveal not only the dimensions of the problem but also the nature of the solution. The huge investigation, via a Royal Commission in 1832, into the operation of the Old Poor Laws is a good early example of the approach. The New Poor Law of 1834, and its application, were significantly shaped by this process of investigation and its findings.

(iii) centralised authority–since the state would be acting to coerce some individuals not to pursue their own best interests, it would have to take steps to ensure that the law was obeyed and not avoided. This would require an efficient system of administration and inspection. Bentham argued that to be efficient, administration should be centralised; dispersal of authority invariably led to a reduction in the strength of intervention. A system of inspection would address the natural inclination of individuals to avoid a law which clashed with their own self-interest. Yet the centralisation of power aroused great controversy in the nineteenth century, and still does today, despite a broad acceptance of the principle in many aspects of government. Traditionally, the centralisation of power was associated with the despotism of absolute monarchy. The traditional bulwark against such abuse of power was to balance central control by reinforcing the authority of the localities. The landed classes, for example, expected to control their own areas via their powers as Lord Lieutenants of the counties; poor rates were levied locally and expended via Guardians of the Poor elected from local dignitaries, and magistrates acted on the basis of local knowledge in the execution of their work. Any move towards centralisation was likely to be opposed in the localities as a usurpation of power. Much of the ineffectiveness of early nineteenth-century social legislation can be attributed to this factor: that the implementation of any Acts of Parliament lay in the hands of a disparate range of local agencies, many of whom did not share Parliament's view of the problem. The case of the New Poor Law, examined below, is a good example of the tension between local and national government. Nevertheless, for Bentham and his followers, state intervention was always coercive and would require a form of central administration and inspection that would ensure its effective and uniform operation throughout the country.

5 EVANGELICALISM

The Industrial Revolution was accompanied by a religious revival. There were many reasons for this. The new middle class sought a set of beliefs that would reinforce their industrial enterprises and they found this in a very active form of religion which stressed the importance of hard work and abstinence. For their part, the labouring poor often looked to religion to replace the traditional community ties which industrialisation destroyed. By the start of the nineteenth century an approach to religion that would become characteristic of the age had emerged, and we may refer to this as evangelicalism.

Religion, the Evangelicals argued, was not to be a once-a-week affair, which absorbed the individual only on a Sunday. Since every action taken by an individual involved a choice between good and evil, the religious dimension was constantly present. Any aspiration to lead a good life would involve a recognition of the essential sinfulness with which human beings were tainted at the time of the Fall in the Garden of Eden. Great emphasis was placed upon conversion and 'justification by faith' which involved the attempt to lead a blameless existence, and an honest recognition of any personal failure to live up to this high standard. Evangelicalism should not be mistaken for a distinct religion; it was rather an approach to Christianity which became popular from about the second half of the eighteenth century onwards. It is often most closely associated with the Nonconformist sects that grew up in this period, most prominently that of Methodism under John Wesley. Wesley felt that the Church of England was too inert as an organisation to make real contact with the growing population in the industrial districts and the countryside. Rejecting formal and ritualistic modes of worship, he evolved a form of service which emphasised the active participation of the congregation. Methodists worshipped in any available location (it became known as the 'religion of barns') and used lay-preachers to pass on a simple message of sin and redemption. By 1850 about half the people who attended religious services attended Evangelical Nonconformist sects such as the Methodists, the Baptists, and the Congregationalists. But Evangelicalism was not restricted to the Nonconformists; there were also Evangelical groups in the Church of England. These pressed to make religion a more active commitment than it had often been in the early eighteenth century. At Cambridge University, the infuential Charles Simeon campaigned for a evangelical clerical profession. In London a group of similarly-minded individuals met at the Clapham house of the banker and Member of Parliament, Henry Thornton. The 'Clapham House Sect' included William Wilberforce, the son of a merchant and a member of Parliament for Yorkshire from 1784 until 1812.

By the middle of the nineteenth century Evangelicalism had become the dominant approach to religion. In some ways we could see this emphasis on moral choice as the spiritual reflection of a society which tended, in economic matters, to stress the role of the individual. The Evangelical ethos was particularly powerful in determining the nature and form that social reform was to take. Above all, it was responsible for the characteristically Victorian view that all social issues were also moral issues and more a matter for the individual rather than the State. The Evangelical view on reform was that it began from within the individual. Each person must make his or her own decision to reform and lead a better life. This view helped to set the outer boundary of State intervention. The State should never, by its actions, prevent the individual from being confronted with the important choices between sin and redemption. Evangelicalism set its face against what today we might refer to as the 'nanny State'. Thus, for example, a Poor Law which encouraged people to live on state benefit would only encourage individuals to make the 'wrong' moral choice and live on the parish without hard work. The role of the State was to protect the vulnerable and to create the appropriate moral environment within which individuals would be encouraged to make the 'right' moral choice.

Given this, it is not surprising that Evangelicals were prominent in those organisations that stressed the importance of moral education, like the Temperance movement, and the Lord's Day Observance Society, formed in 1831, which aimed to make Sunday a quiet and contemplative day that would set the moral tone for the rest of the week. Lord Ashley (who would later become the Earl of Shaftesbury) was its most prominent supporter. Evangelicals were also active in the establishment in 1824 of the Royal Society for the Prevention of Cruelty to Animals. The blood sports, which characterised most public holidays in the early nineteenth century, were seen as degrading to the spectators and leading to a general lowering of moral standards. As the Bishop of Lichfield put it, at the Society's annual meeting in 1866, 'It is not merely for animals that this society is instituted, but it is for ourselves.'

The Evangelical influence upon social legislation can best be seen as an attempt to use State intervention to reinforce the moral autonomy of the individual. Behind it lay a fairly patronising approach to the poor who were seen to be in need of a 'civilising' influence. This view received a real push from the events of the French Revolution, which was interpreted as showing what the poor might do when allowed to think for themselves politically. Later, the advent of Chartism (see chapter IV) would bring the 'Condition of England Question' to prominence in public debate. In the early years of the century, Wilberforce declared that his twin goals were the abolition of slavery (as a moral abomination) and the 'reformation of manners'. The latter he sought to achieve through the Society for the Suppression of Vice, formed in 1802. This took a wide brief, prosecuting those who breached blood sport legislation and also the publishers of radical texts such as Paine's *Rights of Man*. The main objective was the moral state of the labouring poor and the wit Sydney Smith re-named it the 'Society for the Suppression of Vice Among Those With Less Than £500 Per Year'.

6 THE POLITICAL DEVELOPMENT OF THE URBAN MIDDLE CLASS

Free market economics, Utilitarianism and Evangelicalism were all significant in shaping the values and actions of the reformers in this period. Alongside these influences, however, we need to recognise the increasingly important role of the urban middle class. In trying to exert an influence over their world and to define their position in society, this class played a crucial role in determining the nature of state intervention throughout the nineteenth century.

Whatever Bentham's aspirations towards a centralised administration, the traditional diffusion of authority to the localities, which had characterised British political life for many centuries, was maintained in the Victorian period. The Municipal Corporations Act of 1835 was described by one well-placed contemporary as 'a postscript to the Reform Act'. The Act of 1832 had admitted the middle class to the national franchise. This same group was given the authority to control the large towns by the Act of 1835. This abolished 178 boroughs with 'closed' or corrupt local corporations and replaced them with elected borough corporations (town councils). Large towns without corporations could now apply for incorporation. Over the next 20 years, 22 new town councils were established under this legislation, the first being Manchester and Birmingham in 1838. This created a system of elected town councils throughout the country, but the municipal franchise was as narrow as that for parliamentary elections and effectively excluded the working class in the towns. What it did create was a system of local government that was reasonably sensitive to the wishes of local ratepayers. This, however, did not always predispose it to an active role in the field of reform. The voters and officials of the new system were the new middle class, believers in the efficacy of the free market and careful in their expenditure of the ratepayers' money. Both of these characteristics militated against the adoption of large-scale municipal schemes for social reform in the first half of the century. The only reform which the new local authorities were obliged to undertake under the 1835 legislation was the establishment of a Watch Committee to supervise the policing of the area. Other than this, town councils tended to find arguments against schemes that involved a major municipal expenditure. As an example of this, the historian E P Hennock's detailed work on Birmingham and Leeds has stressed the importance of the self-styled 'Economy' parties of small businessmen in the internal politics of the Town Councils of the 1850s.

The development of local authorities threw the whole issue of centralised authority into high relief. When town councils claimed the right to control expenditure in their areas they were really advocating the adoption of local solutions to what were clearly national problems. For example, the issue of law and order was considered of paramount importance in the period. There was a widespread concern that crime rates were on the increase. The numbers of individuals committed to trial for indictable (serious) offences had risen from 4605 in 1805 to 24 303 in 1845. Even allowing for the increasing size of population this was an alarming apparent increase in crime. Chadwick advocated a Benthamite solution in the form of a national police force, that would be centrally controlled by the Home Office. The Metropolitan Police, established in 1829, seemed to be the first step towards this national force, but the move was ferociously resisted in the localities. A centralised police force was seen as the equivalent of a standing army with all the historic associations with despotism. Thomas Attwood voiced a commonly-held view when he described a national police force as 'a species of Bourbon tyranny'. As a result, the development of a police force in the nineteenth century took place in the context of control by local authorities with minimal centralisation. The incorporated boroughs were allowed to establish their own forces under the Municipal Corporations Act. This was extended to the rural areas by the *County Police Act of 1839* and was consolidated in 1856 by the *County and Borough Police Act* which made it compulsory for local authorities to establish local forces. Even with this devolution of power the debate in the local areas over whether or not to establish a local force was often heated. So, even though there was a clear consensus in the middle class that policing should be increased (and this view was partly prompted by the development of the Chartist movement after 1839), a debate still took place on the form that this force should take. As with so many reform initiatives, the recognition that 'a problem' existed did not automatically indicate that a solution had been found.

State intervention in this period can, therefore, be seen as a product of a very particular context of ideas, values, and pressure groups. The way this influenced the legislation and its application may be explored through a number of case studies.

7 Case Study I: The Factory Acts

From the time of their introduction the factories, with their appalling working conditions, attracted the attention of reformers. Pioneering legislation in the form of factory acts in 1802 and 1819 attempted, without success, to limit the working hours of children in the cotton mills. By the 1830s the issue of children's work in the factories, and the brutal treatment that they often endured, had become the focus of a reform movement. For the working people who organised and joined this movement the issue was central to their lives. As one operative from Yorkshire put it to a Select Committee in 1832, 'I would rather see all my children dead and buried, and myself along with them, than see them employed in a mill under the present system.' Yet the working-class objection to the factory was much broader than the campaign for child protection might suggest. Working people entered the factory reluctantly, preferring the greater control over their time that the domestic system of home working allowed. Factory hours were long, monotonous and prescribed by the employer, whereas in the home the work could proceed at the family's own pace. The factory symbolised the extent to which industrialisation was reducing the control that ordinary people had over their own lives. The ruthless exploitation of working-class children in the mills was simply the worst expression of this loss of control. From 1830 onwards, in South-East Lancashire and the West Riding of Yorkshire, the factory operatives formed Short Time Committees to agitate for a ten-hour day for all workers, both children and adults.

The issue attracted a range of support from across the social spectrum. Richard Oastler, the steward of a large landed estate outside Huddersfield, argued that the exploitation of small children in the factories was a standing indictment of industrialisation. The paternalism that had previously bound the landed classes and the labouring poor had been replaced by a relationship in which an employer's obligation towards his employees began and ended with the payment of a wage. Some sympathetic factory owners, like John Fielden, a cotton manufacturer and MP for Oldham, argued that a voluntary system of self-regulation would not work because of the intense competition of the market economy. State intervention into important aspects of factory organisation, Fielden argued, was the only way to enforce a uniform adherence to minimum standards. He had been deeply shocked to discover that in his own mill small children walked 20 miles in the course of a 12-hour shift.

In 1832 a Select Committee, chaired by the MP Michael Sadler, took evidence from the factory districts and recommended a Bill to limit the hours of work of all textile factory operatives to ten per day. Yet this recommendation was rejected as going too far down the road towards the State regulation of private enterprises. Instead, in 1833, a Royal Commission was appointed to investigate the matter, under the chairmanship of the Benthamite Edwin Chadwick. This resulted in the 1833 Factory Act and created sufficient reforming momentum to engender further investigation into this issue. By 1850 five major pieces of legislation had been passed:

(i) The Factory Act of 1833, often referred to as Althorp's Act, was a direct result of this inquiry and it proved to be an enormous disappointment to the Short Time Committees. The Act prohibited the employment of children under the age of nine. Children from nine to 12 were allowed to work a maximum of 12 hours a day and no more than 48 hours a week. Youths from 13 to 18 were restricted to a maximum of 12 hours a day and 69 hours a week. Provision was made for children from 9 to 11 to be given 2 hours of schooling a day.

(ii) 1842 Mines and Collieries Act. This followed a Royal Commission into mining conditions. The act prohibited women, girls and also boys under ten from working below ground.

(iii) 1844 Factory Act, known as Graham's Act. This lowered to eight the age at which children could start work. Women were included as a 'protected' group and their hours, and those of young persons from 13 to 18, were restricted to 12 hours per day. Children under 13 were reduced to a maximum of 3.5 hours per day and schooling was increased to 3 hours.

(iv) 1847 Factory Act, known as the Ten Hours Act, restricted the hours of labour for women and young persons to ten hours per day.

(v) 1850 Factory Act, specified the hours when the work of those covered by the 1847 legislation could take place. They were to work only between 6am and 6pm, with an hour's break for meals, and not after 2 pm on a Saturday.

These five pieces of legislation demonstrate many of the influences at work that were identified earlier. In the style recommended by Bentham, each was based on an extensive parliamentary investigation to identify the 'problem', either by Royal Commission or Select Committee. Similarly, following Benthamite lines, each piece of legislation involved the appointment of a centrally-organised inspectorate to ensure that the Acts were obeyed. Both of these elements were flawed in practice; Select Committees and Royal Commissions generally found what they set out to find, and the inspectors were so few in number (four for the whole United Kingdom under the 1833 Act) that the laws were easily avoided. Despite this, however, the notions of investigation and inspection had become, by 1850, an enduring and positive part of the process of social legisation.

It is easy to feel that conditions in the factories were so bad that any legislation was a step in the right direction. This should not blind us, however, to the recognition of the way in which this legislation was a product of the age. The Benthamite notion of 'rule and exception' is clearly applied. As a rule the State should not interfere in the contractual relationship between workers and employers; exceptionally it might have to. The exceptions were defined as those groups unable to agree a contract of employment as free agents in the labour market; in practice, this meant children and (from 1842) women. It had been the hope of Oastler and the working people who agitated through the Short Time Committees, that the restriction of children's hours would necessarily limit that of the adults they worked alongside. But employers avoided this by using teams of children in relays. Adult male labour remained unprotected by legislation until the end of the century. It was argued that adult men were able to agree whatever contract of employment they liked. In a free market economy it was vital that the State step back and allow individuals to pursue what they regarded as their own best interests.

We may also identify the Evangelical influence at work in this legislation, and the sense that social reform was moral reform. The factory and the mine were seen as promiscuous places where the morals of the young were corrupted. Hence, the linking of reform with education. In

1842 the Mine Commissioners were dismayed to find that women worked underground, cutting coal on a basis of a rough equality with their male counterparts, stripped to the waist and sweating in the heat. They considered this to be unfeminine and the legislation of 1842 and 1844 which declared that women should be protected at work was as much about defining 'acceptable' moral standards as it was about humanitarian intervention. After all, men continued to work underground in these conditions.

The case of the Factory and Mines Acts shows clearly that the influences on legislation, which were identified earlier, often acted to *limit* the extent of intervention. Much of the debate that took place at the time was concerned with identifying an acceptable minimum of State intervention. In 1833, for example, the economist J R McCulloch wrote warmly to the Evangelical reformer Lord Ashley, who was then campaigning in Parliament for a bill to protect factory children;

> I would not interfere between adults and masters; but it is absurd to contend that children have the power to judge for themselves in such a matter.

Here the free market economist and the Evangelical reformer could agree on the limits of intervention. Of course we can still consider the Factory Acts as eloquent testimony to the humanitarianism of people like Ashley. But it is worth remembering that these five Acts applied only to textile factories and mines. The legislation was not extended to factories in other industries until the Factories Acts (Extension) Acts of 1864 and 1867 (which defined a factory as a place employing more than 50 people). Nor were workshops covered by legislation until the Factory and Workshop Act of 1878. What this means is that most people who worked in Britain in the nineteenth century worked in unregulated working conditions, and consequently at great risk to their health and personal safety.

8 Case Study II: The New Poor Law

The Poor Law Amendment Act was introduced in 1834 to deal with the problem of poverty. It was felt that the number of the poor, and the cost to the ratepayer, was rising. Legislation passed in the years 1597–8, 1601 and 1662, had formed the framework of existing provision under what is generally referred to as the Old Poor Law. This had established a system based upon the parish as an administrative unit. The ratepayers in the 15 000 parishes in England and Wales enjoyed a good deal of autonomy over how the poor should be relieved in their area, though there were certain universal characteristics to the system. At the heart of the Old Poor Law was the belief that the poor should work hard. Vagrants were punished severely. Yet it was recognised that if individuals could not work, through no fault of their own, they were entitled to relief from the parish. This was mostly given in the form of money or food (out-relief), although Poor-houses were built to house the sick and the aged who were known as the impotent poor. In the late eighteenth century a large number of rural parishes registered an increase in levels of poverty, partly because the enclosure of land for intensive cultivation robbed the labouring poor of the small pieces of land through which they augmented their meagre wages. The response was the so-called Speenhamland System (named after the parish in Berkshire which fist adopted the scheme). By this, the wages of the poor were supplemented by the parish once they fell below a certain level. This level varied from parish to parish but was typically determined by the size of the labourer's family and the cost of bread in the area.

The Old Poor law was increasingly seen as an anachronism: a hangover from the protective or 'paternalistic' legislation of an earlier age, and out of touch with the needs of an industrial economy. Most importantly, it no longer fulfilled the role for which it was devised. The object of seventeenth-century paternalistic legislation had been to maintain social stability in pre-industrial societies by convincing the poor that the wealthy would fulfil their obligations towards them. The 'Swing' riots of 1830–1 suggested that the rural poor were no longer convinced. In the agricultural districts of the south and east of England, where the 'Swing' riots were most evident (*see page 71*), the cost of relieving poverty through the Speenhamland variant of the Old Poor Law had been soaring since the end of the Napoleonic Wars in 1815.

The task of creating a system of poor relief appropriate for the new age was given to the Royal Commission on the Poor Laws established in 1832. The Commission was chaired by Charles Blomfield, the Bishop of London. Among its 26 members were two particularly significant individuals: the Benthamite, Edwin Chadwick and the economist, Nassau Senior. The Commissioners visited nearly 3000 parishes, and sorted through questionnaires returned by over 1000 parishes, in order to identify the difficulties in the operation of the Old Poor Law. Despite this scientific approach, the investigations served simply to confirm the Commissioners' original belief: that the Old Poor Law was generating pauperism among the able-bodied poor. The system of parish supplements for wages was encouraging a reliance upon relief rather than leading the poor to actively seek work. The report of the Royal Commission, with its evidence collected from the regions, ran to some eight volumes.

The Report of the Royal Commission on the Poor Laws must rank as one of the most important social documents of the nineteenth century since it set the framework for the understanding of poverty, and the administration of its relief, until 1929. The analysis of poverty that it presented, combined an economic perspective with a moral position, in a way that we now look upon as characteristically 'Victorian' in nature.

For an industrial nation to prosper, the report argued, it must have a productive and diligent workforce. The encouragement given by the Old Poor Law for able-bodied workers to live off the parish undermined the development of the 'habits of industry' in the labouring poor. Employers lowered wages secure in the knowledge that the parish would make them up to subsistence level. The availability of artificially cheap labour in certain areas interfered with the operation of the free market. As the report put it 'a Macclesfield manufacturer may find himself undersold in consequence of the maladministration of the poor laws in Essex.' Well-meaning though they were, the parish overseers were upsetting the market mechanism by subsidising labour. The explanation for the apparent increase in pauperisation was essentially moral in nature; inefficient administration of the poor laws was leading the able-bodied labouring poor to make the wrong choice between supporting themselves and living on the parish. In order to lower the poor rates and encourage the able-bodied pauper back onto the labour market the report advised that a law be created which embraced three principles:

(i) the 'workhouse test'. The Commission advised that out-relief be abolished and that poor relief only be available from a system of efficiently run workhouses. The 'test' of an individual's need for assistance would be demonstrated by their willingness to enter a workhouse.

(ii) 'less eligibility'. It was argued that conditions in the workhouses should be less desirable (less eligible) than the worst conditions endured outside the workhouse by workers in employment. Thus nobody would opt for the workhouse if there was the chance of employment on the outside.

(iii) centralisation. The administration of poor relief would have to be uniform or, the argument went, paupers would simply congregate in parishes where relief was given on a lenient basis. Such uniformity could only be achieved by a highly centralised system.

The **Poor Law Amendment Act** of 1834 established a centralised system by making poor relief the ultimate responsibility of a Poor Law Commission based in London, with Chadwick as its Secretary. Parishes were to be grouped together in Poor Law Unions, each with a workhouse and a set of locally-elected Guardians of the Poor (replacing the parish overseers). Twelve Assistant Commissioners were to be appointed to co-ordinate the application of the law in the regions. This degree of centralisation was unprecedented in any area of administration and may be attributed to Chadwick's presence on the Royal Commission. The Act made no reference to the abolition of out-relief and its replacement with the 'workhouse test' nor to the principle of 'less eligibility' for the running of workhouses. Nevertheless, the new

Commissioners were to run the system by a series of directives from their headquarters in Somerset House, and this was to act as a way to reduce local initiative and produce a standardised approach to the dispensation of relief. Encouraged by this central authority, the new Poor Law Unions worked hard to apply both the workhouse test and 'less eligibility'.

Working people were outraged by the Poor Law Amendment Act. Its central concept of poverty as a self-inflicted wound was seen as an insult. In the workhouses which operated under the New Poor Law, less eligibility was achieved by a variety of psychological strategies, which were repugnant to the working community. Families were separated, paupers wore prison-style uniforms and were put to pointless labour, and silence was enforced at meal times. Mothers of illegitimate children were singled out for special treatment; for example, they might be prevented from worshipping with the other inmates. The Old Poor Law had forced the fathers of illegitimate children to support them, but the new law saw illegitimacy as the woman's fault. Under these provisions of 'less eligibility' the workhouse aimed to provide the minimum requirements for life (food, shelter, education) in a form which nobody would consciously choose unless they really had no alternative. Given the regime of the workhouses it was difficult to escape the popular conclusion that people were being punished for being poor.

In fact, people were very often poor for reasons other than having decided to live off the parish. The historian Mark Blaug argues that the parish supplement to wages was only extensively practised in 18 English rural parishes, and that the Report had exaggerated its impact on the system as a whole. In an immature industrial system poverty was caused by economic factors over which the poor had little control. When the trade cycle dipped, it tended to plunge the country into depression and no amount of labour mobility would produce jobs for the large numbers that were unemployed. Nor could this number be contained in the new Union workhouses. For these reasons the practice of giving out-relief continued throughout the nineteenth century. Reasearch on the application of the new law in East Anglia suggests that out-relief was in practice often less expensive than taking the paupers into the workhouse. Out-relief often survived for both practical and economic reasons. The new workhouses became the focus for widespread concern and this culminated in the Andover Workhouse scandal of 1845 when paupers, set to work on bone crushing to produce fertilizer, were said to be supplementing their poor diet by gnawing the gristle from the rancid animal bones. A Select Committee found that dietary levels at the Andover workhouse were below the levels set by the Commissioners, and blamed the Guardians for mismanagement. But it also recognised that the Guardians had simply been following the spirit of directions from the Poor Law Commissioners. Chadwick in particular, was censured for an unbending approach. Under a **Poor**

Law Act of 1847 the Poor Law Commission was replaced by a Poor Law Board under a President who would be a minister of the government (and thereby directly accountable to Parliament). This led to the dismissal of the widely-disliked Chadwick but the historian, Ursula Henriques, concludes that 'there is no indication that this direct ministerial responsibility made any substantial difference to the conduct of the Victorian Poor Law.'

The Poor Law Amendment Act legitimised a particular view of poverty and this proved to be resilient. Poverty was the result of individuals choosing not to work and this, it was felt, must be prevented at all costs since it threatened the social fabric. It soon became the norm to refer to the 'deserving' and the 'undeserving poor'. In practice, the 'undeserving' would be offered the workhouse whereas the 'deserving' might be given out-relief. But this typology involved a judgement on the poor according to middle-class values. In the years to come many Chartists and trade unionists would find themselves defined as the 'undeserving poor', demonstrating the usefulness of this category for exercising control over particular groups.

9 CASE STUDY III: THE PUBLIC HEALTH ACTS

The growth of the large towns in the first half of the nineteenth century (*see page 203*) created major problems for public health. Between 1800 and 1830, for example, the populations of Manchester, Liverpool, Birmingham, Leeds, and Glasgow doubled. This urban expansion took place without planning and was perhaps the most obvious example of the difficulties of basing a society on free market principles. The towns grew up as overcrowded and unhealthy, lacking the sewage systems, refuse disposal and fresh water supplies that we now see as fundamental to health. As the sanitary reformer Sir John Simon put it in 1853, the towns had expanded 'with scarcely more reference to the legitimate necessities of life than if they had clustered there by crystallisation.' As a result, mortality rates increased dramatically in the first half of the century, with a majority of deaths in the large towns being from infectious diseases. In a large city like Manchester well over half the children born in this period did not survive to the age of five. The appearance of cholera in Britain in 1831–2 and 1848–9 added weight to those who argued the importance of cleaning the towns. In 1849, 53 293 died of cholera, and the disease re-appeared in 1853 and 1865, again with devastating effects.

To some extent the scale of the problem can be seen to relate to the level of knowledge available. There was, for example, no agreement over the best way to engineer an effective sewage system, nor was it appreciated until 1848, through John Snow's research in London and that of William Budd in Bristol, that cholera was a waterborne rather than an airborne disease. But despite the accumulation of scientific knowledge, death rates did not drop until the last quarter of the century. The existence of ignorance does not fully explain the difficulties which contemporaries had in dealing effectively with the issue of public health. As Henriques suggests, the reasons were far more complex and relate directly to the social attitudes of the day;

> 'Apathy, the flight of the wealthy from the town centres, the collapse of communal responsibility and communal administration, rather than knowledge, were responsible for the spreading squalor. Overcrowding, filth and disease stole upon the nation like a thief in the night.'
>
> (*Before the Welfare State*, Longman 1979, p 120)

1 *In the light of the structure of attitudes outlined in section 3 of this chapter and in this extract, what do you think were the main difficulties in dealing effectively with the health of towns at this time?*
2 *What do you think Henriques means by the phrase 'the collapse of communal responsibility' in the above passage?*

In a number of the large towns Improvement Boards, sometimes called Street Commissioners, were established to create local improvements. Between 1800 and 1845 nearly 400 local improvement acts were passed by Parliament but their impact on the urban problem was very limited since they tended to focus only on those areas where the wealthier inhabitants lived. The Municipal Corporations Act of 1835 (*see page 49*) recognised that the towns needed an appropriate structure of local authorities to deal with their problems. But public health inevitably required a good deal of money to be spent, since sewage schemes and water systems were large and expensive items. The restricted local franchise meant that the ratepayers acted with a close eye on their pockets. This created a tension between the sanitary reformers and the administrative agencies upon which reform relied.

At the Poor Law office, Edwin Chadwick identified a link between disease and poverty when the Poor Law Commissioners made their fourth annual report in 1838. As a result, when the 1837 Civil Registration Act, which created the office of Registrar-General with responsibility for registering births, deaths and arriages, was passing through Parliament, an amendment was made to the effect that the *cause* of death should be recorded. This would help to create national data on, what Chadwick considered to be, preventable disease. In 1842 he published his *Report on the Sanitary Conditions of the Labouring Population of Great Britain*. This survey of conditions in the large towns identified the cause of much disease as the result of bad drainage, poor ventilation, and an impure water supply. As things stood there was no effective way of removing the rotting organic matter which the report saw as the root cause of infectious diseases (which at that stage were seen to spread through atmospheric impurities). Chadwick advocated the creation of a network of sewers built to the design of the London engineer John Roe. The pipes of these sewers would be small, egg shaped in cross section and made of strong glazed earthenware. Houses could be drained and streets cleaned using the same set of sewers stretching like a system of arteries underneath the streets (arterial drainage). Chadwick also attacked the previous attempts to deal with the problem (by organisations like the London Commissioners of Sewers) as inefficient and, above all, expensive. In true Benthamite style Chadwick recommended the creation of a strong central authority, rather like the Poor Law Commissioners, to deal with the problem nationwide.

As a result of Chadwick's *Report* of 1842, Peel's government established the Royal Commission on Health of Towns under R A Slaney, the Liberal MP for Shrewsbury. Slaney's approach to government intervention embraced many of the elements identified in sections 3 to 5 of this chapter. A gentleman from a landed family, he shared the view of the Evangelical, Lord Ashley, for whom the cities represented a corrupting influence on Christian morality. Although he also accepted the optimism of those who saw the potential benefits of industrialisation, he nevertheless feared the social conflict which, in his view, was engendered by the failure to deal with social problems. A great supporter of the New Poor Law, he wanted public administration rationalised so that it both supported the economy and drew the classes together. This approach gained wide support through the Health of Towns Association, formed in 1844, of which Ashley was a leading member. Sanitary reform presented an opportunity, in Ashley's words, 'to Christianise' the working population.

The report of Slaney's Royal Commission on the Health of Towns confirmed Chadwick's earlier findings on the chaotic nature of the existing administrative machinery for dealing with public health. Nevertheless, there was considerable opposition to the Whig Bill, sponsored in Parliament in 1848 by Lord Morpeth, to establish a central Board of Health. The opposition came particularly from MPs representing urban areas, who were concerned with the threat which a central authority would pose to control of expenditure by the localities, and also from Tory MPs who feared the levying of rates on rural areas to pay for sanitary reform in the towns. From the start, the public health movement found itself opposed by ratepayers and local authorities who objected to control by central government. The reformers attempted to counter this argument by stressing the economic case for sanitary reform. They said that a healthy workforce would be more productive than one prone to sickness; healthy workers would more regularly employed and thus have less recourse to poor relief and charity or to crime. As Slaney explained to the House of Commons in 1848 when defending Morpeth's bill, 'Instead of causing additional expense, it would effect a considerable saving–it would be a measure of economy . . . It would diminish the poor rates, and it would diminish crime, inasmuch as it would remove many of the causes of crime.'

The nature of the final form of the Public Health Act of 1848 reflected this parliamentary struggle. It established a General Board of Health, with three members responsible to Parliament. These were, initially, Lord Morpeth, Edwin Chadwick and Lord Ashley. The General Board was empowered to establish local boards of health following either a petition from at least one-tenth of the local ratepayers or where the death rate exceeded the high figure of 23 per 1000 of the population. In corporate towns the local board of health would be the town council and, where a town was not incorporated, the Board was to be directly elected by ratepayers. These Boards of Health were given very wide powers over issues relating to public health. They were to be responsible for the sewage, drainage and water supply in their areas. They were given the task of approving plans for new roads and for the sanitation of new houses. They could buy up property in areas that needed to be cleared and could provide amenities like parks, public conveniences, and cemeteries.

The 1848 Public Health Act signified a major shift towards central government intervention in an area previously considered outside its jurisdiction. Yet the interventionist element was seriously flawed in the practical operation of the Act. The General Board of Health exercised only the loosest control over the local boards of health. This was an example of 'permissive legislation' in that, once the local boards had been established, the General Board of Health could not force them to undertake any course of action. Rather its role was simply to advise and provide information, through a number of inspectors. Many local authorities, in receipt of advice and information, chose not to be very active.

By 1853, 182 towns had established local boards of health. Of these 71 had plans for sewage and water supply systems but only 13 had put their plans into effect. In both Leeds and Birmingham, for example, the dominance of an 'Economy' group of shopkeepers and small businessmen on the town council, who were keen to minimise local expenditure, prevented any substantial local reform that might raise local rates. The 1848 Public Health Act had excluded London from its provisions since the capital had its own sanitary authority in the form of the Metropolitan Commission of Sewers, established by a separate act in 1848. Chadwick was determined that the power of the Metropolitan Commission should be absorbed under the authority of the General Board. Much of the General Board's time and energy was spent in attempting, unsuccessfully, to bring this about in the face of stiff opposition led by Joshua Toulmin Smith, chairman of one of the sanitary committees in the City of London. Toulmin Smith established the Anti-Centralisation Union which led the resistance to the General Board of Health. In 1853 the opponents of the General Board managed to engineer the resignations of Chadwick and Shaftesbury, and the Board itself was disbanded in 1858. The same year saw the passing of a Public Health Act which empowered local authorities to establish their own sanitary bodies that would be free from central control.

This fractious in-fighting on the application of the 1848 Public Health Act demonstrates two of the points about the general context of reform made in sections 3–6 of this chapter. First, that in this period there were strong social forces working *against* reform, particularly in the form of cost-conscious local authorities, anxious to retain their local autonomy in the face of what they saw as growing centralisation. Even the medical journal, *The Lancet*, celebrated the demise of the Central Board of Health, and saw this as a national reaction against administration from a central authority. 'The truth is', it asserted in 1858, 'we do not like paternal governments'. Secondly, the difficulties faced by sanitary reformers suggests that reform was not simply a matter of using current knowledge to solve a particular problem. By the 1850s developments in the applied science of sanitary engineering had been such that, from a technical point of view, the problems could have been addressed, particularly by the creation of sewage systems on an arterial principle. Also, by 1850, some important principles of administration had been established. The subsequent legislation, (important acts related to public health were passed in 1866, 1871, 1872 and 1875), gradually embraced what was eventually accepted as the essential principle of centralised inspection and management. As the historian Oliver MacDonagh puts it: 'The supreme irony was that the public health act of 1848 failed at precisely the moment when the essential correctness of its main principles was being established.' Yet despite the availability of both the knowledge and the administrative competence to deal with public health, mortality rates remained high. Nor were they noticeably reduced until the last quarter of the century. The death rate of 21.4 per 1000 of the population, recorded by the Office of the Registrar-General in the period 1841–5, had risen slightly to 22.0 per 1000 in 1871–5 and it had not dropped appreciably in the intervening years. MacDonagh argues that 1875 marked the turning point for mortality, with death rates down to 15.4 per 1000 by the first decade of the twentieth century. There were some striking successes, particularly in the cases of some contagious diseases; in 1869 there were 4281 deaths from typhus, by 1885 the number had dropped to 318. Yet, on the whole, Victorian towns remained unhealthy places and the benefits of state intervention to improve the health of the people would not be widely felt until the twentieth century. The historian, George Rosen, sums up the position;

> Most municipalities throughout the Victorian period never came within sight of overtaking problems of community hygiene and health. Nevertheless, enough positive change did take place to yield ascertainable benefits.

10 Conclusion: The Three Rs: Riots, Rates and Rotting Organic Matter

The three case studies suggest the complexity of determining the motivation for, and the nature of, state intervention in the early nineteenth century. Certainly, the two commonest explanations identified in the introduction to this chapter, which see social reform as either flourishing robustly through the growth of humanitarianism or growing feebly as a result of the development of the free market, are both inadequate, in themselves, to the task of full explanation. What is clear is that reform was produced by a variety of factors including the aspiration for 'efficient' government, the need to maintain a productive workforce and the concern that industrialisation should not produce instability by threatening the moral fibre of the nation. These, generally complementary, considerations produced a contemporary debate that was bounded by the question of how authority should be balanced, in practice, between the centre and the localities. Tied into the debate, as a matter of both principle and pragmatic concern, was the issue of the cost of all of this reform to those who had to pay the bill. This produced a context for reform that was by turns enabling and discouraging, as the uneven pattern of reform in each of the case studies demonstrates.

In reviewing this context for reform it is always worth bearing in mind that the 'Condition of England Question', as it was called at the time, was primarily a concern of the middle and upper classes of the day. For the working community, as chapter IV on Chartism demonstrates, both the diagnosis of the ills of industrial society and the prescribed remedy were relatively straightforward. Britain had an undemocratic political system and once this was addressed by extending the vote to working men Parliament could create a better society. The social reformers of the early nineteenth century were attempting to deal with specific problems in ways that consciously avoided such a universal solution. Nevertheless, this did mean that all this social reform activity took place against a backdrop of a working community which was articulating its own alternative programme of reform. As a result, we can identify a clear tension operating in the frame of reference of the middle and upper classes. On the one hand were the difficulties of achieving solutions to huge social problems and, on the other hand, was the potential cost of not addressing these issues. Fear of the consequences of not finding a solution to the 'Condition of England Question', was a recurrent element in the debate over social reform. Whatever benefits industrialisation promised, it also carried the immediate threat of disease (which was not necessarily a respecter of the social class of its victims), and the long-term potential for creating a labouring poor who could not be controlled. It would perhaps be too fanciful to argue that reform, in the mind of the governing classes, was dominated by the 'Three Rs' of 'Riots, Rates and Rotting organic matter'. But it is a reminder that social reform was driven by an association of different elements and that the measures adopted were the outcome of contemporary debate around these recurring themes.

11 BIBLIOGRAPHY

U Henriques *Before the Welfare State* (Longman, 1979), provides an excellent insight to reform in a range of areas, including those presented as case studies in this chapter. Henriques is particularly good at identifying the growth of administration through the often competing demands of central and local government.
O MacDonagh *Early Victorian Government 1830–1870* (Weidenfeld and Nicolson, 1977). This book covers much the same ground as Henriques above, and can be seen as an extended development of the author's long-standing 'intolerability' hypothesis (that reform comes about when circumstances become 'intolerable'). Thus, it stresses the growth of humanitarianism, knowledge, and efficient forms of administration in this period.
A J Taylor *Laissez-faire and State Intervention in the Nineteenth Century* (Macmillan, 1972), summarises the debate that has taken place between historians over this issue.
A Wohl *Endangered Lives. Public Health in Victorian Britain* (Dent, 1983) this is probably the most authoritative book, to date, on the public health issue in the nineteenth century. Wohl is particularly adept at exploring the attitudes and values that lay behind reform initiatives.
A Digby *Pauper Palaces* (Routledge and Kegan Paul, 1978); a good case study of the implementation of the New Poor Law in one area (East Anglia).
A Digby *The Poor Law in Nineteenth-Century England and Wales* (Historical Association, 1982). This short pamphlet gives a good overview of the reform of the Poor Law and the nature of its application.

12 DISCUSSION POINTS AND ESSAY QUESTIONS

A

1 Why did the issue of social reform arise in the 1830s and the 1840s?
2 Why were reformers so often concerned with morality?
3 How far were the reforms detailed in the chapter the result of growing humanitarianism?
4 Was this a period of '*laissez-faire*'?
5 Who was protected by the factory (and mines) acts and why were some groups not protected?

6 Why was the Old Poor Law reformed?

7 Why were the towns and cities a threat to public health?

13 Essay Writing Exercises

Essay topics in this area tend to fall into two categories. These are dealt with, in turn, below and an exercise is suggested to help you to deal with each sort of question.

Essay category one: famous figures

These are essay topics which require you to judge the significance of a particular group or individual in the achievement of reform. For example:

1 Examine the contribution of the Benthamites to the reforms of the 1830s.

2 Discuss the relationship between religion and social reform in the period 1830–50.

3 Assess the importance of one of the following for social reform in the nineteenth century: Edwin Chadwick, Lord Shaftesbury, William Wilberforce.

Exercise A: Creation of a detail bank

In order to respond fully to this type of question you will need to be able to provide basic details on the individuals or groups named in the title: who were they? what were their underlying principles? what specific reforms were they associated with? In fact, because of their involvement in a range of reform movements, biographical notes on Chadwick, Shaftesbury, and Wilberforce will be useful in answering almost any question on nineteenth-century social reform (including those in category two below). Biographical detail on all three people may be found in your local library in standard encyclopaedias or, better still, the *Dictionary of National Biography* for material on Shaftesbury and Wilberforce. *DNB* is a semi-official 'Who's Who' of the past. Using the detail in the chapter as a basis upon which to build your bank of detail, draw up *brief* notes on the lives, and involvement in reform, of these three characters. Any judgements that you make on the influence of these characters will have to incorporate this kind of detail.

Useful back-up reading for this exercise is J R Dinwiddy, *Bentham* (Oxford University Press, 1989), S E Finer, *The Life and Times of Edwin Chadwick* (Methuen, 1952), G Battiscombe, *Shaftesbury* (Purnell, 1974), E Marshall Howse, *Saints in Politics. The Clapham Sect and the Growth of Freedom* (Allen and Unwin, 1973).

If you use the *Dictionary of National Biography* to help you to create this detail bank you might be interested to contemplate this, more general, yet rather intriguing question.

Why do all these social reformers appear in the *DNB* whilst none of the Chartists named in chapter IV appear in this publication?

	Who was he? (With dates)	Was he associated with any particular reform group(s) or organisation(s)? (With dates)	Was he involved in supporting/ achieving any specific reforms? (With dates)	Did he have any administrative responsibility? (With dates)	Can you quote any indicative statements by this person – or by others about him? (Give examples)
Lord Shaftesbury					
Edwin Chadwick					
William Wilberforce					

Leading reformers: detail bank

Essay category 2: the difficulties of reform

The second sort of essay question is one which asks you to explain the reasons for the slow pace of reform. For example:

1 Why were governments so reluctant to tackle the problems of public health in the first half of the nineteenth century, and what were the weaknesses of the 1848 Public Health Act?
2 Was ignorance or indifference the greater obstacle to the improvement of public health in England in the years 1830–50?
3 Why were the efforts of the factory reformers in the years to 1850 so limited in their success?
4 How far would you agree that the Poor Law Amendment Act was 'well intentioned but hopelessly impracticable'?

Exercise B: State intervention as a car

Plan a response to the following essay topic:

Account for the increasing, but still limited, extent of state intervention in social questions in the period from 1830–50.

Having read this chapter you are well placed to answer this question. There are, of course, many different ways to respond to this statement. Nevertheless, there is one golden rule that must be adhered to, whatever your response: your general statements on reasons for intervention, or its lack, *must* be supported by particular examples that illustrate your points. To move between the general and the particular is a very important skill for the historian to develop, and it is much more difficult than it sounds. There are various devices that can legitimately be used to achieve the general-particular balance. There is, for example, the self-disciplining code you can adopt that no general statement will be made unless it can be illustrated in some way. Thus you need to ask of your material not only, 'What are my conclusions?' but also, 'What pieces of legislation/events/people illustrate clearly these conclusions?' Another device, which historians frequently use, is the case study by which general points are explored via extended analysis of one area of study. In this chapter the broad constraints on reform were explained at the start and then developed by looking specifically at factory legislation, the Poor Law, and public health.

The image of state intervention as a car might be helpful here. A number of influences can be seen as pushing on the accelerator, whilst others are furiously applying the brake. There is no doubt that the vehicle is moving forward, but its motion is extremely jerky. Your task is, in the light of what you have read, to identify the feet on the two pedals and to illustrate this by reference to particular reforms. Under 'accelerator' list the positive influences encouraging the growth of

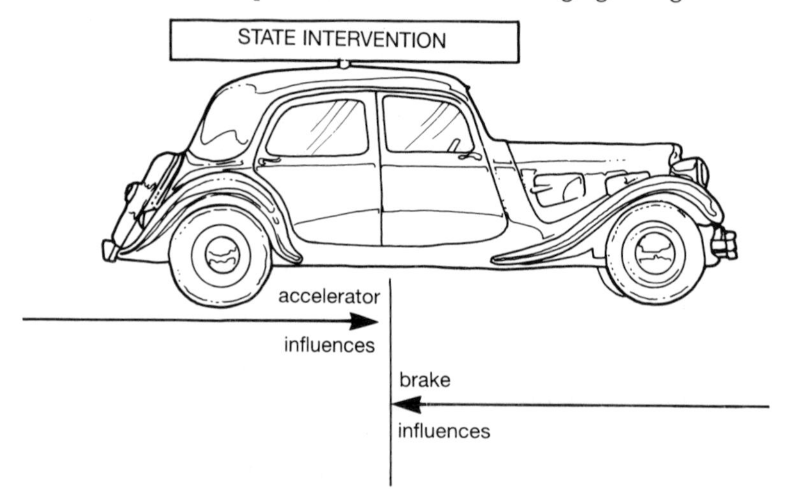

State intervention as a car

state intervention (with examples of reforms that grew from these influences). Under 'brake' list the influences that acted to limit the extent of state intervention (with examples).

14 DOCUMENTARY EXERCISE – THE POOR LAW REPORT OF 1834

Re-read the section of the chapter on the reform of the Poor Law, then read carefully the following four extracts from the report of 1834, and answer the questions that follow.

> a) From the preceding evidence it will be seen how zealous must be the agency, and how intense the vigilance, to prevent fraudulent claims crowding in under such a system of relief. But it would require still greater vigilance to prevent the bona fide claimants degenerating into impostors; and it is an
>
> aphorism amongst the active parish officers that 'cases which are good today are bad tomorrow, unless they are incessantly watched'. A person obtains relief on the ground of sickness; when he has become capable of returning to moderate work, he is tempted, by the enjoyment of subsistence without labour, to conceal his convalescence, and fraudulently extend the period of relief. When it really depends upon the receivers whether the relief shall cease with its occasion, it is too much to expect of their virtue that they shall, in any considerable number of instances, voluntarily forego the pension.

> b) What motive has the man who is to receive 10s. every Saturday, not because 10s. is the value of his week's labour, but because his family consists of five persons, who knows that his income will be increased by nothing but by an increase of his family, and diminished by nothing but by a diminution of his family, that it has no reference to his skill, his honesty, or his diligence–what motive has he to acquire or to preserve any of these merits? Unhappily, the evidence shows not only that these virtues are rapidly wearing out, but that their place is assumed by the opposite vices; and that the very labourers among whom the farmer has to live, on whose merits as workmen and on whose affection as friends he ought to depend, are becoming not merely idle and ignorant and dishonest, but positively hostile; not merely unfit for his service and indifferent to his welfare, but actually desirous to injure him.

> c) In abolishing punishment, we equally abolish reward. Under the operation of the scale system–the system which directs the

overseers to *regulate* the incomes of the labourers according to their families–idleness, improvidence, or extravagance occasion no loss, and consequently diligence and economy can afford no gain. But to say merely that these virtues afford no gain, is an inadequate expression: they are often the causes of absolute loss. We have seen that in many places the income derived from the parish for easy or nominal work, or, as it is most significantly termed, 'in lieu of labour', actually exceeds that of the independent labourer; and even in those cases in which the relief-money only equals, or nearly approaches, the average rate of wages, it is often better worth having, as the pauper requires less expensive diet and clothing than the hard-working man.

d) *Effects on labourers actually relieved*
But though the injustice perpetrated on the man who struggles, as far as he can struggle, against the oppression of the system, who refuses, as far as he can refuse, to be its accomplice, is at first sight the most revolting, the severest sufferers are those that have become callous to their own degradation, who value parish support as their privilege, and demand it as their right, and complain only that it is limited in amount, or that some sort of labour or confinement is exacted in return. No man's principles can be corrupted without injury to society in general; but the person most injured is the person whose principles have been corrupted. The constant war which the pauper has to wage with all who employ or pay him, is destructive to his honesty and his temper; as his subsistence does not depend on his exertions, he loses all that sweetens labour, its association with reward, and gets through his work, such as it is, with the reluctance of a slave.

Extracts from the Poor Law Report of 1834

(i) *Explain what is meant by the term 'relief' as it appears in these extracts.*

(ii) *What is meant by the following:*

'In abolishing punishment we equally abolish reward' (extract c)?

'No man's principles can be corrupted without injury to society in general.' (extract d)?

(iii) *In the view of the Commissioners, how was the Old Poor Law encouraging pauperisation within the working community?*

(iv) *Why, in their view, was this a problem?*

(v) *Why might working people object to this analysis of how paupers are produced?*

IV

THE CHARTIST EXPERIENCE

—

1 INTRODUCTION

Chartism was a movement for Parliamentary reform which ran from 1838 to 1858. During the first ten years of its existence it involved hundreds of thousands of working people, in districts throughout the country. The Chartists' main concern was with agitating for Parliament to accept the 'People's Charter' with its celebrated 'six points':

- *universal manhood suffrage*–that all men over the age of 21 be allowed to vote
- *vote by secret ballot*–so that votes could be cast without fear of pressure from landlords or employers
- *annual Parliaments*–general elections to take place every year instead of every seven years as established under the Septennial Act of 1716
- *equal electoral districts*–constituencies should contain roughly equal numbers of electors
- *abolition of the property qualification for MPs*–at that time a Member of Parliament had to own a certain amount of property
- *payment for members of Parliament*–until 1911 MPs received no salary; an MP had to be a man of independent means or else be sponsored by a patron or party.

Implementation of the first two of these points, it was anticipated, would create a mass-based democracy where voting would be free of the 'influence' which was such an endemic part of the existing system. The idea behind annual parliaments was the development of real and regular accountability of the representatives to the represented. The last three points all signalled a determination on the part of the Chartists to facilitate working-class participation in politics at all levels, not simply as voters but also as members of the House of Commons and of the government. Thus, Chartism contained within it a vision of a political system that was radically different from that which currently existed under the provisions of the Reform Act of 1832. It is hardly surprising, therefore, that when the Chartists made their demands for change, in the form of a petition to Parliament submitted on three separate occasions (in 1839, 1842 and 1848), they failed to persuade the House of Commons to accept the six points.

This failure is at the root of a good deal of the controversy that has always surrounded the movement. Many historians have argued, as many contemporaries did, that the working class in 1839 was not yet 'ready' for full citizenship since its members were uneducated and, by implication, politically immature. From this viewpoint Chartism can be seen as a fragmented movement fired by the hunger of economic depression, given to irrational outbursts of violence, and led by malcontents from the middle classes. It was essentially the politics of hunger on a massive scale. With the movement seen in this light, its failure is seen as confirming the premature nature of the Chartist claims; that they wanted the vote before they were able to use it responsibly. The Chartists wanted too much too soon.

Alternatively, Chartism can be seen as the reflection of a politically-aware working community operating within a well-defined tradition of political activity, and as such essentially rational in its approach. From this point of view, reasons for its failure must be sought outside the movement, in the attitudes of the government and the middle class of the day. To put this another way, Chartism did not fail because the working community was not yet 'ready' for the vote, but rather because they were all too 'ready' in the sense that their aspiration to run the country generated real alarm in the ranks of those currently holding political power. As we will see when we return to the issue of interpretation in section 12, historians tend to be polarised over their explanations of Chartism and its failure to achieve its aims. In order to understand this polarity it is important to reconstruct the movement as it was seen and experienced by the Chartists themselves, as well as taking account of how it looked to others at the time.

Chartism has been described by the historian, Dorothy Thompson, as an 'umbrella movement' which gathered under its shelter a series of smaller movements that had emerged in the 1830s. To understand this evocative image it is important to identify the way Chartism drew upon the experience of the decade that preceded it. The origins and the essential nature of the movement may be sought in three areas:

(i) working-class disillusionment with the Reform Act and its aftermath
(ii) the alternative strategies devised by working-class radicals in the wake of what they saw as the real failure of the political initiative in 1832
(iii) a series of specific issues, notably trade union rights, the failure of the Ten Hours movement, the application of the Poor Law in the North

and the impact of yet another economic depression, which all came together in 1838 to create the immediate circumstances for the emergence of a mass-based movement with very broad political aims.

2 After the Reform Act

The Reform Act of 1832 had engendered extensive support from working people and its passing was greeted with acclaim. However, the sense of euphoria was short-lived. For all the changes the reformed House of Commons looked remarkably like the unreformed House and acted in depressingly familiar ways. Most of the achievements of the 'reforming Whigs' over the next few years were seen to confirm the suspicion that the working community could expect little from the new arrangement, and any suggestion that the Reform Act was simply the first step towards a more democratic society was swiftly dispelled. Notice of this had been given even before the Act was passed.

A *The Swing riots*

In August 1830 a series of riots and disorders began among agricultural labourers in Kent and spread westwards through the countryside with remarkable rapidity. Over the next year the south of the country saw nearly 1400 recorded incidents in what came to be known as the 'Swing' riots after the mythical 'Captain Swing' whom the rioters claimed to follow. Twenty counties from Kent to Wiltshire and north into Lincolnshire reported the activities of the 'Swing' rioters. In fact there was little co-ordination between areas and certainly no central leader. Rather, these were all rural areas hit by the changes in farming associated with the agricultural revolution, responding in similar ways to their situation, encouraged by the actions of labourers in adjacent areas. The corn growing counties of the south saw declining levels of wages in the post-war years and the difficulties for labourers were compounded by the seasonality of their work. The demand for labour in these areas tended to be high in the harvest time of the summer months but low in the autumn and the winter. The specific object of attack by 'Swing' varied from one part of the south to another. Sometimes the new steam threshing machines, which were seen as taking winter employment from the labourer, were destroyed. In other cases the opportunity was taken to get back at the Overseers of the Poor, who were seen to be failing to provide the relief needed by the labouring community. Sometimes the riots involved groups of several hundred; in other cases the firing of hayricks, for instance, was obviously the action of individuals with a grievance against a particular farmer.

The Whigs, in power after the 1830 general election, responded as might have been expected of a group of landowners confronted by labourers refusing to accept their lot humbly. Over 2000 arrests were made. Magistrates were warned not to be lenient even where their personal knowledge of the rioters' circumstances might lead them in that direction. The government set up Special Commissions to try the rioters and in 1831, as the Reform Bill threaded its way through Parliament, 19 rioters were executed and over 1000 either transported or imprisoned. To many observers, including the radical William Cobbett (who was himself unsuccessfully prosecuted for inciting the riots), the ferocity of this backlash suggested that the Whigs would be unlikely to sympathise with the working-class point of view on other issues once the Reform Act had been passed.

B *Actions of the reformed parliament*

The years following 1832 seemed to confirm this point. Administrative historians may celebrate the reforms of the Whig ministries of the 1830s as breaking important new ground in terms of the role of government, but to the labouring population they appeared as an attack on a way of life. The Factory Act of 1833 was a huge disappointment to the working-class factory reformers who campaigned for legal restrictions on the number of hours worked by adults in the textile mills of Lancashire and Yorkshire. The same year saw the passing of the Irish Coercion Act which greatly extended the government's arbitrary power in Ireland. Radical groups in mainland Britain saw this as a rehearsal for a similar move closer to home in the near future. The Poor Law Amendment Act of 1834 was seen to withdraw the 'right' of the poor to outdoor relief. In the same year six farm labourers from Tolpuddle in Dorset were transported for seven years for their attempt to organise themselves as part of a trade union. The case of the 'Tolpuddle Martyrs', as they rapidly became known, clearly signalled the government's determination to prevent the early development of trade union organisation. The Municipal Corporations Act of 1835 was undoubtedly a major piece of legislation. As we saw in chapter III, it introduced local government in the form with which we are familiar today. But to the working community this was simply the extension of a restricted national franchise to the localities. The Reform Act ensured that working people could not participate in national government. The narrow franchise by which town councils would now be elected under the 1835 legislation, ensured that they were similarly excluded from local government. In addition, the urban police forces established by town councils after 1835, were seen as an intrusive element by the working community. In the towns of Lancashire the police forces established in the 1830s were referred to by local workers as the 'plague of blue locusts'.

3 NEW STRATEGIES FOR THE WORKING COMMUNITY

A *The Owenite co-operative movement*

The failure of the Reform Act to bear fruit for the working community led many radicals to seek alternatives to political solutions to improve their situation. Many turned to the co-operative organisations sponsored by Robert Owen. From 1799 until 1829 Owen ran a cotton mill in New Lanark, Scotland. Here he pioneered new techniques of management by persuading his workers to increase production by incentives and involvement rather than threats and punishment. He subscribed to the notion of the 'perfectability of man'. An early socialist, he believed that 'a man's character is is formed *for* him not *by* him'. From this point of view the environment in which people existed determined the kind of people that they were. The problem with industrial society, he argued, was its competitive nature. How much better it would be to base a society on the same principle of co-operation that he had established among his workers at New Lanark.

To this end, between 1821 and 1843 he established six self-sufficient communities in Britain (and one in the USA) based upon the principles of co-operation. Here working people were to be located on the land in communities where they could grow their own food and produce their own goods, sharing their resources and providing their own education and culture. Although none of these communities was very successful they did at least draw attention to what was, from a working-class point of view, one of the paradoxes of industrialisation: that is, despite producing the wealth of the new society by their daily labour, the workers saw only a small fraction of it return to them in the form of wages. Owen, along with a number of other thinkers at the time, argued that 'labour is the source of all wealth'. The Owenite schemes proposed practical ways that this wealth could be returned to its creators. Co-operative societies (and 500 were in existence by 1832) established retail shops where working people could buy unadulterated foodstuffs, with profits conserved in a separate fund devoted to settling members on Owenite communities. A more innovative scheme in 1832 floated the establishment of Equitable Labour Exchanges where the goods which working people produced could be exchanged. These planned to use their own currency based, not on a gold standard, but on the hours of labour taken to produce the goods to be exchanged.

None of these schemes ever met with much success. Only two labour exchanges were ever opened, (in London and Birmingham) and these rapidly failed. Yet, it is noteworthy that such ideas flourished briefly in the wake of the Reform Act. Politically isolated by the Act, many in the working community reacted positively to the Owenite insistence on the importance of labour to production and wealth creation. Many, like William Lovett, who would later become Chartists, were active in Owenite organisations, and the slogan 'Labour is the source of all Wealth' often appeared on banners at Chartist rallies.

B *Trade unions*

Disappointment with the fruits of the Reform Act also led working people back to the familiar organisation of the trade union as a way of improving their position. With the repeal of the Combination Acts in 1824 it was no longer illegal for workers to band together 'in restraint of trade' in order to gain better conditions for themselves. Many organisations that were really trades unions registered themselves as Friendly Societies during the period of the Combination Acts. For example, in 1810, the Loyal Albion Lodge of Button Burnishers had been set up in Birmingham; 'We had a sick and burial club, our only legal hold in those days', a member later recalled, 'but our principal object was to keep up wages'. Similarly many of the older artisan trades like the shoemakers, the printers and the tailors, had well-established national networks and tramping routes whereby their unemployed members could 'go on the tramp' to other areas in search of work with the trade providing lodgings at houses of call. By 1824 it had become a common belief in government that the Combination Acts made the control of unions more difficult for the authorities by pushing union organisation underground and encouraging a tradition of secrecy. With the repeal of the Combination Acts workplace organisations flourished in most trades. It is often difficult to refer to these organisations as trade unions since they were often such temporary and *ad hoc* affairs. Generally, they were made up of small groups of workers in particular towns and districts. Often the groups had little formal organisation, but were simply drawn together by a particular grievance or issue. Once the point had been won the combination would dissolve itself. The historian Richard Price, looking at the organisations of building workers, has argued that before 1850 it was more important among workers that they were 'in union' (with one another) than that they were 'in *the* union'.

This kind of activity was also encouraged by the improvement in trade between 1833 and 1835 and the accompanying demand for labour. There were a number of small-scale strikes throughout the country in 1833 and 1834. More alarmingly for the government, in the wake of the Reform Act, a relatively new kind of trade organisation began to emerge in the form of general unions. These attempted to break away from the traditional forms of combination, based on one trade in one locality. The general unions aimed to unite workers from a number of trades in a cohesive and permanent form of organisation. The way had been shown by the leader of the Manchester cotton spinners, John Doherty, who formed the National Association for the Protection of Labour (NAPL) in 1829. This ran until 1832, had its own newspaper, *The Voice of the People* and accumulated between 60 000 and 80 000 members in its short life. Drawing inspiration from this example, Robert Owen's supporters persuaded him late in 1833 that the Owenite aims could best be achieved by the creation of a general union of all workers. Owen, as a one-time employer himself, had real reservations about trade unions but he was heartened by the belief that his union, the Grand National Consolidated Trades Union (GNCTU), would operate by persuasion rather than direct action and would be open to all, even employers if they wished to join.

The GNCTU, launched in February 1834, probably never attracted a membership in excess of 16 000. It did, however, draw fire from the Whig government, alarmed at the trend towards independent organisations of workers as a class which the GNCTU seemed to represent. The prosecution of the six farm labourers from Tolpuddle, in March 1834, for swearing illegal oaths on being initiated into a union signalled very clearly that the government was unwilling to tolerate this growing form of organisation. The sentencing of the 'Tolpuddle Martyrs' to seven years transportation shocked the working community; the maximum sentence under the Combination Act had been six months at hard labour. In order to effect this prosecution the Whig government revived a piece of legislation passed in 1797 to discourage naval mutinies. The GNCTU took up the cause of the Dorset men and called a protest rally of 35 000 people in Copenhagen Fields, London, but to no effect. Trade unionism, hit by this judgement and by the depression in trade in 1836, began to decline in support.

C *The war of the unstamped*

Even as the Reform Bill was inching its way onto the statute books an illegal newspaper press was beginning to emerge which was critical of the proposed measure. We saw in chapter II how important the free press had been during the 1816–20 period of radicalism. The Six Acts of 1819 had aimed in large part to combat these publications. The legal framework established for the press in 1819 was still in operation in 1830. By this, any publication appearing at less than 26-day intervals and containing news had to bear a government stamp and retail at 7d (3p). By 1831, as part of the growing interest in politics connected with the Reform Bill campaign, various radicals and organisations were beginning to test the effectiveness of the laws. In 1831 Henery Hetherington published his *Poor Man's Guardian* as an outright challenge to authority. Published at only a penny per weekly copy it bore the explicit heading: Published contrary to 'law' to try the power of 'might against 'right'. This paper claimed that the newspaper stamp was a tax on knowledge and carried the significant motto

'Knowledge is power'.

Hetherington's paper was enormously successful and managed to achieve a nationwide sale of 15 000 copies a week despite being London-based. Many other radical papers followed the *Guardian's* lead and the government responded by prosecuting publishers and retailers of the unstamped press. Hetherington himself suffered imprisonment twice although this did not interrupt the weekly publication of the *Guardian* from secret locations. In London alone, 740 vendors of the unstamped press were brought to trial between 1831 and 1836. Eventually the Whig government of Lord Melbourne gave in and lowered the tax to a point where newspapers could retail at 4d (1.5p).

This was a significant victory since it secured a legal status and a lower price for subsequent Chartist publications. In fact, appearing as a stamped newspaper the Chartist paper, the *Northern Star*, published from 1837 onwards, was even entitled to the benefit of free delivery by the Post Office! Perhaps more importantly, success in the War of the Unstamped seemed to suggest that governments of the day did sometimes yield to the pressure that could be applied by a determined and well-organised campaign. Most radical movements in the 1830s were failures and radicals drew as much encouragement as was possible from this isolated success. In addition, many of the radicals who were to shape the nature of Chartism had been involved in the battle for a free press. For example, Bronterre O'Brien, who would be a regular contributor to the *Northern Star*, edited the *Guardian* from 1832. George Julian Harney, who would edit the *Star* in 1845, served his radical apprenticeship as a shopboy for Hetherington in these years.

4 The Immediate Circumstances of 1837–8

Chartism derived its energies from the radical campaigns of the 1830s, each of which contributed in different ways to the nature of the movement. The Reform Bill campaign showed how a successful agitation could use the platform, the press and the 'language of menace' to good effect. It also lent to all subsequent working-class movements a sense of suspicion over how sympathetic the middle class really were to the cause of votes for working men. The various Owenite initiatives, failures though they may have been, emphasised the economic importance of labour. The 'War of the Unstamped' taught that pressure could bring success and the law could, in some cases, be challenged. Each of these agitations, along with the factory movement, pushing for shorter hours through a network of Short Time Committees in Yorkshire and Lancashire (*see pages 50–3*), gave working people the experience of organising themselves, often on a large scale.

This experience was carried into the late 1830s where we may identify three important elements in the immediate circumstances from which Chartism developed in the years 1837–8; economic depression, the application of the New Poor Law to the industrial areas and a renewed campaign for trade union rights focused upon the case of the Glasgow Spinners (*see page* 79).

A *Economic depression*

As we saw in an earlier chapter, mass-based political movements often coincided with a downturn in the trade cycle and the depression that accompanied this phenomenon. Cobbett's famous words, 'I defy you to agitate a fellow with a full stomach', have echoed through much of the historical interpretation of the Chartist movement. Similarly, the view of the Revd J R Stephens, that Chartism was essentially a 'knife and fork' question, has also found a place in traditional accounts. It is indisputable that the periods of maximum support for Chartism (1838–9, 1842, and 1848) were also years of hunger. These, of course, were moments when the existing political structure was seen most clearly not to be working. It was difficult to avoid the view that a system that could provide neither regular employment nor a sufficient wage was ripe for reform.

Economic depression also had an effect on the structure and running of industrial enterprises. In order to maintain profit margins in the face of declining prices, manufacturers often tried to produce more goods for less input by re-organising work. This might involve the introduction of machinery; in a period of underemployment trade unions would be at their weakest. As one Factory Commissioner put it in 1842 when surveying changes in the cotton textile trade of Lancashire:

> the fall in prices stimulated mill owners to lessen the cost of production by making their machinery, by various improvements and increased speed, turn off more work in a given time . . . I have learned that in one mill, the number of spindles which produced 12 100 lbs in 1834 produce 13 300 lbs in 1841 . . .

Depression might provide the employer with the opportunity and the justification to introduce cheaper forms of labour, as a lamp manufacturer explained to a Select Committee in 1833:

> . . . we take as much as we can off the men and have it done in parts by the boys or the women and then give it to the men to finish; which when trade was good the men would not submit to . . . formerly when trade was good we did not resort to that screwing system; if we had done so we should not have had a single workman to work for us the next day.

A depression put particular strains on the small-scale producers since they operated with the narrowest of profit margins at all times, and consequently they were the first to go to the wall. As a result, the periodic dips in the trade cycle encouraged the concentration of industrial concerns into the hands of a smaller number of people. This was the case even in those areas where the domestic system was paramount. For example, in Nottingham's hosiery trade it had been common at one time for the working family to own their own stocking frame, working it in their own home. As time went by, however, ownership of the looms was increasingly concentrated in the hands of a few individuals who then rented them to their workforce. In 1831 there had been 1382 owners of looms in the town, but by 1836 there were only 837. This means that, in this period, 500 owners of one, two and three looms had fallen back into the ranks of the labourers. One firm owned 5000 frames.

The relationship between economic depression and radical movements is a good deal more complex than is sometimes made out by historians. Besides creating the obvious problems of unemployment and hunger, depression tended to speed up the structural changes in production that were implicit in the process of industrialisation. This meant that at periods when they were most vulnerable working people found their lives changed in important ways which they could not control. Chartism was certainly fuelled by unemployment, but the fact that this was manifested in a call for the vote was a reflection of the working community's wish to control their own lives in the face of far-reaching change. This desire to control change was acutely felt at times of depression when those changes came more rapidly.

B *The anti-poor law campaign*

Probably the radical campaign that most influenced the structure and shape of the Chartist movement was the agitation against the application of the New Poor Law in the Midlands, Wales and the North, from 1837. In retrospect, given the growth of unemployment in the industrial areas, the choice of 1837 as a start-up year was a big mistake. As we saw in chapter III, the New Poor Law had been passed with the conditions of the rural south of England in mind. At first it applied only to these areas, but from 1837 a London solicitor by the name of Alfred Power was charged with the responsibility of extending it to the rest of England and Wales. Yet the high levels of unemployment, which were particularly acute in the Yorkshire woollen textile industry, demonstrated the inadequacy of the New Poor Law with its refusal to see poverty as anything other than a self-inflicted wound.

Power also found himself confronted by a highly organised protest movement. Wherever he went in the North he was confronted by angry crowds. The West Riding of Yorkshire and South-east Lancashire had been the focus of agitation for factory reform from 1830 onwards with the formation of the Short Time Committees in the factory districts. These now simply changed their names to Anti-Poor Law Associations and directed their attentions to Power's attempt to apply the new law. Tory radicals, like Oastler and the Revd J R Stephens saw in the creation of workhouses for poor relief, a rejection by the ratepayers of their obligations to the poor. Stephens was a preacher who had been expelled from the Methodists for his involvement in politics. He now ran an independent chapel in Ashton-under-Lyne in Lancashire and applied evangelical 'hellfire and damnation' oratory to the actions of the Poor Law Commissioners.

The anti-Poor Law campaign also introduced Feargus O'Connor to the Yorkshire audience that would be the basis of his personal support during the next decade. The son of a wealthy Irish protestant landed family, O'Connor was trained in law. He had represented County Cork as an MP from 1832 to 1835. A staunch supporter of Daniel O'Connell, O'Connor broke with him when the 'Great Liberator' reached an agreement in 1835 to work with the Whigs in Parliament. In 1837 O'Connor moved to Leeds and started the *Northern Star* as an anti-Poor Law paper. Support for the agitation was extensive and resulted in a Parliamentary motion, put by John Fielden in February 1838, to repeal the New Poor Law. The failure of this motion by a huge margin, 309 votes to 17, provided a powerful impetus for a political movement with a much wider programme. The lesson seemed to be that before individual motions could be successful there would first have to be a complete overhaul of the system of representation. Significantly, 14 of the 20 northern delegates to the first Chartist Convention had been active in the anti-Poor Law campaign.

c *The case of the Glasgow spinners*

Any political movement aiming at mass support needs clear-cut issues to build its case around, since an appeal to principle, in the abstract, will always have a limited impact. What Chartism needed in its early stages were issues that related directly to the everyday experience of the working man and woman and which could readily be related to his or her own situation. The application of the New Poor Law had provided just such an issue, with the government clearly playing the part of the villain of the piece. Another was provided by the case of the Glasgow Spinners.

The county of Lanarkshire, with its focus on the town of Glasgow, was the centre of the Scottish cotton trade. Like its counterpart south of the border it was hit by the depression of the late 1830s. W Hamish Fraser's excellent study of the period has shown that the local employers reacted to this situation by reducing wages and announcing the introduction of larger spinning mules which would require a workforce that was less skilled and therefore cheaper. In response the Spinners' Association, which had emerged during the growth of trade unions in the years after the Reform Act, brought 800 men out on strike in April 1837. The employers decided to fight it out and introduced strike-breaking labour from other areas. One of these strike breakers was shot dead in July 1837. Without any evidence as to their involvement in this or any other violent incidents, the committee of the Cotton Spinners' Association was arrested and five of them were put on trial for murder and conspiracy to intimidate and molest. Within the wider working-class public, facing similar attacks on their own conditions of work, there was a good deal of sympathy for the spinners. It all seemed depressingly familiar, the more so since the 'Tolpuddle Martyrs', to whose case it was widely compared, had arrived back from Australia, following a Royal pardon, in June 1837, to much public acclaim. It appeared that the attack on trade union rights was being initiated again. Nor was it difficult to see the case in political terms. The Sheriff of Lanarkshire, who ordered the arrests, was a Tory by the name of Archibald Alison. He described the spinners' union as 'an example of democratic ambition on a large scale'. In a powerful association of ideas he argued that, 'a committee for assassination was appointed by universal suffrage'.

Certainly strikebreakers, or 'knobsticks' as they were often called, were reviled in the working community. Strikes often involved 'folk violence' against such individuals though this generally took the form of public humiliation rather than physical harm to the individual. In Glasgow there had been attacks on 'knobs' during the lengthy strike, but evidence that the Association had planned such violence, and even sanctioned murder, was, at best, circumstantial. As regular chapelgoers the Spinners' leaders made unconvincing thugs. The jury found the charge of murder 'not proven' but the five men were, nevertheless, sentenced to seven years transportation for conspiring to use 'intimidation, molestation and threats'. The judge's summing-up gives a good insight into the fear of trade unions on the part of the authorities at this time, despite the repeal of the Combination Acts. This was, he claimed:

> a conspiracy, ... by force and violence, to rob the one class of their rights to employ labourers at such prices as the latter were willing to receive, and to rob the other classes of their rights to dispose of their labour, at such prices as may be agreeable to themselves.

The *Northern Star* took a different view, defending the record of the Spinners' leaders and featuring a print of the five convicted men in January 1838. The incident provided a focus for the emergent Chartist movement, to the extent that it was a meeting in Glasgow in May 1838 that saw the launching of the movement.

1 *What are the objections to the Spinners' Association contained in the Judge's summing-up above?*

2 *What are the 'rights' referred to by the Judge in the statement?*

Print from Northern Star, *27 January 1838*

3 *What point is the* Northern Star *making about the Spinners in its print of them?*

4 *Why would the Chartists be keen to champion the cause of the Glasgow spinners?*

In summarising this section it may be useful to return to the image of Chartism as an 'umbrella movement' which drew together a whole series of grievances and expressed them through the demand for the 'People's Charter'. Through such an approach we are able to understand the complexity of the movement and the way it drew on the immediate experience of the working community, without descending into the oversimplification of a one-dimensional 'hunger politics' explanation. Each of the movements, identified in the chapter so far, contributed to the nature of Chartism. They did this in three ways.

(1) First, by influencing the way the working community saw itself, particularly by demonstrating the distance between the classes. The Reform Act damaged relationships between the classes, and the reformed Parliament acted in ways that seemed to injure specifically working-class interests. At the same time the Owenite movement created a sense of the economic importance of labour; 'Labour is the source of all wealth'.

(2) Secondly, these contributory movements extended the range of what the Chartists wanted from reform. In this respect issues like the abolition of the New Poor Law, legal recognition for trade unions, the Ten Hours Act and the freedom of the press are sometimes referred to as part of the 'implicit social Programme' of Chartism.

(3) Thirdly, each of these movements influenced the organisation of the Chartist movement. Much of its strategy, for example, was based on the Reform Bill campaign with its mass meetings and often violent rhetoric. More than this, however, the radical movements of the 1830s created a body of individuals with extensive experience of campaigning and this was to be vital to the development of the movement. The Chartists drew upon a rich radical tradition.

5 The Emergence of Chartism

The 'People's Charter', containing the six points of political reform was first published in May 1838 by the London Working Men's Association which had been formed two years earlier. In the same month the Charter was enshrined in a national petition to Parliament. Signatures to the petition were collected locally by representatives who were elected at mass meetings through the second half of 1838. The representatives met at a National Convention in London in February 1839 which drew the signatures together ready for delivery of the petition to

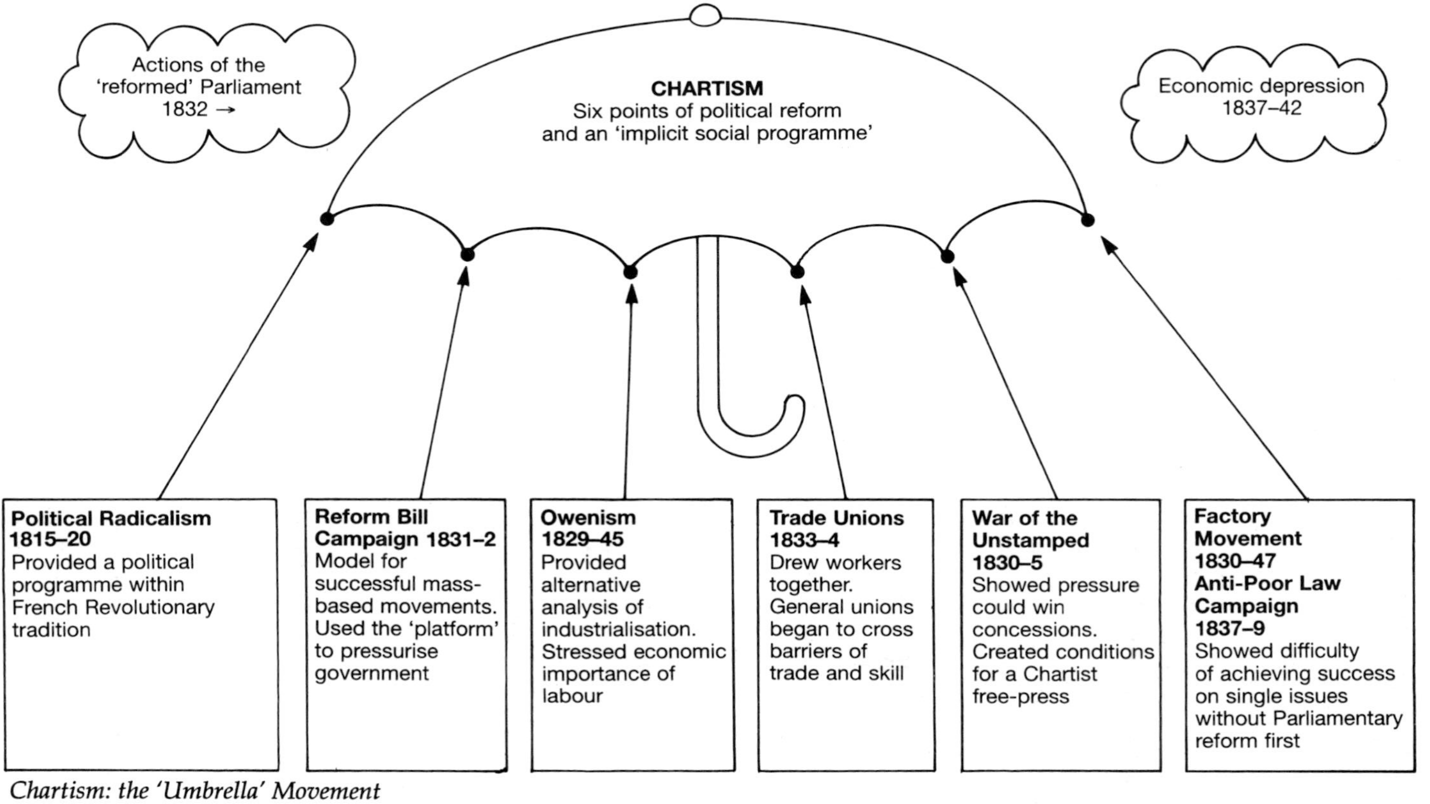

Chartism: the 'Umbrella' Movement

Parliament in June 1839. The Convention also discussed strategy and acted as an administrative centre for the movement as a whole. These three elements, the *Charter*, the *National Petition* and the *National Convention* were the focus of the movement in its first phase. It is worth examining each in turn to identify their origins and main features.

A *The charter*

The People's Charter was drawn up by William Lovett, the Secretary of the London Working Men's Association. Lovett was a cabinet maker by trade and had been involved in a range of radical movements since arriving in London from his native Cornwall in 1821. He had been a leading figure in Owenism in the capital. He had also worked hard to establish a 'Victim Fund' to help those who were arrested for selling the *Poor Man's Guardian*. In 1831, he and a group of radical friends established the National Union of the Working Classes which opposed the Reform Bill, then going through Parliament, seeing it as a limited measure that would not benefit the working community. This organisation was succeeded, in 1836, by the London Working Men's Association. As Secretary of the LWMA Lovett worked with a number of radical MPs to produce a Charter which, it was intended, would form the basis of an Act of Parliament. This was not anything unusual in itself; in 1829 Lovett had assisted radical MPs to draw up a Friendly Societies Act which was subsequently passed by Parliament. Nor by 1838 was there anything new, or unexpected, in the six points of the Charter. Each had formed part of radical demands since 1815. Collectively, they embodied the view which was now widely associated with the work of Thomas Paine (*see pages 13–18*), that individuals had a right to participate in politics and that they should not be excluded from citizenship because they did not own property. The Chartist points were really only a re-statement of the radical programme which had inspired the followers of Hunt and Cobbett in the post-war years. It was now revived in the wake of a Reform Act which had clearly failed to deliver basic political 'rights' to working men.

The Charter was adopted enthusiastically in the Midlands and the North. In these areas the Anti-Poor Law movement had attracted much popular support, a good deal of it inspired by Feargus O'Connor's Leeds-based newspaper, the *Northern Star*. The *Star* endorsed the new movement and encouraged its readership to support the campaign for the Charter.

B *The national petition*

The idea of incorporating the Charter into a massive National Petition to Parliament came from Birmingham. Attwood had reformed the Birmingham Political Union in April 1837, largely to encourage local support for the establishment of a town council under the provisions of the Municipal Corporation Act of 1835. On the crucial issue of universal suffrage Attwood retained his reservations. Throughout 1837 the BPU advocated household suffrage. By this all houseowners would be given the right to vote, rather than only those who owned houses worth £10 or above, as specified in the 1832 Act. Although this would have created a larger electorate, the franchise would still have been based on property ownership and so would have excluded large numbers of working men. As a result working people did not join the revamped BPU in the numbers that Attwood had anticipated. In the eyes of working-class reformers, gradualist approaches to political change had been discredited by the Reform Act and the actions of the reformed Parliament since 1832. It was now male universal suffrage or nothing and in January 1838 Attwood, recognising this, reluctantly adopted the wider franchise as part of the BPU's programme. 'I am now a thorough convert to universal suffrage', he announced, 'and if ever I uttered a word against it I now altogether retract it.' Nevertheless, Attwood retained his reservations on the issue and was to make an early exit from the movement as a result. To demonstrate its newfound conviction the BPU floated the idea of a national petition for universal suffrage. Clearly, Attwood's intention was to place himself at the head of a nationwide agitation as he had in 1831–2.

Again, there was popular support for the idea of a national petition, and for Attwood's endorsement of the scheme. The Birmingham banker had been the foremost agitator for the Reform Act and had been a member of the reformed House of Commons since 1832. His endorsement of universal suffrage represented a clear condemnation of the settlement of 1832 by a respectable public figure who retained enormous popularity for having defied Wellington and the King during the 'Days of May'. The petition was launched at a mass meeting in Glasgow at the end of May 1838. Here the representatives of the LWMA, the BPU and Northern activists like O'Connor and Stephens came together to discuss the way forward. The venue was deliberately chosen to draw attention to the case of the Glasgow spinners and to draw on the enormous public sympathy they had inspired. Here, in front of an audience of 150 000, amid attacks on the New Poor Law and support for trade union rights, the idea was floated of the National Petition that would incorporate the six points of the People's Charter.

As we have seen, Chartism took its programme from the earlier radical movements. In the same way there was nothing new about petitioning for political reform. Such petitions were an accepted part of radical strategy and were perfectly constitutional in their nature. What made this move very different to anything that had gone before was the widely accepted belief that this would be the 'last petition'. This would be a demonstration of popular feeling that would be so strong that no government could ignore it and retain any pretence that it represented 'the people'. This left open the question of what would happen if the petition was rejected. Nevertheless, it was widely-accepted in 1838 that this was to be a last push for change by constitutional means.

A *The Chartist Convention*

The Glasgow meeting of May 1838 also launched the Convention which would meet in London and consist of Chartist delegates, elected at public meetings throughout the country. The delegates would carry the signatures to the petition from their areas and also represent their local 'constituency' in the Convention's deliberations. The similarity between the Convention and the House of Commons was deliberate. British radicals had long toyed with the idea of establishing a national convention, along the lines of that adopted by the revolutionaries during the French Revolution, and always with the intention that such a body would carry symbolic significance. The Convention would be elected by a form of universal suffrage, (in this case, hands raised at public meetings), and so it would represent 'the people' in a way that the House of Commons, elected under the restricted franchise of 1832, could never do. The Convention would meet in London and be a shining alternative to the corrupt Parliament; a kind of 'anti-Parliament', or what many Chartists called the 'real Parliament'. The submission of the petition to the Parliament by the anti-parliament would be an enormously symbolic moment. As O'Connor put it, 'let them attend to the number of 300 000 or 400 000 with a petition on their shoulders to the door of the House of Commons and let them tell the House of Commons that the constituency of England were waiting in the Palace Yard for an answer.'

The work of agitation now proceeded apace. O'Connor launched the Great Northern Union in June 1838. This was based in Leeds but it had branches throughout the north of England. It was O'Connor's intention to re-direct the radical energies in these areas from the Poor Law issue into the wider movement for political rights. By February 1839 the GNU had 62 000 members. Also in June the Northern Political Union was started in Newcastle. Branches of the London Working Men's Association were established in South Wales. Chartism proved to be hugely popular in the valley communities and, by 1839, it has been estimated that there were 25 000 enrolled or committed Chartists in Glamorgan and Monmouthshire. By the end of 1838 there were 76 Chartist associations established in Scotland. Throughout England, Scotland, and Wales locally-based associations were set up to campaign for a common objective. Chartism was formed by the coming together of local organisations and this was a significant element in the nature of the movement. There was always a certain amount of tension between a national and a local organisation, with the tendency towards fragmentation as an ever-present problem. This was exacerbated by communication difficulties between areas and also by the poverty of most Chartists, which made the task of full-time agitation difficult.

Despite this, it was clear from the start that Chartism drew on a rich vein of mass support and in this sense expressed the frustrations and aspirations of the wider working community. This was evident in the mass meetings to elect delegates to the Convention and to collect signatures for the petition. At a meeting in Birmingham in August 1838 200 000 people saw Attwood and O'Connor share the same platform and declare for the same programme. In September, John Fielden chaired a meeting just outside Manchester at which even the unsympathetic *Times*, estimated the attendance at 300 000. In October 250 000 turned out for a similar occasion at Peep Green in the West Riding of Yorkshire. One of the speakers at the September meeting was Robert Lowery, a tailor by trade and a Chartist delegate from Newcastle. In his autobiography he remembers; 'One dense mass of faces beaming with earnestness – as far as you could distinguish faces – then beyond still an enormous crowd but with indistinct countenances.' (In assessing the significance of the large numbers at these meetings it is worth bearing in mind that a Wembley Cup Final crowd today contains somewhere around 90 000 people.) One can only guess at the uplifting experience of attending such a meeting. Certainly for Lowery, the Manchester meeting was an almost transcendental experience; 'There is something in the appearances of such multitudes ... something which for the moment seems to realise the truths of the ancient saying – "The voice of the people is as the voice of God" '.

Meetings like this took their form from the experience of the Reform Bill campaign and the same use was made of the 'language of menace' carefully encased within a broadly constitutional approach. Attwood led the way here and this is significant since he later claimed to have left the movement early because of the violence of its leaders' speeches. At the August meeting he raised the issue of violence himself by saying, 'No blood shall be shed by us; but if our enemies shed blood – if they attack the people – they must take the consequences upon their own heads.' This was by now the tried and tested formula of a mass movement, committed to a constitutional strategy, but utilising violent rhetoric to make its points. There was a widespread belief within the movement that the government might well intervene violently and that if this occurred the Chartists had a constitutional right to defend themselves. The strategies of 'physical force' and 'moral force' were not seen at this stage to be alternatives between which the Chartists would have to choose. Rather both were interwoven into a fundamentally constitutional strategy based on petitioning, with the Convention representing the legitimacy of the Chartists' claim to speak for 'the people'. One of the commonest Chartist slogans was 'Peacfully if we can, forcefully if we must'. Perhaps the concept of 'defensive violence' is summed up best by the slogan carried on banners to meetings by the Newcastle

Chartists (refering to Napoleon's destruction of the Russian capital in 1812); 'If they Peterloo us we'll Moscow them'.

At the same meeting that Attwood made his statement on the use of 'defensive violence', O'Connor identified the importance of the constitutional approach and the possibility of a violent confrontation (his speech is taken from a local newspaper and is reported in the third person):

> He was there representing the wishes and feelings of 3 000 000 of determined minds and stalwart arms. There was not a man among them who was not satisfied to trust the moral power of the nation, even to downbending, even to submission, even to fawning pliability that might be capable of being cited for the purposes of expediency. They were ready to do this, rather than rush into any maddening conflict. They might be sure that the man who was marshalling physical force, would be the first to desert it when it was resorted to. (Cheers) The moral power was that principle of the human mind which taught man how to reason, and when to bear, and when to forbear. But he was not to be understood to imply that he was content to live a slave. No! . . . But when the moral force was expended, and the mind drawn out at last, then, as Mr Attwood had said, if wrong should come from any party, cursed be that virtuous man who refused to repel force by force.

1 *Given what you have read in earlier chapters about popular movements since 1815, why do you think the Chartists felt they could expect a violent reaction from the government?*

2 *What does O'Connor mean by the term 'the moral power of the nation'?*

3 *What is the position of both Attwood and O'Connor on the use of physical force by the Chartists?*

The 53 delegates elected at these, and many other, meetings came together as the General Convention of the Industrious Classes, in London in February 1839. This group met regularly, discussed strategy and sent agitators throughout the country to increase support and to collect signatures for the petition. By June the massive petition with its 1 280 000 signatures was ready for presentation. It was rejected by the House of Commons by 235 votes to 46.

6 THE GROWTH OF TENSION: REJECTION AND REACTION

Tension had grown in the months leading up to the submission of the Charter in June 1839. The government's initial attempts to deal with the Chartist threat had been clumsy. The arrest of the Revd J R Stephens for the violence of his speeches in November 1838 had merely increased working-class support for the Chartists by creating a martyr. Throughout the country working people contributed to the Stephens defence fund. In April 1839 the use of the universally detested Metropolitan Police at Llanidloes in Wales sparked off three days of rioting in the town which had to be supressed by the army. In May 1839 the Convention adjourned to Birmingham to be closer to its basis of popular support as it readied itself for the submission of the Charter.

With this build-up of tension, middle-class support for the Chartists had begun to melt away. By May, 14 of the Convention delegates, all middle-class men, had resigned. They generally cited the issue of violent language used in the speeches of O'Connor, Oastler and Stephens as their reasons for going. In June, when Attwood presented the petition to the House of Commons, his support for the movement was obviously wavering. Despite his own use of the 'language of menace' as recently as the previous August, he now found it necessary to state that he 'washed his hands of any idea, of any appeal to physical force'.

A *Riots in the Bull Ring, July 1839*

On 4 July 1839 rioting broke out in Birmingham, when the Mayor used 60 Metropolitan police to break up a peaceful Chartist meeting in the Bull Ring (a market place). This was particularly unfortunate since the Mayor had been an early supporter of Chartism, to the extent that he was one of the middle-class delegates to the Convention who had resigned the previous March. Middle-class supporters of the revamped BPU had always been more interested in local than in national reform. Birmingham had been given incorporated status in 1838, under the provisions of the 1835 Municipal Corporation Act. This created the structure of local government in the form of a town council with associated powers. Many of the middle-class members of the BPU had been elected to the new town council, and, as a result, their enthusiasm for the People's Charter evaporated. They now saw Chartism, not as an issue of principle, but as a question of public order. The fact that during the Reform Bill campaign the town's middle class had encouraged political meetings in the Bull Ring was also forgotten in the desire to demonstrate their new found authority. The irony of this position was not lost on the Convention. The fortnight of rioting that followed 4 July was exacerbated by news of the rejection of the petition. William Lovett, as Secretary to the Convention, issued a placard condemning the actions of the town council:

> That this Convention is of opinion that a wonton, flagrant and unjust outrage has been made upon the people of Birmingham by a bloodthirsty and unconstitutional force from London,

acting under the authority of men who, when out of office, sanctioned and took part in the meetings of the people; and now, when they share in the public plunder, seek to keep the people in social slavery and political degradation.

For this Lovett was arrested and sentenced to a year in prison. Lovett is often seen as the chief advocate of what is termed 'moral force', that is, strategies of persuasion as opposed to 'physical force'. Yet here he defends the actions of the Birmingham crowd in fighting the police.

1 *Why did the Chartists consider the Metropolitan Police to be an unconstitutional force?*

2 *What does Lovett mean by the phrase, 'now when they share in the public plunder'?*

3 *Using the words of the placard as evidence, what is Lovett's position on the use of violence?*

B *The Newport Uprising, November 1839*

The Convention broke up in disarray in September 1839. An attempt in August to call a general strike, (the 'grand national holiday' or the 'Sacred Month' as it was variously called) had failed. There remained a good deal of support for continuing with the agitation but the failure of petitioning had thown the movement into a state of confusion as to the way forward. The delegates returned to their areas and the movement lost its central direction. From this fragmentation the Newport Uprising emerged as a local initiative.

On the night of 3–4 November 1839 nearly 10 000 men marched from the darkness of the hills surrounding Newport in South Wales. Mostly colliers and iron workers from the valleys, they were armed with pikes and firearms and marched in close military formation, each detachment directed by a 'captain'. Led by local Chartist leaders John Frost, Zephaniah Williams, and William Jones, the advance column clashed with troops firing from the Westgate Hotel in the town square. The Chartists fled leaving between 20 and 30 of their number dead. At their trial Frost, Williams and Jones were convicted of high treason and sentenced to death for attempting to overthrow the state by force of arms. The Whig government, however, had learned the importance of not creating martyrs for the cause, and swiftly commuted the sentences to transportation for life.

The Newport Uprising continues to puzzle historians as much as it did contemporaries. We may see it, as many did at the time, as the violent confrontation that had always seemed likely. The prosecution alleged at the subsequent trial that Newport was to have been the first blow of a nationwide uprising that was nipped in the bud by the swift response of the authorities. On the other hand, many of the Chartist leaders, including O'Connor, suspected it to be a Pentridge-style piece of entrapment (*see page 16*). Defending a plea of not guilty the accused argued that they had simply planned a huge and spectacular demonstration of Chartist strength as a protest against the recent arrest of the local Convention 'missionary', Henry Vincent. Frost and the others were simply the victims of over-reaction on the part of the local garrison.

David Williams, writing his biography of Frost a century later in 1939, accepted this argument and concluded that Newport had really been a 'monster demonstration'. This view was strongly contested by David Jones in his 1985 book *The Last Rising*. He locates the events in their local context and sees the rising as an expression of small mine- and iron-working communities tightly bound together by Nonconformity, radical politics and a tradition of violence. The organisation of the rising was very different from most Chartist activities by virtue of its almost total secrecy. As Jones puts it; 'there was none of the defiant openness and publicity which characterised the wider movement'. Nor did the participants seem to have felt that they were simply part of a 'demonstration'. One Chartist, a 17-year-old cabinet-maker by the name of George Shell, wrote to his parents before setting off, 'I shall this night be engaged in a struggle for freedom and should it please God to spare my life I shall see you soon; but if not, grieve not for me for I shall fall in a noble cause.' Whilst the rising was not part of a nationwide plot, the plan was to take Newport as an inspiration to Chartist groups elsewhere to do the same. The capture of the town would have been followed by a forced march to Monmouth to release Henry Vincent and other Chartist prisoners from the town's gaol.

The Newport Uprising was an unusual event in the history of Chartism and was seen as such by Chartists at the time. In the movement as a whole the issue of violence was never as divisive as historians have traditionally thought. Most Chartists accepted and promoted the right to arm in one's own defence, and to respond if attacked. For example, historians have often seen William Lovett as the apostle of 'moral force' methods, yet even he was prepared to go to prison in 1839 for the right to exercise defensive violence, as we saw in the document extract on pages 89–90. When Chartist violence did occur it was generally in the form of riots where the crowd and the authorities confronted each other in the well-established fashion of the food riot. In fact Chartism, as one of its leading historians, Dorothy Thompson, points out, experienced comparatively little of this 'folk violence'. Throughout the period thousands came together at meetings, both large and small, without involving any great disruption to public order. Unlike many of the movements that preceded it, Chartism was not a secret organisation; it did its business openly and peacefully. At Newport, however, a plot was laid to seize power by force of arms. Small groups of Chartists throughout the country were drawn to this approach. In the wake of Newport there was the arrest of armed Chartists in January 1840, in Sheffield, Dewsbury, Bradford and Bethnal Green, London. But revolution was always a minority interest within the movement. O'Connor had long counselled against such a strategy on purely pragmatic grounds. As the *Northern Star* put it in April 1839, 'the odds are fearful against those who are not trained to arms.' Tragically, Newport confirmed this view. It also gave the government the reason it had been looking for to move firmly against the Chartists. Nearly 500 people were sent to prison for Chartist-related activity between 1839 and 1841. The first phase of the movement was over.

7 Reorganisation: The National Charter Association and 'New Moves'

The Chartist leadership remained remarkably resilient in the face of its setbacks. Plans were immediately laid for reconstructing the movement and gathering signatures for a second petition. Most Chartists accepted that a stronger central organisation was needed to hold together the local initiatives. Encouraged by a series of articles in the *Northern Star*, written by O'Connor from his prison cell in York, the National Charter Association (NCA) was established in Manchester in July 1840. This was to exist for a decade as the most important of the Chartist organisations. By the summer of 1842 it boasted a national membership of 50 000. The experience of the first phase of the Chartist movement led many to reconsider the strategy of simply petitioning for the Charter. Some now argued that the working community needed to demonstrate its readiness for universal suffrage. Whilst in prison Lovett and his fellow-prisoner John Collins, a tool setter from Birmingham, devised a national system of education for the working community. Their scheme included schools for each age group, libraries, community halls, adult education, and teacher training colleges. This represented a remarkable vision of educational provision which was to be financed by weekly contributions of a penny from everybody who had signed the petition. Lovett and Collins argued that a formally educated working class could not long be denied the vote. Henry Vincent emerged from prison certain that the demonstration of overtly respectable behaviour would calm middle-class fears and secure the franchise. He, along with Robert Lowery, encouraged the establishment of teetotal Chartist associations in which working people would take the pledge to abstain from alcohol. Arthur O'Neill, a Nonconformist minister from Glasgow, established a Chartist Church in Birmingham in 1841, arguing that a formal commitment to Christianity by the movement might gain the vote.

These 'new moves', as they were called, aimed to achieve the vote by explicitly 'moral force' strategies. A public demonstration of rectitude by the working class would disarm the major argument against enfranchisement. None of these initiatives ever gained the level of support achieved by the NCA under O'Connor's leadership. O'Connor attacked the 'new moves' but not because he rejected education, sobriety or Christianity. His concern, and that of the NCA, was simply that these strategies were a distraction from the main task of achieving the Charter.

Supporters of these moves also took at face value the reason most frequently given for the Charter's rejection; that the working class were not yet 'ready' for the vote. The NCA argued that, if the vote was a right, as had always been argued by the Chartists, then individuals should not have to qualify for it. Nobody would argue, for example, that one should have to sign the pledge before being entitled to enjoy, say freedom of conscience, or equality before the law. The NCA felt the same point applied to the 'moral force' schemes for achieving the vote. The debate between the various groups within Chartism on the issue of strategy was often acrimonious. Many historians argue that these divisions were disastrous for the future of a movement that was already fragmented by the geographical spread of its support. 'The quarrel thus begun,' remarked Mark Hovell in *The Chartist Movement* (1917), 'was never healed, and exercised a baneful effect upon the Chartist agitation'.

In fact, there has always been confusion around this issue from historians in their interpretions of Chartism. Because the 'new movers' adopted overtly 'moral force' strategies, it is sometimes assumed that the rest of the Chartists were committed to 'physical force' strategies. The Chartists themselves used these two terms and it has been assumed that they represented strategic polarities that were mutually exclusive. Historians have often felt that at this point the mass of Chartists made a mistake in following O'Connor and the NCA, rather than going down the path of moral reform. This is partly because the first real historians of the movement writing in the early twentieth century were members of the embryonic Labour Party which was itself committed to gradual change from within rather than any form of confrontation (see chapter XIII). Thus Mark Hovell, a Labour Party supporter, writing before the First World War, was much taken by Lovett's education scheme. In Hovell's influential history of the movement O'Connor emerges as the villain of the piece, luring working people away from the strategy which might have given the movement success. As he put it; 'It was ... a division between Lovett and a man whose methods of agitation included ... hero-worship, clap-trap speeches, mass demonstrations leading to physical force ideas and even more reckless oratory.' In Hovell's work a crude typology emerged; O'Connor represented 'physical force' and Lovett represented 'moral force' Chartism. Subsequent historians tended to follow Hovell's lead, particularly in the condemnation of O'Connor's leadership. This can be seen, for example, in J T Ward's *Chartism* published in 1975.

O'Connor has fared better at the hands of his biographer James Epstein, who tried in his book, *The Lion of Freedom* (1982), to look at strategy and leadership from the Chartists' point of view. From their position three points need to be borne in mind. First, that petitioning Parliament for the Charter was itself a 'moral force' strategy because it operated within the law and it was an accepted constitutional right which had been widely used over the years. The term 'physical force' was mostly used to denote the kind of overt use of force that had failed so signally at Newport, and it was advocated by only a minority of Chartists. Second, there was broad agreement over defensive violence; that Chartists had a right to defend themselves and that attack was likely. As a result the distinction between moral force and the advocacy of defensive violence was not necessarily as marked as it has seemed to later historians. Thirdly, platform orators used the 'language of menace' as they had in 1832 and, in the context of meetings of many thousands, this was intended to have an intimidatory role. The Chartist case was based on peaceful persuasion, but it utilised all the strategies that were available under that heading.

When Chartism was relaunched as a mass movement with a new petition in 1842, most Chartists chose to follow O'Connor. Epstein argues that this was not because he misled them with his stunning speeches. Rather, O'Connor represented the kind of position that was closest to their own. Petitioning Parliament with massive public support and the hint of menace still seemed the best and quickest way to achieve the Charter and this was the strategy to which the NCA, O'Connor and most Chartists were committed. The Chartists accepted the leadership of a 'gentleman reformer' because his political position mirrored their own. Any leader deviating from this position was likely to be rejected and this was the case with the overtures towards the Chartists made at this time by various middle-class groups.

8 CHARTISM AND CLASS

A *Chartism and the middle class*

Historians of Chartism have often pointed out that the movement always included a number of middle-class men, particularly in its leadership. This is sometimes cited as evidence that Chartism was not really a working-class movement at all, but rather a collection of the discontented from all classes. As historian David Rowe argued 'the Chartist movement ... may be seen as originating less from any new working-class consciousness, than from a radical middle-class element ...' Alternatively, historians like James Epstein, writing on O'Connor, and Dorothy Thompson (*The Chartists* 1984) see Chartism as an expression of working-class political awareness. The issue of relations between Chartism and the middle class is central to any understanding of the nature of the movement.

Take, for example, the first Chartist Convention as it was constituted in February 1839. As a group the Convention was initially less representative of the movement as a whole than it might have been. One well-placed contemporary observer estimated that the initial delegates included 24 working men and 29 from other classes. There are a number of reasons for this. The movements that had preceded Chartism had encouraged some alignment of middle-class and working-class radicals. This had occurred most spectacularly in the Reform Bill agitation. The campaigns against the Factory Act and against the New Poor Law had also created alliances that crossed class barriers. These alliances carried over into the initial phases of Chartism. Also, we should not underestimate the difficulties confronting working men who aspired to be Chartist delegates. Their families had to be supported, and victimisation from employers often followed. Sympathetic 'gentleman reformers' or tradesmen had more independence to act and were often seen to be natural representatives in this respect. Nevertheless, the early months of the Chartist Convention provided this group with an acid test of their support. Unlike previous movements Chartism possessed a clearly defined programme in the shape of the People's Charter. Real support for this became the ultimate test of an individual's commitment to the movement as a whole.

By May 1839, before the Charter was presented, 14 of the middle-class delegates had resigned from the Convention and they were replaced by working men. Also, the public support of Attwood (never a delegate) was clearly wavering. What had brought this about? Resigning delegates complained of the violent speeches from some of the leaders, yet the use of violent rhetoric was by now a well-established tradition within radical movements. As we have seen, Attwood peppered his own speeches with references to defensive violence. The rising tensions of the early months of 1839 may have frightened the middle-class delegates. Alternatively, it may have been their experience of the Chartist Convention that persuaded them to leave the movement. This confronted them with a group of politically-active working men preparing themselves for political power. This was always the dilemma of universal suffrage for the middle class. It was all very well for the Chartists to argue that 'labour is the source of all wealth', but if a society was based on this assumption where would this leave the employers? To put this another way, to what extent was the Chartist concern for trade union rights compatible with the desire of industrialists to run their businesses as they saw fit? If the vote were given to the propertyless, how would they act towards the propertied?

Attwood's view was always that working-class interests could be represented by the election of men of 'productive capital', middle-class men like himself. Universal suffrage would bring this about, with the working class voting deferentially for employers who understood the needs of their workers. Later, looking back on his short flirtation with universal suffrage, he re-iterated his view that the middle class were the natural leaders. 'There is no instance in history in which political movements have been successful without leaders and in almost every instance those leaders were men of wealth and influence.' The working-class delegates to the Chartist Convention saw things rather differently. Referring to the role of the middle class within the movement, one of them asked, 'Did they think they were going to lead the working class by the nose any longer?'.

The supporters with real doubts about universal manhood suffrage, like Attwood, Oastler, and Stephens, soon left the movement. The men of the middle ranks who remained in Chartism accepted that it emerged from within an articulate and self-confident working class. In other words they accepted the full implications of universal suffrage; that the centre of gravity within the political framework would alter radically as a result of its introduction. These men were often from the lower middle class, a group that had been so important in the French Revolution. In this category one might include disaffected professionals, like the Scottish doctor Peter Murray McDouall, elected to represent Ashton-under Lyne at the Convention of 1839, or the lawyer James 'Bronterre' O'Brien, elected for Manchester. Others were shopkeepers, such as linen-draper John Frost of Newport, or beer-house keeper Peter Bussey of Bradford. A few, like O'Connor, were in the 'gentlemen reformer' tradition of Burdett and Hunt. These men remained in Chartism, alongside working-class leaders like Lovett, the cabinet maker and Robert Lowery, the tailor, and hundreds of others from the myriad trades and industries of Britain, because they accepted the implications of the Charter as a political programme. When O'Connor made speeches to Chartist crowds he often wore a jacket of fustian, the cloth of the working man, to symbolise his unity with the audience.

In fact, the Chartists consistently refused to align with middle-class radical groups unless it was on their own terms. Whilst accepting that the support of the middle class would strengthen their case, acceptance of the Charter remained the acid-test of any middle-class movement's sincerity. The Anti-Corn Law League, established in 1839 consistently failed to attract working-class support in any numbers although it established Operative Associations. For the Chartists, the League was a distraction from the task of agitating for the Charter, although the abolition of the Corn Laws remained an important element in the Chartists' 'implicit social programme'. Richard Cobden, leader of the League, wanted working-class support as 'something in our rear to frighten the aristocracy.' The League was happy to have working men as members but would not allow them onto their executive committee. The Chartists were not interested in such a subordinate role.

Nevertheless, the free traders tried twice more to draw in Chartist support by establishing rival political organisations based specifically on the idea of an alliance between the classes. The Leeds Reform Association, launched in 1841 by leading members of the League, advocated household suffrage. The hope was that, following the failure of the petition, and the debacle of Newport, a gradualist programme of step-by step reform might now be more appealing. Its founding meeting was boycotted by most Chartists, and those who attended did so only to insist that the Charter was accepted as the Association's programme. O'Connor dubbed it the 'Fox and Goose Club', suggesting that for the working class to join a political association run by the middle class was rather like inviting geese to join a club run by foxes. The Complete Suffrage Union (CSU) fared little better. Launched early in 1842, to distract workers from the re-vamped Chartist movement, the CSU was started by Joseph Sturge, a corn merchant from Birmingham and a keen member of the Anti-Corn Law League. Sturge was prepared to accept all six points of the Charter but refused to accept the name 'People's Charter' for the CSU's programme. A number of Chartist delegates attended the CSU's conferences in April and December 1842, since the movement remained keen to widen support. In the December conference Lovett moved a resolution, seconded by O'Connor, that the Charter be accepted in name. These two Chartists, who disagreed over so many issues of strategy, were happy to ally on this issue. When the motion was passed by the Conference, packed by Chartists, Sturge and his middle-class supporters left and the CSU was effectively dead.

B *The structure of chartist support*

Middle-class organisations aspiring to lead mass movements now found themselves dealing with a working class which had its own reasonably coherent view of the political and economic world. It was the fact that characters like Attwood, Sturge, and Cobden did not share this view that proved the main stumbling block to co-operation between the classes in the Chartist period. In this sense, the Chartist experience served to clarify existing class differences. A brief examination of the movement's support and ideology may demonstrate this point.

Chartism drew the body of its support from what were called at the time 'the manufacturing districts'. This contemporary term should not be interpreted to mean 'the large towns'. Rather it refers to the, often relatively small, industrial communities which characterised Britain in the early stages of the Industrial Revolution. Asa Briggs suggested in his book *Chartist Studies* (1959), that Chartism recruited better in the older, decaying trades of the increasingly outmoded domestic system rather than among the newer factory workers. Research carried out since his book was published, however, has suggested that it was the size of the community that was more important than the type of industry carried out. Dorothy Thompson (*The Chartists*, 1984) argues that Chartism flourished most extensively in industrial areas 'in which the actual communities were small enough to sustain a unity of purpose, in which communication was easy and in which the authority of church and state was weak.' These might be centres of factory production, mining, the domestic system, or workshop industries. Chartist support came from the home-based handloom weavers, and the factory-based textile workers of South East Lancashire and Lanarkshire (cotton), and the West Riding of Yorkshire (wool). It also drew in the framework knitters of the East Midlands (Nottinghamshire, Derbyshire and Leicestershire), and the metal workers of Birmingham and the Black Country. In all of these the typical work unit was the small workshop. Chartism was strong among the colliers and iron workers in areas like South Wales and the North East of England, the pottery workers of Staffordshire and among the more traditional trades like tailoring, building and shoemaking. What was important, in generating and sustaining Chartist membership locally, was the shared common experience of early industrialisation.

These tightly-knit communities bred a fiercely independent workforce. Early industrial workers expected to exercise a good deal of control over their own working environment. This was partly because British industrialisation began in the domestic system where workers worked in their own homes and determined their own work-pace. There is evidence of the persistence of these attitudes, with workers carrying them into the early factories. For example, there were no formally agreed holidays at this time, but the community would observe particular days as holidays. Employers were expected to fit in with these arrangements and they could expect trouble from their workforce if they did not. In most areas it was common to take Monday as a day of rest. This was known as the observance of 'Saint Monday'. For this reason the Chartists held many of their mass meetings on a Monday.

Many of these communities had undergone a religious revival in the early nineteenth century and there appears to be a link between Chartism and evangelical nonconformity. Many of the Chartists belonged to the Methodists, Baptists or other nonconformist sects. This was also a culture which carried a commitment to self-education. Britain's was a fairly literate workforce with the skills of reading and writing passed down through the generations. As Richard Cobden explained to a Select Committee in 1838, 'the operatives living so much together, and generally having families, there is generally one in the family or connection who can write'. Often the educational role of the family was reinforced by the use of the Sunday school. By 1850 two-thirds of all children in the five to fourteen age group attended a Sunday school. Certainly, the educational achievements of many working people in the years before a formal system of education was introduced, have often been a revelation to later societies who mistakenly associate literacy with formal schooling. Throughout the Chartist period working men defended themselves in court, delivered speeches at mass rallies and penned articles and reports for the many Chartist newspapers that held the movement together.

Within the 'typical' Chartist locality the experience of radical politics reflected the integrated nature of the community culture. One Leicester stockinger's recollections of his workplace provide a fairly typical example of the way politics had entered the mainstream of working-class culture by this period. 'After tea' he remembers, 'a short article would be read from the *Northern Star*, and this would form the subject matter for consideration and chat during the remainder of the day'.

Women were also far more active in Chartism than was recognised by the early historians of the movement. Jutta Schwarzkopf's book *Women in the Chartist Movement* (1991) charts the extensive involvement of women in local Chartist activities. The Chartists themselves adopted a rather ambivalent approach to women's political activity. The Charter specified universal *manhood* suffrage and women were never part of the national leadership of the movement. The Chartist imagery, even that used by the women themselves, also appears to have accepted the notion of the woman's place being in the home. Schwarzkopf argues that the Chartist women adopted a role of pushing for reform on behalf of their menfolk by adopting 'the pose of radical wife and motherhood'. She reminds us that their involvement came at a time when politics was not seen as an appropriate sphere for women. Their extensive participation in Chartism represented a rejection, by working-class women, of the dominant definition of 'proper' feminine behaviour. We know of the existence of over 100 female radical associations formed to agitate for the Charter. The involvement of women in the areas where Chartism was strong testifies to the fact that the movement was to be the expression of integrated communities.

9 THE IDEOLOGY OF CHARTISM

Part of the shared experience of early industrialisation, in the communities from which Chartism grew, lay in the use of common ideas and values by which that experience was judged. The notion that Chartism was a working-class movement suggests the existence of a body of ideas that had currency with working people throughout the country. In other words it was not simply that many different communities experienced, say, the effects of trade depressions, or that they endured the same New Poor Law, or the same downward pressure on wages. Chartism grew because the communities in the different localities *interpreted* their experience in a similar way. This was more likely to happen in the Chartist period than at any previous time. The Industrial Revolution brought an improvement in communications to serve the needs of a developing economy. This reduced the apparent distances between areas and it was not only commodities that were transported but also ideas and news. This created the context within which a national movement could develop. Of course, the dispersal of Chartist support throughout the different localities always posed the problem of fragmentation. Nevertheless, Chartism was always more than a collection of local initiatives.

The Chartist press did more than any other single agency to create a common ideology within Chartism. The *Star* was the most popular of the many Chartist newspapers and, at the height of its popularity in 1839, it sold 50 000 copies a week. But it was only one of scores of newspapers that served the Chartist communities. Thomas Cooper ran four, at different times, in the Leicester region alone. In Glasgow, *The Chartist Circular* appeared, *Mcdouall's Chartist and Republican Journal*, served the Manchester area, whilst *Udgorn Cymru (The Trumpet of Wales)* was published in Merthyr Tydfil and Henry Vincent's *Western Vindicator* served the West Country. Each of these, and numerous others, established their own working-class readership.

There were differences of emphasis within these various publications. The debate over strategy was as lively as might be anticipated in a movement commited to open discussion and freedom of expression. Nevertheless, it is possible to identify a central corpus of ideas that formed the Chartist interpretation of the world. This began with a question, of the kind offered for consideration by the women Chartists of Manchester, in the columns of the *Star* in January 1842.

> Why is it that, in the midst of plenty, we are in such a condition? Why is it that those who are willing to work, that those who have produced everything in society, without whom the factories would not have been built, the machinery made, the railroads constructed, the canals cut, who build and man the ships, who fight the battles, make the hats, shoes and coats, and till the land – cannot get enough to quell the ravings of hunger?

1 *What does this statement tell us about working-class attitudes to the propertied classes?*

2 *The question in the document highlights the importance of the working people; how might an employer have responded?*

3 *On the basis of what you have read so far, how do you think the Chartists would have answered the question posed in the passage?*

4 *What light does this statement cast on the idea that Chartism was based on the 'politics of hunger'?*

In using their six-point political programme the Chartists were echoing earlier movements and drawing on a rich radical tradition. They also accepted the ideological basis of these earlier movements by sharing the arguments put forward by Paine in *The Rights of Man*. The vote was a right which no government could legitimately withold. This and other freedoms were the rights of the 'free born Englishman' which had been confiscated at some point in the past. Thus the Chartists embraced a sense of the past, with historical precedent frequently quoted to back their case. The very term 'People's Charter' was designed to evoke the image of Magna Carta, seen as a medieval protection against tyranny. The continued refusal to admit the working class to the franchise was seen as involving a continuing conspiracy by those who held power. Bronterre O'Brien, writing on the 'Rotten House of Commons' in *McDouall's Chartist and Republican Journal* in 1841, put it as follows:

> What have we gained by the increase in the constituency made by the Reform Bill? – I answer worse than nothing. We have merely augmented the number of our enemies . . . The men who made the Reform Bill were not fools; neither were the middle classes for whom it was made. – the Whigs saw, and the middle classes saw, that the effect of the Bill would be to unite all property against all poverty.

In this passage the complexities of social structure are reduced to a simple equation, 'property against poverty'. This kind of class-conscious statement did not necessarily mean that co-operation between the classes was out of the question. O'Brien himself responded enthusiastically to the early overtures of the Complete Suffrage Union, to the extent that he and O'Connor quarrelled over it. But in any such alliance the distinct position of the Chartists would have to be respected. John Collins shared the willingness of many Chartists for establishing a dialogue with the middle class. As a Chartist delegate to the Leeds Reform Association conference of 1841 and the CSU conferences of 1842, a pastor of the Chartist Church and the co-author of Lovett's founding text for 'education Chartism', Collins was essentially a moderate in his approach. Yet his expressed view was that 'if ever the middle classes united with them again it must be upon the principle of equality.'

The Chartists also claimed to occupy the moral high ground. Many had a background in nonconformity and used this to arrive at a radical reading of biblical texts. The point was frequently made that it was not Christianity that the Chartists opposed, but 'Priestianity'. Many Chartist meetings opened with a prayer and ended with the Old Testament warcry, 'To your tents O Israel'. The Church was seen as a corrupt arm of a pernicious system of government.

To summarise, we may see a sense of class identity expressed in the Chartist movement by identifying four facets. First, a view of the worth of the working class, second, the shared experience of early industrialisation, third, a corpus of ideas through which to interpret that experience and fourth, a sense that the values and interests of the working class were different in fundamental ways to those of other classes. Some of the bitterness of these feelings showed itself in the riots that broke out in August and September 1842.

10 THE 'PLUG RIOTS' OF 1842

The NCA organised the collection of 3 000 000 signatures for the second petition. This was presented to Parliament by a new Convention in May 1842. Assisted again by an economic depression, 1842 was probably the year of Chartism's greatest strength in terms of mass support. This made no difference to the prospects of the National Petition, which was rejected by a Commons vote of 287 to 46. In August, a series of large-scale strikes broke out in the Midlands, Lancashire, Yorkshire, and Lanarkshire. In these the workers used the traditional method of calling a strike; they went from factory to factory inviting the workers to join and to draw the plugs from the boilers, so closing their works. In this way work was stopped in 19 Lancashire towns, where the strikes were led predominantly by powerloom weavers. Yorkshire followed this example, with factories in 29 towns brought to a standstill. There were many clashes between the strikers and the authorities.

These strikes threw the Chartist national leadership into confusion. It was widely assumed that the strikes had been deliberately engineered by employers who were members of the Anti-Corn Law League, in order to engender the sort of crisis that would lead the government to repeal the Corn Laws. Certainly, some of the League leaders had spoken publicly of what they called the 'brickbat argument'. Nevertheless, there is little evidence to support the idea that the League provoked the strikes. Some historians have questioned the Chartist orientation of the strikes. J T Ward, for example, in his book *Chartism* (1974), argues that 'They [the Chartists] could never have organised the strikes; they had only sought to take advantage of disputes caused by industrial troubles . . .'. In fact, it is common to consider industrial organisations, like trade unions, to have been separate and distinct from political movements like Chartism. It is certainly the case that some of the well – established and highly-skilled 'aristocratic' trades held aloof from Chartism. Nevertheless, local studies of the situation in Lancashire and Staffordshire (where 'Plug' activity was strong) have pointed to the difficulty of separating industrial from political agitations, in terms of the people who gave them support. It should be remembered that most workplace organisation at this time was informal. Rather than establishing permanent organisations, groups of workers acted together bound simply by the informal links of the community. The lively agitation associated with the 'Plug' disturbances recalled the boisterous tradition of the food riot rather than the judicious and formalised actions of permanent and continuous trade associations. The 'Plug' disturbances involved workers from many trades and many areas, and lacked the sense of exclusivity, and sectional divisions between the trades, that would characterise the later history of trade unionism (*see chapter VII*). Historians who, unlike J T Ward, argue that Chartism was a movement of the working class (as opposed to simply a loose combination of various disaffected groups) point to the difficulty of distinguishing between 'political' and 'industrial' movements at such moments. Dorothy Thompson writes of the 'close interrelation between the Chartist movement and the actions of the trades in all districts.' The men and women involved in the strikes had also been involved in Chartism, and the strikers frequently argued at their meetings that their objective was to gain the Charter. It would seem that the strikes were led by local Chartist activists, rather than being a centrally orchestrated strategy on the part of the national leadership, many of whom were taken by surprise by the events.

Another round-up of Chartists followed the strikes. If anything, Peel's Tory government was firmer in their dealings with the Chartists than the Whigs had been in 1839. By the end of 1842 around 1500 people had been brought to court for Chartist-related offences. Chartism went into decline. By 1844 the *Northern Star* was failing to reach its break-even point of 4000 sales per week.

Chartism never regained the mass support it had enjoyed in 1839 and 1842. Nevertheless, its fortunes, which by 1844 seemed to be in terminal decline, were revived considerably by the Land Plan. This was a scheme that O'Connor had been contemplating for some time: the creation of rural communities of Chartists. This was to be different from the Owenite communities where the land was held in common. The Chartist Land Company, established in 1845, aimed to create a group of free-holders, each cultivating a patch of land which they owned. Chartists were invited to buy shares in the company, as members of local branches of the Land Company. The scheme was phenomenally successful in attracting support. By 1848 100 000 people were registered subscribers, hopeful that their names would be drawn by lot and their families settled in a Chartist community. Five such communities were established, each with its own impressive facilities of schools, parks and public baths. This was O'Connor at his most visionary, and it is clear from the strength of the response over this issue that he made contact with the aspirations of the world's first industrial working class, to an extraordinary extent. A hunger to return to the land was clearly latent and O'Connor drew this out. The Land Plan would provide an alternative to waged employment and, by absorbing surplus labour, reduce unemployment and raise wages throughout the economy.

Yet the scheme was not a success. Even O'Connor with his boundless optimism was unprepared for the level of support and the Land Company's administration was chaotic. More importantly, the government was openly hostile. In 1848 it instituted a Select Committee to investigate the affairs of the Company in the hope that it would uncover enough scandal to disgrace O'Connor. In the event O'Connor was found to have acted with integrity; in fact the Company owed him £23 000 which he would never recover. Nevertheless, the Company was wound up by Act of Parliament. The reason given was that places in the community were drawn by lot and that this element of chance meant that the Company was not a friendly society as it had claimed. Without the protection of the legislation covering friendly societies the company was technically an illegal body. There seems little doubt that worry and strain caused by running the Company, with his honesty in public question, contributed significantly to O'Connor's subsequent decline into insanity and his early death in 1855.

11 THE THIRD CHARTIST PETITION: 10 APRIL 1848 AND THE FEAR OF REVOLUTION

The popularity of the Land Plan meant that Chartism was flourishing again by 1848. This was the year that European revolutions put political solutions back on the agenda. A number of Chartist candidates had stood in the general election of 1847, in which a Whig government, under Lord John Russell, had been returned to office. In an electrifying campaign, O'Connor was elected for Nottingham. Inspired by this and a revolution in France, a Chartist Convention met in London in April 1848 to organise the delivery of a third petition to Parliament. This was to follow a mass meeting, on 10 April, at Kennington Common in London.

Chartism's last appearance as a mass movement was acted out against a backdrop of events on the mainland of Europe and in Ireland. European developments had always been important to British radicals. The French Revolution of 1789 figured prominently in the imagery of the Chartist movement, though the Chartists were always careful to divorce themselves from the violence of the Terror. The Cap of Liberty was frequently worn by Chartists or used to adorn their placards. The leaders of the French Revolution provided role models for some Chartists. Bronterre O'Brien was a great admirer of Robespierre. George Julian Harney, editor of the *Northern Star* from 1845, modelled himself on Marat. Harney often signed his articles 'L'Ami du Peuple' (the friend of the people), as had Marat. From 1847 Frederick Engels was the Paris correspondent of the *Northern Star*. When in February 1848 he sent word of a revolution in Paris the news was greeted enthusiastically. The National Charter Association sent a three-man delegation with a congratulatory address to be delivered to the new provisional government in Paris.

Radicalism in Ireland had been fairly subdued since the boisterous days of the the Catholic Association (see chapter X) but the failure of the potato crop in 1845 and the subsequent famine in Ireland only added to the Government's fear of a direct response. The famine led to criticism of English absentee landlords, of whom there were many in Parliament and not a few in the Whig administration. Although Chartism was never strong in Ireland, the Chartists were committed to the repeal of the Act of Union and found it easy to make common cause with the new spirit of Irish republicanism. A placard put out by the Chartist Convention on 5 April began; 'Irishmen resident in London, on the part of the democrats in England we extend to you the warm hand of fraternization; your principles are ours, and our principles are yours'.

The authorities found themselves confronted with the prospect of a simultaneous revival of both Chartism and Irish republicanism, in the broader context of turmoil throughout many European capitals. This goes some way to explaining the government's response to the intended meeting on 10 April. Besides the 7122 regular troops, 1231 pensioners and 4000 policemen available in London in April 1848, Russell's government authorised the enrollment of 85 000 special constables, mostly men from the middle class. The meeting planned for 10 April was declared illegal and the Queen was evacuated to Osborne House on the Isle of Wight.

In his book *1848. The British State and the Chartist Movement* (1987) John Saville argues that although the Chartists never intended or planned an armed confrontation for 10 April, this level of response should not be seen as an over-reaction on the part of the government. In the revolutionary context of 1848 the line between defensive and offensive violence seemed thinner than at any time during the Chartist years. Ernest Jones was a lawyer and a recent convert to the Chartist cause who took a leading role in the new Convention. He announced to a meeting on 9 April that 'If the government touch one hair of the head of the delegates – if they place them under arrest, or attempt the least interference with their liberty – every town represented by the delegates would be in arms in less than 24 hours'.

Saville suggests that it is the massive recruitment of Special Constables from within the ranks of the middle class that is the truly striking feature of the whole affair. He calls this 'a closing of ranks among all those with a property stake in the country'. Again the class structure of society seems to have appeared with stark clarity, and there are echoes here of O'Brien's notion of 'all property against all poverty'.

In the event the meeting on 10 April, which went ahead despite the ban, passed off without major incident. Around 20 000 people met on Kennington Common and set off, in an orderly procession, to present the petition to Parliament. The procession was stopped before it reached Westminster. After calming speeches from O'Connor and Jones a small group proceeded with the petition to the House of Commons. A parliamentary committee swiftly declared that, of the five and a half million signatures on the petition, less than two million were genuine. In the light of this the Commons decided not to receive the petition formally.

Such was the relief that the scenes of revolution which Berlin, Vienna, and Paris had witnessed in 1848, were not to be re-enacted on the streets of London, that the anxiety, which had engendered such a massive response in the authorities, swiftly turned to derision.

In the rush to condemn the Chartist Convention as a farce it was forgotten that even Parliament's hurried and hostile calculation of the petition's strength accepted that it contained over one and a half million genuine signatures. Despite the rejection of two previous petitions, Chartism could still muster a huge body of support. Also, rumours of the death of Chartism on 10 April were grossly overstated. The Chartists themselves tended to see 10 April as a moral victory or, in their words, a 'triumph'. Despite the government's apparent determination to provoke a confrontation, the petition had been delivered without bloodshed. The movement continued to grow in many areas until well into the summer of 1848 when nearly 300 Chartists were arrested following riots in Bradford, Manchester and Liverpool. After this the movement went into a slow decline that lasted ten years. Although it never again attracted the kind of support that had characterised 1839, 1842 and 1848, Chartist Conventions continued to meet until 1858.

Yet the myth that Chartism died of shame on the day it was revealed that 'Mr Punch' and 'Queen Victoria' had signed the petition, has proven to be very resilient. This is partly because it reflects the way many contemporaries wanted to see Chartism; as a misguided attempt by the hungry and uneducated to achieve a political citizenship for which they could surely have no real use or understanding. There is much of this condescention in the cartoon that appeared in *Punch* after the Kennington Common meeting.

Similarly when Charles Kingsley, the novelist and Anglican clergyman, depicted Chartism in his novel *Alton Locke*, published in 1850, he used the meeting on 10 April as a way of depicting the folly of the movement. His leading character, a tailor, gives Kingsley's account of the event and the role of the Chartist leadership in the debacle;

A PHYSICAL FORCE CHARTIST ARMING FOR THE FIGHT.

Punch *Cartoon, 1848*

> The meeting which was to have been counted by hundreds of thousands, numbered hardly its tens of thousands; and of them a frightful proportion of those very rascal classes, against whom we ourselves had offered to be sworn in as special constables. O'Connor's courage failed him after all. He contrived to be called away by some problematical superintendant of police. Poor Cuffy, the honestest, if not the wisest speaker there, leapt off the waggon, exclaiming that we were all 'humbugged and betrayed'; and the meeting broke up . . . while the monster petition crawled ludicrously away in a hack-cab, to be dragged to the floor of the House of Commons amidst roars of laughter . . .

1 *What view of the Chartist membership is given in the* Punch *cartoon and in the above extract?*

2 *What is Kingsley's opinion of the leadership of the movement?*

3 *How fair in their analysis of the Chartists do you consider these documents to be?*

4 *What do these two documents tell us about the relationship between the middle class and the working class at this time?*

12 THE FAILURE OF CHARTISM

There is little doubt that whatever its achievements in terms of mobilising large numbers of people towards a particular objective, Chartism must be adjudged an overall failure. The six points of political reform were not brought about until well into the next century, and it is difficult to attribute their acceptance then as in any direct way a result of the Chartist movement. The 'implicit social programme' remained similarly elusive; the hated Poor Law was a feature of British life until the abolition of the workhouse system in 1929; trade unions faced a constant battle for legal status, and working men did not enter Parliament in any numbers until the advent of the Labour Party. Sooner or later all historians of Chartism find themselves facing the central question, 'Why did Chartism fail?'.

Six years after Kennington Common, R G Gammage, a working man from Northampton who had been a local Chartist leader, reflected bitterly on a movement which, he felt, had failed through poor leadership. His *History of the Chartist Movement*, first published in 1854, particularly identified O'Connor as culpable in this respect. Other ex-Chartists shared Gammage's disappointment that the high hopes of the movement had come to nothing, but contested his interpretation of its cause. The Cheltenham Chartist, W E Adams criticised Gammage for concentrating too much on the 'personal squabbles of the leaders' and thereby missing, what he called the 'inspiring light of the movement.' He also expressed the hope that, 'Someday ... a work worthy of the movement will be taken in hand by a competent historian.' It is, of course, a matter for speculation whether or not subsequent historical treatments of Chartism have met these criteria, but these contemporary views are a reminder that our explanation of why Chartism failed depends very much on how we see the movement. *Punch*, Kingsley, and Gammage present us with a movement that was fragmented by disagreement and poorly led. Yet Adams' abiding memory of his experience is of the extraordinary motivation that made people become Chartists.

Modern-day analysis of the reasons for failure tends to fall into one of the two camps identified above; those who see the Chartists as architects of their own doom and those who choose to concentrate more on the 'inspiring light' of the movement. The distinction is really between those who blame Chartism's failure on its internal structure and those who relate its failure to the essentially hostile context in which it had to operate.

Undoubtedly, the simplest way to explain both the rise and the demise of Chartism is to see it as a form of 'hunger politics'. The periods of Chartism's greatest support, when the three petitions were submitted, were also times of economic depression. The period after 1850, when Chartism went into permanent decline, is widely accepted as having witnessed improvements in the standard of living. The link between hunger and the major Chartist initiatives is undeniable, but its significance is more difficult to determine. For example, if Chartism really was driven by despair was it ever a truly rational response to circumstances? Certainly middle-class observers at the time feared the motivation behind Chartism from this point of view. The philosopher Thomas Carlyle, writing in 1839, described it as 'bitter discontent grown fierce and mad'. From this perspective it is easy to sympathise with the accompanying argument that the working class were not yet 'ready' to exercise the vote. Their political immaturity, the argument goes, was best expressed in their willingness to follow 'mob-orators' like O'Connor. In this way the analysis of the leadership also reflects a perjorative view of the 'rank and file' of the movement. It is always worth remembering this point; that any commentary on the leadership also involves a judgement on the 'rank and file' by which it was followed.

Yet the closer we get to the Chartists themselves the less this interpretation seems to fit. As we have seen, Chartism was a predominantly peaceful, constitutional movement. The image of an irrational and uneducated following, ill-equipped to exercise the responsibilities of citizenship, does not accord well with what we know of the Chartists' own commitment to self-improvement and education. Chartism clearly drew strong support from people suffering severe economic hardship. But thinking of the movement as a 'hungry mob' tells us more about the fears of many contemporary observers than about the experience of the Chartists themselves. Speaking in the Parliamentary debate on the Chartist petition in 1842, the Whig politician T B Macaulay argued that 'universal suffrage is utterly incompatible with the very existence of civilisation.' His words echoed those of Edmund Burke who had warned in 1790 of the threat from the 'swinish multitude'. The Chartists, on the other hand, saw universal suffrage in terms of protecting a civilised society. The Scottish newspaper, the *Chartist Circular*, argued that, 'it is the only security against bad laws, and for good government'. Of course the Chartists often translated their demand for the vote as a right into more immediately accessible imagery. After the Charter, as a speaker at one Chartist meeting put it, there would be, 'plenty of roast beef, plum pudding and strong beer by working three hours a day'. Such statements were often delivered 'tongue in cheek' to elicit an ironic response from the audience and cannot be taken as evidence of political naivety.

Hunger was then, as it remains today, a good political educator. Whenever an economic and political system proves incapable of feeding its population, it inevitably runs the risk of having its validity questioned. But hunger has generally been equated with irrationality of behaviour where it has figured in the analysis of Chartism. This has provided a compelling explanation of Chartist failure with a convenient scapegoat in the shape of Feargus O'Connor, the most revered of the radical leaders and the most consistently maligned by historians. Mark Hovell, in his book *The Chartist Movement* (1917), refers to him as a 'blustering, egotistical, blarneying, managing, but intellectually and morally very unreliable Irishman'. Behind this, of course, lies a criticism of the thousands of working men and women who followed O'Connor: Hovell refers to their 'dog-like devotion'. This in itself is seen as a reflection of the underlying irrationality of Chartist motivation. As Hovell puts it, 'Impatience, engendered by fireless grates and breakfastless tables, was the driving force of much Northern Chartism.' Echoing this position, J T Ward, in *Chartism* (1974), finds that;

> The most impressive and moving aspect of Chartist history was that, despite all its charlatans, cowards and crooks, the movement retained the devoted loyalty of so many working men.

This image is extended through the language used to describe working people, who are seen individually as honest simpletons but collectively as a threatening mob. For Ward they are 'humble folk looking to the weekly spelling out of the *Star*' and also, 'The ragged hordes who swept over the Pennines to close Yorkshire mills in 1842'. The tragedy of Chartism, from this sort of perspective, is that O'Connor was allowed to advocate an empty 'physical force' strategy, at the expense of the moderate and conciliatory 'moral force' tactics advocated by men like William Lovett. Middle-class support, which might have been forthcoming, was frightened off by what Asa Briggs refers to as O'Connor's 'oratorical fireworks'.

There are two problems with this analysis. First, as James Epstein's authoritative biography demonstrates, O'Connor was not a 'physical force' Chartist. His Irish experience had taught him that citizen insurgents would fare badly against regular troops. He certainly advocated the Chartists' right to self-defence if they were attacked, but this was a point most Chartists were agreed upon. After all, as we have already seen, Lovett served a prison term for publicly advocating defensive violence in 1839. For O'Connor, the most direct route to the vote was via the Parliamentary petition, and it was to this strategy that he devoted his almost boundless energies. Secondly, middle-class sympathy with Chartism, was always qualified and tentative. As we saw earlier, even when the Complete Suffrage Union adopted the Six Points in 1842, Lovett was prepared to unite with O'Connor to defeat the initiative because both mistrusted the overtures being made. The Chartists wanted political change to take place on their terms and it was this, and not O'Connor's so called 'oratorical fireworks', that frightened many observers.

Nevertheless, there is a well-established tradition of interpreting Chartism as a movement before its time. The regions were too diverse, and the workforce too divided within itself for Chartism to have represented the claim for citizenship of a coherent working class. Many historians prefer to see a class-based society being the result of the more heavily industrialised and urbanised Britain of the early twentieth century. Perhaps Chartism should be seen as the last of the eighteenth-century radical movements, with malcontents from a variety of social groups mobilising the plebeians to challenge the *ancien regime*.

Developing this view Gareth Stedman-Jones, in a provocative essay in 1982, argued that the movement failed because its ideological horizons had been set in the eighteenth century. Confronted with industrial capitalism the Chartists could only draw on Painite radical ideas which defined the aristocracy, rather than the employer, as the villain of the piece. He argued that Chartism lacked a view of social change, its main focus of attack being the unrepresentative state. Thus, when the state began to introduce real and tangible reforms like the repeal of the Corn Laws (1846) or the Ten Hours Act (1847) the Chartist case, that the state was incorrigibly corrupt, began to crumble. Chartism failed because changing circumstances rendered its argument irrelevant to the situation in which working people found themselves.

Stedman-Jones, a left-wing historian himself, has received some energetic rebuffs from other historians who share his broad political persuasion. The argument that Chartism's ideology was inappropriate for the period has particularly been challenged through local studies examining the position of the movement in the localities. Chartism may have pre-dated the major publications of Marx and Engels but this did not prevent working people from understanding that they were being exploited and by whom. The point about the changing nature of the state is perhaps more interesting as a line of analysis. It moves us on to the alternative mode of explanation which focuses on the response of the government to the movement and the context of authority within which Chartism operated.

It is easy to conclude that because Chartism failed it must, *therefore*, have been immature, fragmented, and badly-led. This point is often developed by comparing the failure of the Chartists with the success of the Anti-Corn Law League. The ACLL, the argument goes, was well-organised, directed its energies to a single achievable end, and cultivated the support of Members of Parliament. But the success of the ACLL was not exclusively the result of good organisation any more than Chartist failure was simply the result of bad organisation (*see pages 144–9*). Neither agitation should be divorced from the wider political context in which it was located. The ACLL was largely composed of voters and Peel's conversion to free trade in 1846 was motivated by an awareness of the need to make concessions to a powerful economic and political group in order to reinforce the social compact between the middle class and the aristocracy that had been established in 1832. Peel was also concerned with the immediate issue of the food supply, in the wake of the Irish famine. Chartism, on the other hand, raised the issue of the political status quo in a quite different way. What we can be certain of is that the Whig and Tory governments who rejected the petitions in 1839, 1842 and 1848, feared the consequences of accepting the Charter far more than the dangers involved in turning it down.

Following in the tradition established by E P Thompson, many historians have turned the 'hunger politics' orthodoxy on its head. Here we are back to Adams' 'inspiring light'. Given its circumstances, perhaps Chartism was a pretty impressive movement, so the argument goes. It mobilised thousands, and demonstrated the existence of a working class able to think and act for itself. The 'threat' of Chartism was not that of the 'mob' driven to despair but rather that of a group challenging for power. This challenge was met by a resolute stance from a political establishment reinforced by the political compact of 1832 between the aristocracy and the new wealth of the middle class. In her work, Dorothy Thompson makes the point that far from being a fragmented movement, the Chartists were able to conjure up a degree of cohesion that was truly remarkable. She describes Chartism as 'the response of a literate and sophisticated working class'. Chartist failure was a reflection of the strength of its adversaries, rather than its own inherent weakness. The resolute stance to each petition was born of a confidence in the political settlement of 1832. The army remained loyal and the police force was extended in these years. Chartism as a problem of 'law and order' was less threatening than the prospect of accepting the Charter. Chartism as a movement was very efficiently suppressed, its own commitment to peaceful methods undoubtedly assisting the task of the authorities. Also, it is clear that with the repeal of the Corn Laws and the passing of the long-awaited Ten Hours Act, it became more difficult to assert that only a 'root and branch' change in the political system could bring about improvement. With the end of Chartism working people turned their attention to the achievement of less ambitious, but more obviously attainable, objectives.

13 BIBLIOGRAPHY

Asa Briggs (ed), *Chartist Studies* (Macmillan, 1959). Briggs' volume made the case for the regional study of Chartism and this collection includes studies of the movement in a number of localities. Also included are some good essays dealing with 'national' aspects of the movement (see especially F C Mather on the government and the Chartists and Lucy Brown on relations with the Anti-Corn Law League).

J Epstein *The Lion of Freedom* (Croom Helm, 1982). This book offers a much-needed revision of the orthodox view of O'Connor, and sees him as the leader chosen by a politically-conscious working class.

J Epstein and D Thompson (eds) *The Chartist Experience* (Macmillan,

1982). This collection of essays picks up the regional approach established by Briggs, but pursues a particular theme in each area. See especially R Sykes, on Chartism and trade unions in the North-West. Also contains Stedman-Jones' controversial essay 'The language of Chartism'.

Joe Finn *Chartism and The Chartists* (Hodder and Stoughton, 1992) is a good source for documentary material on the movement.

D Jones *The Last Rising* (Clarendon Press, 1985): a sympathetic and thorough account of the Newport rising.

J Saville *1848* (Cambridge University Press, 1987). This is a systematic treatment of one important year in the life of Chartism. Saville explores the relationship between 'high' politics and the popular movement and challenges the myth that grew up about the meeting of 10 April.

J Schwarzkopf *Women in the Chartist Movement* (Macmillan, 1991). This is a much-needed study of the role women played in the movement.

D Thompson *The Chartists* (Temple Smith, 1984). If you were only ever going to read one book on Chartism this ought to be the one. Dorothy Thompson's book explores the role of particular groups within the movement, particularly in terms of their values and beliefs.

J T Ward *Chartism* (Batsford, 1973). This is the most recent book to provide a narrative account of Chartism. It is sceptical about the claim that the movement's supporters were a politically conscious working class and depicts a movement betrayed by inept leaders and fragmented strategy.

14 DISCUSSION POINTS AND EXERCISES

A *Discussion points*

1 What did Chartism inherit from earlier movements?

2 What was the case *against* universal manhood suffrage in 1839?

3 Argue the case *for* the six points in 1839, (and don't forget annual Parliaments).

4 Who were the Chartists?

5 What role did hunger play in Chartism?

6 To what extent was Chartism a national movement?

7 What was Feargus O'Connor's contribution to the Chartist movement?

8 What was the Chartist attitude towards the middle class?

9 Why was the Land Plan was so popular with working people?

10 Why did Chartism fail?

B *Essay questions*

Chartism remains a fascinating enigma for historians; a movement capable of attracting massive support but which failed to achieve any of the objectives which it set for itself. Most of the questions you will be asked to consider will hinge around this issue, asking for a consideration of the nature of Chartist support and/or an analysis of the reasons for Chartist failure. Here are some examples of this approach;

1 'Its failure stemmed from particularly inept leadership.' Discuss.

2 To what extent did support for Chartism simply reflect the fluctuations in the British economy in the 1830s and 1840s?

3 Did Chartism fail because lower-class unrest was basically a 'knife and fork' question?

4 To what extent did the Chartist movement fail because its programme of reform was totally impractical?

In tackling questions of this kind you need to appreciate the complexity of the issue under scrutiny. What is not called for is an extended list. Thus, for question 1 a list-style answer will respond with something like; 'Well, poor leadership was important in the failure of Chartism, but so were ten other factors and here they are in no particular order... '. However good the list that follows the answer will never get to the heart of the question, which asks you to consider the nature of leadership in the context of the failure of the movement. In order to answer any of these questions you will need more than 'ten reasons for failure'. You will need to arrive at a position on the movement. You should be aware of the range of different positions identified in section 1 and explored more fully in section 12. Consider particularly the relationship between the analysis of the leadership and the way you view the 'rank and file' of the movement. Your interpretation of Chartism's failure will hinge around your view of the nature of the working community and what it was capable of at the time.

B *Exercises*

1 Construct a list of the laws that might have been passed, or repealed, by a Parliament elected on the basis of the Charter. For each item on your list you should explain any evidence from your study of the movement, and its precursors, that supports its inclusion. In doing this remember the image of Chartism as an 'umbrella movement' carrying with it an 'implicit social programme'.

15 DOCUMENTARY EXERCISE – FOR AND AGAINST THE CHARTER

Read this extract from a speech delivered in the House of Commons, 3 May 1842, by T B Macaulay, Whig MP for Edinburgh, on the motion that the House accept the Charter, and also the one that follows from the *Chartist Circular*. Try to answer the questions on the two extracts.

> (1) . . . I believe that universal suffrage would be fatal to all purposes for which governments exist, and for which aristocracies and all other things exist, and that it is utterly incompatible with the very existence of civilisation. I conceive that civilisation rests on the security of property . . .
> . . . I believe that nothing is more natural than that the feelings of the people should be such as they are described to be. Even we, ourselves, with all our advantages of education, when we are tried by the temporary pressure of circumstances, are too ready to catch at everything which may hold out the hope of relief . . . and I cannot but see, that a man having a wife at home to whom he is attached, growing thinner every day, children whose wants become every day more pressing, whose mind is principally employed in mechanical toil, may have been driven to entertain such views as are here expressed, partly from his own position, and partly from the culpable neglect of the government in omitting to supply him with the means and the power of forming a better judgement. Let us grant that education would remedy these things, shall we not wait until it has done so, before we agree to such a motion as this ...

> (2) The Charter defended by *The Chartist Circular*, published in Glasgow, price one halfpenny.

Here are a series of extracts from the leading article in the edition for 2 January 1841 in which each of the six points is considered in turn. This article adopted a popular format in Chartist journalism, that of a dialogue between two parties, one a sceptic and the other a convinced Chartist. They begin with the issue of universal manhood suffrage:

> Do you think it [universal suffrage] essential to obtain and secure good government? I do for the following reasons: – First, because the possession of the franchise is the only difference between a freeman and the Russian serf, who is sold with the land and the cattle. . . It is the only security against bad laws and for good government which otherwise depends upon the caprice and fears of the master class who make the laws; and while the exclusive few have a profitable interest in bad laws, there will be no barrier to tyranny and corruption . . .

Why do you prefer Annual Parliaments to Septennial, as at present? Because we should be enabled, by this means, to get rid of a bad servant at the end of one year, instead of being fixed with him for seven as at present.

But would a man be able, in one year, to obtain an insight into the forms of Parliament, and would it be prudent to dismiss a man as soon as he became useful? This is begging the question; we should not dismiss an honest and capable man, and the sooner a dishonest or incapable one is dismissed the better.

... But would you send men to Parliament not worth a shilling? I doubt whether a man without a shilling would be elected; but the present property qualification is a farce; if a man has money or interest enough to get into Parliament he can purchase a sham qualification for £100. But why should not a poor man, if he has ability sufficient, and the majority of the electors have confidence in him, be elected? If none but rich men are sent to Parliament, the feelings of the poor cannot be fairly represented.

1 *What are the arguments against accepting the Charter, as put by Macaulay?*

2 *What are the arguments in favour of accepting the Charter, as put by the* Chartist Circular?

3 *What does Macaulay mean by 'civilisation rests on the security of property?'*

4 *Can you think of any reasons why the* Chartist Circular *chose to present its case in the form of a conversation between two parties?*

5 *What view of the working community comes through from each of these extracts?*

6 *What light do these documents cast on the failure of Chartism?*

V

PEEL AND THE CONSERVATIVE PARTY

—

1 A CONTROVERSIAL CONSERVATIVE

A strong case could be made for the claim that Sir Robert Peel (1788–1850), Conservative Prime Minister 1834–5, and 1841–6, was the most far-sighted and courageous British statesman of the nineteenth century. To his modern biographer, Professor Norman Gash (*see bibliography pages 159–60*), Peel is also, by virtue of his political ideas and practice, the founder of modern Conservatism. And yet, in December 1845, at the climax of Peel's career, the *Morning Post* – a staunchly right-wing newspaper – could attack Peel in the following terms:

> His whole career since 1842 has been one of insanity or treachery . . . We regard him as the most loathsome of public men. His abilities (which are unquestionable) only add to his odiousness. He prostitutes to the meanest purposes the talents which God has given him . . . That the Tories should ever again have anything to do with him, we can not suppose.

It will be the main objective of this chapter to explain how Peel can be simultaneously regarded as both the villainous betrayer of Toryism and the patron-saint of Conservatism.

2 THE IMPACT OF REVOLUTION

The French Revolution and the Industrial Revolution were the two great events which, in their many ramifications, dominated Peel's whole political career.

By the time Peel first entered Parliament in 1809, the verdict of Britain's political establishment on the revolution in France was unanimous: it had been a disaster for European civilisation. The wars which had followed in its wake (Napoleon was still six years away from his final defeat) were bad enough. But the Terror which had convulsed Paris between 1791 and 1794 had imprinted images on the minds of British politicians that were horrific and impermeable: the mob rampant; the Church desecrated and despoiled; its priests and bishops butchered; and the French aristocracy, either driven into exile or, like Louis XVI and Marie Antoinette themselves, victims of the guillotine. If one question dominated the thoughts of Tories and Whigs alike for most of the nineteenth century, it was this: how could the forces which might seek the destruction of *Britain's* landed aristocracy be neutralised?

To many of Britain's landowners, especially its Tory ones, it was all too easy to identify the forces which they believed threatened them. The Industrial Revolution filled them with profound unease and suspicion. A new world, certainly beyond their control, and probably beyond their understanding, was in the process of being created. When – and how – would the wealthy new factory owners begin to demand their share of power? Could the heathen, ignorant and brutalised workers be tamed? Or would the unnerving cycles of economic boom and slump, to which industrial capitalism was prone, bring down the whole social order in a terrible conflagration?

Peel was frightened of revolution himself. A loathing of the mob, and a bitter contempt for those politicians who agitated the masses, shaped his political outlook until the end. At times, Peel's personal fear of revolution was very real: he twice went so far as to have his country house armed and fortified for fear that it would be stormed, first during the Reform crisis of 1831, secondly at the peak of political unrest in 1842. But his political strategy for coping with such problems was distinctly more sophisticated and constructive than the average Tory's. In particular, his attitude to the Industrial Revolution was positive. While he understood the feelings of those who preferred the order and certainties of traditional rural society, he knew that there could be no going back to the 'Merrie England' which Tory squires remembered – or imagined – so fondly. Furthermore, Peel understood that in its capacity to generate wealth and employment, industrialisation might represent an essential part of the *solution* to the threats of mass poverty and overpopulation which he believed British society was facing. A well-fed workforce would not rush to shed its blood on any barricades. And why should Tories assume that the factory owners were natural radicals and revolutionaries? They were men of property themselves, with much to lose if the mob was somehow unleashed. A government that was responsive to their needs and anxieties would win their support. That government could be a Conservative one.

3 Peel's Early Years: An Apprenticeship in Power

It seems certain that Peel's insight into the constructive potential of industrialisation – and into the Conservative political potential of industrialists – owed much to his own family background. His grandfather was one of the pioneers of the Lancashire cotton industry. Peel's own father, a shrewd and ambitious businessman, built on this success. By the 1780s, he was one of the north-west's wealthiest industrialists. But he had also bought extensive landed property for himself in Staffordshire, and therefore, according to the customs of the age, enjoyed the right to sit as Member of Parliament for Tamworth.

Politically speaking, Peel Senior was an uncomplicated Tory. He was determined that his son Robert should continue to add to the fame and fortunes of the family, and the boy was prepared for a career in politics with an education at Harrow and Oxford University. Young Robert proved to be a quite brilliant student. His prodigious capacity for hard work was complemented by a powerful and rigorous intellect, and a daunting determination to succeed at his studies and in the wider world. He did not have to wait long after taking his 'Double First' at Oxford for an opportunity to enter Parliament. Government patronage – and his father's money – won him the affections of the electors of Cashel, County Tipperary, in Ireland. He was only 21-years-old when he became their MP. It was the start of an astonishing career.

A Chronology of Peel's Career 1809–30

1809 Peel enters Parliament as MP for Irish borough of Cashel.
1810 Appointed Under Secretary for War and the Colonies.
1812 Appointed Chief Secretary for Ireland by Lord Liverpool, the new Prime Minister.
1814 Peel's Peace Preservation Act creates Ireland's first professional police force.
1817 Speaks out decisively against Catholic Emancipation. Rewarded with invitation to become MP for Oxford University.
1818 Resigns Irish Secretaryship.
1819 Appointed Chairman of Currency Committee. Makes himself an expert in the field of banking and finance.
1822 Appointed Home Secretary. Begins extensive reforms of the criminal law.
1827 April. Canning becomes Prime Minister. Peel refuses to serve as Home Secretary, being opposed to Canning's policy of Catholic Emancipation.
1828 January. Wellington becomes Prime Minister. Peel returns to the Home Office.

1829 Peel founds Metropolitan (London) Police. Wellington and Peel (despite his earlier beliefs) force Catholic Emancipation through Parliament, breaking up the Tory Party, and Peel is forced out of his seat representing Oxford University.

1830 Wellington's ministry defeated in the Commons when he rejects all calls for Parliamentary Reform. Peel goes into opposition for the first time in his political career.

1 *What benefits would a government hope to derive from appointing a young man like Peel to high office so early in his career?*

2 *What benefits might Peel derive as a future Prime Minister from the experiences of his first two decades of power?*

In at least one important sense, however, Peel's high-flying early career did not ideally equip him for his later responsibilities: it confined him to a restricted understanding of the business of politics. Hardly ever out of office between 1810 and 1830, he was never able to see the world from the perspective of the backbenches – a limitation which was to have dramatic consequences for Peel and the way in which he treated his own party in the 1840s.

What *did* Peel learn from his two decades' apprenticeship? One of his most important lessons is often overlooked by historians: these years turned Peel into a confirmed authoritarian, for whom a strong executive was the pre-requisite of good government. His response to the disorder endemic in Ireland on his arrival as Chief Secretary in 1812 was symptomatic. He outlawed the dissident Catholic organisation which was leading the campaign for equal civil rights, and created Ireland's first centrally-controlled police force. Similarly, as Home Secretary, his most famous single innovation was the foundation of the Metropolitan Police. In part, this was a response to a crime wave in Georgian London. But just as important to Peel was the fact that its creation gave the executive another arm with which to control popular political dissent. In an age of frequent public disorder, it was thought essential that London – the seat of government – should be secured from the threat of the revolutionary mob.

Hand in hand with such tough-minded Toryism, however, went a cautious leaning towards reform. Much of Peel's time as Home Secretary was devoted to improving prison conditions and streamlining the confused and cluttered penal code, notably by abolishing the death penalty for numerous trivial offences. As D Beales has pointed out (*see bibliography page 160*), the radicalism of such reforms can be exaggerated, and it is true that their main intention seems to have been to make the workings of the law more rational rather than more merciful. But the attitude they embodied is significant. Traditionally-minded Tories had a near mystical veneration for every aspect of the English legal system, no matter how absurd or out of date it might objectively be. Peel was less sentimental. He believed that if the aristocratic constitution was to survive, it had to work efficiently and, moreover, be *seen* to be working efficiently. If that meant pruning anomalies and simplifying legal processes, it was a price worth paying. However cautious and modest his actions were by comparison, 'reform to preserve' might have been Peel's motto as well as Grey's.

Bolder and more significant in its implications for future policy was Peel's increasing involvement in economic affairs. His Chairmanship of the Currency Committee (closely examined by Hilton in his reappraisal of Peel – *see bibliography page 160*) prepared the way for Britain's return to the gold standard, and helped to check the combination of inflation and speculation that threatened Britain's economic stability in the aftermath of the Napoleonic Wars. Just as significant was his work with Liverpool's financial mastermind, Huskisson, in the 1820s. It seems likely that this apprenticeship – as well as his own meticulous reading of the classics of economic theory by Adam Smith (*see pages 142–3*) and others – helped to convince Peel of the case for lowering tariffs and for free trade. Such policies were to be pursued by Peel during his great ministry of the 1840s, with dramatic consequences.

In the meantime, Peel was earning himself the reputation as a master in his own right of complicated fiscal and currency questions. Politicians who understood the arcane but vitally important technicalities of the new 'political economy' were very rare at the time. Peel's expertise in this field helped to make him a central, indispensable figure in early nineteenth-century government.

If one theme unites Peel's growth as a political figure over these two decades, it is his consummate professionalism. His powerful intellect and capacity for sheer hard work made him a superlative administrator. In the Commons, although he was not a brilliant or charismatic speaker, his lucid mastery of his brief and the measured and reasoned style of his exposition of policy won him universal respect, and the vital votes of independent-minded back benchers. In the political confusion that followed the resignation (1827) of Lord Liverpool, it was widely thought that Peel's support for a particular policy – or a particular ministry – would be the decisive factor in its fortunes. In or out of office alike, he would enjoy immense power. Peel knew very well that, with that power, immense responsibility would come. But even he might have been surprised by how onerous and painful his responsibilities would be in the years 1829–32.

4 CATHOLIC EMANCIPATION, THE GREAT REFORM ACT AND THE CRISIS OF EXECUTIVE GOVERNMENT

The crisis over Catholic Emancipation and the Great Reform Act (*see pages 301–4 and 22–8 respectively*) are analysed elsewhere in this book.

What must be considered here is Peel's role in them and what they reveal about his political beliefs and political judgements.

Peel was extremely reluctant to agree to Wellington's desperate request that he take the leading role in piloting Catholic Emancipation through the Commons. The proposal outraged many Tories, who believed that Anglican domination of Irish (and British) politics should be defended to the last.

Peel himself had been, in the past, the most persuasive defender of the Protestants' monopoly of political power in Ireland. For Peel now to throw his weight behind the Catholic cause would constitute an extraordinary political U-turn. It would inevitably do grave damage to Peel's reputation for political consistency and integrity, and might well wreck his career.

Peel was in an extraordinarily difficult position. In private, he had been growing increasingly sceptical about whether anti-Catholic discrimination could remain the linchpin of British rule in Ireland, or be sustained as government policy in the face of growing support for Emancipation in the Commons. But the election of Daniel O'Connell, the Catholics' leader, as MP for County Clare in 1828 gave the question a dreadful urgency (*see pages 303–4*). If Parliament rejected Emancipation, many feared that rebellion would break out in Ireland. Without doubt, Wellington's government would fall-and so confused and divided was the Commons in 1828–9 that no other conceivable government was likely to survive for more than a few weeks. Political paralysis at Westminster combined with civil war in Ireland was an appalling prospect to anyone, but to someone as firmly wedded to the ideal of firm executive government as Peel, it was unthinkable.

Peel felt that he had no choice. He actually introduced the Bill for Emancipation to the Commons. This 'betrayal' of the Protestant cause, and the vilification that rained down on his head as a consequence, was the price Peel believed he had to pay to prevent Ireland collapsing into bloody anarchy. His support for Wellington was instrumental in securing the passage of the Bill, and perhaps saved Ireland from civil war.

The episode is profoundly revealing of Peel's political temper and views. He showed cool judgement, great courage, and a readiness to make considerable sacrifices for higher ends. (His name was indeed dirt in High Tory circles for years to come, and the staunchly Protestant electors of Oxford University forced him out of their prestigious parliamentary seat.) Above all, it shows Peel's attachment to the executive tradition of government – his determination to serve what he saw as the national interest, regardless of the expectations of his fellow Tories.

The Great Reform Act reveals the less constructive side of Peel's approach to politics. His record as Home Secretary had won him the reputation of a cautiously forward-looking, reformist Tory, and he was probably in favour of a modest instalment of parliamentary reform. But the scale of the measure introduced by the Whigs in 1831 staggered and outraged him, and he found himself forced into a position of complete opposition to the Bill.

Some of Peel's Tory colleagues reacted to the Bill as if it marked the end of civilisation itself – or at least of the aristocratic predominance in British politics and society. Peel was less hysterical and more perceptive in his criticisms of it. He rightly warned that – despite the Whigs' promises – their settlement would not be final. He also realised that the Bill would increase the authority of the House of Commons relative to the Lords and the Monarchy, thus making it harder for the executive to do its job and serve the true interests of the nation. Peel had a point: a Commons which had more accurately and forcefully represented the deeply anti-Catholic prejudices of the English people would never have passed Catholic Emancipation.

One feature of the reform crisis particularly disturbed Peel. The Bill had been forced through Parliament in what seemed, at times, like an atmosphere of impending revolution in society at large. Peel himself had gone as far as to have his country mansion fortified, and wrote darkly of preparing for civil war. For all this, the Whigs were to blame – it was they, Peel was convinced, who had recklessly inflamed popular passions, to pressurise the king and the Lords into passing their Reform Bill. Here was dramatic confirmation to Peel of one of his great principles – politics had to be kept out of the hands of the mob.

It is perhaps therefore not surprising that Peel failed to grasp the more conservative objectives of the Whigs' Bill, or to foresee the contribution which the recruitment of hundreds of thousands of middle-class property owners was to make to the defence of the landed constitution in times of future political disorder. In fact, the reformed constitution was to prove the bedrock of political order for the next 35 years – not least during the traumatic disturbances which were to afflict Peel's own ministry between 1841 and 1846.

The Reform Crisis was not to end without testing Peel's high principle of the duty of a politician to serve his king come what may, to breaking point. In May 1832, the Reform Crisis was at its peak. Grey had resigned after William IV refused to promise to create enough Peers so as – if necessary – to force the Bill through the Lords. The king, left without a government, asked Wellington to try and fill the breech. The latter believed that, with Peel's help, it might be possible to form a moderately reformist Tory ministry. But, this time, Peel turned down Wellington's – and the king's – appeals.

By Peel's standards, this was a striking abdication of duty. Wellington certainly felt badly let down, and for some years relations between the two were icy. But Peel believed that, in the debates over Reform, his criticisms of the Whig proposals had been so strong as to make his joining any reform ministry – even one led by Wellington –

look like another breathtaking U-turn. A second 'betrayal' would have brought his political career to an end. It was a sacrifice he was not prepared to make: there were limits to even Peel's commitment to the 'executive tradition' of government.

What was the lasting significance of these years of crisis for Peel? In one important sense, their impact was negative. Catholic Emancipation and the Great Reform Act between them smashed up the Tory Party and inaugurated a decade of Whig political dominance. It would be 1841 before Peel returned to office with a parliamentary majority and was able to pick up the threads of reform and fiscal innovation which he had been helping to spin in the 1820s.

But the events of these years also made it necessary for Peel to redefine his political agenda. As he understood all too well, Catholic Emancipation made it logically impossible to rely solely on Protestant power and goodwill for the government of Ireland. Support from the Catholics would be needed too. Accordingly, the Irish legislation of the 1841–6 ministry would have, as its main objective, the building of an improved relationship with the Catholic Church and the Irish Catholic laity – while, of course, keeping the separatist forces of nationalism firmly in check. Parliamentary Reform itself forced Peel to undertake a redefinition of Tory principles more suitable for – and attractive to – the widened electorate. And as he had feared, it created new problems in establishing a working relationship between the political executive and political parties. Now that 'the king's Ministers' could no longer rely on a block of support from the rotten boroughs to sustain them in office, were they instead to be forced to dance to the tune being played by their party? Peel's answer to this last question – an emphatic and unyielding NO – was to determine the ultimate fate of his great ministry.

Finally, we should not underestimate the psychological impact which these difficult and traumatic years had on Peel. Twice within four years, under the combined pressure of internal divisions and external threat, the authority of the British state had come perilously close to crumbling. For Peel, the great lesson of 1829–32 was that politics had to be kept out of the hands of the mob and that, if concessions were to be made, they had better be made from a position of strength. Whether the shocks of these years left Peel oversensitive to the fragility of the political order, and too quick to sacrifice the interests of his supporters in order to buy off his enemies, are questions to which we will return in sections 8 and 9.

5 THE ROAD TO RECOVERY 1832–41

Between 1832 and 1841, the Tories enjoyed the most spectacular recovery in the history of British party politics.

General Election Results 1832–41

December 1832	Whigs 473	Tories 185
January 1835	Whigs 379	Conservatives 279
August 1837	Whigs 344	Conservatives 314
July 1841	Whigs 291	Conservatives 367

How can the success of this extraordinary fight back be explained?

The Tories' position in 1832 was dreadful: but it was not as catastrophic as first appearances suggest. The heart of their difficulties had been their complete mishandling of the question of parliamentary reform. As the results of the 1831 general election show, even loyal Tory voters must have been driven to vote Whig by the die-hard attitude adopted by the leadership. If Wellington and Peel could only reconcile themselves to the world recreated by the Great Reform Act, Tory voters would feel able to return to their political home.

By contrast, it was Parliamentary Reform alone which had kept Grey's cabinet united, and won for the Whigs a level of electoral popularity unknown for half-a-century. The remaining items on the Whigs' political agenda, like the restructuring of the Anglican Church of Ireland, were likely to lose the party electoral support, and divide it.

It was not long before a major split duly occurred amongst the Whigs. Russell, one of the more adventurous Whigs, floated a plan to divert some of the wealth of the Church of Ireland (which, he argued, was serving little purpose in that predominantly Catholic country) to more obviously useful ends like the building of schools and hospitals. But to hard-line Anglican whigs, such as Lord Stanley and Sir James Graham, such a redistribution of Church property would be little better than robbery. Unable to work with Russell and his Radical friends, they left the party. Eventually, they were to join Peel's front bench.

Such policies, and the divisions they wrought, culminating in Lord Grey's resignation as Prime Minister in 1834, left William IV badly unsettled. His response was a surprise: in November 1834 the king dismissed Melbourne, the new Whig Prime Minister, and installed a minority Conservative government in its place. Peel was to be Prime Minister. Although this minority ministry only lasted for five months, being turned out in April 1835 when the Whigs regrouped their forces, it was not without significance for Tory fortunes. William IV's selection of Peel effectively confirmed his leadership of the party, which some reactionary Tories had been reluctant to accept. It also gave Peel the perfect platform from which to offer the British people an updated version of his political beliefs: the Tamworth Manifesto.

> . . . I will not accept power on the condition of declaring myself an apostate from [traitor to] the principles on which I have

heretofore acted. At the same time, I never will admit that I have been, either before or after the Reform Bill, the defender of abuses, or the enemy of judicious reforms. I appeal with confidence, in denial of the charge, to the active part I took in the great question of the Currency – in the consolidation and amendments of the Criminal Law – in the revisal of the whole system of Trial by Jury – to the opinions I have professed, and uniformly acted on, with regard to other branches of the jurisprudence of the country – I appeal to this as a proof that I have not been disposed to acquiesce in acknowledged evils, either from the mere superstitious reverence for ancient usages, or from the dread of labour or responsibility in the application of a remedy.

But the Reform Bill, it is said, constitutes a new era, and it is the duty of a Minister to declare explicitly – first, whether he will maintain the Bill itself, and secondly, whether he will act upon the spirit in which it was conceived.

With respect to the Reform Bill itself, I will repeat now the declaration which I made when I made when I entered the House of Commons as a Member of the Reformed Parliament, that I consider the Reform Bill a final and irrevocable settlement of a great Constitutional question – a settlement which no friend to the peace and welfare of this country would attempt to disturb, either by direct or insidious means.

Then, as to the spirit of the Reform Bill, and the willingness to adopt and enforce it as a rule of government; if, by adopting the spirit of the Reform Bill, it be meant that we are to live in a perpetual vortex of agitation; that public men can only support themselves in public estimation by adopting every popular impression of the day, – by promising the instant redress of anything which anybody may call an abuse, if this be the spirit of the Reform Bill, I will not undertake to adopt it. But if the spirit of the Reform Bill implies merely a careful review of institutions, civil and ecclesiastical, undertaken in a friendly temper, combining, with the firm maintenance of established rights, the correction of proved abuses and the redress of real grievances, – in that case, I can for myself and colleagues undertake to act in such a spirit and with such intentions . . .

Our object will be – the maintenance of peace . . . the support of public credit – the enforcement of strict economy – and the just and impartial consideration of what is due to all interests – agricultural, manufacturing, and commercial . . .

1 *The Tamworth Manifesto is generally regarded as the first sustained statement of 'Conservative' principles. What does Peel imply were the differences between:*

- **a)** *Conservatism and die-hard Toryism?*
- **b)** *Conservatism and Radicalism?*

2 *The Manifesto was issued on the eve of the 1835 general election. Obviously, Peel wanted to persuade more people to vote Tory! But what particular sectors of the electorate do you imagine he was targetting, and with what particular appeals and promises?*

3 *Look again at pages 120–1 for a brief account of Peel's approach to government in the 1820s. Was there anything* new *about 'Tamworth Conservatism'?*

The form of the Tamworth Manifesto is perhaps as important and revealing as its message. Although the Manifesto was styled as an address to Peel's own constituents, it was in fact designed for immediate release to the national press. A contemporary recorded that it made 'a prodigious sensation'. The Tories had clearly recognised that they had to win round 'public opinion' to their side: the days when they could rely mostly on royal support, rotten boroughs and local influence for a free-hold on power were gone. The Tories were quickly adapting to the political requirements of the post-Reform order.

The Manifesto was by no means Peel's only advertisement for the virtues of Conservative moderation. Between 1833 and 1838, he lost few opportunities to present himself and his party in a responsible and positive light. He refused to adopt a strategy of opposition for opposition's sake. For example, he supported – at the price of a few amendments – the Whigs' Municipal Corporation Act (1835), even though it brought to an end decades of (often corrupt) Tory rule in many boroughs. The controversial New Poor Law (*see pages 55–6*) also had his expert approval, while the Ecclesiastical Commission set up by Peel in 1835 became a model of how Whigs and Tories – with the help of prominent clergymen – could work together to improve the financing and administration of the Church of England. Peel was keeping the promise he had made in the Tamworth Manifesto to approach the general question of reform with an open and unfailingly constructive mind.

But Peel's attempt to capture the political middle ground did not entail – at least as yet – a betrayal of old-fashioned Toryism. Even in the Tamworth Manifesto, Peel had been unequivocal and unyielding in his defence of the Church of Ireland while, in Parliament in 1834, he could dismiss Nonconformist pleas to be admitted to the Universities of Oxford and Cambridge as 'without exception, the most extravagant demand which has been advanced in modern times.' Peel also exploited to the full the 'Compact' which the Whigs, to get themselves back into power, had struck with Radicals and Irish Catholics in 1835. He implied that, in return for this 'extremist' support, the Whigs would allow these supposed subversives and papists to dictate government policy. The lesson to be drawn by the electorate was clear – they had better turn to the Tories to be sure that the true interests of England could be properly defended.

He drove home the attack in the late 1830s. The Whigs were by this stage in severe difficulties. They were struggling to cope with the onset of a major economic depression, which had embarrassing fiscal consequences. With government revenue falling, they repeatedly failed to balance their budgets. Peel insisted that this was rank incompetence. The depression also fuelled the rise of Chartism, with consequent public unrest. Peel showed no mercy, claiming that the Whigs were responsible for the collapse in law and order.

Old-fashioned Toryism had yet to play its best card, however. Sensing in the run up to the 1841 general election that the Whigs' prospects were slight, Russell tried to inject some momentum into their campaign by proposing a significant moderation of the tariffs on corn imports. The promise of freer trade and cheaper bread might win some urban support. But the Tories swooped, claiming that Russell's ultimate intention was the Repeal of the Corn Laws – which would expose rural England to the full blast of foreign competition. A survey of local press coverage of the election campaign strongly suggests that the defence of the Corn Laws was a great vote-winner for the Tories (*see Newbould in bibliography page 160*).

As the election results came out, and the scale of the Tory victory became clear, an observer remarked: 'all turns on the name of Sir Robert Peel'. As Newbould suggests, this claim was an exaggeration. But, with Britain facing a grave economic and social crisis, many voters, old and new, must have thought that Peel's financial expertise, political courage and blend of fair mindedness and firmness were just what the country needed.

Exercise: middle-class support for Peelite Conservatism?

Some historians would claim still more for Peel. Norman Gash, for example, has argued that Peelite Conservatism, with its stress on moderate reformism and its promise of an economic policy which gave full recognition to 'manufacturing and commercial interests' successfully broadened the social base of early nineteenth century Toryism, and recruited many newly enfranchised urban voters to its ranks. The thesis is attractive and plausible. But how far is it confirmed by the following break-down of election results? (*See the table on page 129.*)

1 *If Gash's theory was right, in which types of constituency would Peel's Conservatives have been increasing their support most markedly after the publication of the Tamworth Manifesto?*

2 **a)** *Did the Conservatives in fact make the progress that Gash's theory would have led you to expect?*

b) *In which type(s) of constituency did the Tories actually make the most consistent progress between 1832 and 1841?*

3 *What conclusions might be drawn about the breadth of the appeal made by Peel's party to the electorate between 1832 and 1841?*

Conservative Members of Parliament 1832–41

		1832	1835	1837	1841
	Total	C	C	C	C
English Counties	(144)	42	73	99	124
English boroughs over 2000	(58)	8	16	17	15
English boroughs over 1000–2000	(63)	12	26	26	29
English boroughs below 1000	(202)	63	90	98	111
English Universities	(4)	4	4	4	4
English Total	(471)	129	209	244	283
Conservative majority		−213	−53	13	95
Wales	(29)	13	17	18	19
Scotland	(53)	10	15	20	22
Ireland	(105)	33	38	32	43
Total	(658)	185	279	314	367
Majority in UK		−288	−100	−30	76

As Ian Newbould has pointed out, if Peel's great aim in the 1830s had been to convert his party to a more progressive style of Conservatism so as to win over the 'middle-class voter', he failed. But perhaps *both* Newbould and Gash exaggerate how far Peel tried to solicit the urban middle-class vote. The first priority for the Tory party in the aftermath of the Great Reform Act was to recover those voters who had been alienated by Wellington's ill-judged denial in 1830 of the need for any parliamentary reform. In this respect, the most important passage of the Tamworth Manifesto was Peel's pledge to work with, and not against, the reformed political system. The Tories' second priority was arguably to maximise their support, not in the 62 new borough seats, but in the 62 new county seats created by the Great Reform Act. They thus became the unintended beneficiaries of the Whigs' often-forgotten anxiety to maintain the influence of the landed interest in the reformed political system. The key to the Tory recovery between 1832 and 1841 is not to be found in the larger or even the middle-sized boroughs, but in the smallest English boroughs (often county towns), where they almost doubled their representation, and above all in the English counties, where the number of Tory MPs returned nearly tripled. By 1841, 86 per cent of English county seats were Tory.

The fact that the Tory recovery was rooted in the countryside explains the force of the comment made by a leading Tory in the aftermath of victory. 'I am aware,' he wrote to Peel, 'to what extent our Conservative party is a party pledged to the support of the land, and that, that principle abandoned, the party is dissolved'. Peel did not see it quite that simply. Of course he shared his followers' commitment to the defence of the territorial constitution and the Church of England. But, as he announced to Parliament after his great victory, he resisted the claim that the freedom of manoeuvre of his new government should be restricted by narrow party ties. Peel believed that he could easily justify such an independent stance. He saw himself – in the best traditions of the pre-1832 constitutional order – as the Queen's Minister (Queen Victoria had ascended the throne in 1837), for whom selfless service to the nation came before any other claims or commitments. He was also clear in his own mind that 'land' was only *one* of the great 'interests' which made up the nation. But he did not imagine that his conception of Prime Ministerial responsibility would lead to clashes with his backbenchers. After all, as Peel himself later put it '[in politics], the question only is what, in *a certain position of society*, is the most effectual way of maintaining the legitimate influence and authority of a territorial aristocracy'. Peel's backbenchers, mostly country squires, would indeed have saluted that objective. But, as the next five years were to show, this question was one to which Peel and they were to give progressively discordant and, ultimately, totally irreconcilable answers.

6 Achievement and Arrogance

A *Peel and his ministerial team*

Peel was his Cabinet's linchpin and its moving force. His brilliant protégé, Gladstone, rated him 'the best man of business who was ever Prime Minister'. His range and capacity for hard work was astonishing. Finance was Peel's area of special expertise. But he made sure he was well enough informed to be able to intervene decisively in practically every other area of government too, from Factory Reform to

Foreign Policy. Peel enjoyed a strategic overview of his government's responsibilities and activities that has never been equalled before or since.

Not surprisingly, he sometimes overstretched himself. But his Cabinet colleagues rarely found his promptings and guidance intrusive. Rather, the combination of Peel's rigour in formulating policy and his own readiness to take on board their advice won their loyalty and profound respect. Some, like the young Gladstone, became almost literally his disciples, seeing it as their life's mission to carry on their master's work.

Such a style of government has its weaknesses, however. The sheer professionalism and expertise of Peel and his colleagues bred an arrogant, impatient, even contemptuous attitude towards Tory backbenchers – especially when the latter presumed to criticise the government. Peel gave vent to these feelings in a letter to his wife late in 1845: 'how can those who spend their time in hunting and shooting and eating and drinking know what were the motives of those who are responsible for the public security, who have access to the best information, and who have no other object under heaven but to provide against danger, and consult the general interests of all classes?'

Peel was, doubtless, better informed than his backbenchers. But his judgement was not infallible. And worse, as he himself admitted, he could not or would not lower himself to flatter the vanity of the party rank-and-file with soft words or conciliatory gestures. As early as 1843, a leading backbencher feared that:

> Peel has committed great and grievous mistakes in omitting to call his friends frequently together to state his desires and rouse their zeal. A few minutes and a few words would have sufficed: energy and fellowship would have been infused: men would have felt they were companions in arms; they now have the sentiment of being followers in a drill.

By themselves, Peel's aloofness and intellectual arrogance would not have been seriously damaging to the coherence of the Conservative Party. What made these flaws fatal was the failure of other Cabinet members to compensate for them. Here, the divergent fortunes of Lord Stanley and Sir James Graham are instructive. These two former Whigs were Peel's most significant recruits to the Conservatives' ranks in the 1830s, and both seemed destined to play a key role in the ministry. Stanley was Peel's Secretary for War and Colonies. He loved hunting, horse-racing and shooting as well as any Tory squire, and would have been the natural channel of raw Tory sentiment to the Cabinet. But he found himself progressively excluded from Peel's inner circle, and ultimately became one of the leaders of the old-style Tories against Peel. Instead, it was Graham, the ministry's Home Secretary, who became Peel's right-hand man. He fully shared Peel's elevated ideals of public service, and almost matched his breath-taking industry. But unfortunately, he was even more high-handed and tactless than the Prime Minister and, accordingly was intensely disliked even before the ministry began – in the eyes of its backbenchers – its wholesale betrayal of Tory principles. Indeed, Graham positively relished the bunker mentality which came to characterise the ministry's approach in its final two years.

These flaws of personality, combined with severe failures of man-management, and aggravated by the vigorous assertion of the principle that the Cabinet always knew best, go some way towards explaining why, not five years after coming into power, Peel's ministry – one of the ablest of the century – was to find itself first repudiated, and then destroyed by its own party.

B *Peelite finance*

The catastrophe of 1845–6 would not have been predicted by anybody witnessing the triumph of Peel's first budget (1842). The fiscal problems which Peel faced on coming into power had seemed grave. The deficit he inherited amounted to the vast total (by nineteenth-century standards) of £7.5 million, and had defeated successive Whig attempts to reduce it. The atmosphere of crisis at Westminster was worsened by the deep depression into which the economy as a whole was plunging, the associated resurgence of Chartism (*see chapter IV*) and the rise of the Anti-Corn Law League (*see pages 144–9*). Events seemed to be slipping out of the political elite's control.

In this context, Peel's dramatic introduction in the 1842 budget of an 'income tax' – only ever raised before in times of war – had an all-important psychological impact. Kept secret until the budget speech itself, the very boldness of the proposal matched the mood of national emergency. Peel 'took the House [of Commons] by storm', a contemporary noted. Here at last, many felt, was a leader of vision and political courage, equal to the gravity of the country's needs. Perhaps the secret of Peel's success was the sense of moral urgency which he communicated. He explained that the income tax, levied at the rate of 7d (3p) in the £ on those with incomes of over £150 per annum, would call for a special sacrifice on the part of the wealthier members of society. Every alternative means of raising government revenue entailed taxing those articles of consumption on which the poor depended. How much better, Peel insisted, that the rich should bear this extra burden at a time of national distress.

The introduction of income tax was more than a psychological masterstroke, however. The revenue it was expected to generate would gradually clear the accumulated deficit. It would also give Peel room for manoeuvre in lowering tariffs. The sliding scale on corn duties, dating from the 1820s, had already been modestly reduced. Import duties on raw materials, manufactured goods and (to the annoyance of Peel's agricultural backbenchers) barley, meat and live cattle, could now be cut too.

Peel was convinced that tariff reduction was the key to economic recovery and social stability. Domestic industrial production would be stimulated (e.g. through making raw cotton cheaper to import). The working classes' standard of living would be improved too, with duties on selected food imports cut. As Peel explained, it was one of his great objectives to 'make this country a cheap country for living '. In the long run, it was even possible that the reduced rates of duty might lead to an *increase* in the government's revenues from tariffs – for cheaper goods should encourage extra consumption, and so the government's net revenue from tariffs would actually go up.

To Peel's contemporaries, the national economic recovery which began in 1843 and the astonishing £4 million surplus which Goulburn, his Chancellor, was able to report in 1844, were incontestable evidence of the success of the government's economic strategy.

Peel's budget was not merely a masterly exercise in fiscal management and free trade principles. It marked a decisive shift in the way nineteenth-century politicians thought about the economy and presented economic policy to the nation. It was the first time that government fiscal policy had been conceived as a remedy for poverty and unrest. And, in its immediate political impact, it opened an era in which Budget Day became an event of national significance that could capture the imagination of Westminster and the world beyond. Gladstone, for one, was to take both these lessons to heart.

Peel displayed all his gifts in 1842: political boldness, sheer professionalism and a farsighted social vision. His Budget was one of the greatest triumphs of his career, and perhaps the most characteristic.

c *The authoritarian side of Peelism: mastering the mob*

Economic recovery did not, however, come soon enough to avert a major outbreak of public disorder in August 1842. The background is complex (*see page 102*), but the combination of high unemployment, wage-cuts and the frustrations experienced by the Chartists sparked a spontaneous general strike across a band of northern England, which soon brought much of the industry of Staffordshire, Cheshire, Lancashire and south-west Yorkshire to a standstill. Tens of thousands of workers were on the march, closing down factories and mines wherever they went.

Days of intense anxiety followed for Peel and Graham. Although historians like Gash have praised the 'energy' and 'common sense' of their response, much of what they did and said indicates misjudgement and overreaction. The Home Secretary was convinced – wrongly – that he was facing an organised revolutionary conspiracy aiming at the overthrow of the state. Like Peel, he suspected that the rioting workers were being directed by middle-class agitators from the Anti-Corn Law League, in what a government spokesman described as 'the foulest ... and altogether most dangerous combination [conspiracy] of recent times'. The reluctance of local mayors and magistrates to act decisively against the 'uprising' was taken as further evidence of a massive plot.

The government moved towards something like a state of emergency. Peel and Graham monitored the incoming reports from the trouble centres on an hourly basis, despatching troop reinforcements northwards by railway to back up badly stretched local forces. On several occasions, the troops opened fire, causing deaths in crowds which had refused to disperse. Planned Chartist demonstrations in London were frustrated by the Metropolitan Police and army detachments, with 'ringleaders' being arrested. Peel himself was seriously concerned for the safety of his wife and family in their Staffordshire mansion: for the second time in barely a decade, arms and supplies were stockpiled there, in anticipation of a siege.

This feared attack, however, never materialised and by early September, the crisis as a whole had passed. The rioting strikers returned to work, in part reassured by signs of a good harvest and an upturn in trade, in part demoralised by the hopelessness of their predicament and the government's determined response to their protest. But the collapse of their movement did not signal the end of government-inspired repression.

Scores of strike leaders were imprisoned or transported to Australia. Graham, who had urged that the troops he sent north should 'act with vigour and without a parley' against the strikers (i.e. should not hesitate to open fire) soon set about extending the network of borough and county police forces whose inadequacies had been dramatically exposed by the crisis. Government agents worked long and hard to gather information linking the 'insurrection' to the leaders of the Chartists or the Anti-Corn Law League, with a view to a state-trial. The plan was only dropped when no hard evidence could be found. In fact, none existed.

The events of 1842 do much to bring out the complexity of Peelite Conservatism in its many strands. Even if another 'Peterloo' (*see pages 16–17*) was avoided, the government's heavy-handed response to the strike wave should remind us of its authoritarian roots, and of the exaggerated fear of revolution which always coloured Peel's perception of popular political movements. But Peel went far beyond traditional reactionary Toryism in response to the threat or reality of disorder. Peel knew that more troops and harsher laws were not the real answer. Instead, he believed that the government should do what it could to address the root causes of disorder: it should counteract unemployment and poverty.

In July 1842, as unemployment neared its peak, Peel wrote the following letter to a close political ally who had been worried that Peel had been pushing free trade too hard. In it, the Prime Minister spelled out the thinking behind the government's economic policy.

Whitehall, July 27th, 1842.

> My Dear Croker,
> I can assure you that the difficulty will be to prove that we have gone far enough **in concession** – that is, relaxation of prohibitions and protections – not that we have gone too far. Something effectual must be done to revive, and revive permanently, the languishing commerce and languishing manufacturing industry of this country.
>
> France, Belgium and Germany are closing their doors upon us.
>
> Look at the state of society in this country; the congregation of manufacturing masses; the amount of our debt; the rapid increase of poor rates within the last four years . . . and then judge whether we can with safety retrograde in manufactures.
>
> If you had to constitute new societies, you might on moral and social grounds prefer corn fields to cotton factories; an agricultural to a manufacturing population. But our lot is cast; we cannot change it and we cannot recede.

1. *Explain '. . . and then judge whether we can with safety retrograde in manufactures'.*
2. *How did Peel seek to convince Croker of the depth of the crisis faced by the government?*
3. *What are the letter's implications for the government's future financial policies?*
4. *What light does the letter shed on the contrast between old-fashioned Tory attitudes towards industrialisation and Conservative-Peelite ones?*

The maintenance of social and political order remained perhaps the greatest objective of Peel's ministry, and both his authoritarianism and economic liberalism were calculated to serve that one purpose. But we should not forget that Peel was also motivated, in his response to poverty and recession, by a sense of common humanity and Christian conviction. However much he despised the Chartists' schemes to solve the nation's problems, and however much he feared 'the mob', he was profoundly affected by the reports reaching him of the intense suffering which unemployment brought in 1842 to the country's economic blackspots. When farmers lobbied him, complaining that lower tariffs were hitting their profit margins, he felt exasperated at their selfishness and ignorance. For Peel, the events of 1842 helped to turn his growing commitment to free trade from an intellectual principle into a Christian conviction. He was determined that his fellow man should not suffer from dearth when only selfish, man-made laws were keeping succour out of reach.

D *The arrogance of power*

Over the course of 1844, Peel's intellectual arrogance and political high-handedness significantly increased the tensions between the government and its supporters in the Commons.

In retrospect, even Peel's one supposed triumph of 1844 – the Bank Charter Act – seems to exemplify some of his least attractive qualities. Peel was striving to give some stability to the British banking system, which had been rocked by crisis throughout the 1820s and 1830s. The Act served to restrict the issue of notes, by tying them more closely to the Bank of England's gold reserves. It thereby did much to restore public confidence in the system. Modern historians, however, like Boyd Hilton (*see bibliography page 160*) now believe that Peel's scheme was far too rigid, and his rejection of alternative proposals peremptory. Nevertheless, the Act confirmed Peel's reputation in the eyes of many contemporaries as the greatest expert on banking questions of his age.

Peel's and Graham's approach to factory legislation was just as inflexible – and it proved far less popular. Details of the impassioned campaign led by Lord Ashley, a distinguished Tory backbencher, to improve conditions in mines and factories, and to give special protection to working women and children, can be found elsewhere (*see pages 50–3*). The issue here is the ministry's response to the reformers' case. Neither Peel nor Graham believed they could go even halfway to meet Ashley with the government's own Factory Act (1844). Ashley and his supporters were deeply disappointed that their basic demand – for a maximum ten-hour working day for women and all adolescents – had been rejected. But Ashley was able to swing the mood of the Commons against the allegedly inhuman and un-Christian practices of the factory owners, and a vital amendment was made to the government's bill, restricting the working day to ten hours after all.

Peel was furious. He threatened to resign, and demanded that his backbenchers rescind their vote. Reluctantly they did as they were told. Thus, ultimately, Ashley was defeated, but relationships between Peel and his Commons' supporters were badly soured by the whole affair.

This was disconcerting enough. But the same series of events all but repeated themselves only three months later, over the complicated issue of import duties on sugar. Free traders wanted these to be dramatically reduced. However, influential Tory backbenchers, concerned to protect the interests of British shippers and of British plantation owners in the West Indies, wanted to see sugar imported from the colonies protected by high tariffs against sugar imported from elsewhere. Peel's moderate proposals to reduce import duties went too far for the protectionists, but not far enough for the free traders. A cleverly worded amendment enabled these two contrasting sets of opponents to unite against Peel's bill and it was defeated, with 62 Tory backbenchers voting against the government.

Again, Peel threatened to resign, and again the party was forced into line: the Sugar Duties Bill went through in the form which Peel required. But his harsh and cold attitude towards his backbenchers, when they retreated and agreed to follow the government line, ruined any prospect of genuine conciliation. Even Gladstone, whose admiration for Peel was boundless, commented that 'a great man has committed a great error'.

What issues lay behind these increasingly bitter divisions within the Tory Party? On the questions of factory reform and sugar duties alike, Peel would have claimed that his policies were intellectually correct and his expectation of unquestioning party obedience was politically proper. Intellectually, Peel believed that any government intervention in the free workings of the economy was likely to be for the worse. The relevance of this to factory legislation was clear. Experts warned Peel that the imposition of a ten-hour working day would cripple the cotton manufacturers' profitability. Bankruptcies, mass unemployment and all its miseries would be the consequences. With national economic recovery only just under way in 1844, and cotton production accounting for 80 per cent of British exports, Peel was in no hurry to turn the clock back to the desperate days of 1842. The case with regard to sugar duties was similar: economic theory and recent practical experience had made the virtues of freer trade self-evident to Peel. The privileges accorded to the West Indies interest made the price of sugar – a major factor in the budget of working families – artificially high. Peel remained determined to make Britain 'a cheap country to live [in]': excessive sugar tariffs simply could not be justified.

But economic common sense, at least as Peel saw it, was not the only consideration which determined the Prime Minister's hard line over these questions. Peel believed that his backbenchers needed teaching a constitutional lesson. They had to learn that it was the job of the executive to direct, and of the party to follow. The Cabinet alone had the necessary expertise and information to formulate policy. If backbenchers did not accept its decision in good faith, 'the Queen's government' could not be carried on. By rudely bringing his backbenchers face to face with the prospect of his resignation, Peel hoped to drive home to them the dangerous constitutional implications of their actions, and thus restore discipline.

Unfortunately for Peel and the cohesion of the Conservative Party, many of his backbenchers saw the issues in a different light. By 1844, the overall direction of the government's economic policies was causing much concern: the course being charted seemed to lead away from protectionism and inexorably towards free trade. This was the very opposite of the policy which the Tories had been elected to pursue in

1841. The appalling thought was dawning on some Tories that Peel might be ready to abandon the Corn Laws themselves! After all, the man who had abandoned the Irish Protestants in 1829 was capable of anything.

Neither were Peel's backbenchers convinced by his increasingly self-regarding constitutional arguments about the duty of the Party to follow the Executive. To them, the Conservative Party existed to defend distinct interests in the nation, of which 'the land' was the greatest of all. Yet Peel seemed more eager to please the Tories' enemies, like the middle-class mill owners, than to satisfy his supporters.

Finally, there was Peel's style. Tory backbenchers were invariably men of wealth and standing and their pride and sense of dignity had been repeatedly affronted by Peel's dictatorial attitude. No less than Peel, they lived by principles of honour and personal consistency. They were *gentlemen* and should not be made to reverse their votes or betray their constituents even at the command of a Prime Minister. Their judgement, loyalties and feelings deserved respect and understanding. But Peel showed them neither. The worst of the problem was that Peel seemed to have little appreciation of the depth of offence he was causing. He could joke in a letter to a friend that he was regarded by many as very obstinate and very presumptuous: but, he went on, 'the fact is, people like a certain degree of obstinacy and presumption in a minister. They abuse him for dictation and arrogance, but they like being governed'. The events of 1845 and 1846 suggest that Peel's backbenchers had much less taste for 'being governed' than Peel imagined.

7 Ireland: Coercion, Conciliation and Consequences

A *Coercion*

It was always likely that Peel's government would clash with the forces of Irish nationalism. Since the mid-1830s the Tories had been denouncing the Whigs for their readiness to do deals with Irish Catholic MPs at England's expense, and in the election campaign of 1841, they had re-emphasised their traditional role as the stalwart defenders of the Anglican Church in Ireland and England. But the sheer scale of the movement which the Catholics had organised by 1843 in response to the Tories' election victory was a surprise. Daniel O'Connell, the great Irish Nationalist leader, was now campaigning for the Repeal of the Act of Union itself. A series of mass meetings, each attended by up to half a million demonstrators, revealed the startling extent and militancy of anti-British feeling. There were even plans afoot to set up an independent Irish Parliament in Dublin. This seemed certain to claim the right to speak for the people of Ireland, and then go on to repudiate the Act of Union itself. By the summer of 1843, the Repeal movement was representing a greater threat to the authority of the British state than Chartism ever had.

The challenge brought an unyielding and sternly authoritarian response from Peel. In a chilling parliamentary announcement, he made it clear that he would crush any attempt to break the Union with armed force. Wellington, for one, was eager to send in the troops. Ireland was on the brink of civil war.

When the crisis point came, Peel acted with decisiveness and cool judgement. He banned the next proposed 'monster meeting', due to be held at Clontarf in October 1843, and had O'Connell arrested for sedition, tried and then imprisoned. Peel's actions could have provoked a rising. But as he had guessed, O'Connell shrank back from the bloody prospect of armed rebellion, and agreed to the meeting being called off. This was a turning point in O'Connell's career. Although he was soon to be released from prison on appeal, he never recovered his full authority, and the Repeal movement fell into decline and division. Peel's tough-minded brinkmanship had scored a clear victory: the Tory die-hards were proud of him.

B *Conciliation*

As his response to the disorders in mainland Britain in 1842 had already shown, there was a lot more to Peel than mere Tory authoritarianism. Peel explained to Graham a few days after O'Connell's arrest that, 'mere force, however necessary the application of it, will do nothing as a permanent remedy for the social evils of [Ireland]'. Accordingly, he put in train a series of measures designed to bring long-term peace and stability to Ireland.

This package of measures constituted a brave and farsighted departure in the policy of British governments towards Ireland. It is one of the tragedies of Peel's career, however, that their actual impact on the Irish problem was, in fact, minimal, while their impact on British politics was disastrous.

C *The objectives of Peel's programme and its impact on Ireland*

Catholic Emancipation (*see pages 303–4*), which made it possible for Catholics to become MPs, had made it essential that the British state win over the loyalty of the Catholic majority in Ireland. The key to this, Peel believed, was establishing a good working relationship between the British government and the Irish Catholic Church. It was widely acknowledged that Catholic priests had played a central part in mobilising the mass movements which had pressed with such force for Emancipation in the 1820s and for the Repeal of the Union in the early

Peel's Plan of Conciliation	
Legislation/Action	*Description/Comment*
Lord Heytesbury replaces Lord de Grey as Lord Lieutenant of Ireland, 1844	De Grey had been a hard-line defender of the Protestant Ascendancy. Heytesbury, by contrast, was happy to follow Peel's policy of giving equal opportunities to Catholics when making government appointments.
The Devon Commission 1844	Lord Devon, a progressive landowner, was appointed to chair an inquiry into how Irish agriculture in general and landlord-tenant relations in particular could be improved.
Charitable Bequests Bill 1844	This made it easier for Catholics to endow their Church with land or money in their wills.
Maynooth Bill, 1844–5	Maynooth College was a Catholic seminary where priests were trained. The Bill made a grant of £30 000 for building improvements, and almost tripled its annual grant from the government.
The Irish Colleges Bill, 1845	Colleges, free of denominational religious control, were to be set up in Cork, Galway and Belfast.

1840s. Peel was now determined to win the priests away from Irish nationalism and if possible to convert the Irish Catholic hierarchy into supporters of British rule in Ireland.

The Charitable Bequests Act advertised the goodwill of Peel's government to the Catholic Church: but the increased grants to Maynooth were the keystone of Peel's scheme. He was convinced that this Catholic seminary, badly underfunded as it was, attracted an inferior (i.e. more potentially subversive) social class into the priesthood. He believed that the harsh and miserable conditions at Maynooth itself then converted the young trainee priests (in Peel's own words) into 'sour malignants' and 'spiritual firebrands', all too ready to spread disaffection and nationalism throughout their future parishes. The cure of these ills, Peel was convinced, was more generous provision for the college. A better, more conservative class of trainee-priest would be attracted, and, while at Maynooth, would learn to be grateful to their Westminster benefactors – and come to see any agitation against British rule as a crime and a sin. Ireland's Catholic priests were to be transformed from the recruiting sergeants of nationalism into the Union's first line of defence.

Peel also hoped to check the spread of nationalism amongst the laity. The first move here was the replacement of Lord de Grey by Lord Heytesbury as Lord Lieutenant in 1844. This was designed to inaugurate a new era in the government of Ireland. Peel had been getting increasingly annoyed at how, with de Grey's connivance, the Protestant minority had continued to enjoy a near monopoly of political power and government patronage in Ireland, thus frustrating much of the promise of Catholic Emancipation. Such a situation was to Peel 'unjust ... dangerous ... and utterly impracticable'. Ireland could no longer be governed by such means. With Lord Heytesbury's arrival in Dublin, Peel could now be sure that a serious attempt would be made to recruit Catholics into the magistracy and the civil service. As well as making British rule in Ireland less foreign in appearance, it would end the dangerous process by which educated Irish laymen, finding no hope of their advancement in service to the Dublin government, turned, disaffected, to the service of the nationalist cause instead.

The reform was linked to the next stage of Peel's plan – the founding of new colleges of higher education in Cork, Galway and Belfast. This should ensure that there would soon be more educated Catholic Irishmen fit to compete for government jobs in particular and to make successful professional careers – as lawyers and doctors, for example – in general. Peel's ultimate aim was to foster the growth and prosperity of a new middle class in Ireland, which would be sympathetic to British rule and would set the standards and values for the rest of Irish society to follow. This might take decades to come to fruition: but at least the colleges would meet the long-standing Catholic grievance that Ireland's only existing university (Trinity College, Dublin) was almost exclusively Anglican in its intake. Finally, the Devon Commission would lay the foundations of a transformation of landlord/tenant relations, and thus make possible the rejuvenation of rural Ireland, which had become desperately impoverished because of overpopulation and under-investment.

Peel was attempting something like a programme of what the twentieth century would call 'social engineering'. If his visionary plans had come to fruition, he believed that the whole of Irish society would have been set on the path to stability, liberalism and 'modernisation'. But, even before the Famine devastated Ireland (*see pages 305–6*), Peel's programme was foundering. It is true that the Maynooth Bill was welcomed by most Catholic bishops: but in years to come the priests educated at Maynooth persisted in feeling greater sympathy towards their downtrodden and impoverished parishioners than towards the British state which had oppressed their Church for so long. The hierarchy of the Church had, anyway, soon lost confidence in Peel when they saw his plans for higher education. The bishops had wanted a Catholic university of their own. Peel had flatly refused to consider the idea. They did not take this lying down, and managed to wreck Peel's plans. His new colleges were designed to be 'unsectarian' and thus free from religious controversy. Instead, the bishops argued that they would therefore be free from Christianity itself, 'godless' places which no young Catholic could attend without putting his morals and his very soul in jeopardy. The effect of this denunciation was that the Catholic laity boycotted the colleges. And, despite the best of intentions, when the Devon Commission reported, its depressing mass of facts and figures merely served to bring home how intractable the problem of rural poverty in Ireland was, and its modest suggestions to increase the rights of tenants vis-a-vis their landlords were attacked by Whigs and Tories alike.

It is hard not to conclude that Peel's Irish policy was a failure. It was bold and imaginative and, by the standards of traditional Toryism, constructive and generous. But the government's attempted rapprochement with the Catholic Church had largely broken down by 1846, and Peel's hopes for education and land reform came to little or nothing at all. Yet it seems unlikely that Peel could have done more. The resistance offered to his initiatives, at Westminster and in Ireland, is an indication of the yawning chasm between his practicable means and his visionary objectives.

D *The impact of Peel's Irish policies on British politics*

The positive impact of Peel's policies in Ireland was negligible: by contrast, their negative impact in Britain itself was tremendous. Maynooth was the problem. British Protestants, both inside and outside the established Church, united to attack Peel's proposal to increase the state funding of the Catholic seminary with a vehemence and intensity that staggered Peel. *The Times* led the way, accusing Peel of 'forcing [Romanism] on the nation', denouncing Maynooth as 'a name and a thing above all odious and suspicious to England'. Over one million and a quarter signatures were collected in a petition urging him to change his policy. In the House of Commons, itself, Peel had to rely on Whig support to get the Maynooth Bill through. Maynooth provoked the worst Tory rebellion against Peel so far, with the party dividing 149 votes against, 148 for. It became law in April 1845, but its passage left the Tory party shattered.

How can we explain the popular fury outside Parliament, and the bitter antagonisms within? Catholicism was widely despised and loathed in Victorian England. It was believed to be alien, superstitious and backward-looking. *Irish* Catholicism was still worse: it was the engine of disloyalty and rebellion, as the career of O'Connell proved. The Irish themselves were widely regarded as racially inferior, incorrigibly violent and brutishly ignorant. Yet Peel was proposing to increase state support for Maynooth Seminary, the very centre of Irish papist subversion!

Peel's backbenchers found this very hard to swallow. As many had reiterated on the hustings in 1841, one of the main functions of the Tory Party was to uphold the privileges of the Anglican religion and keep Catholics in their place. Peel had recently shown himself a poor friend of Anglican causes: he had abandoned plans to guarantee the Church of England the major responsibility for the education of factory children and he refused a government subsidy to a church-building programme for the rapidly expanding industrial towns of the Midlands and the north of England. But when it came to doling out tax-payers' money for the training of Catholic priests in Ireland, Peel seemed only to happy to oblige! For many backbenchers, this was one betrayal too many.

Peel regarded such sentiments with withering contempt. He stuck to his great principle that it was the duty of the Queen's minister, regardless of party pledges or connections, to do what he believed was in the best interests of the nation. To Peel, the Maynooth Bill was the centrepiece of his government's Irish policy through which he hoped to bring lasting peace to Ireland and to put the Union on a new and much firmer foundation. With such a prize at stake, the prejudices and pledges of his backbenchers could be discounted, and their cries of treachery ignored.

By May 1845, the feelings of mutual distrust and dislike between Peel and his backbenchers had bitten deep. Writing to a friend, he made a list of his ministry's achievements: industrial recovery was underway, Chartism had been defeated, the working classes were better-off, and the nation's finances restored to a good order. 'But', he concluded with exasperated irony, 'we have reduced protection to agriculture, and tried to lay the foundations of peace in Ireland, and these are offences for which nothing can atone'. Quite simply, he no longer cared about whether his party held together. Graham was even more fatalistic, not merely expecting but actually hoping that the 'country gentlemen' would 'give us the death blow'.

This mood – embattled, exhausted, but stubborn and self-righteous – was now to characterise the upper reaches of the Conservative leadership until the very end. It is the frame of mind in which people who see themselves as heroes seek to do great deeds and make great sacrifices. It was the frame of mind in which Peel and Graham approached the Repeal of the Corn Laws.

8 The Anti-Corn Law League

The Anti-Corn Law League became a legend in Victorian politics. Founded in Manchester in 1838, only eight years later it had apparently pressurised a Conservative administration into a complete U-turn on one of its central policy commitments: agricultural protectionism. The League's success was taken as proof of the irresistible power of rational argument when combined with popular mobilisation, and every successive Radical pressure group regarded it as their model and inspiration. But on closer examination, the success of the Anti-Corn Law League is surprisingly open to doubt.

Its greatest advantage was the basic intellectual power of the free trade argument. From Adam Smith onwards, political economists argued that 'laissez-faire' policies, opening markets to unfettered competition and thus driving prices down, served the interests of the consumer best. A flexible and industrious producer, too, had much to gain in a dynamic and expanding economy. These were the lessons learnt in turn by Huskisson, Peel and Gladstone. So compelling was the argument, that, even without the League, the Corn Laws – which protected the British farmer from foreign competition by imposing a prohibitive tariff on corn imports – were probably doomed.

In the late 1830s, the case against the Corn Laws was taken up by the Anti-Corn Law League. The League turned it into a passionate and brilliantly organised middle-class crusade. The main reason for the League's growth was the widespread support it enjoyed amongst northern manufacturers. They identified the Corn Laws as the root cause of the economic depression which was having such a devastating impact on the cotton industry at the time. There were two main strands to their analysis. First, by keeping corn imports from the European continent out, the Corn Laws indirectly crippled Britain's potential export markets – for foreign landowners and their labourers, deprived of *their* most attractive export market, were too poor to buy British manufactured goods. Secondly, the Corn Laws were blamed for keeping the price of bread artificially high. Bread was the basic foodstuff for working-class families. If its cost fell, such families would have more money to spend on manufactured goods themselves – or alternatively, factory owners would be able to cut wages without forcing their workers towards starvation. In either case, self-interest clearly played a major role in explaining the manufacturing classes' support for the League: their increasingly large donations to its funds were, in effect, a good business investment.

But the appeal of the League went beyond material calculation. The cry for 'cheap bread' gave the League the appearance of a campaign for social justice. Nonconformists felt that the crusade against the Corn Laws was sanctioned by God himself: for was it not written in the Bible that '[he] that withholdeth corn, the people shall curse him; but blessing shall be upon the head of him that selleth it'? The most idealistic saw in universal free trade the prospect of establishing the reign of peace between nations, arguing that the free exchange of goods and the pursuit of mutual advantage would draw the peoples of Europe ever closer together in shared prosperity and understanding. Such sentiments help to explain the righteous passion with which committed Leaguers pursued their cause.

The League's activists, however, were also pursuing an underlying political agenda. The Corn Laws were a godsend to those radicals who had been consciously searching for an issue around which to mobilise popular support for their continuing assault on the landed aristocracy. 'Never yet,' a Radical exulted, 'had the people a fairer battleground than on the question of the Corn Laws'. They were intellectually indefensible, economically ruinous, and immoral and un-Christian too. To a League journalist, the Corn Laws were 'the outwork of the citadel of corruption ... If we can bombard this outwork until we gain admission, we shall plant the banner of rational liberty upon the ruins of the despotism of the aristocracy'. In other words, the League was an instrument of class war, led by bourgeois militants as convinced as any Marxist revolutionary of the justice of their cause and the right of their class to rule.

But, however startling and annoying the League's growth between 1838 and 1845 was to the defenders of the 'territorial constitution', a close analysis of its fortunes would have made it difficult to forecast its ultimate success. All the indefatigable optimism and resourcefulness of Richard Cobden, its most prominent leader, cannot disguise the fact that, until 1844 at least, it mostly stumbled from failure to failure, flirting with catastrophe en route. Its numerous shifts of strategy reveal Cobden's genius for improvisation, but they just as surely indicate the number of dead-ends down which the League travelled, however energetically. Indeed it is far from clear that the League was near to attaining its goal right until the very end.

For the sake of simplicity, the various stages of the League's campaign have been tabulated as follows:

Stage	Year	Main Tactic	Success?
1	1838 onwards	Propaganda – spread by pamphlets, lecture tours and the League's own newspaper. Main target areas were northern industrial towns and southern agricultural districts. The power of the League's argument was by itself expected to force the abolition of the Corn Laws	Very limited – League nearly bankrupt in 1839. Chartists convince many workers that League is a front for wage-cutting factory owners. Farmers and farm-labourers resent intrusion of League activists, and distrust their arguments.
2	1841	A shift to direct involvement in party politics. Cobden convinces other leaders of the League of the need to win a majority in Parliament to ensure Repeal. A committed free trader was to be selected to fight every by-election. Only gradually does Cobden accept that the League must focus its efforts on the most winnable borough seats.	Narrow defeat of Cobden at Walsall by-election early in 1841 shows League can fight electoral battles effectively. Cobden later returned as MP for Stockport. But General Election of July was a crushing victory for Toryism – and protectionism. No prospect of Conservative majority being undermined. Free trade candidates defeated in promising looking seats (e.g. Leeds, Bradford).

Stage	Year	Main Tactic	Success?
3	1842	Lack of political progress and depth of recession mean desperate remedies considered. Closer co-operation with moderate Chartists? A tax strike? A lock-out, creating mass unemployment, and the threat of revolution, to force the government to repeal?	None of these plans got far. Chartists remained suspicious of predominantly middle-class League. Illegality of tax-strike, and obvious dangers of lock-out strategy, help Cobden block these extreme proposals.
4	1843	A breakthrough. *The Times* acknowledges the League as 'A Great Fact'. But strategy still uncertain: Cobden considers that the 'agricultural districts of the south will carry our question'.	Fund-raising achievements are impressive. But no sign of significant electoral progress. Cobden's latest agricultural campaign proves abortive, and by-election results continue to be mixed.
5	1844	Cobden discovers significance of requirements (laid down in Great Reform Act) for prospective voters to register on electoral rolls. League channels its energies into a) ensuring *its* supporters *are* properly registered b) getting known supporters of protection, wherever possible, disqualified.	League morale and activity high – but how many seats were susceptible to such (dubious?) practices.

Stage	Year	Main Tactic	Success?
6	1845	Cobden realises that, by buying property in county constituencies valued at 40s (£2) p.a., League supporters can, in effect, buy themselves more votes in parliamentary elections. All League's propaganda and legal machinery now directed to organising the purchase of enough votes in key constituencies to buy control of them.	Tremendous successes in South Lancashire and West Riding of Yorkshire (Feb. 1846) by-elections. But how many seats were vulnerable to such tactics? Cobden convinced that this was the key to victory, but few modern calculations put numbers above 30. If so, League still a long way off from building up a major presence in the Commons.

1 *Based on the above information, make a brief assessment of the electoral track-record of the League and the Parliamentary threat it posed to Peel on the eve of the Repeal of the Corn Laws.*

Only when we have considered the significance of the Irish potato blight (*see page 149*) in precipitating the Repeal of the Corn Laws, and Peel's overall assessment of the interests of the 'territorial aristocracy', will we be able to judge how important the immediate political threat posed by the League in 1845–6 was in determining Peel's calculations. But of one thing we can be certain already. In its *wider* political objectives, the League failed. Britain was to remain for the rest of the century a country which was ruled by the landed aristocracy and its friends. Until the First World War men of commerce and industry were a rare sight in any Cabinet, Conservative or Liberal. Not the least reason for this is that few industrialists shared Cobden's confidence or class consciousness, instead preferring local pre-eminence – and making more money – to the distractions and uncertainties of a political career on the national stage. The Anti-Corn Law League was a vanguard whose army – if it had ever been there – melted away on the morrow of victory.

It is also notable that the items on the Radicals' hidden agenda – like the disestablishment of the Church of England, or a reform of the Land Laws (so as to make it legal for the aristocracies' great estates to be broken up and sold off) – never made much progress. Indeed, for almost two decades after 1846, Victorian Radicals would struggle to find another issue to unite their own forces and to mobilise the people.

With the Repeal of the Corn Laws the 'outwork of the citadel of corruption' had indeed been given up by the enemy. But the bastion of aristocratic power seemed to have remained perfectly intact – as Peel, of course, had intended it should.

9 THE REPEAL OF THE CORN LAWS

Peel was a politician of courage and vision, but even he must have felt daunted by the scale of the disaster which began to overtake Ireland late in 1845. In mid-October he learnt that a mystery disease, which had already ruined mainland Europe's potato crop, had finally reached Ireland.

This 'Potato Blight' seemed certain to have a quite catastrophic effect, because the potato was the staple diet of the bulk of the Irish peasantry. So it proved: between 1845 and 1851 Ireland lost over two and a quarter million people through disease and starvation or emigration

Whether the British government could have done much to alleviate this tragedy over these years may be doubted. It is, however, clear that the centrepiece of Peel's supposed cure for the famine – the Repeal of the Corn Laws – was to have a far greater impact on the history of mainland Britain than it was ever to have on the history of Ireland.

A *Peel's motives for repeal*

At the onset of the crisis, Peel made an unequivocal and apparently compelling connection between the impending disaster in Ireland and the need for the Corn Laws to be repealed. 'The remedy [for the failure of the potato crop],' he insisted, 'is the total and absolute repeal for ever of all duties on all articles of subsistence'. It would be intolerable, he insisted, to allow the Corn Laws to obstruct the passage of foodstuffs through Ireland's ports when a whole nation was facing starvation.

But for once, Peel's cabinet colleagues were not convinced by Peel's logic. It does indeed seem faulty. First, as they pointed out, it was quite within the British government's powers to suspend the Corn Laws in Ireland *temporarily*. Indeed, this course had clear advantages: suspension could be speedily effected, while full Repeal would entail the recall of Parliament. Repeal would also bitterly divide the Conservative Party. Secondly, the sceptics knew that the earlier failure of the European potato crop meant that practically every alternative continental supply of food had been used up: there were no stockpiles of grain waiting to be imported into Ireland, and anyway the Irish peasantry were too impoverished to afford what reserves there were. To put the matter with brutal simplicity, Peel's proposal to repeal the Corn Laws would not save the life of a single Irishman or Irishwoman.

It is hard to avoid the conclusion that Peel was using Ireland's impending catastrophe as a pretext, or cover, for the implementation of a policy upon which he had already decided upon for completely separate reasons. His contemporaries suspected as much, and the element of duplicity they detected in his presentation of the case for Repeal added to their sense of outrage at being 'sold'. The Potato Blight was the occasion, and not the cause, of the Repeal of the Corn Law.

We cannot be certain as to when Peel first came to regard the Repeal of the Corn Laws as desirable. Dr Hilton has suggested that Peel's work with Huskisson, on the revision of the Corn Laws between 1825 and 1828, may have been decisive in persuading him of the ultimate desirability of Repeal. He certainly made no unequivocal defences of 'protectionism' thereafter, and left it to his colleagues to make the full-blooded assaults on Russell's proposed tariff reforms which helped the Tories win the 1841 election. Peel was biding his time, and keeping his options open.

However, Peel felt his options diminishing rapidly once in power, for the Corn Laws became progressively less and less defensible. Britain's economic recovery after 1842 was interpreted by Peel and others as incontestable proof of the merits of free trade. Therefore, to Peel's intellectual conviction that free trade was best, was added the evidence of experience that it was a cure for social distress. This lesson was put into practice with supreme confidence in the 1845 budget, in which over 400 remaining important duties were abolished. But this only left the Corn Laws even more exposed as an unjustifiable anomaly. As one well-informed insider noted in his diary, in August 1845, 'everybody expects that he means to go on, and in the end to knock the Corn Laws on the head... but nobody knows how or when he will do [it]'.

These pressures alone, however, cannot explain the urgency and determination with which Peel was to drive Repeal through, regardless of the cost to himself or to his party. The answer lies in Peel's growing fears for the long term well-being of British society. Peel had thought deeply about the course of Britain's social development since the Industrial Revolution, and was more confident than most other right-wing politicians about the capacity of the old landed order to survive in the new Britain. But, although reconciled to industrialisation, he did not regard all its consequences as benign. And by 1845, he had become convinced that Britain was heading for a double disaster, each indirectly brought about by industrialisation, which could only be averted by the Repeal of the Corn Laws.

The first potential disaster was demographic. Britain's inability to feed her rapidly expanding population by her own agricultural resources had been an underlying anxiety for governments since the late 1810s. Between then and 1841, Britain's population had grown by almost 50 per cent. In one of his earliest skirmishes over agricultural protection in 1842, Peel had explained to the Commons that 'I have a deep impression, a firm conviction, that population is increasing more rapidly than the supply of provision in this country... '. The Irish famine itself, and the associated revelations of how easily the whole European food supply network could be overstretched, served to confirm Peel in his free trade convictions. Only by opening Britain's ports permanently to foreign corn would increased continental production be stimulated, and entirely new sources of supply be opened up.

The second potential disaster was political. Here, the Anti-Corn Law League was the problem. It seems unlikely that Peel's main anxiety was about the League's *immediate* electoral prospects (*see page 148*). But Peel *was* appalled by the wider political impact which the League was having, and its potential to do still greater damage to the stability of British society. To Peel, the League was a foul and reckless revolutionary conspiracy, no better than the Political Unions of 1830–2, the Chartists, or even the Jacobins of revolutionary France. He knew that the fundamental objectives of its leaders were the break-up of the 'territorial constitution' and the overthrow of aristocratic rule. The Corn Laws – or, as League propaganda styled them, the 'Bread Tax' – were all too potent a symbol of the unacceptable face of aristocratic power around which anti-aristocratic feeling could be whipped up. As Peel wrote to a friend early in January 1846, 'the worst ground on which we can *now* fight the battle for institutions, for the just privileges of Monarchy and landed Aristocracy, is on a question of food'. He had earlier warned Prince Albert, that the Anti-Corn Law League 'had made immense progress, and had enormous means at [its] disposal'. Therefore, by repealing the Corn Laws, Peel would in his own words, 'remove the contest entirely from the dangerous ground upon which it has got – that of a war between the manufacturers, the hungry and the poor against the landed proprietors [and] the aristocracy, which can only end in the ruin of the latter'.

Peel was determined to defuse the class struggle which Cobden and his friends were waging. At a stroke, Repeal would destroy the platform on which the Radicals were mounting their agitation, and would give the lie to the Chartists' old claim that a Parliament dominated by the landed classes was by definition incapable of legislating in the interest of the nation as a whole. Above all, Repeal would be done when and how Peel and Parliament chose. It would not be conceded by a routed aristocracy desperate to appease the clamour of the mob. Thus, the integrity of the executive tradition of government would be maintained.

This was the real case for Repeal – one which, to sophisticated Conservatives, might seem incontrovertible. But months of agonised and acrimonious debate would be required before Peel could persuade his Cabinet colleagues that they had no choice but to press for Repeal, and before Parliament could be persuaded to pass it.

B *A chronology of repeal*

15 October 1845	Peel writes to the Lord Lieutenant of Ireland, stating that the 'remedy' for the potato blight is the Repeal of the Corn Laws.
1 November	Peel opens Cabinet debate with memorandum suggesting Repeal as possible response to likely Irish famine. Protracted and difficult discussions follow; Graham apart, Cabinet unconvinced.
22 November	Lord John Russell, Leader of the Whigs, announces his conversion to the total Repeal of the Corn Laws.
Late November	Peel gradually wins over majority in Cabinet for Repeal. Secret import of maize from America arranged.
5 December	Lord Stanley and Lord Buccleuch still refusing to accept Peel's case for Repeal. Convinced that only a unified Cabinet could carry the measure, Peel resigns. Russell tries to form a pro-Repeal Whig ministry.
20 December	After difficult negotiations with leading Whigs, it becomes clear that Russell is unable to form a ministry. Peel sees this as a moment of destiny. He becomes the 'Queen's Minister' again, determined to press on with Repeal regardless of the cost. In fact, only Stanley refuses to join the reconstituted Cabinet.
22 January 1846	Peel introduces Bill to Repeal the Corn Laws into the Commons. Bitter debates follow, in which Lord George Bentinck and Benjamin Disraeli lead the assault on Peel from the Conservatives' own back benches.
15 May	Peel has majority of 98 in favour of Repeal in final vote in Commons. But Whig support essential: 241 Conservatives vote against Repeal – only 112 for.
June	House of Lords, heavily influenced by the Duke of Wellington, vote for Repeal.
26 June	Hard core of irreconcilable Tory protectionists join forces with Whigs, Radicals and Irish MPs in vote against Irish Coercion Bill: 'a blackguard combination' (Wellington). Government defeated, and Peel resigns the following day. Russell becomes the new Prime Minister.

c *The opposition to repeal*

By the end of 1845, Peel was well used to expressions of dissent and dissatisfaction on his backbenches. But the savagery and longevity of the rebellion provoked by his proposal to repeal the Corn Laws caught him by surprise. Why was the Tory reaction so furious?

By late 1845, Peel's backbenchers had had enough of being bullied and duped. His behaviour over the Factory Act and the Sugar Duties had been offensive, and the U-turn over Maynooth was obnoxious – but Repeal was intolerable. The Tory Party believed it stood for two great principles, in whose cause it had fought and won the 1841 general election: the defence of the Anglican Church and of the landed interest. Peel had had the brazen affrontery to abandon both within the course of one year.

To rank-and-file Tories, the Corn Laws were not just a package of tariffs protecting agriculture: they symbolised aristocratic, landed predominance in British society, and were at the heart of what made the nation great. A leading Tory journalist explained the deeper significance of the Corn Laws to a friend in 1843: 'I look farther, much, than the mere questions of prices of corn and rates of wages... [what is at stake] is the existence of a landed gentry, which has made England what she has been and is, without which no representative government can last; without which there can be no steady mean (middle way) between democracy and despotism... [the Repeal of the Corn Laws] would mean the overthrow of the existing social and political system of our country.' Yet only three years after this was written, the cotton-barons of Manchester had triumphed over the good Old England of squire and parson – and the enemy had been aided and abetted by Peel!

The depth of the anger which Peel faced in early 1846 was terrible: but this cannot explain how the backbenchers' revolt was transformed into a permanent break in the party. To understand this, we must turn our focus to the English counties. By 1845, the Tory heartlands of the shires were in revolt. The farmers had long been anxious at the free trade tendencies of Peel's policies, and in 1844 they had founded the Central Agricultural Protection Society to defend their interests. As Peel became more equivocal in the defence of the Corn Laws, the 'Anti-League', as the Protectionists' organisation soon became known, grew more militant. County MPs who were reluctant to join the attack on Peel were told to present themselves for re-election by their constituents. They were invariably 'de-selected'. Convinced Protectionist MPs, on the other hand, were emboldened to continue their assault. Thus, the Anti-League's organisation, tenacity and its concentrated bitterness first helped to inspire the Tory backbench revolt, then to sustain it, and finally to ensure that, after Repeal was passed, the party would depose Peel and turn him and his followers into political outcasts. The consequence of this for the structure of politics at

Westminster was dramatic. For the rest of the 1840s and most of the 1850s, the House of Commons would be divided into three main groupings: the Whigs and their allies; the Peelites; and the old Tories.

The parliamentary leaders of the Protectionists played a vital role in determining the depth of these divisions. In some of the most savage debates the Commons has ever seen, Peel was mercilessly harried and hunted down. Lord George Bentinck and Benjamin Disraeli were his two most venomous foes. In Bentinck, son of a Duke and king of the turf, the fury of rural England found its ideal mouthpiece – relentless, utterly convinced that right and honour was on the protectionists' side and apoplectic in the face of Peel's reptilian treachery. And in Disraeli, the Tory backbenchers discovered a parliamentary genius whose brilliant sarcasms could wound, torment and humiliate Peel in a way they had not thought possible.

The Protectionists would not call off their assault until Peel was crippled. Repeal itself could not be stopped: the Whigs in the Commons and the Lords mostly favoured it and would join the Conservative frontbenchers to give the bill a majority. But Peel himself could be. In June 1846, 69 of the most embittered backbenchers joined forces with Whigs, Radicals and Irish Catholics to defeat the Irish Coercion Bill and overthrow Peel's ministry. As they had hoped, his resignation ended Peel's career as a political leader. Four years later, he died after a riding accident, in some eyes a sort of martyr – to others, the foulest of villains. But what the Protectionists could not have guessed, in their blind passion, was that the split which they were helping to bring about in the Conservative Party was to keep it out of effective power for the best part of 30 years (*see pages 338–40*).

D *The case for the protectionists*

Historically, the Protectionists have received 'a bad press' for their actions in 1846. Bentinck is sometimes presented as little less than insane in the violence of his attacks on Peel, while Disraeli, notoriously, was supposedly driven by personal vendetta against Peel (*see pages 335–8*). The Protectionists as a whole are damned for bad economics and bad politics: the Repeal of the Corn Laws opened the door to three decades of unparalleled economic growth and social stability, while they condemned themselves and their party to almost thirty years of impotence and near-unbroken opposition. A prophecy which Peel's lieutenant Graham had made early in 1845 seemed to have come completely true: 'the old High Tories will not see that they can only govern on Peel principles in a Reformed Parliament, and if they reject the only man who has the wisdom and capacity to lead them through the difficulties of the Age in which we live, they must be content to see power transferred to their political opponents'.

But the strength of the Protectionists' case should not be underestimated.

- Peel was widely regarded to have made – for the second time in his career – a complete U-turn on the most important and bitterly disputed question of the day. He lived in an age which expected the highest standards of integrity and consistency from its politicians. However much Peel might argue that he had only acted in the service of the national interest, to those who had supported him in 1841, believing they were supporting protection, he was a 'rat' – and as such, only fit to be treated as a traitor and an outcast.
- Peel argued that Repeal would not only be good for the consumer and the manufacturer, but for the farmer too. Agriculture could benefit from the expanding urban markets which would soon – thanks to Repeal – be moving even faster out of recession. By adopting the techniques of 'high farming' – heavy investment in better drainage and fertilisers, for example – farmers could cope with foreign competition. But in this analysis, Peel proved over-sanguine. High farming required high investment which many farmers could not afford. And from the 1870s onwards, grain from the Russian Steppes and the North American Plains were to send British agriculture spiralling into profound depression. Social historians date the decline of the British aristocracy to the late nineteenth century. Perhaps Peel was a less skilful defender of the 'territorial constitution' than some historians have imagined?
- If Peel was over-optimistic about the capacity of British agriculture to respond to world competition, he may have been too pessimistic about the threat posed to the aristocratic order by the Anti-Corn Law League. Wellington, for one, detected an element of 'panic' in Peel's behaviour in 1845/6. Perhaps, as Bruce Coleman has suggested (*see bibliography page 159*), Peel's experiences between 1829 and 1832 – when Parliament had come terribly near to losing control of events – had made Peel oversensitive to the threat of popular pressure, and too anxious to defuse crises with concessions that were in fact premature and overgenerous. If Peel saw the Anti-Corn Law League as a conspiracy to equal the Jacobins of Revolutionary France in their destructive and subversive power, he was wrong.
- Peel seemed to ignore the constraints which the Great Reform Act placed on the executive's freedom of manoeuvre. Before the Great Reform Act, Prime Ministers had been able to rely on the rotten boroughs to provide them with a core of votes to help them carry their policies in the Commons. Their abolition in 1832 left the executive searching for new means of support. In fact, as Disraeli realised, the backing of 'party' would now be required if Prime Ministers were to enjoy stable parliamentary majorities. But Peel had spent too long as an 'executive man' under the old system to find tolerable – or perhaps even to understand – the new rules of the game. Thus, Graham's prophecy can be reversed: it was in fact impossible to govern 'by Peel Principles' in a Reformed Parliament, where 'Peel Principles' entailed a contempt for the sentiments and loyalties of party, and a high-handed style of executive government which appeared oblivious to the fact that the Reform Act had ever happened.

By presenting a more balanced account of the issues at stake when Peel and the Protectionists clashed, it becomes possible to identify some of Peel's political blindspots more clearly. He failed to appreciate the strength of the protectionists' case, the intensity with which they were committed to it, or the true consequences of his course of action. The most immediate of these was the destruction of the Tory Party. He was warned by Cabinet colleagues that Repeal would smash the Tories and thus leave Britain at the mercy of Whigs and Radicals. It was lucky for the old aristocracy that, instead, they ended up facing the not very terrible figure of the cautious Whig leader, Lord Palmerston. But it was a lesson which the future Tory leaders, Disraeli and Salisbury, took to heart. Both of them made it their top priority to keep the Conservative Party united. By contrast, in 1845–6 Peel gave every impression that he could not care less about its fate. Peel has some claim to be one of the worst party managers ever to lead the Tories.

10 ASSESSMENT

A *Peel and the conservative tradition*

Not surprisingly, Peel's place in the Conservative tradition remains a matter of controversy. Lord Blake, in his well-known history of the Conservative Party (*see bibliography page 159*) denies Peel a place in the 'Hall of Fame': after all, the split for which he was, Blake believes, mostly responsible, crippled the Conservatives as a political force for almost three decades. But Norman Gash has a rather different emphasis. According to him '[Peel's] place as the founder of modern Conservatism is unchallengeable ... His central achievement was to refashion the principles of Toryism for a new age'. Gash continues: 'only on the basis of [Peel's] principles could a party of the right in the conditions of Victorian political life obtain and retain power'. Until recently, Professor Gash's views tended to dominate Peel scholarship. But in recent years, this 'orthodoxy' has come under increasing attack. The most radical challenge to Gash's interpretation of Peel has come from Dr Hilton (*see bibliography*).

Hilton's arguments are complex and difficult, and only two elements can be noted here. First, Hilton has given us a fresh interpretation of Peel's way of thinking. Whereas Gash finds Peel to be a great pragmatist, always learning from experience, and a master of politics as 'the art of the possible', Hilton sees Peel's whole approach as dogmatic and divisive – and underpinned less by rational calculation than Christian commitment. Peel's faith in the free market was in part the product of highly intellectual theorising, in part sprung from his conviction that laissez-faire capitalism was God's means of punishing the thriftless and vicious, who did not deserve to be *protected* by the state from the consequences of their actions.

Secondly, and in direct contrast to Gash, Hilton insists that 'Peel was not the founder of the Conservative Party, but the progenitor [father] of Gladstonian Liberalism.' This claim may appear to be perverse, but in fact it makes a lot of sense. Gladstone always revered Peel as his greatest political teacher. From Peel, he learnt how fiscal policy – the delicate interplay of free trade, tariffs and income tax – could be deployed to strengthen economic prosperity and social harmony. Gladstone's attitude towards the power and function of the executive owes much to Peel too: Gladstone, like Peel, was supremely confident that there was no political problem that a courageously and expertly – directed executive could not resolve. His Irish policies, in particular, can be seen as a direct continuation of Peel's. Equally, Gladstone was single-minded in his determination that the executive should not be made the servant of any class or selfish party interest. Above all, he derived from Peel an urgent sense that the strength and justice of executive government be communicated to the people: or in Hilton's words, to 'persuade the toiling masses that there was a moral energy at the centre of the state which was not indifferent to their fears and aspirations'

Peel himself saw this as his central responsibility. In one of his final defences of the Repeal of the Corn Laws, he said:

> If I look to the prerogative of the Crown, if I look to the position of the Church, if I look to the influence of the aristocracy, I cannot charge myself with having taken any course inconsistent with conservative principles, calculated to endanger the privileges of any branch of legislature, or of any institutions of the country. My earnest wish has been, during my tenure of power, to impress the people of the country with a belief that the legislature was animated with a sincere desire to frame its legislation upon the principles of equity and justice. I have a strong belief that the greatest object which we or any other government can contemplate should be to elevate the social condition of that class of the people with whom we are brought into no direct relationship by the exercise of the elective franchise

There can be little doubt that Peel was a great and farsighted conservative – but a conservative with a small 'c'. It is much less easy, however, to assess his contribution to the Conservative Party, and its ideology and practice, in the nineteenth century.

We will consider later in this book the often-made claim that Disraeli eventually learnt that it was only on Peelite principles that a Conservative Party could rule in Victorian Britain (*see pages 364–5 and 367–8*). But if we draw up any list of the most salient characteristics of Peelism – great technical expertise in the arts of government, a taste for big bills and finding bold solutions to major problems, and a distrust and loathing of the dynamics of popular politics – we should note now that we have to look very hard to find much trace of these in Disraeli's political practice. And although the Disraelian Conservative Party did begin to attract to its banner the middle-class manufacturers and men of commerce to whom Peel had (largely unsuccessfully) appealed, this tendency was much more a process of repulsion from the perceived excesses of Gladstonian Liberalism than a question of attraction to anything Peelite about Disraeli. Only as a free trader did Disraeli become a Peelite, but as everyone else was a free trader in mid-Victorian Britain, it was not a policy with which Disraeli was going to win many votes, or carve out a distinctively Conservative identity. Perhaps it is Salisbury, with his sometimes paranoid suspicions about the threat from the mob, his instinctive authoritarianism and guiding belief that the Conservative Party should become the natural home of all men of property, who owes more to Peel. But it is hard not to conclude, as Hilton has suggested, that Gladstone has a stronger claim to the Peelite mantle than any Conservative.

B *Peel, statesmanship and mid-Victorian England*

Just as Gash's claims for Peel as the founding father of modern Conservatism have been under attack, so are his claims for the achievements of Peel's statesmanship. Gash has argued that it was Peel above all others who guided Britain out of the social and political turmoil of the 1830s and 1840s towards an era of stability and prosperity. For most – although not all of his career – Peel did live up to his ideal of statesmanship: a commitment to serve the interests of the nation with courage and foresight, abjuring all temptations to satisfy personal advantage, and if necessary, ignoring the claims of party. But has not Gash tended to exaggerate Peel's achievements? His Irish policies ended in failure. Even the connection between his tax and tariff reforms, and Britain's economic recovery, is open to doubt. Some economic historians believe that the cycle of boom and slump which characterised the early nineteenth-century economy went on regardless of government policy. Peel certainly overreacted to the threat posed by the Chartists and the 'general strike' of 1842. He may well have overreacted to the threat posed by the Anti-Corn Law League too.

But above all, the focus on Peel as the all-conquering hero of these years of crisis detracts from the contribution made by the Whigs to securing Britain's difficult transition to mid-Victorian stability. Peel's doctrinaire laissez-faire beliefs left little room for factory reform, and his sympathies with the grievances of Nonconformity were very limited. In both cases, the Whigs were to prove more sensitive to the needs of the nation as a whole than Peel. In particular, his dogged resistance to the Whigs' Bill for Parliamentary Reform highlights the negative, authoritarian streak in Peelite Conservatism.

Late in 1848, having retired from the political front rank, Peel reflected on the question of why the British state had survived the revolutionary upheavals of that year so much better than had the continental monarchies. He concluded, with an element of self-congratulation, that the main reason was because the Repeal of the Corn Laws had demonstrated to the British working classes that an aristocratic parliament could respond to their needs, even at the cost of sacrificing its own material interests. The British state was just and was seen to be just. But Peel should also have asked himself what the Great Reform Act had contributed to the survival of the established order. The middle classes, who in their tens of thousands offered their services as special constables to face the Chartists in 1848 (*see page 105*), had not been impressed enough by the principles of Tamworth Conservatism to back Peel in any great numbers in 1841. But Grey's bold extension of the franchise – the scale of which had outraged and amazed Peel – had successfully recruited enough of the forces of 'property and respectability' to the side of the aristocracy to see the British state and its 'territorial constitution' through the crisis of the 1840s. As Professor Beales has stressed, there was no *one* architect of the prosperity and stability of mid-Victorian Britain. Peel achieved much: but perhaps the Whigs achieved more? It was they who had had to fight for Parliamentary reform – and indeed, it was they who provided most of the votes by which the Repeal of the Corn Laws was finally carried.

11 Bibliography

Professor Norman Gash's work dominates the field. His *Sir Robert Peel, The Life of Sir Robert Peel after 1830* (Longman, 2nd edn 1986) is the second volume of a great biography. It looks intimidatingly bulky, but the most ambitious A-level students should certainly study the analyses to be found there of key episodes such as the 1842 Budget, the Maynooth Crisis and the Repeal of the Corn Laws. Gash has distilled many of his ideas in a superb chapter on the Conservative Party in his *Reaction and Reconstruction in English Politics 1832–1852* (Oxford University Press, 1965). He has also written two very useful, brief essays with A-level students in mind in *Modern History Review*: 'Sir Robert Peel and the Conservative Party' (February 1990) and 'Peel and Ireland' (April 1992).

Students will also find much of interest in the three following surveys: Robert Blake *The Conservative Party from Peel to Thatcher* (Fontana, 1985); Robert Stewart *The Foundation of the Conservative Party 1830–1867* (Longman, 1978); and Bruce Coleman *Conservatism and the Conservative Party in Nineteenth Century Britain* (Edward Arnold, 1988).

Gash's work has recently been subject to historical revisionism, and the A level student is fortunate to have two excellent syntheses of modern Peel scholarship available in easily accessible forms: Paul Adelman's *Peel and the Conservative Party 1830–1850* (Longman's Seminar Studies, 1989) and E J Evans *Sir Robert Peel: Statesmanship, Power and Party* (Routledge Lancaster Pamphlet, 1991). There is also a very stimulating article by David Eastwood in *History Today* March 1992 ('Peel and the Tory Party Reconsidered').

Important revisionist articles in scholarly journals include D Beales 'Peel, Russell and Reform' (*The Historical Journal, 1974*). I Newbould 'Sir Robert Peel and the Conservative Party, 1832–1841: A Study in Failure?' (*English Historical Review*, 1983) and Boyd Hilton's difficult but crucial 'Peel: A Reappraisal' (*The Historical Journal*, 1979).

For the Anti-Corn Law League, the A level student should start with either chapter 29 of E J Evans *The Forging of the Modern State* (Longman, 1983) or P Adelman *Victorian Radicalism*, chapter 1 (Longman, 1984): two masterly exercises in compression.

12 DISCUSSION POINTS AND EXERCISES

A *This section consists of questions or points that might be used for discussions (or written answers) as a way of expanding on the chapter and testing your understanding of it:*

1. What talents did Peel display, and what lessons did he learn during his years in government up to the crisis over Catholic Emancipation?
2. What was Peel's role in the crisis over Catholic Emancipation and Parliamentary Reform, and how did these events help shape his later career?
3. How can we explain the Conservative electoral recovery between 1832 and 1841?
4. What made Peel's 1842 Budget such a success?
5. What problems were posed by political disorder in Britain in Peel's great ministry, and how did he cope with them?
6. Why did relationships between Peel and his backbenchers deteriorate in 1844?
7. 'Coercion, then conciliation'. Expand this description of Peel's Irish policy.
8. Why did the Anti-Corn Law League want to repeal the Corn Laws, and how did they set about trying to achieve their objective?
9. Why did Peel want to Repeal the Corn Laws?
10. Why did the Repeal of the Corn Laws split the Conservative Party?

B *Essay questions*

1 'A great statesman but a poor party leader'. Discuss this evaluation of Peel.
2 'A Conservative is a Tory who has learned to live with the Industrial Revolution'. Discuss.
3 'The root of Peel's difficulties lies in his attempt to govern through a Reformed Parliament according to pre-reform rules'. Discuss.
4 Why, twice in Peel's career, did he find himself having to make a complete U-turn on the most important political issues of the day?
5 Why did Peel become the most hated man in British politics?
6 'Peel's achievements have been exaggerated'. Discuss.

13 DOCUMENTARY EXERCISE – COBDEN AND PEEL

Although they had been political and personal enemies, Peel went out of his way to praise Cobden as the true architect of the Repeal of the Corn Laws in the closing passage of his final speech on the issue. Peel's subsequent fall from power prompted an extraordinary letter from the League's leader. Cobden suggested that Peel call a general election immediately, campaigning on the slogan 'Peel and Free Trade', and thus put himself at the head of a new political movement that would break up the old party system. Cobden explained his thinking as follows:

> My object in writing is ... to draw your attention from the state of parties in the House, as towards your government, to the position you hold as Prime Minister in the opinion of the country. Are you aware of the strength of your position with the country? If so, why bow to a chance medley of factions in the Legislature, with a nation ready and waiting to be called to your rescue? Few people have more opportunities forced upon them than myself of being acquainted with the relative forces of public opinion. I will not speak of populace, which to a man is with you; but of the active and intelligent middle classes, with whom you have engrossed a sympathy and interest greater than was ever possessed by a minister. The period of the Reform Bill witnessed a greater enthusiasm, but it was less rational and less enduring. It was directed towards half a dozen popular objects – Grey, Russell, Brougham, etc. Now the whole interest centres in yourself. You represent the Idea of the age, and it has no other representative amongst statesmen. You could be returned to Parliament with acclamation by any one of the most numerous and wealthy constituencies of the kingdom. Fox [the Whig leader at the end of the eighteenth century] once

> said that 'Middlesex and Yorkshire together make all England'. You may add Lancashire, and call them your own. Are you justified towards the Queen, the people and the great question of our generation, in abandoning this grand and glorious position? Will you yourself stand the test of an impartial historian?

Cobden went on to try and anticipate Peel's possible objections:

> Do you shrink from the post of governing through the bonafide representatives of the middle class? Look at the facts, and can the country be otherwise ruled at all? There must be an end of the juggle of parties, the mere representatives of traditions, and some man must of necessity rule the state through its governing class. The Reform Bill decreed it, the passing of the Corn Bill has realised it.

1 *Explain what Cobden means when he writes to Peel: 'You represent the Idea of the age'. How does he justify this claim?*

2 *In what respects might Peel have been flattered and tempted by Cobden's appeal?*

3 *Re-read the last 7 lines of the extract ('Do you shrink . . . has realised it'). What did Cobden believe the Radicals had achieved with the Repeal of the Corn Laws?*

4 *Peel, in his reply, politely rejected Cobden's proposal. Can you suggest why?*

5 *'Cobden had completely misunderstood Peel's underlying reasons for repealing the Corn Laws, and the strategic political significance of Repeal'. Do you agree?*

VI

FOREIGN POLICY 1815–70

—

1 INTRODUCTION

THE Foreign Office was, without doubt, the most consistently and inherently demanding of all the great offices of state in the nineteenth century. No occupant of the post with any inclination to indolence could remain there for long without acquiring, willingly or otherwise, more dedicated habits of work. Other offices might be made more challenging or exacting by individuals who brought to them particular enthusiasm or administrative skills. A good example of this is that of Peel's galvanising effect upon a rather lethargic and low profile Home Office in the 1820s. Foreign Secretaries however had no need to seek out new fields to conquer; they faced an enormous burden of work on a daily basis, all year round. Lord Palmerston, who was Foreign Secretary for a total of some 16 years during the period 1830 to 1851, was often considered by some of his contemporaries to be a rather frivolous figure, more given to chasing after potential romantic conquests than to working on his despatches. In fact he faced a crippling schedule, customarily working 12 or even 16 hours a day. He even resorted to the use of a specially constructed table which allowed him to work standing up, for fear that he might fall asleep if he worked for long in a seated position!

Contrary to what might be supposed, Foreign Secretaries rarely left London and hardly ever travelled abroad. The circumstances which took Lord Castlereagh to the continent in 1814 and 1815 were exceptional. Canning conducted foreign policy from London, using representatives (most notably Wellington), when direct contact was needed. Palmerston generally travelled abroad only when he was out of office. In fact, Foreign Secretaries were the only Cabinet Ministers who routinely remained at their desks throughout the parliamentary recess. The strain which all this imposed was undoubtedly one of the factors which brought about the suicide of Castlereagh in 1822. For a decade he had combined the Foreign Office with another of the more demanding government posts, that of Leader of the House of Commons, at a terrible cost to his general health and in particular to his mental stability.

The pressures of the office were made worse by the poor quality of the clerks upon whom the hard-pressed Minister was compelled to rely. As with other Government Departments, clerical posts were filled by a mixture of patronage and individual introductions gained through social connections. Few of these appointees had any genuine appetite for the sustained workload imposed at the Foreign Office and they deeply resented attempts, such as those made by Palmerston in the 1830s, to impose a strict regime of work upon them. Those who were valuable to a Foreign Secretary faced such severe overwork that one of Castlereagh's best assistants, Edward Crooke, suffered a breakdown during a diplomatic mission in 1814.

Communications, or rather the lack of them, played a major role in the conduct of foreign policy. Before the availability, on any significant scale, of railways, steamships, and the telegraph, Foreign Secretaries had to contend with lengthy delays before they could receive details of developments abroad, or make their wishes known to ambassadors and representatives. In 1830, despatches from Paris took at least two days and sometimes three to arrive; from places such as Madrid or St. Petersburg they might take between ten days and two weeks; from Washington or Constantinople the waiting time was around a month; from South America the delay was some three months and from China up to seven months. All this meant that any British Foreign Secretary was compelled to rely heavily upon his representatives, on the spot, to take responsibility and make their own decisions. Such decisions frequently had to be made on the basis of instructions which might have been given many months before and in quite different circumstances. Depending on the particular situation, it might even fall to military or naval personnel to make important decisions of a diplomatic nature. In some areas of special significance or sensitivity, ambassadors were given extraordinary powers of independent action. The High Commissioner in the Far East had the authority to declare war on China, whilst on various occasions the Ambassador to the Porte (Constantinople) was given the power to summon the Fleet to the Dardanelles to back up his diplomatic manoeuvres.

The Foreign Secretary also needed to be constantly aware of the opinion of the Monarch when considering his policy. Even by 1815, the power of the Crown to interfere in domestic political issues was becoming limited and this trend was confirmed and accelerated by the effects of the Reform Act of 1832. On the other hand, foreign policy was seen as an area of continuing, legitimate concern for the monarch, who had the constitutional right (indeed duty) to see diplomatic despatches before they were sent. This right became the crux of a great contest between Palmerston and the Crown from 1846 until 1851.

The monarch had the right not only to see despatches, but also to make alterations to them. During the reign of William IV, Palmerston, though regarding the practice as tiresome, accepted the need to submit his papers in the normal way and accepted alterations when they were made. When Queen Victoria came to the throne in 1837 however, he took the opportunity to change the procedure. Instead of sending all despatches for approval, he began to send only a selected number, justifying this by claiming that he was sparing the 18-year-old Queen an unnecessary burden of work. Since his relations with the Queen were entirely cordial at this time, it is likely that Palmerston was, at least, partially sincere in this claim as well as fulfilling his preference for a freer hand. After her marriage in 1840 however, the Queen (who had not realised what Palmerston was doing) demanded to see all of the despatches in strict accordance with her rights. In this she was prompted by her new husband Prince Albert who, in addition to considering himself an expert on international affairs, had a personal dislike of Palmerston. The potential confrontation was not put to the test at this stage because the Whig Government lost office following the General Election of 1841 and Lord Aberdeen, who had been Foreign Secretary under Wellington in 1828–30, returned to the post in Peel's new Conservative Government. The Royal couple approved of both Aberdeen and his policies but when the Whigs returned in 1846, Palmerston found to his annoyance that many of his despatches were being altered, some substantially. His response was to become highly selective in the material which he submitted for approval. Victoria and Albert were soon demanding the removal of Palmerston from the Foreign Office, a demand which the Prime Minister, Lord John Russell, felt unable to meet because of Palmerston's influence in the Cabinet and his popularity in the House of Commons. The Crown did not triumph until 1851, when Palmerston unilaterally declared British approval of Louis Napoleon's coup d'etat in France. This cost the support of many of his Cabinet colleagues and the Prime Minister, Lord John Russell, asked him to resign.

Questions of trade and commerce always weighed heavily in the balance whenever foreign policy issues were being considered. As an island nation, Britain had for centuries recognised the importance of protecting trade routes and trading rights. Such imperatives had become inextricably interwoven with the question of national security. These concerns focused most immediately upon the issue of the Low Countries and their freedom from domination by another major power. This was both an economic and a strategic question since it affected the flow of goods into and out of Britain as well as the fear of possible invasion. The significance of the Dutch ports to British interests stretched back to the middle ages; of more recent importance to Britain was her Indian Empire, the source of many commodities and a seemingly limitless market for manufacturers. The defence of routes to the Far East, and the security of India itself, added a new dimension to Britain's relationship with the Turkish Empire, a trading partner since the sixteenth century and now a key strategic area for communications with the Indian Empire.

The defence of British interests on such a global scale necessitated both a strong navy and the will to use it when other diplomatic methods failed. The power of the navy had made it possible for Britain to bombard Copenhagen in 1807 and capture the Danish Fleet, thus preventing it from falling into French hands. In 1840, Palmerston ordered a naval blockade of Naples in order to force the Neapolitan Government to reverse a law which had effectively excluded British merchants from the sulphur trade. Such methods were understandably unpopular with other countries and were generally the last resort. In the latter instance, Palmerston had tried for three years to influence the Neapolitan Government by more conventional diplomacy.

Finally, the makers of British Foreign Policy had always to take account of, even if they did not always bow to, domestic political considerations. As a constitutional state, Britain had developed far freer and much more influential institutions than existed elsewhere in Europe at this time. Parliamentary opinion, the press and even the public, could all influence decision-making, as could the powerful merchant and commercial interests. The need to consider such pressures, which by their very nature tended to shift or even redefine themselves radically from time to time, meant that British policy had to be flexible in method, even if it remained consistent in its broadest aims.

The fundamentals of British interests did indeed remain constant when viewed in general terms. Britain aimed to maintain peace and stability in Europe; this was necessary for continuity of trade and because wars were expensive. British prestige as a global power demanded that her possessions and her citizens be protected as far as possible from violation. However, the securing of these objectives could be achieved by a variety of means. Palmerston sought to maintain British interests in the Low Countries in 1831 by threatening war against France unless French troops were withdrawn from Belgium. On the other hand, in 1832, he allied Britain with France and approved the re-entry of French troops into Belgium in order to pressurise the Dutch. It is hardly surprising that the nations of Europe and beyond viewed Britain with a mixture of envy, grudging admiration and distrust British friendship was a source of much potential benefit, but it was not a factor to be relied upon for all seasons.

2 CASTLEREAGH AND THE VIENNA SETTLEMENT

The Congress of Vienna was convened to establish a peace settlement after 20 years of European war. It took place over an 18-month period from October 1814 to May 1815. It had been preceded by many months of diplomatic discussion between the coalition powers, headed by Britain, Russia, Prussia and Austria, which were then in the process of defeating the French Empire. Guided by Napoleon's military genius, France had swept away the old order in Europe and constructed an Empire which had extended, before collapsing, from the Atlantic to Moscow. The work of the victorious allies was therefore one of reconstruction; the dilemma which faced them was – how far was this reconstruction to be a work of restoration and how far was it to be innovation?

Castlereagh, the British Foreign Secretary from 1812, entered into these negotiations with some advantages. It was British economic power which had made the last coalition against France possible and had held it together. Moreover, Castlereagh's specific objectives in Europe were limited and geared to the overall need to produce a peace which would be permanent. In pursuing this aim Castlereagh enjoyed virtually a free hand. Lord Liverpool, the Prime Minister, painfully aware of how much the war had cost the nation (the National Debt had risen from £234 million in 1793 to £834 million), was fearful of a resumption of hostilities and prepared to agree to almost anything to avoid it. Parliament had little knowledge of, and probably even less interest in, the affairs of Europe, being entirely engrossed in domestic problems.

Castlereagh's main concern was with the position of France. He had a delicate balance to achieve. On the one hand, he wished to ensure that France could be contained in future; on the other hand he did not wish to cripple her since she was needed in the longer term to counterpoise the growing power of Russia. His policy was based upon a memorandum drafted in 1804 by Pitt, in which the late Prime Minister had proposed that Prussia be allowed to expand in North and West Germany whilst Austria expanded in Italy. These expansions would compensate for any Russian movements to the west. At the same time Belgium would be combined with Holland to provide greater security against France. So far as the treatment of France itself was concerned, Castlereagh was chiefly concerned that the allies should not impose an unwanted government on the French people, a move which he was sure would make instability in France inevitable and therefore another war certain. Initially he agreed with Metternich, the Austrian Foreign Minister, that the best solution would be to negotiate a satisfactory peace with Napoleon and allow him to continue to rule. Only when this option became impractical did he turn reluctantly to the idea of restoring the Bourbon monarchy.

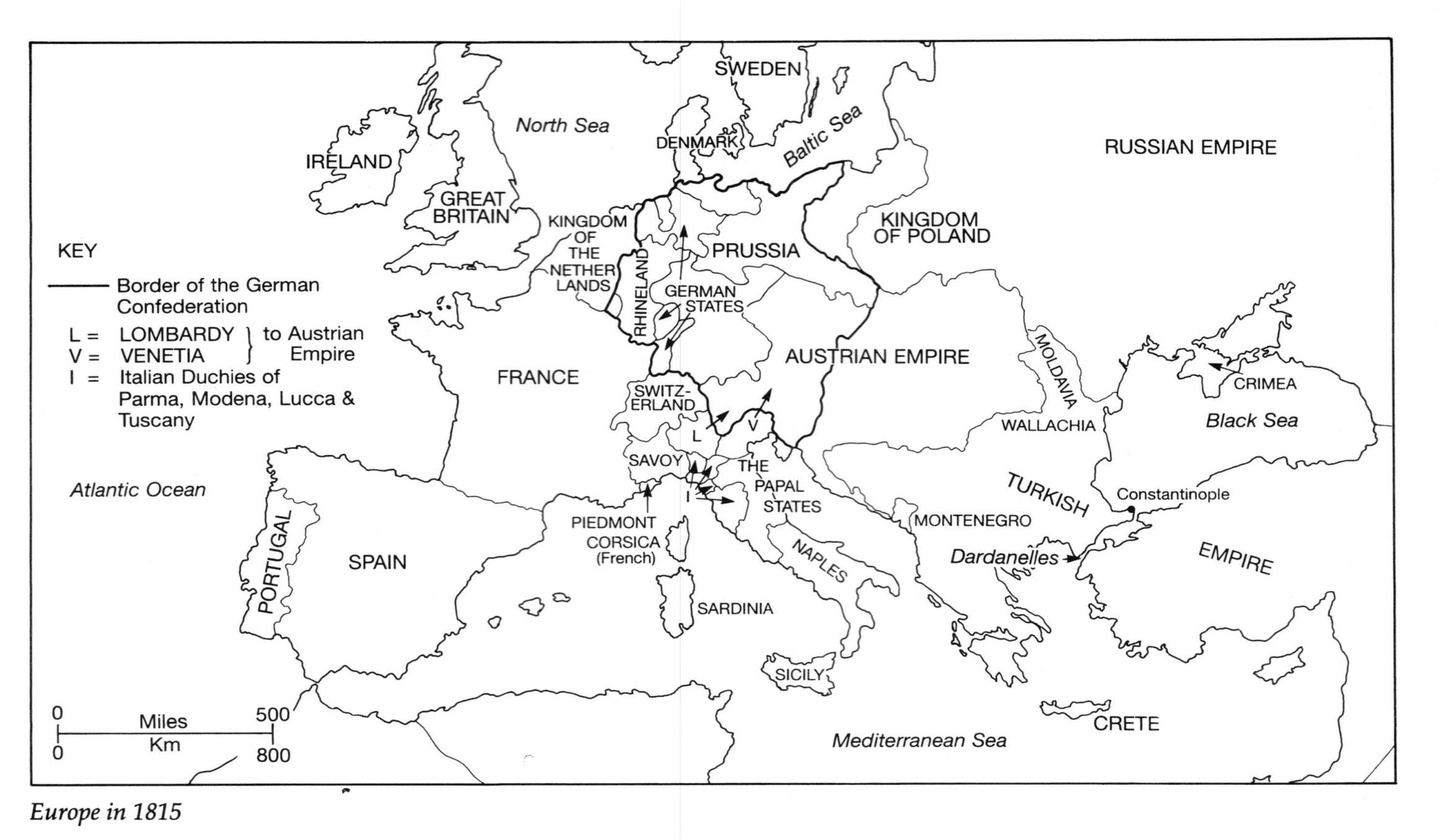

Europe in 1815

Castlereagh's gains for Britain were established early in the diplomatic discussions. Under the Treaty of Chaumont (March 1814), the allies agreed to continue their collaboration for as long as necessary to defeat France and then to maintain their alliance for a period of 20 years afterwards to defend any settlement. In addition the enlarged and independent Holland, which was so important to Britain, was agreed upon. In the First Treaty of Paris (30 May 1814) – which followed Napoleon's overthrow and the return of the Bourbon King – France surrendered Tobago, St. Lucia and Mauritius to Britain. In the Vienna negotiations Britain obtained the union of Belgium and Holland, as prescribed by Pitt. This had the further benefit of compensating Holland for colonial losses, such as the Cape Colony, to Britain. In addition to the Cape, Britain gained Heligoland in the North Sea, Malta and the Ionian Islands in the Mediterrean, and Ceylon.

In his efforts to ensure that France would be peaceful in the future, Castlereagh pressed for a moderate settlement. This he achieved in the First Peace of Paris. However, all this was put at risk by the return of Napoleon to France in March 1815. The enthusiasm with which he was received bore out all Castlereagh's fears about the inadequacy of the Bourbons. The flight of Louis XVIII to Ghent showed just how fragile the restoration was and how little affection the monarch enjoyed amongst the French people. The defeat of Napoleon at Waterloo, welcome though it was, left the allies with little alternative but to reinstate Louis XVIII and Castlereagh faced demands from the Prussians for Alsace and Lorraine, as well as other French territory, and heavy reparations. Castlereagh was determined to resist any penal settlement which would offend the dignity of France and set up a permanent, destabilising sense of grievance. He enlisted the support of the Tsar and with this he managed to persuade the Austrians to adopt a moderate line. In this way he was able to compel the Prussians to give up their more extreme demands. The final settlement, although tougher than that of May 1814 – the French faced an indemnity of 700 million francs as well as other penalties – was undoubtedly more favourable to the French than would have been the case had it not been for Castlereagh's efforts.

3 Britain and the Defence of the European Settlement 1815–41

A *Castlereagh and Canning*

During the first dozen years following the peace settlements of 1814–15 British Foreign Policy was dominated by two men of very different styles and temperaments. Lord Castlereagh continued as Foreign

Secretary until his suicide in August 1822 when he was succeeded by George Canning, a man as flamboyant and extrovert as Castlereagh was colourless and introvert. Nor were these differences of personality the only factors involved. Castlereagh saw diplomacy as essentially a private and secret world in which public involvement and pressures could only affect outcomes adversely. Canning, on the other hand, gloried in the public speeches he gave on the subject and lost no opportunity, short of risking national security, to publicise his policy. Certainly contemporaries saw the accession of Canning as marking a great change in British policy. The comparison between the two men and their conduct of foreign policy, which began almost as soon as Castlereagh died, has fascinated historians ever since and formed the basis of a regular line of questioning for A level Chief Examiners in particular! In general the trend in most recent commentaries has been to suggest that the differences between them, in terms of actual policy, were largely exaggerated.

In fact, meaningful comparisons between Castlereagh and Canning are far more difficult than is commonly supposed. Both were disciples of the great Pitt and both entered politics as his proteges. Canning had already served as Foreign Secretary between 1807–09 and Castlereagh had been Secretary for War and the Colonies. The two men fought a duel in 1809 – in which Canning was slightly wounded – after Canning had attempted to have Castlereagh removed from his post. After this, however, their circumstances when in office differed very markedly. Even though both men occupied the office of Leader of the House of Commons at the same time as the Foreign Office, the implications were by no means the same. The leadership of the Commons was a key post whenever the Prime Minister of the day happened to be in the House of Lords as was the case with Lord Liverpool. During his tenure of the post, Castlereagh faced a series of domestic crises as the leading speaker for the Government in the Lower House. His attention could never be focused entirely upon international affairs to the exclusion of all else – even in Vienna in the early months of 1815, he was being pressured by Liverpool to return home as soon as possible to reassert Government authority over an unruly House of Commons. Canning faced no such extreme pressures in the calmer domestic waters of the 1820s. Nor did he face the task of reconstructing Europe after the dislocating effects of more than two decades of war.

As we have seen, the question of protecting the peace settlement had occupied the mind of Castlereagh even before the defeat of Napoleon was secured. The commitment to future collaboration, contained in the Treaty of Chaumont, was reaffirmed and given concrete form in the Quadruple Alliance, signed on the same day as the signing of the Second Treaty of Paris in November 1815. Under this arrangement Britain, Russia, Austria and Prussia agreed to uphold the settlement and to confer together whenever necessary. This was regarded by

Castlereagh as the fundamental basis of future peace and the best means of rendering obsolete the Tsar's brainchild of a 'Holy Alliance'. The Holy Alliance was an idea which implied the intervention by the abolutist powers – i.e. Russia, Prussia and Austria – on almost any pretext and was regarded by Castlereagh as dangerous as well as 'sublime mysticism and nonsense'. He intended that the Quadruple Alliance should be primarily a safeguard against any French attempt to avenge their recent defeat. He envisaged that congresses would be summoned only to deal with really major crises. He viewed the subsequent congresses at Aix-la-Chapelle (1818), Troppau (1820), and Laibach (1821), with a mixture of apprehension and distaste as representing a distortion of the fundamental concept of the Alliance. At Aix-la-Chappelle, although the Quadruple Alliance was renewed, a new Quintuple arrangement was also signed bringing France back into the diplomatic fold. Castlereagh welcomed this in itself, but saw the danger of a new 'Holy Alliance' emerging. His response was to issue, in May 1820, the famous State Paper, in which he clearly distanced Britain from the principle of intervention in the affairs of other nations unless the general peace of Europe was manifestly at risk:

> The principle of one state interfering by force in the internal affairs of another, in order to enforce obedience to the governing authority, is always a question of the greatest possible moral as well as political delicacy ... to generalise such a principle ... or ... to impose it as an obligation is ... utterly impracticable and objectionable ... No country having a representative system of government could act upon it ... The importance of preventing the Low Countries ... being melted down into the general mass of French power, whether by insurrection or by conquest, might enable the British Government to act ... but upon all such cases we must admit ourselves to be, and our Allies should in fairness understand that we are, a power that must take our principle of action ... from those maxims [rules], which a system of government strongly popular, and national in its character has irresistibly imposed upon us. We shall be found in our place when actual danger menaces the system of Europe, but this country cannot, and will not, act upon abstract principles of precaution. The Alliance which exists had no such purpose in view in its original formation ... if it had, most assuredly the sanction of Parliament would never have been given to it ...

1 *What is the significance of Castlereagh's reference to possible British intervention in the Low Countries?*

2 *What contribution does this extract make to an understanding of the conduct of British foreign policy at this time?*

The State Paper also underlined the limited nature of the British view of her obligations: the guarantee of the territorial settlement for a period of 20 years and the exclusion of the Napoleonic dynasty from power in France. The document, circularised to all the major British embassies abroad, but typically not made public by Castlereagh, was his direct answer to the 'Troppau Protocol' of 1820, in which Russia, Prussia and Austria had committed themselves to intervention against revolution in terms broad enough to allow it in almost any event.

When Canning came back to the Foreign Office in 1822 after an absence of 13 years, British foreign policy was, therefore, already significantly distanced from the aims of the absolutists in Europe. Canning published the State Paper of 1820 and adopted it as the basis of his policy. It is possible that Canning himself had played some part in the drawing up of the State Paper; at any rate he made no alteration to the instructions which Castlereagh had drafted for the Verona Congress of 1822, which the latter had been preparing to attend at the time of his death. Canning had to face the immediate problem of the Tsar's desire to intervene in Spain to restore absolutism and destroy the liberal constitution achieved by means of a revolution in 1812. He proceeded exactly as Castlereagh had intended by resisting the proposal, through his representative the Duke of Wellington. He failed to prevent a French army entering Spain to restore autocracy, but, with an eye on British economic interests, he made it clear that while Britain would not fight over Spain itself, she would most certainly do so if any attempt was made to reimpose control over the Spanish colonies in South America, which had previously declared their independence from Spain. This was of far greater long-term significance for Britain and the autocrats of Europe did not press the matter further.

In Portugal however, Canning adopted a different line. Here, the clash between constitutionalism (the governing of a country by means of a constitution) and absolutism (the governing of a country by the absolute will of an individual), resulted in Canning sending a British fleet to Lisbon in 1824 to protect the constitutionalist King John from the absolutist pretentions of his younger son Miguel. After some lengthy and complicated internal political wrangling in Portugal, Canning ended up sending 5 000 British troops to Portugal in 1827, to ensure the succession of John's granddaughter, Maria, and the acceptance of a liberal constitution for the country. Canning had therefore established a pragmatic theme to British policy which would be taken up and developed by Palmerston in the 1830s.

B *Palmerston*

Palmerston became Foreign Secretary in the Whig-led Coalition government which took office in 1830, having previously served in the Tory administrations of Liverpool and Wellington. His break with the

Tories was of very recent origin and, although he had long experience of government, little of it was at Cabinet level. Politically he was known as a Canningite, having remained loyal to Canning in joining the 1827 coalition and his resignation from Wellington's government in 1828, was due to a dispute between this group (led by Huskisson), and the Prime Minister. Palmerston's first speech of any significance on the subject of foreign policy came on 1 June 1829, when he roundly condemned Wellington's policy towards Portugal and Greece. The case of Greece is explored more fully in the next section. So far as Portugal was concerned, Palmerston criticised the Government for its inaction in the face of a coup d'etat in 1828 which had removed Queen Maria and replaced her with Dom Miguel. This reversed the outcome engineered by Canning in 1827.

This speech established Palmerston as a major Parliamentary figure. Not that there were many MPs assembled to hear it; foreign affairs did not interest members very much in the normal course of events. However, Palmerston took the trouble to have his speech printed and widely circulated in order to ensure its effect. When Wellington's government fell in November 1830, Palmerston was more or less a certainty for some appointment, but his placing at the Foreign Office was widely greeted with scepticism and even derision. He was not the Prime Minister, Lord Grey's first choice as Foreign Secretary, and he was still seen by many as too much of a lightweight politically. However, he had a strong advocate in Princess Lieven, the wife of the Russian Ambassador and Palmerston's former mistress. Also, as a former Tory, he looked less alarming to the various European Courts which were nervous at the prospect of a Whig-dominated government in Britain, something which, from their point of view, was an unknown and potentially radical quantity with which to deal.

As Foreign Secretary, Palmerston encountered, from the outset, a series of significant challenges to the Vienna Settlement. These came in the form of a succession of revolts throughout Europe which threatened the arrangements made at Vienna. The revolts occurred as a chain reaction following the overthrow of the Bourbon dynasty in France, in July 1830. This was followed by revolts in Belgium and Switzerland. These were successful, partly because of the support they attracted from Britain and from the new liberal monarchy of Louis-Philippe in France. Elsewhere in Europe there were uprisings in both Italy and Poland. Neither was successful since both were too far removed from British and French influence to benefit from it to any great degree. The influence of the Holy Alliance, in the shape of Austria in Italy and Russia in Poland, was too strong to allow any upturn in nationalist feelings to upset the status quo. Austria was determined to maintain her predominance in northern Italy against the threat of any form of Italian nationalism, while Russia ran Poland as part of her sphere of interest, control of which was not to be curbed by any nationalist movement. Palmerston's response to these events and pressures was governed principally by his perception of their likely effects on British interests. He had no wish to offend either the Austrians or the Russians and had no desire to intervene. In the case of Belgium however, Palmerston was resolved that any change in the settlement affecting the Low Countries must be one which was consistent with British interests. In this context, it meant that French influence should not be expended, as that would be a potential threat to Britain. The union of Belgium and Holland had seemed practical enough in 1815. However, underlying differences of language and religion had fed a whole range of social, economic and political grievances on the part of the Belgians and thus led to large-scale disturbances in 1830.

Palmerston decided from the time he took office that the only long-term solution to the Belgian crisis lay in the creation of an independent and neutral Belgium. Within days of becoming Foreign Secretary, he wrote to the British representative in Brussels:

> His Majesty's Government consider the absolute and entire separation of Belgium from Holland to be no longer a matter for discussion, but to have become, by the course of events, an established . . . irreversible fact.

In reaching this decision, Palmerston was not moved by any idea of the justice of the Belgian case. Indeed he revealed in a despatch to the Prussians, in December 1830, that he would have preferred to maintain the union of Belgium and Holland had that option been in any way practicable. What he feared was that somehow Belgium might end up in a union with France. This was totally out of the question from the British point of view. Even an arrangement which left Belgium with any semblance of dependence on France was unacceptable.

Palmerston was assisted in his handling of the Belgian crisis by two factors. First, the new French King was still unsure of his position at home and apprehensive about how his accession was viewed by the Holy Alliance powers. The last thing he wanted therefore, was to have bad relations with Britain. Second, there was a ready-made villain to hand in the shape of William I of Holland. Palmerston was convinced that William's stupidity and intransigence were at the root of the crisis and believed that the Belgian grievances would not have escalated into irreconcilable differences had it not been for the King's attitude. He was therefore resolved, if necessary, to coerce William into accepting Belgian independence. Initially things did not look promising for Palmerston. He was successful, with Louis-Philippe's support, in persuading Austria, Russia and Prussia to accept the basic principle of Belgian independence. However, the Belgian decision to offer the new throne to Louis-Philippe's son, the Duke of Nemours, and the intervention of French troops to support the Belgians against William's troops in 1831, left Anglo-French relations hanging over a precipice.

Palmerston, however, rose to the occasion. He secured Louis-Philippe's agreement not to support his own son as the future King of Belgium and brought forward a compromise candidate in the form of Prince Leopold of Saxe-Coburg. The latter had a British connection as a widowed son-in-law of George IV; he was also about to be married to Louis-Philippe's daughter. Palmerston believed Leopold to be sufficiently pro-British to serve his purpose. When the French entered Belgium in support of Leopold in 1831 Palmerston warned them off with the threat of war, and secured a withdrawal of French troops. The following year, however, with William still refusing to come to terms, he adopted the Canningite tactic of allying himself with a rival (i.e. France) in order to avert a clash. Thus it came to be that British and France jointly blockaded the Dutch coast, whilst the French, this time with Palmerston's approval, sent their troops to expel the Dutch from Antwerp. The finer points of the final settlement of Belgian independence were to drag on for several years before the eventual signing of the Treaty of London in 1839, which effectively secured all Palmerston's aims.

In the case of Portugal Palmerston worked to reverse the coup d'etat of 1828. Again he collaborated with France, even sanctioning the use of the French fleet, which went to Lisbon in 1831. Palmerston hoped to keep the pressure on Dom Miguel and, when Queen Maria's father Pedro intervened on his daughter's behalf, Palmerston allowed him to enlist troops in Britain, a move which needed a change in the law since it was illegal for British subjects to serve in foreign armies. Queen Maria was finally restored to her throne in 1833. In Spain, Palmerston faced even more complex problems as the tangled web of Spanish politics drew liberals and absolutists into conflict. This situation was complicated by the decision of the Holy Alliance powers to support the abolutist pretender Don Carlos. Palmerston's answer was to negotiate a Quadruple Alliance in 1834, between Britain, France, Spain and Portugal. The four powers undertook to exclude the absolutist claimants from the thrones of Spain and Portugal, and Palmerston claimed the creation of a 'counterpoise' to the Holy Alliance. Despite this however, Palmerston did not lose sight of the need to work with the Holy Alliance powers whenever British interests were best served by doing so. Nowhere was this need more evident than in the complicated situation which had developed in south-eastern Europe involving the Turkish Empire and its European territories – the 'Eastern Question'.

4 BRITAIN AND THE EASTERN QUESTION 1815–70

A *The problem*

By 1815 the status of the Turkish Empire as a 'sick man' was well-established. The essence of the problem, from the viewpoint of the great powers of Europe, was that a Muslim and Asiatic power was imposing a notoriously-vicious rule upon millions of Christians in a large area of south-eastern Europe. The European powers had never accepted the Turks as equals, but as the corrupt and decaying empire weakened in the eighteenth century no commonly acceptable policy could ever be found which would allow a consensus to emerge on how to deal with the problem. On the one hand, the wish to see fellow Christians liberated inclined the great powers to welcome signs of decline in Turkey; on the other, there was a fear that conflicting interests amongst the powers themselves would lead to war if Turkey collapsed without there being any agreement on how to fill the 'power vacuum' which would be created on her demise. As Turkey declined, so the European powers were faced with a long-term problem for the balance of power and the stability of international relations.

In the eighteenth century Britain had attached relatively little importance to the question of the future of Turkey. The volume of British trade with Turkey was reasonable but not huge. When Russia defeated Turkey in a war in 1774 and imposed a punitive peace treaty on the Turks, the event aroused little interest in Britain. This should be compared with the situation in France, where the need to protect a valuable source of foreign trade with Turkey caused the French to protest vehemently to the Russians. The increasing importance of the Indian Empire towards the end of the century gradually began to change this relative British indifference and the loss of the American colonies in the 1780s prompted a general reconsideration of the security of British imperial possessions. The major event which changed British perceptions dramatically, however, was the invasion of the Turkish dependency of Egypt by Napoleon at the end of the 1790s. This threatened British links with the East and forced a response. Napoleon was expelled by British military and naval power from Egypt, but the lesson was not forgotten and the future of Turkey thus became an issue for British interests at the Vienna Congress.

By the time the Vienna Congress met, the situation surrounding British attitudes towards Turkey was complex. Castlereagh saw the need to safeguard Turkey but he also wanted to fit Turkey into the wider needs of the balance of power in Europe. The overwhelming priority was to prevent the resurgence of an expansionist France and the key to this was the power of Russia. However, Castlereagh was also anxious that Russia should not become too strong. To guard against this the strategic positions of the countries bordering Russia were crucial. Turkey, with its hold on south-eastern Europe and on the Straits of the Dardanelles (*see map on page 168*) was clearly a major element in this complicated calculation. To make matters even more confused Britain had to recognise that the French might, at some point in the future, again become a threat to British interests. The future of Turkey had thus become an issue which bore upon British interests in a number of different ways: the security of the Indian Empire and commercial interests both there and elsewhere in the Far East; the balance of power in Europe and the maintenance of European peace and stability.

B *The Greek revolt*

Perhaps the greatest potential threat to the future viability of the Turkish Empire, and one which lay largely outside the control of the Great Powers, was the danger of internal revolts against Turkish rule by subject peoples. The Greeks had long been simmering in resentment at Turkish control and, in 1821, they rose in revolt. The rising commenced with a brutal massacre of Muslims, including the execution of 12 000 Turkish troops who had surrendered to the Greeks at Tripolitsa. Turkish retaliation followed. Greek religious leaders were hanged in Constantinople and most of the occupants of the Greek island of Chios were butchered. The Greeks declared themselves to be independent in January 1822.

The reaction in Britain to the Greek revolt was confused. Popular sentiment was largely with the Greeks, but at higher levels of politics opinions were more varied. Castlereagh, recognising the extent to which the Greeks looked to the Russians as fellow Orthodox Christians for support, urged the latter to act with restraint. At the same time, he warned the Turks that Britain would not support them if they provoked a war with Russia. The feelings of the Russians were running high however, after the hangings in Constantinople and by mid-1821 Russia and Turkey were close to war. The neutralist approach which Castlereagh had adopted looked unlikely to be enough to prevent hostilities from breaking out and it was in this climate that Castlereagh and Metternich, the Austrian Chancellor, met for what proved to be the last time, in Hanover in October 1821. In fact they found that little general agreement was possible on the Greek issue. Austria was broadly sympathetic to Russia and in any case if Britain and Austria had appeared to collude too closely it might have had the opposite effect to that which was intended, by provoking the Russians rather than restraining them. The failure to find a joint approach to the Greek revolt did not depress Castlereagh greatly; more importantly he had revived relations with Metternich, which had been strained since he had dissociated Britain from the Troppau Protocol.

What benefits might have accrued from this renewed collaboration between Castlereagh and Metternich must remain hypothetical.

Castlereagh's suicide meant the end of diplomacy based upon personal relationships. To Metternich the advent of Canning as Foreign Secretary was the signal for him to retreat to the security of a closer Russian connection. For his part, Canning had no desire to seek an allied approach to the Eastern Question at that time. His personal sympathies were with the Greeks, and in 1823 he accorded them formal recognition as 'belligerents' rather than 'rebels'. However, his main concern was with the best interests of Britain and in any case he had to contend with the influence of Wellington, who was suspicious of revolts of any kind. The King was also less than enthusiastic about Greek claims. When the Tsar tried to promote joint intervention, Canning refused to agree. When Tsar Alexander died at the end of 1825, however, Canning saw the opportunity for a new relationship with Russia. The new Tsar, Nicholas I, proved far less enthusiastic for congress-style diplomacy and far more willing to engage in direct negotiations. This suited Canning and he despatched Wellington to Russia with the object of securing a bilateral agreement on Greece. The outcome was the Protocol of St Petersburg of April 1826. Under this, Britain and Russia agreed that Greece would become an autonomous state, though still under Turkish suzerainty. This agreement was followed by the Treaty of London in July 1827 – by this time Canning was Prime Minister – and the French were also brought into the discussions. The three powers now agreed to an alliance which would force the Turks to accept Greek autonomy or, if the Turks remained obdurate, would aim to secure Greek independence.

Canning died in August 1827, but the policy which he had set into motion followed its own momentum under his successor, Lord Goderich. The Turks refused an armistice and decided to quell the revolt. To do this the Sultan was forced to rely on the power of his Egyptian vassal, Mehemet Ali. Mehemet Ali's forces in Greece were being supplied and reinforced from Egypt and the allied navies were sent to sever this supply line. This resulted in the Battle of Navarino, in which the Turkish-Egyptian fleets were destroyed in October 1827.

At this point a complication set in from the British side. In January 1828, the Duke of Wellington replaced Lord Goderich as Prime Minister. He appointed Lord Aberdeen as Foreign Secretary. Aberdeen, a classical scholar of some repute, was personally sympathetic to the Greeks but Wellington, alarmed by the growing weakness of Turkey, apologised to the Sultan for the sinking of his fleet and distanced Britain from the dispute. The Sultan meanwhile repudiated a previous agreement which he had made with the Russians and declared a holy war. This act of lunacy had the inevitable effect of causing the Russians to declare war on Turkey in April 1828. The war was a predictable disaster for the Turks and the Russians imposed a peace settlement, the Treaty of Adrianople, in September 1829. Under the terms of the settlement Turkey had to agree to what amounted to a

Russian protectorate over Moldavia and Wallachia, which are situated in a vital position at the mouth of the River Danube, (*see map on page 168*). Thus Turkey had to give up control of an important strategic position as well as submitting to various other conditions, such as Serbian autonomy under Russian protection and commercial concessions.

To Britain these arrangements seemed to portend the break-up of Turkey on Russian terms. The agreement said nothing on the subject of Greece, but Wellington and Aberdeen now felt that the issue could not simply be left with the 1826 proposals of autonomy for the Greeks with continuing Turkish suzerainty. To Wellington this seemed to offer yet further room for Russian pressure in the future. In fact the fears of Wellington and Aberdeen were largely groundless, since the Russians had actually concluded in 1829 that the preservation of Turkey would serve their interests better than the setting up of a series of possibly unpredictable independent Balkan states. This, however, was not known at the time, and Britain was not the only country to draw the wrong conclusions from the Treaty of Adrianople.

Wellington's solution to this dilemma was to perform a complete about-face on the Greek question and opt for outright Greek independence. In this he was supported now by the Austrians who also feared Russian intentions. Metternich had objected to the more limited plans initiated by Canning in 1826; now he joined with Britain in supporting the more drastic option. The three allied powers, Britain, France and Russia, met in London in February 1830 to discuss the Greek question and no difficulty was encountered in agreeing to the basic principle of independence. The three powers themselves guaranteed the borders of the new nation, under arrangements which left Northern Greece and the island of Crete – previously a major centre of revolt – still in Turkish hands. It was these proposals which stirred Palmerston, who was much more pro-Greek than Canning had been, into a strong condemnation of Wellington's policy.

c *Mehemet Ali, Palmerston and the London Convention*

The settlement of the Greek crisis did not bring about any respite for the Turkish Empire. On the contrary, the use which the Sultan made of Mehemet Ali to subdue the Greeks ushered in the next phase of the Eastern Question and led to new difficulties for British policy. Mehemet Ali had received Crete as a reward for his abortive services, but he was not satisfied with this. He was anxious to secure Syria and the city of Damascus. In 1831 he sent his son Ibrahim to attack Palestine. Ibrahim had been his father's general in Greece and was a seasoned and effective campaigner. He made short work of the Sultan's forces. By the end of 1832 he had defeated the last army that Turkey could field against him and looked set to seize the whole

Empire. The Sultan, no doubt recalling Wellington's conciliatory attitude in 1828, now swallowed his pride and appealed to Britain for help.

Since the end of 1830, Palmerston had been Foreign Secretary and he now had to respond to this appeal. Despite his position on the particular issue of Greece, Palmerston was not anti-Turkish as such. In any case, as has already been seen, Palmerston's reaction to events was governed almost entirely by his perception of how they affected British interests. In this instance his instinct was to help Turkey. He was anxious to avoid any further extension of Russian influence and did not want to see Mehemet Ali gain at the expense of Turkey, since he feared the influence of the French behind the rising power of the Egyptians. In the event however, Palmerston's ideas did not convince the Cabinet, which refused to agree to his pleas for intervention on behalf of the Sultan. The reasons for this refusal by the Cabinet were complex. Some Whigs were naturally Francophile and did not share Palmerston's suspicions of France; some saw Mehemet Ali as a reformer and therefore preferable to the Sultan; some were worried about over-extending British resources at a time when the navy was already involved in the blockade against Holland. Palmerston was therefore compelled to inform the Sultan that no aid could be expected from Britain. Palmerston was under no illusion as to the seriousness of the decision. In later years he wrote:

> There is nothing that has happened since I have been in this office which I regret so much as that tremendous blunder ... Grey, who was with me on the point, was weak and gave way, and so nothing was done in a crisis of the utmost importance to all Europe ... (1838); and then in 1840; I humbly venture to think ... that no British Cabinet at any period of the history of England ever made so great a mistake in regard to foreign affairs.

The Sultan was left with no alternative but to swallow even greater quantities of pride and turn to the Russians. In the words of one of his own officials it was much as 'a drowning man clings to a serpent'. Palmerston hit the same note with his own comment, 'the Russian Ambassador becomes chief Cabinet minister of the Sultan'. The help of Russia was decisive but it came at a price. A Russian squadron entering the Bosphorous in February 1833 was enough to convince Ibrahim to retreat. He was too good a general to risk a clash with the Russians. In April, 6000 Russian troops landed opposite Constantinople and the security of the Sultan was assured. This still left Ibrahim in a strong position so long as he made no further moves forward. The Russians forced the Sultan to sign the Treaty of Unkiar Skelessi in July 1833 before withdrawing her troops. Under this the two countries agreed to mutual assistance in the event of an attack on either one of them and the Turks agreed to close the Dardanelles to all warships whenever the Russians wished. This latter agreement was supposed to be a secret provision, but Lord Ponsonby the British Ambassador at Constantinople, found out about it almost immediately and notified Palmerston.

With Mehemet Ali checked, but still in a strong situation, the French now urged the Sultan to make concessions to his protege. Palmerston, trying to make the best of a bad job and salvage something of British prestige from a sorry affair added his voice to this advice. In public he defended the intervention of the Russians whilst behind the scenes he ordered Ponsonby to persuade the Sultan not to ratify the Treaty of Unkiar Skelessi. When this failed he sent strong protest notes to Turkey and to Russia but he still did not criticise the Russians publicly and even defended them in the House of Commons. Privately however, Palmerston was outraged and worried by what had occurred. The Russians had achieved an unprecedented degree of influence with Turkey, while Mehemet Ali, with his French connections, had gained Palestine, Syria, Aleppo and Damascus as concessions from the Sultan. What incensed Palmerston most of all was that now the Turks were pledged not to make any foreign policy decisions without consulting Russia. His anger was given a bitter twist by the belief that it was the stupidity of his own Cabinet colleagues which had brought this disaster about.

In the immediate aftermath there was little that Palmerston could do to remedy the situation. He did his best to restore relations with the Sultan and in 1838 agreed to help Turkey, still fearful of Mehemet Ali's intentions, if the latter declared his independence from the Empire. This was less than the Sultan had hoped for since he was harbouring the idea of a pre-emptive strike against Mehemet Ali and had wanted an offensive agreement with Britain to support this, but it went some way to breaching the Turkish-Russian entente. Finally, in April 1839, the Sultan, now aware that he was dying and determined to have revenge upon Mehemet Ali before his demise, launched an attack on Syria. It was a complete failure and the Sultan died in July. At that the Turkish fleet promptly sailed to Alexandria and surrendered to Mehemet Ali. Palmerston had done nothing to incite the Sultan to this attack and had even instructed Ponsonby to make it clear to him that he could not expect British support if he did make a move. Nevertheless, once the Sultan had disturbed the status quo, it created a situation of both danger and opportunity for Palmerston. There was the danger that the conflict might escalate into a European war; there was the opportunity for him to undo the damage done in 1833.

Palmerston now embarked on a lengthy process of diplomacy in which he showed considerable skill as well as enjoying a fair degree of luck. He accepted a call from the French to send their respective fleets jointly to the Dardanelles in order to impress the Russians who might be expected to intervene as things went badly for the Turks. At the same time he proposed an international conference of the five great powers. He then secured a separate Anglo-Russian agreement under which the Russians agreed to modifications in the Unkiar Skelessi Treaty and Britain agreed to support the expulsion of Mehemet Ali from Syria. In this way Palmerston isolated the French and curbed the power of Mehemet Ali (whom he thoroughly detested) whilst overturning the Unkiar Skelessi provisions.

It was not all plain sailing. France threatened war and the pro-French elements in Britain (including those within the Cabinet) gave Palmerston a hard time. He held fast to his conviction however, that the French would not fight to keep Mehemet Ali in Syria. He had a major stroke of good fortune when the Syrians themselves revolted against Ibrahim and loosened his hold upon the region. The result was two conventions which secured virtually all that Palmerston could have hoped for. The London Convention – which the French refused to sign – expelled Mehemet Ali from Syria and he was subsequently compelled under threat from the Royal Navy to return the Turkish Fleet. (As compensation for the loss of Syria he was recognised as the hereditary ruler of Egypt.) The Straits Convention was signed in 1841. Under this, the major powers and Turkey agreed that the Straits (i.e. the Bosphorous and the Dardanelles) would be closed to all warships while Turkey was at peace. These arrangements restored Britain's vital interests in the Eastern Question. The French were diplomatically outmanoeuvred and their protege Mehemet Ali was removed as a future threat. By the 1850s Egypt was one of the weakest provinces of the Turkish Empire. Moreover, Britain was once again regarded as the saviour of Turkey and Russian influence had declined.

D *The Crimean War, 1854–6*

The next great crisis of the Eastern Question was created not by anything which occurred within the Turkish Empire, but rather by the deterioration in relationships between the great powers themselves. There was no one single factor involved and the issues largely lay outside British control. The Holy Alliance powers, Austria, Prussia and Russia drifted apart due to the dislocating effects of the revolutions in Europe during 1848–9. The Austrians resented having to rely on Russian support to crush their own rebels in Hungary. At the same time the Austrians were increasingly worried about future Prussian intentions in the German States. For their part the Russians regarded the French Emperor Napoleon III, who had created the Second French Empire by coup d'etat in 1851, as a 'non-legitimate' sovereign. Napoleon, sensitive to any suggestion that he was not a bona-fide monarch, duly reciprocated the Tsar's dislike. At the same time Anglo-Russian relations, which had become excellent during the 1840s, began to founder in mistrust. Thus when Napoleon III, seeking to increase his popularity at home, chose to raise the issue of French rights of protection over the Roman Catholic monks in the Holy Places – which dated back to the 1740s – all the ingredients for war were present.

Of all the developments which contributed to the outbreak of the Crimean War in 1854, the breakdown of Anglo-Russian relations was perhaps the most serious. In both 1826 and 1839 it had been the willingness of first Canning and then Palmerston to secure the co-operation of Russia and the willingness of the Russians to respond, which had opened the door to settlement. Although Palmerston retained a watchful eye on any sign of expansion of Russian influence he was never fundamentally anti-Russian. The signing of the Straits Convention meant, so far as Britain was concerned, the restoration of the old status quo and the prospect of sound long-term understanding with Russia. This was certainly the view which Lord Aberdeen took when he returned to the Foreign Office in 1841 following the fall of the Whig Government in the General Election. When the Tsar visited London in 1844, it coincided with a period of extremely bad relations between Britain and France, which was giving rise to genuine fears that there might be war between them. Peel and Aberdeen took the opportunity to seek a closer understanding with the Russians. This took the form of an agreement that both powers would seek, as their first aim of policy, to preserve the integrity of Turkey, but if that should prove impossible they would consult each other on how to proceed. In the longer term it might have been better if these talks had never taken place. To the Tsar, they seemed to guarantee that he had an understanding with Aberdeen, who became Prime Minister at the end of 1852. However, in Britain, the publication of the details in 1854 led to claims that Russia had intrigued over a long period to bring about the dismemberment of Turkey.

A number of factors caused the breakdown in Anglo-Russian relations. The brutal intervention by Russia to assist Austria to put down a revolt in 1849 angered public opinion, which was always inclined to be anti-Russian anyway. The British blockade of Greece during the Don Pacifico affair, (*see page 199*), which was carried out without giving notice to the other great powers, offended the Russians. Turkey, anxious now to retain the security of British protection, reqularly expressed concern about future Russian aggression. Finally, the Tsar himself, apparently feeling that he had a complete understanding with the British, frequently threw out ideas concerning hypothetical occupations of Egypt (by Britain) and Constantinople (by Russia), which sowed confusion and doubt about his aims.

It was, however, the intervention of France over the Holy Places which stirred the Tsar into action. In March 1853 he sent Prince Menshikov to Constantinople. His mission was to force the Sultan to repudiate the concessions to France and to gain further rights for

Russia as protector of all the Orthodox Christians within the Turkish Empire. In addition a Russo-Turkish defensive alliance was demanded. The Sultan agreed to withdraw his concessions to France, but was persuaded by the British Ambassador, Lord Stratford de Redcliffe, to reject all the other demands. This naturally angered Menshikov and he departed from Constantinople in protest, as he had previously threatened to do if Russian requirements were not met in full. In July Russia occupied Moldavia and Wallachia whilst at the same time the Tsar stated that he wished not for war but merely to secure recognition of Russian religious rights. The occupation of Moldavia and Wallachia, which bordered the Austrian Empire, alienated the Austrians who mobilised troops in response. Turkey however, acting on British advice, did not resist. Britain, France and Austria now joined in contructing a peace formula which became known as the Vienna Note. The three powers hoped by this to pacify the Russians by reaffirming Russia's right to sail her ships in the Black Sea and through the Straits into the Mediterranean, and by obtaining further guarantees from the Turks that decisions relating to the Turkish rule over Christian subjects would not be made without reference first to either France or Russia. At first the Tsar appeared satisfied, but an attempt by the Sultan to modify the terms so as to make them less humiliating, undermined this agreement and by October 1853 the situation remained deadlocked.

As the crisis drifted on, it was Turkey which took the initiative. At the beginning of October 1853, the Sultan demanded that Russia withdraw her forces from Moldavia and Wallachia. When the Russians predictably refused to comply, Turkey declared war. At first Britain, along with France, made an attempt at neutrality, but when the Turkish fleet was totally destroyed at Sinope at the end of November 1853, the pressure for British intervention grew. Public opinion was already violently anti-Russian and the Sinope victory was presented in the press as 'barbarism' following allegations (probably false) that the Russians had massacred the Turks after they had already surrendered. The British and French fleets entered the Black Sea in January 1854. The Russians asked for clarification of Anglo-French intentions and, receiving no satisfactory reply, withdrew their ambassadors from London and Paris. At the end of February Britain and France demanded the withdrawal of Russian troops from Moldavia and Wallachia and, receiving no response, made a treaty of alliance with Turkey on 12 March 1854. On 28 March war was declared by Britain and France on Russia.

None of the great powers had really anticipated that a major war would result from a dispute over the Holy Places. With the possible exception of France, none of the powers saw any likely benefits which might accrue. The war resulted from the general confusion and indecisiveness wich beset European diplomacy in the early 1850s. Nowhere was this more obvious than in Britain; indeed the British position was probably decisive in as much as it confused both the Russians and the

Turks. In the former case, the Tsar was misled into thinking that Britain was not prepared to fight; in the latter case, the Sultan was misled into thinking that British intervention was almost a formality. That such misconceptions could arise was due to the lack of firm control over foreign policy, which in turn resulted from the confused domestic political situation.

This destabilisation of British foreign policy began at the end of 1851, when Palmerston was forced to resign from the Foreigh Office. His fall was prompted by his incautious private approval of Louis Napoleon's coup given to the French Ambassador in London. This was at odds with the official government policy which ordered a neutral response to the seizure of power. Unfortunately, the French Ambassador in London, who was an illegitimate son of Napoleon Bonaparte and a supporter of the new regime, had lost no time in informing Paris of Palmerston's personal approval. There was no stopping such a matter from leaking out, especially since the British Ambassador in Paris did not like the coup and complained about the contradiction. The Queen and Prince Albert had long been in conflict with Palmerston and now that he had alienated the Cabinet, he could not survive. The Cabinet scarcely had time to adjust to life without Palmerston before it too fell, brought down by Palmerston's condemnation in the House of Commons of an ineffectual defence policy. For most of 1852, foreign policy resided in the hands of Lord Malmesbury who took office in a stop-gap Conservative administration. Palmerston knew Malmesbury well and had long connections with his family, so he frequently advised the new Foreign Secretary from behind the scenes. The new government, however, could not last. At the end of 1852, Lord Aberdeen became Prime Minister, forming a Whig-Peelite coalition, in which Palmerston, still beyond the pale so far as the Foreign Office was concerned, became Home Secretary.

The new government had a wealth of talent and experience at its disposal, but in terms of foreign policy it contained a fatal overdose of riches. In his biography of Palmerston, Jasper Ridley, observes that to have Palmerston in the Cabinet, but not at the Foreign Office was an arrangement likely to produce the worst possible results. Palmerston was certain to try to impose his influence in the conduct of foreign affairs. However, he faced powerful forces within the Cabinet. Lord John Russell, who went to the Foreign Office initially, was a former Prime Minister; his successor Lord Clarendon was a former diplomat, profoundly anti-Turkish and dominated by the greater figures around him; the Prime Minister, Lord Aberdeen, was a former Foreign Secretary and, (though he himself denied this), was identified in most minds, with a quite different approach to foreign policy. If this were not enough, the Chancellor of the Exchequer was William Ewart Gladstone, now a formidable figure and deeply opposed to what he saw as the immorality of Palmerston's attitude to foreign policy.

In these circumstances it is hardly to be wondered at that British foreign policy went through a confused and ineffective period. Palmerston strove to secure a tough but clear policy of resisting any Russian expansion and supporting Turkey, but since he was not at the Foreign Office he was unable to direct and control this policy with any consistency. Clarendon, as Foreign Secretary, was suspicious of the Turks, believing that they were trying to entangle Britain in their quest for self-preservation. He failed, however, to control the activities of the British Ambassador at Constantinople, Lord Stratford de Redcliffe, who constantly urged the Sultan to resistance and hinted at British support which was far from assured. Both Aberdeen and Clarendon doubted the wisdom of leaving Stratford at Constantinople but they failed to act, thus reinforcing the Sultan's faith in Britain. When the news of Sinope broke in Britain, it was shortly followed by Palmerston's resignation. This was universally interpreted as a protest against the Government's pacific attitude towards Russia. In fact it had nothing whatever to do with foreign policy, but was the result of proposals for parliamentary reform being floated by Russell, to which Palmerston was opposed. Palmerston wished to see a tougher British line, and so did nothing to correct the misinterpretation of his actions. Thus although Aberdeen sent a strong note of protest of Russia after Sinope, the Tsar could interpret Palmerston's departure as evidence that his 'understanding' with Aberdeen remained intact, Palmerston's resignation was short-lived. He rejoined the Cabinet after only ten days out of office, but the confusion did not end. If anything, the fear that Aberdeen's docile approach would be disastrous, led Palmerston to over-compensate and take a much more hostile attitude towards Russia than would have been the case had he had control of policy in his own hands. Not until Palmerston became Prime Minister in 1855 was some kind of consistency restored to the conduct of British Foreign Policy.

The Crimean War degenerated into a costly stalemate. Despite allied victories at Balaclava and Inkerman the British public became angry at the lack of a decisive breakthrough and the reports of losses due to cholera amongst the troops. The heroic, but futile, debacle of the Charge of the Light Brigade further alienated public opinion. By the end of January 1855, the pressure on the Government was becoming impossible to resist. A motion to set up a parliamentary committee to enquire into the conduct of the war, in effect a motion of no confidence in the Government, was carried by 305 votes to 157 and the Government resigned. Though the Queen shrank from facing the fact at first, it was clear that, Palmerston, whether he merited it or not, was the only man who retained sufficient prestige to form a new administration.

The end of the deadlock came towards the end of 1855, hastened on by the death of Tsar Nicholas I and the accession of Alexander II. The new Tsar was deeply concerned about the internal condition of Russia and anxious to end the war if reasonable terms could be secured. Peace was eventually made in the Treaty of Paris in March 1856. Russia accepted the demilitarisation of the Black Sea and gave up control of the mouth of the Danube which she had secured in 1828. Turkey was now formally admitted to equal status with the European powers and the Sultan, for neither the first time nor the last, gave notice of his 'generous intentions towards the Christian population of his Empire'. All the great powers attended the Paris Conference and they all pledged themselves to respect the independence and territorial integrity of the Turkish Empire.

The peace terms effectively ended the Russian threat to Turkey for the time being. Russian influence had taken a severe blow and in contintental Europe it was now France which was once again regarded as the leading power. Palmerston continued to dominate British politics until his death in 1865 and so long as he lived the Eastern Question remained a settled issue. Only when Gladstone came to the premiership, with his emphasis on moral virtue and non-intervention, did the provisions of the Treaty of Paris come under challenge from the Russians. Alexander II cultivated the French after 1856 as the best way of overcoming the threat of continued Anglo-French collaboration. How far this policy would have got him was never really put to the test since the outbreak of the Franco-Prussian War in 1870 gave Russia the ideal opportunity to reverse the clauses of the Treaty relating to the Black Sea. Alexander promised the German Chancellor, Bismarck, that Russia would remain neutral in return for support over the Black Sea and the latter was quite prepared to agree. With France embroiled in war and Britain more isolationist under Gladstone than she had been for generations, there was little danger in a unilateral declaration by the Tsar that the clauses of the Treaty relating to demilitarisation and neutralisation would no longer be observed. Gladstone responded with a note rebuking the Russians, but took the matter no further. Early in 1871 a conference of the European powers accorded formal ratification to the Russian action. Within a few years a new crisis would bring Europe once more to the brink of war over the future of the Turkish Empire.

5 The Changing Scene in Europe 1841–70

The diplomatic triumph of Palmerston in 1839–41 marked the end of the post-Vienna phase of European co-operation which has been commonly termed the 'Concert of Europe'. Although British policymakers were guarded in their attitude to Russia during this period and were willing, when it seemed useful, to work with France to achieve British aims, the basic assumption seems to have been that it was France which needed to be watched the more closely. The Greek question and the Eastern Crisis of 1839 were both resolved, in the last analysis, by Anglo-Russian collaboration. In the latter case, the achievement of British aims involved the isolation and humiliation of France. Despite often high levels of anti-Russian feeling amongst the British public and press, hatred of Russia was rare at government level. On the other hand, although British radicals generally maintained a sentimental francophilia, the French reputation as the natural source of revolutionary ideas and activity, made France an object of suspicion in British political circles, where Whigs and Tories were in more basic agreement about political fundamentals than might appear to be the case from their clashes over such issues as political reform.

There were practical reasons, too, for Britain's emphasis on co-operation with Russia. Of all the continental powers, Russia alone seemed to be in any meaningful way an equal. Even France was feared more for her capacity for a future resurgence, than as an immediate threat. Russia's military power seemed in many ways to be an ideal complement to British naval and economic power and, so long as Britian could see sufficient safeguards against an excessive expansion of Russian influence, the advantages of co-operation seemed far to outweigh other considerations, such as the unpopularity of Russia in the public mind. These safeguards against inordinate Russian expansion were to be found primarily in the positions of Turkey, Austria and Prussia, in that order of significance. Although 1841 can be seen as the last occasion on which these ideas operated in practical diplomacy, the assumptions which gave rise to them continued to condition British thinking in the 1840s. Even after 1850, the restoration of a Napoleonic regime gave rise to a swell of anti-French hysteria great enough to allow Palmerston to bring down the Government in February 1852, with the argument that not enough was being done to guard against the new French threat.

On the surface, the impact of the revolts which broke out in Europe in 1848, ought to have confirmed the status quo. Both Russia and Britain were virtually untouched by these events. Indeed, in Britain, the Chartist fiasco marked the beginning of a more stable period in domestic politics. Thus while France, Austria, Italy and the German States were racked by revolution, Britain and Russia seemed to be havens of strength and stability. In practice, however, far from underpinning the status quo, the events of 1848 hastened the demise of Anglo-Russian understanding. Palmerston was far from happy to see Austria in turmoil, since in his mind the principal function of that ramshackle empire was to provide a check on Russia. The Russian intervention, crushing the Hungarian revolt in 1849, though it restored the integrity of the Austrian regime, seemed to stand Britain's diplomatic assumptions on their head whilst at the same time raising the Russophobic tendencies of the British public to fever-pitch. Suspicion, fear and detestation of Russia were fatally high when events began to shape the crisis which would lead ultimately to the Crimean War.

The war did not bring about the death of the Concert of Europe – rather it demonstrated that it was already dead. Britain pressed for tough terms in the Treaty of Paris. Palmerston did not follow the conciliatory approach to France which Castlereagh had adopted at Vienna; he rather opted to pile diplomatic humiliation on Russia's military defeats. The terms of the peace settlement ensured that Russia would become a revisionist power, bitter and resentful at the limitations which had been placed on her freedom of action and seeing Britain as the power against which she now needed to intrigue, in order to restore her pride.

The consequences of the Crimean war were far-reaching for more than just Anglo-Russian relations. The Austrians failed to support the Russians in 1854 and even threatened to intervene against them in 1855. This ended forever the closeness which had endured between them since 1815. The Russians turned to the French, ironically the instigators of the original crisis, as their best hope for diplomatic leverage in the future. The Austrians were fatally weakened, which left open the opportunity for Prussia to show its strength. First the Danes and then the Austrians were swept aside in the 1860s; then the French were crushed in the Franco-Prussian war of 1870–1. The Treaty of Frankfurt which ended the hostilities was a humiliation for France and demonstrated to Britain that a new diplomatic reality had been established in Europe, without any reference to her position.

British impotence in the face of the rise of the new German Empire, established under Prussian leadership, was an indication of the extent to which British objectives had been achieved in the past by prestige and skilful diplomacy along with a good deal of bluff. In the 1860s British bluff was increasingly called by those who were supposed to fold up in the face of it. When the Poles revolted against their Russian masters in 1861, Russell, now Palmerston's Foreign Secretary, and Palmerston himself, both protested to the Russians but were ignored. When Prussia threatened the Danes in 1863, Palmerston and Russell were both forthright in their support for Denmark. None of this, however, impressed the Prussian Prime Minister, Bismarck, and when war came between Prussia and Denmark in 1864, the Danes, found themselves abandoned and Palmerston staved off a censure motion from Disraeli by a bare margin. This rebuff to British prestige was obvious and disconcerting to contemporaries. Both Palmerston and Russell, in this last phase of their long careers, were striving to maintain the integrity of the Vienna Settlement which they saw still as forming the fundamental basis of relations between the European powers. In France, however, Napoleon III was calling for a new European congress, obstensibly to discuss the Polish Question, but in reality to revise the whole settlement of 1815. To Britain this was unacceptable. As Palmerston put it: 'Russia would ask to get back all she lost by the

Treaty of Paris; Italy would ask for Venetia and Rome; France would plead geography for the frontier of the Rhine; . . .'. These were just the more significant issues which would arise in the general turmoil which would ensue. British rejection of a new congress in 1863 alienated the French and weakened Britain's position in the Danish crisis. Shortly before his death Palmerston wrote a letter to Russell in which he emphasised his continuing concern about the aggressive tendencies of France and Russia and suggested that, notwithstanding what had happened over Denmark, the European balance might be best served by the emergence of a stronger Prussia to act as check against both.

Palmerston finally died in October 1865 and was succeeded by Russell, the most senior of his colleagues. But Russell, old and close to retirement, was himself soon replaced by Gladstone, who led the Liberals to their 1868 election triumph. As Prime Minister Gladstone was determined to exercise a strong control over foreign policy. He had been a long-term critic of Palmerston's approach and was committed to the idea of raising the conduct of policy, domestic and foreign, to a higher moral level. He disapproved of interventionism and foreign 'entanglements', preferring to emphasise the rights of all nations to equality in international affairs. These principles led Gladstone into conflict with Disraeli, who became leader of the Conservatives in 1868. Although critical of him at times, Disraeli was in fact a great admirer of Palmerston. When the latter died, Disraeli was anxious to adopt the mantle of the Palmerstonian tradition himself and incorporate its public appeal into the image of the Conservative Party. Gladstone's low-key response to the Russian action in overturning the Black Sea Clauses in 1870, his neutrality in the Franco-Prussian War and his willingness to submit to international arbitration in a dispute with the United States, (*see page 195*), all convinced Disraeli that Gladstone was undermining British prestige and seriously weakening her international position.

By 1870, the European balance of power had altered in a way which had considerable implications for Britain. The German Empire had emerged in the middle of Europe as the most powerful military force on the continent, replacing France. This German Empire would be economically strong and substantially impervious to British pressure. Russia was strongly anti-British, while France was resuming her traditional anti-British stance, a process which would be confirmed, as the century proceeded, by the colonial rivalries which would spring up between the two countries, Russia and France would be driven closer together, initially by their dislike of Britain and then held together by their fear of Germany. Britain would be left largely isolated from these developments, yet having vital interests affected by them.

6 BRITAIN AND CHINA

Whilst these developments were taking place in Europe, Britain's position as a global power was involving her increasingly with the world outside. In the Far East, Britain's involvement in India caused her to take a long-term interest in affairs in Afghanistan and Persia, since both bordered India. In 1839–42 Britain intervened directly in Afghanistan to ward off a Russian-inspired attack by the Persians. In the process of this intervention, Britain deposed the existing Afghan regime and imposed another. The new regime proved unpopular and was itself removed by a popular rising, in the course of which a British force of 15 000 was massacred leaving only one survivor. This humiliation could not go unavenged and the following year (1842) another army was despatched from India. It occupied Kabul, the Afghan capital, burnt down a bazaar and two mosques, removed the sacred gates of the city and sent them to India, from which, it was falsely claimed, they had been stolen some 800 years previously. Once honour had been restored, however, Britain took a more cautious line on Afghan affairs.

In China British intervention was more positive and consistent. The reasons for this were economic. Britain's Indian Empire depended heavily on the trade in opium as a source of revenue. Sales to China, where the importing of opium had been illegal since 1800, helped to balance the heavy imports of cotton into Lancashire. By 1833, 55 per cent of British exports to China was illegal opium. When the Chinese finally decided to clamp down on the trade in 1836, a clash with Britain was inevitable. Relations with China were always a source of difficulty. Formal diplomatic relations did not exist either with Britain or any other country for that matter. The Chinese took the view that their Emperor ruled the entire world and that they were the superior race above all others. It followed that diplomatic relations, which implied some form of equality, were out of the question. British attempts to send an ambassador to Peking foundered on the humiliating ritual expected of those being received by the Emperor. This involved a series of nine prostrations before him. Such pretensions angered the British traders all the more since they appreciated how weak the Chinese were in military and naval terms.

The clash finally came in 1839, when Britain refused to hand over, to the Chinese authorities, officers of ships carrying opium. The ensuing war was a disaster for the Chinese. A British force blockaded Peking and forced a surrender. China was compelled to pay an indemnity; a number of ports were designated as treaty ports and opened to British traders; British consuls had to be allowed in certain cities including Canton and Shanghai; Hong Kong was ceded to Britain and the Chinese were forced to accept that foreigners accused of breaking

Chinese law could be tried only under the law of their own country. Palmerston was criticised for this policy by radicals but Peel's government stuck largely to the same line in the Treaty of Nanking in 1842. After this humiliation the Chinese were reduced, for a while, to a resentful compliance.

Meanwhile, the French became involved. Under a treaty signed in 1844, France became the official protector of Roman Catholics in China. As time went by the Chinese became increasingly reluctant to honour their undertakings to Europeans and a series of violent clashes followed. Finally, after an incident in 1856, when a ship sailing under a British flag was boarded, several attacks were made on European factories and a French missionary was murdered in Kwangsi province, an Anglo-French force set out to put the Chinese firmly in their place. By the end of this campaign in 1858, Peking had been seized and the Emperor's summer palace burned down. The Chinese were forced to accept western embassies in Peking and the legalisation of opium imports. These demonstrations of Chinese weakness also encouraged other countries, such as Russia and Japan, to demand and obtain concessions, making China another area of potential conflict between the great powers in the future.

7 Britain and the United States

Another area of increasing importance for British policy was the United States. Relations with the ex-colonial Americans were always fraught with difficulty. British assumptions about her maritime rights, and especially her use of blockades against those with whom she was in dispute, led to clashes with the Americans who resented what they saw as a high-handed and arrogant British attitude. In 1812 this led to a war which lasted until 1814 and included the famous defeat of British forces at New Orleans which, bizarrely, occurred after peace had actually been signed without the knowledge of the combatants. In the course of the war much had occurred to stoke up bitter feelings for the future. The British burned the President's official residence in Washington – the white-wash repairs giving rise to its future popular name; the Americans burned Toronto. Little was resolved for the future by the Peace of Ghent which ended the official hostilities. Fishing rights remained in dispute. The territorial boundary between the USA and Canada was still undefined. Many Americans still harboured grudges against Britain going back to the War of Independence. Andrew Jackson, the victorious general of New Orleans, who became President in 1828, hated the British because his brother had been killed and his home destroyed by British forces when he was 11-years-old.

Although Canning co-operated with the Americans in 1823, over the question of the future of the Spanish colonies, relations remained strained. The famous 'Monroe Doctrine', proclaimed by the US President, James Monroe, in 1823, suited British interests by declaring US opposition to further European colonisation on the American continent but, in the absence of a final agreement over the US/Canadian border, could be seen as anti-British. This was rather galling to Britain since, in practice, it was the British Navy which would have had to enforce the Monroe Doctrine if it had ever put to the test by another European power – the Americans themselves lacking the strength to do so. Palmerston constantly feared that the United States would take some unilateral action over the Canadian border and by the 1840s Anglo-American relations were in a parlous state. In addition to the traditional areas of contention, a new dispute arose when slaves aboard an American ship, the 'Creole', mutinied and took refuge in the British port of Nassau in the Bahamas. The United States demanded the return of the offenders but were refused on the grounds that no extradition treaty existed.

Lord Aberdeen was determined to settle matters amicably with the United States once and for all. To this end he sent Lord Ashburton, a banker with significant business connections in the USA, to negotiate with Daniel Webster, the American Secretary of State. The result was the Webster-Ashburton treaty of 1842 which finally settled the border issue in the north-east, between Maine and New Brunswick, set up the extradition treaty and promised co-operation over the slave trade. Palmerston condemned the terms as conceding too much to the Americans, but received little support even from public opinion.

The treaty still did not create a new climate in Anglo-American relations such as Aberdeen was hoping for. Fears about American encroachments further west remained and the slavery issue was too emotive a problem on both sides of the Atlantic to allow for an easy solution as long as the institution remained in existence. Even so, in the years before the American Civil War, relations did improve to the extent that the young Prince of Wales was allowed to make a visit to the USA (in early 1860, following a trip to Canada. The Civil War, however, put new stresses and strains on Anglo-American relations. Opinions in Britain were divided between those who supported the Union and those who wished to see the Confederacy succeed in its attempt to set up a new nation. With hindsight it is too easy to see the issue primarily as a matter of freeing slaves and abolishing the institution of slavery. At the time the situation was far more complex. To begin with, the issue of slavery was very much played down by the American President, Abraham Lincoln, in the immediate period before hostilities commenced. He continued to enforce the Fugitive Slave Law which meant the return of runaway slaves to their masters even when they had taken refuge in 'free' states; he repeatedly denied, during the first 18 months of the war, that it was being fought on the issue of slavery; he did not abolish slavery until the Emancipation Edict of January 1863.

Palmerston was sympathetic to the claim of the Confederacy that individual states which had entered the Union freely had a legal right to leave it freely. He did not wish to go to war with the Union over the issue, but he suspected that certain elements in the US Government, led by William H. Seward, the Secretary of State, were intriguing to heal the internal divisions in the country by trying to involve the US in a war with foreign powers. Seward was notoriously anti-British and Palmerston sent reinforcements to Canada as a precaution. As soon as the Civil War began in 1861, Palmerston and Russell agreed to recognise the Confederacy as a belligerent and to receive, unofficially, Confederate representatives. This fell short of recognising the Confederacy as a sovereign power, but it was a clear enough sign of preference. When the Union suffered an unexpected reverse in the first major battle of the war at Bull Run, Virginia, in July 1861, Palmerston indulged in some witticisms at Lincoln's expense. However, although by the end of 1861 he was feeling fairly certain in his own mind that Lincoln would not be able to compel the seccessionist states to return to the Union, he still made no official move to recognise the Confederacy.

The main crises of the war, from the British point of view, came over two separate incidents. First, the removal, by the Union Navy, of two confederate envoys, Mason and Slidell, from a British mail steamer, the *Trent*, off the coast of Cuba, late in 1861, nearly led to disaster. It was fortunate perhaps, on this occasion, that communications across the Atlantic took sufficiently long for tempers on both sides to subside. In the end the Union Government, declaring that the naval officer who had seized Mason and Slidell had exceeded his authority, agreed to release the two men. The second incident involved the building of a warship for the Confederacy at a shipyard in Birkenhead. The Union Government found out about the project and protested to Palmerston that this was a breach of neutrality. The Government carried out an enquiry but could find no proof for the accusation. Palmerston and Russell therefore decided to allow the order to be completed. Just before completion, the Union's Ambassador in London, Charles Adams, received concrete proof of the Confederate involvement and submitted it to Russell. By the time the new evidence had been evaluated and a decision made it was too late. On 31 July 1862 orders were sent to Birkenhead to impound the ship, but she had already sailed two days before and, as soon as she was outside British territorial waters, she raised the Confederate flag and assumed the name *Alabama*.

The *Alabama* was eventually sunk by the Union Navy in the summer of 1864, but not before she had done considerable damage to Union shipping. The Union Government, suspecting that the British Government had secretly connived at the escape of the ship in the first place, demanded compensation. Palmerston treated this claim with contempt and the matter remained a bitter bone of contention until 1872 when, following Gladstone's decision to accept international arbitration in the case, Britain paid $15 million in gold to the United States as damages. Anglo-American relations remained shaky despite this settlement. The sensitivity between the two countries, always more pronounced on the American side, ensured that it took very little to excite ill-feeling. Residual anti-British feelings, reinforced by the influx of Irish migrants meant that American politicians could always resort to a round of anti-British rhetoric if all else failed to bring them support. This situation was not to change significantly until the turn of the century.

8 CONCLUSION: PRINCIPLES, POLICIES AND PERSONALITIES FROM CASTLEREAGH TO GLADSTONE

Castlereagh's biographer, C J Bartlett, used the phrase 'New Diplomacy' to describe his conduct of policy with regard to European affairs. He justified this by arguing that Castlereagh himself saw his diplomacy as representing a very different approach to that of the eighteenth century. To Castlereagh the 'old diplomacy', characterised by intrigues and short-sighted jostling for advantage, had 'poisoned the public health of the body politic of Europe, but which has happily in latter years been in great measure banished, at least from the councils of the Quadruple Alliance'. Bartlett, however, accepted that Castlereagh's conduct of policy was a peculiarly personal one, 'the most personal ever pursued by a British Foreign Secretary'. It was based upon his personal relationship with foreign statesmen and rulers and it could not have been adopted by Canning even if he had wanted to do so – which he did not – because he did not have Castlereagh's prestige and was not trusted, most noticeably, by Metternich.

The death of Castlereagh, just before the Vienna-Verona meetings in 1822, clearly illustrates both the strengths and the weaknesses of his methods. Had he lived, the discussions might have resulted in Britain, Austria and Russia working together over the Greek crisis and reaching agreement over wider matters, including Spanish America. Metternich, however, only had faith in Britain so long as Castlereagh was in control of policy. Equally, Castlereagh relied heavily on the reciprocal effect of his relationships. Had Metternich died or lost office or if the Tsar had died, all his planning would have been at risk. Canning was bound by no such considerations. Where his predecessor had aimed to find a European basis for settling the problem of the future of the Spanish American colonies he acted unilaterally, although he invoked a largely illusory concept of Anglo-American co-operation to cover this fact up. With the Russians, he could make no progress while Alexander lived but, once he was dead, he approached the new Tsar directly and without attempting to develop a concerted European approach as Castlereagh would have instinctively striven for. Canning was not interested in developing allied responses to potential international problems before they arose; he preferred to devise strategies to cope with situations as they occurred, acting either unilaterally if necessary, or with whichever party seemed appropriate or feasible in each case. This did not mean, however, that he was in any sense isolationist or zenophobic. As his biographer, Wendy Hinde, observed, 'Canning believed passionately in England's greatness, but he did not think she could or should stand isolated and alone.'

The respective merits of Castlereagh and Canning were extensively debated in the 1920s and 1930s by two giants of British diplomatic history, Professors Webster and Temperley. Webster lauded the diplomatic skills of Castlereagh, seen at their best, he argued, in the question of Spanish America. Temperley, on the other hand, advanced the claims of Canning, with his apparent virtues of liberalism and constitutionalism. It was a fascinating academic wrangle but its main long-term effect was to convince most subsequent writers that the differences between Canning and Castlereagh had been over-stressed, at least in terms of their overall aims, if not in terms of their methods and personalities. In other words, just as Castlereagh's supposed preference for absolutism was a myth, so too was Canning's for liberalism.

A generation or so after his death, Canning had become a revered figure and his handling of foreign policy came to be seen as a model by politicians of very different temperaments and approaches. Palmerston, Aberdeen, Peel and Disraeli all referred to Canning or invoked his memory in reverential tones. During his tenure of office, however, there were regular doubts expressed about his conduct of policy. Wendy Hinde has suggested that Canning only survived at all as Foreign Secretary because of the loyal support of Lord Liverpool. George IV hated Canning because of the latter's adherence to the Queen during the great divorce scandal and once expressed the view that Canning was no more capable of conducting foreign policy than a baby. There were other, less prejudiced, critics. Wellington had championed the appointment of Canning to the Foreign Office and indeed it was largely due to the influence of the Duke that Liverpool was able to persuade the very reluctant King to accept him. Before long, however, Wellington grew alarmed at Canning's approach. The latter's blatant efforts to popularise foreign policy, the openness (and regularity) of his public speeches, his unprecedented habit of publishing large amounts of diplomatic correspondence all caused anxiety to the more conservative-minded elements in the Cabinet. It was a matter of style and temperament more than political philosphy, but it convinced contemporaries, critics and admirers alike, that Canning had brought about some substantive change in the conduct of affairs.

The contrasts between Canning and Castlereagh were to some extent replicated in a later generation by the conflicting personalities and policies of Palmerston and Aberdeen. Where Palmerston was open and flamboyant, Aberdeen was shy and retiring; where Palmerston was thick-skinned and rarely took criticism to heart or held a grudge, Aberdeen was sensitive and insecure. Palmerston outdid even Canning in the mass publication of diplomatic documents and even resorted to publishing articles in the press. Aberdeen despised and distrusted such methods. He was also a poor speaker compared to Palmerston. These differences of personality, however, were not the limit of the divergences. Whereas it is reasonable to argue that the differences in approach between Canning and Castlereagh were fairly minimal in terms of policy, this would not be a tenable position to take in relation to Palmerston and Aberdeen.

Palmerston's basic approach to foreign relations was nationalistic. That is not to say that he, any more than Canning, was zenophobic, but rather that he operated on the sole principle of seeking British advantage in any given situation. Aberdeen was fundamentally more internationalist in outlook. Moreover, whereas Palmerston, though not in any sense a warmonger, wanted to avoid war for practical reasons, Aberdeen felt a deep moral aversion to war that went to the very roots of his character. This aversion to war left him far more willing than Palmerston ever was to consider the viewpoints of other countries. It was not that Palmerston could not see or understand the attitudes of others – he simply did not conceive that it was any business of his to consider them except in so far as they might affect his own intentions for the advancement of British interests. Similarly, when it came to preparations for war or using the threat of war, Palmerston had no compunction about using either as a valid lever to get what he wanted. To Aberdeen, the doctrine of preparing for war to ensure peace was an immoral concept – to Palmerston it was commonsense so long as it worked.

R T Shannon, in his biography of Gladstone, argued that British foreign policy in this period was characterised by three, initially separate and competing traditions. One, developed by Palmerston, was based upon a combination of Whig/Liberal ideas of constitutionalism, reinforced by radical and nationalist concepts; another was the Manchester School tradition of Cobden and Bright which saw international peace and harmony as resulting from the adoption of the mutually beneficial principles of free trade; whilst the third was more internationalist than the first and more pragmatic than the second and was epitomised by Aberdeen and Peel, having been derived from Castlereagh. According to Shannon, Gladstone eventually produced a synthesis of the Aberdonian and Manchester School approaches which were, in a sense, natural allies.

It is important to note that all of these traditions or 'schools' proceeded upon an assumption of British moral superiority. Even Cobden and Bright assumed that Britain had to demonstrate moral leadership for the benefit of other nations. Nor was Palmerston so entirely without principles as may be thought. In his dealings with China, for example, an area where he has received particular criticism, he never sought exceptional privileges for Britain over other nations – only for equal opportunities for all Western nations. He assumed that British superiority in manufacturing would enable British traders to win any competition based on fair and equal conditions. Moreover he was a stickler for international law and was always most reluctant to put himself in the position of having acted illegally. He routinely sought legal advice before taking action and having received it, he framed his subsequent policies around the need to observe it.

9 Bibliography

M E Chamberlain *British Foreign Policy in the Age of Palmerston* (Seminar Series, Longman, 1980) Aimed at A level students and contains a useful introductory section on Castlereagh and Canning as well as documents.

There are also three biographies which provide detailed information on foreign policy issues which can be set within the context of domestic politics:
C J Bartlett *Castlereagh* (Macmillan, 1966).
Wendy Hinde *George Canning* (Purnell, 1973).
Jasper Ridley *Lord Palmerston* (Constable, 1970)

10 Discussion Points and Essay Questions

A *Discussion Points*

1 Whose conduct of foreign policy was the more effective in securing British interests – that of Castlereagh or Canning?

2 Was Palmerston a supreme diplomat or a muddler who was occasionally lucky enough to acquire a good result?

3 On balance, did British diplomacy prove beneficial or detrimental to weaker powers during the period 1815–70? (This might be discussed as a general proposition or in relation to specific cases – e.g. Greece or Spain etc.)

4 Were Britain and Russia doomed to clash eventually over the Eastern Question?

5 Was Britain right to support the Sultan of Turkey, rather than Mehemet Ali, in 1839?
6 How important was Britain's status as a constitutional monarchy in terms of the conduct of foreign policy during the period 1815–70?
7 How much responsibility should Britain take for the outbreak of the Crimean War?

B *Essay questions*

1 Did the death of Castlereagh in 1822 mark the beginning of a fundamental change in the conduct of British foreign policy?
2 How consistent was British policy towards the Eastern Question during the period 1815–70?
3 'An opportunist and a bully, rather than a great statesman'. Is this a fair assessment of Palmerston in his handling of foreign policy issues?
4 Account for the increasing antagonism in Anglo-Russian relations between 1815 and 1854.
5 'The Arbiter of Europe'. How far did Britain fulfil this role in the period 1830 to 1870?

11 DOCUMENTARY EXERCISE – THE DON PACIFICO DEBATE

The following documentary extracts relate to one of the most famous parliamentary debates of the nineteenth century, which has become known as the 'Don Pacifico debate'. The immediate cause of the debate was a motion from a radical MP, JA Roebuck, supporting Palmerston's conduct of foreign policy. Palmerston was coming under increasing criticism for his decision to support the claim of David Pacifico for compensation from the Greek government following losses he sustained to his property in Athens during anti-Jewish riots in 1847. Pacifico was a Jew who had been born in Gibraltar and was therefore a British subject. From early childhood he had lived in Portugal and had become a naturalised Portuguese subject. He originally went to Athens as the Portuguese Consul but was dismissed for an attempted fraud against the Portuguese Government. When he had first arrived in Athens he had used his Gibraltarian origin to secure a British passport and, with this security, he decided to remain in Athens after his dismissal. When his property was attacked, Pacifico applied to the British for help and it was the failure of lengthy attempts to secure redress for him which led Palmerston in the end to sanction a blockade. In fact, Pacifico's case was only one of a number of strains between Britain and Greece which led to this action and the criticism of Palmerston stemmed from more than just his championing of Pacifico. It was rather the result of doubts about his handling of foreign policy over many years which came to a head with this issue. The debate raised the whole question of British intervention in the affairs of other nations. It raised issues of morality, the true nature of British interests and of Palmerston's fitness to conduct British foreign policy. Palmerston defended his policy thus:

> I believe that the principles on which we have acted are those which are held by the great mass of the people of this country. I am convinced that these principles are calculated, so far as the influence of England may properly be exercised with respect to the destinies of other countries, to conduce to the maintenance of peace, to the advancement of civilization, to the welfare and happiness of mankind ... It is a noble thing to be allowed to guide the policy and to influence the destinies of such a country ... while we have seen ... the political earthquake rolling Europe from side to side – while we have seen thrones shaken, shattered, levelled; institutions overthrown and destroyed – while in almost every country of Europe the conflict of civil war has deluged the land with blood, from the Atlantic to the Black Sea, from the Baltic to the Mediterranean; this country has presented a spectacle honourable to the people of England, and worthy of the admiration of mankind ... I contend that we have not in our foreign policy done anything to forfeit the confidence of the country ... I therefore fearlessly challenge the verdict of this House, as representing a political, a commercial, a constitutional country is to give on the question now brought before it; whether the principles on which the foreign policy of Her Majesty's Government has been conducted, and the sense of duty which led us to think ourselves bound to afford protection to our fellow subjects abroad, are proper and fitting guides for those who are charged with the Government of England; and whether, as the Roman, in days of old, held himself free from indignity when he could say *'civis Romanus sum'*; so also a British subject, in whatever land he may be, shall feel confident that the watchful eye and the strong arm of England, will protect him against injustice and wrong.

1. *To what is Palmerston referring when he speaks of 'the political earthquake rolling Europe from side to side'?*
2. *How far could Palmerston have substantiated the claim that his principles were 'held by the great mass of the people'?*
3. *In what ways might an opponent of Palmerston have been able to criticise the arguments which Palmerston put forward in this extract?*

VII

VICTORIAN VALUES

—

1 INTRODUCTION

IT is always difficult to identify the 'dominant values' which operated at a given moment in the past since, by definition, any society encompasses a variety of differing views and beliefs, many of them in conflict. This has already been seen, most sharply, in chapters II and IV, where working people have been identified as expressing their own view of the economic and political system in movements like Chartism. Similarly, chapter III explored the many different views, held by the wealthier classes in Victorian society, over the issue of State intervention to deal with social problems. The emergence of Liberalism and Conservatism in the mid-Victorian period, each with very different ideologies and social bases of support (chapters VIII and XI), is also a reminder of the plurality of society and the multiplicity of social viewpoints current at the time. Nevertheless, for all this apparent diversity, it may still be possible and useful for historians to identify a broad framework of ideas and assumptions which mid-Victorians, or at least those who possessed wealth and exercised authority, might have held in common. This could particularly assist an understanding of the attitudes adopted towards working-class behaviour and organisations in this period. It will also highlight why the Victorians had so much difficulty in coming to terms with the very different economic and social circumstances of the later nineteenth century, when some of the certainties of the mid-Victorian period began to disappear (*see chapters XIII and XIV*).

By the middle of the nineteenth century it had become clear that important changes had taken place in the economic and social life of the nation. The twin processes of industrialisation and urbanisation were rapidly transforming Britain from an agrarian society of small and relatively isolated settlements into a 'modern' society of large towns containing industries that catered for a national and an international market. Above all, it was evident to the mid-Victorians that the dominant values of the new society were essentially those of the burgeoning middle class whose enterprises formed the basis of Britain's industrial expansion. This was not, however, a swift 'takeover' of power by the new middle class; a sort of bloodless revolution. The traditional ruling groups, the aristocracy and the landed gentry, remained very much in evidence as authority figures in both national and local politics. For example, it was not until 1885 that the number of Members of Parliament whose wealth derived from trade and industry outnumbered those from landed backgrounds. As we will see elsewhere in this book, British governments remained predominantly aristocratic until the early part of the twentieth century. Yet there was no disguising the growing economic importance of industry and commerce. The repeal of the Corn Laws in 1846, by a Parliament rooted fimly in the land, signalled a recognition of the significant presence of the new middle class.

This chapter will analyse the social relations of mid-Victorian society by exploring the values of the British middle class. As will be seen, their outlook was essentially optimistic because they pictured themselves in the vanguard of progress. Yet this huge optimism was always counterbalanced by a great fear of social instability. This was understandable enough, given the closeness of the Chartist experience, but the concern bit far deeper. In pre-industrial society order had been maintained by the role of the landowner, who traditionally acted not only as employer but also as a magistrate and the dispenser of charity and largesse in times of hardship. These roles were socially significant because they revolved around the personal ties between rich and poor. There is no need to romanticise this 'paternal' system since within it rich and poor often found themselves at odds. Yet within the small and highly localised communities of seventeenth-and eighteenth-century society, stability of sorts could be maintained by the paternal relationship: an acceptance of an obligation towards the poor by the wealthy and in return, a due deference towards authority by the poor.

Industrialisation dispensed with much of this. In the large towns that were emerging by 1850 the face-to-face relationships of the older society were neither possible nor deemed desirable. The table on page 203 shows the very rapid growth of towns and cities, particularly in the second half of the century. Many contemporary observers felt that the sheer size of these centres of population created fundamental problems in the maintenance of social order and stability.

In the mushrooming towns the Church struggled to gain a foothold. A religious census taken for England and Wales in 1851 revealed that only about half the population attended any organised form of worship on a Sunday, and in the large towns attendance was very much lower (for example, 24 per cent for Birmingham). At the same time, the ethos of individualism, upon which the new industrial society was based, divided individuals one from another and placed them in active competition. Employers were no longer 'responsible' for their employees in the way in which it was felt they had been in the paternalistic rural communities that preceded the Industrial Revolution. The new

	1841	1851	1861	1871	1881	1891
Birmingham	183	233	296	344	437	478
Belfast	70	87	122	174	208	256
Cardiff	10	18	33	40	57	83
Glasgow	275	345	420	522	587	658
Manchester	235	303	339	351	462	505
Leeds	152	172	207	259	309	368
Nottingham	52	57	75	87	187	214

This table shows the growth of large towns, 1841–91 (population is given in thousands).

(Source: B R Mitchell and P Deane, *Abstract of British Historical Statistics* 1962).

society was a free market economy of individuals actively pursuing their own best interests.

So, the major problem for mid-Victorian society was this; how was public order and morality to be maintained in a society which, by its very nature, challenged or threatened the traditional mechanisms by which they had been achieved in the past? In order to understand how this question was addressed at the time we need to examine three important areas, as follows:

(i) The role ascribed to the individual in nineteenth-century society. This was a society based, economically, upon competitive individualism. As was seen in chapter III, approaches to social reform stressed the importance of individual morality. Many Victorians argued that the economic and moral health of society was simply a reflection of the decisions made by its individual members.

(ii) the Victorian attitude to women, since the family was seen as the focus for social regeneration;

(iii) the attempt, in the third quarter of the century, to establish a new relationship between the middle class and the working class. This involved both the 'taming' of popular culture and a movement towards making the 'respectable' workman into a full citizen by legalising his unions and giving him the vote.

We will take each of these areas in turn.

2 The Individual and Society

Victorian society was built upon 'individualism'. This dominant characteristic was evident in many spheres of life. Economically, many Victorians followed the late eighteenth-century economist Adam Smith, with his argument on the congruence of public and private virtue (*see page* 42). His belief in the importance of a competitive market place recurred in many aspects of Victorian social life. In the realm of social reform, as we saw in chapter III, the Utilitarians argued that whilst the government should intervene to correct the worst abuses of industrial society, it should never do so in ways that restricted individual initiative in the economic sphere. In a similar way the Evangelicals argued that public morality was simply a reflection of the private morality of the individuals who made up society. Every individual faced the choice between good and evil in every decision that he or she made. The moral health of any society was the sum total of these choices.

The importance of individuals making the right choice was a frequent subject of both Victorian literature and art. In Charles Dickens' *Oliver Twist* (1837), the prostitute Nancy faces a moral dilemma of classic Victorian proportions. Should she help Oliver to escape or comply with the wishes of her evil lover Bill Sykes? Victorian readers would have been cheered by her decision to act 'correctly' (though, of course, for Nancy this had tragic consequences). The possibility of redemption by this means was one of the messages conveyed by the artist William Holman Hunt in his painting 'The Light of the World' (plate 1, page 215) first shown in 1854. This shows Christ holding a lantern and knocking on the door of the soul. Hunt was inspired by lines in The Book of Revelations which begin, 'Behold I stand at the door, and knock; if any man hear my voice, and open the door, I will come unto him ...'.

1 *Victorian viewers of the painting pointed out that the door in the painting had no handle. What might Hunt have symbolised by this?*
2 *How optimistic a painting is this?*

The consequences of making the wrong moral choices were great. The artist Robert Martineau depicted the middle-class nightmare of personal and family ruin in his painting 'Last Day in the Old Home' (1862), in which a family undergoes eviction (plate 2, page 216).

1 *What clues does the artist give to indicate why the family faces financial ruin?*
2 *What indications are given here of the respective roles of men and women in Victorian society?*
3 *What is the significance of the children in this picture?*

Even the developing physical sciences seemed to carry the same message. When Charles Darwin's work on evolution, *The Origin of Species and Natural Selection*, appeared in 1859, it was widely interpreted as indicating that the living world consisted of species in competition with each other and that the weakest (those unable to make the 'right' choices) world perish. By the middle of the nineteenth century, competitive individualism was accepted as a fact of life verified by Nature.

This focus on the individual was central to the way Victorian society saw itself. It was an approach underpinned by the belief that a free market economy (economic individualism) had an almost limitless capacity to improve the quality of life. The Victorians looked forward to the consumer society, when goods which their forebears had considered luxuries would be freely available. They also felt that the free market would bring universal peace when nations who traded together would do so on the basis of mutual understanding. By the middle of the nineteenth century the equation between industrialisation and progress was widely accepted and this view survived any doubts and fears raised by the debate on the 'Condition of England' question in the 1840s. This development was encouraged by the continued growth of the economy after 1845. Investment in the railways during the 1840s gave a much needed boost and, in the view of a number of historians, among them Eric Hobsbawm and S G Checkland, this relaunched the Industrial Revolution. The period from the mid-1840s until the 1880s saw the expansion of heavy industries such as engineering, coalmining, textiles and shipbuilding (where steam-driven iron and steel ships took over from wooden sailing ships by 1880). These were all industries which required a high level of capital investment, technological innovation, and a disciplined workforce. This image of a burgeoning economy is a popular view, though the economic historian Francois Crouzet has counselled against seeing the 1850s and the 1860s as years of unmitigated growth. He reminds us that, 'Between 1846 and 1874 the years of recession were as numerous as those of expansion, and the slumps of 1857, 1862, and 1868 were hardly less severe than those of 1826, 1837, or 1842.' Despite these qualifications to the idea of a 'mid-Victorian boom', it remains clear that the early hopes of an expanding industrial economy, inspired by the Industrial Revolution, were justified in the light of continuing economic growth at home and, particularly, of investment overseas. As the first industrial nation Britain was in a position to export its technology, skills and capital to the developing economies throughout the world.

Viewed from the City of London or the industrial centres of the Midlands and the North it must have seemed as if the globe was being transformed into a huge inter-locking economy with Britain as its pivot. This was the period when Britain assumed the title of the 'Workshop of the World' and such was the confidence in the ability to compete internationally that protectionism was abandoned. The triumph of free trade, which was signalled by the abolition of the Corn Laws, represented a major shift in economic attitudes by the Victorians. In 1840 some 1146 articles attracted customs duties; by 1860 this had been reduced to 48 articles. Above all, this reflected a belief in the capacity of British industrialists to continue to lead the world.

For many, this optimism was encapsulated by the 'Great Exhibition of the Works of Industry of All Nations' held in 1851. The exhibition was a celebration of industrial achievement and, although all nations were invited to exhibit their wares, over half the goods on display were from Britain or the Empire. It was housed in a magnificent prefabricated structure of glass and iron which covered 18 acres of Hyde Park and could accommodate 30 000 people with ease. Albert, the Prince Consort, was deeply involved in the organisation and this fact alone was significant. The patronage of royalty indicated the achievement of a new respectability for commerce. The Duke of Wellington headed a long list of distinguished patrons. The Great Exhibition was a huge success attracting over six million visitors of all classes during its six-month duration. Queen Victoria attended on no fewer than 30 occasions and working men and women arrived by the trainload from all parts of the country on day excursions organised by Thomas Cook. The interest from all sections of society suggested to many that industrial enterprise had the potential to unite social groups around agreed objectives. This was rather a romantic view for, after all, the third Chartist petition, and the fear of revolution that had surrounded it, was barely three years away. Nevertheless, the Exhibition was widely perceived as representing the 'visibility of progress'. In this way it was seen to confirm the potential of the new individualism and to herald a society built upon the values of the industrial middle class.

The Victorians considered theirs to be an open society, offering great opportunity for those who were prepared to work hard. The new middle class saw themselves as 'self-made', unlike the aristocracy who had been born to wealth and power. In the many biographies that appeared at this time and which were devoted to the new 'Captains of Industry', it was invariably the common or universal human qualities that were celebrated. Probably the book that caught the spirit of the moment best was Samuel Smiles' *Self Help* which appeared in 1859. In this work Smiles, who at the time was the Secretary of a railway company, analysed the lives of successful men (women appear only in supportive roles as the wives and mothers of the famous). Each was revealed as owing his success to personal discipline and hard work. The implication was clear to Smiles and to the readers who had purchased 150 000 copies by 1889, making this an international bestseller. As Smiles put it 'What some men are, all without difficulty might be. Employ the same means and the same results will follow.'

Yet Smiles' book was rather more than a 'How to be successful' manual. It was also an affirmation of individualism. In his words:

> National progress is the sum of individual industry, energy and uprightness, as national decay is of individual idleness, selfishness and vice. What we are accustomed to decry as great social evils will, for the most part, be found to be but the outgrowth of man's own perverted life; and though we may endeavour to cut them down and extirpate them by means of Law, they will only spring up again with fresh luxuriance in some other form, unless the conditions of personal life and character are radically improved.

1. *What does Smiles suggest might limit the effectiveness of State intervention in matters of social reform?*
2. *What kinds of social reform would you expect Smiles to favour on the basis of this statement?*
3. *In what ways might an individual be able to demonstrate to observers that his or her 'personal life and character' was of an acceptable level?*
4. *Consider why the Victorian middle class were so keen on the ideas put forward by Samuel Smiles.*

This quotation gives us a good insight into the importance of 'respectability' in the Victorian frame of mind. Personal improvement was seen as the basis of national advancement. The successful middle class argued that they were coming to dominate society not by accident of birth as was the case with the aristocracy, but rather as a result of personal endeavour and moral rectitude. In this calculation wealth and position were seen as a reflection of the moral worth of the individual. The leaders of commerce and industry offered their values as the means of social progress and their life experiences as exemplars of what could be achieved. The concomitant to this, of course, was that any hint of moral impropriety by an individual could 'ruin' him or her. Hence the familiar Victorian concern to maintain a high moral tone in all aspects of everyday life, and the scandal that ensued if this image was dented.

3 The 'Angel in the House': Victorian Definitions of Femininity

Victorian society was highly patriarchal (male-dominated) in its nature. This is not to suggest that patriarchy was the product of industrialisation; it was rather that industrialisation extended the role and significance of patriarchy in important ways. For the Victorian middle class the cornerstone of morality was the stable family unit and its guardian was the dutiful wife. Feminist historians have drawn our attention to the way femininity was re-defined during the first three quarters of the nineteenth century in such a way that women were seen as the 'Angel in the House'. The phrase is taken from a poem of the same name published in 1854 by Coventry Patmore, who was inspired to write by his relationship with his wife Emily Andrews Patmore. In this poem women were seen as the moral regenerators of their menfolk. Their task was to marry and to provide a stable homelife for the male breadwinner. In this position as homemaker and childraiser it was the woman's role to keep the family on the 'straight and narrow'. Men, it was argued, were essentially weak creatures who might be easily led astray. Public morality was considered to be women's responsibility: if they created a good domestic environment men would behave well. Thus individualism was underpinned by a domestic role for women.

Patmore's poem clearly struck a public chord for, despite being a poor poem, it sold better than any other poetic work except Tennyson's *Idylls of the King*. In fact, like Smiles' writing on the role of the individual, Patmore was simply expressing a widely-held view; in this case, that a woman's place was in the married home in a supportive and subordinate role to her husband. This was a version of gender that drew heavily on the Evangelical revival of the early nineteenth century (*see pages 46–8*). The Evangelicals felt that individuals were confronted by the choice between good and evil, sin and redemption, in their every action. In their view a man was more likely to make the right choice consistently if he had a wife and family to support. It was a short step from this to the belief that it was a woman's duty to ensure the morality of her menfolk.

Thus, the threat to morality which industrialisation constituted was partly countered by an emphasis on the family as the basic unit of social life. This 'ideal' of femininity was based on the experience of middle-class married women. Since this was, in fact, a minority of women, the ideal was at odds with the reality of most women's lives. The Victorians spoke of 'separate spheres' for men and women; women's being the private sphere of the home and men's being the public sphere of commerce and politics. They convinced themselves that this was based on essential physiological differences between the sexes and, after Darwin, evolutionary theory was used to support this. Men and women, it was held, had evolved differently and possessed inherently different characteristics. The Scottish biologist Patrick Geddes explained in his book, *The Evolution of Sex* (1889), that it was pointless attempting to legislate for equality between the sexes. As he put it, 'What was decided among the prehistoric *protozoa* cannot be annulled by act of parliament'.

Despite these appeals to science the Victorians were simply engaged in redefining the role of women in a way that fitted their dominant values and the needs of a society which felt that it required a moral anchor. This construction of femininity which marooned women in the home, is often referred to by historians as 'domestic ideology'. Of course, the working-class family often depended on the earnings of the wife, and so this is sometimes seen, erroneously, as an ideal that was applied only to the experience of middle-class women. In fact, domestic ideology defined the boundaries of all women's lives, irrespective of class. For the working-class woman it meant that her role as a wage earner was seen as subsidiary to that of a man's. Employers argued that women in the workplace had stepped outside their 'proper sphere' and were therefore simply transitory workers on their way to fulfilling their true destinies as wives and mothers. As such it was considered perfectly legitimate to pay them less than men. They were also excluded from certain jobs that were considered unfit for women. As we saw in chapter III the 1842 Mines Act prohibited women's work underground. The historian Angela John has explored the reasons for the exclusion of women from underground work in her book *By the Sweat of Their Brow*. She rejects the common argument that this reflected a growing humanitarianism. Instead, she sees the Act as expressing part of a broader anxiety to re-define the role of women in society as a whole. In a similar way, without the formal intervention of legislation, women found themselves excluded from skilled work throughout industry. In 1851 nearly 75 per cent of the women who worked did so in three types of occupations, domestic service (37 per cent), textiles (18.5 per cent), and dressmaking (18 per cent) all of which were seen as 'fit work for women'. All were very poorly paid.

The ideal of femininity that was being developed in these years was clearly at odds with the reality of life for working-class women. Nevertheless, working-class women still found assumptions being made about them that referred in some way to the ideal. The Chartists, for all their undoubted radical zeal, had campaigned for universal *manhood* suffrage and pushed women to the margins of the movement. The trade unions, as formal organisations of skilled workers, emerged as a male preserve. Trade unionists found it useful to demand that a man's wage should be a 'family' wage, that is to say an income on which a working man could allow his wife to stay at home. By the middle of the nineteenth century, definitions of male and female roles seem to have cut across class divisions and been accepted at all levels of society.

The law reinforced these gender roles. In the eyes of the law, to quote a contemporary legal authority, 'A husband and wife are one person and that person is the husband.' On marriage a woman gave up any title to personal property and this was immediately transferred to the husband. Under the New Poor Law of 1834 a wife could be refused admission to a workhouse if her husband declined to enter. She could also be refused permission to leave if her husband wished to remain inside. The role of women as the guardians of public morality was enshrined in the bastardy clauses of the 1834 legislation which defined illegitimate children as the responsibility of the mother, rather than the father as had generally been the case with the Old Poor Law.

In fact, women who fell below the exacting standards set for them by this evangelical morality could expect little sympathy. It is worth remembering that despite the numerous social problems that industrialisation created, for the mid-Victorians it was prostitution that was considered 'the Great Social Evil'. Studies undertaken in the middle of the century suggested that prostitution was growing in the cities. There was evidence available at the time which suggested that women were being forced into prostitution by economic circumstances, such as the need of a single parent to maintain a family on a low wage. The social investigator Henry

Mayhew showed in 1849 that, in the 'sweated' needlework trades of London, wages were so low and work so difficult to obtain that women sometimes took the option of selling themselves. Nevertheless, the orthodox middle-class view remained that prostitution was essentially a moral issue and that some women simply took the wrong moral choice. Mayhew calculated that London alone supported 80 000 prostitutes in the early 1850s. The medical journal *The Lancet* argued that in the capital one house in every sixty was a brothel and one in every sixteen women was a prostitute. These 'guesstimates' were doubtless wildly inaccurate but they do reflect a growing sense of morality threatened by a decline of virtue and this was an important factor in reinforcing the dominant belief in woman's role as homemaker. The Contagious Diseases Acts of 1864, 1866 and 1869 embodied this same concern. Originally these were devised as a means of controlling the spread of venereal disease in garrison towns. The Acts forced prostitutes to register with the police and to undergo medical examination and treatment. The historian Judith Walkowitz has argued in her book, *Prostitution and Victorian Society*, that this legislation was an attempt to legislate for respectability. By creating prostitutes as an 'outcast' group, 'correct' feminine behaviour was clearly signalled. Women who sold sex were failing to fulfil their primary role as women; that is to say they were not acting as moral guides to men, whose susceptibility to temptation was seen to be endemic and, in that sense, excusable.

Patmore's poem, with which we began this section on domestic ideology, makes this point clear;

> Ah, wasteful woman, she who may
> On her sweet self set her own price,
> Knowing man cannot choose but to pay,
> How has she cheapen'd paradise;
> How given for nought her priceless gift,
> How spoil'd the bread and spill'd the wine,
> Which, spent with due, respective thrift,
> Had made brutes men, and men divine.

1 *What is the meaning of the line, 'Knowing man cannot choose but to pay'?*

2 *What criticism of the prostitute is being offered here?*

3 *What light does the passage cast on Victorian attitudes to women?*

This view of women can also be seen in some of the most popular paintings of the day. The Pre-Raphaelite group, which gathered around Dante Gabriel Rossetti, William Holman Hunt and John Everett Millais in London in the 1850s, generally depicted women as Madonna-figures or as whores. In their highly acclaimed pictures women appear as remote and unattainable, as figures to be admired, or as individuals who have made the wrong moral choice and thus failed to fulfil their role and destiny. Rossetti's 'Beata Beatrix' (plate 3, page 217) depicts Beatrice, the wife of the Italian poet Dante, at the point of death. It is thought to be Rossetti's tribute to his own wife, who had herself recently died but it clearly has a wider significance as a very particular representation of femininity. For this reason, the artist described the work as 'an ideal of the subject'. By contrast, 'Found!' (plate 4, page 218) by the same artist (begun in 1854 and unfinished at the time of his death in 1882) presents the common Victorian image of the 'fallen' woman. Here, a country drover, taking a calf to market, discovers his lost love on the streets of the city, where she has taken to prostitution. The drover is intended to represent what the painter conceives as the honest simplicity of the rural working class. For this purpose he is given a smock of a sort that had not been worn by farm workers for several decades. The woman is clearly ashamed of her position because she recognises the degree of personal failure involved. Here the accepted roles are being reversed, the man is attempting to retrieve the woman from the folly of her ways. The 'innocent' calf in the background, on its way to market to be slaughtered, is also an important part of the artist's message. Such images en-couraged the view of women as victims, actively conspiring in their own downfall.

The Contagious Diseases Acts, however, gave rise to a widespread reaction from Victorian women, challenging what were becoming the accepted images of women. A movement for the repeal of the Acts was led by Josephine Butler, who argued that the Acts blamed women, by implication, for the spread of venereal disease. The men who employed the women's services were apparently deemed to be blameless. The Ladies Association, established by Butler in 1870, saw the Acts as an extension of the arbitrary authority of the police and an infringement of the civil liberties of women. Any woman identified by the police as a prostitute was subject to the provisions of the legislation and, as Butler argued, this meant that the law invaded the privacy of *all* women. Thus the debate over the conflict between personal freedom and public health took place around contemporary assumptions about gender roles. Butler, the wife of a clergyman from Liverpool, confronted head-on the assumption that women 'caused' prostitution. In 1871 she gave evidence to a Royal Commission appointed to investigate the operation of the Contagious Diseases Acts:

> It is quite the fashion I find, in London among the upper classes, to talk of this subject as if women were tempters, harpies, devils, while men are wholly innocent and in every case the tempted, and legislation, following out this idea, has in almost all cases been protective for men and punitive for women.

1 *Compare the statement above with the view expressed in Patmore's poem cited on page 210. In what ways does Butler question Patmore's analysis?*

2 *What does Butler mean when she refers to the legislation as 'punitive', and what are her objections to it?*

The extensive agitation against the Contagious Diseases Acts gave rise to the first popular feminist movement. Between 1870 and the repeal of the Contagious Diseases Acts, Butler orchestrated the collection and delivery of 17 367 petitions to Parliament containing 2 606 429 signatures, calling for the abolition of this legislation. This is evidence enough that women did not passively accept the role that mid-Victorian society assigned to them. Similarly, the notion of separate spheres, domestic and public, was questioned. Unsuccessful attempts were made to 'tack' female suffrage onto Disraeli's Reform Act by proposing that the term 'adult person' be substituted for 'adult male'. The vote rapidly became an objective of women's suffragist groups, drawn particularly from the middle class. These proved more successful in gaining admittance for women to local, rather than national, politics. In 1869 the Municipal Franchise Act gave women ratepayers the vote in municipal elections. From 1870 they could also vote in elections for school boards, from 1888 for County Councils and, from 1894, for parish and district councils. Despite this, the idea that politics was an unfit interest for a woman remained entrenched. The issue of votes for women in national elections was debated in every session of Parliament from 1870 to 1885 but it was not until 1929 that women would gain the vote on an equal footing with men. The argument against female suffrage invariably invoked what was called the 'natural role of the sexes' and promoted the idea of 'separate spheres'.

The family was seen as the cornerstone of Victorian society; its location, the home, became idealised in the literature of the day. One of the most popular songs of the period was 'Home, Sweet, Home!', written in 1823 and sung repeatedly for a century around the pianos in middle-class parlours. Victorian novels were written to be read aloud to the family, with sexual details carefully coded for adult readers. Family life was identified as a bulwark against moral decay and at its heart was the 'angel in the house'. In 1858 the artist Augustus Egg made the break-up of the family the theme for his series of three paintings, entitled 'Past and Present' (plates, 5, 6 and 7, pages 219–20). In the first of these two children (symbolically building a house of cards) look on as their father receives the news of his wife's adultery. The second picture shows the children without their parents; the mother has deserted the home and the father has killed himself. In the third picture Egg shows the woman sheltering homeless under Waterloo Bridge with her illegitimate child. The paintings emphasise the importance of family life and also its fragility. The family could be destroyed if the woman made the wrong choice. As in most of these Victorian sermons on the family, the responsibility for moral rectitude is placed firmly with the woman. The part that men might play in adulterous relationships, or the large number of middle-class men who used the services of prostitutes, did not feature extensively in the debate on morality.

It was a widespread belief, among the middle class in the towns, that social stability depended upon the re-fashioning of working-class attitudes around these middle-class notions of morality and the role of the family.

4 RELATIONS WITH THE WORKING CLASS

If the new middle class were to re-construct society in their own image they had to draw the working class into their way of thinking. Samuel Smiles felt that the lessons of *Self Help* were as relevant to the working community as they were to the middle class:

> That there should be a class of men who live by their daily labour in every state is the ordinance of God, and doubtless is a wise and righteous one; but that this class should be otherwise than frugal, contented, intelligent, and happy is not the design of Providence, but springs solely from the weakness, self-indulgence, and perverseness of man himself. The healthy spirit of self help created amongst working people would more than any other measure serve to raise them as a class, and this not by pulling down others, but by levelling them up to a higher and still advancing standard of religion, intelligence, and virtue.

1 *Why does Smiles consider that the working class should be 'frugal'?*

2 *What does he mean by the term 'self-help' in this passage?*

The mid-Victorian middle class set itself the task of encouraging the working class to help itself. In many ways this was the outcome of the 'Condition of England' debate). As we saw in chapter III, the predominant feeling that social legislation would be unnecessarily intrusive and only act to hamper the free flow of market forces put the onus for action firmly onto the individual. The role of the middle-class reformer lay less in campaigning for specific legislation and rather more in inculcating the importance of thrift, abstinence and self improvement by educating those sections of the working class who were inclined to listen.

By the middle of the century middle-class observers had come to see the working class as divided firmly into two parts: the 'respectable' and the 'rough', or the 'deserving' and the 'undeserving'. Along with this was an awareness that Victorian society depended, for the generation of wealth, upon the hard work of the working people. We can see in the art of the period a romanticised image of the 'deserving' working class. Ford Maddox Brown's famous painting 'Work' (plate 8, page 221), shown in 1865, depicts workmen digging a sewer in Hampstead. The picture shows all levels of Victorian society, from gentlemen to vagrants, but symbolically the knot of robust workmen occupy the centre of the picture. Meanwhile, two middle-class philanthropists,

Thomas Carlyle, the political writer (bearded) and F D Maurice (co-founder of the Working Men's College, an adult education venture), look on with approval. The painting was commissioned by the Leeds businessman, Thomas Plint, who paid 400 guineas and specified much of what appears on the canvas. An evangelical woman carries tracts for distribution, whilst ragged children are cared for by their elder sister. Representing, as it does, Plint's view of the world, it gives a good insight into the middle-class perception of the role of the hard-working sector of the working class and the contrast with the 'undeserving poor, who also appear. Similar points are made in William Bell Scott's 'Coal and Iron', (plate 9, page 222) first shown in 1860. This shows workers in the Tyneside shipyards. While the men work, one of their children looks on, having come to the yard to bring her father his lunch.

1 *What view of the working class is conveyed by Scott's painting?*
2 *Why might the painter have chosen the shipyards to depict labour in this way?*
3 *What is the significance of the child in this picture?*

Whilst claiming to admire the working class of this popular image, the Victorian middle class frequently depicted the problems of the day in terms of what they referred to as the 'undeserving' poor. In 1842 Chadwick's *Sanitary Report* referred to the inhabitants of the worst slums as 'the natives of an unknown country'. By the 1850s it was common to refer to the 'residuum', that part of the labouring poor that was beyond hope of redemption and which, it was felt, threatened to contaminate the rest of society. As the historian Gertrude Himmelfarb puts it in her study of nineteenth-century attitudes to poverty, 'It is significant that the same words – "residuum", "refuse", "offal", – were used to denote the sewage waste that constituted the sanitary problem and the human waste that constituted the social problem'. (*Idea of Poverty*).

We can determine two strands in the approach adopted towards the working class at this time: to police and control the 'rough' working class and to make citizens of the 'respectable' working class. This can best be seen in operation by exploring four areas of interaction between the classes: (a) popular culture, (b) the approach to trade unions, (c) the working-class franchise and (d) education.

A *Popular culture and 'rational recreation'*

The patterns of leisure which the labouring classes carried with them into the world's first industrial nation came to be seen as inappropriate to the nature of the new society. The fierce independence of the working community expressed itself most clearly in its defence of when and how it worked. In most trades, for example, it was customary to take Monday off; the observance of 'St. Monday' as it was known at the time.

1 *The Light of the World*, William Holman Hunt

2 *The Last Day in the Old Home*, Robert Martineau

4 *Found!*, Dante Gabriel Rossetti

3 *Beata Beatrix*, Dante Gabriel Rossetti

5 *Past and Present No. 1*, Augustus Egg

6 *Past and Present No. 2*, Augustus Egg

7 *Past and Present No. 3*, Augustus Egg

8 *Work*, Ford Madox Brown

9 *Iron and Coal*, William Bell Scott

Similarly, the year was traditionally punctuated by a series of unofficial holidays. These were loosely built around the religious calendar but were celebrated in boisterously secular ways. Many of these holiday activities had their origins in the smaller communities of an earlier age where they had helped to defuse social tension, by allowing a collective outburst of energy. Take, for example, the street football played in the town of Derby on Shrove Tuesday and Ash Wednesday. Any of the inhabitants were free to participate and there were often a thousand people on each side, the goals were a mile apart, at either end of the town, and the public streets were given over to the game for two days. In Kidderminster, on the first Monday after Michaelmas, a 'lawless hour' took place in which the inhabitants would gather on the streets and throw harmless missiles such as cabbage stalks at each other.

The mid-Victorian objection to this sort of activity was expressed in moral terms. Popular culture, much of it built around the consumption of alcohol and blood sports such as dog-fighting and bull-baiting, was easy to portray as hedonistic, cruel and drunken. As such, it was out of joint with the serious tone of public life as desired by the new middle class. Yet more than this, the inherent irregularity of the older popular culture was at odds with an industrial society's requirement of a disciplined workforce, whose presence at work could be guaranteed. Also, boisterous crowd activities involving the whole community might have been acceptable when the community was small, but when they took place in the large towns that had grown up by the middle of the century they were seen as a threat to public order. The urban middle class, running their own town councils since the Municipal Corporations Act of 1835, suppressed the crowd celebrations by use of, first the army and then the new police. For example, the annual street football in Derby was declared a breach of the peace and its participants prosecuted in 1846. The Cruelty to Animals Act of 1835 banned bloodsports, (except foxhunting which, since it involved the wealthier classes, was not deemed morally degrading) and this provided a good basis for prosecuting participants in many of the traditional pastimes.

Yet it was not enough simply to suppress the older popular culture; an alternative was sought that would be more in keeping with the spirit of the age. Evangelical reformers in particular argued the need for 'rational recreation'; leisure activity that would be educational, morally uplifting, and peaceful. The focus of social life, they believed, should shift from the public house and the community to the home and the family. As Smiles put it 'Home is the first and most important school of character'. Drinking was discouraged by the development of temperance societies through which men and women of all classes were called upon to sign the pledge to abstain from alcohol. Perhaps the most significant development in this area was the establishment of the United Kingdom Alliance for the Suppression of the Traffic in Intoxicating

Liquors (commonly known as the United Kingdom Alliance) in 1853. This brought together the local temperance societies organised from the 1830s onwards, into one, large, national, organisation. The Temperance movement always saw itself operating against a backdrop of potential alcohol-induced social disorder. Cardinal Manning, the Roman Catholic Archbishop of Westminster, and a great supporter of the United Kingdom Alliance, argued that without the efforts of the reformers drink would create, 'a heaving, seething mass of discontented, disaffected, moody passionate socialists; regarding the rich with hate, brooding over the "tyranny" of capital, and ready to bury the social edifice in ruins'.

The middle class also promoted educational initiatives among the working class. They supported the development of Mechanics' Institutes which provided evening classes for working people. Thrift was encouraged by the establishment of savings banks and working people were encouraged to join Friendly Societies through subscriptions to which they could insure themselves against the misfortunes of unemployment, old age, or the death of a bread-winner. By 1874 there were about 32 000 Friendly Societies with a total membership of about 8 million people.

There can be little doubt that the tone of public life was changing in these years. This was reinforced by the extension of the police force. Many of the boroughs had introduced their own forces under the provisions of the Municipal Corporations Act (*see page 49*). In 1856 the County and Borough Police Act extended provision to the counties and, in effect made uniformed police forces compulsory in both rural and urban areas, under the control of the local authorities. This was an important development since it signalled that the traditional ways of maintaining order, that of paternalism reinforced by the parish constable, had been replaced by an authority that would have a more formal and constant presence within British society. One of the main objectives of the local police forces, as they assumed their duties in the 1860s and the 1870s, was surveillance of the streets in working-class areas. Prosecutions involving drunkenness increased nationally from 75 000 in 1857 to over 200 000 in 1876.

Nevertheless, in interpreting these changes, two important qualifications should be borne in mind. First, that the rational recreationalists were not totally successful in their aim of reforming the leisure of the poor. A cursory inspection of any large town today will reveal, in the opulent architecture of the public houses built in the Victorian period, evidence enough that the pub remained at the heart of much of working-class life. Secondly, the historian Gareth Stedman-Jones has warned against employing a mechanistic model of 'social control' to explain those changes that did take place in popular culture in these years. It was not the case, he argues, that the working class simply had middle-class values thrust upon them and were manipulated and cajoled away from their earlier pastimes. This creates the image of an ignorant and passive working community, an image which Stedman-Jones rejects. Rather, much of the pressure to change popular culture came from within the working class itself. A newly class-conscious working community, which recognised the truth of the old Chartist slogan 'knowledge is power', undertook self-improvement as a way of gaining control over their own lives and not to simply 'ape' their 'betters'.

What was emerging in the mid-Victorian period was a new relationship between the middle class and the working class. After the turmoil of the Chartist years the middle decades of the century appear to be characterised less by class strife than by shared values and beliefs. This shift in social relations has been interpreted in a number of ways by historians. Many historians on the political left have seen this as a refashioning of class relations. Edward Thompson has argued that the failure of Chartism led working people to focus on more limited but achievable objectives like legal status for unions, improved working conditions and the vote for a limited sector of the working class. As he puts it 'the workers, having failed to overthrow capitalism, proceeded to warren it from end to end.' Thus, for Thompson, and most historians on the left, class conflict did not disappear after Chartism, it simply took a different (and generally less belligerent) form.

Similarly, Eric Hobsbawm identified the emergence of a 'labour aristocracy' from about 1850 onwards. This was a better-paid sector of the workforce whose skills were essential to industrial development as the British economy moved into a new phase of expansion. As a result, a range of groups of workers (engineers, boiler makers, iron workers, miners, the building trades and so on) were able to establish effective and lasting trade union organisation. From the 1840s onwards, large federated unions began to appear in these trades. The classic 'new model union' was the Amalgamated Society of Engineers formed in 1851. By 1867 the ASE had 33 000 members in 308 branches and financial resources of £140 000. The early historians of trade unionism, Sydney and Beatrice Webb, writing in 1894, dubbed these large organisations 'new model unions' and the label has stuck.

After 1850 the characteristic working-class activist was not the platform orator of the Chartist movement but rather a full-time official of a large union, working through negotiation to improve conditions for his members. This made for a less heroic and less ambitious labour movement with the aim shifting from the grandiose and universal attempt by the Chartists to change society, to the more limited objective of legal status for trade unions. Nevertheless, this strategy met with some success. Trade unions had been legalised by 1875 and, for good measure, the vote had been conceded to a proportion of the working community. Hobsbawm's work on the labour aristocracy was developed in local studies of Edinburgh and London. Here, it is argued, the skilled workers were able to improve their living and working conditions through trade unions, membership of Friendly Societies, and co-operative societies. By the 1860s, 14.4 per cent of the workforce received weekly wages 40–50 per cent higher than those of common labourers. Nevertheless, it is argued, the skilled worker still represented a distinctly working-class culture built around working-class values that were still much at odds with those of their employers. For example, the 'new model' unions resisted the use by employers of systematic overtime and piecework, both of which tended to increase the pressure on the individual worker to be more productive, and thus decrease the total amount of work available. They also resisted the introduction of unskilled labour, such as that of boys or women, into areas of work that had previously been the preserve of skilled labour (labour dilution). Employers objected to this as an intrusion into their 'right' to manage their businesses and an infringement upon the operation of the free market.

Nevertheless, the 'labour aristocracy' theory of how class relations developed has been criticised as misunderstanding the position of the skilled workers and the role of their characteristic organisations. The skilled worker, the opposing argument runs, was more concerned to establish the distance between himself and the unskilled worker than to fight for 'workers rights'. It would be more appropriate, from this point of view, to refer to 'working classes' rather than the 'working class'. The 'new model' unions adopted high subscription rates (a shilling a week was normal) that would deliberately exclude the less skilled, and in the workplace insisted that certain jobs were the exclusive province of the skilled worker. From this point of view, the emergence of an 'aristocracy of labour' represented, less a continuation of class war by other means, and more a re-affirmation that nineteenth-century society was a hierarchy of many social layers and not a polarity between two groups, the working class and the middle class.

Liberal historians tend to celebrate the middle decades of the nineteenth century as witnessing the birth of a society based on consensus values that tied together these various social layers. 'This was a cultural change', says F M L Thompson, 'a sign that sections of the working class were settling down to urban living and to industrial work, incorporating these conditions into a normal and accustomed pattern of living, carving out for themselves an honourable place in the new society.' Similarly, Harold Perkin argues that the period saw the 'rise of a viable class society within which conflict could be contained without threatening the overall stability of a society based on competitive individualism.'

This is a view deeply influenced by hindsight; we know that mid-Victorian society continued as a stable entity until the very different economic pressures of the late nineteenth century produced social disruption on a par with that of the 1840s. What is likely to be missed by any interpretation which focuses exclusively on mid-Victorian stability is the contemporary fear, amongst wealthier sections of society, that the social fabric might tear apart at any moment. This led to a search for areas of agreement between the classes and this is perhaps best illustrated by examining more closely the changing legal status of trade unions between 1850 and 1875 and the extension of the franchise in 1867 and 1884.

B *Trade unions 1850–75*

The development of 'new model' unions was simply an extension of some of the characteristics evident in trade unions earlier in the century. They were generally established through the federation of unions already in existence. Three quarters of the membership of the Amalgamated Society of Engineers, at its inception, came from the Society of Journeymen Steam Engine Makers established in 1826. The amalgamated societies stressed the role of trade unions as Friendly Societies, providing sickness and unemployment benefit. From their high subscription rates they were able to build up reliable funds. From 1875 to 1879 the ASE paid out £350 000 in unemployment benefit.

The new model unions appointed full-time officials to organise their affairs. Concerned to protect funds, these big societies preferred negotiation to strikes as a way of settling their differences with their employers. As Robert Applegarth, General Secretary of the Amalgamated Society of Carpenters and Joiners (formed in 1860) advised his members, 'Never surrender the right to strike but be careful how you use a double-edged weapon'. Strikes did not disappear in this period but they ceased to be a union's first weapon. The centralised organisation of the new unions reinforced the movement towards moderation since decisions to strike could be officially taken only at district or national executive, rather than local, level.

The unions that came to prominence in the middle decades of the century identified the achievement of legal status as their prime target. Since the repeal of the Combination Act in 1824 it had no longer been an offence to belong to an association acting 'in restraint of trade' but in reality the unions enjoyed only a quasi-legal existence. Employees could still be criminally prosecuted for breach of contract when undertaking strike action. In addition, under an amendment to the repeal of the Combination Act passed in 1825, 'molestation' of other workers was deemed a crime. It was left to the courts to define what molestation amounted to but it was clear by the middle of the century that unions did not yet have the right peacefully to persuade workers to join a strike or a union. Besides this, in 1867, in the case of Hornby v Close, the unions found that their funds were not protected at law. It had been widely assumed that since unions performed the role of Friendly Societies, and registered as such, their funds were protected by the Friendly Societies Act of 1855. But when the Boilermakers attempted to sue a dishonest official for the return of union funds the judgement was returned that unions were not seen by the law to be Friendly Societies, and their funds were not protected.

The push for full legal status was led by the London Trades Council, formed in 1860. This group later known as the 'junta', consisted of the leaders of five new model unions; William Allen of the ASE, Applegarth of the ASCJ, Daniel Guile of the Ironfounders, Edwin Coulson of the Bricklayers and George Odger of the shoemakers. In 1868 the first Trades Union Congress was held in Manchester with 34 delegates representing 118 367 members. The TUC, held annually, acted to draw together the campaign to amend the labour laws.

Despite its conciliatory approach, this group encountered the traditional opposition to the unions as organisations that restricted the freedom of the individual in a society committed to individualism. Public concern was aroused in 1866 by the 'Sheffield Outrages'. A series of violent attacks were made by saw-grinders on fellow workers who refused to be bound by their local union. As a result a Royal Commission was appointed, in 1867, to investigate the whole issue of trade unions. The 'junta' of new model unionists co-ordinated much of the evidence presented to the Royal Commission and this tended to stress the advantages to society of a well-organised and amenable trade union movement. They were assisted in this respect by the presence on the Commission of two middle-class supporters of the new unions, Frederic Harrison, a radical lawyer, and the author and MP Thomas Hughes. The unions presented themselves as being very different organisations to the strike-prone radical organisations of popular demonology. As a result the Royal Commission recommended that unions be given the same protection for their funds as Friendly Societies, though it stopped short of recommending the amendment of the law on molestation. This was short of the full legal status desired by the trade unionists. Nevertheless, many had expected the report to be more clearly hostile to trade unions. Pushed on by the Parliamentary Committee of the TUC, Gladstone's Liberal government, and then Disraeli's Conservative government, subsequently passed a number of Acts which accorded the unions the status they sought.

1871 Trade Union Act, (Liberal) – registered trade unions were given full legal status and accorded the same legal protection for funds as enjoyed by Friendly Societies. (*See also pages 266–7*)
1871 Criminal Law Amendment Act, (Liberal) – restricted the right of picketing; the unions organised extensively in opposition to this act arguing that the Liberals had given with one hand only to take away with the other by their two pieces of legislation in 1871.
1875 Conspiracy and Protection of Property Act, (Conservative) – conceded the right to peaceful picketing, repealing the Criminal Law Amendment Act. (*See also pages 335–6*)
1875 Employers and Workmens Act, (Conservative) – breach of contract was no longer a criminal matter.

By 1875 the unions had gained full legal recognition of their right to exist and to act on behalf of their members. This brings us back to the issue of interpretation. What light do these changes cast on the broader issue of social relations in mid-Victorian society? The first point to make is that the legalisation of the unions did not mean that they were approved of by all classes. The criticism of unions as organisations that restricted the freedom of the individual was often made as trenchantly in the 1860s and 1870s as it had been in the 1840s. The following statement by the firm of Messrs W B and N Smith of Birmingham presented to the Royal Commission was a fairly typical example of the continuing case made, by employers, against the unions:

> The object and rules of the policy of the council of such trades unions as have come under our observations has been with respect to wages, to raise them artificially; with respect to the hours of labour to limit them; with respect to apprenticeship, to keep down the number, with respect to piecework, to prevent it altogether; with respect to overtime, to prevent it as far as possible by increasing the cost; with respect to non-union men to prevent their employment.

1 *What is meant by the suggestion that trade unions raise wages 'artificially'?*

2 *What objections are being raised to trade unions in this passage?*

Nevertheless, the new model unions, utilising the channels of public opinion and Parliamentary lobbying, had presented themselves as the acceptable face of trade unionism. The new model unions still represented a view of the social and economic world that was identifiably working class, as can be seen from William Allen's comments to the Royal Commission on the polarity of interests between masters and workers (*see page 236*). Against the notion of an unrestrained marketplace, where wages would be determined by the free-play of economic forces, the unions spoke of the 'rights' of their members; for example, the 'right' to work or the 'right' to 'a fair day's wage for a fair day's work'. Nevertheless, they publicly accepted enough of the dominant values of mid-Victorian society to render them acceptable. We may list points of contact between the unions and the dominant values of mid-Victorian society that we identified earlier in the chapter.

competitive individualism – by 1850 the trade unions accepted the permanence of the existing economic system. The failure of the Owenite initiatives of the 1830s meant that little reference was now made to socialist alternatives until the late nineteenth century (*see page 423*). Whilst the unions continued to stress the importance of labour to production, and worked hard to raise wages and restrict labour supply, there was a general acceptance by leaders like Allen and Applegarth that it was the market that ultimately defined what was possible. This did not mean that they unquestioningly accepted capitalism and its fundamental tenets but rather they recognised that it was here to stay.

thrift – the unions stressed their Friendly Society role in providing benefits for their members;

self-reliance – the trade unionist who could draw benefits from subscriptions paid into the union would never be a drain on public or charitable funds;

sobriety – the new unions dropped the custom of holding trade union meetings in public houses; they discouraged drinking at work; many of the leaders were prominent in the Temperance movement;

moral probity – as Allen put it to the Royal Commission in 1867: . . . we have a controlling power over them (the members); if men misconduct themselves through drinking or anything of that kind, we have the opportunity of dealing with them, and we do our best to keep them up to the mark so far as regards their position.'

domestic ideology – the unions argued that a reasonable wage was one that enabled a working man's wife to remain at home and look after the home; as the TUC put it in 1877, 'wives should be in their proper sphere at home, instead of being dragged into competition for livelihood against the great and strong men of the world.'

Moreover, formal unions represented only a small proportion of the workforce. The concession of legal status held the promise of benefits in terms of social stability. If trade unions were officially recognised by the law they would be inclined to abide by the law. Also, if their funds were protected and they were permitted to expect a continuous existence they would be less inclined to resort to strike action which could threaten their existence. This lesson had been learned early in the period, when a national lock-out cost the ASE £40 000 in strike pay to their members. The 1867 Royal Commission on Trade Unions reported that the ASE, with total funds of £459 000, had expended only £26 000 in strike relief over a ten-year period (i.e. 6 per cent of its assets) whilst the ironfounders with 10 000 members and total funds of £210 000 had spent only £5300 (2.5 per cent of its assets) supporting strikes over the period. This made a good case for protecting the unions in law.

Trade unions in the mid-Victorian period continued to represent the interests of their members, often in conflict with the views of their employers. To return to Stedman-Jones' criticism of the notion of 'social control', some broader points might now be made. The legalisation of the unions did not signal the existence of either consensus throughout society nor the neutralising of a once radical force. It was simply that, the advantages of formalising the role of trade unions were seen at this point as outweighing the disadvantages of forcing them into an effectively illegal existence. As the *Times* (which was no friend of the unions) put it, 'Trade Unions will continue to exist, and to number half a million members, whether they are protected by Act of Parliament or not.'

C *A working-class franchise, the reform acts of 1867 and 1884*

The same kind of analysis applied to the enfranchisement of the 'respectable' working class. The Parliamentary machinations around the issue of extending the franchise are discussed elsewhere in this volume. For the mid-Victorians, concerned to construct social stability within a society encompassing vast social differences, the case was being put in both 1867 and again in 1884, that this could best be achieved by admitting a section of the working class into what would be a restricted, formalised, and controlled democratic structure. Even under the clauses of the 1884 Act (which was seen at the time to have conceded 'manhood suffrage') it is unlikely that more than six men in every ten would be able to exercise the vote. Nor were the cumbersome registration procedures, that restricted the franchise in practice, the result of badly devised legislation. Quite the reverse was true: they represented an attempt to extend the franchise in a way that would minimise the numbers of working men able to vote.

For their part, trade unionists saw the vote as a vital element in bringing about change in the labour laws and they formed the basis of the Reform League established in 1863. Although committed to universal suffrage, the Reform League made it clear from the outset that it would happily co-operate with John Bright's middle-class Reform Union which aimed for a more limited franchise. The Reform League also accepted the view of middle-class reformers that it was only 'registered and residential' workingmen who should be enfranchised. In this way they accepted that they were more likely to achieve success by accepting the parameters of the debate as established by the middle class. But labour now added its numerical strength to the argument for a reformed electoral system. When the Liberal Bill was rejected in June 1866 the Reform League held a number of rallies in Trafalgar Square. When a similar meeting in Hyde Park in July was banned the crowd tore down the railings of the Park and rioted. When the League planned a meeting in the Park on 6 May 1867, to coincide with Parliament's discussion of Disraeli's Reform Bill, 15 000 special constables were enrolled to deal with potential disturbances. At 6 pm 100 000 people were led into Hyde Park by the Reform League.

This demonstration passed off peacefully but had presented the House of Commons with clear alternatives: enfranchise a section of the workforce or watch it return to the boisterous mass-based agitations of the Chartist days with all their potential for disruption. The historian Royden Harrison believes that Disraeli took the 'Hyde Park Railway' to reform and was influenced by the popular agitation to extend the provisions of his bill. Other historians, like Maurice Cowling and, more recently, John Walton, have been more sceptical, focusing on the Parliamentary wrangles as the really decisive factor for settling the issue (*see also page 346*). Nevertheless, the extensive public debate that surrounded the reform of the franchise suggests that, far from being the passive recipients of the decisions of Parliament, organised labour played an active part in determining the way those decisions were taken.

Through the extension of the franchise, one part of the working community became formally involved in the political life of the nation. Their involvement was encouraged by the development of modern party structures. The National Union of Conservative and Constitutional Associations (1867) and the National Liberal Federation (1877) competed for the support of the new working-class voters, and with some success. As Engels wrote to Marx despairingly in 1868, 'Everywhere the proletariat are the rag, tag and bobtail of the official parties.' For the moment organised labour saw its advantage in supporting existing parties, most notably the Liberal Party under Gladstone. In 1874 two working men were elected as official Liberal candidates, both trade unionists and miners. Alexander Macdonald and Thomas Burt elected for Stafford and for Morpeth, respectively, were referred to as Lib-Labs.

The entry of working men to Parliament seemed to confirm the success of labour's change of strategy in the third quarter of the nineteenth century. The adjustment of the political and legal system to allow trade unions a formal role and, for some working men at last, the vote, acted to preserve the peace of the realm. It enabled the mid-Victorians to reflect that the era heralded by the 'Great Exhibition' was one of progress induced by economic change. But class did not disappear as a significant social divider in this period; rather a negotiated compromise was arrived at between potential protagonists. The historian Trygve Tholfsen has questioned Professor Burns' description of the period as 'The Age of Equipoise'. Instead he sees mid-Victorian Britain as 'a stable culture in a state of inner tension'. In this period it became clear that Britain was being re-fashioned in the image of the developing middle class and that their characteristic values derived from a commitment to economic individualism. The defeat of Chartism as a mass-based movement, followed by economic improvement, allowed the middle class to arrive at a sort of negotiated compromise with labour. In the process public life was transformed. But the apparent stability that was created was short-lived and the period from 1880 to 1914 witnessed a resurfacing of overt class conflict in the face of economic change and social re-alignment (*see chapters XIII and XIV*).

D *Education*

The promotion of education was always a major reforming interest of the Victorians. In a society that was reluctant to blame its own economic system for the origin of its social problems, it naturally followed that a great emphasis was placed on the importance of education. An educated population would be free of the ignorance that led individuals to make the wrong moral choices. By the middle years of the century, middle-class observers were promoting education as a universal panacea that would provide the answer to the problems of poverty, disease, crime and disorder. This was understandable given the emphasis upon the role of the individual in the social context.

Nevertheless, the same commitment to individualism restricted what was seen as the State's role as a provider of education for the poor. This was seen as the proper province of voluntary agencies, most notably the religious and charitable bodies. In the city slums many of the initiatives to save children from joining the ranks of the 'dangerous classes' involved the establishment of 'ragged schools', often co-ordinated by Lord Shaftesbury's Ragged School Union established in 1844. Voluntary initiatives were supported by government funds and these had been controlled from 1839 by the Committee of the Privy Council on Education. By 1861, government expenditure on education ran at £800 000 per year. Linked with the grants to schools was a system of school inspection. The findings of the Newcastle Commission, established in 1858 to investigate the education of the poorer classes, led to the introduction of what was called 'The Revised Code'. By this, school grants would be linked to attendance levels and examination results.

Thus by the 1860s a system of schooling of sorts was in existence. But there was growing concern that this particular combination of state funding and voluntary endeavour was not achieving the desired results. The provision of schools was haphazard and, in 1869, Inspectors' reports suggested that in the large towns less than a tenth of the child population were in schools. W E Forster's Education Act of 1870 divided the country into 'school districts' generally corresponding with boroughs in urban areas and parishes in rural areas. Each district was to ensure the existence of sufficient schools to provide an elementary education for its children. The districts were to be managed by elected School Boards and provision was made to finance schools from local rates as well as by government funding. By this, the role of both the state and local government in the provision of education was increased. In 1876 education became compulsory for children to the age of ten (*see also pages 354–5*).

The debate surrounding education was intensified by the movement towards a wider electorate; a large proportion of which would consist of working-class men. In a famous statement in the House of Commons in 1867 Robert Lowe, a Whig, who as Secretary of the Council of Education had been responsible for the introduction of the Revised Code, pointed out the importance of educating the electorate to the Conservative government. 'I believe that it will be absolutely necessary to compel our new future masters to learn their letters.' The idea that the Reform Act of 1867 created the perceived necessity of 'educating our new masters', of course, over-stressed the impact that the changes in the franchise were to have on the structure of politics. The working-class voter was far from being the 'new master' as Lowe had suggested. Nevertheless, the link between citizenship and education was widely recognised, and in this respect was a position shared between the classes. After all, as we saw in chapter IV, the Chartists, under Lovett's and Collins' guidance, had called for an efficient national system of education in 1840 (*see page 92*). Through education the Chartists aimed not only to earn the vote but also to use it effectively; thus endorsing the popular slogan that 'Knowledge is power'. The educational reformer James Kay-Shuttleworth argued in 1877 that 'the destiny of a free country is mainly the consequence of the degree of intelligence and virtue that the people possess,' and drew attention to 'the relation which elementary education bears to the political training of the working class and their fitness to discharge the duties of electors to the Commons House of Parliament'.

For this reason a crude 'social control' interpretation, of the sort that Stedman-Jones objected to in relation to popular culture, fits uneasily into the analysis of the development of a more formal education system at elementary level. It was certainly the case that the political parties, and middle-class reformers generally, saw educational reform as a way of defending the position of the 'respectable' working class from the incursions of the 'dangerous classes'. Also, the curriculum adopted in the schools undoubtedly reinforced the values we have identified in this chapter as characteristically Victorian. In the words of Kay-Shuttleworth in 1877, 'Education necessarily embraces a religious training.' The schools also reproduced the gender distinctions and conceptions of 'respectability' and self-help that had become so much a part of public life by 1875. Smiles' book and others of the same genre were frequently given as prizes to 'model' pupils. Yet the working community had always seen education as linked with their own emancipation rather than as the instrument of their subordination. Trade unionists, like Robert Applegarth, had long argued the necessity for a national system of education for working people. From this point of view the Act of 1870 could be seen as part of the fruits of the new relationship between the classes that had emerged in the mid-Victorian period, and as an achievement that could be built upon. Nevertheless, the economic changes of the last quarter of the century were to indicate the fragility of the relationship between the classes, and this will be examined in chapter XIII.

5 Bibliography

Steven Adams *The Art of the Pre-Raphaelites* (1992). A helpful introduction to this important group of artists, who in many ways embodied the values of the period.

Asa Briggs *Victorian People* (Penguin, 1985). A series of lively essays on important individuals who are often neglected. The essay on Robert Applegarth is a particularly good study of a mid-Victorian trade unionist.

Francois Crouzet *The Victorian Economy* (Routledge, 1990). This is a welcome attempt to provide an overview of economic change in the period. In the process Crouzet challenges a number of the standard interpretations.

Robert Gray *The Aristocracy of Labour in Nineteenth Century Britain* (Macmillan, 1981). A good summary of, and commentary on, the 'labour aristocracy' debate.

Angela John *By the Sweat of Their Brow* (Routledge, 1984). A feminist re-interpretation of the role of women working in the mines and the way this was portrayed in the 'reforming' movements of the time. This book is also a good text for chapter III on the 'Condition of England Question'.

Frank Mort *Dangerous Sexualities* (Routledge, 1987). A very good study of the relationship between dominant values and attitudes to sexuality in the nineteenth century. It also points up similarities between nineteenth-century attitudes to prostitution (particularly the Contagious Diseases Acts) and twentieth-century attitudes to AIDS. Part One of this book would also be useful reading to support the points made in chapter III.

Richard Price *Labour in British Society* (Croom Helm, 1986). An exploration of the changing relationship between labour and capital in the mid-Victorian period.

Judith Walkowitz *Prostitution and Victorian Society* (Cambridge University Press, 1980). This book looks at the way prostitutes were portrayed as an 'outcast' group in the period, as part of the notion that women were seen, in the dominant values of the day, as the guardians of morality.

J K Walton *The Second Reform Act* (Routledge, Lancaster Pamphlet 1987), usefully summarises the historiography of the Act of 1867.

6 Discussion Points and Essay Questions

A

1 Why was the Great Exhibition identified so strongly with progress?

2 What were the main threats to social stability in the early-to mid-Victorian period?

3 What mechanisms were open to the mid-Victorians for the maintenance of social stability in their society?

4 Why were the middle class so concerned with the individual?

5 Why were women seen as 'the angel in the house'?

6 Why was prostitution seen as 'The Great Social Evil'?
7 Why were the Victorian middle class concerned about working-class leisure patterns?
8 How far should we see the attempt to influence patterns of working-class leisure as an exercise in 'social control'?
9 In what ways did the trade unions support the idea of 'self-help'?
10 What were the economic and moral objections raised by some Victorians to trade unions?
11 What were the advantages of full legal status from the trade unions' point of view?
12 Why was the Education Act of 1870 passed?

B *Essay questions*

1 How and why did the nature of trade unionism change between 1833 and 1875?
2 Discuss the main successes and failures of British working-class movements from 1833–75.
3 Given the supposed finality of the 1832 Reform Act, why did further reform of Parliament take place in 1867? (In answer to this question, also read section 5 of chapter XI.)

7 DOCUMENTARY EXERCISE – A LEGAL STATUS FOR TRADE UNIONS

The legalising of trade unions presents a good opportunity to explore the interface between the classes and to consider how strategies for the achievement of social stability might have looked at the time. In the mid-Victorian period, as we have seen, trade unions were finally given the legal status that had previously been denied to them. Yet, the objectives of the unions remained generally antagonistic to those of the employers. Besides this, for a society committed to the freedom of the individual the collective nature of the unions seemed particularly threatening. In the chapter you have read this was illustrated by the statement of the employers Messrs. WB and N Smith of Birmingham (*see page* 229). Below is a series of extracts from the evidence given to the Royal Commission on Trade Unions in 1867 by William Allen, the General Secretary of the 'model' union, the Amalgamated Society of Engineers. Read these carefully and consider the advantages and disadvantages of awarding the unions legal status from the point of view of an employer. Points may be arranged in two columns.

> Q. What has been the effect of the union upon the men that are members of it as to social position, or character, or skill?

Allen I think it has been the means of decided improvement in their position and character generally; for we have a controlling power over them; if men misconduct themselves through drinking or anything of that kind, we have the opportunity of dealing with them, and we do our best to keep them up to the mark so far as regards their position.

Q. Do you find that the possession of very large funds, and the fact that they belong to a very powerful organisation, such as your society is, tends generally to make the members of your society disposed to enter into . . . a dispute . . . ?
Allen I should say that the members generally are decidedly opposed to strikes and that the fact of our having a large accumulated fund tends to encourage that feeling amongst them.

Q. Why should you prevent a master from employing boys who can do the work?
Allen We have a perfect right to say to him, 'If you employ a certain number of boys beyond what we conceive to be a proper number, we will not work for you'.

Q. A proper number means the number that you like?
Allen What the men think is right.

Q. You set your face against competition in labour by the free admission of boys?
Allen We endeavour to prevent an over surplus of labour in our market by the admission of boys.

Q. But the interest of the employer and the employed is to work together is it not?
Allen There I differ. Every day of the week I hear that the interests are identical. I scarcely see how that can be, while we are in a state of society which recognises the principle of buying in the cheapest and selling in the dearest market. It is their interest to get the labour done at as low a rate as they possibly can, and it is ours to get as high a rate of wages as possible and you can never reconcile those two things.

VIII

GLADSTONE PART I: FROM TORY TO LIBERAL

---

1 INTRODUCTION

WILLIAM Ewart Gladstone (1809–98) was at, or near, the centre of British political life from the 1830s to the 1890s. He came into Parliament, as a Tory, immediately after the Great Reform Act (1832), and retired as the Liberal Prime Minister, in 1894. The Parliament he first entered was overwhelmingly aristocratic and Anglican: when he resigned from his fourth premiership more than 60 years later, Britain was something approaching a democracy and the rise of Labour was only just over the horizon.

Hand in hand with these tremendous political changes had gone a social and economic revolution which transformed Britain, within Gladstone's lifetime, from a predominantly rural society into a land of town-dwellers. The urban population had grown from a mere third of the total around the time of his birth to fully four-fifths of the total by the time of his death. Gladstone, with other politicians of his generation, had to learn how to cope with the unprecedented social and political problems caused by urbanisation and industrialisation. But the unparalleled prosperity and self confidence of Britain in the 1850s and 1860s suggested that industrialisation and urbanisation had a benign as well as a threatening political face.

Gladstone and the Liberal Party were the most obvious political beneficiaries of this transformation. His years as Chancellor of the Exchequer (1852–5 and 1859–66) firmly established his position in the front rank at Westminster, while the Whigs and Liberals – with whom Gladstone finally joined up in 1859–were rarely out of office in these decades.

The Liberal era culminated in Gladstone's own great first ministry (1868–74). By this time, he had established a political power base outside Westminster, in the rapidly expanding towns of the industrial North. After a brief 'retirement', Gladstone came back to power again in 1880. But when, in 1886, Gladstone decided on a radical solution – Home Rule – to what he saw as the injustice of British domination of Ireland, he split the Liberal Party. He was never to enjoy the full confidence of the British electorate again.

Gladstone was no mere spectator of the great political and social changes that transformed Victorian England. But the exact nature of his contributions remains a matter of intense debate. Two interrelated questions loom large: how is Gladstone's transformation from reactionary Toryism in the 1830s to apparently radical Liberalism in the 1880s to be explained, and what was the place of principle, as opposed to ambition, in his career?

It is no longer possible to see Gladstone as his first great biographer John Morley did in 1903. For Morley, Gladstone's political life was a pilgrimage from prejudice to enlightenment: blessed with a generous and open mind and an elevated soul, Gladstone was forced by the experience of government to abandon his first principles and shed his prejudices. In fact, most of Gladstone's instincts, and many of his objectives, remained essentially conservative. Neither can we simply accept the picture painted by JL Hammond in *Gladstone and the Irish Nation* (1939), of a man driven by a vision of justice, whose sense of mission put him above the miserable calculations of self-interest that are the lot of the ordinary politician. Gladstone was not a saint, whatever some of his supporters seemed to believe. Recent historians of 'high politics', like Michael Bentley, have stressed that Gladstone was as hard-headed, anxious for power and ruthless as any other politician. But this picture of Gladstone is itself arguably rather one-dimensional. The most recent scholarship on Gladstone (*see bibliography page 295*) would suggest, rather, that, while acknowledging the role of ambition, we need to put principle, and above all, religious belief, at the centre of his personal progress and political practice.

2 THE MAKING OF A CHRISTIAN POLITICIAN

A *Anglican foundations*

Gladstone came from a wealthy commercial background. His father was one of Liverpool's richest merchants, and between 1818 and 1827 was one of that city's Members of Parliament. He made sure his son received the best of educations. At Eton (1821–7) and Oxford University (1828–31), where he capped his academic career with a brilliant degree, Gladstone established a reputation as one of the most talented men of his generation. The Duke of Newcastle became his patron and, late in 1832, eased him into the Commons through one of the pocket boroughs effectively left intact by the Great Reform Act. He was not yet 23-years-old.

Politics was not the only career which Gladstone had considered. He was a deeply committed Christian, and had thought very seriously about ordination in the Church of England. But, searching his soul, he doubted whether he had recieved a clear call to serve Christ in the Church, and, as his father had hoped, decided to try to make his way to the forefront of public life in politics instead.

In no sense, however, did this mark a repudiation of Gladstone's religious ideals. Indeed, he believed that the best way in which he could serve the Church of England was through politics. In the 1830s, the young Tory Gladstone was convinced that there was a conspiracy by Whigs, Radicals and Irish Catholics to destroy the Anglican Church of Ireland and undermine the Church of England. He soon became, in the words of the Whig intellectual and politician Macaulay, 'the rising hope of those stern and unbending Tories' on the right of the party, who believed that the privileges of the Church had to be defended at all costs.

His major contribution to the struggle was a book, *The State in its Relations with the Church* (1838). This was an elaborate defence of the principle of Establishment, i.e. the idea that the Anglican Church should be the only church officially recognised and supported by the State. Anglicanism, it argued, was the only true religion, and the ideal society would be one in which all citizens were Anglicans.

Critics found much that was purely negative, and even dangerous, in this vision. Macaulay wondered what room there was for Nonconformity in Gladstone's Britain, and pointed out that in Ireland, the attempt to impose Anglicanism on an overwhelmingly Catholic population had led to more riots that conversions. Gladstonian Toryism, if it had ever been put into practice, would have made for a deeply reactionary, repressive style of government.

Over the following two decades, Gladstone's growing experience of practical politics was to make him realise that his early Church-State principles were untenable. By 1845, he had come to see that the hope of making Anglicanism the religion of Irishmen was a fantasy. Furthermore, in the 1850s, he began to recognise the scale and quality of the Nonconformist contribution to British Christianity.

In important respects, however, he remained true to his early beliefs. Practically speaking, he worked hard to defend the integrity and extend the influence of the Church of England. More fundamentally, he held to his conviction that the state had a duty to choose between right and wrong, and that society might yet be infused with Christian zeal, and purpose. These beliefs were to shape the practice and objectives of his statesmanship to end of his days. Underpinning all of this was his personal faith. Here, an intense and pervasive sense of sin was balanced with a conviction that it was within our powers to discern

God's purposes for us, and that we should throw ourselves into the battle against evil and injustice. He was to bring the same passion and zeal – and, in his opponents' eyes, fanaticism – to his political crusades of the 1870s and 1880s, as he had brought to his High Tory defence of the Establishment in the 1830s.

B *Peelite transformations*

It was not Gladstone's passionate religious convictions which first brought him to Peel's attention, however. What impressed Peel about Gladstone was his manifest political and administrative ability. Gladstone's maiden speech confirmed that his brilliant Oxford reputation was well-merited, and as early as 1835 he was given office as Under-Secretary for War and the Colonies in Peel's first brief ministry. When Peel returned to power in 1841, Gladstone served at the Board of Trade and he was promoted to Cabinet rank in 1843. But his career suffered a major set-back in 1845, when he startled his contemporaries by resigning over the Maynooth question (*see pages 140–3*). Gladstone reluctantly agreed with the government's decision to increase its grant to the Irish Catholic Seminary at Maynooth. It was justifiable as part of Peel's strategy to detach moderate Catholics from nationalist extremists. But the Maynooth grant was in clear opposition to rigid principles he had spelled out seven years earlier in his treatise on Church and State, and Gladstone believed that personal honour and public consistency required his resignation.

However, the experience of working in Peel's great administration had a profound impact on Gladstone's future political career. He had made his name as an immensely able and industrious minister. As Peel's Home Secretary had remarked, 'Gladstone could do in four hours what it took any other man sixteen hours to do, and he worked sixteen hours a day'. Furthermore, the business of government helped to give Gladstone's political life a new meaning and purpose. Ministerial responsibilities themselves proved to be a joy, not a burden. He found great intellectual pleasure in mastering the details of a brief, a pleasure compounded by his sense that his work was a form of service to the state, and thus worthy in God's eye.

Gladstone still gave the ends to which he worked Christian significance. The steady reduction or abolition of the tariffs on hundreds of articles may seem a singularly dry and dreary administrative task. For Gladstone, however, the progress towards Free Trade had a moral and Christian content. At the most general level, the creation and preservation of wealth – which Free Trade would facilitate – was a Christian duty. More specifically, as the state's interference in the workings of the economy decreased, so greater responsibility would be thrown on the individual. The free market would be an instrument of Providence, rewarding the virtuous and thrifty, and punishing the vicious and spendthrift.

Above all, Free Trade was welcome as a means of securing social harmony and justice. The Repeal of the Corn Laws was the ultimate demonstration to worker, industrialist and landowner alike that the state served no vested interest, but rather the whole community. This model of the right use of executive power, soothing away agitation and doing what was right, regardless of the political cost to those in office, was to remain with Gladstone throughout his career in politics.

3 FROM CONSERVATIVE TO LIBERAL

The immediate price which Gladstone paid in 1846 for his support of Peel was the loss of his protectionist patron, the Duke of Newcastle. But the academics and clergymen who elected Oxford University's very own MP came to his rescue. Between 1847 and 1865, Gladstone sat for this most prestigious of all constituencies. These years saw his transition from Peelite Conservative to radical-tinged Liberal, and his discovery that he had a popular political power base. They also cover his first and most successful years as Chancellor of the Exchequer (1852–5 and 1859–65) when he established his position as one of the most dominant mid-Victorian political figures.

A *Gladstone as Chancellor*

As a loyal Peelite, Gladstone had followed his leader into political exile in 1846 (*see pages 153–4*). But his administrative skills and rhetorical power in the Commons remained widely admired. In the confused politics of the 1850s, Whig and Conservative Prime Ministers alike attempted to recruit him to their ranks, believing that his adhesion would greatly increase their ministries' stability. Lord Aberdeen's coalition (1852–5) made the first successful bid, and Gladstone became Chancellor in December 1852. His colleagues expectations of him were amply fulfilled when, in 1853, Gladstone produced one of the century's most celebrated budgets.

The following extracts, from Morley's classic *Life of Gladstone*, give some indication of the style in which Gladstone approached his first budget, its political sensitivity, and its impact.

> Thirteen, fourteen, fifteen hours a day he toiled at his desk, Treasury officials and trade experts, soap deputations and post-horse deputations, representatives of tobacco and representatives of the West India interest, flocked to Downing Street day by day all through March. If he went into the city to dine with the Lord Mayor, the lamentable hole thus made in his evening was repaired by working till four in the morning upon customs reform . . . and budget plans of all kinds.

> The budget was vital for the survival of Lord Aberdeen's ministry. The position of the government in the House of Commons was notoriously weak. The majority that had brought them into existence was excessively narrow. It had been well known from the first that if any of the accidents of a session should happen to draw the Tories, the Irish, and the radicals into one lobby, ministers would find themselves in a minority.

Gladstone introduced his Budget on 18 April 1853. His speech lasted four and three-quarter hours; but his audience seem to have been anything but bored. Lord Aberdeen wrote to Prince Albert:

> the display of power was wonderful; it was agreed in all quarters that there had been nothing like the speech for many years, and that under the impression of his commanding eloquence the reception of the budget had been most favourable.

The Prime Minister also expressed his pleasure and gratitude to Gladstone:

> While everybody is congratulating *me* on the wonderful impression produced in the House of Commons last night, it seems only reasonable that I should have a word of congratulation for *you*. You will believe how much more sincerely I rejoice on your account than on my own, although most assuredly, if the existence of my government shall be prolonged, it will be your work.

Gladstone must have been particularly pleased to have received a letter of praise from Peel's widow. He replied as follows:

> I know the recollections with which you must have written, and therefore I will not scruple to say that as I was inspired by the thought of treading, however unequally, in the steps of my great teacher and master in public affairs, so it was one of my keenest anxieties not to do dishonour to his memory, or injustice to the patriotic policy with which his name is for every associated.

As an expert political commentator noted in his diary, the speech had:

> raised Gladstone to a great political elevation, and what is of far greater consequence than the measure itself, has given the country assurance of a man equal to great political necessities and fit to lead parties and direct governments.

1 *Why was Lord Aberdeen, the Prime Minister, so pleased with Gladstone's success? In what other respects do these extracts help us understand why*

Whig and Tory leaders alike were eager to recruit Gladstone to their ministerial teams?

2 *What light does Gladstone's note to Peel's widow shed on his political loyalties and objectives?*

3 *How did the 1853 budget mark a turning point in Gladstone's career?*

The principles of Gladstone's budget were impeccably Peelite. *Laissez-faire* and retrenchment were its keywords. The state should interfere with the natural progress of the nation's economic life as little as possible, and cut its own spending to a minimum. In practice, this meant the reduction or abolition of tariffs, the elimination of bureaucratic waste, and keeping a tight rein on defence expenditure.

The scope of Gladstone's budget was impressive. Income tax, despite its unpopularity, was maintained at 7d (3 p) and the threshold above which it was to be paid lowered from £150 to £100. But Gladstone projected its ultimate abolition in 1860, anticipating that extra revenue would be generated by continued economic growth and the increasing consumption of 'luxuries' like beer and tobacco on which duties still fell. But almost 300 other duties were lowered or abolished. The relative contribution made to the Exchequer by direct and indirect taxation was carefully balanced to reflect the respective abilities of the propertied classes and the working man to pay. If government was seen to be even-handed, spreading the burden of taxation fairly between rich and poor, class harmony would be promoted and the state's authority more readily accepted, even amongst those who had no vote. Here, as elsewhere, Gladstone was following Peel.

Gladstone had relished playing the role of Chancellor, and helped to make Budget Day into a great piece of political theatre. His contemporaries believed that the budget had displayed a combination of precision, professionalism and far-sightedness to rival Peel himself.

However, Gladstone was never the easiest of colleagues. The Crimean War 1854–6 (*see pages 182–7*), which he believed could have been avoided, wrecked his plans for retrenchment and made him struggle to balance the books. His ill-temper was aggravated by the threat of a Committee of Inquiry into the government's mismanagement of the war, and he resigned in 1855.

B *Gladstone's progress towards the Liberals*

Gladstone was out of government for four long years, eventually returning as a Liberal Chancellor of the Exchequer in 1859. But there was nothing inevitable about Gladstone ultimately throwing his weight behind the Liberal cause. On three occasions in the 1850s, Lord Derby, the Conservative Party leader, tried to tempt him back to his Tory roots. But each time, and with some reluctance, Gladstone turned him down. Why?

- Gladstone could not stomach the prospect of working with Disraeli. They were not merely rivals for pre-eminence: they came to loathe each other. Gladstone believed Disraeli's immorality and opportunism threatened to corrupt British politics. Disraeli, in turn, regarded Gladstone as an insufferable and self-deceiving prig.
- Gladstone was highly ambitious, and was desperate to be in government. But the Tories practically never *were* in government. They lost every general election between 1841 and 1874! Purely for the sake of his own career, there was only one choice for Gladstone: the Liberals.
- Gladstone was also supremely conscious of his energies and abilities, which out of office (as he was for most of the 1850s), were going to waste. He shared with Peelite friends–and Radicals–an anxiety that vital British institutions–the ancient Universities, the Civil Service, and the Army–needed shaking out of their privileged complacency. The British performance in the Crimean War (1854–6) certainly gave no cause for confidence. Only a party with a stable parliamentary majority and a broad popular mandate would be strong enough to take on the vested interests which were clogging up the arteries of national life. The 'Liberal Party' seemed capable of doing the job. By contrast, the Tories lacked both the power and the will to execute vital reforms.
- Finally, in three vital policy areas, Gladstone was nearer to the Liberal way of thinking than he was to the Tories.
- First, religious policy. In the 1840s, Gladstone had had to abandon his early hopes that a revitalised Church of England might come to dominate the religious life of the whole nation. Instead, he was learning to live with, and make the most of, religious pluralism. British Liberalism, which combined a core of tolerant Anglicanism with distinctive Nonconformist influences, was ideally constituted to help Gladstone get the best out of all the strands of British Christianity. It was certainly more spiritually vital than mid-century Toryism.
- Secondly, economic policy. The 1853 budget had established Gladstone's reputation as Peel's political heir. Gladstone felt that the Tories could not match the Liberals in their commitment to the principles of Free Trade and retrenchment–a suspicion which Disraeli's shifty and abortive Budget of 1852 had confirmed (*see page 340*). The Liberals offered the best platform for the defence – and extension–of the principles of Peelite finance.
- Thirdly, foreign policy. Gladstone took a great interest in Italian

culture and politics. Until 1860, Italy was split up into a dozen states and provinces. They were mostly backward, sometimes despotic, and almost all dependent – directly or indirectly– on Austrian force to keep Italian nationalist and liberal forces down. Gladstone deplored this situation, and gave his full support to the cause of moderate Italian nationalism. Whigs and Radicals felt the same: but the Tories seemed either lukewarm or opposed to Italian unification. In April 1859, fighting broke out in northern Italy. Two months later, Gladstone joined leading Peelites, Radicals and Whigs at a meeting to express their solidarity with the Italian nationalists, and to co-ordinate their own efforts to bring down Derby's minority Tory government. Most historians regard this as marking the foundation of the Liberal Party. A new era in British politics – and in Gladstone's career – was about to open. Within weeks, Gladstone was back in government, as Palmerston's Chancellor of the Exchequer.

c *Chancellor again 1859–65*

Gladstone was to be Palmerston's Chancellor for six years. His budgets of the 1860s continued the themes of *laissez-faire* and retrenchment proclaimed in 1853. Already by 1860, import duties had been abolished on all but 15 articles. Income tax was raised to 10d (4 p) – but only as an emergency measure, to cover the financial mismanagement and military extravagance which Gladstone claimed had characterised government while he was out of office! To sweeten this pill, Gladstone promised its progressive reduction–which he was to achieve (income tax was at 6d by 1865). But for all his forecasts, its abolition was to prove elusive: little wars and war-scares just seemed to keep on happening.

There were some new features in the budget, like the abolition of paper duties, with its wide-ranging political consequences (*see pages 249–50*). Also important was a Treaty with France (1860) for mutual tariff reduction. This was negotiated, under Gladstone's auspices, at a time of great international tension between the two countries. Many, including Palmerston, believed war a distinct possibility. To Gladstone, the impetus the Treaty would give to trade was less important than the prospect that greater trade would 'bind the two countries together by interest and affection'.

But Palmerston did not share Gladstone's internationalism, or his hopes that the threat from France was to be so easily or cheaply defused. Accordingly, to his Chancellor's dismay, he decided to press on with a programme of naval construction and fortification which seemed set to wreck the prospects of tax reduction. The debate in

Cabinet was intense and recurrent. Despite repeated threats of resignation, the iron clad ships were built. Gladstone retreated – and stayed in office.

What had Gladstone achieved as Chancellor in the 1850s and 1860s? He had made Liberalism synonymous with Free Trade, and low-taxing, low-spending government, as well as supremely competent administration. His own reputation rose higher, and spread wider. Gladstone's technical expertise was admired by the political elite, while his tax cuts left more money in ordinary people's pockets. He was becoming a popular hero.

But on closer inspection, the scale of Gladstone's achievements invites qualification. The passion and drama with which Gladstone presented his budgets was remarkable. But their contents, in essentials, were not. Gladstone was the inheritor rather than the creator of a tradition of public finance. In the history of liberal political economy, Peel, for his political courage, and even Liverpool's financial expert Huskisson, for his intellectual boldness, have greater claims to fame.

Has too much been claimed for this tradition anyway? Economic historians now dispute how far Free Trade contributed to Britain's economic recovery in the 1840s and 1850s. The natural cycle of slump and boom may well have progressed without Peel's encouragement. Even if Peel can claim to be one of the architects of mid-Victorian prosperity, Gladstone as Chancellor cannot. Rather, it was his good fortune to be responsible for administering the government's finances for much of the boom of the 1850s and 1860s. Then, a uniquely dynamic economy guaranteed the Chancellor his surpluses: he had the pleasant task of deciding how to give them away. Gladstone was a superb administrator, with a remarkable vision of the social and moral implications of his policies. His Chancellorships elevated him to the threshold of party leadership. But we must not forget that he was lucky enough to be in the right place at the right time.

D *The People's William*

With his second spell as Chancellor (1859–66), Gladstone's place near the top of British politics was secure, but he remained a strangely isolated figure. All acknowledged his great talents. But many – Whigs as well as Tories – found his arrogance and self-righteousness practically intolerable. He was also highly unpredictable. Salisbury, the future Conservative Prime Minister, wrote that 'no psychologist that has ever existed' could fathom his motives. Less kindly, Clarendon (before long to be Gladstone's Foreign Secretary!) put the rumour about that a leading medical authority had claimed that Gladstone was so imbalanced that he would die insane.

The explosive growth of popular support for Gladstone in the 1860s made such suspicions and resentments largely irrelevant for the progress of his career. He became 'The People's William', building up an extraordinary personal relationship with large sections of the British middle and working classes.

In chapter VII, the rise of the labour aristocracy, with its new model unions has been traced. From the early 1860s, Gladstone was in contact with their representatives, and was invariably impressed by their sense of 'responsibility' – for example, by their thrifty desire to make use of his newly established Post Office Savings Bank. Equally important, the labour aristocracy believed they had an ally in Gladstone.

We can trace something of Gladstone's feelings as this relationship developed from the following extracts from his diaries. The first recalls some of the scenes attending his headline catching visit to Tyneside in 1862. The second records an anxious moment of reflection following similar triumphs in Bolton, Liverpool and Manchester in 1864.

> 8 Wed [October, 1862]
>
> Reached Gateshead at 12 and after an address and reply embarked in the midst of a most striking scene which was prolonged and brightened as we went down the river at the head of a fleet of some 25 steamers amidst the roar of guns and with the banks lined or dotted above and below with great multitudes of people. The expedition ended at six, and I had as many speeches as hours. Such a pomp, I probably shall never again witness: circumstances have brought upon me what I do not in any way deserve.
>
> 14 Fri. [October, 1864]
>
> Off at 9 to Manchester. There, taken first, by the Mayor and Town Clerk, to M'Lachlan the Photographer. Then to the Town Hall to receive Address. Spoke an hour in reply.
> Then to the Exchange: some 8000 persons–said a word. Then to the Mayor's Luncheon: and at 2 to the Free Trade Hall, where some 6000 persons, some said 7000, were present. Distributed the Prizes and Certificates: and spoke I suppose 45m with considerable effort from the vastness of the crowd.
> Reached Worsley at 5.0 pm: and so ended in peace an exhausting, flattering, I hope not intoxicating circuit. God knows I have not courted them: I hope I do not rely on them: I pray I may turn them to account for good. It is however impossible not to love the people from whom such manifestations come, as met me in every quarter.
> A pleasant and calm evening and not too early rest. Somewhat haunted by dreams of halls, and lines of people, and great assemblies.

1 *What evidence is there in these passages that Gladstone was becoming 'The People's William'?*

2 *Why was Gladstone anxious about his growing popularity? How did he reassure himself? How convinced are you by his self-justification?*

This ability to short-circuit the little world of the high political elite, combined with his proven administrative powers, made him the likeliest successor to the Liberal leadership. But the virtuous passion of his followers was more than a means to his personal advancement. Gladstone knew that it could be tapped and channelled, to reinvigorate and energise the executive and give it the strength to tackle problems which, since the fall of Peel, it had mostly seemed too feeble to face.

The emotional and moral roots of Gladstone's hold over his popular audience has been sensitively explored by historians like Vincent (*see bibliography, page 295*). In part, the working men who thronged to see him were simply flattered by his presence: Gladstone was one of the very first nineteenth-century politicians to condescend to address the people at all. But what made Gladstone unique was his moral grandeur. The people sensed Gladstone's passionate commitment to justice, and he flattered their growing sense of personal independence and moral integrity by inviting them to share the trials of his fight for what was right.

We can understand something of the impact Gladstone was having on his newly discovered audience from the following Address presented to him by some representatives of the working men of York in 1864.

> You have spoken words that have sunk deep into the hearts of every working man in every corner of the land. We thank you from our inmost souls. We look upon you as a powerful and consistent advocate of our cause, and may God preserve your life. That you may continue to be the sound and impartial statesman–the friend of the poor, seeking simple justice to all – is the fervent wish and desire of the working men of this ancient city.

Gladstone was beginning to earn something of the reputation of a Radical. The abolition of paper duties, finally forced through by Gladstone in 1861, was important here. These 'taxes on knowledge' had long been resented by radicals, for they tended to put the price of newspapers beyond the reach of the working classes, and left *The Times* with an unhealthy position of dominance in the formation of public opinion. The fact that the House of Lords at first resisted Gladstone's plans only added to his reputation as an opponent of privilege.

The popular press proved eager to repay Gladstone for ending the near-monopoly of *The Times*. They gave his speeches and public tours generous and approving coverage. With the circulation of the *Daily*

Telegraph – then a Liberal paper – leaping to 150 000 in 1861 (more than twice that of *The Times*). Gladstone could afford to lose the latter's support. Particularly important was the role of the rapidly expanding radical provincial newspapers like the *Leeds Mercury* and the *Newcastle Chronicle*. These were to become the essential means of communication between Gladstone and his new audience, and powerful local opinion formers in their own right.

By now, Gladstone's colleagues were becoming alarmed. Whigs prided themselves on their responsiveness to the genuine grievances of the people, but they had no time for demagoguery, and viewed popular excitement with the greatest suspicion. To some, it seemed as though Gladstone was set on becoming the mob's pet. Their worst fears were confirmed in 1864 when he made the following startling declaration: 'every man who is not presumably incapacitated by some consideration of personal unfitness or of political danger is morally entitled, to come within the pale of the Constitution'. For a moment, Gladstone had sounded like an advocate of manhood suffrage, and in the uproar that followed it was easy to miss the significance of the potentially severe limitations to his proposed extension of the franchise.

Palmerston, for one, was furious. He expressly denied that 'every sane and not disqualified man [had] a moral right to vote'. After all, as he had earlier quipped, it was the unhealthy characteristic of democracies that the scum always came to the top. Gladstone was upbraided: his speech had been fit for a radical agitator, not a member of the Queen's Cabinet.

Gladstone professed himself to be perplexed. He denied attempting to whip up popular pressure to force the Cabinet to adopt his own preferred policies. The extension of the franchise would anyway be a just and essentially conservative act: the labour aristocracy, in its maturity and responsibility, merited the privilege of the vote. To deny them would risk their alienation and might ultimately turn them into enemies of the existing constitution. A concession now, he implied, would cement class harmony as surely as had the Repeal of the Corn Laws, or his own budgets.

Only Palmerston's death in 1865 ended this battle of wills. Lord John Russell took over as the Liberal leader, with Gladstone as his deputy. 'Little Johnnie', who had been one of the Whigs' heroes in the crisis surrounding the Great Reform Act, hoped to end his career with a matching triumph, and gave Gladstone the job of devising a new measure for Parliamentary Reform.

If Gladstone had managed to pass his Second Reform Bill in 1866, his career as the People's William would have been fully consummated. But some right-wing Whigs, bewildered and resentful at Gladstone's radicalism and unpredictability, helped to defeat his Bill and split the Liberals. It was only Disraeli's extraordinary political manoeuvrings which secured a (surprisingly Radical) instalment of parliamentary reform in 1867. (*For this see pages 341–8*). Whatever the risks he took, Disraeli had certainly humiliated Gladstone and exposed the tensions within the Liberal Party. Before we examine how successfully Gladstone reunited the various strands of Victorian Liberalism, we need to examine its make-up.

4 THE LIBERAL PARTY: COMPONENTS AND TENSIONS

On Russell's retirement (1867), Gladstone became leader of the Liberal Party. His proven executive capacities and the unique bonds joining him to the Liberal rank and file made his claims irresistible. But the party which he led was an unstable creation. By modern standards it was hardly recognisable as a party at all. There was no national membership and no annual national conference. Elections themselves might be fought on a 'cry' (e.g. 'Disestablishment' in 1868 – *see page 256*) which committed each MP to vote for a particular bill, but there were no official party manifestos. It needed someone of Gladstone's charisma to transcend these deficiencies, and give 'party' the cohesion necessary to support any programme of legislation.

A *Whigs*

Until the 1890s, the core of the party was provided by the Whigs. The ideal Whig was a wealthy aristocratic landowner who could trace his family line, and political allegiance, well back into the eighteenth century, or even beyond. The Whigs believed that they were born with a right to rule, and even after Gladstone became Liberal leader, they could expect to fill half or more of the seats in Cabinet. In fact, this should not surprise us, for Gladstone had profoundly elitist theories of government which would have shocked his radical allies, and he was always pleased to be able to surround himself with talented aristocrats.

The Whigs' effortless self-confidence was the fruit of their sense of tradition, service and achievement. It was the Whigs' duty to lead the people and protect their freedoms – listening to their grievances, interpreting their wishes and moderating their demands. They were also obliged to uphold the framework of law and order which protected the rights of property and prevented liberty from sliding towards anarchy. The Whigs believed that it was because they combined a love of order with political sensitivity and imagination that the country had been spared a bloody revolution, not least in 1831–2. Instead, Britain had enjoyed a unique combination of constitutional progress and social and economic improvement. The political stability, class harmony and unparalleled prosperity of Mid-Victorian Britain were the fruits of a

Whig civilisation – so the Whigs believed.

Gladstone shared some of these values and this sense of achievement. The Whigs respected his superb administrative skills and knew that his mastery of the public platform and the press gave their party access to sources of political support that they were incapable of mobilising themselves. The more perceptive sensed his reverence for tradition and aristocracy, and trusted his judgement that radical means could serve conservative ends. His influence over Radicals and Nonconformists was the best hope of containing the threat to property, hierarchy and the Establishment which these outsiders were held to pose.

In other Whigs, however, suspicions of Gladstone grew. His arrogance and high Tory origins had made him insufferable enough in the 1840s and 1850s. But his transformation into the People's William in the early 1860s was too much for them to stomach. He seemed to be pandering to the masses like a demagogue. His radical lurches were as rash as they were unpredictable. Clarendon, the Foreign Secretary (1865–6 and 1868–70) could not contain his bile and paranoia. According to him, Gladstone's 'insatiable desire for popularity' made him 'a far more sincere Republican than Bright [a Radical leader], for his ungratified personal vanity makes him wish to subvert the institutions and the classes that stand in the way of his ambition.' Gladstone's High Churchmanship was another problem. It ran against the grain of traditional Whiggery, with its suspicion of 'superstition' and clerical power.

It is hardly surprising that Stanley, the leading Tory, wondered how long Gladstone and the Whigs could work together. 'His colleagues detest him, and make little scruple in saying so ... [and] he is complained of as overbearing and dictatorial ... ' It was to be more than 20 years before the Gladstone/Whig fault line was to generate the political earthquake of the party split of 1886, but the dangers and tensions were there from the start.

B *Radicals and Nonconformists*

The Whigs' anxieties over Gladstone were compounded in the 1870s and after by their fears of the growing influence of Radicalism and Nonconformity within the Party. Radicalism is notoriously difficult to define. Not all Radicals were Nonconformists, although there was a considerable overlap between the two categories. In general Radicals were the fiercest in their denunciations of aristocratic abuses and inefficiency. They believed that, in alliance with the working classes, they could transform society so that individual effort might be fully rewarded, and privilege and inherited power smashed.

Since the 1840s, Nonconformists had also been growing more politically assertive. Emboldened by the startling 1851 census, which revealed that nearly half of English and Welsh churchgoers were dissenters, Nonconformist leaders like the Congregationalist minister Edward Miall decided that their voice deserved to be heard more widely and listened to more carefully. With only 38 out of 656 MPs Nonconformists in 1852, they had some work to do.

For 200 years, Nonconformists had suffered discrimination at the hands of the Establishment. The Test and Corporation Acts had only been repealed in 1828 (*see page* 23). Other examples of religious inequality still rankled, leaving Nonconformists resentful of the stigma of second-class citizenship. They were effectively barred from entry to the Universities of Oxford and Cambridge until the 1850s. They even had contribute to the upkeep or development of Anglican churches through a compulsory rates payment until 1868.

Through their own agitation and Whig sympathy and parliamentary support, they had succeeded in having most of the offending legislation removed from the statute books by the time of Gladstone's First Ministry. But one fundamental grievance remained: the status, privileges and wealth of the Established Church of England. Miall's Liberation Society (founded in 1853) aimed at its disestablishment and disendowment, i.e. the breaking of its links with the state and the redistribution of its assets. Here, most Nonconformists parted company with the Whigs. The Whigs believed that a reformed state church could still be a great force for good in society – indeed, in an ideal world, Nonconformists might rejoin it. Furthermore, they argued that some state control of the Church was needed to keep its more extreme elements (they were thinking of some of Gladstone's High Church friends) under control. Anglican fears that Nonconformists might ultimately take over the Liberal Party and disestablish the Church were to help undermine support for Gladstone in the 1870s and 1880s.

Disestablishment was the most important objective of Radicals and Nonconformists, but it was by no means the only one. Numerous political pressure groups sprang up in mid-Victorian England, incidentally providing the Liberals with some much needed organisational backbone. Inspired by the vision of preachers who believed that Britain could be transformed into a truly Christian society, Nonconformists saw it as their duty to drive down manifestations of sinfulness and purify the land. The United Kingdom Alliance aimed to vanquish drunkenness by closing down public houses. The National Education League urged the creation of a nationwide system of free and compulsory primary school education, combating vice by combating ignorance. Others campaigned against capital punishment or state-licensed prostitution (implicitly sanctioned by the Contagious Diseases Act).

The Nonconformists' ambition and self-confidence had various roots. They were certain of the God-given righteousness of their cause and of its ultimate victory. Their numbers were still growing: a religious revival swept Wales in the 1860s stirring the valleys and breaking the hold of Anglican Toryism over the counties. Nonconformist businessmen dominated the political life of most of the great northern towns, and generally enjoyed the support of their workers, who by and large shared their dissenting beliefs. Religious affiliation, indeed, was far more important than class in determining political outlook in mid-Victorian Britain, and to be a Nonconformist factory owner, grocer, artisan or machine-hand was, in all likelihood, to be a Liberal. Employer and employee often shared the same moral and social vision, regarding themselves jointly as the agents of progress, working in harmony to produce the nation's wealth. The aristocracy by contrast, supposedly idle and decayed, contributed nothing. Model housing developments for their workers, or parliamentary support in the 1860s for pro-trade union legislation, were the practical expressions of class harmony. The brotherhood of man was no pious cliché for many a Nonconformist industrialist. Against such an alliance, the citadels of aristocratic inefficiency and privilege – like the army and the civil service – could surely not hold out unreformed for long.

That Gladstone, passionate Anglican that he was, became the popular hero of Nonconformity is one of the more puzzling paradoxes of mid-Victorian politics. In part, Gladstone's intentions were simply misunderstood. Gladstone's enthusiasm for the disestablishment of the Irish Church, for example, was taken by many Nonconformists (and some worried Whigs) as evidence of an unspoken desire to disestablish the Church of England. In reality Gladstone would do all he could to avoid such a catastrophe. There were, however, real and powerful reasons for the mutual attraction of Gladstone and Nonconformity. They shared a religious zeal and moral earnestness unusual even in the Victorian era. Both believed that making Britain into a more just and truly Christian society should be the ultimate aim of political life, and in Nonconformity, Gladstone believed he had found an ideal instrument for his evangelical mission. Its classlessness matched his own ideal of social harmony and selflessness, and its organisations reached into many dark corners of the land – notably the big industrial cities – where, sadly, the established Church had failed to penetrate.

Gladstone had less in common with the out-and-out Radical: his instincts were in many ways traditionalist. But Gladstone did not see mid-victorian Radicalism as a threat. For one thing, its internal divisions made its power less ominous than the Tory press liked to pretend. But more positively, in two important respects, Gladstone and the Radicals shared common ground. First, Gladstone was an energetic reformer and, as he grew older, a progressively bolder critic of aristocratic privilege and selfishness. Secondly, the fundamental objectives of the Radicals were not in fact drastic social revolution or the pillage of the rich through punitive taxation – contrary to what Conservatives like Salisbury put about! They wanted nothing less than a better world. Their social programme was subsumed within a vague, universal humanitarianism. Gladstone's crusades for justice in Ireland (1868–9), the Balkans (1876–8), South Africa and Afghanistan (1879–80) and Ireland again (1886) moved them as no secular plans for land reform or county councils could ever do. For Gladstone touched their souls.

How were these various shades of Liberal opinion reflected in the Parliamentary Liberal Party? If a broad definition of the term 'Whig' is adopted, including great landowners and landed gentry as well as members of aristocratic families, just over two-fifths of Liberals in the Commons in 1874 can be called Whigs. By comparison, only a little over one-third of the Parliamentary Liberal Party were industrialists and merchants. Some of these would themselves be significant landowners: they were certainly not all radicals and/or Nonconformists. It is misleading to try and split the Liberal Party at Westminster into distinctive camps, especially ones at war with each other.

It is often assumed that the Whigs were in retreat, numerically and politically, throughout the Gladstonian era. But T A Jenkin's recent analysis (*see bibliography page 295*) of the balance of forces within the parliamentary party in 1880 suggests otherwise: indeed there was even a slight increase in the size of the aristocratic – landowning bloc relative to the rest. The Whigs seem to have been the largest Liberal social group in the Commons until 1885. Although the northern industrialists and their workers were the most dynamic section of the national party, they were far from dominating the party at Westminster. The fact that only 64 of the 382 Liberal MPs returned in 1868 were Nonconformist makes the gap between provincial and parliamentary Liberalism even more explicit.

These facts invite reconsideration of some of the received ideas about Gladstonian Liberalism. Given the numerical weakness of Radicalism at Westminster and its internal divisions, it seems likely that the decline of the Whigs as a political force has been pre-dated, and its inevitability exaggerated. It follows that the analysis of the internal dynamics of the Liberal Party in terms of Radical/Whig tensions needs reassessment. In particular, we need to reconsider the role of Gladstone himself.

The diversity, and potential incoherence and instability of the forces which made up the Gladstonian Liberal Party are striking. Historians inevitably focus on Gladstone to explain how it was all held together. He was the keystone of the Liberal arch. With his understanding of the Nonconformist conscience, his pre-eminence as the People's William, his financial radicalism and his desire to uphold the role of the aristocracy and Church Establishment, he uniquely was connected to all of the disparate strands of mid-Victorian Liberalism. But there is another side to the picture. At times – and increasingly often as Gladstone grew older – he could be a force for disruption. His very ambiguities bred misunderstanding and suspicion. He was never as Radical as his most energetic supporters imagined: ultimately he was guaranteed to disappoint them. Yet his very readiness to build bridges to Radicalism and Nonconformity, combined with his personal unpredictability and unfathomability, could all too easily make him a figure to bewilder and antagonise the Whigs. These tensions and misunderstandings were to unravel in the two decades following Gladstone's accession to the Liberal leadership.

5 Gladstone Comes to Power

Gladstone's task after the debacle of 1866–7 (*see pages 250–1*) was to reunite the Liberal Party and to win the forthcoming general election. He could not have found a better 'cry' for either purpose than the proposal to disestablish the Irish Church. The injustice of imposing an alien, Protestant institution on the overwhelmingly Catholic people of Ireland had become so blatant by 1868 that even few Conservatives could be found to defend it. The policy clearly had great appeal in Ireland itself, where in the elections the Liberals enjoyed one of their best performances of the century. But it was also designed to appeal to and reunite the various sections of the mainland party. To Nonconformists, it marked the first stage of a process that they hoped would climax in the disestablishment of the Church of England itself. To the Whigs, it would remove an absurdity whose unpopularity was a threat to law and order in Ireland. Radicals could celebrate an attack on a grotesquely privileged institution. All could join with Gladstone in a crusade for what was right. Gladstone himself had recognised since the Maynooth crisis of 1845 (*see pages 142–3*) that the only hope which might justify the existence of an Established Church in Ireland – that it might begin to convert the Catholics to Protestantism – was forlorn. It was far better to rescue the Church of Ireland from its false position, as much for the sake of the good name of Anglicanism as for the sake of the people of Ireland.

The general election produced an overwhelming Liberal majority: 387 seats against the Conservatives' 271. The call for Irish disestablishment had been the greatest vote winner, but the promise of land reform in Ireland, educational reform in Britain, and cheaper and more efficient government in general (firmly associated with Gladstone's name) had also made their mark. But this was by no means an agreed party manifesto, and some observers were soon wondering how long the Liberal Party would hold together.

The Cabinet was clearly weighted towards the centre-right of the party, although Gladstone did make one concession to Radical and Nonconformist sentiment in its construction. John Bright, a Quaker, veteran Anti-Corn Law League campaigner and ardent supporter of Parliamentary Reform, was made President of the Board of Trade.

Gladstone was to struggle hard, and unsuccessfully, to retain his services, despite his manifest ineptitude. But elsewhere, a high order of administrative skills, combined wherever possible with an aristocratic background, were the main conditions of entry for would-be ministers. Amongst the leading Whigs were the Earl of Granville and the Marquis of Hartington (soon to be promoted to Foreign Secretary and Chief Secretary for Ireland respectively). Lowe at the Exchequer and Goschen as President of the Poor Law Board seemed set to outdo Gladstone as proponents of retrenchment. Cardwell, at the War Office, was (Gladstone apart) the leading Peelite. Although most of the different strands which made up the Liberal Party had a voice in the Cabinet, the predominance of the Whigs, who occupied a total of seven out of the fifteen seats in Cabinet, is unmistakable.

Gladstone was to describe this Cabinet as 'one of the best instruments for government ever constructed'. His ministry certainly produced an exceptional volume of legislation and reforms, fearlessly taking on vested interests and deep-rooted problems. The cabinet was united and even-handed in its approach, brushing aside the special pleading of friends and opponents alike, with surprisingly little thought for electoral consequences. In part, this reflected a confidence, bordering on arrogance, that the Liberals were the natural party of government. The Tories, they believed, were too stupid, incompetent and selfish to win the confidence of the country. But they were also guided by a sense of duty, public service and self-sacrifice which would strike many modern politicians as quaint.

6 GLADSTONE AND IRELAND 1868–74

All these qualities would be brought to bear on the problem that was to dominate the ministry's first year, and, ultimately bring it down. Gladstone had placed Ireland at the forefront of his campaign: 'Ireland is at your doors. Providence has placed her there.' The people of Britain had answered Gladstone's call, and given him a popular mandate to end the abuses of British rule. Accordingly, the most important elements of Protestant power in Ireland were to come under attack in Gladstone's first ministry. These were the imposition on the Catholic majority of an alien church; the iniquities of the Protestant-dominated system of land owning; and the discrimination suffered by Catholics in education. Gladstone described these as the three branches of the tree of the Protestant ascendancy: 'a tall tree of noxious growth ... darkening and poisoning the land so far as its shadow can extend'. Gladstone, strengthened in his power and convictions by popular support, was now to take an axe to that tree.

The Irish Church Disestablishment Bill was Gladstone's own work, and a great technical feat in itself. As well as ending the Church of

Ireland's official status as the national church there, it aimed to reduce its endowments, redistributing about a third of its annual revenue to non-religious ends, like the improvement of workhouses or hospitals. The Lords tried to haggle over the terms offered and block the bill's progress, apparently ready to defy the clear popular mandate enjoyed by the Liberals in the Commons. A major constitutional crisis seemed inevitable. But behind-the-scenes negotiations, involving the Whig leader Granville and the Conservatives' leader in the Lords, as well as the Archbishop of Canterbury and Queen Victoria, defused the conflict. The Conservatives made most of the concessions. In July 1869, the bill to disestablish the Irish Church was passed.

Gladstone's motives for putting disestablishment on the political agenda when he did, remain controversial. Towards the end of his life, Gladstone was to identify 1868 as one of the golden moments of his career, when he had sensed that public opinion was ripe to be shaped and channelled to put right a long-standing injustice.

At the time, however, Gladstone seemed more concerned by the threat which he believed that the Fenians (revolutionary Irish Nationalists) were posing to law and order, and to the security of the Empire. 1867 had seen an upsurge in Fenian violence in mainland Britain and even an Irish-American incursion into Canada. Gladstone believed that only just laws would secure for the British government the support of moderate Irish opinion and leave the extremists isolated and impotent. These fears help to explain the earnestness and intensity with which Gladstone was to declare, on the eve of forming his first ministry, 'My mission is to pacify Ireland.'

Not all historians have been convinced by Gladstone's analysis of the situation, or of his own motives. In particular (as we have already noted) Gladstone's proposed solution to the Irish question was tailor-made to meet the immediate political needs of the Liberal Party. In his book *Politics without Democracy*, Michael Bentley has deflated Gladstone's heroic posturings brilliantly: Gladstone's real mission, he writes, was not so much to pacify Ireland as 'to pacify the Liberal Party.'

We must, however, be careful before assuming that political calculation and ambition can fully explain what Gladstone was about. If the quest for power, and power alone, was the fundamental driving force behind Gladstone, his determination to *continue* his mission with the Irish Land Act and especially the Irish Universities Bill becomes hard to understand. For as Gladstone knew very well, Land and Education were issues which would aggravate the stresses within the Liberal Party as surely as the disestablishment of the Irish church had soothed them.

The Irish Land question was as complicated as it was intractable. Gladstone himself, despite his massive reading into the subject, never seems to have grasped the sheer variety of Irish farming and land-holding practices. But he was convinced that 'the social and moral influence' of Irish landlords could be raised to that 'happily held as a class by the landlords of [England]'. If the British state could establish fair ground rules for landlord and tenant alike, and remedy legitimate grievances, the Irish might come to show to their superiors the deference and respect which Gladstone's tenants on his own estates at Hawarden doubtless displayed to him. The tenants of Hawarden, however, unlike their Irish counterparts, were not embittered by a growing conviction that the landlords' forefathers had stolen that land from their own forefathers in a brutal war of colonial conquest centuries earlier.

Gladstone struggled to appreciate the nationalist dimensions of the Land Question. He had little more success in negotiating the domestic political difficulties it raised. Here, it was the Whigs whose anxieties had to be eased. The Whigs were, by definition, landowning aristocrats, many of whom had extensive Irish estates. Therefore, the defence of the 'rights of property' – for example, the right to charge tenants a market rent and to be free to evict in the event of non-payment – was to many of them a matter of both self-interest and principle. Even those without Irish connections feared that if the rights of tenants were artificially extended in Ireland, radicals would soon be clamouring for similar innovations in mainland Britain. Palmerston himself had summed up the general rule: 'tenants' right was landlords' wrong'.

Gladstone's original plans for his Land Bill were quite ambitious. The problem was how to make a legal reality of the Irish tenant farmer's belief, entrenched in local tradition but ignored by contract law, that he was a co-proprietor of the land he farmed. Gladstone believed that the solution was to extend the customs of Ulster to the rest of Ireland. 'Ulster custom' gave the tenant greater security from eviction. Furthermore, should the Ulsterman decide to leave his farm, he would both receive compensation for any improvements he had made to the property (e.g. better drainage) and, most important, a payment from the new tenant for his share or 'interest' in the property.

By the time Gladstone's Cabinet colleagues had finished with their amendments, the Bill's intended scope was much reduced: the idea of extending 'Ulster custom' throughout Ireland was dropped, although where it was already practised it was now to be given the force of law. For the rest, the main concession was to provide compensation for eviction. An amendment forced on the Bill in the Lords even restricted the scope of this to extreme cases where the rent could be proved to have been 'exorbitant'. For all that Gladstone convinced himself that the Act would help bring about an era of happiness and social stability in Ireland, its progressive dilutions reduced it to a feeble measure.

The failings of the Act are, indirectly, a testimony to the power of the Whigs within Gladstone's Cabinet, and his capacity to defer to them. Nevertheless Gladstone's readiness to consider radical departures from the basic rights of property owners left many Whigs uneasy about what Gladstone would try out on them next. Indeed, Gladstone had got the worst of all worlds: undermining his colleagues' confidence in his judgement while failing to satisfy the expectations which the promise of legislation had created in Ireland.

A similar pattern repeated itself in 1873, when Gladstone finally brought the Irish Universities Bill before Parliament. The Irish Catholic hierarchy had long complained that their flock lacked a suitable university. Trinity College, Dublin, was the preserve of the Anglican elite, while the Catholic bishops themselves had damned the Queen's Colleges (founded by Peel) as 'godless', and as such, places which no Catholic could attend without jeopardising his soul. Instead, they demanded a properly endowed Catholic university, where the faith and morals of students could be protected and nurtured.

Gladstone never intended to give the Catholic hierarchy all that they wanted. He knew it would be a political impossibility: neither Whigs nor Nonconformists would stand for it. Furthermore, Gladstone had his own purposes to serve. He wanted to foster the creation of an independently-minded Catholic professional class, free from undue clerical influence, and fit to share in the leadership of Irish society. 'We *know* what we ought to give them whether they will take it or not,' he wrote.

Gladstone's Bill proposed a total restructuring of the Irish university system. A new, religiously-neutral University was to be created. Existing colleges – Anglican, Presbyterian or Catholic – could attach themselves, if they were prepared to accept central direction from the new University's Governing Body, which would set the examinations and award degrees. An unusual feature of the new University was that it would have no Professors to teach theology, modern history or philosophy. By these restrictions on potentially controversial subjects, Gladstone hoped to minimise the risk of sectarian strife breaking out.

Despite making the issue a vote of confidence, the Bill was defeated by three votes in March 1873. Gladstone offered to resign, but Disraeli preferred to wait for a general election rather than become, again, the vulnerable Prime Minister of a minority government. Despite this reprieve, Gladstone's ministry never recovered its momentum.

The Whigs and the Irish Liberals between them had brought about the Bill's defeat. The Whigs regarded it with a mixture of indifference and hostility. Many thought that Gladstone's restrictions on the syllabus were bizarre and anti-intellectual. Others, having studied the constitution of the proposed new University, feared that it would soon be dominated by the Catholic Church. The Protestant ascendancy had been bad, but the Whigs were not going to dismantle it to make way for a Catholic one, which would be infinitely worse. Hartington for one believed that Gladstone was always too ready to make concessions to the Catholics, and dangerously blind to the threat which the power of their priesthood, especially if it was allowed to get entrenched in the education system, might pose to progress and freedom in Ireland. This divergence of views on the Irish problem was to reach a dramatic climax 13 years later, when Hartington led the Whig revolt which ended Gladstone's plans to give the Irish Home Rule.

By contrast, the Irish Liberals revolted because they believed Gladstone had conceded too little to the Catholic case. They were here following the lead of the Irish Catholic hierarchy, which had refused to endorse a bill which failed to endow their own university. When added to the disappointing Land Act, this made Gladstone's boast that 'there is nothing that Ireland has asked and which this country and this Parliament have refused' look increasingly hollow. The Irish drew the natural conclusion: Ireland could not expect to have its true needs recognised or satisfied until she had her own Parliament in Dublin. Accordingly, 60 MPs sympathetic to Home Rule were returned by the Irish electorate in the 1874 general election. By the end of the decade, there were very few Irish MPs left who called themselves Liberal.

Despite this disturbing trend, Gladstone believed that his mission to pacify Ireland had been seen through to a successful end. His self-congratulation was premature. It is true that, from 1871, agrarian outrages fell into steep decline, and that the Fenians were moving away from a strategy of violence and insurrection. But it is hard to trace these improvements to the impact of Gladstone's legislation. The disestablishment of the Irish Church won Gladstone the goodwill of the Catholic bishops, but the inadequacy of his university proposals as surely lost it. Equally, how little the 1870 Land Act actually eased the plight of the desperately vulnerable small tenant farmers was revealed by the agricultural depression of the late 1870s, and the savage Land War that followed (*see pages 275–7*). Given the political constraints on Gladstone, in his cabinet, party and parliament, it might be argued in his defence that it is unlikely that anyone could have done more. But his capacity for self-delusion – amazed and outraged by the Catholic bishops' rejection of his university scheme, convinced until 1881 that his 1870 Bill had settled the Land question – invites us to doubt the accuracy of both his diagnosis and prescription. Far from having solved the Irish problem, it is arguable that the most significant, albeit unintended consequence, of the Irish legislation of his first ministry, was the growth of the Home Rule party.

7 THE DOMESTIC LEGISLATION OF GLADSTONE'S FIRST MINISTRY

A *Introduction*

Gladstone was personally responsible for little of the domestic legislation of 1868–74. Although the nine or ten major Acts of Parliament which crowd these years can be regarded as collectively embodying many of the principles of Gladstonian Liberalism, it is important to recognise that Gladstonianism and Liberalism were not one and the same thing. Gladstone's rhetoric could appear radical, but in practice his most passionate commitments were Peelite. He wished to modernise the nation's great institutions the better to preserve them, and at all times to defend the public good against the selfishness of powerful minorities. These objectives, and his lack of real enthusiasm for some of his ministry's most important reforms, invite a disconcerting conclusion: Gladstone put the conservatism into Gladstonian Liberalism.

A readiness to reform the inefficient and antiquated institutions of the state was evident in the Judicature Act (1873), which dramatically streamlined the operations of the Upper Courts of Law. Similarly, Robert Lowe, Gladstone's Chancellor of the Exchequer, increased the professionalism of the Civil Service by introducing recruitment by examination (as opposed to appointment by patronage) into most departments (1871).

Constitutionally speaking, the most important of the attacks on the old order was the Ballot Act (1872) which introduced secret voting. John Bright, the leading Radical, had long campaigned for this reform. He explained some of his reasons in his 1868 election address

> Whether I look to the excessive cost of elections, or the tumult which so often attends them, or to the unjust and cruel pressure which is so frequently brought to bear upon the less independent class of voters, I am persuaded that the true interest of the public and of freedom will be served by the system of secret and free voting.

Gladstone admitted to a 'lingering reluctance' to abandon the old system of open voting. His instinctive conservatism is also evident in his defensive response to Radical and Nonconformist demands for the opening to non-Anglicans of all teaching posts at Oxford and Cambridge Universities. The cause of religious equality here conflicted with Gladstone's own commitment to protect the interests of the Church of England. He was only able to maintain some privileges for Anglicans in his University Test Act (1871) with the help of

Conservative votes against his own backbenchers. Gladstone was disappointing some of those Radicals and Nonconformists who had made him their hero.

B *The Education Act 1870*

This pattern of voting across party lines, with its unhappy implications for Liberal unity, had first been seen during the passage of the Education Act (1870), perhaps the most important and controversial of all the domestic legislation of Gladstone's First Ministry. A string of Royal Commissions of Inquiry in the 1860s had made it commonplace amongst politicians of both parties that the British educational system was inadequate. Neither the Church of England-run National Schools nor the Nonconformists' British Schools had kept pace with the rapidly growing urban population. The implications of this were awful. How was Britain to retain its industrial lead with a largely ignorant, illiterate and innumerate workforce? Moral and spiritual peril seemed an even greater danger. To grow up in ignorance was to grow up incapable of self-improvement, and perhaps to be left languishing in godlessness, vice and criminality. The 'dangerous classes' had to be tamed. The 1867 Reform Act gave these fears greater urgency. Robert Lowe, one of the main opponents of Parliamentary Reform, had remarked pointedly that 'it will be absolutely necessary to compel our new masters to learn their letters.'

Although the problem was therefore recognised to be extremely pressing, it was equally obvious that any attempt to remedy it would involve grave political difficulties. Some all-embracing, national education scheme was widely called for. Yet this would entail a major extension of the role and power of the state in an age which deplored the idea of government intervention in society, and valued 'voluntaryism' – the ideal that the best way to meet social needs was through voluntary local initiatives – very highly. Any national scheme was also bound to be expensive.

Above all, education was a religious battlefield in which Anglicans and Nonconformists vied for the upper hand. Church of England schools outnumbered their rivals by roughly 3:1. Anglicans, organising themselves into the National Education Union (1869), were determined that this lead be maintained, and with it the distinctive religious identity of their schools. The Radical/Nonconformist-influenced National Education League (1869) by contrast, pressed for the absorption of the Anglican schools within a new nationwide system in which education would be free, and free of religious bias. The fact that many Whigs supported the Union, while many Radicals, notably their future leader Joseph Chamberlain, were prominent in the League, shows how vulnerable to fragmentation the Liberal Party was on this issue. Nevertheless, the government took the problem on.

The Education Act was mostly the work of W E Forster. He aimed to supplement the existing voluntary system rather than replace it, thereby saving money and continuing to draw on the energies of voluntaryism. The Education Department would find out which areas lacked adequate schools. There, elected School Boards were to be set up, empowered to raise money to build new ones.

Forster believed that he could solve the religious difficulty by allowing each School Board to decide the nature of the religious instruction to be given in its area. This was coupled with a 'conscience clause' to allow, for example, a Nonconformist parent to withdraw their children from lessons in which Anglican religious instruction was being given.

In fact, Forster had underestimated the sectarian fervour of Victorian Britain. There was widespread unease that a dangerous precedent was being set up for Irish primary education: the idea of possible future School Boards there providing Roman Catholic instruction with money raised in local taxes appalled many Liberals. But it was the Nonconformists who felt especially outraged by Forster's bill. It proposed to increase the amount of state aid given to existing Anglican schools. Where schools did not as yet exist, if Anglicans were in a local majority, they would be fully entitled, under the Act's provisions, to levy a rate on Nonconformists through a 'School Board', forcing them to contribute to the building of a Church of England school to 'fill in the gap'. As far as the Nonconformists could see, far from dismantling the Established Church's network of elementary schools, Forster seemed set on entrenching and extending it.

Compromise of a sort was finally reached in Parliament with the acceptance of an amendment put forward by a leading Whig MP, Cowper-Temple. His idea was that 'Board Schools' should base their religious lessons on a broad and simple bible-based Christianity. There was to be nothing distinctively Anglican or Nonconformist in style about the instruction offered.

Not all Liberals, however, could support this. Gladstone himself agreed only very reluctantly: he wrote that in accepting it, he had 'never made a more painful concession to the desire for [party] unity'. He feared that 'Cowper-Temple religion', as he dismissively called it, would dilute the eternal truths of the Anglican faith and prove too lukewarm to inspire zeal or fervent belief. Radicals regretted that attendance was to be neither compulsory nor free. Hard-line Nonconformists felt badly let down too. The Government's education legislation had failed to advance the cause of Nonconformity. Instead, in vote after vote, Nonconformists had been left in a minority, outnumbered by a broad front of Anglican Liberals and Anglican Conservatives. They felt this humiliation deeply. Temporarily at least, there was a rupture between the party leader and his Nonconformist foot-soldiers.

Any judgement of the importance of the 1870 Education Act must be carefully balanced. It is typical of Gladstonian Liberalism in its scale, ambition and political courage. It met the responsibility of the executive to serve the national interest, however difficult the task. Although it was only a stage in the extension of educational provision in nineteenth-century Britain (elementary education was not made compulsory until 1881, and was not free until 1891), it was a vital one, for with Forster's Act, the state had come near to recognising a duty to provide some education for all.

Clearly this principle would have dramatic social consequences. It advanced the great Liberal aim of empowering individuals to make more of themselves and their talents. Gladstone, however, had little interest in the social dimensions of education policy. His preoccupation was with its religious implications, and especially the need to uphold the teachings and influence of the Church of England in the nation's schools, which the increased state-grant for Anglican schools had helped to strengthen. The creation of a 'meritocracy' with 'equality of opportunity' was never one of his objectives. He remained too attached to principles of hierarchy, deference and aristocracy for that.

c *Army reforms*

Gladstone's belief in aristocracy did not preclude him from attacking privilege, especially where it posed a threat to the national good. His vigorous support of Cardwell's programme of army reforms is a striking example of this. Amateurism and incompetence were undermining the army's strength, as its poor performance in the Crimean War had shown. Cardwell, the Minister for War, was a Peelite to his fingertips. He examined the problem dispassionately, and by redesigning the whole pattern of regimental service, organisation and command, was able both to save money and leave the army a more efficient fighting force.

The most important reform was the abolition of purchase, i.e. the practice by which wealthy young men, often with aristocratic connections, could buy themselves into the officer class, regardless of their fitness for command. This struck Cardwell and Gladstone as a gross abuse: potentially, the interests of the nation might be jeopardised by the selfishness and incompetence of the privileged few. But the few were well represented in the Lords and on the Tory backbenches in the Commons. They put up prolonged and vehement resistance to Cardwell. Gladstone ultimately had to invoke the Royal prerogative to bypass the Lord's obstructionism, a controversial manoeuvre which infuriated the military-aristocratic elite.

The affair had significant consequences. It marks a turning point in Gladstone's relation with 'the classes' i.e. the upper ten thousand of Victorian society. Gladstone was appalled by the 'folly and selfishness' which 'the classes' displayed in the conflict over army purchase. From now on, Gladstone showed an increasing readiness to align himself with the people – or 'the masses' – against 'the classes'. Although he still believed in the ideal of aristocracy, there seemed to be fewer and fewer aristocrats ready to devote themselves to the service of the nation. Instead, he believed that the aristocracy, corrupted by wealth, was becoming obsessed with the defence of privilege and the pursuit of pleasure. The masses, by contrast, had the keenest moral sense and the truest appreciation of the needs of the nation. The Bible itself taught, so Gladstone believed, that the poor were 'better and wiser than the rich'.

This radical rhetoric, one of Gladstone's great themes of the 1870s and 1880s, reached its climax in the speech made in June 1886 to the electors of Liverpool (*see exercise pages 298–9*). It helps explain why Gladstone seemed such an extremist to many of his contemporaries – at times like an agitator talking the language of class war. This doubtless added to the appeal of the People's William. But his populism worried the Whigs, while 'the classes' in general began to regard him with fear and loathing.

D *Trade union reform*

The fact that Gladstone came to value the political judgement of the masses more and more did not mean that he singled out the working classes for any acts of legislative favouritism. This is clearest from the thrust of his Trade Union reforms. Despite the emergence of the self-consciously respectable New Model Unions of skilled workers (*see page 225*) many Victorians continued to regard Trade Unions with great suspicion. Some industrialists believed they were a menace to profits, while the Sheffield Outrages – where an overzealous trade union official had tried to encourage a non-member to join up by blowing up his house with gun-powder – received great publicity. These problems had prompted Disraeli to appoint a Royal Commission of Inquiry. Its findings in 1867, largely sympathetic to the cause of responsible trade unionism, formed the basis for the Liberals' legislation.

The Trade Union Act (1871) was designed to establish their legal rights beyond doubt. But the Criminal Law Amendment Act (1871), especially as interpreted by Justices of the Peace, made picketing practically impossible, and consequently the organisation of effective strikes very difficult. Gladstone can be seen here trying, not completely successfully, to balance the competing claim of employer and employee while above all defending the rights of the individual. Peaceful collective bargaining was sanctioned; but intimidation and violence were quite prohibited.

Gladstone had clearly resisted the temptation which might have been strong after the Second Reform Act to do organised labour any special favours. Gladstone believed that it was the instinct of all groups in society – from the aristocracy to the working classes – to 'exaggerate their rights', as he put it. It had been one of the prime functions of government since the days of Peel to challenge such pretentions. The speed with which Disraeli made his bid for working-class support with the Conspiracy and Protection of Property Act of 1875 (*see page 355*), which repealed the Criminal Law Amendment Act, reveals how far he operated on different political principles.

E *Towards defeat*

In fact, the legislation of Gladstone's first ministry had annoyed a wide range of sectional interests with heroic impartiality. The trade union legislation doubtless cost working-class votes in the 1874 election. Some workers had already been annoyed by the Licensing Act of 1872. This restricted the opening hours of public houses and authorised magistrates to close some down in areas where there were too many. Drunkenness was a blight on Victorian society, but Conservatives were able to make great play with this supposed example of moralising interference by the government with the freedom of the working man to pursue his pleasures. Not surprisingly, the Act also turned the large and influential Brewers' and Publicans' trades against the Liberals. Yet the United Kingdom Alliance, the important Nonconformist temperance pressure group, regarded the legislation as much too mild: they had wanted local councils to be given the power to enforce total prohibition. Other Nonconformists, stirred up by Chamberlain, were still fuming about the Education Act. By 1874, the commitment of Nonconformist and working-class activists to the Liberal cause was weaker than it had been for a decade.

Gladstone had given the Establishment a battering too. Privilege had been forced into retreat in the Civil Service and Army. Die-hard Anglicans resented the fate of their Church in Ireland, Oxford and Cambridge. Property-owners were anxious at the implications of the Irish Land Act in particular and the rise of Radicalism in general. Disraeli's claim that the ministry had 'harassed every trade, worried every profession, and assailed or menaced every class, institution and species of property in the country' struck a chord. Even moderate Liberals wondered what Gladstone would do next. Some outrageous concession to Irish Catholics or British Nonconformists was unfairly, but widely feared.

Gladstone and his ministers had simply been too busy. Competence in government rather than perpetual legislative innovation was what the electorate expected. But after a decade of Palmerstonian stagnation, such a programme was precisely what Gladstone believed the country had needed. He was convinced, in his own words, that the 'vital principle of the Liberal Party is action'. Legislative activity kept it together.

But when the country tired of its exertions, and came to fear to what purposes its energies would be put next, it was time to seek some peace and stability. In 1874, even Disraeli looked a safer bet than Gladstone.

Gladstone's first ministry had marked a departure from Palmerston's style in foreign policy too. In place of the bluster and belligerence of Pam's 'gun-boat diplomacy', Gladstone sought compromise and conciliation – notably over the *Alabama* affair (*see pages 194–5*). Many observers, however, regarded this performance as spineless. Disraeli made great play of the Liberals' supposed inability to stand up for British interests in the world (*see pages 349–51*). The Conservatives, he claimed, were the truly patriotic party. The skill with which Disraeli draped himself and his party in the Union Jack was not the least of the reasons why Gladstone was defeated in 1874.

8 DOCUMENTARY EXERCISE – THE GENERAL ELECTION OF 1874

The Liberal electoral defeat of 1874 surprised many politicians and political commentators. Gladstone' own diagnoses, made in a letter to his brother, in part blamed the indiscipline of the government's radical and nonconformist critics. 'But', Gladstone continued, 'more immediately operative causes have determined the elections. I have no doubt what is the principal. We have been borne down in a torrent of gin and beer. Next to this has been the action of the Education Act of 1870 and the subsequent controversies'.

The analysis offered to Gladstone by a Whig colleague, Lord Halifax, was rather different

> As far as I can make out people are frightened – the masters were afraid of their workmen, manufacturers afraid of strikes, churchmen afraid of the nonconformist . . . and in very unreasoning fear have all taken refuge in Conservatism.

The third analysis comes from Frederic Harrison – an intellectual and journalist of strong Radical convictions

> The real truth is that the middle class, or its effective strength, has swung round to Conservatism. Conservatism no doubt . . . of a vague and negative kind; but its practical effect is an undefined preference for 'leaving well alone'. When we look at the poll in the City of London, in Westminster, in Middlesex, in Surrey, in Liverpool, Manchester, Leeds and Sheffield, in the metropolitan boroughs and in the home counties, in all the centres of middle-class industry wealth and cultivation, we see one unmistakable fact, that the rich trading class, and the comfortable middle class has grown distinctly Conservative.

There are no special causes at work in these great constituencies. Beer has no influence with the merchants, shopkeepers and citizens of London . . . The Conservative Party has become as much the middle-class party as the Liberal used to be, as much and more. The sleek citizens, who pour forth daily from thousands and thousands of smug villas round London, Manchester and Liverpool, read their Standard and believe that the country will do very well as it is. There is nothing now exclusive about the Conservative Party. Conservatism has opened its arms to the middle-classes, and has reaped its just reward.

1 **a)** *Re-read pages 263–5 and explain how the Liberal Party had been damaged by the Education Act.*

b) *What does Gladstone mean when he claimed 'we have been borne down in a torrent of gin and beer'? Why was the 'drink interest' a tempting and easy target for Gladstone?*

2 *How far do Halifax and Harrison converge in their analysis of the Liberal defeat?*

3 *Which analysis or analyses, if correct, would be the most dangerous for the future prospects of Liberalism? Which do you find most convincing, and why?*

4 *Can you identify any important causes for the defeats which are not mentioned in these extracts?*

9 Discussion points

A *This section consists of questions or points that might be used for discussion (or written answers) as a way of expanding on the chapter and testing understanding of it.*

1 In what respects had Gladstone moved away from his early High Church Toryism by the time of the Repeal of the Corn Laws?

2 What policies did Gladstone pursue as Chancellor under Aberdeen and Palmerston, and how did his performance as Chancellor advance his career?

3 'Gladstone's move towards the Liberals owed more to opportunism and rivalry with Disraeli than to questions of principle'. How far do you agree with this?

4 How did Gladstone emerge as 'The People's William', and with what political consequences?

5 Why did the Whigs feel so ambivalent towards Gladstone?

6 What qualities did Victorian Nonconformity add to Victorian Liberalism?

7 'The 1870 Education Act served the national interest much better than it served the political needs of the Liberal Party.' Do you agree?

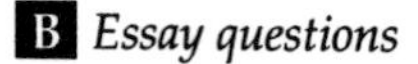

B *Essay questions*

1 Given the contrasts and tensions between Gladstone and the constituent parts of the Liberal Party, how can we explain his emergence as party leader in 1868?

2 'A heroic failure'. Is this a fair verdict on the Irish legislation of Gladstone's first ministry?

3 What was 'Liberal' about the non-Irish domestic legislation of Gladstone's first ministry?

A bibliography for Gladstone can be found at the end of the next chapter.

IX

GLADSTONE PART II: POLITICS AS CRUSADE

—

1 RETIREMENT?

GLADSTONE was 65-years-old when his first ministry came to its end. Had anyone foretold that he had another 20 years ahead of him at the centre of British politics, Gladstone would have been startled and incredulous. He wanted – at least he told himself he wanted – to retire. Had he not travelled far enough already in his political lifetime, and (although a sense of his own worthlessness in the face of God would have checked the reflection), achieved much? What more had he to offer? And surely death itself could not be too far away?

More immediate political considerations pushed him towards retirement. The election defeat by Disraeli had been a crushing reversal. Gladstone himself had determined the timing of the election, and he had devised the 'cry' – a promise to abolish income tax – on which the Liberals had fought it. Tax-paying voters seem to have been sceptical about the promise – after all, it was not the first time Gladstone had made it – while to the hundreds of thousands of voters below the income tax threshold who had been enfranchised by Disraeli in 1867, it offered no benefits at all. Gladstone's 'gift' for discerning the moods and needs of the British people appeared to have quite deserted him. Neither could he see any way to restore the unity of his party. He was himself exasperated by the sniping and self-importance of many Radicals. His own religious ideals made the prospect of future co-operation with Whigs or Nonconformists on contentious issues like education reform remote. The increasingly thankless and difficult job of party leader could be done better by someone else.

Gladstone's religious ideals constituted powerful personal reasons for retirement too. A part of him longed to 'be out of the dust and heat and blast and strain, before I pass into the unseen world'. With more time for 'spiritual leisure', he would be able to 'cultivate the poor little garden of [his] soul'. Therefore, with thoughts of mortality, and hopes of salvation – and in the shadow of political failure – Gladstone resigned from the leadership of the party in December 1874.

He was not to be given much time for spiritual leisure, however: God, it seemed, had other plans for him. Politics had always been a Christian vocation for Gladstone, and it was, he believed, a Call to rejoin His service in the world that brought him out of retirement. The political issue which offered Gladstone the platform for his return to politics was the agitation which many of his old political allies had raised against Disraeli's handling of the Eastern Question. Gladstone's friends were aghast at Disraeli's support for the Turks who had repressed, with appalling ferocity, Christian uprisings in their Balkan empire. Ghastly details of massacre and rape were soon filling the columns of British newspapers. Disraeli's reaction to these stories – initially dismissive and flippant, and never deviating from his insistence that Turkish power be upheld – scandalised his opponents and precipitated the 'Bulgarian Agitation'. Nonconformists joined with High Churchmen, radicals and intellectuals in demonstrations and meetings all over England. They could not believe that the British state would support so bestial and anti-Christian a regime as that of the Ottoman Turks.

Gladstone was not at first at the forefront of the agitation, but he soon saw its potential. In August 1876, he wrote to Granville: 'good ends can rarely be attained in politics without passion: and there is now, the first time for a good many years, a virtuous passion'. In September, he published a pamphlet on *The Bulgarian Horrors and the Question of the East* which burned with righteous anger at the Turks' crimes and at Disraeli's complicity in them. Within a month it had sold over 200 000 copies, and made Gladstone the effective leader of the Agitation.

In practical terms, the Agitation was a failure. Disraeli affected a languid scorn for Gladstone's production: 'Vindictive and ill-written – that of course. Indeed in that respect of all Bulgarian horrors perhaps the greatest'. More to the point, the government's policy was not altered and by January 1878 public opinion actually appeared to be swinging behind the Turks. Disraeli's threat of armed intervention forced the Russians to back down, and the Congress of Berlin (June-July 1878) marked a clear check to Russia's ambitions (*see page 392*). Disraeli returned from the Congress in triumph, claiming that he had secured 'Peace with Honour'.

But the Agitation did have a dramatic impact on the fortunes of Gladstone and the Liberal Party. Over its course, Gladstone had reforged the links with militant Nonconformity and Radicalism which had been eroded by the disappointments of his first ministry. The masses had, as in 1868, shown that they could be elevated in a great quest for justice, thus confirming in Gladstone's mind a pattern of politics-as-moral-crusade to which he was to return with great success in 1879–80 and less happily in 1886. Above all, the Agitation had served to bring Gladstone back to the forefront of politics. If Gladstone's opponents in the Liberal Party had hoped that Disraeli's apparent triumph in 1878 would force Gladstone into retirement again, they were to be disappointed. In fact, the practical failure of the Bulgarian Agitation made it essential, in Gladstone's own eyes, that he stand his ground until other means could be found of vanquishing the abominable Disraeli. He would not have long to wait.

The celebrated Midlothian Campaigns of 1879–80 (named after the Scottish constituency for which Gladstone stood in the 1880 general election) reinforced Gladstone's union with Nonconformity and Liberalism, and brought his battle with Disraeli to a climax. Gladstone deployed a striking range of approaches to capture the imagination of the voters within the constituency – and beyond. There were cavalcades through the streets of Edinburgh, and whistle-stop tours of the countryside, with speech after speech to the thronging thousands. Then, nineteenth-century mass-communications took over. Every word would be recorded by the reporters on the campaign, telegraphed to London, type set in the massive steam presses of Fleet Street (and in the presses of the great provincial dailies too) and printed verbatim across acres of newspaper column for a nationwide readership the following morning. Never had British politics been so theatrically exciting and never had one man so impressed himself on a wider constituency. It is remarkable that Gladstone, who celebrated his 70th birthday in the middle of the campaign and had entered politics almost 50 years earlier as an opponent of the Great Reform Act, should have seen so clearly the means by which the wide electorate created by the Second Reform Act could be mobilised and given a sense of direction.

The content of his speeches was a sustained assault on Disraeli's foreign policy and style of government. Crucially, it was now possible to criticise the government without appearing unpatriotic, for Disraeli could be held responsible for incurring defeats abroad. His representatives in Afghanistan and South Africa had independently promoted expensive, bloody and mostly unsuccessful military campaigns to extend British power in their corners of the Empire (*see pages 360–1*). Even if these had been more successful, Gladstone claimed that Disraeli's foreign policy would have failed to serve Britain's national interest. Further imperial acquisitions would make for an overextended Empire, increasingly difficult and expensive to maintain. But anyway, Disraeli's gambles had failed.

To strategic misconception and tactical incompetence, Gladstone added a charge of moral dereliction. Disraeli was behaving as if oblivious to the rights of other nations and peoples. The emotional peak of Gladstone's denunciations was reached in a celebrated speech to the women of Dalkeith on 26 November 1879. He described the actions of British troops burning down Afghan hill villages in reprisal raids, and contemplated the dreadful consequences.

> The women and children were driven forth to perish in the snows of winter. Is not that a terrible supposition? Is not that a fact which . . . rouses in you a sentiment of horror and grief, to think that the name of England, under no political necessity, but for a war as frivolous as ever was waged in the history of man, should be associated with consequences as these? . . . Remember the rights of the savage, as we call him. Remember that the happiness of his humble home, remember that sanctity of life in the hill villages of Afghanistan among the winter snows, is as inviolable in the eye of Almighty God as can be your own.

The onset of economic depression in 1879 allowed Gladstone one last but telling twist of the rhetorical knife. Unemployment was at levels unknown for 30 years. 'Beaconsfieldism', as he dubbed the Disraelian system, was to blame here too. (Disraeli had been created Earl of Beaconsfield in 1876.) His foreign policy had not merely been a moral disgrace – it had been extravagant and expensive as well. The tax payer had had to foot the bill, creating, Gladstone claimed, a severe downturn in demand. Disraeli was not fit to manage the nation's finances.

In Midlothian, Gladstone made a combined appeal to the national interest and the consciences and pockets of the electorate that proved irresistible. In the light of the economic depression, and the lack-lustre campaign fought by Disraeli (*see page 362*) the Conservatives might have been heading for defeat anyway. But when the Liberals returned to power in 1880, with an 84 seat majority, most contemporaries saw it as Gladstone's triumph.

2 GLADSTONE AND IRELAND 1880–2

A *Introduction*

To Queen Victoria's dismay, Gladstone became Prime Minister for the second time in April 1880. Although he had not fought the Midlothian campaign as party leader, its spectacular success led Hartington, who had succeeded him in the post in 1875, to concede that only Gladstone had the authority to lead the Party. But lead it where? For, in contrast to 1868, the Liberals had not fought the election on any positive legislative programme: instead, Gladstone had conducted a triumphant crusade against the evils of Beaconsfieldism. Indeed, he imagined that once the political system had been purged of Disraeli's crimes and its health restored, he could retire at last.

Gladstone's expectations were to be frustrated in two ways. First, the momentum of imperialism proved very hard to reverse. Britain's position in South Africa and Afghanistan only stabilised after tortuous manoeuvres and negotiations (*see pages 401 and 404*). Worse, Gladstone was to find himself, much against his will, ever more deeply embroiled in the tangled affairs of Egypt and the Sudan (*see page 397*). The impossibility and expense of unravelling the imperial commitments bequeathed by Disraeli was not the least of the reasons for the Liberals' loss of office in 1885. But secondly, and still more seriously, the Irish problem erupted with a violence and intensity that was unparalleled, and quite unexpected. In the Irish Land League (*see page 276*) Gladstone's government arguably faced the United Kingdom's most threatening revolutionary mass movement ever.

Gladstone had no premonitions of the coming crisis as he assembled his cabinet. With one duke, one marquis and four earls, its centre of gravity once again leaned towards the Whigs. This reflected both the predominantly landowning and cautious tone of the parliamentary party, as well as Gladstone's well-established preference for rule by aristocracy. The main controversy was the issue of representation for the party's Radical wing. In 1877, Joseph Chamberlain, the most prominent, ambitious and dynamic of the Radical leaders, had set up the National Liberal Federation. This was designed to co-ordinate the local constituency organisations, pressurise the party in Westminster into adopting more Radical policies, and propel Chamberlain, its President, into the Cabinet. In fact, many leading Radicals, suspicious of Chamberlain's style, refused to join the organisation. But this did not stop its President from claiming that the NLF's campaign had been instrumental in winning 60 seats at the general election.

Gladstone himself regarded what he took to be Chamberlain's shallow careerism with a mixture of condescension and distaste. Only reluctantly did Gladstone agree to making him President of the Board of Trade. Over the course of the ministry Chamberlain was to feel increasingly patronised and underestimated by Gladstone – or 'Grand Old Man', as his awe-struck colleagues now referred to him. Chamberlain's personal exasperation, as well as his political frustrations, go a long way to explain his decisive rejection of his leader's proposal of Home Rule for Ireland in 1886.

B *Ireland: the Land League and the Land Act (1881)*

The late 1870s and early 1880s were grim times to be a tenant farmer in Ireland. The combined effects of a worldwide fall in agricultural prices and a series of appalling harvests brought even the more prosperous farmers near to destitution, while many of the impoverished tenants of the desperately overcrowded West were literally starving. Evictions for non-payment of rent reached record levels: from 1879 to 1883, 14 600 tenants were evicted – more than the total for the previous 30 years.

The Land League was created in 1879 as a response to this crisis. Its immediate purpose was to protect tenants from eviction and to secure reductions in rent. In the long term, militant Land Leaguers aimed at an end to landlordism itself and the establishment of peasant ownership of the land they farmed. At the helm of the League were the Fenian organiser Michael Davitt and, its leader from October 1879, Charles Stewart Parnell, the most tenacious of the Irish Home Rule MPs. Crucially, the organisation and its leadership were in place before the agrarian crisis reached its peak: the anger of the evicted and destitute could be channelled into political action rather than dissipated in despair.

This fusion of agrarian mass movement, revolutionary Nationalism, and Parliamentary agitation marked, as its leaders recognised, a 'New Departure' in the history of Irish Nationalism. The 'New Departure' entailed a considerable change of style for the Parliamentary Home Rule Party. It became more intransigent, more violent and more disciplined. Its old leader, Isaac Butt, had failed to instil either unity or a sense of purpose into its ranks. Parnell, partly by sheer force of personality, and partly through the authority his leading role in the Land League gave him, was able to make himself its virtual dictator. He exploited to the full the leverage which a threatening mass movement gave him. The Home Rulers' behaviour in the Commons was designed to echo the violence and extremism of their Irish followers. Furious outbursts earned many a suspension, while obstructionism – the art of debating every clause of an unwelcome bill to delay its passage for as long as possible – was worked up from the level of an irritant to that of a strategy. But for major alterations in the rules of Parliamentary procedure, the Commons would have ground to a halt. However, Parnell's ultimate aim – unlike some of the Land League's other leaders – remained to work towards the ultimate goal of Home Rule by Parliamentary means.

In 1880, the Irish Secretary Forster introduced his Compensation for Disturbance Bill. It was designed to soften the blow of eviction for non-payment of rent. To Parnell, this was an example of what the Liberals could be pressurised into conceding. But the Tory-dominated Lords' rejection of the Bill necessitated a shift in strategy. It was the signal for an explosion of agrarian outrages. The League's campaign of rent strikes, intimidation, boycotts and violence escalated dramatically. This 'Land War' aimed not only to break the will of the land-owner, but to make the government of Ireland itself impossible. As Chamberlain had noted on hearing of the Lords decision: 'The bill is rejected, the civil war is begun'.

Liberal reactions to the worsening situation in Ireland were divided. Whigs saw the problem as one of law and order – agitators needed to be locked up, suspending their civil rights if necessary, before any concessions were made. Radicals, by contrast, believed that social injustice was the root cause of Ireland's miseries. The only chance for peace and progress was if the blight of landlordism and the grievances of the tenants were removed.

W E Forster, the Chief Secretary for Ireland, saw that the best prospect for ending the Land War – and for maintaining Liberal Party unity – was to combine elements of both strategies. Accordingly a Coercion Act was passed in February 1881, followed shortly by the Second Irish Land Act (introduced April 1881).

The scope of both Acts was dramatic. The first, as was said at the time, practically enabled the Dublin government to imprison anybody it pleased, for as long as it pleased. The second, presented by Gladstone to the Commons with an astonishing mastery of argument and detail, finally conceded the legendary 'three Fs' for so long demanded by the Irish tenantry: 'fair rent' (to be determined by a sympathetic rent tribunal, and not by market forces); 'fixity of tenure' (making it impossible to evict a tenant who was paying his 'fair rent'); and 'free sale' (recognising the right of an outgoing tenant to receive a payment for his 'interest' in the property from the incoming one).

The main objective of the Act was to meet the grievances of the more moderate tenants and thereby drive a wedge between the Land League's radical leadership and a good part of its rank and file. The leadership's ultimate objectives were ideological, i.e. nationalistic. But the preoccupations of the rank and file were more materialistic – they were desperate for land, or at least for greater security and lower rents. The Act, especially by establishing Land Courts in Ireland to fix 'fair rents', held out the prospect of survival, and better, to the bigger tenant farmers. If the Land Courts could be successfully brought into operation, the Land League would probably disintegrate.

However much it unsettled some Whigs, the Land Act certainly put the leadership of the Land League in a dilemma. Many of their supporters clearly welcomed the Act, and it could be presented as a major concession wrung from the government. Yet in doing so, the leadership would probably be endorsing their own political extinction. The alternative was to organise a boycott of the Land Courts to frustrate the Act's operation. But given its popularity, could such a strategy be either defended or sustained? Parnell, characteristically, tried to avoid any commitment either way. Forster, however, was convinced that the League was conspiring to sabotage the workings of the Act. He persuaded Gladstone that the only way to end the violence and guarantee the free access of the tenantry to the courts was to smash the League by interning its leaders, including Parnell, and outlawing the whole organisation. This was done in October 1881.

The decision to imprison Parnell in Dublin's Kilmainham gaol was probably a mistake. He himself commented: 'Politically it is a fortunate thing for me that I have been arrested, as the movement is breaking fast'. The government had secured for Parnell the dignity of martyrdom just as the tenants were flocking to the Land Courts. But worse, there was a dramatic rise in serious crimes of violence in the Irish countryside. The internment of the League's leadership had created local power vacuums which were bloodily filled by out-and-out terrorists pursuing their deadly vendettas. As F S L Lyons, the great historian of modern Ireland has remarked, 'the country was never more in need of firm leadership than during those months and the only man who could provide it was locked up in jail'.

Forster, increasingly desperate, called for even more severe powers to round up terrorist suspects. But he was now losing the confidence of his Cabinet colleagues, who had no stomach for extending an illiberal policy which had already clearly failed. They agreed with Gladstone to a major change of strategy. Negotiations were opened with Parnell to see if his release could be used to help rescue Ireland from descent into total anarchy. The so-called 'Kilmainham Treaty' followed: the terms of the Land Bill were to be extended to leaseholders and tenants in arrears, thereby bringing over one quarter of a million more peasants within its scope, and coercion was to be dropped. Parnell, for his part, committed himself to work for rather than against the Land Act, to denounce and try and rein in the activities of the terrorists, and to inaugurate a new era of co-operation between the Home Rulers and the Liberal Party in general. Forster, who regarded Parnell as no better than a terrorist himself, was appalled by the deal, and resigned.

Parnell made the appropriate statesmanlike speeches on his release, while the passage of the Arrears Bill in July 1882 met most of his own expectations. Then came the horrific assassinations of Lord Frederick Cavendish (Forster's replacement) and T H Burke (a senior civil servant) in Dublin's Phoenix Park. Many feared that this would bring the new Anglo-Irish understanding to a tragic end and not surprisingly, a new and extremely severe Coercion Act was soon passed. But, in response, Parnell – who had been genuinely appalled by the assassinations – confined himself to theatrical obstructionism in the Commons. He was now more and more convinced that the constitutional path to Home Rule was the only one.

Gladstone's evaluation of Parnell changed radically over these months. Before having him locked up, Gladstone had denounced him as an agent of anarchy. Yet one reason for his release was the belief that he could help the government to restore law and order. Perhaps Gladstone had realised that there was a wide gap between Parnell's sometimes blood-curdling rhetoric (which was needed to keep his more extreme supporters satisfied) and his instinctive caution, social conservatism and constitutionism. In 1883 Gladstone wrote to Earl Spencer, the new Lord-Lieutenant of Ireland: 'Though Parnell is a Sphinx, the most probable reading of him is that he works for and with the law as far as he dare.'

In the long run, this was to open up the intriguing possibility of working formally with Parnell to maintain good government and social stability in Ireland. As one unintended consequence of the Land Bill had been a further erosion of the status and authority of the Irish landlords, even Gladstone was to be forced to accept that the natural rural hierarchy of his dreams could not be created there. Gladstone's supposed 'conversion' to Home Rule is in fact the logical working out of the policies of 1881 and 1882. For in the crisis of 1885–6, Gladstone was convinced that Parnell and the Nationalists were the only potential source of legitimate authority in Ireland. Forster was retrospectively proved correct when he had stated in 1882 that Parnell's release marked 'a tremendous step towards Home Rule'.

3 Problems with Imperialism and Radicalism 1880–5

If Gladstone expected some relief from his difficulties when he turned from Ireland to consider imperial affairs, he was to be disappointed. In the Midlothian Campaign, Gladstone had promised to reconstitute British foreign policy along Liberal lines. Peace was to be the ultimate objective. By working in close co-operation with the other leading European powers, respecting the rights of other nations and peoples, and keeping a careful eye on expenditure, the dangerous and extravagant adventurism which had characterised Disraeli's foreign policy, could be avoided. The immediate priority, was to roll back the frontiers of Beaconsfieldism, and reduce British commitments in South Africa and Afghanistan.

Exercise

Read the following pages of chapter XII taking notes on Gladstone's foreign policy, and its effectiveness, under the following headings:

a) Afghanistan, 1880 and 1885 (see pages 403–4)

b) South Africa, 1880–4 (see pages 400–1)

c) Egypt, 1882–5 (see pages 397–8)

d) The Sudan, 1882–5 (see pages 398–9)

Then discuss and make notes on the following questions:

1 *In what respects did Gladstone's foreign policy between 1880 and 1885 leave him open to attack from the Conservatives?*

2 *Why, given the principles which he had spelled out in the Midlothian campaign, would Gladstone find it hard to make political capital even out of his successes?*

In the spring and summer of 1885, Gladstone and his ministry seemed to be afflicted on every front. In a further unhappy echo of Gladstone's campaign against Beaconsfieldism at Midlothian, the Liberals discovered the price which – literally – would have to be paid for their misfortunes: £10 million in extra taxes. The Chancellor of the Exchequer's revelation horrified and dismayed his Cabinet colleagues.

Party morale was low enough already. The Radicals lamented that events in Ireland, Egypt and the Sudan between them had squeezed out most of the reforms they had wanted from the legislative timetable. Even the one that had got through – the Third Reform Act (*see pages 371–3*) – had not gone according to plan. Salisbury, the Conservatives' leader, had blocked its passage through the Lords until vital concessions concerning the redistribution of seats had been made. These were to prove greatly to the Conservatives' advantage. The Third Reform Act had left the Whigs worried, too, as to the role they would have to play in the new electoral system. They rightly feared that Liberal constituency organisations would prefer to adopt Radical candidates rather than men of their own type to fight the new single member constituencies. The Whigs were, finally, in retreat in the Liberal Party.

The situation in Ireland was deteriorating too. After two relatively quiet years, disorder was spreading at an alarming rate. The old Whig/Radical divisions opened up. The Lord Lieutenant of Ireland, Earl Spencer, argued for the necessity of coercion; Chamberlain insisted that this had to be moderated and counterbalanced by a more constructive approach, in particular by devolving to the Irish greater responsibilities for local government. The Cabinet could not agree and there was deadlock.

The government was finally defeated on its Budget in June 1885 by a surprising – and short-lived – alliance of Conservatives and Irish Nationalists. The predominant feeling in Cabinet was one of relief. For the six months it would take to compile the new electoral registers required in the wake of the Third Reform Act, Britain was ruled by a minority Conservative government under Lord Salisbury.

1885 was to bring one other disappointment for the Liberals in general, and the Radicals in particular. Chamberlain had hoped that the 1885 elections, which were finally held in November, would be a Radical triumph. In his 'Unauthorised Programme' and a series of speeches, he unveiled a package of proposals targeted at the newly enfranchised agricultural labourer. Elective county councils were to be created, with powers of compulsory purchase, to buy up parts of larger estates and sell the land off, on attractive terms, to create a new class of small-holders. Progressive taxation and 'Death Duties' were to be introduced, to pay for free education and better housing for the poor. There were hints about the possible disestablishment and disendowment of the Church of England, which would release more funds for the common good.

Chamberlain's campaign had a tremendous impact – but at least as much to the Conservatives' advantage as to the Liberals'. It is true that he seemed to catch the imagination of the farm workers: the Liberals made big gains in the counties. But Liberal losses in the middle-sized boroughs – their traditional strongholds – were greater. Salisbury had delighted in denouncing Chamberlain as a 'Sicilian Bandit'. Gladstone, trying to distance himself from the Radical assault, insisted that the Radicals' Programme had no official status. But middle-class, Anglican England was unconvinced. Instead, it was frightened for its property, and its Church. The Liberals lost over 25 seats to the Conservatives in November 1885, and Chamberlain was widely blamed for the setback. By the end of the year, having suffered the rejection of his local government scheme for Ireland and the failure of his 'Unauthorised' programme, Chamberlain had every appearance of being a coming man whose time had somehow gone.

4 GLADSTONE AND IRELAND: THE HOME RULE CRISIS 1885–6

The Liberals' misfortunes were by no means the most striking feature of the 1885 election, however. This was the return of 86 hard line Nationalists – and not a single Liberal! – for Irish constituencies. Parnell could no longer be dismissed as an unrepresentative extremist: he spoke for the majority of the Irish people. What made Parnell's success particularly significant was that 86 was precisely the majority which the Liberals had over the Conservatives at Westminster. The Irish could make Gladstone Prime Minister again: or they could block him. That simple arithmetical fact lay behind the political drama of the next months.

A Chronology of the Home Rule Crisis

1885 November	General Election results – Liberals 335; Conservatives 249; Irish Nationalists 86
17 December	Gladstone's supposed 'conversion' to Home Rule leaked to the press by his son.
1886 26 January	Liberals and Irish Nationalists vote together to end Salisbury's 'caretaker' administration. Gladstone forms his third ministry – but without Hartington, who disagreed with Home Rule.

26 March	Chamberlain, finding Gladstone irrevocably committed to Home Rule, leaves the Cabinet.
8 April	Gladstone introduces the Home Rule Bill into the Commons.
31 May	Chamberlain chairs meeting of Radical Liberals who commit themselves to vote against the Bill.
8 June	Home Rule Bill defeated by 30 votes, with 93 Liberals (led by Hartington and Chamberlain), voting against Gladstone. Gladstone calls a general election.
July	General elections results – Gladstonian Liberals 196, Tories 316, Liberal Unionists (i.e. anti-Home Rule Liberals) 74; Irish Nationalists 83

These were momentous events. The split in the Liberal Party became permanent and helped to ensure that the following two decades of British politics would be Tory dominated. The Irish question, of course, is still 'unsolved' today. It is hardly surprising, therefore, that historians continue to debate the merits of Gladstone's plans, the exact nature of his motivation, and the motives of his rivals – inside and outside the Liberal Party – over these crucial months.

A *Gladstone's motives*

For those historians who focus on 'high politics' as their means of analysis, the events of these months are like the moves of some vast and intricate game. Each player, Gladstone not least, strives to maximise his advantage relative to every other, and tactical flexibility is all, principle nothing. The ultimate object of the game is not to implement a policy but to hang on to, or win, power.

By these lights, Gladstone's 'conversion' to Home Rule served a variety of self-interested purposes. It was the price of parliamentary power, securing for his party the necessary Irish support. More subtly, by bringing the question of Home Rule to centre stage, Gladstone was inventing a reason for his own survival as party leader, for he, as no one else, had made Ireland into a mission. Hartington and Chamberlain, his potential rivals, would be left stranded. This high political rivalry had an ideological dimension too. Gladstone was tired of the timidity and barrenness of Whiggery, and anxious about the materialistic and 'socialistic' aspects of Chamberlainite Radicalism. A victory for Gladstone would commit the party to an altogether bolder and purer vision. Here Gladstone's vanity and capacity for self-delusion come to the fore. As Randolph Churchill jibed, he was an 'old man in a hurry', craving one last triumph to crown his political career, oblivious to the process by which he invariably chose the path which led him to maximum personal advantage, all the while hearing only the voice of duty and providence calling him on.

However, the emphasis which this interpretation places on the rivalry between Gladstone and Chamberlain is misleading. The cohesion and strength of Radicalism within the Parliamentary Liberal Party during the 1880s has been exaggerated, and with it the threat posed by Chamberlain to the party leadership. Furthermore, Chamberlain's own star seemed to be waning in 1885. There was no need for Gladstone to use Home Rule to stave off a non-existent threat from the left.

This leaves undefended the cruder charge of opportunism: that Home Rule was the price Gladstone was prepared to pay for 86 Nationalist votes. Unfortunately some of the vital evidence here is thoroughly ambiguous. For example, Gladstone definitely hoped that the Home Rule question could be solved on non-party lines. In mid-December, he let it be known to Salisbury that the Liberals would support a Conservative Home Rule scheme, arguing that this would serve the national interest best, not least in securing a safer passage for the bill through both Houses of Parliament. Gladstone was prepared to sacrifice the prospect of office if he could thereby help to advance legislation which he believed was vital for the well-being of the United Kingdom. Surely this marks the very opposite of political opportunism? But Salisbury clearly thought otherwise. Indeed, he was reportedly 'sickened' by Gladstone's 'hypocrisy' in making the offer. For Salisbury realised that his party would be smashed to pieces if he were to try and push Home Rule through. He was not going to replay Peel and 1846, and consign the Conservatives to another lengthy spell in the political wilderness. As far as Salisbury could see, Gladstone had, not for the first time, conveniently confused the national interest with the interests of the Liberal Party.

Perhaps a less equivocal defence of Gladstone's integrity can be found. If the policy of 'Home Rule' can be shown to be a logical development of long-established Gladstonian principles, the charge of opportunism might be rebutted. One of the foundation stones of Gladstone's view of politics was his belief in nationality. All peoples had a God-given right to freedom and independence, and when, conscious of their nationhood, they rose up to claim that freedom, it was a crime and a sin to oppress them or to aid their oppressors. Gladstone had followed this principle in the Balkans, in South Africa, in Afghanistan and in the Sudan. With Home Rule, Gladstone was merely applying the same principle to Ireland.

But this still does not account for the timing of Gladstone's concession. Why was British rule in Ireland justifiable in 1880 but intolerable in 1885? There were several reasons. The Irish people's sense of nationhood, inspired by Parnell, had grown dramatically over these years. They had spoken unequivocally in the 1885 election: the scale of the Home Rulers victory was to Gladstone 'a very great fact indeed'. Their vote was also a verdict on British rule. Gladstone more than anyone hoped to bring peace and justice to Ireland, and he had believed that the reforms of his first and second ministries would convince the Irish people that the Union of 1800 (*see page 300*) might yet be made a 'union of hearts'. But the strength of the National League was proof that he had failed.

Gladstone's historical perceptions were changing too. The more Irish history he read, the more he became convinced that the Union had been a tragic mistake, and equally, the better he understood the Irish Nationalists' resentment of British misgovernment. He described Britain's rule in Ireland as 'a sad exception to the glory of our country', and a 'broad and black blot' upon its Empire's history. It was a sin which had to be atoned for.

What finally crystallised these sentiments, and made Gladstone determined to act, whatever the odds, was the fear which gripped him towards the end of 1885 that Ireland was again on the brink of anarchy. His contacts, like the senior Dublin civil servant, Sir Robert Hamilton, repeatedly warned him that unless he took a bold initiative 'social dissolution' and 'revolution' were inevitable. Home Rule alone could avoid the oncoming catastrophe.

It was time to draw on the insight which had prompted Parnell's release in 1882, and recognise Home Rule itself as the only legitimate instrument by which social order could be upheld in Ireland, and the ultimate integrity of the Empire be maintained. Home Rule was now, as Gladstone put it, 'a source not of danger but of strength – the danger . . . lies in refusing it'.

B *The Home Rule Bill*

Gladstone introduced the Home Rule Bill into the Commons on 8 April 1886. In its scale and ambition it was the greatest piece of legislation he had ever devised. It was not a bill for Irish independence. As Matthew (*see bibliography, page 295*) has said, Gladstone's 'mission was still to pacify Ireland, not to liberate it'. But the only way to pacify Ireland was to give Ireland its own Parliament, so that the Irish could teach themselves the arts and responsibilities of self government. Accordingly, the Dublin Parliament which Gladstone envisaged was to have considerable powers – for example, over law and order, and taxation. But defence, foreign affairs and trade were to be left in the hands of the Imperial Parliament at Westminster. Ireland was to have no representatives there, although being expected to contribute 1/15th of the total requirements of the Imperial exchequer.

The Home Rule Bill was accompanied by an even more complicated Land Purchase Bill, enabling tenants to buy out their landlords on very generous terms, with loans from the British treasury to finance the scheme. This bill was widely seen as a gigantic bribe to buy off the otherwise inevitable opposition of the Lords. Gladstone's calculation was that the prospect of a Treasury sponsored buy-out would prove irresistible to the landowners of Ireland. After all, their land, thanks to the League's Land War, his own Land Courts and worldwide agricultural depression, was returning less and less money for more and more trouble. It was the most effective way to neutralise the class which Gladstone had identified as 'the bitterest and most implacable of our political adversaries'.

Both Bills were to fail. Indeed, the Land Purchase scheme proved so unpopular that Gladstone withdrew it before it could be voted on. Home Rule itself was lost by 30 votes in early June, with Hartington and Chamberlain leading the Liberal rebels.

So much analysis is often devoted to the underlying motives of the rebels that the substance of their criticisms tends to be overlooked. The Home Rule Bill was Gladstone's biggest bill, but it wasn't his best. Perhaps the Irish Question, as conceived by Gladstone, was fundamentally insoluble.

Its critics spotlighted a series of flaws in design that might well have made it unworkable. It seemed quite impossible to stabilise the constitutional status of Ireland at some half-way house between Union and Independence. No one could offer any meaningful guarantees that the Irish would not regard Home Rule as a mere staging-post on the journey to full nationhood. The projected removal of all Irish MPs from Westminster in Gladstone's Bill was held to make ultimate separation more likely.

The fate of Ulster posed a major problem too. Some predicted that Protestant Ulster would rebel rather than accept rule from Dublin. It was the wealthiest and most industrialised part of Ireland, whose commercial ties with the British mainland and the Empire beyond were far more important to it than any ties to the south. Would a Dublin parliament nurture or destroy its prosperity? More serious was Ulster's religious grievance. Parnell and Gladstone both mistook the genuine anxiety of the Protestant community for the bigotry of a few extremists in the Orange Order. The way in which the National League's propaganda played on the historical injustices suffered by Irish Catholics seemed to add substance to the slogan that Home Rule would mean Rome Rule. For those in Ulster who believed that the Nationalists' ultimate aim was full independence, Home Rule was a profound threat to their prosperity and culture.

Prejudice and bigotry do have their part to play in explaining the vehemence of the reaction to Gladstone's proposals, however. Even moderate Whigs who prided themselves on their breadth of sympathies and tolerance perceived Catholic Ireland through spectacles warped by racial and religious contempt. Most Tories were a good deal worse: Salisbury was to sneer in May 1886 that the Irish were no more capable of self-government that Hottentots.

Imperialism was important for opponents of Home Rule, both as an ideology and as world strategy. What business had the backward, violent and superstitious Irish to turn their back on the civilising influence of the richest and best governed country in the world? Radicals like Chamberlain and Bright were appalled by the consequences for Britain's status as a world power if she were seen to back down before a gang of 'ruffians' and 'assassins'. And the prospect of separation raised the fearsome danger of an Irish alliance with some future continental enemy of Britain.

c *The break up of the Liberal Party*

All these complaints, common to Liberal dissident and Tory alike, were explicit in the Parliamentary debates which raged over April, May and early June. But there were significant underlying motives for the Chamberlainite and the Whig secessions which must briefly be examined.

Ambitious and unsentimental as he was, self-interest must be placed near the centre of any analysis of Chamberlain's actions in 1886. He knew that if Gladstone were allowed to make Home Rule into the Liberals' new crusade, his own plans for domestic reforms, as outlined in the Radical Programme of 1885, would be sidelined indefinitely. Chamberlain was also convinced that Home Rule would be a vote loser, probably inside Parliament and certainly with the British electorate. It would be best if he distanced himself from the debacle that was closing in on Gladstone. The rejection of Home Rule would surely precipitate Gladstone's retirement, when the party would turn to men with fresh ideas who were untainted by any Irish infatuations – men like Chamberlain, perhaps?

Hartington and the Whigs present greater interpretative difficulties. Hartington wanted to be Prime Minister, and was the natural leader of any centre coalition – an outcome quite conceivable in early 1886. But it is not necessary to explain his opposition to Home Rule in terms of opportunism: he had long been committed to pursuing coercion first, and concession only second, as the way forward in Ireland.

Even more than most Whigs, Hartington was exasperated by Gladstone's readiness to make concession after concession to the Irish Catholics. As far as Hartington could see, they were neither deserving nor grateful. But Gladstone's fund of generosity was as inexhaustible as the Irish problem itself appeared insoluble. That, Hartington concluded, was not a recipe for rational politics. As with Chamberlain,

Hartington expected Home Rule to be rejected, Gladstone to retire and the Liberal Party to be restored to saner leadership – in this case, his own.

For the Whigs as a whole it has been argued that Home Rule was more the occasion than the cause of their break-away. Radical pressure was supposedly rising inexorably in the party, and with it, the challenge to the rights of property. In this analysis, 1886 becomes the moment when the class tensions within the Liberal Party were finally resolved, and the Whigs – wealthy, privileged and anxious – made their long-expected move towards the Conservative ranks.

However attractive this interpretation may seem, it is vulnerable to a variety of criticisms. The debate over the Second Land Act in 1881 had raised the threat to the rights of property owners far more directly than anything in the Home Rule Bill, but the party had survived that episode pretty much intact. Furthermore, the analysis is based on an exaggerated estimation of Chamberlain's prospects – not good early in 1886 – and the threat from Radicalism in general. But one fact above all makes an interpretation of the Liberal break-up as being determined by a Whigs vs Radical fault-line implausible: the party did not split along left/right lines! Many 'moderates' ended up staying with Gladstone, while 'Radical Joe' led 30 of his followers into the same lobby as Hartington's Whigs and Salisbury's Tories.

What pressures could have forced Chamberlain and Hartington to move in the same direction? Both were anxious about the repercussions of Home Rule for British imperialism and national security. Neither wanted to sacrifice Ulster's Protestants to 'Rome Rule'. But most important of all, the events of 1885–6 had finally convinced them that Gladstone's style of leadership was simply intolerable.

Seventy-seven years of age, Gladstone was increasingly a stubborn and self-deluding old man, deaf to warnings or criticisms even from close friends. 'I fear,' one remarked 'that the time has passed when he can listen as he used to do. Generally, disagreement with him produces sorrow that people can be so blind as not to see the truth . . .' His management of colleagues was distant and dictatorial. So obsessive and self-righteous was Gladstone's pursuit of justice for Ireland that he had hardly felt any obligation to consult with leading colleagues before his 'conversion' to Home Rule was made known. In particular, he had made no attempt to keep Hartington or Chamberlain in the picture. Gladstone staggered Harcourt, his Chancellor of the Exchequer, in late January 1886 when he revealed that he was ready to press on, if necessary, without support from either of them. In fact, he would, he mused later, have been 'prepared to go forward without anybody'.

Radical and Nonconformist activists might well be enraptured by such heroism, but to many Whigs it looked more like blind and destructive fanaticism. Gladstone's election speeches for Home Rule could only have confirmed Whigs' anxieties that he was ready to betray every principle of progressive but moderate, rational government that they held dear (*for one such speech, see the exercise on pages 298–9*). Gladstone was no longer channelling the virtuous passions of the people – drunk on his own words he had become the slave of King Mob, and of his own terrible sense of mission.

D *Defeat*

The chances of a majority for Home Rule slipped away between April and June, despite a variety of concessions and promises from Gladstone. On 31 May, a vital meeting of disaffected Radicals took place, under Chamberlain's chairmanship, to decide on the lengths they would go to to oppose the Bill. Swayed by a letter from Bright, who was particularly anxious at the prospect of consigning the Ulster Protestants to the mercy of the Irish nationalists, they agreed to vote against it. That meeting determined the outcome of the vote: a majority of 30 against the bill, including 93 dissident Liberals.

Gladstone threw himself into the following general election with awesome vigour for a man of 77 years, convinced that the people would respond to his call as they had done in 1868 and 1880. His optimism again suggests a slackening grasp on political reality. It is true that his own campaign produced echoes of the revivalist fervour of Midlothian. His hold over the party's radical activists had already been demonstrated by his remarkable capture in May of the National Liberal Federation – Chamberlain's own power base – for Home Rule. But the commitment of Liberal enthusiasts did not compensate for the alienation of the electoral middle ground and the decisive desertion of the Liberal Unionists. With the latter, Gladstone fell victim to a masterstroke of opportunism by Salisbury. He promised that Conservative constituency organisations would not put forward their own candidates against any defecting Liberal Unionists. This stiffened the latter's resolve in the last weeks of Westminster arm-twisting and helps to explain how 78 of them held on to their seats in the election. The Gladstonian Liberal party was reduced to 191 MPs, as against 316 Tories. The 83 Parnellites, now firmly locked to Gladstone, could not begin to bridge the gap. Home Rule, for now, was dead. It was not obvious that the prospects for Gladstonian Liberalism were any healthier.

5 EPILOGUE: THE DECLINE OF GLADSTONIAN LIBERALISM

Just as the failure of the Bulgarian Agitation had made it imperative for Gladstone to stay on in politics so that the fight for justice could be continued, so the defeat of Home Rule was treated as a temporary set back and any thought of retirement postponed into the indefinite future. But Gladstone's position as Liberal leader became increasingly paradoxical. For the break up of 1886 had purged the party of most of its Whigs, leaving it more consistently Radical in outlook than it had ever been before. Yet Gladstone had either no interest in, or a positive antipathy towards, the main items on the Radical agenda. The climax of the uneasy marriage of Gladstone and Radicalism came at the meeting of the National Liberal Federation in Newcastle 1891. Gladstone reluctantly gave his endorsement to the whole Newcastle Programme – a ragbag including the introduction of death duties, free elementary education, parish councils, concessions to the powerful temperance lobby and disestablishment for Wales and Scotland – in return for the party committing itself to Home Rule as the number one priority.

What enthusiasm there ever had been for Home Rule in the party and amongst the electorate was now waning. Admittedly, some radical Liberal Unionists re-attached themselves to Gladstone, appalled by the ruthlessness with which the Conservatives were applying their policy of coercion. But, in 1889, disaster struck the Irish Nationalist camp. For a decade, Parnell had had as his mistress the wife of Captain O'Shea, one of the Irish Home Rule MPs. This man now decided to divorce his wife at last, and the ensuing squalid revelations in the courts ruined Parnell's reputation. Gladstone knew that his Nonconformist supporters would be appalled by the scandal, and strongly recommended that Parnell stand down as the leader of the Home Rulers. His refusal split the party into Parnellites and anti-Parnellites, the latter with the full backing of the Irish Catholic hierarchy behind them. In an extraordinarily bitter campaign, the Parnellites were crushed and their leader drove himself into the ground. In October 1891, he died, an exhausted, broken man.

This was the unpropitious background to Gladstone's last attempt, in 1893, to force a Home Rule Bill through Parliament. The Liberals had won the 1892 general election, but the big majority which he had been expecting, failed to materialise. They had 273 seats, only 4 more than the Tories, and with 46 Liberal Unionists in the new Parliament, Gladstone would be completely reliant on the support of 82 Irish Nationalist MPs. Although the Second Home Rule Bill passed through the Commons by a majority of 45, its rejection by the Lord's was as overwhelming as it was predictable: 419 votes to 41.

The final parting was near. Gladstone wanted to dissolve Parliament and fight one last election on the issue of justice for Ireland. His cabinet colleagues refused. They were convinced that Home Rule was a vote loser, and were exasperated by the way Gladstone's increasingly obsessive commitment to Ireland was blocking all other legislation.

There were other differences. Imperialism was in the ascendant, and tensions between the great powers were growing, with predictable consequences: the Admiralty was demanding a large increase in naval spending. Gladstone, reflecting that he had spent 60 years of his political life in 'a constant effort to do all I could for economy and for peace' could not accept such 'mad' proposals, despite the fact that they had won the support of the rest of the Cabinet. This was the issue on which, (with his hearing and eyesight increasingly failing) in March 1894, he chose to resign.

Gladstone seemed quite out of step with the political demands of the time. He himself felt more and more like a 'survival' from another era. Not one of the principles of Gladstonian Liberalism appeared relevant to Britain's needs as the turn of the century approached. The pressures of imperialism had been undermining the ideals of Midlothian almost from the moment of their utterance. Retrenchment was also retreating in the face of the rise of Labour: a new generation of Liberal thinkers was emerging, who were convinced that the state had the means and the duty to ameliorate poverty – and thus keep Socialism at bay (*see page 453*). Gladstone, however, could not abide any interference in the workings of the free market. For example, he had regarded pressure for a statutory eight-hour working day in the early 1890s as an ominous sign that even 'the working masses' had been warped by that spirit of self-interest which had long since corrupted 'the classes'. He seemed blind to the probability that the Liberals' survival as a major political party would depend on their success in retaining their support. The Conservatives might have capitulated to the politics of class interest: but the Gladstonian Liberal Party would not.

But even Gladstone could not freeze the process of social change in Britain. By the 1890s, it had become, predominantly, a horizontally-divided class society. The remarkable alliance of ranks and interests which had provided the social underpinning of Gladstonian Liberalism, had irreparably broken up. Whig aristocrats, moderate Anglican landowners, Nonconformist men of commerce and industry, radical artisans and progressive intellectuals no longer shared a common language or purpose. It had been the miracle of Gladstonian Liberalism to make them believe for so long that they had.

But the lessons of the following two decades did not all serve to show the Grand Old Man up as a hopeless anachronism. The chaos and impotence into which the Liberal cabinet fell after his departure was a painful reminder of how far his personal authority and political crusades had been necessary to keep the party together and electorally successful. The Tories were to enjoy crushing victories in the 1895 and 1900 elections.

When the Liberal recovery came, with their great electoral victory of 1906, it was inspired by political passions which Gladstone would have understood well. The denunciation of the crimes of British Imperialism in South Africa, during and after the Boer War (1899–1902), and the fervent defence of Free Trade, threatened by Conservative plans for Tariff Reform (*see page 459*), recalled the golden age of Gladstonian

Liberalism. In power, the Liberal ministries were to experience major constitutional conflict with the House of Lords, which would have confirmed all Gladstone's suspicions about the selfishness of the privileged 'classes'. The First World War itself was seen by many Liberals as dreadful fulfilment of Gladstone's dire warnings of the consequences of militarism and imperialism. Regarded by his bewildered and exasperated colleagues in his final years as the 'Grand Old Madman', he was soon after his death being invested instead with the authority and dignity of an Old Testament Prophet.

6 Assessment

A *Was Gladstone a fraud?*

It seems unlikely that historians can ever write with real certainty about what motivated Gladstone. As we have seen, a variety of interpretations are compatible with the mass of available evidence. He was without doubt capable of considerable self-deception, loathe to acknowledge even to himself the sheer strength of his ambition, or the intensity with which he enjoyed power and adulation. He was also a compulsive myth-maker, forever seeing himself embattled against the forces of darkness.

Beaconsfieldism was a Gladstonian myth, in which he endowed Disraeli with almost superhuman power as the architect of a whole system of depravity. Gladstone could conjure up unlikely allies too. He eulogised the political judgement of the 'masses' with ever increasing fervour. But the record shows that they were a fickle lot, swept away in Gladstone's own phrase (he was blaming the influence of the drink interest) in 'a torrent of gin and beer' in 1874, turning bullishly patriotic in 1878, and not even very keen to help Gladstone atone for the nation's sins against Ireland in 1886.

Ultimately, Gladstone became a myth himself. By the late 1870s his country house was receiving train loads of pilgrims, who gathered up the chippings from his celebrated tree felling sessions like so many splinters from the true cross. It is not surprising that the object of such adulation found it hard to keep a grip on reality. His face was on pictures, plates and cups – and Tory bedchamber pots. Well might Randolph Churchill despair that in an 'age of advertisement', Gladstone sold himself to the public with greater flair than Colman's sold their mustard.

But all his ambition and all his political craft does not mean he was a great humbug, as Churchill believed, or the 'arch-villain' of Disraeli's letters. For, as Gladstone himself put it, 'politics are at once a game and a high art'. Unless the game is played, with all its calculations, excitements and tactical ruses, even perhaps with a degree of ruthlessness, it cannot be won. But the high art is vital too, or politics becomes merely a demoralising and unprincipled race for power. The high art is the grasp of strategy and ultimate purpose, the sense of how the available means can be shaped to serve higher ends. Gladstone knew that power without principle was corrupting – such he believed was Disraeli's fate. But principle without power was impotent. Gladstone's mastery of the platform and of high political manoeuvre – and (to Churchill's distaste and jealousy) of the consumer-style politics of the age of the mass electorate – guaranteed he would never be that.

The high art of politics was given its content by Gladstone's Christian vision, and its dynamic by his sense of Providence and calling. These ideas are largely alien to our age. Cynicism comes easily when someone tells us that he or she is acting as a servant of the Lord: we are tempted to see only a charlatan or a fanatic. But these beliefs were simply a part of everyday reality for many Victorians. Sin was a burden they lived with, while the hope of salvation, and a sense of the Providential order of the world sustained them. Gladstone simply felt these things with a greater than usual intensity. It is our historical responsibility to enter that world and try to empathise with its now peculiarly foreign mentality.

B *Was Gladstone a conservative?*

Once in his later career, the great painter and critic Ruskin charged Gladstone with being a political 'leveller'. Gladstone's reply was emphatic. 'Oh dear, no! I am nothing of the sort. I am a firm believer in the aristocratic principle – the rule of the best. I am an out-and-out inequalitarian'.

Gladstone believed in aristocracy as both a political ideal and a social practice. The Whigs were always well represented in his Cabinets, and no one valued more highly the tradition of disinterested public service embodied in their great families than Gladstone. The Gladstones themselves were the biggest landowners in Flintshire. In letters to his son, Gladstone left him in no doubt as to the 'serious moral and social responsibilities' which owning the estates entailed. 'Nowhere in the world is the position of the landed proprietor so high as in this country, and this is in great part for the reason that nowhere else is the possession of landed property so closely associated with definite duty'. Gladstone believed that the 'principle source' of Britain's 'social strength', and 'a large part of true Conservatism', was the ownership of landed estates by the same family from generation to generation, and he made it clear that it was his son's duty to continue this tradition. No Tory could have made a higher case for the place of landed wealth in the life of the nation.

But what was 'true conservatism', and how far was the Conservative Party able to defend it? Gladstone believed it was the responsibility of the nation's leaders to protect what was best in Britain's pre-industrial past – its aristocratic government, its constitutional liberties, its Established Church – and give them new life in the Britain being created by the Industrial Revolution. Far from being incompatible with these aims, Gladstone's Liberalism – his programme of retrenchment and reform – was essential to its achievement. These were tasks which he believed the Victorian Conservative Party, after its repudiation of Peel, was incapable of fulfilling. Disraeli had seen to that – but even his death did not cure the disease. Instead, the Conservatives increasingly became the vehicle of 'class preference', determined above all else on the defence of property and privilege. Salisbury's Conservatives, he feared, would never have repealed the Corn Laws. They had no spirit of self-sacrifice, and little sense of where the national interest lay.

Peel remained the model Conservative for Gladstone. His administrative expertise, his defence of the public interest and his commitment to free trade were each to become characteristic of Gladstonian Liberalism too. But although these are major components of that political practice, they by no means exhaust its definition. Peel's notion of individual freedom focused on freedom from economic oppression: the imposition of tariffs on the people. It did not extend to freedom from political inequality or from religious discrimination. He would have been startled by Gladstone's desire to extend 'the pale of the constitution', and his emergence as the hero of Nonconformity. The confident certainty in the fruits of progress which characterise Gladstone's speeches of the 1860s, and the ringing denunciations of British imperialism which is the theme of the later 1870s and 1880s would have been foreign to him too. As we have seen, Gladstone put the conservative in Gladstone Liberalism (*see page 262*); but, he grafted mighty branches of Liberalism onto the trunk of Peelite Conservatism too.

c *Was Gladstone a failure?*

For a politician of Gladstone's energy, longevity, vision and administrative power, his legislative record is in some respects mixed. The scale and control evident in his great bills on the Irish Church, the Irish Land Question and, for all its flaws, the Home Rule Bill itself, are remarkable. Yet it remains unclear what they achieved. The Second Irish Land Act, superficially Gladstone's most complete Irish triumph, was a measure to which Forster only won him round with some difficulty. Although its political objective was partly achieved, its social and economic consequences were more dubious. The Home Rule Bill itself was, of course, lost (at least partly because of Gladstone's miscalculations and style of presentation); but it is by no means certain that it would have worked had it been passed. Gladstone's 'mission to pacify Ireland' was a sometimes misguided, sometimes heroic, failure.

Gladstone's domestic record is equivocal too. His greatest triumph was as Chancellor of the Exchequer. But even here commentators, dazzled by the brilliance of his performance, have tended to neglect the good fortune he enjoyed. Economic booms sustained Gladstone's give-away budgets. On Parliamentary Reform, he was comprehensively outmanoeuvred by Disraeli in 1866–7, while in 1884–5, Salisbury was allowed to determine the shape of the redistribution of constituencies, to the Conservatives' lasting electoral advantage.

Gladstone played little part in designing the great (non-Irish) reforms of his first ministry; his second was notoriously barren of any comparable achievements; while after 1886, his all-consuming passion for Home Rule left him, and the Liberal Party as a whole, with little time or energy for anything else.

Some of his greatest political triumphs were derived from his interventions in the field of foreign policy. His contributions to the Bulgarian Agitation, and above all his Midlothian Campaign, offered perhaps the most thrilling and uplifting spectacles of nineteenth-century British politics. But their impact on foreign policy is hard to trace. Disraeli triumphed in Berlin in 1878, contemptuous of Gladstone's ravings, while Gladstone himself found the imperial entanglements he inherited in 1880 all too inescapable. Overall, and perhaps unfairly, foreign and imperial policy was perceived as the Liberals' Achilles heel. Gladstone's name was associated with the humiliations of the Alabama settlement and the catastrophe at Khartoum, rather than the resolute brinkmanship of Penjdeh, or – an achievement which Gladstone found deeply embarrassing – the annexation of Egypt.

Were Gladstone's successes then, after all, largely confined to the 'game' of politics, rather than its 'high art'? No one doubts that Gladstone played the game with as much skill as any of his contemporaries. His cultivation of provincial Liberal support in the early 1860s, the masterly way in which he reunited the party after the debacle of the Second Reform Act, and the brilliant and innovative style of his Midlothian campaigns, reveal a political mind of extraordinary flexibility and penetration.

As this range of examples shows, Gladstone was completely at home in the rarified world of 'high politics' and equally comfortable amidst the people and on the platform in the world of 'low politics'. No one had a better grasp of how these two worlds could be fitted together, and presented to each other. Gladstone was the first politician to move freely between the two worlds and he became, in the 1860s and 1870s, their sole mutual interpreter. By tapping the 'virtuous passion' of the people, he was able to infuse energy and purpose into the undisciplined yet stagnant Parliamentary scene which was reluctantly bequeathed to him by Palmerston. By presenting the conflicts of Westminster as a battle between good and evil, he engaged the rapidly expanding electorate in the political process in a way which had meaning for them, so that they became the excited partisans, as Vincent remarks, 'in a demonstrably superior cause'.

Legislation, in fact, was not the ultimate goal of Gladstonian politics. The process became an end in itself. Gladstone made mass politics into a crusade against sin. In doing so, he imposed some shape and purpose on the unknowable and potentially threatening electorate enfranchised by the Second and Third Reform Acts. He was able, at his greatest, to turn the voters' attention away from their immediate material preoccupations and elevate them towards the pursuit of higher ideals. In doing so, perhaps Gladstone went some way towards making the elector a part of that Christian Commonwealth of which he had dreamed in *The State in its Relations with the Church.* Failure is not the best word to describe a political career of such essential consistency, intense drama and intriguing complexity.

7 Bibliography

E J Feuchtwanger's *Gladstone* (Macmillan, 1989) is a comprehensive and accessible biography. Shorter accounts can be found in the following: Paul Adelman's *Gladstone, Disraeli and later Victorian Politics* (Longman, 1983); Martin Pugh's *The Making of Modern British Politics 1867–1939* (Basil Blackwell, 1982) – a brilliant chapter; and Michael Winstanley's *Gladstone and the Liberal Party* (Routledge, 1990) – a superb and up-to-date synthesis, which, however, does not aim to cover the Irish dimension in much depth. John Vincent's classic, *The Formation of British Liberal Party 1857–68* is marvellous on the context and structure of Gladstonian Liberalism (Harvester, 1976).

A Level students should know that Gladstone has been the subject of much outstanding – but difficult – historical research over the past decade. R T Shannon's massive half-completed biography, *Gladstone 1809–1865* (University Paperbacks, 1984) and the ongoing edition of *Gladstone's Diaries*, with searching introductions by H C G Matthew (partly collected in *Gladstone 1809–1874* [Oxford University Press, 1988]), together summarise much of this. But they are not easy reads themselves!

There are also wide-ranging review articles in *Parliamentary History* by J P Parry (Vols 3 and Vol 10 pt. 2) and A Warren (Vol. 9 pt. 1). This chapter is indebted to Dr Parry in particular whose ideas are more fully expounded in *Democracy and Religion: Gladstone and the Liberal Party 1867–1875* (Cambridge University Press, 1986), and now in his *The Rise and Fall of Liberal Government in Victorian Britain* (Yale, 1994). T A Jenkins' *The Liberal Ascendancy, 1830–1886* (Macmillan, 1994) is briefer and more accessible.

8 DISCUSSION POINTS AND EXERCISES

A *This section consists of questions or points that might be used for discussion (or written answers) as a way of expanding on the chapter and testing understanding.*

1. Why did Gladstone's publication of his pamphlet on *The Bulgarian Horrors and the Question of the East* mark a turning point in his career and in the history of the Liberal Party?
2. What clues does the Midlothian campaign give us as to what made Gladstone such an effective politician?
3. What was the significance of the Second Irish Land Act?
4. Why did the Land Act pose problems for the Land League, and how did the government unintentionally help the League's leaders out of their difficulties?
5. What was the 'Kilmainham Treaty' and why did it arguably mark 'a tremendous step towards Home Rule'?
6. How powerful were Chamberlain and the Radicals between 1880 and 1885?
7. 'Opportunism veiled by self-deception: this is the key to Gladstone's conversion to Home Rule'. How fair is this assessment?
8. What were the underlying reasons for
   a) Hartington's and the Whigs', and
   b) Chamberlain's rejection of Home Rule?

B *Essay questions*

1. Why did Gladstone's second ministry achieve so much less than his first?
2. 'Between 1868 and 1885, foreign policy was the area of greatest electoral weakness for the Gladstonian Liberal Party'. Discuss. (Readers should study the relevant parts of chapters VI and XII before attempting this question.)
3. Why did Gladstone fail to solve the Irish Question?
4. Why did Gladstone try so hard and for so long – and at such cost – to solve the Irish Question?
5. 'Gladstone hijacked the Liberal Party and subordinated it to his own – wilful and destructive – sense of mission'. Is this a fair assessment of Gladstone between 1876 and 1894?
6. 'An old, wild and incomprehensible man'. [Queen Victoria on Gladstone, 1892.] Why did so many of the Victorian upper classes come to fear and loathe Gladstone?
7. What was Gladstonian about Gladstonian Liberalism, and to whom did it appeal?

8 'Gladstone's achievements have been exaggerated.' Discuss.

9 What consistency, if any, is there in Gladstone's career from the 1830s to the 1890s?

9 ESSAY WRITING – SUMMARISING YOUR ARGUMENT

One of the first things a Sixth Form historian is told about A Level essay writing is that 'telling the story' is bad, and that analysis and argument must be put at the centre of his or her essays. This is indeed a crucial skill – but it is also one of the most difficult to learn. What strategies can the student adopt to try and master it?

One good exercise is to write down a concise summary of your argument in no more than three or four sentences: the enforced brevity will leave you with little time for narrative. This can be an excellent basis for class discussion, with each student reading out his or her compact answer. Students often underestimate how much they have to learn from each others' bright ideas! You should also be on the alert for answers which miss the point of a question or stray into irrelevance: identifying the mistakes of others is a good way to build up your own skills.

Take question 4: Why did Gladstone try so hard and for so long – and at such cost – to solve the Irish question? A compact answer might run as follows:

> 'Gladstone, as a Liberal, was determined to put right injustice and end discrimination, and by the late 1860s he recognised that Ireland's religious inequalities and social problems called out for redress. His first attempted solution did not go deep enough, but by the 1880s he more fully appreciated the damage which British rule had done there. He became convinced that it was his mission, and his God-given opportunity, to do all he could to put right the wrongs of the past. The almost religious fervour with which Gladstone conceived of his task, and the gravity of the situation in Ireland in the 1880s, explains the urgency and determination with which Gladstone pursued his ultimate solution – Home Rule.'

In which respects is this a rather one-sided summary of Gladstone's approach to the Irish Question?

After discussion and mutual criticism, the writer of the first compact answer might have been tempted to modify his answer as follows:

> Gladstone was a supremely accomplished politician, and it is hard to avoid the conclusion that making it his 'mission to pacify Ireland' suited his own purposes very well.

'Disestablishment' won the Liberals the 1868 general election, and he may have hoped that 'Home Rule' would do the same in 1886: it certainly had the effect of keeping the Liberal Party under his control! But there was another side to Gladstone – his concern to put right injustice and rectify the wrongs for which British power was partly or wholly responsible, be it in the Balkans, South Africa, Afghanistan – or Ireland. This sense of mission – fired by religious fervour or driven by blind obsession, it is hard to say – as well as the gravity of the situation in Ireland in the 1880s, explain the perhaps reckless determination with which Gladstone pursued his ultimate solution to the Irish problem: Home Rule.

Having established the thrust and range of your argument, before either planning or writing your essay, it should be much easier to ensure that the essay does not stray into pure narrative or irrelevance.

10 DOCUMENTARY EXERCISE-GLADSTONE ON THE 'CLASSES' AND THE 'MASSES'

The following passage is an extract from a speech Gladstone made at the conclusion to his 1886 election campaign.

> [The Liberals] are opposed throughout the country by a compact army, and that army is a combination of the classes against the masses. I am thankful to say that there are among the classes many happy exceptions still. I am thankful to say that there are men wearing coronets on their heads who are as good and as sound and as genuine Liberals as any working man that hears me at this moment. But, as a general rule, it cannot be pretended that we are supported by the dukes, or by the squires, or by the Established clergy, or by the officers of the army, or by a number of other bodies of very respectable people. What I observe is this: wherever a profession is highly privileged, wherever a profession is publically endowed, it is there that you will find that almost the whole of the class and the profession are against us . . . in the main, gentlemen, this is a question, I am sorry to say, of class against mass, of classes against the nation; and the question for us is, Will the nation show enough unity and determination to overbear, constitutionally, at the polls, the resistance of the classes? It is very material that we should consider which of them is likely to be right. Do not let us look at our forces alone; let us look at that without which force is worthless, mischievous, and contemptible. Are we likely to be right? Are the classes ever right when they differ from the nation? ('No.') Well, wait a

moment. I draw this distinction. I am not about to assert that the masses of the people, who do not and cannot give their leisure to politics, are necessarily, on all subjects, better judges than the leisured men who have great advantages for forming political judgements that the others have not; but this I will venture to say, that upon one great class of subjects, the largest and the most weighty of them all, where the leading and determining considerations that ought to lead to a conclusion are truth, justice, and humanity, there, gentlemen, all the world over, I will back the masses against the classes.

Let me apply a little history to this question, and see whether the proposition I have just delivered is an idle dream and the invention of an enthusiastic brain, or whether it is the lesson taught us eminently and indisputably by the history of the last half century. [Gladstone went on to list ten subjects, including the abolition of slavery, Parliamentary reform, the triumph of Free Trade, the disestablishment of the Irish Church and the destruction of Beaconsfieldism which together had 'formed the staple employment and food of our political life for the last 60 years'.] On every one of them, without exception, the masses have been right and the classes have been wrong. Nor will it do, gentlemen, to tell me that I am holding the language of agitation; I am speaking the plain dictates of fact, for nobody can deny that on all these ten subjects the masses were on one side and the classes were on the other, and nobody can deny that the side of the masses, and not the side of the classes, is the one which now the whole nation confesses to have been right.

1 *Suggest reasons why Gladstone had earned the opposition of '... dukes, ... squires, ... the Established clergy [and] the officers of the army.'*

2 *According to Gladstone, what superficial advantages do the classes have over the masses in forming political judgements? Why, on the most important questions, would Gladstone still 'back the masses against the classes'?*

3 *What bearing does Gladstone's speech have on the Home Rule question?*

4 *How might the style and content of Gladstone's speech have inspired his mostly working-class audience?*

5 *Why might some Whigs have been infuriated by Gladstone's survey of 'the history of the last half century' and his 'classes against the masses' rhetoric?*

6 *'The Irish problem radicalised Gladstone'. Discuss.*

X

IRELAND FROM THE UNION TO PARTITION

—

1 INTRODUCTION: THE IRISH QUESTION AND THE ACT OF UNION

On 1 January 1801, the previously separate kingdoms of Great Britain and Ireland became a single state under an Act of Parliament which unified them into a 'United Kingdom'. Under this Act of Union, the separate Irish Parliament was abolished and representation was merged into the Imperial Parliament at Westminster. In this new parliament, Ireland was represented by 100 MPs in the House of Commons and by 4 bishops and 28 other peers in the House of Lords. The Act of Union further provided that the Anglican Church of Ireland would be recognised as the official church within Ireland and that free trade between the two countries would be maintained.

The principal explanation for this major constitutional step is to be found in the immediate situation in which the British Government found itself in the late 1790s. War had been declared on revolutionary France in 1793 in order to counter both French expansion into the Low Countries and the influence of revolutionary ideas, but in neither objective had there been much success. On the contrary, the power of France appeared to be increasing, to the extent that it seemed to threaten the very security of Great Britain itself. Ireland, ruled by a British administration, was resentful of British domination and divided internally between Catholics and Protestants, with the latter themselves divided between Anglicans and Dissenters. Thus it was an obvious target for French subversion, or even invasion. Indeed, a French expeditionary force had actually been sent to Ireland in 1796, but few of the ships had completed the voyage and those that did failed to land because of bad weather. When a rebellion broke out in Ireland in 1798, it came as no real surprise to the British government, which had long-feared such an eventuality.

The revolt was engineered by a group calling itself the 'United Irishmen'. It was led by a young Dublin barrister, Wolfe Tone, who was an admirer of the French Revolution. The 'United Irishmen' aimed to create a democratic and republican Ireland, free of both British control and religious divisions between Roman Catholics and Protestants. The movement, however, failed to secure much influence in Ireland as a whole. Its strength lay mainly in the north-eastern counties of Ulster and, when the rising began in May 1798, it was soon crushed. The revolt was supported, rather belatedly, by the French who this time sent two separate expeditions. One was defeated by a naval squadron. The other landed, but was forced to surrender by the British Army. Tone, who had been in France organising the intervention at the time of the initial rising, was captured with the French forces and later committed suicide in prison.

Although the rising was a total failure, the British Prime Minister, William Pitt, could no longer ignore the threat posed by a hostile and unstable Ireland. As the Irish historian, Professor JC Beckett observes, 'From the British point of view the union was little short of a military necessity'. Nevertheless, the Act of Union was intended not only to make Ireland easier to govern but also to try to create a more stable situation in which some of the traditional tensions and grievances of Ireland could be reduced or eliminated. This hostility stemmed primarily from the fact that Ireland was a country in which the overwhelming majority of the population were Roman Catholics, whilst the majority of land was owned by English Protestants, many of whom did not even reside on their Irish estates. In addition, British administration had, since the seventeenth century, sought to identify Roman Catholics as political enemies of the constitution, denying them political rights.

During the eighteenth century most of the laws against Roman Catholics (the so-called 'Penal Laws') had been repealed. However, in 1801, when the Act of Union came into operation, the most obvious reminders of the 'Penal Laws' were still in existence. These were the parliamentary oaths which MPs and peers had to swear upon admission to Parliament. These oaths (which had also applied to the recently defunct Irish Parliament) specifically required the swearer to renounce central tenets of Roman Catholic doctrine and thus constituted an insuperable barrier in political life for Roman Catholics.

It was Pitt's intention to follow up the Act of Union with further legislation to amend the parliamentary oaths which prevented Catholics from taking seats in Parliment. In this aim he was thwarted by the intransigent opposition of King George III. Pitt resigned, as did his two principal assistants in Irish affairs, Lord Cornwallis, the Lord-Lieutenant of Ireland, and Lord Castlereagh, the Chief Secretary, as well as several others who supported his position. The failure to grant a revision of the oaths, or 'Catholic Emancipation' as the issue became known, ruined any hope that the Union would be accepted in Ireland

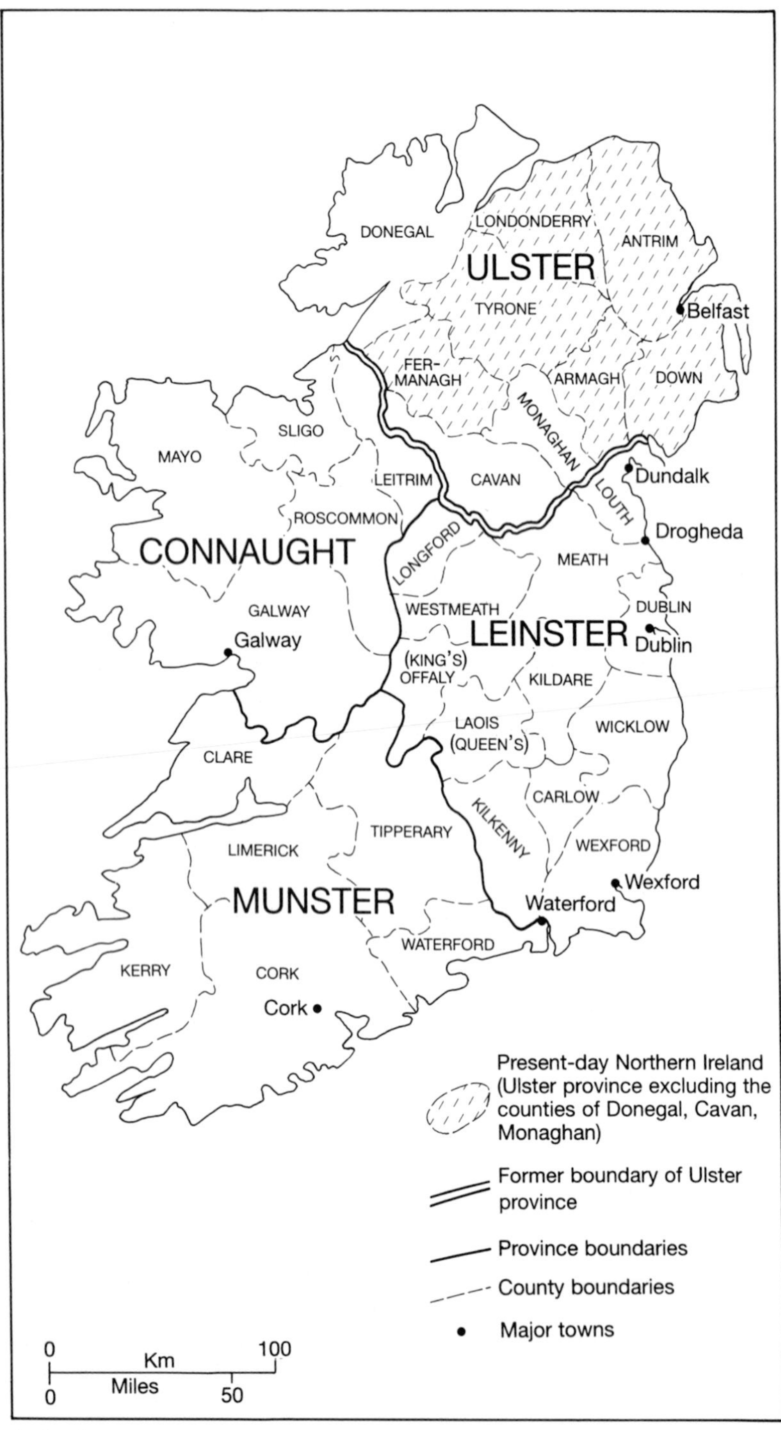
DONEGAL
LONDONDERRY
ANTRIM
ULSTER
TYRONE
Belfast
FER-
MANAGH
ARMAGH
DOWN
MONAGHAN
SLIGO
MAYO
LEITRIM
CAVAN
Dundalk
LOUTH
ROSCOMMON
Drogheda
CONNAUGHT
LONGFORD
MEATH
GALWAY
WESTMEATH
DUBLIN
Galway
LEINSTER
Dublin
(KING'S)
OFFALY
KILDARE
LAOIS
(QUEEN'S)
WICKLOW
CLARE
CARLOW
KILKENNY
TIPPERARY
LIMERICK
WEXFORD
Wexford
MUNSTER
Waterford
WATERFORD
KERRY
CORK
Cork
Present-day Northern Ireland (Ulster province excluding the counties of Donegal, Cavan, Monaghan)
Former boundary of Ulster province
Province boundaries
County boundaries
Major towns
0
Km
100
Miles
0
50

Ireland

as a whole. The demand for Catholic Emancipation became a banner behind which to rally Irish opinion (and not exclusively Roman Catholic opinion) in the three decades following the Union.

2 From Union to Famine 1801–45

A *Daniel O'Connell and Catholic Emancipation*

At first, the reaction in Ireland to the failure of the British Government to grant Catholic Emancipation was one of disappointment rather than angry rebelliousness. There was also an increasing realisation, on all sides, that the political momentum was running in favour of Catholic Emancipation. There was a strong body of opinion in the House of Commons in favour of the 'Catholic claims' and many of the leading politicians who emerged after 1801 also supported reform. In these circumstances it appeared prudent to await the natural progress of events which must, in the course of time, deliver Catholic Emancipation without the need for a militant campaign which might stir other, less acceptable, ambitions.

This gradualist approach was totally disrupted by the arrival on the Irish political scene of a dynamic new force which transformed the entire situation. Daniel O'Connell, born in 1775, a successful barrister and a Roman Catholic, had already made a name for himself opposing the Act of Union. After its passing he continued the attack, urging its repeal. O'Connell came to realise that repeal was impossible without the presence of Roman Catholic MPs at Westminster and he diverted his efforts to emancipation, with the specific intention of using it as a springboard for a greater nationalist campaign. O'Connell was not only a nationalist – he was also a populist. It was immensely important to him that emancipation not only be won, but be won by a popular campaign which involved the mobilisation of the masses in Ireland. Such a victory would provide the momentum for the greater victory to come – the end of the Union and the restoration of an Irish Parliament.

As O'Connell's prestige grew, so the dilemma posed by Catholic Emancipation became more complicated. The Tory governments which dominated British politics up to 1830 were divided on the issue and could only maintain their unity by making it an 'open question' and abstaining from any debate within the Cabinet. In Ireland there was suspicion of O'Connell's motives and methods. However, in 1823, O'Connell launched what turned out to be the decisive factor – the Catholic Association. Although containing some upper-class members, this was essentially a mass movement. It was organised at parish level and rested on the authority of the local Catholic priests and O'Connell himself. By devising the 'catholic rent', collected by the priests at a rate of a penny a month, O'Connell ensured an immense operating fund for the movement which he could deploy virtually as he saw fit. Against such a formidable organisation the British governments after 1823 could offer only a divided and temporising opposition. When O'Connell personally challenged the continued exclusion of Roman Catholics from Parliament by standing as a candidate in at the County Clare election in 1828, the whole edifice of die-hard resistance crumbled. Wellington and Peel, two of the most prominent opponents of reform in the past, were obliged to swallow hard and bring in Catholic Emancipation the following year (*see pages 121–2*).

At first sight the triumph of 1829 seemed to be complete. It was a personal victory for O'Connell whose prestige and oratory had given the movement its direction; it was a popular victory for the Catholic Association whose size had contributed an irresistible momentum. To this extent 1829 was all that O'Connell could have hoped for. And yet it was also a flawed victory – at least in terms of O'Connell's future aspirations. To begin with, the concession of Catholic Emancipation came complete with a sting in its tail: in order to offset the impact of emancipation on the future structure of the House of Commons, Peel devised the simple expedient of raising the Irish franchise qualification from 40s (or £2) freehold to £10. At a stroke this drastically reduced the size of the Irish electorate and the vast majority of those excluded were Roman Catholics. Although the Reform Act of 1832 **did** re-extend the franchise in Ireland to some degree, it maintained the £10 franchise and thus the post-1832 electorate remained smaller than that of 1829. Thus, O'Connell was deprived of the substantial number of supporters in the House of Commons which he had counted upon to spearhead a new attack on the Union. Furthermore, he could no longer count upon the support of British politicians for his aims: many Tories and all the Whigs had supported emancipation, but none of them supported the repeal of the Union. British politics, once fatally divided, now spoke with one voice on the constitutional future of Ireland.

B *The decline of O'Connell*

The momentum for repeal which O'Connell assumed would follow from Catholic Emancipation simply failed to materialise. The reasons, however, were not entirely due to the unfavourable scene in British political circles. As the more perceptive members of the Wellington government had foreseen, the admission of a limited number of Roman Catholic MPs, including O'Connell himself, had the effect of removing them from Ireland itself, at least for substantial periods of the year when Parliament was sitting. Even O'Connell, whatever his talents, could not solve the problem of being in two places at once! As he adjusted to life in the House of Commons, he could not help but slacken his grip on affairs in Ireland.

In the 1830s O'Connell waited in vain for constitutional reform of the

Anglo-Irish connection to fall into his lap. It failed to do so and, when the Conservatives, under Sir Robert Peel, came to power following the general election of 1841, O'Connell was forced to recognise that repeal of the Union was unlikely to be achieved purely by parliamentary pressure. Belatedly, he attempted to revive the 'monster' meetings of the old Catholic Association, in the hope that popular demonstrations would be as effective as they had been in the 1820s. This time, however, the situation was quite different. Peel headed a strong government which was determined to maintain the Union. The Whig opposition were themselves no supporters of repeal. Peel had his own agenda for Ireland (as exemplified by the Maynooth Grant and his Irish Universities policy – *see pages 138–42*) and his aim was to bind Ireland more securely to the Union rather than to slacken the ties. Moreover, O'Connell no longer enjoyed unlimited sway in Ireland itself. During the inactive period of the 1830s, younger Irish radicals had grown impatient with O'Connell and his gradualist approach. This movement, 'Young Ireland', urged more extreme methods and a more complete separation of Ireland and Great Britain than O'Connell had ever envisaged.

In 1840, O'Connell had produced a plan for a restored Irish Parliament. To support this scheme, 1843 was designated by him as 'Repeal Year' with plans for a monster meeting at Clontarf near Dublin at the end of the year. The Government, fearing general disorder if the meeting went ahead, banned it, and O'Connell, who was always basically law-abiding at heart, accepted the ban. Despite this, O'Connell was arrested on a charge of sedition in 1844 and sentenced to a year in prison. His conviction was quashed by the House of Lords on appeal and he was released after serving only 14 weeks. The experience, however, was enough to break his spirit for continuing the struggle. He was nearly 70 and his health was failing; the attacks on him by 'Young Ireland' added to his disillusion. Bitter and broken he finally left Ireland in 1847 and died in Genoa in the same year. However, even before this, O'Connell's campaign, Peel's policies and the dreams of 'Young Ireland' had all been rendered largely irrelevant by the devastating catastrophe which struck Ireland between 1845 and 1851 – The Great Famine.

3 Famine and Fenians

It is almost impossible to exaggerate the impact which the Great Famine has had upon Irish history. In the space of half a decade the population of Ireland was decimated by death and emigration. No official censuses were held in Ireland until 1851, but the population in 1845 has been estimated to have been as high as 9 million, thus comprising nearly a third of the total population of the United Kingdom. The

Famine reduced this population to around 6 million and it continued to fall thereafter under the impact of a sustained pattern of emigration. The whole demographic condition of Ireland was therefore radically altered. At the end of the nineteenth century, Ireland was the only part of Europe to have a lower population than it had had in 1800.

The Great Famine changed more than just the population structure of Ireland. It bit deeply into the consciousness of the nation. Strictly speaking, there was no famine in Ireland during these years – only the potato crops were blighted and this was part of a Europe-wide disease pattern. In fact, vast quantities of food were being produced in, and even exported from, Ireland throughout the whole of this period. What led to mass starvation was the Irish peasantry's dependence on potatoes for subsistence. The Irish peasant farmer barely used cash; he grew cereals to pay his rent and lived off the potato, which was the only crop which could be grown in sufficient quantities on the small plots of land which he farmed for his own subsistence. This pressure on land was partly the result of the old 'Penal Laws', which had originally insisted on the splitting up of the estates of Irish Roman Catholics amongst all their sons upon the death of the father. It was also the result of the massive population explosion which had occured since the middle of the eighteenth century, ironically aided by the potato, which, when healthy, was an excellent and easily cultivated source of nutrition.

The loss of potato crops in successive blights from the summer of 1845 until 1851 spelled disaster for the Irish peasant families unless some safety net could be put in place. Unfortunately, the principles of the New Poor Law (*see page 55*) were almost entirely irrelevant to Ireland, where there was very little scope for raising poor rates amongst the higher classes who were themselves hard pressed for cash much of the time. The current economic wisdom was strongly against any use of large-scale government intervention, which was the only hope for many of the Irish people. Limited public works schemes were eventually set into motion and private charity did some good, but these efforts were on entirely too small a scale to meet the need. The result was that up to a million Irish men, women and children perished from starvation and disease in the midst of plenty. Perhaps as many as two million more fled from Ireland, some only to perish on the hazardous voyage to North America. Many thousands made it only as far as the industrial towns of Britain where they lived in squalor, resented and feared by the indigenous population.

The political effects of the famine were immense. The repeal movement was halted; Young Ireland was discredited and its members dispersed, some to remote areas of the globe: O'Connell was dead and no leader of similar stature would emerge until the era of Parnell began in the late 1870s. In the immediate aftermath of the famine, the nation was too crushed and exhausted to consider a political agenda. The loss of

Young Ireland, in particular, left a vacuum among the ranks of what would have been the rising generation of politicians. An abortive fiasco of a revolt (barely meriting the term rising), in 1848, had been Young Ireland's contribution to the year of general unrest in Europe, marked by the so-called 'Revolutions' in France, Austria and elsewhere. Its leaders were arrested and imprisoned or else fled abroad to escape the authorities. They joined a flow of emigration directed primarily to the United States, where a huge Irish population was beginning to take shape. Emigration had been an increasing trend in Ireland even before the famine years; the effect of the famine was to so increase this trend that the Irish population in America quickly began to outstrip in size and wealth the population of the mother country. These Irish-Americans developed a tradition of violent hatred for Britain as the Cause of Ireland's misfortunes.

From the ashes of Young Ireland a new movement for Irish national freedom slowly began to take shape. In 1858, James Stephens, a former member of the Young Ireland movement, founded the Irish Republican Brotherhood. It became the inner element in a wider organisation, with branches not only in Ireland and Britain but also in Irish communities in the United States, which became known as the 'Fenians'. The term derives from the Old Irish word 'Fene' which means 'the people'. Stephens, and to some extent his movement too, existed for many years in a kind of fantasy world in which the establishment of a fully independent Irish Republic was held to be on the verge of becoming reality. The Fenian Oath enshrined this myth: 'I, xxxx, in the presence of Almighty God, do solemnly swear allegiance to the Irish Republic, NOW VIRTUALLY ESTABLISHED... '. The Fenians started their own newspaper, *The Irish People*, in 1863, and Stephens began calling himself, 'Chief Organiser of the Irish Republic'. In reality, the Fenians made little progress. Stephens travelled to the United States on regular missions to awaken and sustain support among the exiled Irish there; branches were also established in South Africa and Australia. Despite all this however, the Fenians never became a truly national movement in Ireland itself. Stephens regularly promised a rising in Ireland, but year after year it failed to materialise.

When the Fenians finally rose in 1867 the result was a debacle which left the movement in ruins. The attempt was heavily sponsored by Irish-Americans, some of whom (veterans of the American Civil War) actually travelled to Ireland to take part. There was some sporadic fighting, but the organisation and internal security of the movement was amateurish and chaotic. Stephens was arrested and sent to prison and although some of his American collaborators contrived to rescue him and take him to the United States, his career was effectively over. However, the Fenians were saved from being a total failure by three factors. First, the rising had an effect on the leading British politician, Gladstone. He had been concerned about the moral implications of the state of Ireland for some time: the Fenians did enough to ensure that he publically declared his interest in the future of Ireland (*see page 257–8*). Secondly, the aftermath of the rising created a viable set of martyrs for future generations to revere. Thirdly, in their failure, the Fenians managed to focus the attention of more mainstream Irish politicians on ways to improve Ireland's situation by less extreme methods. These last two factors hinged upon the fate of three 'Fenians' who attempted to rescue some of their comrades from a police van taking them for trial in Manchester. They killed (probably accidentally) a police officer in the course of the rescue. The trial and execution of the 'Manchester Martyrs' for the murder of the policemen galvanised Irish political opinion in a way the the Fenians themselves had never been able to achieve. From this renewed interest in political solutions sprang the concept which was to dominate Irish politics until the outbreak of the Great War in 1914 – Irish Home Rule.

4 THE HOME RULE OPTION

The essence of the Home Rule solution for Ireland lay in the idea that, whilst it might be impracticable to aim for the complete separation of Ireland from Great Britain, it was reasonable and attainable to seek a compromise position. Such a compromise would involve the granting of internal self-government to Ireland, within the continuing union of the two countries. Such a solution had been envisaged by O'Connell in his idea for a federal relationship. The problem with this concept from the outset was that it seemed to some to offer too little, whilst to others it seemed to offer too much. For those who sought an independent Irish Republic, it was a cowardly betrayal of Ireland's true destiny. To those who placed the protection of the Union before all else, it was the thin end of a wedge which would ultimately be used to drive the two countries apart.

Nevertheless, the failure of the Fenian rising in 1867, left the way open for a more moderate movement to take the stage in Irish politics. The man who did most to develop the idea of Home Rule, before it was eventually taken up by Gladstone, was Isaac Butt. Butt was an improbable leader of Irish Nationalism. Like O'Connell, he was a lawyer, but there the similarities ended. Butt was an Anglican (the son of a vicar in fact) and in his early political career he was looked on as a staunch Tory. Moreover, he was from Ulster and was to some extent influenced by the Protestant Orange Order and its extreme anti-Roman Catholicism. As he grew older however, his views began to change. In 1848, impressed with the sincerity of the Young Ireland movement, if not with its political ideals, he defended some of them in court. After this he rather fell out of the political limelight, but the case of the 'Manchester Martyrs' brought him back to political prominence as he agreed to defend them at their trial. Subsequently he supported an unsuccessful appeal for an amnesty for the condemned prisoners, on the grounds that whilst their actions might have been wrong, their motives were selfless and sincerely held.

These actions by Butt gave him some degree of credibility amongst the extremists, although in reality he had almost nothing in common with them. This credibility, in addition to the genuine respectability which Butt exuded, gave him a sufficiently broad political appeal to build an Irish National Party with a viable base in the House of Commons. In the 1874 general election, in the wake of general disappointment with Galdstone's Land Act of 1870 (*see page 258–9*), the Home Rule Party won 60 seats, almost double what Butt had expected. It was now a significant force in British politics.

5 The Rise of Parnell

It was at this point, with the Irish Party developing, but as yet unproven as a political weapon, that a new, dynamic and aggressive Irish leader arrived upon the scene. Charles Stewart Parnell was born in 1846, the son of a substantial Protestant landowner in County Wicklow. He was educated in England and went on to Cambridge University, where he refused to complete his degree after being temporarily suspended following a street brawl. He entered Parliament at a by-election in 1875, not it appears because of any great interest in politics, but because he was rather at a loss for any alternative career. All this would appear to make him an even less likely a leader of Irish nationalism than Isaac Butt, but in this case the appearance is deceptive. Although coming from the landowning, Protestant gentry, Parnell's family traced its descent back to Sir John Parnell, who, at the time of the Act of Union, had bitterly opposed the policy, stressing instead the distinctive claim of Ireland to a separate identity. Not only that, but on his mother's side he was descended from a famous American General, Charles Stewart, who had fought against Britain in the War of 1812. Both sides of his family tradition, therefore, gave to Parnell a decidedly anti-British cast of mind. This was reinforced by his own character and personality. He had deeply resented being sent to school in England, where he had felt both alienated and regarded as inferior. He had a violent and rebellious side to his nature which led him to disregard conventions and to take risks. He was also capable of great loyalty once his passions (which were often intense) were roused. Finally, he could display tremendous personal charm and had immense powers of persuasion. These made him, in turn, the object of great loyalty and passion amongst those who fell under his influence.

Once embarked, however casually, on a political career, Parnell soon showed himself to be an adept and ruthless politician. He quickly became the leader of a small group of the more radical Irish MPs and organised them in disruptive tactics in the House of Commons. His oratorical skills developed rapidly and he soon made himself a force to be reckoned with not only in the House but in Ireland at large. Even before Butt died in 1879, Parnell was universally recognised as the most dynamic force in Irish politics. After the general election of 1880, he succeeded to the leadership of the Irish National Party and proceeded to mould it into a formidable parliamentary force. It has been said that, in the 1880s, no British Prime Minister could take office or decide policy without considering how Parnell might choose to use the powerbase which he had built.

Parnell's rise to prominence in Parliament coincided with the return of bad conditions on the land in Ireland itself. The agricultural depression, as we saw in chapter IX, had led to a dramatic increase in the number of convictions for non-payment of rent. In 1879, the Irish nationalist leader, Michael Davitt, founded a Land League, which pledged itself to defend, with violence if necessary, the tenant-farmers from eviction. Davitt persuaded Parnell to become President of this Land League and the latter now drew close to the extremist fringes of Irish politics. He established contacts with the Fenians in the United States and, though he refused to go so far as to join the Irish Republican Brotherhood, he generally recast the Irish National Party in the mould of an anti-landowner, pro-tenant force with an ambiguous attitude to violence. It was all very different from the image that Butt had originally intended. This populist approach, combined with his own powers of oratory and persuasion, raised Parnell to unparalleled heights of popularity, even of adoration, in Ireland, surpassing even O'Connell's position in its passion and intensity. By the early 1880s he was being openly referred to a the 'uncrowned King of Ireland'.

The revived land agitation inspired by the Land League forced Gladstone to renew his interest in Ireland. The concession of his 1868–74 ministry – disestablishment of the Irish Church and the 1870 Land Act – had been significant in British terms (*see pages 257–61*), but had had little impact in Ireland. In 1881, he produced a more extensive Land Act which went much of the way to meeting the grievances of the Irish tenant-farmers (*see pages 275–7*), but he accompanied it with a Coercion Act, allowing detention without trial, to curb the activities of the Land League. This allowed Parnell, who privately admitted the likely effectiveness of the new Land Act, to go on condemning the British Government in inflammatory speeches. Gladstone responded by issuing a warrant for Parnell's arrest and imprisoning him in Dublin's Kilmainham Jail. This 'martyrdom' played into Parnell's hands. His popularity reached even greater heights and at the same time he was able to scale down his entanglement with the extremists without appearing to be weakening his nationalist zeal.

Parnell was soon released from jail under the so-called 'Kilmainham

Treaty'. Under this, entirely unofficial, arrangement Parnell undertook to use his influence to end the violence against landowners and to accept the Land Act as a final settlement of the land question. For its part the British Government agreed to deal with the problem of rent arrears and to extend the fair rent clauses of the Land Act to include leaseholders, who had previously not been protected. The Irish leader still faced a delicate political balancing act however. On the one hand, he recognised that some kind of collaboration with Gladstone and the Liberals was probably the only hope of securing constitutional reform for Ireland; on the other hand, he could not afford to appear too conciliatory or he might start to compromise the goodwill of the political activists in Ireland who still hankered after an Irish Republic. Publicly, Parnell appeared to support the Home Rule solution, but he frequently hedged this commitment with qualifications which gave the strong impression that he saw Home Rule as merely the first step to complete separation. His position was made more difficult by the Phoenix Park murders in 1882, which occurred shortly after his release from Kilmainham. The Irish Secretary, W E Forster, had resigned in protest at Parnell's release, and was replaced by Gladstone's nephew, Lord Frederick Cavendish. Shortly after arriving in Dublin, Cavendish, along with his assistant, an Irish Roman Catholic named Burke, were hacked to death, in Dublin's Phoenix Park, by a terrorist group wielding surgical knives. With Cavendish and Burke died any hope, in the short term, for any new initiatives on the Irish Question.

In 1883 and 1884, Parnell kept a fairly low profile politically. This was partly due to events in his personal life. For some years he had been involved in a love affair with a married woman. The fact that she had been about to give birth to his child (which died shortly after being born), had been one of the factors which had prompted Parnell to abandon his Kilmainham martyrdom in 1882. Another reason for his 'semi-retirement' was that the success of the Land Act had left him little room for manoeuvre, unless he adopted an extreme position. A final reason was that he was facing financial problems. Nevertheless, he returned to active politics in 1885, with a powerful speech, in which he demonstrated the ambiguity of his views on the long-term relationship between Ireland and Great Britain:

> It is given to none of us to forecast the future . . . it is impossible for us to say in what way or by what means the national question may be settled . . . We cannot under the British Constitution ask for more than the restitution of Grattan's Parliament [i.e. the 1792 constitution], but no man has the right to fix the boundary to the march of a nation. No man has the right to say to his country – 'Thus far shalt thou go and no further' . . . while we struggle today for that which may seem possible for us . . . we shall not do anything to hinder or prevent better men who may come after us from gaining better things.

1 *What is the implication of Parnell's reference to 'gaining better things'?*

6 THE FAILURE OF HOME RULE

Late in 1885 Gladstone finally reached the conclusion that only Home Rule could resolve the future of Ireland. The reasons for his conversion are not entirely clear. Certainly he was disappointed that his Irish policy to date had still not 'pacified' Ireland as he had pledged himself to do in 1868. Equally it is clear that he was looking for a new 'moral' cause with which to stimulate the Liberal Party. Finally, he was no doubt influenced by Parnell's decision in the 1885 general election to switch Irish Party support to the Conservatives, in the mistaken belief that their leaders were prepared to contemplate some kind of compromise on Home Rule. Whatever Gladstone's reasoning, when his new position became public, Parnell, unabashed, immediately swung back behind the Liberals. When Gladstone introduced the Home Rule Bill early in 1886, Parnell gave it his support and even ventured to suggest that it represented the fullest expectation for Irish national identity that he could conceive.

The Home Rule Bill produced a split in the Liberal Party, which ensured its ultimate defeat in the House of Commons (*see pages 281–8*). It was, in any case, a seriously flawed bill. Gladstone was proposing that Ireland should have no representation at Westminster, whilst in matters of foreign affairs, defence and external trade, Ireland would remain subject to the Imperial Parliament. Parnell was disappointed by the loss of the bill, but reassured by the continued commitment of Gladstone to the principle of Home Rule. Whatever he said in public, it is clear that Parnell did not really believe that Home Rule would be the last word for Ireland. So long as the Liberal Party remained pledged to the idea, it seemed that sooner or later it must become a reality and, as such, a useful extension of Irish independence upon which to base further developments. Parnell was now content to bide his time until conditions should favour a further attempt. Although the House of Lords was bound to be implacably opposed to such a reform, the peers' opposition to constitutional changes could be overcome, as it had been in 1832 and on other occasions, by the threat, implied or explicit, to create new peers. Gladstone was determined now to remain in politics until the cause was won.

Parnell's waiting game strategy was upset in the late 1880s when his high-risk lifestyle finally began to catch up with him. In 1887 *The Times* published a series of letters, allegedly written by Parnell, which implied that he had, at least, approved of the Phoenix Park murders. Parnell denounced the letters as forgeries, but he did not sue *The Times* and doubts about his dubious political connections grew amongst the

Liberals. Finally, in 1889, after repetitions of the allegations in *The Times*, Parnell did at last resort to legal action. He sued the newspaper for libel and in the ensuing court case a journalist named Piggott, under cross-examination by Parnell's lawyer, admitted to having forged the letters. Piggott later committed suicide. Parnell won the case and his political standing seemed unassailable, as even those who were generally critical of him joined in an ovation when he returned to the House of Commons. It was to be a short-lived triumph however. Parnell's earlier reluctance to sue *The Times* in 1887 had been partly due to his concern that his private life would not stand up to public scrutiny. His long-standing love-affair was with Mrs Katherine O'Shea, the wife of a fellow Irish Nationalist MP, Captain William O'Shea. Parnell had long since come to regard Mrs O'Shea as his wife in all but name and for many years her husband raised no objection to the relationship. Katherine was the heiress to a considerable fortune and both she and Parnell hoped that Captain O'Shea would agree to an uncontested divorce in return for a reasonable financial settlement. However, in 1890 O'Shea started divorce proceedings claiming adultery and named Parnell as the guilty party.

Divorce hearings at that time were held before a judge and jury and evidence was heard in a manner similar to that of a criminal trial. The revelations about Parnell's relationship with Mrs O'Shea created a scandal of immense proportions. Almost overnight Parnell went from being the object of virtual adoration in nationalist Ireland to being the subject of bitter controversy. The priests of the Roman Catholic Church at once denounced him as an adulterer; families were split over whether to support him or not; the Irish National Party was also divided about its response. Gladstone, who was himself a devout churchman and also headed a party which relied to an extent on the support of the Nonconformist churches in Britain, stated that if Parnell were to continue as leader of the Irish Party, his own leadership of the Liberals would be rendered 'almost a nullity'.

Parnell himself never had the least doubt that he should continue as leader, but by a majority of 54 to 32 he was overthrown when the issue was put to a vote of the Irish MPs. Neither Parnell nor the minority which supported him would accept this verdict and the party was therefore split into two bitterly hostile factions. Parnell tried to rally support for his diminished group by public speeches and by fighting by-elections. But his candidates were defeated and his speeches became more and more extreme. He began to appeal openly to the revolutionary and violent traditions of Irish national feeling. All the time he was struggling against the power of the priests who were denouncing him from the pulpits as the agent of the devil or even the devil himself. The strain began to tell on his health, which had always been fragile. He suffered from a long-term, incurable kidney complaint and finally, with his general condition debilitated by fatigue, he collapsed completely. He died at Hove, with Katherine (whom he had since married) at his side, to conclude a tragedy of Shakespearian dimensions.

The death of Parnell did not ease the dissensions within the Irish Party. If anything, it actually exacerbated them in the short term as the Parnellites mourned their lost 'King' – hounded, as they saw it, to his grave by traitors and bigots. Soon, however, there was a hopeful distraction on the horizon. Gladstone returned to power in 1892, at the head of a minority government which depended for its majority on Irish Party support (*see page 289*). Gladstone at once proceeded to introduce a new Home Rule Bill, and this time it achieved a safe passage through the House of Commons. There was never any doubt, however, as to what the verdict of the House of Lords would be. The peers threw out the Bill by the largest majority ever recorded in the House up to that time. Although Gladstone was in favour of taking on the Lords over the issue, he could not persuade the rest of his Cabinet to support him, and the second Home Rule Bill was thus consigned to the scrap-heap of history along with its predecessor.

Although there was natural disappointment with this outcome, the reaction in Ireland was generally muted. Many had seen this result as inevitable anyway; the second Land Act was benefiting the tenant farmers; most of all perhaps, Ireland was too fatigued by internal division and too disillusioned by the tragedy of Parnell, to rouse from political apathy. There was, too, a fundamental change slowly creeping over the country. Gladstone's 1881 Land Act, had made provision for a policy of land-purchase, funded by Government loans, aimed at enabling tenant farmers to buy out their landlords. The Conservative Government of Lord Salisbury approved of the concept, which they saw as calculated to cement Ireland more firmly into the Union, by removing one of the most fundamental popular grievances. The Conservatives, therefore, not only continued the policy; they greatly extended it, both during the period 1886–92, and subsequently between 1895 and 1905. This policy created a class of peasant proprietors, naturally disinclined to revolutionary or even nationalist politics. This approach, known as 'killing Home Rule with kindness', worked in combination with the introduction of popularly-elected county councils in 1898, which signalled the end of the dominance of the old landlords in local government.

In these circumstances, it is not surprising that Ireland entered upon a relatively peaceful period between 1893 and the introduction of the third Home Rule Bill in 1912. Political apathy ruled the day. National pride and aspirations found their expression, increasingly, in a great cultural revival which emphasised the importance of restoring the status of the Irish language which had long been in decline; Irish sports began to flourish; Irish literature, dance and music recruited new enthusiasts. This movement was marked by the formation of organisations such as the Gaelic League, founded in 1893, and by the expansion of earlier groups such as the Gaelic Athletic Association (1884). Even so, despite the apolitical tone of the cultural revival, nationalism of this kind could not be wholly divorced from a political context. The fundamental message of the revival was anti-British. It condemned so-called 'West Britonism' and advocated a separate Irish consciouness. It required only a change in the political climate to harness this sense of a separate Irish identity to a new and specifically Irish political agenda.

7 THE LIBERAL REVIVAL AND THE 'NEW NATIONALISTS'

The alliance of Conservatives and Liberal Unionists, which formed the Unionist Coalition Government of 1895–1905, hoped to bury the issue of Home Rule once and for all. The Land Act of 1903, usually known as 'Wyndham's Act' after George Wyndham, the Chief Secretary for Ireland, substantially completed the transfer of land from landlords to tenants, which was the cornerstone of the Unionist strategy by which Ireland was, in Gladstonian terminology, to be 'pacified'. The Irish Home Rule Party was in two minds about this process. On the one hand, they could hardly condemn the end of the hated 'landlordism', on the other, they recognised that with its passing they had lost one of their most potent political weapons. They consoled themselves with the thought that the Liberal Party remained pledged to the introduction of Home Rule and waited on events.

In 1906 this policy of patience appeared to have paid off when the Liberals won a great victory in the general election. The Liberals now had so great a parliamentary majority that they could, if necessary, contemplate a constitutional clash with the House of Lords if the peers proved obstructive to measures passed with massive support in the Commons. This was the situation which Gladstone had dreamed of, but never achieved, after his conversion to Home Rule. Unfortunately for the Irish Party, his successors had inherited his pledge but not his commitment. From the outset the Liberal Government was determined not to allow Irish affairs to dominate their administration. Although the policy of Home Rule was not abandoned, it was no longer to be the primary objective as Gladstone had desired. The Liberals now preferred to embark upon a general policy of social reform, before considering any fundamental constitutional change. This was an exact reversal of Gladstone's priorities. Nor was there much that the Irish Party could do to force the issue. The Government was not dependent on Irish support and was aware that Home Rule had never aroused much support or even interest among the English electorate, to whom social and economic issues were of far more importance.

In the meantime, in Ireland itself, new forces were taking shape which would ultimately control Irish detinies and destroy the Irish National Party. A labour movement was growing, under the control of James Connolly, an ardent socialist and trade union organiser. Connolly was imbued with the Marxist belief that socialism could only be achieved when a country was sufficiently industrialised for the industrial workers (or proletariat) to be strong enough to overthrow 'capitalist oppression'. He believed that Ireland had remained largely agricultural because it was subservient to the wider needs of the British economy. Therefore, to Connolly, Irish independence was essential if Ireland was to ever reach the stage at which a socialist state could be established. In aiming for a Socialist Workers' Republic, and in linking that idea with trade unionism, Connolly made a major breakthrough in the cause of Irish nationalism. He won over the urban working classes in Dublin to republicanism and, therefore by definition, to separatism. This provided a new and important political driving force for independence from Britain.

Connolly's movement, with its newspaper, the *Workers' Republic*, and its group of activists – the Citizen Army – was opposed by another new nationalist force, Sinn Fein, (meaning 'we ourselves,' or 'ourselves alone'), founded by Arthur Griffith in 1905. This movement, through its paper *The United Irishmen*, rejected socialism, violent revolution and the constitutional approach of the Irish National Party. Instead, Griffith advocated a system of peaceful resistance in which a voluntary parliament would be formed to administer the country in defiance of the British Government. In effect this meant simply carrying on as if Ireland was already independent and ignoring British institutions, such as the courts and civil administration, as though they did not exist. The essence of Griffith's policy was a kind of federal solution, similar to that which had been proposed by Daniel O'Connell years before. He did not want a republic and he did not want the overthrow of capitalism. Rather he sought to create conditions in which capitalism could flourish more to the benefit of the Irish people.

Apart from these two open organisations, there remained the underground groups dedicated to the Fenian tradition, such as the Irish Republican Brotherhood. Though republican, the IRB had no clearly defined political philosophy: it was romanticist, not Marxist, and it therefore had little natural affinity with Connolly's movement, while its commitment to violence repelled Griffith. Thus there were serious areas of division between the various strands of the new nationalism and in these circumstances, the Irish National Party faced little in the way of a concerted challenge to its continued domination of Irish politics in the short term.

In 1909 the situation in the wider British political arena began to change dramatically. The crisis over the 1909 budget (*see pages 469–71*) resulted in some momentous developments for Ireland. The general election at the beginning of 1910 saw the Liberals lose their overall majority in the House of Commons. From now on they were to be a minority government, with the Irish Nationalist MPs holding the balance of power. This was followed by the passing of the Parliament Act of 1911 (*see page* 472), which deprived the House of Lords of its indefinite veto over legislation. These changes put Irish Home Rule right back at the top of the political agenda again. During the Budget Crisis, John Redmond, the Irish National Party leader, had opposed a proposal to increase whisky duties on the grounds that it would adversely affect Irish distilleries; during the crisis over the Parliament Act he had based his support for the Government on the assurance that Irish Home Rule would be a priority once the curbing of the powers of the House of Lords had been achieved. In his negotiations with the Liberals he had made it clear that the Irish would act to disrupt Government policy if Home Rule remained on the shelf.

Redmond's threat of disruption was in many ways a bluff since there was no alternative government in prospect from which he might expect to obtain Home Rule. It was however a bluff which was not called. The Liberal commitment to Home Rule, though no longer Gladstonian in its intensity, was nevertheless genuine. This was not to say, however, that the Irish Party could simply present its demands and expect them to be met in full. Asquith, the Prime Minister, intended to introduce a modest measure that could not reasonably be represented as a staging-post to separatism. Other leading Liberals, like Lloyd George and Winston Churchill, believed that a separate deal for the largely Protestant Ulster counties would have to be devised in the end. Asquith knew they would face fanatical opposition from Ulster itself, along with strong resistance from the Unionist Party in Britain. The Parliament Act, which was the key to overcoming opposition in the House of Lords, was in reality something of a mixed blessing. It ensured that a Home Rule Bill could be passed, but since the peers could reject the Bill twice before being constitutionally compelled to accept it on the third occasion, it also meant that there would be a minimum period of two years, before enactment, during which passions would be whipped up to fever pitch.

8 THE ULSTER CRISIS 1912–14

The third Home Rule Bill was introduced into the House of Commons in April 1912. It was a modest enough proposal which left considerable control of Irish affairs (including control of revenue) with the Westminster Parliament – a limited devolution of self-government. To Redmond it was barely acceptable and could only be sold to the more extreme INP members as a starting-point for future progress. To the Unionists it was entirely unacceptable for the same reason. Bonar Law, the Unionist leader, was provoked into an extreme stance when, in July

1912, at a huge Unionist rally at Blenheim Palace, he observed that he could 'imagine no length of resistance to which Ulster can go in which I should not be prepared to support them'. Asquith responded by calling Bonar Law's speech 'reckless' and 'a complete grammar of anarchy'.

In this bitter atmosphere the Bill passed the Commons for the first time, eventually completing its stormy passage in January 1913. There was great disorder in the House during the debates – verbal abuse was common and in one incident a book was thrown at Churchill. The verdict of the Commons was immediately reversed in the Lords. The whole process then had to be repeated with totally predictable results. By August 1913 the Bill had been passed once more through the Commons, only to receive its routine rejection by the peers. A proposal for a constitutional conference in September 1913 foundered on the intransigent positions taken by the opposing forces. The most that the Ulster leader, Sir Edward Carson, would accept was Home Rule excluding the whole of the nine counties of Ulster which would include Cavan, Donegal and Monaghan, all of which had Catholic majorities. These were impossible terms for Redmond and the most that Asquith would concede was a reasonable degree of autonomy for Ulster, within the general Home Rule package.

While attention had been focused on the fate of the Home Rule Bill at Westminster, events had been moving in Ireland itself. Ulster opinion had been hardening into die-hard resistance well before the introduction of the Bill and, in Sir Edward Carson, it found an able and articulate leader. In September 1912 Carson drew up a 'Solemn League and Covenant' whose signatories pledged themselves to resist a Home Rule Parliament in Ireland should one ever be set up. Over 470 000 people signed this Covenant – some of the more passionate using their own blood as ink. In January 1913 the Ulster Volunteer Force was set up and soon numbered 100 000 men. This provoked the setting up of a nationalist counterpart organisation, the Irish Volunteers, a body pledged to support Redmond, but which was quickly and predictably infiltrated by the Irish Republican Brotherhood. With two such bodies bent upon diametrically opposed objectives, the long-heralded risk of civil war began to assume a concrete form.

In December 1913, Asquith's government resorted to a ban, by Royal Proclamation, on the importation of arms and ammunition into Ireland. Neither of the two para-military forces were as yet armed, at least not openly or extensively, and the precaution seemed wise as well as justified. At the same time Asquith was also preparing to extract more concessions from the Irish National Party, in the hope that the opposition in Parliament to Home Rule could at least be diminished. This could only be done by putting pressure on Redmond. First he was induced to accept the idea of considerable autonomy for Ulster and then the actual exclusion of Ulster altogether for a temporary period –

initially set at three years, but almost immediately doubled to six. The latter concession compromised the whole concept of Ireland as a single unit and can be seen as the first concrete move towards the idea of partition, but in reality it was a gesture Redmond could afford at that point, because it was obvious that Carson would never accept any temporary exclusion. Carson duly obliged by rejecting the proposal as soon as Asquith put it forward.

In March 1914 the Government was rocked by the so-called 'Curragh Mutiny'. The Government had long been uncomfortable with the thought that if it came to a confrontation with the Ulster Unionists, it would depend, for the enforcement of Home Rule, on an army which was dominated by officers of Anglo-Irish Protestant background who were overwhelmingly anti-Home Rule in their sentiments. In a misconceived attempt to lessen the risk of widespread resignations from the army, the Secretary of State for War, Seely, agreed with General Sir Arthur Paget, the Commander-in-Chief in Ireland, that officers whose homes were actually in Ulster could be allowed a temporary leave from duty. At this point the only moves being proposed were precautionary measures to secure arms depots and communications in Ulster as the Bill was still in the course of its third passage through Parliament. Even so, there were rumours that the Government was about to order the arrest of the Ulster leaders (they had been considering this for some time), and Paget, in briefing his officers, was deliberately pessimistic, suggesting that Ulster would be 'in a blaze by Saturday'.

As a result, 58 officers, including a Brigadier-General, resigned. Action against the defectors was impossible because sympathy for them was widespread throughout the army and even strong in the navy. The Government was forced to conciliate the rebels and Seely even went so far as to grant, on his own authority, an undertaking that, in effect, force would not be used against the opponents of Home Rule. Seely paid for this absurd concession with his job, but the damage was done. The Government appeared weak and indecisive. The Ulster Volunteers were encouraged to proceed with a venture to arm themselves. In April a series of landings of armaments took place at Larne, Bangor and Donaghadee. There was no interference from the authorities and the Ulster Volunteers were thus transformed into a well-armed and formidable army. It was only a matter of time before the Irish Volunteers reponded. In June, guns for the Nationalists were landed near Dublin (this time in the face of official intervention which left three dead and nearly 40 injured), and, although it was by no means as successful an effort as the Ulster landings, it still left considerable quantities of arms in the hands of the nationalist force.

Meanwhile, the Home Rule Bill was heading inexorably for the Statute Book. Asquith, Bonar Law and Carson had agreed by June that an Amending Bill would be introduced as an addition to the main legislation to incorporate some form of compromise. This in itself was of little use, however, since there was no agreement as to what these amendments should be. Furthermore, any amendments had either to be accepted by or imposed on Redmond and the Irish National Party. In late June the Government produced its first attempt at an amending bill. The main proposal was for the exclusion of the Ulster counties from the Home Rule Bill for a period of six years, with each county voting separately for its own destiny. This idea had already been refused by Carson and the House of Lords reponded by amending the proposal to provide for the automatic exclusion of all nine Ulster counties on a permanent basis, a solution that the Government could definitely not agree to.

Encouraged by King George V, the politicians convened a constitutional conference at Buckingham Palace on 21 July 1914. Asquith and Lloyd George represented the Government; Redmond and John Dillon the INP; the Unionist Party was represented by Bonar Law and Lord Lansdowne, with Carson and James Craig representing the Ulster Unionists. The conference was intended to reach decisions in two stages: first to debate the area of Ulster to be excluded; secondly to debate the terms of exlusion, whether they were to be temporary or permanent, and, if the former, then for how long. In the event the discussions deadlocked on the first stage and so the second stage was never even considered. The conference broke up after three days to be followed two days later by the nationalist gun-running coup. Barely a week later the European crisis came to a head and Britain was at war with Germany.

The crisis of war overtook the Irish Question at a crucial point. All sides in the constitutional conference realised that some kind of compromise was inevitable. Carson, in particular, was far more moderate in private than he was prepared to be in public. If the parties had been forced to continue the negotiations, a constitutional settlement would almost certainly have been reached. In the event, the war enabled all sides to agree to shelve the issue in a way which virtually guaranteed the renewal of the crisis at some later date. The Home Rule Act was passed as an all-Ireland measure but was accompanied by a Suspensory Order which made it inoperable for the duration of the war. This was just about the worst outcome, short of actual civil war, which could possibly have been contrived to the Ulster Crisis.

9 WAR, REBELLION AND PARTITION 1914–21

Initially the First World War seemed to have a positive effect upon Anglo-Irish relations. Support for the war was almost universal at the outset, with the fate of 'little Belgium' seeming to represent the interests of all small nations in their relations with those greater than themselves. In comparison to the threat of German militarism even British rule seemed, or could be made to seem, comparatively benign. Ulster, already intoxicated with its Britishness and loyalism, rushed to the colours in a frenzy of unbridled patriotism. In the rest of Ireland the reponse was less passionate but nevertheless Catholic Ireland also answered the call and marched to slaughter in France and Belgium. Probably never before in her history had Ireland seemed to be so much at one with Britain.

For John Redmond the war seemed the ideal opportunity for nationalist Ireland to demonstrate her loyalty to the Crown and cement, by her valour in arms, the future of Ireland under Home Rule. Even before the war he had secured, for political reasons, a strong grip over the running of the Irish Volunteers organisation. Now he threw them into the fray. First he declared that the Volunteers would defend Ireland against invasion, thus releasing the regular army to fight the Germans in Flanders. He then went further and urged them to fight overseas. In a speech intended to reassure opinion in England of Irish loyalty he argued passionately for an extension of the Volunteers commitment to the war effort:

> This country at this moment is in a state of war, and the duty of the manhood of Ireland is twofold. Its duty is at all cost to defend the shore of Ireland from foreign invasion. It has a duty more than that, of taking care that Irish valour proves itself on the field of war as it always has proved itself in the past. The interests of Ireland . . . are at stake in this war. This war is undertaken in defence of the highest principles of religion and morality and right . . . go on drilling and make yourselves efficient . . . then account for yourselves as men, not only in Ireland itself, but wherever the firing line extends.

This was dangerous for Redmond. He was tolerated rather than respected by the leaders of the Volunteers and he was no Parnell in terms of his popular appeal.

Support for the war split the Volunteers. The majority, reflecting the overwhelming sentiment of public opinion, sided with Redmond and followed the path of loyalty to the Empire. A minority, however, broke with Redmond, seeing the pro-war stance as collaboration with the enemy and a betrayal of Ireland's claim to nationhood. Their isolated, minority position drew them closer to Connolly's 'Citizen Army'. Herein lay the origin of the Easter Rebellion in 1916. To these dissident nationalists the danger which Britain faced in Europe was an opportunity to strike for freedom. A small organising committee comprising Tom Clarke, Sean McDermott, Patrick Pearse and James Connolly planned the rising. Pearse in particular was deeply committed to the idea that Ireland's future could be redeemed only by a 'blood sacrifice'. To that extent, even if the intended revolution failed, it would have purged the soul of Ireland which had been compromised by collaboration with the British oppressors.

The rebellion was ill-timed, ill-planned and chaotically executed. Many of these failings were not entirely the fault of the revolutionary leaders themselves. They were obliged to keep their plans secret, even from some of the key personnel involved, in order to maintain security. They counted on support from Germany in the form of an arms shipment, organised by Sir Roger Casement, a former British Civil Servant, which in the event was intercepted. Casement himself was arrested and later executed for treason. Even the Commanding Officer of the dissident Volunteers, Eoin MacNeill, a Professor of History at University College, Dublin, was not informed of the planned rising until the last possible moment. MacNeill was horrified to learn of the intended Easter Rising which he considered premature and doomed to failure. When he learned that arms from Germany were going to be available, he reluctantly agreed to support the revolt, but, when news of Casement's arrest came through, he immediately reversed his decision and did everything he could to abort the coup attempt. He cancelled the Volunteers' planned route marches for Easter Sunday which were supposed to be the launching-pad for the rising. The revolutionary leaders got round this obstruction by rescheduling the marches and the rising for Easter Monday.

The Easter Rising was doomed from the start. It was centred entirely on Dublin, the number of rebels actively mobilised was too few and they were inadequately armed. The declaration of Irish Independence was read by Patrick Pearse to a small, largely bemused crowd, outside the General Post Office, the headquarters of the rebellion:

> In the name of God and of the dead generations from which she receives her old tradition of nationhood, Ireland, through us, summons her children to her flag and strikes for her freedom ... supported by her exiled children in America and by gallant allies in Europe, but relying first on her own strength, she strikes in full confidence of victory ... We declare the right of the people of Ireland to the ownership of Ireland and to the unfettered control of Irish destinies, to be sovereign and indefeasible ... we hereby proclaim the Irish Republic as a Sovereign Independent State, and we pledge our lives and the lives of our comrades in arms to the cause of its freedom, of its welfare and of its exaltation among the nations ... The Republic guarantees religious and civil liberty, equal rights and equal opportunities to all its citizens ... cherishing all the children of the nation equally, and oblivious of the differences carefully fostered by an alien Government, which have divided a minority from the majority in the past ...

1 *What is the significance of the references to 'exiled children' and 'gallant allies' contained in the Proclamation?*

2 *What is the purpose of the guarantees which the Republic offers?*

3 *Do you agree that the British Government had tried to divide communities in Ireland as the Proclamation alleges?*

Even if the attempt had attracted immediate and widespread popular support, the odds would have been against the rebels. In the event their rising flew in the face of popular feeling and was almost universally condemned by the Irish people. Nevertheless, the rebels held the British Army at bay for the best part of a week and, although many saw no actual fighting at all before surrendering, some fought with great skill and courage against overwhelming odds before they were killed or captured. This was glorious defeat when compared to the Fenian Rising, and its potential for exploitation was immediately apparent to the Irish National Party, who urged leniency for the captured rebels upon the British Government.

These pleas fell on largely deaf ears. Admittedly, of over 70 death sentences initially passed, the great majority were commuted to terms of imprisonment, but any executions were likely to be controversial, given the nature of Irish history. In the end, 14 of the leaders, including Pearse and Connolly, were shot; one further execution took place of a rebel who had killed a policeman whilst resisting arrest. As the executions progressed, so the mood in Ireland began to change and the fears of the Irish MPs grew. In May 1916 John Dillon pleaded again with the Government:

> I admit they were wrong . . . but they fought a clean fight . . . no act of savagery or act against the usual custom of war that I know of has been brought home to any leader . . . the great bulk of the population were not favourable to the insurrection . . . . What is happening is that thousands of people in Dublin . . . are now becoming infuriated against the Government on account of these executions . . . feeling is spreading throughout the country in a most dangerous degree.

The policy of executions brought about a most profound change in the atmosphere in Ireland. Few ordinary people knew much about the revolutionary leaders or their aims. The rising was popularly known as the 'Sinn Fein' rebellion although in fact Sinn Fein had had no involvement in it. Gradually, however, the leaders and those they had led were transformed into heroic figures. When the captured groups of rebels had been marched to the Dublin docks to be shipped off to prison on the mainland, they had needed army protection from angry mobs of mothers, fathers, wives and sisters of Irish soldiers fighting in France and Belgium, who had tried to attack them as cowards and traitors. Now these same people, for the most part, were demanding their release. The Government was, of course, in too difficult a position, at a crucial stage in the war, to adopt a lenient policy towards those who had committed treason. Nevertheless, it is impossible to escape the conclusion that, had the executions not been carried out, the subsequent course of Irish history might have been very different.

The rebellion and its aftermath polarised attitudes in Ireland beyond recall. To Protestant Unionist opinion, the rebels were traitors who had got what they deserved; to Catholic nationalist opinion, they had become heroes and martyrs. From this point onwards, the prospect of achieving an all-Ireland settlement by concensus was virtually extinguished. In 1917 Asquith, alarmed that the Irish Question might sour relations with the then still neutral United States, offered immediate Home Rule with a provision for the exclusion of the six north-eastern counties of Ulster where the Protestant majority was substantial. The Government also sponsored a Convention to discuss the long-term future of the six counties. This had no chance of success. The Sinn Fein party, which now comprised an alliance of Griffith's original organisation and the remnants of the 1916 rebels, refused even to attend. At the end of 1917, the remainder of the rebels interned on the mainland were released as a goodwill gesture but, though welcomed in Ireland, it did little to improve the image of the British Government. In 1918 the Government, now headed by Lloyd George, put the seal on the failure of its Irish Policy by seeking to extend conscription to Ireland. Even the Irish National Party opposed this move, but its show of resistance to British authority came too late to save it from the backlash of opinion in nationalist Ireland which was now moving firmly in support of Sinn Fein.

The 1918 general election marked the end for the Irish National Party. It was decimated as a political force winning only 7 seats against the triumphant 73 won by Sinn Fein. The result was not, in fact, as overwhelming as it appeared on the surface. Barely two-thirds of the electorate voted and less than 50 per cent of the votes cast went to Sinn Fein. Also there was considerable illegality in some of the elections, with Sinn Fein activists voting many times over, often on behalf of electors who were dead. Even allowing for this, however, there is little doubt that the result reflected a genuine demand in Ireland for a substantial degree of independence from Britain. The elected Sinn Fein candidates refused to take their places at Westminster, preferring instead to constitute themselves as Dail Eireann – the Assembly of Ireland – claiming to represent the only legitimate legislative authority for the country.

The main organisers of the independent Dail were Griffiths, Eamon de Valera, (a commander from the 1916 Rebellion, originally sentenced to death but reprieved mainly because of his American citizenship), and Michael Collins, a junior figure in the Rebellion, who had emerged as a leader of those interned on the mainland. De Valera, who had been elected as President of Sinn Fein in October 1917, became the leader of the illegal government whilst Collins doubled as Finance Minister and organiser of the military arm of the nationalists – the Irish Republican Army. In the early months of 1919, as the victorious allied powers assembled at Versailles to discuss the peace settlement, the Irish leaders hoped that American goodwill and the principle of self-determination of nations, upon which the peace settlement was supposed to be based, would ensure that their claim to independence would be forced upon the British Government. This was a forlorn hope. The American president, Woodrow Wilson, needed the co-operation of the British Prime Minister, Lloyd George, at the Paris Peace Conference and was not prepared to alienate him on behalf of Ireland.

In an atmosphere of disappointment the situation quickly deteriorated. Local groups of IRA men soon began to take independent action to secure arms and explosives. Before long acts of terrorism became commonplace. The British Government responded in kind. Additional men were drafted into the Royal Irish Constabulary; they were known, due to the use of ex-army khaki to supplement the standard police uniform, as the 'Black and Tans'. The police, reinforced by the 'Tans' and by a specially recruited unit of ex-officers known as the 'Auxiliaries', met terror with terror and, between 1919 and 1921, Ireland writhed in agony as these two groups of increasingly ruthless fighters battled for supremacy. The Dublin Government of de Valera had scarcely any control over the IRA; Lloyd George's Government was hardly much better placed with the 'Black and Tans'. Pressure for a resolution of the situation began to mount from many quarters. The British Government, seeking a policy of international co-operation in the post-war world, was acutely aware that its policy in Ireland was the object of international contempt; the press in Britain was increasingly critical of the actions of the 'Tans'; there were demands from the Church of England and from King George V for peace; not least, the IRA were running out of both human and material resources to continue their campaign and the Irish Government itself was willing to seek a settlement.

Lloyd George had already offered a legislative solution in the form of the Government of Ireland Act of 1920. This had proposed Home Rule for Northern and Southern Ireland separately, with a Council of Ireland drawn from the two parliaments to oversee an eventual reunification. This was broadly acceptable to the Ulster Unionists who obviously had no intention of co-operating with the Council of Ireland idea. It was quite unacceptable to the nationalists, however, and this led to the final irony in the Home Rule saga: Ulster, so long the rock upon which Home Rule had foundered, now prepared to embrace Home Rule for itself. In June 1921, the King, scorning the threat of assassination, opened the first Northern Ireland Home Rule Parliament and used the occasion to deliver a plea for peace. De Valera immediately responded and an armistice was signed early in July. Months of negotiations then ensued and Griffith and Collins headed a delgation to London to complete the final agreement.

The 'final settlement' of the Irish Problem, if it can really be so termed, was arrived at in a manner typical of the confused and off-the-cuff approach which had always characterised British government of Ireland. Lloyd George, determined to secure a settlement to restore his sagging prestige, offered Dominion status to Southern Ireland along with an amazing offer to place Northern Ireland under the Dublin Government for a limited period. Collins and Griffith were as delighted as they were stunned, and accepted at once. The proposal was, however, vetoed by the Unionists in the Government and Lloyd George, ducking and weaving with a skill remarkable even by his own accomplished standards, swiftly withdrew the idea of forcing Ulster into a temporary union with the South. Instead, he threatened to renew the war and prosecute it ruthlessly to a conclusion, unless the offer of Dominion status, minus the North, was accepted at once. While the Irish negotiators attempted to grasp this sudden reversal, Lloyd George offered a final twist entirely of his own devising. A boundary commission would be set up to arrange a final settlement of the North-South border and, Lloyd George hinted, this commission would set a boundary so limiting to the North that it would ultimately be compelled to accept reunification.

Whether Lloyd George really believed that such a scheme could ever be brought to fruition, or whether he simply threw it in to sweeten the pill knowing it would never happen, is impossible to determine. The offer had the desired effect. Collins and Griffith agreed to accept the formula despite their well-founded doubts as to how it would be received in Dublin. In doing so they condemned the new 'Irish Free State', as it was called, to a period of civil war. Collins was assassinated at the hands of those who saw the 'Anglo-Irish Treaty' as a betrayal. The offer of Dominion status, though a major advance over anything previously offered, involved continued Irish membership of the British Empire and the sworn allegiance of the legislature and government of the Free State to the British Crown. This, even more than the loss of the territory in the north (which many regarded as temporary), was too much for some nationalists to bear. Although the Dail eventually ratified the Treaty by a narrow majority, opposition to the settlement in the Free State was bitter and ended only by the ruthless action of the new administration.

Many loose ends were left over to plague later generations. The Boundary Commission disappeared in 1925, leaving many areas of South Armagh, South Down and Fermanagh, where there were Catholic majorities, under Northern control. Thus a discontented, substantial majority was left inside the borders of Northern Ireland. The Council of Ireland was a dead duck from the start, since the Government of Northern Ireland refused to have anything to do with it. The right of the Irish parliament to speak for a united Irish Republic was effectively recognised in the Anglo-Irish Treaty. Since no such Irish republic existed, this scarcely seemed significant at the time, but it later became the basis of the claim of the Irish Republic, founded in 1949, to constitutional jurisdiction over all of Ireland. The IRA, which refused to accept the settlement, was ruthlessly hounded by the new Free State Government. Many of its members were imprisoned, some were executed and many fled to the United States. However, though the IRA was defeated, it was not eradicated and survived, embittered, to continue its struggle through succeeding generations.

10 BIBLIOGRAPHY

J C Beckett *A Short History of Ireland* (Hutchinson, 1979 6th Ed.). This is excellent introductory reading, especially for those wishing to set the topic in a longer-term context going back to the Middle Ages. Only the last two (of six) chapters cover the period from the Act of Union.
Grenfell Morton *Home Rule and the Irish Question* (Seminar Series, Longman, 1980). Primarily aimed at A level students and useful for an interesting range of documents. Part One contains a brief but useful review of the first half of the nineteenth century, while the bulk of the book deals with the Home Rule issue.
Nicholas Mansergh *The Irish Question 1840–1921* (University of Toronto Press, 1965). This is a major work which covers the topic through a series of themes rather than chronologically. It requires a detailed factual knowledge before being tackled. Complex and demanding, but very rewarding for those who can cope with it!
S R Gibbons *Ireland 1780–1914* (Evidence in History Series, Blackie, 1978). Based mainly on primary and secondary extracts with a linking text to explain and introduce the topics. Again, it needs a good factual grasp to begin with in order to get the best out of it.
R F Foster *Modern Ireland 1600–1972* (Viking, 1993), has contributed much to our understanding of Anglo-Irish relations.

11 DISCUSSION POINTS AND ESSAY QUESTIONS

A *Discussion points*

1 Was the Act of Union doomed to failure from the outset?

2 Does Daniel O'Connell deserve to be regarded as the 'Great Liberator'?

3 Could Britain have done more to help Ireland during the 'Great Famine'?

4 Were the Fenians a failure or a success?

5 How great a leader of the Irish was Parnell?
6 Did Gladstone ever really understand the Irish Question?
7 Was Home Rule the right solution for the Irish Question on any of the three occasions it was attempted?
8 Was the Easter Rising a 'just cause' or an 'act of treachery'?
9 Was there any alternative to the policy pursued by the British Government to deal with the Irish Question between 1919 and the end of 1921?

B *Essay questions*

1 What was the impact of the Act of Union on Ireland between 1801 and 1829?
1 Assess critically the contribution of Daniel O'Connell to Anglo-Irish affairs.
2 Account for the failure of the first two Home Rule Bills of 1886 and 1893.
3 'In the final analysis his career must be considered a disastrous failure for Ireland.' How fair is this verdict on Parnell?
4 Account for the divisions which had emerged in Irish Nationalism by 1914.
5 Was the partition of Ireland in 1921 inevitable?

12 Documentary Exercise

i) John Redmond, speaking in 1907, based his demand for the future self-government of Ireland on the concept of Home Rule:

> The national demand, in plain and popular language, is simply this, that the government of every purely Irish affair shall be controlled by the public opinion of Ireland and by that alone. We demand this self-government as a right. For us the Act of Union has no binding moral or legal force. We regard it as our fathers regarded it before us, as a great criminal act of usurpation, carried by violence and by fraud . . . we declare that no ameliorative reforms, no number of Land Acts. . . . no redress of financial grievances, no material improvement or industrial development, can ever satisfy Ireland until Irish laws are made and administered upon Irish soil by Irishmen . . .

James Connolly, writing in the *Workers Republic* in February 1916, explained why he rejected the concept of Home Rule as irrelevant to the needs of Ireland:

> What is a free nation? A free nation is one which possesses

absolute control over all its internal resources and powers.... Is that the case of Ireland? If the Home Rule Bill were in operation would that be the case of Ireland? To both questions the answer is: no, most emphatically, NO! A free nation must have complete control over its own harbours, to open or close them at will ... Does Ireland possess such control? No. Will the Home Rule Bill give such control ... it will not ... A free nation must have full power to nurse industries to health either by government encouragement or by government prohibition of the sale of goods of foreign rivals ... Ireland ... will have no such power under Home Rule ... A free nation must have full powers to alter, amend, or abolish or modify the laws under which the property of its citizens is held in obedience to the demand of its own citizens ... Every free nation has that power; Ireland does not have it, and is not allowed it by the Home Rule Bill ... all the things that are essential to a nation's freedom are denied to Ireland now, and are denied to her under the provisions of the Home Rule Bill, and Irish soldiers in the English Army are fighting in Flanders to win for Belgium, we are told, all those things which the British Empire, now as in the past, denies to Ireland.

1 *What is the basic difference between Redmond and Connolly in their views on the concept of Home Rule?*

2 *How do you account for the differences between the views they express, (a) using the evidence in the documents, and (b) using your own knowledge?*

3 *Compare Connolly's comment about Irish involvement in the First World War with the comments made by Redmond in the extract on page 321. How do you account for the differences in tone and viewpoint?*

ii) John Redmond reflected on the record of British Government in Ireland during the same speech in 1907:

... our claim to self-government does not rest solely upon historic right and title. It rests also ... upon the failure of the British Government in Ireland for the last hundred years ... In every civilised country in Europe the population has increased, in Ireland, in the last sixty years, it has diminished by one-half ... There has been a Coercion Act for every year since the Union was passed; there is today in existence a law which enables the Lord-Lieutenant, at his arbitrary discretion, by the stroke of a pen, to suspend trial by jury, personal liberty, freedom of discussion, and the right to public meeting all over Ireland ... There have been since the Union three insurrections, all of them suppressed in blood, with sacrifices untold in the prison cell and upon the scaffold ... it is the history of constantly-recurring famines every few years ... A history of industries deliberately suppressed by British Act of Parliament, and not one finger lifted in the last hundred years to advance industrial prosperity . . .

1. *Explain the charges which Redmond is making against British Government in Ireland.*
2. *In what ways could the British Government be defended against these charges?*

XI

DISRAELI, SALISBURY AND THE CONSERVATIVE PARTY

—

A DISRAELI AND THE CONSERVATIVE RECOVERY

1 INTRODUCTION: THE AFTERMATH OF THE REPEAL OF THE CORN LAWS

THE Conservatives dominated British politics for most of the last quarter of the nineteenth century. Their ascendancy owes much to the two great leaders of these decades: Benjamin Disraeli (Prime Minister in 1868 and 1874–80) and Lord Salisbury (Prime Minister in 1885, 1886–92 and 1895–1902). One object of this chapter will be to compare and assess their relative contributions to the Tory success story. But before this can be done, it will be necessary to examine, briefly, the condition and prospects of the Conservative Party in the years after Peel's fall in 1846. For only then will the extraordinary and quite unpredictable scale of the Conservatives' recovery and triumph later in the century be apparent.

For most of the first half of the nineteenth century, the Tory Party had had a distinct identity and political function, which guaranteed it – with some exceptions, like the 1830s – widespread support. In an age of economic and political revolution, the Tories stood for order, tradition and hierarchy. People who were fearful of threats to the constitution or to the established Church looked automatically to the Tories to defend them. Not least, the 'landed interest' saw the party as its bulwark against change.

Peel (Conservative Prime Minister 1834–5 and 1841–6) had no intention of subverting the world the Tories held dear. But he believed it was in the national interest, and the interest of the aristocracy itself, for the traditional order to be defended with greater flexibility and imagination. Stubborn and undiluted resistance to change would be self-defeating. In particular, Peel believed it was time the government recognised the vital contribution industry was making to the life of the nation. By 1846, he had concluded that the Corn Laws – which had given special protection to agriculture since before the Napoleonic Wars – could no longer be justified. With Whig help, Peel repealed them in 1846.

His backbenchers felt utterly betrayed. Repeal broke every promise they had made to their rural constituents, and seemed to threaten farmers with economic ruin. In some of the most bitter debates ever heard in Parliament – in which Benjamin Disraeli emerged as the unlikely champion of the protectionists – the Conservative Party was rent in two. Peel's own backbenchers overthrew his leadership, and the most embittered helped to vote him out of office. They then reconstituted their party along protectionist lines.

The consequences of this were catastrophic for the Conservatives. For, in destroying Peel, they condemned themselves to almost three decades in the political wilderness.

There were various reasons for this. Firstly, practically all the men of administrative talent – the 'brains' of the party – followed Peel. Voters knew that there was not enough ability and experience left in the party for a competent Cabinet to be formed out of its leading members. Secondly, by expelling Peel, they had reduced themselves to a narrowly agrarian party, incapable of speaking for the wider nation. Although the land had been at the core of the old party, wealthy financiers and merchants, as well as a few great industrialists, like Peel's own father, had supported the Tories in the past. But they would not give their votes to a mere rump of 'agricultural fanaticks'.

But underlying these deficiencies of personnel, ideology and policy was a problem of image. The Tories appeared to be resentful and backward-looking reactionaries. The Whigs, the Liberals and their Peelite friends were optimistic and positive-thinking by comparison: in a word, they stood for progress. And the fact was that the Whigs matched the mood of mid-century Britain so much better. The 1850s and 1860s were the great 'years of expansion'. Free trade worked: the British economy dominated the world as no other had done before, or has done since. The fruit of this prosperity was unparalleled social harmony, and a confidence about the prospects of future progress which is hard for us even to imagine. It must have been all the more striking to Victorians, coming after the despair of the late 1830s and early 1840s, when at some awful moments Britain had seemed on the verge of social disintegration.

Having jettisoned Peel, the Tories apparently had nothing to say of relevance to a Britain newly at peace with itself. The Tory backbenchers' gut instinct had been that industrial society was not viable, and they had turned their back on the world created by Manchester. But Manchester represented the future – and it worked! The Tory Party would have to find means of coming to terms with the new Britain, otherwise it faced extinction. Its leadership accordingly had to provide it with a new electoral strategy and a refashioned ideology and image.

This, in their contrasting but ultimately complementary ways, Disraeli and Salisbury were to do. By 1900, the Conservative Party had been transformed into a mass political party, more confident in its handling of an increasingly democratic electorate, and drawing up to half of its backbenchers from the ranks of business and commerce, including more than a few Nonconformists among them.

But if there is one story more extraordinary than the recovery and transformation of the Tory Party in the last quarter of the nineteenth century, it is Disraeli's rise to the leadership of that party between 1846 and 1868.

2 An Outline of Disraeli's Early Political Career

A *The rise of a scoundrel*

The Conservative Party has never had a less likely leader than Disraeli. He was a Jew by birth (1804) in an age when anti-semitism was far more widespread and 'respectable' than it is today, and when Conservative backbenchers were overwhelmingly Anglican and fiercely committed to the defence of the privileges of the Church of England. His background was literary rather than landed: his father was a celebrated author and 'man of letters'.

To these disadvantages of birth were added deficiencies of education – at least by the standards set by other Victorian Prime Ministers. For Peel and Gladstone, Harrow and Eton, and then Oxford University, had proved excellent springboards for their political careers. By their mid-twenties, they were already moving towards the inner circle of the Tory Party. Disraeli, by comparison, spent an undistinguished adolescence at a string of obscure private schools, followed by three dreary years as a solicitor's clerk. This was hardly a fast lane into the world of high politics.

Disraeli was not only the great outsider of Victorian politics: he was its great latecomer. He had turned 40-years old before he won any recognition as a significant figure in the House of Commons. But Disraeli was not easily put off. Lord Blake, in his great biography (*see page 381*) has characterised the young Disraeli as a man of 'immense ambition consumed with an almost insolent determination to make his mark'. He was convinced of his own genius and desperately wanted the rest of the world to acknowledge it. Quite where or how he was to do this seemed almost irrelevant.

Instead, Disraeli managed to convince most of those in respectable society that he was a blackguard and a scoundrel, shamelessly ambitious and utterly untrustworthy. For 15 years, until his marriage in 1839 to a wealthy widow 12 years his senior – an event which gave badly needed stability to both his emotional and financial affairs – he lived recklessly, stretching even the accommodating morality of late Regency England up to and beyond breaking point.

He got involved in the promotion of shady South American mining companies and in the launching of a new daily newspaper – both of which landed him chronically in debt. After suffering a nervous breakdown he went on a sixteen-month tour of the Mediterranean and experienced an intriguing variety of sexual and narcotic delights, of the sort that would keep one of today's tabloid newspapers busy with exposés for months. If all Victorians had had 'Victorian Values', Disraeli would never have become Prime Minister.

His flamboyant style, brilliant conversation and spectacular appearance (one outfit featured 'green velvet trousers, silver buckles, lace at his wrists, and his hair in ringlets') created a sensation – not always agreeable – wherever he went. His love life, too – which included a passionate and public affair with the wife of a baronet – further increased his notoriety. However, in the early 1830s a more definite interest in politics began to emerge. He fought and lost three elections as an independent Radical with Tory sympathies. In 1834 he made his breakthrough into serious politics, when he found a powerful patron: the former Tory Lord Chancellor, Lord Lyndhurst. Lyndhurst had recognised that the wider franchise of the post-Reform Act had made 'public opinion' an ally for which Whigs and Conservatives alike would have to compete. In Disraeli, he knew he had found a writer and journalist of great power and little scruple. So Lyndhurst hired him. The relationship between Lyndhurst – something of a rogue himself – and the young Disraeli, grew deeper. Disraeli was soon Lyndhurst's friend, confidant and secretary. The fact that Disraeli shared his mistress with the ageing but still vigorous ex-Lord Chancellor did not go unremarked by disapproving contemporaries.

With Lyndhurst's backing, Disraeli was soon making the right contacts. In 1835, he became a member of the aristocratic Carlton Club which also served as the Conservative Party's Headquarters and in 1837, with the help of a good deal of bribery, he was elected MP for Maidstone. The Commons was now to provide Disraeli with a new stage on which to make the sensation he craved. But Disraeli's first years in the Commons were neither happy nor successful. His maiden speech was nothing short of a disaster. His dandified appearance, flamboyant manner and florid rhetoric provoked sections of the House to shout him down. He soon learnt that this new stage required a new style, and he began to acquire the virtues of dullness and sobriety.

His ambition remained, however. No sooner was Peel Prime

Minister (August 1841), than Disraeli was writing to him begging for office. Peel had many more urgent or deserving calls on his patronage, and no government post was found. Had Disraeli enjoyed greater fortune, it is hard to imagine that his attitude towards Peel over the next few years would not have been very different.

B *'Young England' and the Origins of Disraelian Conservatism*

Disraeli had to find other ways of making his mark. A young group of aristocratic Conservative MPs soon fell under his spell. They called themselves Young England.

Young England was as much a dining club as a parliamentary faction. Its members delighted in each others' wit and gaiety. It had no political programme but it believed in resurrecting a style of aristocratic paternalism quite different from Peel's cold and unsentimental brand of Conservatism, which seemed obsessed with theories of political economy at the expense of any feeling for community, deference or tradition.

Young England's aristocratic members were in part the audience, in part the inspiration for Disraeli's ideas about the true nature of Toryism. According to Disraeli, England's history was in large part the story of the battle between a selfish Whig oligarchy on the one hand, and the Tory aristocracy of England, supported by and representing the English people as a whole, on the other. Disraeli insisted that, despite the apparent liberality of the Great Reform Act, the Whigs were a great threat to the freedoms and traditions of Englishmen. To Disraeli, the widely-hated new Poor Law and the local government 'reforms' of the mid-1830s were examples of this. The Whigs were conspiring with doctrinaire Radicals to strip the traditional rulers of the English counties and boroughs – the aristocracy and gentry – of their proper influence and power. The ordinary people of England would thus be left at the mercy of a harsh, unfeeling centralising state. Just as bad was the Whigs' attack on the Anglican Church in Ireland. The parliamentary alliance struck up between the Whigs and Irish Catholics in 1835 (*see page 127*) enabled Disraeli to caricature them as the un-English party ready to sacrifice other people's privileges and property to stay in power. Disraeli's strategy here – however unfair – clearly anticipates his later attacks on Gladstone's Liberal Party, which Disraeli portrayed as a 'front' for the operations of Radical subversives, dependent for its hold on power on Irish and Nonconformist votes.

All this cleared the ground for a major redefinition of what the Tory Party stood for – a redefinition which Disraeli was to draw on, with profit, in the 1870s. The Tory Party was, 'the national party . . . the really democratic party of England'. Here is the origin of the concept most closely associated with Disraelian Conservatism: Tory Democracy.

Its vagueness and ambiguity has been much remarked on – but these were strengths as much as weaknesses. Disraeli did not of course mean that the Tories should be the instruments of a transfer of power to the working classes. But he was implying that the Tories were the natural leaders of the people and that the party should trust their instinctive patriotism and conservatism. Such ideas must have seemed startling and novel to Disraeli's audience in the 1830s. To most Tories then, standing up to the threat posed by 'democracy' was the only strategy that made political sense. But Disraeli seemed to be suggesting that the best way to defeat the Whigs was to outflank them by seeking a popular alliance against the exclusive and self-serving Whig elite.

Disraeli was soon developing these ideas, and communicating them to a wider audience. In the 1840s, he produced his celebrated trilogy of Young England novels: *Coningsby* (1844), *Sybil* (1845), and *Tancred* (1847). Together they constitute an analysis of the 'Condition of England' in the troubled 1840s, and a vision of how English society might be refashioned along more harmonious lines.

Class conflict and the chances for survival of the aristocratic order were Disraeli's great themes. Some Tories believed that Chartism had simply to be crushed, and that industrial capitalism threatened social stability and the political power of the landed classes. Disraeli was neither as negative nor as pessimistic. It was true that England had become, in his words, 'two nations, ignorant of each others' habits, thoughts and feelings: THE RICH AND THE POOR'. But Disraeli believed he had identified the remedies for social disintegration. First, a more charismatic style of political leadership was required, to guide the people and convince them that those in power understood their needs and problems. Secondly, at the local level, he demanded a more paternalistic approach from the wealthy to the poor: factory owners had just as big a responsibility to their workers as landed aristocrats had towards their 'peasants'. Through the provision of schools, churches and better housing, class conflict would be dissolved and the platform of radical agitation destroyed. Thus would a true spirit of community, in the parish, and in the nation, be restored.

What was the significance of these novels for Disraeli's future? Robert Blake, Disraeli's great biographer, believes they have little importance. Their essential function was to amuse and entertain. Disraeli's social vision was an uneven mixture of brilliant intuition and feudal fantasy. In no way do the novels constitute a basis for practical politics. As far as Disraeli did have a political purpose, so Blake believes, it was to villify Peel for his supposed failings. This was merely a personal vendetta which Disraeli had been pursuing since Peel had turned down his bids for a post in the government.

Recently, however, John Vincent has argued that there is much more to the trilogy than this. Of course, the reader who expects to find a blue print in them for the social legislation of Disraeli's ministry of 30 years later will look in vain! But Disraeli's cast of mind, and points of reference, remain very similar. We will find, in the 1870s, a concern for the rights of labour and the living and working conditions of the poor. We will find, in Disraeli's style of leadership, an attempt to capture the public imagination with a calculated flamboyance and theatricality. Not least, we will find that Disraeli still believed that the statesman's greatest function was to create a spirit of community, so that English society could live in harmony with itself, and be spared the aggressive individualism of Liberals, the class-rancour of Radicals, and the self-righteous separatism of Nonconformity. Thus, society would recover its true nature as one large extended happy family. The Young England trilogy remains the single most important source for the myths and imagery which constitute Disraelian Conservatism.

3 DISRAELI VS PEEL: THE PARLIAMENTARY DUEL 1844–6

In terms of practical politics in the 1840s, the impact of Young England as a parliamentary faction was very limited. But through Disraeli's trilogy, their ideas had a wide impact on the Victorian public. Key phrases and arguments passed into currency of political debate, where they enjoyed greater resonance and longevity than any politician's 'soundbite' does today. Disraeli was beginning to perform one of the functions of the statesman in the age of the popular press: he was helping to shape the public mind.

Personally, Disraeli's career began its upturn in the Commons too. By 1844, Tory backbenchers were becoming infuriated by Peel's arrogance and dictatorial ways. Twice that year he had demanded that they reverse their votes and thereby undo defeats they had previously inflicted on the government. When Disraeli defiantly proclaimed that he had no intention of 'changing my vote within 48 hours at the menace of a minister', he was greeted with great applause. Disraeli had arrived.

The inarticulate squires who peopled the backbenches had made a perplexing discovery. Disraeli's race, his manner, and his scandalous lifestyle as a young man, must have raised feelings of profound distaste and suspicion amongst these backwoodsmen. But he alone seemed able to give voice to their more urgent feelings of anger and resentment towards Peel. Peel had appeared unassailable – the complete master of his brief, speaking with the authority of a man who had spent three decades at the centre of public life. But he could not cope with Disraeli's insinuating, drawling sarcasms. Whether reminding the House of Peel's questionable behaviour at the time of Catholic Emancipation, prophesying the Repeal of the Corn Laws or mocking

Peel for his U-turn over Maynooth, Disraeli, again and again, made Peel squirm – a spectacle which delighted the Tory squires. Observers were stunned to see the great statesman reduced to 'nervous twitchings', and quite incapable of hiding his deep annoyance as his tormentor stirred the House to 'delirious laughter' at his expense.

Disraeli's campaign was to culminate in the bitter debates over the Repeal of the Corn Laws and the defeat of Peel's ministry (*see pages 149–56*). The style of his attacks made them all but unanswerable. Many commentators, however, have found them lacking in substance. They have speculated that Disraeli was motivated by despair at his own prospects and a desire to revenge himself on the man who had baulked his career. In fact, there is a consistent and plausible theme of constitutional argument running through the speeches. Disraeli's claim was that Peel, by betraying the principles on which he was elected and ignoring the claims of party, was undermining the whole parliamentary system. Peel associated himself with a different tradition of government, asserting that it was the first duty of the Prime Minister and the executive to serve the sovereign, and through the sovereign, the interests of the nation as a whole, even if this meant riding roughshod over party interests and loyalties. Such a theory may have been practicable in the era before the Great Reform Act: but the development of party government in the Victorian era suggests that Disraeli was a lot more perceptive about the way in which the Victorian constitution was evolving than Peel.

In Disraeli's eyes, probably the most damaging of Peel's deficiencies was his lack of vision, imagination and charisma. Disraeli here amplified his arguments in *Coningsby*. Instead of creating public opinion, Peel was following it: to be more precise, when he repealed the Corn Laws he was letting the arguments of the Anti-Corn Law League dictate the government's economic policy. Peel had not merely betrayed his followers and tried to subvert the function of party: he had abdicated the greatest responsibility of leadership itself and had left the people to create their own leaders – or as Disraeli put it, to 'fashion their own divinities'.

Disraeli's attacks on Peel may well have been motivated by personal dislike. But it is wrong to dismiss them as *merely* personal. For it was Peel's defects of personality as much as the demerits of his policies, which made him in Disraeli's eyes unfit to lead the party or to govern the nation.

4 THE YEARS OF FRUSTRATION 1846–65

Although Disraeli had been the outstanding speaker on the Protectionist side in the debates over Repeal, he had not been the recognised leader of the Tory rebellion. In the Commons and in the

Lords, Lord George Bentinck and Lord Stanley respectively had supplied the vital qualities of aristocratic pedigree and unquestionable personal integrity – qualities which Disraeli manifestly lacked – to sustain the morale of the Protectionist backbenchers and to transform their revolt into a permanent break with the Peelites.

The Peelites had no great desire for reunification anyway. The Conservatives' commitment to Protectionism made them, in Peelite eyes, unfit to govern: the Tories had reduced themselves to an agricultural rump incapable of representing the national interest. The Whigs, by contrast, had a broader political vision and a wider social base, and could anyway be kept on the path of good government by their reliance on the votes of the 100 or so Peelites for their parliamentary majority.

Even when, by the early 1850s, most Conservatives had come to accept the irreversibility of Repeal, the detestation and moral revulsion which Disraeli inspired amongst the Peelites remained. Peel's early death in 1850 had made his political martyrdom of 1846 the more poignant in retrospect and Disraeli's vicious personal attacks on him the more unforgivable. Furthermore, all the old suspicions about Disraeli's untrustworthiness and boundless ambition had been compounded by his recent rise within the Conservative ranks. To a leading Peelite, he was 'a Jew Adventurer [and a] rogue capable of anything for a party or personal object'. Even Stanley, who became the Conservative Party leader in 1846, had to admit that Disraeli was 'the most powerful repellent we could offer to any repentant Peelites' who might be thinking of returning to the fold.

The Tory backbenchers themselves retained a residual distaste for him, which held back his emergence as the Conservatives' official leader in the Commons until five years after the crisis over Repeal. The departure of the Peelites had left the Conservative front bench so denuded of talent that to have tried to deny his actual pre-eminence would have been absurd. Even so, the depth of resistance which Disraeli's rise encountered suggests that it is inconceivable, for all his immense talent and ambition, that Disraeli could ever have become leader of his party but for the catastrophe of 1846. And when Disraeli surveyed the political scene in the 1850s, he must have wondered whether his efforts on the party's behalf would ever be rewarded.

The Crisis of Mid-Victorian Conservatism

- Between 1841 and 1874 the Tory Party did not win one general election (*see pages 332–3* for the reasons).
- On three occasions – in 1852, 1858 and 1866 – the Tories *did* take office. But these were minority governments entirely dependent for their power on internal Whig divisions. On each occasion the Whigs soon reunited to turn the Tories out.

- When the Tories did get into power, they faced the contradictory tasks of legislating to please their own backbenchers and to prove to the electorate that they were a genuine national political party and not a mere agricultural pressure group.
- For example, when Disraeli was made Chancellor of the Exchequer in 1852, he could not return to protectionism: such a move would immediately reunite the opposition groups in the Commons, and the government would be defeated. But his attempts to find subtler means of keeping his backbenchers happy were denounced by Whigs and Peelites as unorthodox, and the Tories were defeated anyway. This was the time when Gladstone launched an overwhelming attack on Disraeli's budget, opening three decades of often bitter public rivalry between the two. By contrast, Gladstone's own budget, the following year, was a brilliant success.
- In 1859, Disraeli tried to improve the Tories' image with a modest proposal to extend the franchise. But his Cabinet colleagues diluted it even more, so as not to frighten the Tory backbenchers. The consequence was that Disraeli's Reform Bill ended up looking so half-hearted that neither Whigs nor Radicals (and the Tories' minority government needed the support of some members of these groups in the House of Commons if it was to survive), nor the wider electorate, could summon any enthusiasm for it. Soon, the Tories were out again.
- Worse was to come. Palmerston's spell as Prime Minister was a disaster for the Tories. He kept his Radical left-wing reined in, thus preventing any unsettling domestic legislation, while his aggressive, headline-catching foreign policy guaranteed him massive popular support. The Tory Party seemed redundant. Derby, Disraeli's 'chief' seemed to agree, and was quite happy for Palmerston to remain in power.
- Disraeli's real breakthrough only came with 'Pam's' death in 1865. His replacement was the aged Lord Russell – vain, unreliable, petulant and impulsive. Russell was anxious to cap his political career with a second instalment of parliamentary reform. This would disturb the more cautious Whigs. Even better, his heir-apparent was not a Whig at all but Gladstone – intense, unpredictable, and showing Radical tendencies. It looked at last as though Conservative fortunes were going to pick up!

5 THE SECOND REFORM ACT – A LEAP IN THE DARK?

A *The social and political background*

It seemed inevitable that Palmerston's death would bring major changes to Westminster. But no one could have predicted all the extraordinary twists and turns of party politics that the next three years were to bring. That Russell and Gladstone would make a bid for Parliamentary Reform was expected. That in doing so they would run the risk of frightening off some of their more cautious supporters, split their party and lose office, was always possible. But that Derby and Disraeli would then bring before Parliament their own Reform Bill, one more radical than Russell's and Gladstone's, and in the course of its passage through the Commons, accept amendment after amendment until a total of over one million new electors were enfranchised, was inconceivable. But incredibly, the Conservatives, the natural party of reaction, were to do just this, and so revolutionise the Constitution. At the end of this tale, the emergence of the 'Jew Adventurer' Disraeli as Prime Minister and leader of England's landed, Anglican party, was ample confirmation that the world had been turned upside down.

By the mid 1860s, a degree of consensus existed that a further, moderate instalment of Parliamentary Reform might be prudent. It was widely believed that the make-up and attitudes of many members of the working class had undergone a profound transformation since the days of Chartism. They deserved the vote, not as a right, but as a well-merited privilege. Of course, there was no question of making Britain into a democracy. But it would be safe to bring the 'labour aristocracy' (*see page 225*) within the franchise. These were reckoned to be sober, upright and thrifty citizens. Victorians thought it was vital to distinguish between them and the feared and despised 'residuum' – the unskilled and semi-criminal proletarian under-class. The habits of the latter were drunken, violent and improvident. They took no interest in the life of the nation, and had they been foolishly given the vote too, would either have sold it for beer, or become prey to demagogues. Quite how the franchise could be set to bring the virtuous within 'the pale of the constitution' while leaving the rest outside was a thorny technical problem, which was to trouble Gladstone and genuinely conservative Conservatives alike.

There was less consensus about what purposes enfranchisement should serve. The conservative argument, found amongst both Tories and Whigs, would have been familiar to Earl Grey in 1830. It was foolish to continue to exclude intelligent, responsible and property-owning elements of society from the Parliamentary process: it was the surest way to turn them into revolutionaries. Liberals like Gladstone and the more progressive Whigs agreed with this, but added some more positive notes to the argument. Under Palmerston Parliament seemed to have grown sleepy and the executive passive. A widened electorate might re-energise politics.

Radicals like Bright put this last point more aggressively. Two decades before, they had been convinced that the Repeal of the Corn Laws was bound to lead to the political dominance of the progressive middle class. In fact, the aristocratic constitution had proved exasperatingly resilient. Cabinets were no less aristocratic in their make-up, the Commons remained dominated by landowners and/or relatives of Peers in the Lords, and the distribution of seats still left the great industrial towns under-represented. The sort of enfranchisement the Radicals wanted was a good deal more far-reaching than anything Gladstone, let alone the Conservatives, would happily contemplate. It was designed to inaugurate a new era of far-reaching institutional reform which would show no mercy to the bastions of the old order such as the Anglican Church, the ancient Universities or the Army. These ambitions made it all the more surprising that Disraeli was to make so many concessions to the Radicals in the final weeks of the Reform Bill's passage through the Commons.

B *Liberal failure, Conservative opportunity and Disraelian triumph*

When Gladstone began to prepare the Liberal Reform Bill in 1866, he hit a variety of problems. It proved very difficult to construct a measure that would siphon off the respectable working classes and leave 'the residuum' behind, not least as the level of rents or rates – the two most obvious measures by which to set the franchise – varied so much from region to region. To complicate the matter further, it was discovered that up to a quarter of the electorate were already from the working classes: mid-Victorian prosperity had brought them within the £10 borough franchise of the 1832 Reform Act. Gladstone grew nervous. If the threshold were to be set at £6 annual rent, he calculated that another 250 000 workers would be added to the electorate. This would make it possible for the working class to dominate many boroughs, a prospect which the Whigs would find intolerable. So, in his Bill, Gladstone settled on a £7 rental franchise which would enfranchise 100 000 less than first intended. Reducing the county occupation franchise from £50 to £14 would add about 170 000 to the county electorate, but they were reckoned to be middle class, safe and generally Liberal.

Gladstone's caution was poorly rewarded. In June 1866, encouraged by Disraeli, some 30 Whigs rebelled and defeated the Bill. Their motives were mixed. Their leading spokesman, Robert Lowe, feared that Gladstone had still gone too far, and that the rule of property and intelligence, which had been the glory of the Victorian parliament, would be swept away by a democratic torrent of corruption, demagogy and naked class-interest.

Others, while sharing these anxieties, were especially concerned about the way in which Gladstone (whose personal arrogance was offensive in itself) seemed to be leading Palmerston's party down unwelcome, unpredictable Radical paths. By rejecting his Reform Bill they would slap him down, and open up the possibility of reconstructing party allegiance and leadership along more conservative lines.

Derby and Disraeli were pleased to find the Liberals collapsing into division and confusion. But they had to be very careful about how they played the rest of their hand. Many Whigs now expected the creation of a coalition government of conservative-minded Liberals and liberal-minded Conservatives, who together could resist any radical demands. Such a 'fusion', however, had few attractions for either of the established Conservative leaders. Derby feared it would result in a dilution of the traditional Tory commitment to defend the privileges of the Church of England. Disraeli knew that it would end any possibility of his succeeding the ageing Derby as party leader. The negotiations with the Whig defectors came to nothing. The Conservatives' distinctive identity – and Disraeli's ambitions – were therefore preserved, and a minority Conservative government took office in late June.

What would be the new government's attitude to parliamentary reform? To hard-line Conservatives like Cranborne (soon to be Lord Salisbury on his father's death) the answer was obvious: resistance. What was the purpose of Conservatism if not to defend the constitution? Derby, however, was more flexible. After all, he had been a Whig as a young man, serving in Grey's reforming ministry of 1830–4. Unless the party seized this latest opportunity to prove itself capable of responsible but progressive legislation, it might be doomed to extinction. The mounting popular agitation, although in no sense forcing Derby to embrace reform, kept the issue on the agenda. It also made it likely that, if the Conservatives were to fall without settling the issue, Gladstone would return with a vengeance, and, driven on by a Radical head of steam, deal them a blow from which they might never recover.

By October 1866, Derby had won Disraeli round to the merits of taking up reform. As in 1852 and 1859, Disraeli was given the unenviable task of constructing a measure that would satisfy the Cabinet, his own backbenchers and the majority opposition. It is Disraeli's greatest claim to political genius that he managed to do just that.

The progress of Disraeli's Bill through Cabinet and Commons was anything but straightforward, however. The heart of Disraeli's proposal for Parliamentary reform – household suffrage for the boroughs – was dramatic and apparently simple. In fact, at least at first, elaborate safeguards were built in to it to contain the threat of working-class electoral power. Fancy franchises, such as for investors in Savings Banks, and plural voting, would give the wealthy and educated extra weight in the borough constituencies. But hard-line ministers, led by Cranborne, were deeply suspicious of Disraeli's readiness to gamble on household suffrage. They thought that the safeguards were too fragile to survive Commons' amendments, or to be much use in practice, and threatened to resign. At first, Derby and Disraeli backed down. But the much tamer proposals which Disraeli tried to substitute for the household suffrage scheme left the Commons unimpressed. The Parliamentary Conservative Party feared that the Cabinet's timidity would give Gladstone the opportunity to get back into power and do his worst. Thus emboldened, Derby and Disraeli decided in March 1867 to return to their original plans, confident that the repercussions of the die-hards' inevitable resignation would not shatter the party.

The Conservative backbenchers' fear and loathing of Gladstone perhaps blinded them to the full implications of the course of action they had invited their leaders to take. Having 82 less seats than the opposition in the Commons, the government would have little control over the progress of their bill, or its final shape.

The Bill which Disraeli introduced into the Commons on 18 March had enough safeguards in its clauses to keep the total number of new voters down to around 400 000. Yet after a three-month barrage of Liberal and Radical amendments, this number was to be almost tripled. Disraeli casually jettisoned the elaborate schemes for fancy franchises and plural voting. One amendment alone, enfranchising 'compounders' in the boroughs – i.e. those who paid their rates indirectly through higher rents – made possible the enfranchisement of 400 000 extra voters. Cranborne seemed to have had his worst fears confirmed: so all consuming was Disraeli's lust for power that there was no concession to the forces of democracy he was not prepared to make as the price of his staying in office. Even a year after these events Cranborne was still seething with fury, as the following letter to a local Conservative organiser shows:

> As far as I can judge the one object for which the Conservative party is striving heartily is the premiership of Mr Disraeli. If I had a firm confidence in his principles or his honesty, or even if he were identified by birth or property with the Conservative classes in the country – I might . . . work to maintain him in power. But he is an adventurer and as I have too good cause to know, he is without principles and honesty.
>
> Mr Disraeli's great talent and singular power of intrigue make him practically master of the movements of his party. It was shown as clearly as possible last year. The conversion of the Cabinet and the party to household suffrage was a feat which showed that there was nothing strong enough in either to resist his will. For all practical purposes Mr Disraeli for the time being at least is the Conservative Party . . .

> The worst alternative that can happen is his continuance in power . . . In an age of singularly reckless statesmen he is I think beyond question the one who is least restrained by fear or scruple.

1 *On what general, and on what specific, grounds did Cranborne regard Disraeli with such suspicion?*
2 *Why do you think Cranborne believed it would be dangerous for the Conservative cause if Disraeli continued in power?*
3 *What light does the letter shed on personal and ideological tensions within the upper reaches of the Conservative Party at this time?*

Cranborne may have only slightly exaggerated the degree of Disraeli's ambition. But his attack offers us no explanation of how Disraeli got away with this supposed betrayal of Conservatism.

All contemporaries agreed that his was a dazzling Parliamentary performance. Disraeli managed to give the impression of being in calm control even when he was being rushed into improvisation and concession. He could conjure up statistics to befuddle critics, or, in the turn of a phrase, make 'household suffrage' sound homely, solid and respectable, rather than forbidding, democratic and revolutionary. In stark contrast to Peel, he kept in close touch with his backbenchers, who the more happily accepted his authority. Disraeli warned them that defeat would mean dissolution, and dissolution, election. Election, in turn, would mean Gladstone. Instead, they could enjoy the spectacle of Gladstone reeling under the impact of their leader's jibes and sarcasms. To some Tories, seeing Gladstone outmanoeuvred and outwitted at every turn of the debate was itself worth the price of reform. Furthermore, the exercise of power and the pleasure of being on the winning side were novel and intoxicating experiences for his party too. The Conservatives had achieved nothing for over 20 years. Now the party was, at last, showing that it could govern, and deal decisively with a thorny problem which the Liberals had proved themselves incapable of solving. They could claim to be a national party again.

For all Cranborne's evident disgust, Disraeli might therefore be said to have satisfied the political needs of his party. His performance had certainly secured his own position within the party as Derby's successor. But had he satisfied the needs of Conservatism – the long-term interest of the propertied classes, which the Conservative Party was supposed to defend?

C *Revolution?*

Fear of revolution haunted nineteenth-century Conservatism. If Disraeli's actions in 1866–7 can be shown to have been motivated by a desire to defuse the threat of revolution, they might be vindicated as prudent concessions which averted a major crisis. After all, the conservatism of the Great Reform Act of 1832 both in intention and impact, is widely acknowledged (*see pages 23 and 30*).

It is true that in 1866–7 Bright and other Radicals built up a mass movement for reform. They aimed to exert popular pressure on Westminster and, through their 'monster demonstrations', coerce the MPs into conceding a substantial increase in the franchise. The activities of the Reform League and the Reform Union were certainly on Derby's and Disraeli's minds. But it is very difficult to detect any sense in their letters or diaries that they were being forced to concede household suffrage by any perceived threat of revolution. Given the nature of the Radical agitators, this is hardly surprising. The most violent incident of their whole campaign occurred in Hyde Park, in July 1866, when the attempt to impose a ban on a pro-reform working class demonstration led to skirmishing with the police and the demolition of some park railings. This hardly compares with the atmosphere of crisis created by the riots of October 1831, and the conspiracies of the Days of May (*see pages 26–9*).

Pressures originating in the world of 'low politics' should not be given too much prominence in any explanation of the passing of the Second Reform Act. The ultimate Act, in all its superficial radicalism, is better understood as the outcome of a classic of 'high political' struggle: the price of the Conservatives holding onto power, of Disraeli's victory over Gladstone, and, not least, of Disraeli's emergence as Derby's certain successor.

D *Tory Democracy*

Was the Second Reform Act therefore an extraordinary gamble, a 'leap in the dark', as Derby himself described it, motivated by personal and party ambition? Disraeli insisted not. He claimed it was an expression of 'Tory Democracy': his belief that the working people of England were naturally Conservative, and that the Tories should learn to 'trust the people'. As Disraeli explained in a speech in October 1867, the party could, with a little flair and imagination, strengthen the bonds between ruler and ruled by legislating to promote their welfare and by appealing to popular sentiments of 'loyalty to the throne, reverence for the Church and the desire to promote the greatness of the Empire'.

Robert Blake is convinced that Disraeli was here indulging in retrospective self-justification. Derby, not the supposed visionary, Disraeli, had first pressed the case for reform, and the extraordinarily-widened franchise of 1867 had been forced on the Conservatives as the price of staying in power. But Blake here risks neglecting the *context* of beliefs and assumptions within which these political manoeuvres took place.

By 1867, the belief had taken hold in Conservative and Liberal circles alike that many amongst the working class – especially the residuum – were instinctively Tory. Cranborne himself, although deeply sceptical of this view, recalled in a later analysis of the passing of the Second Reform Act the 'vague' arguments that were 'floating very loosely in men's minds' that 'the poorer men are, the more easily they are influenced by the rich; a notion that those whose vocation it was to bargain and battle with the middle class [factory owners] must on that account love the gentry; (and) an impression ... that the ruder class of minds would be more sensitive to traditional emotions'.

This 'vague' argument had been 'floating' in Disraeli's mind since the 1830s! He now found that many of his backbenchers shared it. No wonder he wrote to a close friend early in 1867 that the Second Reform Act would '[realise] the dream of my life and [reestablish] Toryism on a national foundation'. For Disraeli, the existence of the working-class Tory was, and always had been, the keystone of his vision of England as a 'Tory Democracy'.

There is thus more than 'retrospective self-justification' to the address which Disraeli gave to an audience of Edinburgh working men in October 1867.

> I have from my earliest public life been of opinion that this assumed and affected antagonism between the interest of what are called the Conservative classes and the labouring classes is utterly unfounded ... I have always looked on the interests of the labouring classes as essentially the most conservative interests of the country. The rights of labour have been to me always as sacred as the rights of property, and I have always thought that those who were most interested in the stability and even in the glory of a State are the great mass of the population, happy to enjoy the privileges of freemen under good laws, and proud at the same time of the country which confers on its inhabitants a name of honour and of glorious reputation in every quarter of the globe ... Do not listen to those who pretend to you that society is to be revolutionised because the people are trusted. Do not listen to those who tell you that you have been invested with democratic rights, and that, therefore, you must effect great changes in the fortunes and form of one of the most considerable nations and Governments that ever existed. Be proud of the confidence which the constituted authorities of the country have reposed in you, by investing you with popular privileges: prove that you know the value of such privileges: and that you will exercise them to maintain the institutions of your country, and to increase its power, its glory and its fame.

1 *To what evidence might Conservatives who were sceptical about 'Tory Democracy' refer, to prove that '[the] assumed – antagonism between the Conservative classes and the labouring classes' was* not *'utterly unfounded'?*

2. *How did the Radicals hope the newly enfranchised working men would use their votes? How did Disraeli try to counter this appeal?*
3. *When you have read section 7 (pages 351–6), assess how well Disraeli kept his promise to look after 'the rights of labour' as well as he did 'the rights of property'.*

It is true that Tory Democracy was not a programme of political action – the unplanned, piecemeal nature of the social legislation of Disraeli's second ministry proves otherwise – but it was more than a slogan. Disraeli's belief in Tory Democracy helps to explain the confidence and self-assurance with which he embraced household suffrage.

E *Redistribution: a safety net*

Disraeli could not be *certain*, however, that the workers he was enfranchising would turn out to be Tory voters, amenable to traditional influences. The Second Reform Act was, in that sense, a leap in the dark. But Disraeli provided a skilfully woven safety net: the Redistribution Act which accompanied the extension of the franchise was profoundly Conservative. Of the 52 seats to be reallocated, 25 went to the counties where the Conservatives usually did best, and where the extension of the franchise had been relatively slight. The agricultural labourer would have to wait until 1885 for the vote. London, the Midlands and the North remained seriously under-represented. If Tory Democracy did *not* work, the Liberals might win more *votes* in the industrial centres, but as these tended to be Liberal already they would not win many more *seats*. And future Conservative successes in working-class constituencies in Lancashire and London suggest that Disraeli's instincts about working-class political loyalties were not without foundation.

Disraeli was guided in his handling of the Second Reform Act as much by a mixture of sociological intuition and well-concealed caution as by risk-defying ambition. But we must not claim too much credit for Disraeli as a Conservative statesman, for he showed no anticipation of the most conservative consequence of his legislation. The Second Reform Act radicalised the Liberal Party. Gladstone's first ministry was emboldened by the popular mandate it won in the 1868 general election to undertake an ambitious programme of legislation. For many voters, however, it proved too energetic. A process of reaction set in and, in a series of by-elections, several constituencies where the comfortable middle classes predominated, swung over to the Conservatives. Disraeli went on to win the 1874 general election. In fact, the Second Reform Act had opened an era in which the Conservative Party became the bastion of the anxious suburban bourgeoisie. This was a development Disraeli had not planned for, did not understand, and might not have welcomed even if he had.

6 Disaster and Recovery

When ill-health finally forced Derby to retire in February 1868, Disraeli succeeded him as Prime Minister and Party Leader. The latter's breath-taking personal Parliamentary triumph in 1867 had guaranteed his succession. But Gladstone was soon regrouping his forces. In March, he announced his support for the disestablishment of the Irish Church (*see pages 256–8*), and went on later that year to fight a triumphant electoral campaign on the issue. The scale of the Conservative defeat (271 seats to 387 Liberals) was shattering. There was little evidence in the larger boroughs, as Salisbury rather cruelly pointed out, of 'the eternal gratitude of the artisans'. The Second Reform Act suddenly looked like a disastrous gamble. Disraeli's critics were not soothed by what they saw as his half-hearted resistance to the Irish Land Act which the Liberals pushed through in 1870. Disraeli was also ill, and seemed strangely uninterested in providing the fighting leadership the party needed. A meeting of Tory grandees early in 1872 all but concluded that he had to go.

Against this background, Disraeli's celebrated speeches of 1872 at the Free Trade Hall, Manchester and Crystal Palace, take on extra significance. He reasserted his authority within the party and silenced his critics. More importantly, he spelt out the issues on which the Liberals could be beaten, and developed his vision of what Conservatism meant. Together, these speeches mark one of the turning points in Disraeli's career.

Disraeli's attack on Gladstonian Liberalism in 1872 was expertly judged. Indeed, some of his themes are echoed to this day in Conservative Party broadsides against the Left. Disraeli identified the government's weakspots, and scored hit after hit. Gladstone was presented as the (more or less) respectable front-man for a party which, in its ultimate intentions, was in fact subversive of all that was best about England and her institutions. The Liberal radicals, Disraeli asserted, were conspiring to undermine the Church of England, the House of Lords, and the Monarchy itself. Disraeli also claimed that the Liberals were incapable of defending the interests and prestige of England abroad. In fact, with its obsession about cutting defence spending, which would weaken colonial ties, and exaggerated regard for the rights of all peoples except the English, Liberal policy spelled the disintegration of Empire.

Only the Conservatives could be trusted as the guardians of England's destiny. It went without saying (although Disraeli repeated it) that they would uphold every branch of the ancient constitution. Disraeli argued that the era of constitutional reform was passing. The true interest of the working classes now lay in the pursuit not of more political power, but in improvements to their material well-being, like better housing. Echoing the paternalistic themes of Young England, Disraeli claimed that the Conservatives had the welfare of the working classes closest to heart. Class harmony could be secured by reinvigorated social policy.

Binding the nation together was the great objective of Disraelian Conservatism. Disraeli realised that one of the most effective ways of achieving this was by a direct appeal to the spirit of national self-confidence which was nearing its peak in mid-Victorian England. In the absence of opinion polls, the historian cannot be sure, but rhetoric like this seems to have struck home: 'I express ... my confident conviction that there never was a movement in our history when the power of England was so great and her resources so vast and inexhaustible. And yet, gentlemen, it is not merely our fleets and armies, our powerful artillery, our accumulated capital, and our unlimited credit on which I so much depend, as upon that unbroken spirit of her people, which I believe was never prouder of the Imperial country to which they belong'. Disraeli was putting his trust in the people, and dedicating the Conservative Party to their services.

Some historians, notably Lord Blake, have looked on these speeches with a degree of scepticism: their rhetoric might be suggestive, but they offered little in terms of concrete policy. It is quite true that Disraeli preferred to paint with a broad brush, and it would be difficult to trace the details of his later social or foreign policy to the impressionistic sketches offered in 1872. But such criticism misses the mark. Perhaps modern political parties, with their detailed manifestoes and elaborate policy studies, enter government with carefully planned programmes ready for implementation. In the nineteenth century, however, the electorate merely expected a statement of general principles and some indication of the direction which legislation might take. Disraeli's gestures were sufficient to do this.

It is equally mistaken to dismiss such speeches as *mere* rhetoric. Politicians then and now establish their own identify, and the identity of their parties, as much by what they say and how they say it, as by what they do. The experience of more than two decades in opposition had left Disraeli in no doubt about the effectiveness of the Liberals' image as the party of free trade, prosperity and executive competence. Disraeli somehow had to rival this unassailable reputation without seeming merely to imitate it. This he achieved in his speeches of 1872.

The distinctive Conservative identity which Disraeli manufactured combined a promise to re-establish constitutional stability and to promote social harmony, while offering a commitment to defend and enhance Britain's status as a great power. With these great themes, the Conservatives could at last claim to be a national party again, and a viable alternative government.

The Conservatives' greatest asset, however, was not Disraeli's skill as an image-maker: it was Gladstone. Since becoming the Liberals' leader, he had broken decisively with the Whig traditions. Whereas Palmerston had kept the Radicals on a tight rein, Gladstone at times seemed to identify himself with their cause and speak their language. Abroad, the difference was even more striking. Palmerston had known how to treat foreigners, especially the Greeks and the Chinese. He had conducted diplomacy in a style that reminded the world (and the electorate) that Britain was a mighty power. Gladstone deplored this dangerous and expensive mixture of bluff and belligerence. But his internationalism and readiness to seek compromise could be made to look weak in comparison.

There were, perhaps, two faces to Disraelian Conservatism: the positive one of 'Tory Democracy' and the negative one of 'anti-Gladstonianism'. By the end of Gladstone's first ministry, Disraeli was emphasising the latter. The Liberals he argued, were incapable of upholding England's institutions or international standing: the previous five years would have been the better for 'a little more energy in our foreign policy and a little less in our domestic legislation'. The electorate seemed to agree, and returned Disraeli with a 110-seat majority (*see pages 267–9* for more on the 1874 general election).

7 DOMESTIC AFFAIRS 1874–80: A TORY DEMOCRACY?

A *The Cabinet*

In sharp contrast to the problems of the 1850s, the Cabinet which Disraeli was able to assemble in 1874 was a strong one. The Foreign Secretary, the 15th Earl of Derby, (the son of the Conservative Party's leader between 1846 and 1868) was seen by many as a potential Prime Minister. Sir Stafford Northcote, at the Exchequer, had mastered the rules of Peelite finance as Gladstone's Private Secretary in the 1840s. Although his budgets were never inspired, his orthodoxy and competence were undoubted. At the India Office, Lord Salisbury began to moderate his distaste for Disraeli: he was to succeed Derby as Foreign Secretary in 1878. His sheer intellectual power and reputation for the unwavering defence of true Conservative principles strengthened the Cabinet and the cause of party unity.

Disraeli's only surprise was the appointment of RA Cross as Home Secretary. As a Lancashire-based lawyer and banker, he was to bring invaluable knowledge of urban problems to a Cabinet which was otherwise unmistakably aristocratic and landed in outlook. In his Departmental work, he combined the virtues of industry, efficiency and precision, and was responsible for most of the social legislation for which Disraeli's second ministry is celebrated. Cross was arguably the ministry's greatest success.

Cross himself was rather less impressed by his Prime Minister. On taking office in 1874, he was surprised to discover that, despite Disraeli's famous pronouncements on social and imperial issues, he had no legislative schemes ready to put before the Commons. Characteristically, Disraeli was to rely on others to flesh out the rather vague promises made in 1872.

Even so, the achievements of 1875, were considerable. Blake has described the Acts of that year as 'the biggest instalment of social reform passed by any one government in the nineteenth century'. These included a Public Health Act, consolidating a variety of existing legislation, a Sale of Food and Drugs Act, which aimed to improve standards of purity for consumers, and a Factory Act, extending the protection the state offered to women and children by further limiting the hours they could work. Disraeli put his own weight behind an Agricultural Holdings Bill designed to ease tensions between landlords and their tenants. Most important of all, there was major legislation on working-class housing and trade union rights (*see pages 355–6*).

However, as Paul Smith has demonstrated in his now classic study, *Disraelian Conservatism and Social Reform*, on closer analysis this impressive looking list is revealed as rather less than a programme of full-blooded Tory paternalism. Instead, much of the legislation was a pragmatic response to practical problems which both parties recognised, and which might just as well have been passed by the Liberals. There was little that was far-reaching or innovatory about the legislation. Much of it was 'permissive', not compulsory, leaving it to the local authorities to decide whether a bill would be implemented. For example, the provisions of the Sale of Food and Drugs Act became operative only where a town council was ready to appoint trained analysts to report on incidents of adulteration. As a contemporary critic noted, the chances of cost-conscious councillors going to this expense were slight – not least as a fair number of them might be the very shopkeepers most likely to be hit by the analysts' findings!

Even greater practical deficiencies were apparent in one of Cross's most significant pieces of legislation – the Artisans' Dwelling Act. The deplorable quality of much working-class housing had become – and was to remain – a major preoccupation of Victorian politicians. Slums were held to be the breeding grounds of vice and criminality. The well-being of society, even the future of the English race, was supposedly at stake.

This sense of urgency was ill-matched by the detail of Cross's actual legislation. Local authorities were given the power of compulsory purchase over property certified as unhealthy by a medical officer. But central government offered little help with the expense of slum clearance or the rebuilding that would follow, to make the proposition attractive. Councillors well knew that the ratepayers' likeliest response to the increases in local taxes inevitably entailed by any such programmes would be to vote them out of office. Not surprisingly, only 10 out of 87 eligible authorities took up the powers offered to them by Cross. Here again, the promise of Disraelian social reform was not matched by the reality.

It is easy to list the deficiencies of the ministry's social legislation: but perhaps it is historically more valuable to understand the constraints and inhibitions under which Disraeli and Cross were operating.

Politically speaking, Disraeli knew that he had to tread carefully. Not one of the Acts passed in 1875 or 1876 was of the scale, or provoked anything like the controversy, of the 'big bills' which the Liberals specialised in. They were described by a sympathetic backbencher as 'suet-pudding legislation ... flat, insipid, dull but ... very wise and very wholesome'. Disraeli knew very well that the electorate had suffered more than enough legislative excitement at the hands of Gladstone. Further instalments of major reform would have been a poor reward for Conservative voters.

There were also deeper, long-term reasons for avoiding major changes. From the 1830s, Disraeli had been quick to defend the autonomy of local government against the threat of central direction by Whitehall bureaucrats. He had not now become Prime Minister to undermine the power of ancient borough corporations and county magistrates. They constituted a part of the 'aristocratic settlement' which he was sworn to defend. Disraeli firmly believed that power should be left in the hands of those who, by tradition, legitimate influence and local knowledge, were best equipped to exercise it.

These old-fashioned Tory beliefs were reinforced by shifts in Tory thinking on economic policy. By the 1870s Tory and Liberal ideas on taxes, tariffs and state intervention were practically indistinguishable. Liberals and Conservatives alike believed in the ideal of a low-taxing, small-scale state. Underpinning this was a basic philosophical belief, that the dignity and identity of human beings were inseparable from their freedom, as individuals, to make their own choices and assume responsibility for their own lives. Cross put the matter succinctly. The very 'starting point' of the Conservative's social legislation was the principle that 'it is *not* the duty of the government to provide any class of citizen with any of the necessities of life'. The origins of the Welfare State obviously cannot be traced back to the social policy of Disraeli's second ministry.

C *Special cases: shipping and education*

On occasions, however, political calculations did temper the rigours of *laissez-faire* economics. The Merchant Shipping Act (1876) was designed to make it difficult for unscrupulous ship owners to overload their ships and thereby put their crews' lives at risk. Disraeli had at first been reluctant to interfere with the owners' rights to make their own business decisions, reminding the Commons that 'the maintenance of freedom of contract is one of the necessary conditions of the commercial and manufacturing greatness of the country'. But Conservative MPs representing ports warned him that working-class feelings were running high, and a furious protest in the Commons by the Liberal MP Samuel Plimsoll, the leading campaigner for sailors' interests, focused much sympathetic public attention on the issue. Disraeli had to concede that government time and support would be found for Plimsoll's proposals to prevent the overloading of ships. However, the Lords still managed to weaken the bill: the final act 'was far from ensuring the safety of the merchant seaman, and did very little to promote his general welfare', as Paul Smith concludes.

The Education Act of 1876 is another example of apparently progressive social policy which was in reality motivated by narrow political calculations. It had the effect of making compulsory the education of children up to the age of ten: a marked increase of state power at the expense of parental freedom. The Conservatives were not inspired by any desire to encourage social mobility. They did not aim to create an educational ladder to help the ambitious sons (let alone the daughters!) of the working classes rise to the ranks of the middle classes. Rather, in Cross's words, the object of education for the great mass of the people was to make them 'more fit to do their duty in that station of life to which they are called'.

What finally drove the Conservatives to legislate was a determination to reverse some unwelcome and unanticipated side-effects of the 1870 Education Act (*see pages 263–5*). This had left the network of overwhelmingly Church of England 'Voluntary Schools' intact. But it had opened the possibility of setting up non-Anglican 'Board Schools' where existing voluntary establishments were failing to do the job. These new schools were to be run by popularly elected 'boards' – hence their name.

Board schools were widely hated in Conservative ranks. Their religious teaching was not specifically Anglican and they were often controlled, through popular election, by Dissenters. Worse still, the different way in which they were financed gave the Board Schools an advantage. Board Schools were paid for out of the rates. The Voluntary Schools were much more dependent on the small fees paid by their pupils. Low attendance and difficulty in collecting subscriptions meant that many of them were too poor to provide their catchment areas with the 'efficient' education required by the 1870 Act. There was therefore a danger that the better-resourced Board Schools would increasingly take over the provision of education.

In these circumstances, making attendance at all schools compulsory was the easiest way of guaranteeing the Voluntary Schools an adequate income, through the parental fees, and so staving off the threat from the Board Schools. Preserving the Voluntary School system would also save rate-payers' money (Board School expenditure was hitting them hard), and offer 'a better security for moral and religious teaching'. The Voluntary Schools would remain, indirectly, a great source of strength to the Church of England, the local squire, and the Conservative interest in general.

The 1876 Education Act reveals traditional Conservatism at its most inventive: working with the grain of Liberal legislation to uphold the power of the gentry and to preserve the political cohesion of the rural communities which remained the great bulwark of Conservatism.

D *Disraeli and Tory Democracy*

The picture that has so far emerged of the social legislation of Disraeli's second ministry has led many historians to doubt the depth of his commitment to Tory Democracy. There was indeed much that was piecemeal, ineffectual, reluctant or partisan about Conservative social policy between 1874 and 1876. But given the fiscal and intellectual constraints under which Disraeli had to work, it is perhaps surprising that anything significant was achieved at all. At least, Cross had made a sustained and wide-ranging effort to convert the vague pledges of 1872 into concrete legislation.

Neither was Disraeli a mere passive observer of Cross's works. The strength of Disraeli's own commitment to the principles of Tory Democracy is most apparent in his decisive intervention in support of the Conspiracy and Protection of Property Act (1875). This Act dramatically improved the rights of workers in industrial disputes. It prevented trade unions from being prosecuted for conspiracy when they organised strikes and it also legalised peaceful picketing. It thereby rectified all the deficiencies which working-class leaders had complained of in the Liberals' legislation of 1871 (*see pages 266–7*). When considered with the Employers and Workman Act (1875), which removed the threat of imprisonment from working men for breaking their contracts, Paul Smith has argued that they constitute 'easily the most important of the government's social reforms'. Yet without Disraeli's support for Cross, in a hostile and sceptical Cabinet, the Conspiracy Bill would have been sunk before it even reached the Commons.

Why was Disraeli so determined that the Conservatives should get pro-trade union legislation onto the Statute book? Undoubtedly pure political calculation played a large part. To have made concessions to the working classes which Gladstone had denied them was quite a coup. But Disraeli was not merely thinking of short-term tactical advantage. He wrote to two intimate friends that he expected the Act to 'gain and retain the Tories the lasting affection of the working classes ... It is one of those measures, that root and consolidate a party.

We have settled the long and vexatious contest between capital and labour'.

There is something unrealistic and fanciful about this claim. It is more likely that, by removing a point of contention between the working classes and their Liberal allies, he unintentionally paved the way for their reconciliation, thus undermining the electoral calculations behind 'Tory Democracy'. Furthermore, Disraeli's dreams of having at last settled 'the contest between capital and labour' were soon to look ridiculous. Class tensions increased markedly from the late 1870s onwards, becoming one of the dominant issues in politics (*see page 376*).

But Disraeli's political judgement is not at issue here: his intentions are. His sincerity is notoriously difficult to judge, but it is possible that Disraeli was at his most sincere precisely when he was at his most visionary and idiosyncratic. His obsession with Britain's prestige as an Asiatic, Imperial power is one example of this. His hopes to ground Conservatism in the affections of the working classes is another. The excitement Disraeli expressed at the passing of his trade union legislation, and the centrality which he accorded it in securing the Conservatives' future successes can perhaps be explained if Disraeli is seen as fulfilling in his own mind, the desire to make One Nation of England's Rich and Poor, which he had expressed 30 years earlier in *Sybil* and which remained, for Disraeli, the great mission and opportunity of Conservatism.

Yet even the immediate electoral impact of his social legislation is hard to trace. Instead, the Conservatives attracted more and more middle-class voters, in flight from Gladstonian Radicalism. Under Salisbury they were to become the bastion of the interest of property, and the party of resistance to working-class demands.

The rise of the New Unionism and militant mass labour (*see pages 423–8*), made the old Disraelian appeals to national solidarity and class harmony sound absurdly old-fashioned. Salisbury's stark talk of class war seemed to fit social reality much more closely, although a good deal less comfortably. By the turn of the century, the Conservative Party was more the voice of high finance and big business than of the English counties, whose supposedly natural cohesion was a model for Disraeli of what all social relations should be. Disraeli may well have believed in 'Tory Democracy', and the legislation of his second ministry did something to make a reality of the promise of his rhetoric: but in the evolution of Conservative Party social policy towards the working classes, it represents not a beginning but a dead end.

8 FOREIGN POLICY 1874–80: THE PURSUIT OF POWER

A *Disraeli – the imperialist*

Disraeli believed in the greatness of Great Britain. He was determined that she should play a role in European and World Affairs that reflected her wealth and the extent of her Empire. Disraeli also had an acute sense of national self-interest, and was single-minded, even ruthless, in his defence of it. Unlike most of his contemporaries, he refused to let any idealism or considerations of a higher morality shape his foreign policy. He cared only for power and prestige.

The details of Disraeli's foreign policy can be found elsewhere in this book (*see chapter XII*). The focus in this chapter is on the domestic impact of European and Imperial affairs. In his great speeches of 1872, Disraeli had declared his intention to defend Britain's imperial power and standing in the world. He also invited the working people of Great Britain to take pride in their country's imperial destiny. It seems likely that Disraeli struck a rich vein here for the Conservatives: the last quarter of the century saw many displays of belligerent nationalism and popular imperialism, culminating in the Queen's Diamond Jubilee in 1897 and the general election in 1900 (*see page 377*). Disraeli had successfully draped his party in the Union Jack and cast the Liberals in the role of un-English subverters of the Empire.

In terms of increasing the Conservatives' popular appeal, this was a triumph of the first order. But what, exactly, were Disraeli's attitudes to Empire? Undoubtedly it was the mystery and glory of India which seduced Disraeli's imagination. The preservation of British control there was the guiding theme of his foreign policy, and his European diplomacy should be seen from that perspective.

Disraeli was a passionate imperialist. But, unlike Joseph Chamberlain, later Colonial Secretary, he was not systematic or aggressively expansionist in his imperialism. There were no great plans for colonial development or closer colonial co-operation. As with social policy, he preferred to let others work out the practical implications of the visions he had sketched. It was one of Disraeli's misfortunes that he was not to find agents of the judgement and reliability of RA Cross to do his work in the outposts of Empire.

B *Disraeli and the Eastern Question*

In his handling of the Eastern Question, however, Disraeli was, at least at first, to show notable insensitivity to the feelings of many Victorians. The Eastern Question was arguably the most complex of all the problems faced by European diplomats in the nineteenth Century. The seemingly irreversible decay of the Ottoman (Turkish) Empire, and the Turks' oppression of the Christian races of the Balkans, encouraged not only these peoples' longing for freedom and nationhood, but also the desire of the Russian Empire to expand southwards at the expense of the Ottomans. British involvement in the Question stemmed from the conviction that Russian gains might ultimately make the Suez Canal, that lifeline to India, vulnerable. More generally, British prestige and influence in the Eastern Mediterranean and Central Asia were felt to be at stake.

To Disraeli the issues were very clear cut. 'Constantinople,' he wrote 'is the key to India'. This assessment may have been dubious strategically: nevertheless, it remained the fulcrum of British foreign policy under Disraeli. The consequence was that Britain was committed to uphold the integrity of the Ottoman Empire.

The stark simplicity of Disraeli's conclusion, and his conviction that the defence of Britain's great power status was his overriding duty, made it impossible for Disraeli to understand, let alone sympathise with, those who challenged his policy. His problems began in June 1876, when news reached London that the Turks had killed thousands of Christians, with appalling brutality, in repressing a rebellion in Bulgaria. As the details became public, a massive agitation galvanised the ranks of Radicals and Nonconformists. Disraeli, however, was casually dismissive of the stories of Turkish atrocities. Liberal newspapers, he implied, were merely trying to whip up political feeling against the government and its pro-Turkish policies, and their reports were based on nothing more than 'coffee-house babble'. It was one of the worst-judged utterances of Disraeli's career: the phrase sounded callous and heartless, and provoked an intensification of the 'Bulgarian Agitation'. The blunder revealed one of Disraeli's weaknesses as a politician: an insensitivity to the passionate moral earnestness that inspired the political commitments of many Victorians.

All Disraeli could see in the opposition's campaign was a sickening exhibition of self-righteous moral indignation. Worse, because its scale convinced the Russians that Britain was too divided to take any effective action to restrain their ambitions, it encouraged Russian designs on Constantinople and thus made the horrors and expense of war the more likely. The two sides of the Agitation faced each other in profound and mutual incomprehension, each believing they alone represented what was best in, and best for, Britain. Few popular political debates in Britain before or since have been conducted with the venom and spirit of loathing that marked the debate over the Eastern Question in 1876–8.

In the end, it was a debate Disraeli won. Although the agitation had a dramatic effect on the future of the Liberal Party (*see pages 272–3*), if anything it stiffened Disraeli's determination to stand firm against Russia. In fact, Gladstone struggled to maintain the momentum of 1876. His opening blast – the celebrated pamphlet on *The Bulgarian Horrors and the Question of the East* – had sold 200 000 copies in one month. But the follow-up, published in January 1877, sold only 7000. Gladstone had to curtail a planned Commons campaign against the government because of lack of support and fear that his 'unpatriotic' line would damage his reputation and split the party. To some observers, the Liberal Party in 1877 seemed almost as divided as it had been in 1866–7.

Public opinion, with a little prompting from Conservative activists, began to surge behind the Turks, whose rearguard action against the Russians was seen as heroic. In the absence of opinion polls, politicians looked to the outcome of by-elections – and even the popularity of music hall songs – as indicators of their changing levels of support. Both types of omen augured well for the Conservatives. Indeed, the most popular song of the season has added a concept to the language of political analysis:

> We don't want to fight, but, *by Jingo* if we do,
> We've got the ships, we've got the men, we've got the money too,
> We've fought the [Russian] bear before, and, while Britons shall be true,
> The Russians shall not have Constantinople.

The spirit of Jingoism, i.e. chauvinistic, belligerent patriotism, which the international crisis had produced amongst sections of the working class, was ample confirmation of the belief Disraeli had expressed in 1872: that the nation took pride in its imperial greatness and would trust the Conservatives to defend it.

The changing national mood, and the renewal of the Russian advance towards Constantinople, brought about a decisive crisis in Cabinet. Here, the government had been very badly divided. At one extreme was Disraeli, certain that there was only one way to inhibit Russian expansionism: she had to be convinced that Britain would go to war if Britain's vital interests in the eastern Mediterranean were threatened. To Disraeli, diplomatic warnings would not suffice. Men and ships had to be despatched to the potential war zone, ready to fight. At the other extreme was Derby, the Foreign Secretary. He was appalled by Disraeli's belligerence, arguing that such a provocative display was bound to be counter-productive.

Disraeli eventually won the Cabinet debate, just as the 'jingoes' had triumphed in the music hall. It was agreed the peace terms imposed by Russia on Turkey in the Treaty of San Stefano in March 1878 (*see page 391*), were excessive. Disraeli persuaded the Cabinet to call out the reserve and move troops from India to Malta, with the intention of securing a strategic base deep in the eastern Mediterranean (six warships had already been dispatched to Constantinople to dissuade the Russians from seizing the city). Derby finally resigned.

His replacement was Lord Salisbury. This might seem surprising. For most of 1877, Salisbury had been an ally of Derby in the Cabinet debates and, in the past, he had harboured the deepest suspicions of

Disraeli, seeing him as an opportunist and adventurer (*see pages 344–5*). But Salisbury had gradually come to appreciate Disraeli's fundamentally Conservative instincts, and his courage and keen sense of the national interest. Salisbury and Disraeli were to make a good team.

Thus, Disraeli emerged victorious out of the political crisis in Cabinet. That he did so with a former bitter enemy at his shoulder is testimony that, even in old age, he could deploy impressive powers of persuasion and political manoeuvre. It marks one of the greatest – and least often recognised – triumphs of his career.

Disraeli was to cap these successes in Cabinet with a diplomatic triumph over the Russians. In the face of British resolution and Austrian opposition, they backed down. The Tsar agreed to renegotiate, under international supervision, the terms of his treaty with the Turks. Thus, at the Congress of Berlin, in the summer of 1878, Russia was forced to abandon many of her gains. The British were also allowed to take control of Cyprus, from where any future threat to her interests in the Eastern Mediterranean could be speedily countered. Salisbury had done much of the ground work for the final settlement but Disraeli won the public acclaim for having achieved 'Peace with Honour'.

The crisis had established Disraeli's credentials as a national leader as nothing previously had. He seemed to have fulfilled the promise he had made to Queen Victoria in June 1876: 'I think not only peace will be maintained, but that Her Majesty will be restored to her due and natural influence in the government of the world'. If Disraeli had called a general election on his return from Berlin, there is every chance that the Conservatives would have won.

But reality broke in with a vengeance from November 1878 onwards. Disraeli was to enjoy a reputation for effortless and masterful statesmanship for less than six months.

c *Imperial debacle*

To Disraeli's surprise and considerable displeasure, in late 1878 and for most of 1879, Britain found itself involved in difficult, protracted and expensive colonial wars in Afghanistan and South Africa. In neither case does Disraeli bear much direct blame for the blunders and setbacks which did much to discredit his government. His indirect responsibility is harder to assess.

In Afghanistan, most of the problems were caused by Lord Lytton, the Viceroy of India. Disraeli had appointed Lytton in 1876, thinking that his ambition, imagination and theatricality would impress the Indian princes and reinforce the image of imperial rule projected by the Queen's new title, Empress of India. But Disraeli got more theatricality than he bargained for. Lytton lacked the judgement and tact needed to handle the complex and delicate situation developing in neighbouring Afghanistan. His aggressive policy, pursued without proper consultation with London, led first to the humiliation, and then to the massacre of British forces. Misadventure and blunder also characterised Britain's imperial activities in South Africa. The new governor, Sir Bartle Frere – like Lytton, acting contrary to his orders – wanted to 'teach the Zulus a lesson'. Instead, the incompetently-led British forces were themselves outmanoeuvred, outnumbered, outwitted – and defeated. Reinforcements and a new commander had to be despatched before British prestige was restored.

The bloody shambles into which imperial policy had collapsed in Afghanistan and South Africa put a severe drain on the Exchequer and dented British self-confidence – and Disraeli's reputation as a foreign-policy wizard. Gladstone exploited these reverses, as well as questioning the arrogant and racist prejudices which had led to them in the first place, in his brilliantly managed campaign at Midlothian in the winter of 1879–80 (*see pages 273–4*). There is little doubt that his speeches and the publicity they received were a major factor in securing for the Liberals their victory in the following general election.

Gladstone's charge that Disraeli was the evil architect of a reckless plan of imperial expansion was electorally powerful. But it was probably unfair. In one sense, it flattered Disraeli by exaggerating the coherence of his imperial vision. Gesture and improvisation – not cold and calculated blueprints for aggression – were at the heart of Disraeli's imperial style. Furthermore, on analysis, Disraeli is revealed to be the victim as much as the villain of the piece. Disraeli's wretched predicament was in large part the consequence of the misjudgement and incompetence of his subordinates. Both Lytton and Frere had acted rashly, and against orders. Given the distances involved, and the recognised need for imperial pro-consuls to make their own decisions in emergencies, it was natural to allow Lytton and Frere a good deal of room for initiative. But they took too much.

Disraeli cannot be acquitted of all responsibility, however: it was characteristic of his style of cabinet government to devolve even important decision-making to his subordinates. He almost invariably left them to do the job of working out how his own vague aspirations and promises were to be put into practice. Furthermore, Disraeli's speeches of 1872 had implied that the Conservatives would seek to uphold the might and splendours of the Empire. The appointment of Lytton and Frere, both aggressive and self-reliant imperialists, was a natural corollary. Given their dispositions, the loose structure of executive control and the climate of expectation Disraeli had created, the humiliations of 1878 and 1879 might be classed as accidents waiting to happen. They thus shed important light on the weaknesses of the Disraelian style of government.

9 Disraelian Conservatism: An Assessment

A *Defeat*

The ministry's misadventures in Afghanistan and South Africa, so brilliantly exploited by Gladstone, were amongst the main reasons for the Conservatives' defeat in the 1880 general election. The fact that Britain was experiencing a sharp economic downturn added to their difficulties. Even so, the scale of the defeat surprised Disraeli: the Conservatives' total of 238 seats was their second worst performance of the whole Victorian era, only a handful better than that of 1847, when the party was still reeling from the breach with the Peelites.

The seriousness of the Conservatives' position in 1880 has perhaps been obscured by the knowledge that they were only six years from entering a period of dominance in British politics that was to last for two decades. But in 1880, Tory Democracy, as a political philosophy, or as an electoral strategy, seemed to have been shown up as one of Disraeli's less happy inspirations. In the election, the Conservatives had only won 36 of the 159 most populous boroughs. For all Disraeli's good spirits in the aftermath of defeat, there was an awful possibility that the conservative ministry of 1874–80 would prove to be a mere interlude in a world made for – and largely populated by – Liberals.

Evidence was also to hand that the Conservative Party was not, after a promising enough start, adapting well to the changed political conditions created by the Second Reform Act. The National Union of Conservatives and Constitutional Associations (NUCCA), founded in 1867, had been designed to bring the Conservative message to the working-class electorate and to create a larger role in the party for its increasing number of middle-class recruits. In fact, it had met much resistance from the party's landed establishment, its activists all too often being made to feel like second-class citizens.

Even more disturbing, the electoral campaign of 1880 had shown that no one in the ranks of the Conservative elite was capable of bridging the gap between the party at Westminster and the newly-enlarged electorate. This was especially true of Disraeli, who had been ennobled in 1876 as Lord Beaconsfield. The Manifesto he prepared for his party was eccentric and lacklustre, and even if constitutional convention had allowed a member of the House of Lords to go on tour, drumming up votes, it is inconceivable that the increasingly frail Prime Minister could have begun to match Gladstone's performance at Midlothian. It was one of Disraeli's greatest political weaknesses, that for all his superlative performances in the Commons, he had never been able to conjure up the magical oratorical displays on the public platform that were Gladstone's speciality. Gladstone made himself the People's William. Disraeli was never the People's Benjamin.

In defeat, Disraeli seemed tired, old and increasingly infirm.

Bronchitis, asthma, gout and insomnia had been taking their toll for some years and a chill he caught in 1881 proved fatal. The electoral prospects for Conservatism on his death were, at best, uncertain. The experiment in Tory Democracy seemed to have been suspended and the Liberals were expected to waste little time before introducing a Third Reform Act, which would extend to the counties the household franchise established in the boroughs in 1867. Disraeli had been particularly concerned before his death by signs that the agricultural depression had opened divisions in the county community between landlord and tenant farmer. The Liberals would be well-placed to benefit from any disintegration of the rural hierarchy; it was feared that the greatest bastion of traditional Toryism was about to be undermined.

The Conservatives were not, however, in total despair. Many expected that tensions between the Whigs and the Radical wing of the Liberal Party were bound to worsen. Sooner or later the Whigs would have had enough, and realise that their future lay with the true friends of property and the constitution – the Tories. Gladstone himself might prove to be his enemies' trump card. He was ever more arrogant, frighteningly unpredictable and – many insiders seriously believed – half-mad. Who could put up with him for long? Anyway, his supposed lack of patriotism and susceptibility to radical adventures would doubtless soon discredit him again with moderate Liberal voters.

By 1886, these predictions had been in many ways fulfilled. But the greatest damage which was inflicted on the Liberals in the 1880s came from a largely unexpected quarter: Ireland. The sustained scale and violence of the Land War that was to be waged there, and the ruthless determination with which a reinvigorated Home Rule Party set about achieving its objectives, staggered Conservatives, Whigs and Radicals alike. When Disraeli had complained that 'hard times' had wrecked the Conservative cause in Britain, he could hardly have guessed what agrarian depression and its social and political consequences would do to Liberalism in Ireland.

B *Gladstone, Disraeli and the historians*

Gladstone's judgement on the contributions of his departed rival to Victorian Conservatism is of more than passing interest. He loathed Disraeli, believing that his influence on public life had been wholly bad. He had corrupted his party, until it was no longer capable of speaking with the voice of authentic Conservatism, as its extraordinary performance in 1867 had shown. Disraeli had also tried to corrupt the public, exciting their baser, chauvinistic impulses and encouraging reckless imperialist adventures and gross extravagance. In his shamelessly opportunistic pursuit of personal power and his craving for the superficial and treacherous glitter of great-power prestige, Disraeli had put the achievements of Peelite Conservatism – and its heir,

Gladstonian Liberalism – in jeopardy. Even in death, Gladstone could not extend charity to his foe. Disraeli's preference for a modest private funeral was judged by Gladstone to be contrived and drew from him the following comment: 'As he lived so he died – all display, without reality or genuineness'.

Given such sentiments, the qualities which Gladstone found he could praise in his opponent must indeed have been striking. Gladstone identified three: Disraeli's understanding and control of his party; his genius as a parliamentarian; and his immense political courage, which had sustained him as he battled against hopeless odds in the 1850s, through to the striking, but morally dubious triumphs, of 1867 and 1877–8.

The implication of Gladstone's analysis is obvious: Disraeli had a mastery of the baser arts of politics, but was utterly deficient in the moral vision and intellectual integrity which the statesman needs to make good use of that power – statesmen like Gladstone, of course. It is striking how, until recently, modern historians have tended to endorse Gladstone's assessment. Even Lord Blake, in his marvellous and generally sympathetic biography of Disraeli, often leaves the reader with the impression that he was the supreme political illusionist for whom principle and policy were subordinated to power and prestige.

Disraeli's concept of the function of government is also foreign to twentieth-century commentators. Today, legislation is the natural end of political activity: accordingly, the nineteenth-century Prime Ministers who tend to win our admiration and respect are Peel and Gladstone. Both of them demonstrated a supreme facility for working out practicable solutions (and sometimes impracticable ones!) to the most complex problems: at the height of their powers they achieved an unparalleled strategic overview of their ministries' whole legislative programmes.

Notoriously, Disraeli lacked these skills. But it is too easily forgotten that his objectives were different. In 1874, he reminded his Cabinet colleagues that: 'We came in on the principle of not harassing the country'. The country, he believed, had had enough of big bills. Such an attitude may be unheroic, but it is unhistorical to condemn it as selfish or backward looking. There is more to politics than 'reforms' and the execution of legislative programmes.

c *Opportunism, pragmatism and principle*

What of the common charge that Disraeli was an unprincipled opportunist? It is true that even Disraeli's closest collaborators doubted his political sincerity. Disraeli's drawling, ironic manner, and mask of uninterestedness clearly provoked suspicion. But actual U-turns in Disraeli's political career are not easy to find. The dropping of protectionism?: yet Disraeli's attack on Peel was essentially a question of personality and loyalty to party. The adoption of Parliamentary reform?: yet from the 1840s Disraeli had been privately convinced of the untapped Tory potential of the working classes. His supposed adoption of the Peelite strategy of reinforcing Conservatism by recruiting the property-owning middle classes?: evidence that Disraeli was actively soliciting such support in the 1850s, the 1860s, or the 1870s, is patchy.

Furthermore, the dividing line between 'mere' opportunism and 'responsible' pragmatism is narrow: the concessions which it might be prudent to make to protect an interest or secure an objective are a matter of judgement. In 1848, Disraeli wrote to Derby, in words strangely reminiscent of Peel (*see page 130*), that the function of the leader of the Conservative Party was 'to uphold the aristocratic settlement of this country'. This was 'the only question at stake, however manifold may be the forms which it assumes in public discussions and however various the knowledge and labour which it requires'. In the 1830s and 1840s, Peel had given himself hardly less freedom in defining what was necessary for the defence of the aristocratic settlement. Disraeli was merely to show more flexibility and inventiveness in working to achieve the same end. And it is not the least of his achievements that, unlike Peel, he held his party together in the process.

The suggestion that, at his core, Disraeli was a 'conviction politician' might invite disbelief, but here even Lord Blake seems to concur: 'through all the labyrinthine twists and turns of his bewildering policy, [the defence of the aristocratic settlement] remained to the end his guiding purpose'. A moment's reflection will show how the work of Disraeli's 1874–80 ministry was indeed tailored to this objective. The Education Act was designed to uphold the ascendancy of squire and parson in rural England: the very deficiencies of the Artisans Dwelling Act, leaving the powers to implement policy (or not) with the local authorities, reflected Disraeli's anxiety at the dangers which centralised, authoritarian, bureaucratic government spelled to the independence of the local communities. The objective of Disraeli's trade union legislation was to ensure social harmony; his foreign policy, with its stress on imperial greatness, invited all classes to identify with the nation and share its triumph. The message was the same throughout: Liberalism had a disintegrating effect; Conservatism an integrating one. And for Disraeli, the landed interest, gentry and aristocracy together, stood at the apex of the national community, guaranteeing its stability; the very embodiment of its historical continuity.

D *Jewishness, aristocracy and genius*

One of the most difficult puzzles of Disraeli's career is how this great outsider came to invest so much energy and ingenuity in the defence of the aristocratic settlement. There is some truth in the hostile picture that Disraeli was a snob and a successful social climber, anxious to defend the world of title and privilege which, whatever its reservations, he had conquered with his wit and brilliance. After all, Tory grandees clubbed together in 1848 to set him up in Hughenden Manor, with its 750 acres. Disraeli could then live the life of the country gentleman: an inescapable prerequisite for any Conservative Party leader.

To many Conservative voters, the aristocratic settlement was attractive because it seemed that the best guarantee of the life of civilised comfort, leisure and privilege which propertied Victorians led. Disraeli probably shared and respected such straightforward self-interest. The wider values of freedom and paternalism, secured and promoted by the existing order, doubtless had their appeal too. But how did Disraeli come to feel *he* belonged to this world?

Here, Paul Smith and John Vincent (*see bibliography, page 381*) have recently shed some light on Disraeli's psychological make-up. Disraeli was obsessed by his Jewish background. Jewish themes and heroes repeatedly crop up in his writing. Vincent bluntly presents Disraeli as a 'racial thinker' convinced, in the words of one of his fictional heroes, that 'all is race; there is no other truth'. Reconciling these beliefs with his social and political ambitions was a feat which only a mind as unorthodox and inventive as Disraeli's could have managed.

There were three aspects to the myth which Disraeli spun to construct a coherent identity for himself. First was an entirely fanciful account of his own family's descent from an ancient aristocratic line of Spanish Jews. This was compounded by a belief in the superiority in the Jewish race as a whole, which, unlike the native races of Europe, had not debased themselves and their blood by promiscuous intermarriage. Finally, Disraeli argued that the Christian Church was no more than a continuation of the best traditions of Judaism: he could take pride in it as 'the only Jewish institution that remains'.

Together, this singularly peculiar concoction of pure invention, racial prejudice and religious fantasy, helps to explain the profundity of Disraeli's attachment to the Anglican, aristocratic settlement of Victorian England. For him, the religion of his forefathers now found its best expression in the Anglican church on his Hughenden estate, and by right of his blood and his faith, he could feel at least the equal of the greatest Tory grandee at the Carlton Club.

There was one final ingredient to Disraeli's personal philosophy: the cult of genius. Romanticism had had a profound impact on the young Disraeli, especially the idea that a single individual, if endowed with a unique and shattering talent, could refashion whole civilisations. Disraeli's fictions abound in such creatures. He had announced in *Coningsby* that 'brains every day become more precious than blood. You must give [to the people] new ideas, you must change their laws, you must root out prejudices, subvert conviction, if you wish to be great'. Disraeli saw himself as a genius: that, as much as his Jewishness, gave him the right to rule, and, if he chose, to flout and overturn Victorian values.

Lord Blake suggests that Disraeli's genius had a timeless quality which would have made him at least as at home in the Parliaments of the Hanoverian or modern era as he was in his own. Blake is surely right to put Disraeli's political brilliance near the centre of his portrait: but we must not underestimate how far Disraeli's eccentric racial and religious theories would make him an unique and puzzling figure in *any* era.

E *Disraeli and the middle classes*

While acknowledging that Disraeli was in many respects an exotic and unorthodox figure, until recently most historians have felt confident in placing him in direct continuity with Peel, as a politician whose chief task was to integrate the increasingly conservative middle classes into the continuing rule of the aristocracy. It is undoubtedly the case that this process of political assimilation and subordination was the most important long-term political development which occurred during the period of Disraeli's leadership of the Conservative Party. But recently, historians have begun to question both how far we should regard Disraeli as the true heir of the Peelite style of government, and whether Disraeli consciously set out to recruit middle-class support for the Conservative Party. Indeed, John Vincent has gone so far as to argue that 'Disraeli did not like the middle classes [and] he did not seek to encourage them ... He appears not to have foreseen on any scale the growth after 1868 of late Victorian suburban and commercial Toryism.'

Such a claim might sound exaggerated. But contemporaries and insiders noted it too. In the 1870s Derby remarked that it was peculiar that 'the Premier [Disraeli] neither likes nor understands the middle class ... though [it is] the strength of our party'. None of Disraeli's legislation was designed to appeal to the middle class. Indeed, Disraeli's two greatest legislative coups – the Second Reform Act and the Conspiracy and Protection of Property Act – were more likely to have startled and discomforted it. Disraeli can take little credit for the fact that the cumulative effect of Palmerston's death, the Second Reform Act and Gladstone's first ministry drove tens of thousands of middle-class voters from the ranks of the Liberals into the surprised but grateful arms of the Conservative Party. To secure the 1874 Conservative landslide, all Disraeli had to do was to promise to do nothing, except to reverse the processes of social and Imperial disintegration upon which Gladstone had supposedly embarked.

If Disraeli had little regard for, or understanding of the middle classes, we should not be too surprised. Unlike Peel and Gladstone, he did not trace his roots to their ranks, and in contrast to Palmerston or

Gladstone, he did not solicit their support with regular tours of the northern industrial towns. Disraeli knew the world of Westminster and of fashionable society. At Hughenden, he came to know the world of the gentleman squire: he took the responsibilities of being a leading figure in the County of Buckinghamshire seriously, apparently enjoying the responsibilities of the Quarter Bench, and capable of rhapsodising about the cool shade of the woodlands. If he saw society in terms of community, paternalism and deference, it was because that constituted much of his actual social experience. The aristocratic settlement was a reality to him, and he a part of it. But Disraeli was in many ways a foreigner to the new land into which industrialisation and urbanisation had been turning England.

F *Was Disraeli a failure?*

In 1981, John Vincent published a brilliant and provocative essay which dared to ask the question: *Was Disraeli a Failure?* (*see bibliography, page 381*). He pointed out that, for all Disraeli's much advertised political genius, he lost five out of the six general elections he fought as a senior Tory. He also had an unmatched record in misjudging the public mood, forecasting victory in the general elections of 1857, and even of 1868, while being surprised by the victory of 1874, and the defeat of 1880.

Bruce Coleman mounts a yet more severe attack in *Conservatism and the Conservative Party in Nineteenth Century Britain*. He concludes that it is 'doubtful' whether 'anything which can properly be called Disraelian Conservatism' ever existed. For all his exotic personality and showy rhetoric, he left the party largely unchanged. In fact, according to Coleman, Disraeli should be a villain in the eyes of all thinking Conservatives. By destroying Peel, he destroyed the party's only chance of power in the 1850s. And simply by being Disraeli – the unscrupulous, unprincipled 'Jew Adventurer' – he was the single greatest obstacle to the long predicted but long-awaited absorption of the Whigs. Only under Salisbury would the Conservatives re-establish themselves as the party of property and resistance.

It is probable that Coleman underestimates Disraeli's case. Peel has been too generously treated by historians. For completely understandable reasons (*see pages 153–5*) many Conservatives felt that in 1846 he had got what was coming to him. Disraeli was only the political hitman: we should admire his professional skill rather than complain about his morals or motivation. Then, against all the odds, having achieved a position of prominence in his party, Disraeli managed to steer it away from the ghetto of protectionism and, over the next two thankless decades, he not only kept it alive but within sight of power, despite playing in a political game where the odds were stacked against the Conservatives.

He only had one real chance, in 1867, to change the game's rules, and he seized it with breathtaking skill. Thereafter, apart from remoulding the image of the party in his speeches of 1872, his greatest triumph was in 1878, when his brinkmanship, first in Cabinet, and then at Berlin, earned British diplomacy a triumph which, objectively, British arms did not merit.

These are significant achievements, but they are mostly transient in nature, or triumphs in adversity. To identify Disraeli's long-term contribution to Conservatism, we have to return to the world of political images. John K Walton, in his brief but penetrating survey of Disraeli's career, concludes that 'there is much to be said for the view that Disraeli's contribution to the ... fortunes of the Conservative Party is much more to do with ideas, slogans, rhetoric and presentation than with specific policies and actual legislation'.

This might be at one with Disraeli's own assessment of his political role. For he had, in his own words, always 'recognised imagination in the government of nations as a quality not less important than reason'. Disraeli was a compulsive myth maker: about himself, about his party, and about the English nation. However shallow their roots in reality, they have had an extraordinary potency and durability. This is what John Vincent means when he writes that of all the Victorian Tories ('a dull lot') 'Disraeli alone had the literary creativity which lies at the heart of politics'.

With his unique blend of constitutional, paternalistic and imperial themes, Disraeli made it possible for the Conservatives to project themselves as the National Party again, for them to be believed, and not least, for them to be elected.

For Bibliography, Discussion Points, Essay Questions and an Essay-writing exercise on Disraeli, see end of chapter.

SALISBURY AND CONSERVATIVE DOMINATION

1 LORD SALISBURY: A REACTIONARY CONSERVATIVE

Disraeli's successor as Conservative Party leader was Lord Salisbury – his former enemy and more recent ally. They are a remarkably contrasting pair. Below you will find some details of Salisbury's family background and early career.

Born: 1830 **Died:** 1903

Family Background:
An aristocrat of impeccable pedigree. His family's fortunes were founded in the sixteenth century by William Cecil – Elizabeth I's greatest minister.

Religion:
A solemn and profound Anglican.

Education:
Eton (badly bullied) and Oxford (very clever, but too highly strung to take exams).

Style:
Awkward and badly dressed as a young man. In later life, a figure of natural authority, exuding reassuring calm. But always aloof. Doesn't like Westminster or High Society. Only really happy in the privacy of his stately home at Hatfield.

Reputation:
A man of principle and unquestioned integrity.

Early political career:
Family influence secures his unopposed return as MP for Stamford in 1853. Appointed Secretary of State for India in 1866, but resigns over Disraeli's Second Reform Act, 1867.

Prime Minister:
1885 (minority government), 1886–92, 1895–1902.

Writings:
No novels or poetry. But a regular contributor to Conservative journals, producing expert commentaries on foreign and domestic affairs. Famous for his scathing attacks on Disraeli's opportunism.

As a comparison make a note of the headings in bold type, and make your own biographical box highlighting some details of Disraeli's career and style.

It would be difficult to imagine two more contrasting political outlooks than those of Disraeli and Salisbury. Salisbury was essentially pessimistic. To him, human beings were mainly driven by greed – or fear. Mankind's lot could not be easily improved, least of all by governments. Their overriding domestic responsibility was to uphold law and order. As to 'Tory Democracy', Salisbury hated and feared the masses, and believed that industrial society was inevitably divided into antagonistic classes. In the long run, he could not see how the aristocracy could retain its power and wealth in the face of the democratic onslaught, but he was determined to fight a long and bitter rearguard action on its (and his own) behalf. Ultimate defeat could be postponed – perhaps for decades – if the Conservative Party would fulfil its function of organising and defending the interests of property against the attacks of Radicals and Socialists. It was to this task that Salisbury dedicated his political life. He was to surprise himself by the extent of his own success.

2 Crisis Years 1884–6

Salisbury knew that the best means of strengthening the forces of resistance was to recruit from the enemy those voters and parliamentarians in the Liberal ranks who were unwilling to follow Gladstone down his increasingly hazardous and unpredictable paths. The brinkmanship and far-sightedness which Salisbury displayed between 1884–6 were vital to the success of this strategy.

A *The Third Reform Act 1884–5*

Few commentators could have predicted that Salisbury would turn the Third Reform Act into a Tory triumph: yet that is what he did. The prospect of further Parliamentary reform was full of menace for his party, not least because the logic of the Liberals' proposals was hard to resist. By 1884, Disraeli's Second Reform Act had begun to seem like a job half done. He had generously conceded the vote to the ordinary householder in the boroughs. But on what grounds had the county householder – the agricultural labourer – been denied equal treatment? Most Liberals believed that it was high time that this anomaly was corrected. Equally, Disraeli's Act had failed to give a fair share of parliamentary seats to the rapidly expanding industrial centres of the North, the Midlands, or of London. When Gladstone finally took up the reform issue in 1884 he clearly intended to redress both these grievances.

The Conservatives had good reason to be worried. Perhaps 20 years earlier, giving the agricultural labourer the vote would have caused them little unease. But since then, the pro-Tory political loyalties of rural constituencies had been undermined in a variety of ways. The introduction of the secret ballot in 1872, and much stricter legislation outlawing bribery, in the Corrupt and Illegal Practices Act of 1883, had between them ruled out the landlords' more blatant methods of arm-twisting. Worse, the combination of agricultural depression from the late 1870s onwards, with the spreading into the countryside of militant nonconformity and farm labourers' trades unionism, had begun to break up the timeless patterns of deference and communal solidarity which landed Tories had once taken for granted. The country constituencies – for long the core of the Tory Party's parliamentary representation – seemed vulnerable to Liberal attack as they had never been before.

The post-reform prospects for Conservatism in the urban constituencies seemed even worse. Peel and Disraeli had tried, in their different ways, to swing urban votes towards the Conservatives. But hardly any of the big cities offered safe habitats for Tory candidates. To many Conservatives, it must have seemed that the creation of more borough seats was as good as the creation of more Liberal MPs.

Pessimism came naturally to Salisbury, but for once he was probably not exaggerating the Conservative predicament when he prophesised that, if the Liberals were allowed to put their ideas for Parliamentary reform directly into practice, the Conservatives might find themselves excluded from political power for decades to come.

In reality, Salisbury was able to force the Liberals to accept vital changes to their plans. Risking a major constitutional crisis, he used the Tories' built-in majority in the Lords to block the advance of the Liberals' Reform Bill. Salisbury insisted that he be allowed a major say on the redistribution of constituencies as the price of allowing the bill to proceed. Anxious to bring the clash to an end, Gladstone reluctantly agreed.

When the ensuing cross-party negotiation had finished, it seemed at first as though Salisbury had got little out of them. The enfranchisement of the rural householder was to go ahead. Small boroughs with populations of less than 15 000 were to lose both their MPs, and those with populations between 15 000 and 50 000 would lose one. Salisbury was ready to let these traditional bulwarks of Conservatism disappear! With 142 seats now available for redistribution, the major cities would at last receive something like their fair share of Parliamentary seats: the very rough rule of thumb was that every 50 000 of the population should be represented by one MP.

What did Salisbury get out of all this? Paradoxically, his masterstroke was his acceptance of the long-standing radical demand for single-member constituencies. This meant that the old electoral map, dominated by two-member constituencies, had to be torn up. It was agreed that the new constituency boundaries would be fixed so that, as far as possible, each new seat represented a distinct economic and social interest. Salisbury exploited this principle with insight and ruthlessness. He made sure that rural communities were cleansed of the 'corrupting', predominantly Liberal, influences of industry, which had often spilled over the old county boundaries. No less important, he saw to it that, in the big cities, middle-class suburbs were cordoned off from working-class areas. They would then be able to elect their own MPs. This was a vital breakthrough for urban Conservatism. Acute observers of the political scene had noted as early as 1868 – and certainly by 1874 (*see pages 268–9*) – that there were islands of middle-class Conservatism waiting to be exploited in most of the big cities. But all too often this 'villa Toryism' was submerged at election time by the weight of popular Liberalism in the overlarge, two-seater urban constituencies. Salisbury was giving 'villa Toryism' the chance to make itself heard loud and clear at election time.

The electoral consequences were striking. In formerly radical cities like Leeds and Sheffield, after 1885, the Conservatives regularly took two or three of the five seats. And in London, which had received almost 40 seats in the 1885 Redistribution Act, the Conservatives were to win, in 1895 and 1900, no fewer than 51 out of the total 59 seats. In 1859 and 1865, they had won none at all!

B *Home Rule 1885–6*

Salisbury's response to the threat posed by the Third Reform Act had begun as a damage limitation exercise and developed into a fundamental recasting of the whole electoral system which proved distinctly advantageous to the Conservatives. His handling of the Home Rule Crisis of 1885–6 was no less masterly. This time, however, his objective was to maximise the damage which the Liberal Party seemed intent on inflicting on itself.

Gladstone's apparent readiness to capitulate to Irish Catholic pressure in general and Parnell in particular (no better than a terrorist in the eyes of many) seemed to prove what Conservative propagandists had been saying about the Liberals for years: they were the un-English party, the party of 'disintegration', incapable of upholding the rights of property owners, and unfit to be trusted as guardians of the interests of the British Empire.

Salisbury was ruthless in maximising the advantages he had been given. He made his intentions plain in December 1885, contemptuously brushing aside Gladstone's suggestion that, for the good of the nation (or so Gladstone claimed), he take up the cause of Home Rule himself, regardless of the damage he might do to his party. Salisbury had absolutely no intention of splitting the Conservatives, and thereby giving the Liberals a free hold on power for years to come, as Peel had done in 1846.

When Gladstone's Home Rule Bill had been defeated in the Commons in June 1886, and a general election called, Salisbury did all he could to deepen the split in the Liberal ranks. He instructed local Conservative Party associations not to oppose defectors from the Liberals with their own candidates. This helped to secure the return of 78 Liberal Unionists. Gladstone's hopes that the Liberal opponents of Home Rule would either fade away or, shame-faced, rejoin his ranks, were to be disappointed. Indeed, most went on in 1895 to join up formally with the Conservative Party, together calling themselves the Unionist Party. But this happened on Salisbury's terms, not theirs.

In the meantime, the election of July 1886 was a total triumph for

Salisbury. When the seats of the Liberal Unionists were added to those of the 316 Conservatives who were returned, he had an effective majority of about 120 over the combined forces of Gladstonian Liberals and Irish Home Rulers. After Disraeli's heavy defeat only six years earlier, many Conservatives had feared it would be decades before they might again enjoy such a majority. But this victory was much more than any swing of the electoral pendulum: for Salisbury (with Gladstone's unwitting help) had smashed the Liberal Party – the dominant force in British politics for four decades. The Conservatives now entered two decades of political ascendancy.

3 SALISBURIAN CONSERVATISM IN POWER 1886–92 AND 1895–1901

A *The virtues of doing nothing*

With such a large majority the Conservatives could have kept Parliament busy with a dynamic legislative programme. Nothing could have been further from Salisbury's intentions. He disliked legislation on principle. Too many 'big bills', he believed, proceeded on the assumption that every political problem, no matter how complex, had a solution. The sorry state of Ireland, after two decades of Gladstone's earnest attempts at 'pacification', was evidence enough to confirm Salisbury's basic attitude that legislative interference generally made problems worse.

Salisbury's intellectual conviction that it was best to do as little as possible while in government was given added weight by party political considerations. He was highly sensitive to the fact that the upper and middle classes – increasingly the natural supporters of the Conservative Party – had been repelled by the endless barrage of legislation with which Gladstone Liberalism had 'harassed' them. 'All legislation', he wrote, 'is rather unwelcome to [these classes], as tending to disturb a state of things with which they are satisfied'. Salisbury concluded, therefore, that 'our Bills must be tentative and cautious, not sweeping and dramatic'. He was to prove as good as his word: his 13 years as Prime Minister produced only three significant items of legislation.

1. The Local Government Act of 1888. This established elective county councils, thereby ending the landed gentry's centuries' long monopoly of regional power through their rule as magistrates.
2. The introduction of free elementary education in England, 1891.
3. The Workmen's Compensation Act, 1897. It enabled workers to claim compensation from their employers, as of right, for injuries suffered at work.

Short as the list is, Salisbury would have preferred it to be shorter still. He approached the problems of local government and education with grudging pragmatism: if he didn't legislate, a future Liberal government probably would, and Liberals would certainly show less tenderness to Tory interests than Salisbury. For example, by reforming local government on his own terms, Salisbury could do something to preserve the influence of the old authority figures in the counties – the Justices of the Peace – rather than risk them being completely swept away in some future torrent of radicalism and democracy. He could also ensure that the administration of the Poor Law, and the raising of local taxes to finance this primitive form of social security, would not be given to the newly-created, popularly-elected authorities. In Salisbury's phrase, 'the cat' was not to be 'put in charge' of the 'jug of cream'.

Salisbury's thinking on education was similar. The predominantly Anglican-run voluntary schools were again, by 1891, struggling to match the quality of education offered by the rate-subsidised Board Schools. By abolishing all fees for elementary education, and increasing the funding from central government, Salisbury could put the Church of England schools on a much sounder financial footing. His legislation also pre-empted Radical Liberal plans to review the whole system and perhaps incorporate the fading voluntary schools in a new national organisation outside the Church's control. The Church of England had long been the Conservatives' friend, and Salisbury was determined to uphold its influence.

Of all the legislation for which his ministries were responsible, Salisbury was least enthusiastic about the Workmen's Compensation Act. This seemed to interfere in the contractual relationship between employer and workman in a way wholly advantageous to the latter. Under it, most workmen were now guaranteed compensation for any injury suffered at work, without having to prove that their employer had been negligent. The inspiration behind the Act was Joseph Chamberlain. The ex-Radical had become Salisbury's Colonial Secretary in his 1895 ministry, when the Liberal Unionists had at last formally joined the Conservatives. Chamberlain hoped that this legislation would form a part of a much larger package of social reconstruction, including Old Age Pensions. He believed that if Salisbury's government made imaginative concessions to the working classes, they could be kept out of the socialist camp. Salisbury disagreed. He believed that the more concessions the wealthy made to the workers, the more the workers would demand. Resistance, and the defence of the free market, was the best strategy for the Conservatives and their Liberal Unionist allies. The Workmen's Compensation Act was the only concession Salisbury was prepared to make to Chamberlain to keep him happy. It was just enough, for soon, the Boer War (*see page 403)* would be fully absorbing 'Radical Joe's' destructive energies.

B *The social context of Salisburian Conservatism*

Readers may have been puzzled by mention of Joseph Chamberlain as an influential Cabinet colleague of Salisbury. Salisbury himself had described the former leader of Liberal Radicalism as a 'Sicilian Bandit' as late as 1884. But Chamberlain's transition from the Conservative's 'enemy number one' to a central figure in the Unionist hierarchy exemplifies a much broader shift of political allegiances which was crucial for the fortunes of Salisburian Conservatism.

The Liberals had flourished in the 1850s and 1860s, when economic growth was unprecedented, social harmony was unquestioned, and Gladstone's dreams of building a classless Christian Commonwealth seemed eminently practicable. By the 1890s, this mood had largely disappeared. Britain's economic supremacy was under challenge from Germany and the United States. Furthermore, the rise of militant, unskilled trades unionism, sometimes inspired by outright socialism, began to give the flavour of 'class-war' to industrial relations. Salisbury's brand of Conservatism, with its emphasis on uncompromising resistance to radicals and socialists, increasingly seemed to make sense to many old Gladstonians. This was a tendency which Chamberlain himself noted in 1894:

> Information obtained from a great number of constituencies . . . and confirmed by other correspondence, shows that the electors are much more interested at the present time in social questions and the problems connected with the agitations of the Labour Party than they are in any constitutional subject [e.g. Reform of the House of Lords]. There is much more searching of heart among the most moderate, and above all the wealthier Gladstonians. The men who have anything to lose are getting uneasy now that they see that Gladstonianism is not likely to be confined to an attack upon Irish landlords or British millionaires [the Liberal budget of 1894 had introduced Death Duties] but will probably result in an onslaught on capital generally.
>
> The resolutions of the TUC [Trade Union Congress] . . . amount to universal confiscation in order to create a Collectivist State. It is true that this is at present an unauthorised programme, but the policy of the Gladstonian leaders has been, and still is, to invite popular pressure in order that they may yield to it . . . in doing so, they will risk a further secession of all that remains to them of wealth, intelligence and moderation.

1. *According to Chamberlain, for what reasons would the 'wealthier Gladstonians' be thinking of voting Conservative in the next general election?*
2. *What long-term problems would be caused to the Gladstonian Liberal Party if it lost the backing of wealthy industrialists?*

Such feelings help to explain how many businessmen, even those from Nonconformist backgrounds, came to vote Conservative in the 1890s and how some even found themselves sitting on the Conservative backbenches in the Commons.

But this long delayed consummation of Peel's dream – that the Conservative Party should become the natural home of all men of property, whether their wealth was landed, financial or industrial – cannot by itself explain the electoral popularity of Conservatism in the last two decades of the nineteenth century. How were *the masses* persuaded to vote for the Conservatives?

This is a much disputed question. Three main explanations have been offered: there is probably truth in all of them. Firstly, social historians point to the growing size of the lower middle classes in later Victorian England. This group includes office workers, shopkeepers, insurance salesmen and elementary school teachers. It has been suggested that they were especially responsive to Salisbury's appeals for a union of all ranks of the educated and propertied against 'the mob'. Although they were often hardly better off than the working classes, they had a keen sense of their superior status. A Conservative vote was their way of asserting their own sense of identity with the wealthy – and it just as surely registered their anxiety at the danger of slipping backwards into the ranks of the poor.

Secondly, it is probable that the Conservatives enjoyed a surprising amount of success in those quarters where Salisbury least expected it: the working classes. Election results from Lancashire and the East End of London suggested the existence of a 'slum Toryism' at least as virulent as the 'villa Toryism' of the suburbs. Disraeli had been the first to appreciate how much Conservatism could gain electorally from identifying itself with the glories of empire and the spirit of patriotism – especially as the Liberals made it so easy to have themselves smeared with accusations of spinelessness, defeatism and doing England down.

The post-Disraelian Conservative Party had no hesitation in continuing with this strategy. The death of General Gordon at Khartoum in 1885, for which Gladstone was universally blamed, confirmed the negative stereotype of Liberalism's weaknesses. The Golden and Diamond Jubilees of 1887 and 1897, which coincided with Salisbury's premierships, were as much celebrations of the might and breadth of Britain's Empire as of Victoria's long reign. They helped to reinforce the association of Conservatism with imperial glory. By 1900, even Salisbury seemed to have appreciated the political capital to be extracted from popular chauvinism. He called an early general election in the middle of the Boer War, at the height of a period of patriotic fervour. The Conservatives and their Liberal Unionist allies reaped splendid rewards. They won 402 seats, reducing the Liberals, who were bitterly divided over the war, to a wretched 183 MPs. Contrary to the premises of Salisbury's life's work, Toryism and democracy seemed distinctly compatible.

The third strand of explanation has been offered by Martin Pugh (*see bibliography page 380*). Disraeli had appreciated that it was essential for Toryism to penetrate deep into popular culture if it was to survive in an age of mass politics. In 1883, inspired by this vision, some friends of his founded The Primrose League. Its objective, according to its charter, was to promote 'Tory principles – viz. the maintenance of religion, of the estates of the realm, and of the Imperial Ascendancy of Great Britain' through a 'true union of the classes'. The Primrose League was to embody Disraeli's idea that the English nation was one great and happy extended family.

Pugh is the first historian to draw out the full significance of the League's extraordinary popularity. By 1891, it boasted a membership of over one million. Through a stream of events and entertainments – dances, brass bands, visits to stately homes, 'magic lantern' shows, perhaps featuring pictures from distant parts of the Empire – it engaged ordinary men – and women – in a Conservative political culture in a way that Salisbury could never dream of doing. He would have regarded the League's festivals and junketings with incredulity and distaste. But at election time, the League did crucial work in spreading propaganda and mobilising the Conservative vote. No less important, its more diluted political activities between elections were instrumental in building up a bedrock of popular attachment to Conservatism.

According to Pugh, the League 'formed the vital bridge between [the party's] parliamentary leaders and the [rapidly expanding] mass electorate'. It marked an essential development in the range and style of popular Conservatism, which Salisbury had done little to sponsor, but from which he was to derive much benefit.

4 Salisbury in the Conservative Tradition

According to Michael Bentley (*see bibliography page 7*) Salisbury was 'the most formidable politician the Conservative Party has ever produced'. Evidence for this is not hard to find: Salisbury's electoral record is the most impressive of any political leader in the Victorian era. The victories he scored in 1886, 1895 and 1900 were all by large, even massive margins, while the defeats of 1885 and 1892 were close enough to leave the Liberals deeply compromised in their reliance on the Irish Nationalists for working majorities.

But there is an element of exaggeration about Bentley's claim. Salisbury himself was reluctant to take too much personal credit for the Tories' electoral dominance. Instead, he argued – with much truth – that 'Mr Gladstone's existence was the greatest source of strength which the Conservative Party possessed'. Beyond this, it must not be forgotten that the social changes which characterised later Victorian Britain – especially the rise of the lower middle classes, and the threat perceived as being posed by an increasingly militant working class – were singularly conducive to the Conservative triumph. Of course, Salisbury showed much skill in exploiting the changing social climate – his warnings about 'disintegration' and class war were well-judged to maximise the Conservatives' appeal to anxious property owners. But he was far from infallible. For example, his complete neglect of popular and working-class Conservatism could have proved very expensive. Salisbury's political vision was clear, piercing, unillusioned and in many respects far-sighted, but it lacked breadth, generosity and imagination.

A concluding comparison with Peel – and of course with Disraeli – should shed some light on what Salisbury contributed to the success of nineteenth-century Conservatism. He learnt much from both. He shared with Peel a tough-minded authoritarianism and contempt for the masses. For both of them, the French Revolution and the guillotine were the monstrous shadows hanging over aristocratic politics: the great problem was to keep the masses in order. The best prospect for this was, Salisbury and Peel agreed, to unite all the forces of property under the Conservative banner.

But Salisbury rejected two of Peel's most fundamental beliefs. First, he lacked Peel's confidence that a well-informed and bold executive could master most problems to which it set its mind. To Salisbury the main function of government was to maintain law and order and uphold the workings of the free market and the rights of property. No great legislative schemes ever fell from Salisbury's pen. Secondly, he absolutely rejected Peel's notion – exemplified in the great crises of 1845 and 1846 – that the Conservative executive might have to sacrifice the unity of the Conservative Party to the interests of the nation. To Salisbury, the true interest of the nation and the interests of the Conservative Party were indistinguishable. The Conservatives represented wealth, religion, intelligence, order – civilisation itself.

Salisbury vehemently rejected important elements of the Disraelian legacy, too. He deplored Disraeli's opportunism and adventurism, which had reached their ruinous climax in the signally un-Conservative Second Reform Act. The notion of a 'Tory Democracy' struck Salisbury as a contradiction in terms. As to 'trusting the people', the only thing that Salisbury believed the people could be 'trusted' to do – if given half a chance – was to plunder the property of their betters. While Disraeli's dream was to make the two nations of Britain – 'the rich' and 'the poor' – into one, it was the premise of Salisburian Conservatism that these two nations were necessarily divided and embattled. It was, Salisbury believed, the main responsibility of the Conservative Party to keep the poor from the throats and pockets of the rich. Salisbury's and Disraeli's visions of what British society could and should be like could hardly have been more different.

Yet Salisbury's succession as Conservative leader marked less of a discontinuity in Conservative political practice than might have been expected. In foreign affairs, he shared with Disraeli an unashamed conviction that British interests had to be defended, by war if necessary, and without reference to the higher principles of morality about which Gladstone got so worked up. Salisbury also well understood that the electorate were more likely to be impressed by successful assertions of British power, than by any gracious concessions and high-minded compromises.

At home, Disraeli's declining taste for political adventures ensured that Salisbury was more or less able to continue where Disraeli had left off: like Disraeli, he was determined not to 'harass the country' with legislative interference. Indeed, Salisbury was to extend this lesson to the point where the defining characteristic of his administrations was their domestic inertia.

Luckily for the Conservatives, Salisbury's and Disraeli's differences proved oddly complementary. Disraeli had targeted the working classes as potential Tory voters: by contrast, he had neglected and even despised the middle classes, although their flight from Gladstonian Liberalism was the key to Tory success in the later nineteenth century. Salisbury's strategy was the reverse: oblivious to the potential of working-class Toryism, the linchpins of his strategy were 'resistance to socialism' and the cultivation of 'villa Toryism'. Nevertheless, to his incredulity, the phenomenon of working-class Conservatism not only persisted, but grew. Disraeli's hopes that a Conservative political culture might capture the imagination of large sections of the lower classes was realised – a process in which the Primrose League, and imperialist rhetoric and celebrations, had a large role to play. Thus, Disraeli's and Salisbury's political blind spots were cancelled out: between them, in a way which neither of them as individuals would have thought possible, they were able to attract *both* working-class *and* middle-class voters to the Tory ranks. In that sense, the credit for the achievement of Tory hegemony in the last quarter of the nineteenth century should be jointly shared. But it is just as important to recognise that both individuals benefited greatly from changes in the social structure and dynamics of later Victorian Britain which neither of them properly understood, and which were indeed, in some respects, hidden from both of them.

5 Bibliography

R Blake *The Conservative Party from Peel to Thatcher* (Fontana, 1985), B Coleman *Conservatism and the Conservative Party in Nineteenth Century Britain* (Edward Arnold, 1988), M Pugh *The Making of Modern British*

Politics 1867–1939 (Basil Blackwell, 1982) chapter three, and Paul Adelman *Gladstone, Disraeli and Later Victorian Politics* (Longman, 1983): all have much of interest on Disraeli and Salisbury. For Disraeli alone, R Blake *Disraeli* (Eyre and Spottiswode, 1966) is the modern classic. It looks dauntingly bulky but is in fact very readable, has an excellent index, and its conclusion is only ten pages long! John K Walton *Disraeli* (Routledge, 1990) is a very stimulating brief survey. John Vincent's *Disraeli* (Oxford University Press, 1990) is mainly about the novels. His article in *History Today*, (Oct. 1981) 'Was Disraeli a failure?', should not be missed. See also P Smith *Disraelian Conservatism and Social Reform* (Routledge, 1967), Smith's essay on Disraeli's psychological makeup in *Transactions of the Royal Historical Society*, 1987 and Richard Shannon *The Age of Disraeli, 1868–1881, The Rise of Tory Democracy* (Longman, 1992). On the Reform Acts, D G Wright *Democracy and Reform 1815–1885* (Longman, 1970), J K Walton *The Second Reform Act* (Routledge, 1987) and Paul Adelman's article 'The Peers vs. The People' (*History Today*, February 1985) are all very useful.

6 Discussion Points and Exercises

A *This section consists of questions or points that might be used for discussion (or written answers) as a way of expanding on the chapter and testing understanding of it.*

1. How did the Tories come to find themselves in the political wilderness at mid-century, and why was it so hard for them to get out of it?
2. What aspects of Disraeli's background and early career make his ultimate emergence as Conservative Party leader surprising?
3. What was distinctive and significant about the political views which Disraeli developed in the 1830s and 1840s?
4. How effectively did Disraeli exploit the political opportunities which came the Conservatives' way in the 1850s?
5. Why did Palmerston's death in 1865 mark a turning point in the fortunes of the Conservative Party?
6. How did the Conservatives come, so successfully, to push through the Commons a Reform Bill *more* radical than that of Gladstone's?
7. What was the significance of Disraeli's speeches of 1872 for his own career and for the fortunes of the Conservative Party?
8. How far did the Second Reform Act and the social legislation of Disraeli's second ministry (1874–80) embody his vision of a 'Tory Democracy'?
9. What difficulties did the Eastern Question cause for Disraeli in domestic politics, and how well did he cope with them?

10 Why did the Conservatives lose the 1880 general election? What were the prospects for a Tory recovery on Disraeli's death a year later?

11 Why have modern historians often tended to underrate Disraeli?

12 What dangers did the Third Reform Act present to the Conservatives, and how did Salisbury turn the Act to his own advantage?

13 How did the Home Rule crisis benefit the Conservatives?

14 Why did Salisbury's ministries pass so little legislation?

15 How did Salisburian Conservatism manage to win unexpected electoral popularity?

B *Essay questions*

1 'An unprincipled opportunist'. Discuss this view of Disraeli.

2 How Conservative were the intentions and consequences of the Second Reform Act?

3 'The main reason why the Conservatives won the 1874 election was because Disraeli was not Gladstone and Gladstone was not Palmerston'. Discuss.

4 'All image, no substance'. Assess this view of Disraeli.

5 Was Disraeli a failure?

6 What did Disraeli learn from Peel and Peelite Conservatism?

7 What was 'Disraelian' about Disraelian Conservatism, and to whom did it appeal?

8 What did Salisbury contribute to the Conservatives' dominance of British politics in the last quarter of the nineteenth century?

9 'Mr Gladstone's existence was the greatest source of strength which the Conservative Party possessed'. (Salisbury). Discuss.

7 ESSAY PLANNING – A CHRONOLOGICAL APPROACH

The key to a good A level essay is a good plan, and a good plan has three qualities. First, it must be comprehensive, identifying the essential issues and information relevant to a particular question. Secondly, it must have at its core an argument which addresses the question set. And thirdly, it must enable the essay to have shape, movement and coherence – the essay must be more than a string of big facts and bright ideas.

A strategy for working out the argumentative core of an essay is discussed in chapter IX. Here, the focus will be on the first and third objectives: comprehensiveness and shape.

Consider the following title: 'Was Disraeli a Failure?' Cast your mind back over the topic, and jot down – in any order – as many of the really important facts and areas which simply must be considered. Your list could end up looking something like this:

Second Reform Act. Foreign Policy – e.g. Congress of Berlin. Domestic Policy – e.g. Artisans' Dwellings Act. Peel. Afghanistan and South Africa. Trade Union Reform. Free Trade Hall and Crystal Palace Speeches (1872). 1874 election. 1868 and 1880 electoral defeats. 1846–67 – lack of success. Novels – the Young England Trilogy (1840s).

This recall of information was easy enough. But how to give your list shape and coherence? The obvious strategy is to reorganise the list in chronological order:

- **Novels** – The Young England Trilogy
- **Peel**
- **1846–67** – lack of success
- **Second Reform Act**
- **1868 general election**
- **1874 general election**
- **Domestic policies:** – Artisans Dwellings Act (1875)
  – Trade Union Reform (1875)
- **Foreign Policy:** – Congress of Berlin (1878)
  – Afghanistan and South Africa (1879)
- **1880** – electoral defeat

Of course, this is not an essay plan! To base your essay on this alone would be to invite that most fatal of all essays (failure guaranteed!) – the general narrative. But we are nearer to a decent plan than you may think.

Look again at the original question. 'Failure' is a less straightforward term than we might imagine – was Disraeli a failure (or a success) *by whose standards? by what criteria? and over what period of time?* We know that Disraeli rose to be leader of the Conservative Party and Prime Minister from – by nineteenth-century standards – a relatively obscure background. And we know that, despite only one electoral victory to show for a lifetime in politics, the Conservatives were to enjoy great success in the two decades after Disraeli's death. What credit – if any – can Disraeli take for this? By thinking a bit harder about the scope and terms of the question, we open up some new perspectives and lines of enquiry. In particular, we can see that a full answer will require something on Disraeli *before* his parliamentary duel with Peel, and something on the Conservatives' fortunes *after* Disraeli's death.

The next stage in converting our list into a plan is a crucial one. How can the information in our table be given a structure and a focus so as to answer the question set? Let's assume that we are aiming to write a seven paragraph essay – about the length that a good candidate should be able to manage in 45 minutes by the end of his or her A level studies. So, split the chronological list into seven blocks, one for our 'pre-Peel' paragraph, five for the chronological core we have already identified, and one more for our section on Conservatism after Disraeli's death.

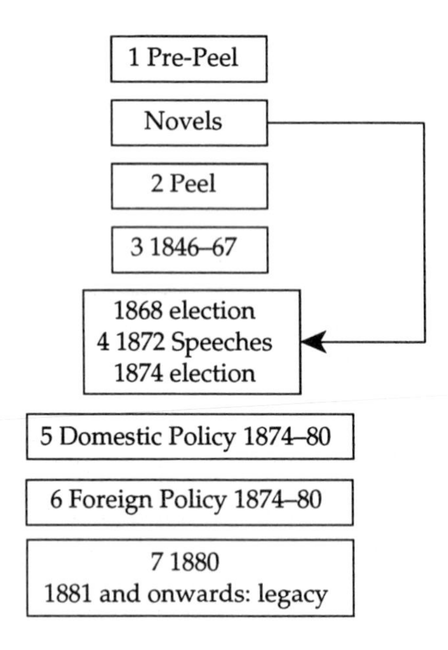

Two things must be said about the list. Firstly, it is sometimes necessary to cheat, shifting an easily movable block out of its strictly chronological sequence to help simplify the plan. Here, 'novels' can be made to fit in with another major statement of Disraeli's political ideas: the speeches of 1872. Secondly, the boxing of the dates suggested here is by no means the only practicable solution to the task of organising the information. For example, 'Peel' could easily be fused with the aftermath of his fall, the barren years of '1846–66', or the election defeat of 1880 could be directly linked to Foreign Policy 1874–80, especially to the imperial misfortunes of 1879. Whatever pattern you decide upon, the intellectual task remains the same: to present the information contained in the boxes to the reader so that each forms a part of the answer to the question to be tackled. So, what is the analytical thrust of each box to be?

1 *Disraeli's unusual background. Why was it unlikely that he should ever have become a Conservative leader? His own ambition satisfied – so, in this sense at least,* not *a failure.*

2 *'Assassination' of Peel the key to his rise – departure of the Peelites makes Disraeli's accession to ranks of leadership inevitable.* But, *success for Disraeli meant failure for (perhaps disaster for?) wider interests of Conservatism?*

3 *Two decades in wilderness. How far Disraeli's fault? (see 2) Could anyone have done better? Achievement of Second Reform Act. Brilliant opportunism. Serves Disraeli's interests well. But does it serve the broader interests of Conservative Party?*

4 *1868 election results suggests not or at least not yet (see 3). Disraeli to retire/be retired? But he bounces back with speeches of 1872. These expand/add to some of the themes of Young England. Vital role of Disraeli as image maker for modern Conservatism. But does he win 1874 election? Or does Gladstone lose it?*

5 *Disraeli's 1872 speeches vaguely gestured to social policy as means of achieving/consolidating class harmony. But how successful in practice? Account for limitations of legislation. Assess success or failure.*

6 *Disraeli had promised in 1872 to make England count again as a world power. Succeeds at Congress of Berlin? How? How far? Fails in Afghanistan etc. Why?*

7 *1880 horrid defeat. Does it reveal bankruptcy of Disraelian Conservatism? How far were Salisbury's successes based on his own distinctive analysis/political skills? How much do they owe to Disraeli's legacy?*

Two advantages of a chronological approach to planning should be evident here. With a little thought, the essay can be made to flow smoothly from paragraph to paragraph, developing an overall coherence and sense of movement. Secondly, the conclusion of the story (defeat, death and legacy) is also the ideal vantage point for a general evaluation of Disraeli's career.

You should not necessarily write out all these questions when planning your essay. But questions like them should be in your mind. The answers which you give to them will be the key to converting your chronological outline into an analytical argument – and analysis and argument are, of course, the key to A level success.

XII

FOREIGN POLICY 1870–1914

1 INTRODUCTION

Two events occurring in 1869 and 1870–1 were to have a massive, formative effect on the nature and conduct of British foreign policy in the late nineteenth century and early twentieth century. The first was the opening of the Suez Canal in 1869. The second was the Franco-Prussian War which began with the French declaration of war in July 1870 and ended with the total defeat of France and the surrender of Paris to Prussian forces at the end of January 1871. The former event ushered in a period of estrangement and bitterness between Britain and France which eventually threatened to lead to war between the two countries. The latter event changed the balance of power decisively in Europe and meant that, ultimately, the traditional policy of containment pursued by Britain in relation to the strongest European power would be aimed at German rather than French expansionism.

The Suez Canal project was developed by the French, who were keen to link the Mediterranean with the Indian Ocean. By 1858 a company had been organised and work commenced in 1859. The British attitude to all this was one of suspicion as Palmerston was inclined to distrust French motives in most situations. To his mind the completion of the scheme was primarily beneficial to the French and might threaten the route to, and hence security of, India.

The opening of the Canal in 1869 brought an increase in trade with the Middle East and Asia. As Palmerston had foreseen, the French merchant fleet expanded and French influence over the region and in the Turkish Empire in general increased. A restoration of Britain's position, however, soon became possible owing to the financial difficulties of the Egyptians, who were the majority shareholders in the Canal in partnership with the French. In 1875, the Khedive of Egypt, reduced to the verge of bankruptcy, offered over 175 million shares in the Canal for sale in Paris. Disraeli, the British Prime Minister, acting without parliamentary authority, borrowed £4 million from the bankers Rothschilds and bought up the entire block. By this move the British Government became, overnight, the largest single shareholder. British influence and power in Egypt was further secured in the early 1880s, when British troops intervened to crush an internal revolt. By the beginning of 1883 Britain was in effective occupation and control of Egypt, to the bitter fury of the French. This set in motion a period of intense rivalry between Britain and France, as the latter attempted to compensate herself for the loss of Egypt by expansion elsewhere in Africa.

The significance of the Franco-Prussian War was not evident to most British contemporaries. Accustomed as they were to centuries of French continental supremacy, it was not easy for the British to perceive a fundamental change in the balance of power. Indeed, as A J P Taylor pointed out, in his *Struggle for Mastery in Europe*, the inclination of the British was to regard the Prussian victory as helping the maintenance of the balance of power. Gladstone, the Prime Minister, made it clear that the key issue so far as Britain was concerned was the security of Belgium and in this he was supported even by Disraeli. The fact that the transfer of Alsace and Lorraine from France to the German Empire took place without consulting the inhabitants of those provinces stirred Gladstone's conscience, but he never contemplated intervention. Any remote prospect of British support for France was effectively ended by the publication in *The Times* of details of a proposal, by the French foreign minister Benedetti in 1866, for a treaty between France and Prussia which would have allowed France to occupy Belgium. The German Chancellor Bismarck was the source of the leak and his action was well-calculated to reinforce Britain's traditional fears of French ambitions.

The emergence of Germany underlined a growing British isolation from the other European powers: Russia had been estranged by the harsh peace terms insisted upon by Palmerston at the end of the Crimean War; France, who might have been expected to seek British friendship as security against the new might of Germany, was alienated by imperial rivalry; Austria was increasingly under German influence and entered the Dual Alliance with Germany in 1879; Germany initially had no particular conflict of interest with Britain but, in the longer term, Kaiser Wilhelm II's pride and ambition led to a naval expansion which seemed to threaten British interests more directly than any other single development in the period up to 1914. In 1881 the Dual Alliance became a triple arrangement through the inclusion of Italy. In 1894 the French sought security in an alliance with the Russians. Strategically this was aimed against Germany, but the stimulus for the growing diplomatic entente between France and Russia had originally been their joint detestation of Britain quite as much as any fear of German power. Since both Russia and France resented Britain's global position, the prospects for co-operation with this power block did not look promising.

Abstinence from alliances did not mean total isolation from European affairs. It was never practical or desirable for Britain to adopt a truly isolationist role. The concept of 'Splendid Isolation', if it has any useful meaning at all, should be taken as referring to the fact that Britain felt that she could afford to stand apart from the power blocks emerging in Europe, retaining her freedom of action in a period when the other great powers were significantly decreasing their own. In this sense 'isolation' meant no more than the traditional policy of 'non-entanglement' espoused by every authority from Castlereagh to Gladstone in the period 1815 to 1870. Nor should the term 'splendid' be taken to imply an increase of power in the strategic sense. Rather, it was that sense of moral superiority over other nations which had for generations underlied the basic principles of British foreign policy. Thus, as will be shown in this chapter, Britain collaborated with the great powers (and the lesser ones) as and when it served her interests to do so.

Britain entered into only one formal alliance during the period up to 1914, with Japan in 1902. This was a reflection of two realities which Britain finally faced up to at that point. The first was the enormous global burden of empire which Britain rapidly accumulated at the end of the nineteenth century. The strain which these added responsibilities placed upon British resources was colossal, and was made even more acute by the need to withstand any erosion of naval superiority such as that posed by the expansion of Germany's navy. An alliance with another, if lesser, naval power might alleviate this strain. The second was the realisation in the period 1895–1902, that British 'splendid' isolation was in danger of turning into a genuine isolation, possibly leading Britain into the role of an outcast nation. In February 1896, the First Lord of the Admiralty made a speech in which he referred to British isolation being 'self-imposed'. One of the tasks of this chapter will be to examine how Britain emerged from her isolation.

2 Britain and the Eastern Question 1870–1914

A *The Bulgarian crisis and the Congress of Berlin*

The outbreak of the Franco-Prussian War in 1870 gave Russia the opportunity to realise the objective which had been at the heart of her diplomacy since the end of the Crimean War – reversing the imposition of the Black Sea Clauses of the Treaty of Paris of 1856 (*see page 187*). In that treaty, Palmerston had insisted on the neutralisation of the Black Sea, so that Russian warships could not sail on its waters. From the Russian point of view the Black Sea Clauses were a humiliation.

Compulsory disarmament of this kind had never been imposed on a great power in any previous peace settlement. The Russians could hardly help but contrast this harsh treatment with the relative leniency accorded to France in 1814–15 after years of warfare in which all Europe had been thrown into turmoil. Palmerston, however, would not consider the Russian complaints. He accepted that it was a humiliation, but to his mind 'Russia has brought this humiliation upon herself'.

Not all Palmerston's contemporaries agreed. Among those opposed to the treaty was Gladstone. In his view the treatment of Russia was too harsh and when the Russian repudiation came in 1870 his main concern, as British Prime Minister, was not that Britain had lost an essential strategic advantage, but that, in acting unilaterally Russia had failed to observe the moral imperative of changing treaties by agreement rather than force. Gladstone's doubts were overcome at a conference in London in March 1871, proposed by Bismarck. Russia was formally freed of her restrictions in the Black Sea in return for her acceptance that international treaties could not be changed unilaterally. This suited Gladstone but not Disraeli, who, settling comfortably into his increasingly nationalistic attitude, foresaw a renewal of the threat to Constantinople.

In July 1875 revolts occurred in the two Turkish provinces of Bosnia and Herzogovina (*see map on page 394*). These two provinces were primarily inhabited by Serbs who wanted union with the autonomous province of Serbia. The Serbs traditionally regarded Russia as their principal ally – a role the Russians themselves were usually willing to play. This was precisely the kind of situation feared by Disraeli, who took over as Prime Minister in 1874 following the Conservative general election victory. Public opinion was likely to favour Christian subjects rebelling against their Turkish overlord, yet Disraeli was convinced that British interests demanded the maintenance of Turkey's territorial position. He feared that a weakened Turkey would allow further Russian expansion which would, in turn, threaten Britain's position in the Eastern Mediterranean. Disraeli found it increasingly difficult to hold to this course however, since the revolts spread to involve Montenegro and Bulgaria. In the latter region the Turks suppressed the rebels with their customary barbarity but also with rather less typical efficiency. Exaggerated reports of the massacres soon reached London and a political storm erupted (*see page* 272).

From the beginning of the crisis Disraeli favoured a strong line against any Russian intervention and in support of the preservation of Turkey. He accepted the need for reform within the Turkish Empire but hoped that the Turks could be persuaded to reform themselves. He had a great distrust of nationalism, seeing it not as an agent of reform, but rather as a destroyer of institutions. Initially Disraeli was not deeply alarmed by the revolts in Bosnia and Herzogovina since these regions bordered the Austrian Empire and seemed unlikely to involve Russia. Therefore when the Austrian Foreign Minister, Andrassy, produced a peace plan at the end of December 1875, in conjunction with Germany and Russia, Disraeli, although annoyed that he had not been consulted, agreed to associate Britain with the proposals. The Andrassy Note, as the plan became known, required that Turkey accept an armistice and carry out land reforms in the rebellious provinces. The Turks accepted the plan although they made no moves to carry out the proposed reforms.

The problem with the Andrassy Note was that the Turks never had any intention of delivering the promised reforms. Forcing them to do so was the next logical step. Early in May 1876 Bismarck and Andrassy met Gorchakov, the Russian Foreign Minister, in Berlin to formulate the Berlin Memorandum. Since the three parties involved were hardly agreed themselves about how to proceed, the Memorandum produced little that was new. It did, however, contain an implied threat, inserted by Gorchakov, to the effect that if the proposals failed there would have to be 'the sanction of an understanding with a view to effective measures'. This was a rather muted threat of intervention but it was enough to alert Disraeli. The new proposals were transmitted to the governments of France, Italy and Great Britain for approval, but whilst the first two agreed to it, the British government turned it down flat. Instead, the British Mediterranean fleet was ordered to Besika Bay in the Eastern Mediterranean to protect Constantinople. (*see map on page 394*).

In the Balkans, things now went from bad to worse. The Bulgarians rebelled at the end of May 1876 and, at the beginning of July, Serbia and Montenegro declared war on Turkey. Now Disraeli was really alarmed. Bulgaria, bordering on the Black Sea, was an obvious area of Russian interest and the Serbian and Montenegran forces were largely commanded by Russians. Moreover, Disraeli's room for manoeuvre at home was rapidly diminishing. His Foreign Secretary, Lord Derby, was the son of the former Prime Minister under whom Disraeli himself had served, and was an influential figure. He was opposed to intervention and, though he did not dissent from the basic aims of Disraeli's policy, he thought his leader's methods were dangerous. Disraeli was a strong Prime Minister and could cope with Derby's opposition so long as he held the bulk of the Cabinet with him. However, the tide of public opinion against the Turks was now threatening to undermine cabinet confidence.

Disraeli's initial reaction to the first reports of the 'Bulgarian atrocities' in June 1876 was to dismiss them as exaggerations. He was encouraged in this by the British ambassador to Constantinople who was fiercely pro-Turkish and played down the seriousness of the massacres. In fact, the press estimates of deaths were considerably inflated

(25 000 according to reports – nearer 12 000 in reality), but this counted for little in the face of the barbarities visited by the Turkish soldiers on defenceless women and children. There was a chorus of protest from the Liberals and public opinion was soon firmly set in an anti-Turkish stance. Worse was to come. Gladstone was moved to come out of retirement and join the political fray once more. His pamphlet *The Bulgarian Horrors and the Question of the East* appeared, in the autumn of 1876, to widespread public acclaim. Disraeli could mutter resentfully about 'designing politicians' who produced pamphlets which were 'vindictive and ill-written' but he could not alter the reality of the fact that majority opinion in Britain now wanted to see the Turks taught a lesson, even if that meant allowing the Russians to go in and do the job.

The inevitable clash between Russia and Turkey came in April 1877 when the Tsar, losing patience with Turkish failure to implement reforms, declared war. Disraeli could do nothing but declare British neutrality and remind the Russians not to violate Constantinople or interfere with any key British interests. Contrary to popular expectation the Turks gave a surprisingly good account of themselves in the war. The Turkish troops fought with great bravery and resource, holding out at the fortress of Plevna for nearly six months. They were eventually overrun and the Russian advance from then on was swift, but Russian plans for a quick war were in ruins and fickle public sympathy in Britain rapidly swung round to the Turkish side. By January 1878 Disraeli felt confident enough to warn the Russians that any alterations to the 1856 Peace of Paris could not be made without the general consent of the great powers. In February the British fleet moved towards Constantinople to discourage any Russian advance on the capital. Realising that their diplomatic position was rapidly crumbling, the Russians hurriedly forced the Turks into a peace settlement – the Treaty of San Stefano – signed on 3 March 1878. Under the terms of the Treaty (*see map on page 394*), Serbia, Montenegro and Romania were to become independent with increased territory; Russia was to gain new territory in the Caucasus; Bosnia and Herzegovina were to be granted home rule, while Bulgaria was to become an autonomous principality, greatly enlarged and initially administered and garrisoned by the Russians. The Turks signed the Treaty in the hope that Britain would rescue them from this awful humiliation.

Strictly speaking, the terms of the Treaty of San Stefano did not directly threaten British interests. Constantinople remained untouched; the navigation of the straits was unaffected; the Suez Canal and Egypt were not threatened. Nevertheless, the treaty represented a massive extension of Russian power and Britain was not the only country to react angrily. The Austrians were equally outraged and joined Britain in calling for an international conference. For Disraeli, San Stefano was a justification of the policy he had tried to pursue all along. In the

House of Lords, (he had been created Earl of Beaconsfield in 1876), he denounced San Stefano as substantially against British interests:

> The Treaty of San Stefano completely abrogates [cancels] what is known as Turkey-in-Europe . . . it creates a large State which, under the name of Bulgaria, is inhabited by many races not Bulgarians. This Bulgaria goes to the shores of the Black Sea and seizes the ports of that sea; it extends to the coast of the Aegean . . . The Treaty provides for the government of this new Bulgaria, under a prince who is to be selected by Russia; its administration is to be organised and supervised by a commissary of Russia; and this new State is to be garrisoned, I say for an indefinite period, but at all events for two years certain, by Russia . . . The Sultan of Turkey is reduced to a state of absolute subjection to Russia . . .

1 *What significance do you attach to Disraeli's complaint that many non-Bulgarians were to be included in the new State?*

2 *Why was Disraeli so concerned about the geographical extent of Bulgaria in relation to the Black Sea and the Aegean?*

3 *In what ways, according to Disraeli, would Russia be able to influence Bulgaria?*

When Bismarck added his voice to the demand for an international conference and offered Berlin as a neutral venue, the Russians knew they had little option but to agree. They tried to play for time by raising technicalities about the scope of the proposed discussion, and Disraeli used the delay to good effect, calling up the army reserves and redeploying troops from India to the Mediterranean. These actions provoked a minor crisis in the cabinet as Lord Derby strove to maintain a more neutralist line. Derby was opposed to any action which might imply the threat of war and, finding that Disraeli was also proposing to secure British control of Cyprus for the future, he at last resigned, to be replaced by Lord Salisbury. Disraeli scarcely noticed the departure of Derby. He had long since taken to conducting foreign policy personally. Salisbury himself had doubts about Disraeli's handling of foreign affairs, but by early 1878 he was convinced that Disraeli's strategy was at least better than Derby's and for the time being he devoted himself to carrying out the Prime Minister's wishes.

The Congress of Berlin was a result of Bismarck's determination to support the Austrians. The Russians, sensing that a coalition was forming against them, knew from the start that they would have to make concessions. Disraeli was determined to go into the conference with the essentials already agreed. At the end of May he secured agreement from the now resigned Russians that the 'big Bulgaria' concept would be abandoned. Early in June he concluded a treaty with the Turks under which Britain agreed to defend Turkish interests against Russia, in return for the purchase of Cyprus, which he planned to use as a military and naval base. Obtaining Cyprus meant that Disraeli was prepared to concede the Russian gains in the Caucasus. Finally, Disraeli agreed a mutual support policy with the Austrians, under which Britain accepted Austrian occupation of Bosnia and Herzegovina. It should be emphasised that although Disraeli set out the basic aims of policy in these matters, it was Lord Salisbury who actually conducted the negotiations and worked out the precise details of the agreements.

With this degree of preparation it was hardly surprising that the Congress of Berlin went off smoothly enough. The Turks, elated that their 'play dead' policy at San Stefano had paid off so spectacularly, promised reforms and religious liberty for all their subjects. They possibly even meant it at the time! 'Big Bulgaria' was divided into three: an independent Bulgaria; a partly autonomous state to be known as Eastern Rumelia; and Macedonia which reverted to full Turkish control. Serbia, Montenegro and Romania became completely independent, but with only modest extensions to their territory. The threat to Constantinople was removed and Turkey remained 'in Europe'. Disraeli returned to London claiming 'peace with honour'. Few contemporaries disputed his claim at the time.

B *From Berlin to Sarajevo*

In retrospect it is almost too easy to be critical of the Berlin settlement and of its chief inspiration – Disraeli. Most of his ideas either collapsed quickly or can be seen as contributing to later problems. Within the Balkans themselves the treaty sowed the seeds of future confrontations. Serbia and Montenegro resented the extension of Austrian influence and the curtailment of their own ambitions. The Bulgarians too were angered by the settlement, as were the Greeks and the Romanians – all these had hoped for territorial expansion that had failed to materialise. Russia and Austria had both strengthened their positions but equally both now had a lot more to lose in the region and were even more jealous and suspicious of each other. Russo-German relations had taken a turn for the worse. Bismarck's idea of a power block of the three emperors of Germany, Austria and Russia (the Dreikaiserbund) was fatally weakened and in the following year Germany decided to conclude a 'dual alliance' with Austria. Although Bismarck made subsequent attempts at a rapprochment with Russia relations between the two countries never really recovered. Most damning of all to Disraeli's reputation, in the short term, is the fact that the Bulgarians soon proved to be totally unwilling to play the role of a Russian satellite and entered a union with Eastern Rumelia in 1886. This union was made in the face of Russian opposition and supported by Britain and Austria as a barrier to Russian expansion, an exact reversal of the 1878 policy.

Disraeli's policy needs, however, to be seen primarily in the context

The Balkan Settlement under the terms of the San Stefano Treaty, March 1878

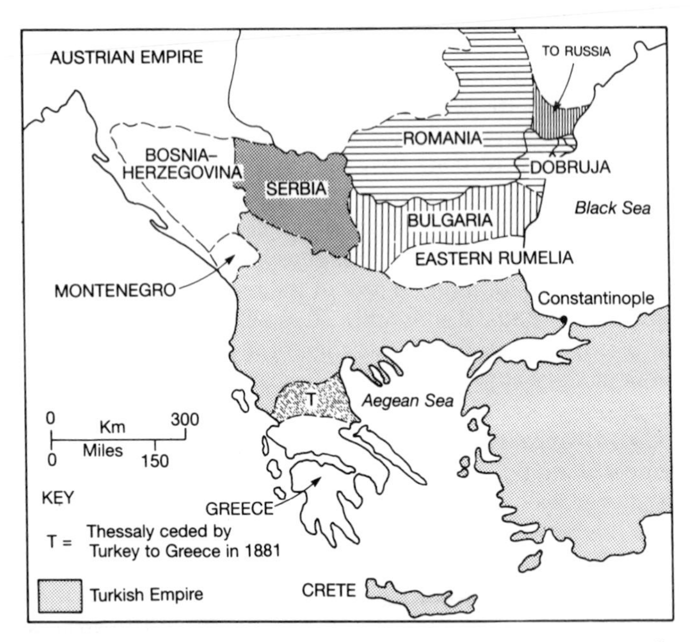

The Balkan Settlement under the terms agreed at the Congress of Berlin, June 1878

of the situation in 1878. It is easy enough to cite Salisbury's observation in 1885 that Britain had 'backed the wrong horse' at Berlin. It is less easy to suggest what might have been the alternative 'right horse'. It was universally assumed in 1878, even by the Bulgarians, that the proposed 'big Bulgaria' would be pro-Russian! The disenchantment which developed between Russia and Bulgaria could scarcely have been foreseen. Moreover, in securing Cyprus, it could be argued that Disraeli made it possible to protect British interests in the Eastern Mediterranean without the need for similar intervention in the future. So far as driving a wedge between Russia and Germany was concerned, while it was not a prime object of Disraeli's policy, it appeared at the time to be a welcome opportunity to guard against the revival of a latter-day 'Holy Alliance'. Finally, although Disraeli's hopes for internal reform of the Turkish Empire appear on the surface to be naive, the new Sultan, Abdul Hamid II, had granted Turkey's first-ever constitution early in 1877 and appeared to have the credentials for the role of reformer. It turned out that Abdul Hamid's flirtation with constitutionalism was a brief one. At the time, however, the fact that he had granted a constitution at all must have seemed miraculous.

The securing of Cyprus and the subsequent occupation of Egypt left Britain in a strong position. The Suez Canal route to India and the Far East meant that the long-standing significance of Constantinople was diminishing even by 1878. It is noticeable that Disraeli referred as often to the importance of the Canal as he did to that of Constantinople. Subsequently, the importance of the Canal came even more to the fore as the growing dominance of steam shipping concentrated more and more trade in that direction. It is not surprising therefore that although there was continued activity within the Balkans, Britain played a relatively low-key role in events there after 1878. In the resumed Bulgarian crisis of 1885–6, as has been noted, Britain eventually agreed with the Austrian viewpoint that a big Bulgaria would hold off Russian aggrandisement. Lord Salisbury, Prime Minister between 1886–92 and 1895–1902, became convinced, with the passage of time, that Turkey was on the verge of disintegration and was determined not to tie Britain into permanent defence of the indefensible. He was helped in this by two factors. Firstly, the Turks never again became popular with British public opinion as they briefly had in Disraeli's time. Secondly, the Turks themselves became disenchanted with Britain's role as their protector. As time went on the Berlin 'triumph' seemed increasingly hollow.

In the years leading up to the outbreak of war in 1914, British policy towards Turkey and the Balkans essentially resolved into two aims. The first was to prevent, curtail or contain any outbreaks of conflict in the Balkans. The second was to counteract the growing influence of Germany in the Turkish Empire. Neither of these was a particularly easy objective. The influence of Germany in the Turkish Empire was already increasing in importance well before 1895. Military contacts between the two had been established as far back as 1881, when German officers had begun reorganising the Turkish army. Turkey increasingly sought closer links with Germany in the hope of filling the void left by Britain's abdication of the role of protector. Wilhelm II had already paid a state visit to Turkey in 1889. In 1898 he returned, this time for a pilgrimage to the Holy Land. During this visit he assured the Turks of German friendship 'at all times'. In 1899 rail concessions were granted to a German company for a link connecting Berlin with the Persian Gulf. This led to a growth of German economic influence which seemed to threaten British interests and also those of Russia. It was a contributing factor to the eventual co-operation which emerged between Britain and Russia in their 'entente' of 1907. From the strategic point of view German military influence in Turkey posed a potential threat to the security of Egypt and the increasingly important Persian Gulf. Likewise the Straits, though no longer the primary object of attention, assumed a greater significance if they were likely to fall under German control.

So far as the politics of the Balkans was concerned, Britain could do little more than seek to co-operate in a general peacekeeping role. In the Bosnian crisis of 1908–9, during which Austria unilaterally converted her occupation of Bosnia-Herzogovina into full annexation, Britain sought to placate the Turks and restrain the fury of the Serbs who had deluded themselves into thinking that the provinces would eventually become part of Serbia. However, when Italy declared war on Turkey in 1911, without a shred of justification other than her desire for a North African empire, Britain, like the other powers, took no action. Italy seemed to occupy a key position in the Mediterranean and the risk of losing her friendship was seen as unacceptable. The defeat inflicted on the Turks by Italy increased tension in the Balkans and contributed to the formation of the Balkan League in 1912. This group, comprising Greece (the prime mover), Serbia, Bulgaria and Montenegro, temporarily set aside their differences and attacked Turkey, inflicting a heavy defeat on her. This was too much for the great powers and Britain sponsored a conference in London which imposed a peace settlement which attempted the effectively impossible task of satisfying the members of the League whilst at the same time protecting the integrity of Turkey. The result was that the members of the League fell out amongst themselves and Bulgaria attacked Serbia. All the others supported the Serbs and the Bulgarians were defeated. Turkey took the opportunity to attack Bulgaria and gain back territory from her. The Treaty of Burcharest finally put an end to this chaos in August 1913, but by this time Britain was becoming totally disenchanted with the thankless task of attempting to bring some kind of order to the region.

To some extent the Germans now felt the same way. Both Austria and Russia had behaved recklessly at times throughout the series of crises. The only hopeful development at all had been that Britain and Germany had been more or less forced to work together to restrain them. Britain had tried to use her recently-found closeness to Russia to urge moderation; the Germans had tried to use their longer-standing relationship with Austria, to do the same. It has to be said that neither effort was particularly successful. By 1914, although Britain (along with the other powers) had secured acceptable guarantees about the German-sponsored railway expansion in the Turkish Empire, the Eastern Question remained essentially unresolved. A terrible price was paid for this on 28 July 1914, when a Bosnian Serb, embittered by the continued Austrian possession of Bosnia-Herzogovina, assassinated the heir to the Austrian throne and set in motion a chain of events which would embroil the Great Powers in a catastrophic war.

3 IMPERIAL EXPANSION 1870–1914

A *Egypt and the Sudan*

Once the British Government had become the largest shareholder in the Suez Canal, there was an obvious obligation to protect that investment. In the late 1870s continued financial mismanagement in Egypt seemed to threaten the whole stability of the region. Initially Britain did no more than join with France to demand that the Sultan of Turkey depose the incompetent ruler of Egypt, the Khedive Ismail, and provide a more efficient administration. This he did, but resentment at what was seen as foreign interference led in 1881 to a coup, led by an Egyptian army officer. The new Khedive appointed a new ministry to placate the rebels but, fearing for his long-term safety, he appealed to Britain and France for help. Gladstone was by now Prime Minister once again and his immediate reaction was against intervention. However, when riots broke out in Alexandria and Europeans became the object of attack it was no longer possible for the British Government to stand aside. Gladstone was anxious to collaborate with the French over intervention and he secured French agreement to a proposal for a joint fleet to make a show of strength at Alexandria. Once there, however, it became apparent to the commanders that a military intervention on land would be required. At this point the French drew back. They had been conducting separate negotiations with the rebels and feared that any major entanglement in Egypt would detract from their main obsession – the recovery of Alsace and Lorraine from Germany. Britain had therefore to proceed alone or withdraw. Gladstone chose the former course. Alexandria was bombarded and the Suez Canal was seized. In August 1882 a large British force landed at Port Said and proceeded to crush the Egyptian rebel forces.

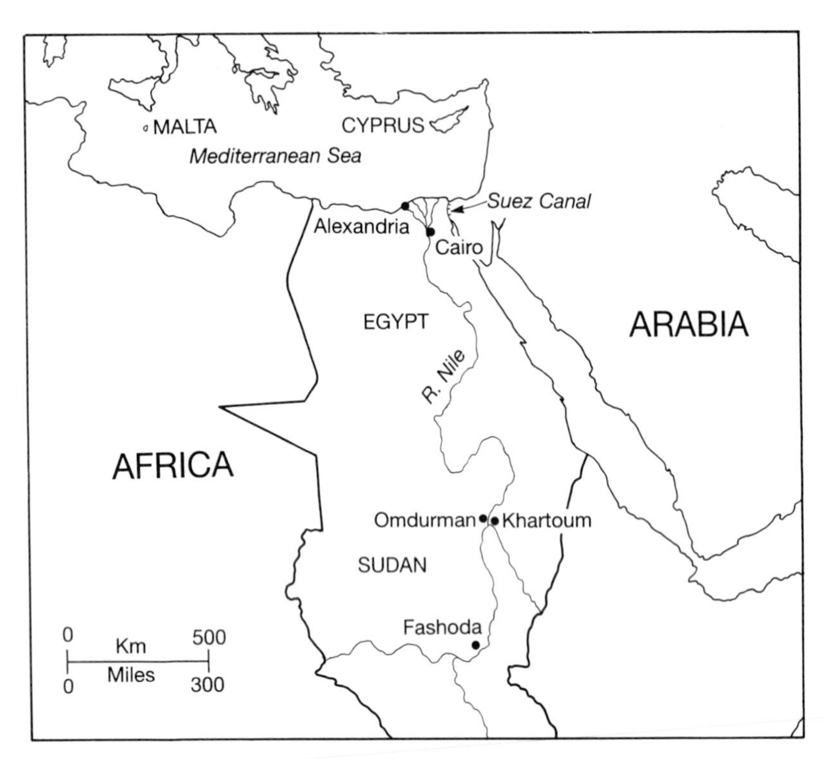

British Expansion in Egypt and the Sudan

Gladstone had no wish to remain in Egypt but equally he had no means of withdrawing, at least in the short term. The state of the country was so bad that a British withdrawal would have plunged it into total anarchy. Sir Evelyn Baring (later Lord Cromer) was despatched to become Consul-general and to take over the Khedive's administration. The French were informed that they had forfeited their rights to a role by backing out at the crucial time. For some time the official British line was that the occupation was only temporary. Gladstone began negotiations to set up an international board of control in 1882 and finally, in 1885, a body was appointed, comprising representatives from Britain, France, Germany, Austria, Russia and Italy in equal numbers. The board, however, could not disguise the completeness of British military control, and British statesmen ultimately came to regard Egypt as part of the Empire.

Soon after Britain assumed control a further complication set in. Egypt itself was a colonial power in the Sudan, having ruled there for 60 years, suppressing the slave trade but generally acting in a repressive manner. The Sudanese rebelled in 1883 under the inspiration of Mohammed Ahmed, a former civil servant and slave trader, who had proclaimed himself 'Mahdi', the 'divinely guided one', sent to convert the world to Islam. In 1883 his forces defeated the British-led Egyptian army. Gladstone believed that Britain had taken on more than enough already and had no wish whatever to get involved in the Sudan. On the other hand he could hardly stand by and see the Egyptians there massacred. He decided on a policy of protected evacuation and the Government despatched General Charles Gordon to oversee the withdrawal from Khartoum. It was a poor choice and the Government itself was not clear as to his exact role. Gladstone clearly saw him acting as an advisor and was not too keen on sending Gordon at all. He was a public hero for crushing a rebellion in China in 1860 and had already been governor of the Sudan (1877–80), during which time he had acted ruthlessly against the slave trade. He was known to favour resistance to the Mahdi.

It was not surprising, therefore, that Gordon soon forgot about evacuation once he arrived at Khartoum, calculating that public opinion and the weight of feeling in the Cabinet would ensure that a relief expedition would be sent. Gladstone, who was furious with Gordon, (and probably with himself for agreeing to send him in the first place) was all for leaving him to his fate, but eventually, in February 1884, the Cabinet agreed in principle to send help. There then followed months of wrangling over the size and scope of the force and whether or not a minister should accompany it. In the end the force under General Wolseley arrived two days after the death of Gordon in Khartoum in January 1885. Public opinion was outraged and Gladstone got most of the blame. Gladstone had enjoyed the affectionate nickname of the 'Grand Old Man', or 'G.O.M'. Now he found his fortunes reversed; he became the 'M.O.G.', the 'Murderer of Gordon'. Gladstone eventually decided to abandon the Sudan to the Mahdi in spite of demands for revenge for Gordon and the protests of the Egyptians. The Queen reflected the general tone of public opinion when she observed that 'Mr Gladstone and the Government have Gordon's innocent, noble, heroic blood on their consciences'.

The Mahdi died later in 1885 but clashes continued between the Egyptians and the Mahdi's successor, the Khalifa. In 1896 it was decided to send a military force under General Kitchener to reconquer the Sudan. This change of policy was partly due to the increasing awareness of the Sudan's key position in controlling the waters of the Nile which were fundamental to Egypt's economy. Also, by now, other countries were showing some interest in Sudan, particularly France. Kitchener slowly secured Anglo-Egyptian control. He defeated the forces of the Khalifa in April 1898 and then again in September 1898 at the Battle of Omdurman. He went on to capture Khartoum and forced the Khalifa to go into exile. Finally, in November 1898, he forced a French expeditionary force to retreat from Fashoda, a small outpost on the Upper Nile some 375 miles south of Khartoum (*see page 398*). British supremacy over the entirety of Egypt and Sudan was secured.

B *Southern Africa*

Ever since the period of the Napoleonic Wars, Southern Africa had been of considerable interest and concern to Britain. The Cape had been in British hands since the Vienna Congress and had formerly been of key importance in the sea route to the East. With the opening of the Suez Canal and the rise of steam shipping its significance in that respect had declined, but the potential wealth of mineral resources available more than made up for this. Because British administration was entrenched in the Cape Colony it was always likely that circumstances would promote extensions of British influence. The descendants of the original Dutch settlers of the Cape, the Boers (farmers), had left the Cape in a series of migrations to escape British rule in the 1820s and 1830s. In the 1850s the British had given up attempts to maintain sovereignty over the Boers and had recognised two independent areas – the Transvaal Republic and the Orange Free State (*see map below*). Britain controlled Cape Colony itself and Natal, which bordered both the Boer States to the south-east and separated them from the sea. From the late 1860s, Britain proceeded to extend northwards. A protectorate was established over Basutoland in 1868 and Griqualand West was annexed in 1871. These moves were designed to prevent expansion of the Boer Republics.

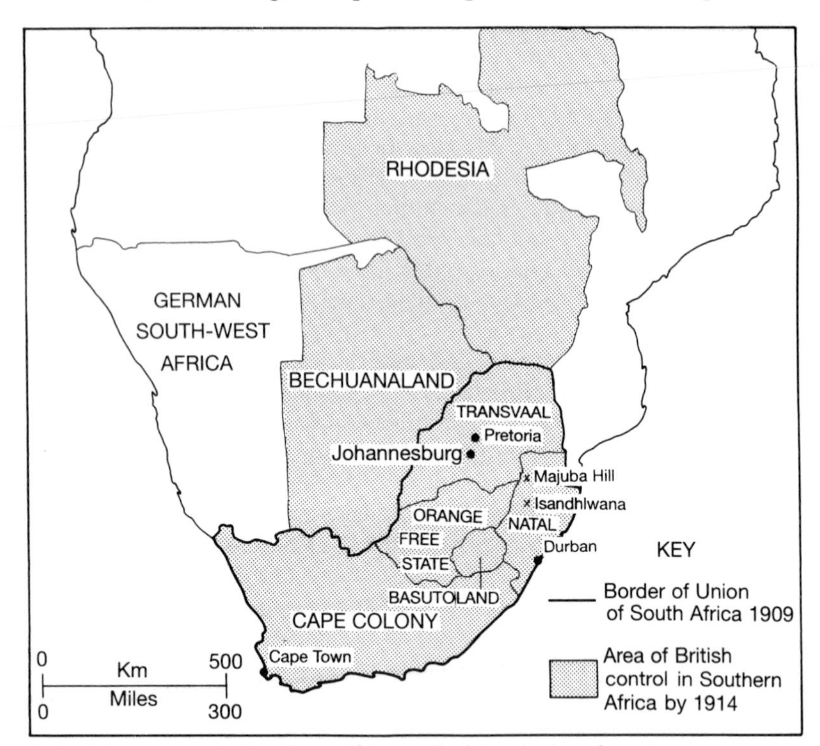

British Expansion in Southern Africa in the late nineteenth century

When Disraeli returned to power in 1874, he was already converted to the idea of Empire, a concept for which he had previously shown little inclination. His Colonial Secretary, Lord Carnarvon, was an enthusiast with a strong desire to turn his leader's vague utterances on imperialism into reality. Carnarvon was determined to annexe the Transvaal in the hope that such a move would facilitate a federation of South Africa. He decided to send Sir Theophilus Shepstone, a former Lieutenant-Governor of Natal, to Transvaal to see if such a coup might be possible. Fortune favoured Shepstone. His visit coincided with a disastrous financial crisis in Transvaal and an uprising by the Zulu nation. The Boers swallowed their dislike of British influence in the face of their immediate need for protection. Annexation followed in 1877, quickly followed in turn by a war against the Zulus which the new Governor of the Cape encouraged. The war was successful in the end but not before a British force had been massacred at Isandhlwana in 1879. Disraeli, beset by economic problems on the home front and war in Afghanistan, was angry at the way things had gone in Southern Africa but could do little to influence events from so far away.

Once the threat of the Zulus had disappeared the Boers were less than happy to remain under British control. Gladstone, who had roundly condemned Disraeli for events in Southern Africa, was disposed to let them have their independence, but he failed to move fast enough for the Boers who attacked British forces in 1881 and inflicted a defeat at the battle of Majuba Hill. Gladstone was embarrassed but stuck to his resolve and granted the Boers independence in the Pretoria Convention of 1881. When the Boers subsequently complained at a clause requiring them to recognise British 'suzerainty' it was removed in the Treaty of London of 1884, although British control of Transvaal's foreign policy was retained.

Further extension of British influence up into East Central Africa in the 1880s, was primarily the result of the activities of Cecil Rhodes. Rhodes was born in Britain, but went to Natal at the age of 17. He made a fortune in the diamond mines of Kimberley and the gold mines of Transvaal. He conceived a great vision of British imperial greatness in Africa which would encompass the entire length of the continent, linking, by rail, the Cape with Cairo. In 1885, Rhodes persuaded the British Government to take over Bechuanaland (now Botswana) arguing that it was under threat from the Germans. Believing that gold deposits were still waiting to be found further north, Rhodes then set about securing concessions from the chiefs of tribes living in present-day Zimbabwe and Zambia. This expansion did not proceed altogether peacefully. The Ndebele, furious at what they saw as broken pledges and bad faith, rose in 1893 and again in 1896. The Shona, previously a subject people of the Ndebele, who originally had collaborated with the British, joined in the second revolt.

In 1889 Rhodes secured a Charter for his British South Africa

Company, which effectively gained control of these regions. There had been considerable opposition to the granting of a Charter in Britain, especially from religious groups who preferred that the Government itself take responsibility. Rhodes, however, argued that the Company option involved no expense to the taxpayer, only to the shareholders of the company, and his view carried the day. The BSA Company developed into a powerful organisation with what amounted to its own private army. It was backed by some of the richest organisations in the world including Rothschilds. De Beers and Consolidated Goldfields. It not only controlled the land but also obtained mineral rights and the right to tax the African people. Although its powers were controlled by the British Government, in practice it had virtually sovereign rights. When Rhodes became Prime Minister of the Cape in 1890 his power and influence seemed to have reached limitless proportions.

There was, nevertheless, still one remaining barrier to Rhodes' vision of the future. The Boer states needed to be brought under full British control, especially the Transvaal with its great mineral wealth. These states were now completely encircled by British-controlled territory, but were highly resistant to any extension of their connection with Britain. Indeed, they were increasingly resentful of the obligations imposed under the Treaty of London. The means of bringing them to heel, however, already existed. Many British miners and engineers had been drawn to Transvaal by the prospect of the wealth to be obtained from mineral exploitation. The Boers had been more or less obliged to allow in these 'Uitlanders' (or foreigners) because of the expertise they brought to what was essentially an agricultural economy. The Boers, under the leadership of Paul Kruger, the President of the Transvaal, were determined to retain control, and subjected the Uitlanders to heavy rates of taxation and various restrictions, including virtual exclusion from political rights. The complaints of the Uitlanders at their treatment formed a natural basis for a possible revolt within the Transvaal, as well as constituting an argument for British intervention to free what were mainly British subjects from oppression.

The British Government was reluctant to intervene directly in the Transvaal. In 1894 the prospect of a Uitlander revolt prompted the Colonial Office to specifically rule out any British intervention in support. When Joseph Chamberlain became Colonial Secretary in 1895, however, the position of the Colonial Office became rather more ambiguous. Chamberlain was an enthusiast for both expansion and greater unity in the Empire, which he saw as the only basis for Britain's long-term prosperity and strength. When Rhodes planned support for a rising of Uitlanders in Johannesburg at the end of December 1895, Chamberlain took no action even though he undoubtedly knew of Rhodes' intentions. In the event the whole thing was a fiasco. The rebellion was aborted at the last moment and the invasion force of Company police, led by Dr Jameson, was easily overcome by Kruger's troops. Chamberlain was heavily implicated and faced a parliamentary enquiry which he managed to survive; Rhodes was compelled to resign as Prime Minister of the Cape and Jameson ended up in prison. The affair assumed a wider diplomatic significance due to the involvement of Germany in the aftermath. The confidence of the Kruger Government had been boosted by the proximity of a German presence in South-west Africa (now Namibia) since 1884. The Kaiser, always anxious to cut an impressive figure on the diplomatic stage, sent a telegram to Kruger congratulating him on handling the crisis without having to seek outside help. This implied that Germany considered herself free to intervene, an attitude which could not be tolerated by the British Government. Britain demanded an explanation from Germany and put a naval force to sea, the like of which had never been previously seen. The Kaiser was forced to offer a conciliatory 'explanation' of his action, but Anglo-German relations were seriously damaged by the episode.

War between Britain and the Boer Republics eventually broke out in 1899. It was an ugly war in which many Boer women and children perished from disease in British camps and Britain's international reputation was badly tarnished. It caused division at home between those who supported the war and those, like the young David Lloyd George, who saw it as a bullying act of aggression. It was finally ended in May 1902 by the Peace of Vereeniging. The two states became self-governing colonies in 1907 and the Boers were sufficiently reconciled to the situation to enter the Union of South Africa in 1910. In bringing about the Union the British Government had to face squarely the issue of the political rights of the Africans. In Cape Colony Africans were not excluded from the franchise, if they met the required qualifications. Although their rights were maintained in the Cape, the constitution of the Union excluded them from the franchise elsewhere. This issue split opinion in Britain. The preference of the Liberal Government in 1910 was clearly in favour of opening up the whole franchise to qualified Africans, but this view found little support amongst whites in South Africa and, despite an appeal from the Prime Minister, Asquith, the Union Bill passed unamended.

c *Afghanistan*

In Afghanistan Britain had maintained a low profile since the Kabul fiasco of 1841 (*see page 191*). In 1876, Disraeli's appointment of the imperial expansionist, Lord Lytton, as Viceroy of India, led to another debacle. Disregarding his instructions, Lytton sponsored a new British mission to Kabul aimed at extending British influence and forestalling the Russians. At first the mission appeared to be a success, but disaster struck in September 1879 when the entire group was massacred. When Gladstone returned to power in 1880 he was able to reverse the 'forward' policy in Afghanistan. Lytton was recalled and a brilliant campaign by General Roberts ensured a dignified withdrawal. The emergence of a strong ruler in Afghanistan made that country a viable independent state and helped Gladstone to achieve his only clear-cut reversal of what he termed 'Beaconsfieldism'. In 1885, Gladstone achieved in Afghanistan another of his rare foreign policy successes. The Russians had captured the town of Penjdeh and seemed set to expand their influence further. But with the full backing of the House of Commons, which granted him £11 million in war credits, Gladstone made it clear that any further moves would be resisted by force. In the face of such resolution, the Russians backed down. For once, Gladstone had matched Palmerston in his assertive defence of British interests. It was not, however, a role in which he felt comfortable.

4 Rivalries, Alliances and Ententes 1900–14

A *The end of isolation?*

As was noted in the introductory section to this chapter, the concept of Britain as a power in 'Splendid Isolation' as the nineteenth century came to an end, is one which needs careful qualification. The distinctive feature of British foreign policy in the 1890s was not so much that Britain was more isolated as such, but rather that she became alienated from so many other powers at the same time. To the longer-standing difficulties surrounding Anglo-French and Anglo-Russian relations was added a serious dispute with the USA over the exact location of the border of Venezuela with British Guinea and the brush with the Germans over the 'Kruger telegram' incident. The dispute with the Americans was bad enough to provoke threats of war from Washington whilst the clash with the Kaiser upset the prevailing assumption of harmony between Britain and Germany. It was the universality of hostility towards Britain in the late 1890s which prompted some contemporaries to point to what they saw as dangerous, rather than splendid, isolation in Britain's position in the world.

The chief advocate of an alliance with a continental power as a way of retrieving the situation was Joseph Chamberlain, the Colonial Secretary (1895–1903). Chamberlain believed that Britain's future security rested on two elements: the integration and development of the Empire and an alliance with Germany. To Chamberlain (and he was far from being alone in this opinion), Germany and Britain were 'natural' allies for a wide variety of reasons ranging from economic linkages to racial and cultural similarities. He proposed an alliance with Germany on three occasions: March 1898, November 1899 and January 1901. However, as will be seen in the following section on Anglo-German rivalry, on each occasion the initiative failed to deliver the intended result. Neither Lord Salisbury, who acted as Foreign Secretary as well as Prime Minister from 1895 to 1900, nor Lord Lansdowne who took over the Foreign Office in 1900 shared Chamberlain's confidence in the German option. This was not because they were anti-German but rather because they realised that the forces promoting such an alliance were superficial. Nevertheless, they did recognise the need to do something about Britain's unpopularity in the world.

Salisbury was anxious to improve Anglo-French relations after a near catastrophe in 1898, when Britain and France had come close to war over an incident at Fashoda in the Sudan (*see map on page 398*). A French expeditionary force had occupied this out post in 1898 after an epic march north from Central Africa lasting two years. Kitchener was ordered to secure its removal once Khartoum had been taken, and he duly did so, enforcing a French retreat. Public opinion on both sides became frenzied. Both governments would have welcomed a better relationship but such was the depth of feeling, on the French side especially, that there was little hope of moving much beyond limited colonial compromises at first. Progress was more feasible in other directions.

The Venezuelan border dispute between Britain and the USA had come as a shock to both sides. The Americans, however, did not really want a war over the issue and agreed to settle matters through an arbitration tribunal based in Washington. Both sides in fact had good reasons to look for a more harmonious relationship. The USA wanted to proceed with a long-desired project for linking the Pacific and Atlantic with a canal at Panama. They were determined that such a venture must be under their sole control, but under an agreement with Britain dating back to 1850, the British had equal rights to share in the undertaking. Preliminary discussion to amend the 1850 treaty began in 1899 and the outbreak of the Boer War later in the year made Britain particularly keen to see a successful outcome. In the end Britain agreed to cede to the USA full control of the project in return for guarantees about freedom of access to the canal for other powers. These negotiations were not straightforward and continued until the summer of 1901 before a new treaty was agreed. Nevertheless, there was never any real doubt about the outcome. Lansdowne was a strong advocate of Anglo-American friendship and was prepared to make almost any reasonable concession to secure it. A treaty was eventually signed in November 1901 and with it Anglo-American relations were set on a new course for the new century.

In the Far East Britain had two objectives: the security of her trade with China and the maintenance of peace without which trade could not flourish. Both these objectives seemed to be most compromised by the activities of the Russians. Britain suspected Russian ambitions in Persia, Afghanistan and China, whilst the extension of rail networks inside Russia itself (largely funded by French money) seemed to offer a threat even to India. Britain was not alone in fearing Russian intentions in the Far East. The Japanese did as well. Their particular concern was to hold primacy in Korea, then a Chinese dependency and directly opposite her own coastline. In 1894 the Japanese went to war with China in order to establish Korea as a buffer-state, free of Chinese influence. In this they succeeded. They also gained extensive concessions in northern China. This appalled the Russians, who wished to dominate China themselves.

The Russians managed, in 1895, (with unusual efficiency) to organise a European coalition consisting of themselves, the French and the Germans to force the Japanese to hand back their gains to the Chinese. This was achieved without the participation of the British, which was indicative of the extent to which Britain could be marginalised whenever the other powers acted in concert. However, the Japanese were still determined to realise their aim of bringing Korea under their own influence, while the British were concerned to find a way to counter the growing Russian hegemony in the Far East. Thus the seeds of an Anglo-Japanese alliance were sown. The Japanese made the running. There were two possibilities for them. They could reach an agreement with the Russians over Korea or they could link up with the British to counter Russian power. In the autumn of 1901 they began to explore both avenues simultaneously. They approached the Russians via the French but made no progress. Britain, on the other hand, saw an opportunity and took it. Fearing that the Russians might make up their minds to reach an agreement, the British entered into an alliance with Japan in 1902. The terms were straightforward. If either power was at war with a third party, the other would maintain strict neutrality; if either power was at war with two other powers the other would come to their aid; both powers asserted their special interests in the region and Britain recognised Japan's claims in Korea.

This arrangment suited both parties well. Britain, like the Japanese, had tried in the past to reach an agreement with the Russians to respect each others' interests but without success. Neither country wanted war with Russia except as the last resort, (the Japanese were as surprised as everyone else when they crushed the Russians in the war of 1904–5); on the contrary both believed that the alliance made war with Russia less likely. Apart from the Russians themselves, the real losers were the French. They had been hoping for a Russo-Japanese deal because it would have been less dangerous for them and would have increased the pressure on Britain to improve relations with France, something the French Government had long desired but had no idea how to achieve. Now France had the worst of both worlds. There was an increased chance of their being drawn into a conflict with Britain, whilst the British were freer than before to remain aloof from European 'entanglements'.

However, although the Anglo-Japanese Treaty took the pressure off

Britain to a considerable degree, this did not mean that there was any reduction in the British desire to improve relations with France. Initially the French reaction to the Anglo-Japanese Alliance, though full of polite diplomatic vagueness, was predictably hostile. However, once their indignation had worn off; the French had to face realities. Unless they could reconcile Japan and Russia and detach the Japanese from the British (both forlorn hopes) they had to effect an Anglo-French reconciliation. Thus events in the Far East made an Anglo-French 'entente' or 'understanding' as near to inevitable as perhaps anything in human affairs can ever be, since the British also hoped for better relations with the French. Britain did not regard the Japanese Alliance as in any way anti-French and the French reaction to it was seen as a genuinely unfortunate by-product of an otherwise entirely happy arrangement. The biggest stumbling-block was likely to be French public opinion. Here the three-day visit of King Edward VII in May 1903, proved to be the catalyst. The visit was an unexpectedly huge success. Parisian crowds which turned out on the first day to boo and chant *'Vivent les Boers!'* returned to see the King off on the final day chanting *'Vive le Roi!'*. The climate of Anglo-French relations thawed dramatically. In July 1903 the French President visited London and the British Foreign Secretary, Lord Lansdowne, began serious talks with the French Ambassador. It was not easy going. Much distrust remained on both sides, particularly with the French who had the added difficulty that agreement with Britain meant recognising the British position in Egypt – an emotional obstacle for French opinion. The French therefore went through agonies of indecision while the British chaffed at the delay.

It took nine months to settle the details of the Anglo-French Entente which was signed on 8 April 1904. It would probably have taken much longer, had not events in the Far East served to force the French to take the plunge. On 8 February 1904 Japan declared war on Russia and launched an immediate attack on Russian ships at Port Arthur. This attack was the direct result of the continued failure of the Japanese to secure Russian recognition of Japanese primacy in Korea. Fearing that the Russians intended to extend their influence into Korea, Japan opted for a pre-emptive strike. The French nightmare became reality. From using delay as a bargaining tactic in the negotiations, the French Foreign Minister, Delcassé, hurried now to get them completed. The terms of the entente were as follows: Egypt and Morocco would be mutually recognised as British and French spheres of influence respectively. In each the 'open door' principle of free economic access would be adopted for a period of 30 years. In secret articles, Britain and France agreed to set up a Moroccan protectorate if this policy broke down, (meaning if the Sultan of Morocco was overthrown), in which France would share Morocco with Spain who would receive a small coastal strip opposite Gibraltar on condition that it remain unfortified. Finally, various disputes affecting Newfoundland, Madagasgar and

Siam were resolved. The comprehensive nature of the agreements meant that all the serious 'flashpoints' through which Britain and France might previously have come into conflict were resolved.

The cumulative effect of the alliance with Japan and the understandings reached with the USA and France transformed Britain's diplomatic position. The policy of rationalisation (making limited concessions in order to achieve objectives) and detente (reducing tension by eliminating areas of conflict) could now be applied to what seemed the most difficult area of all – Anglo-Russian relations. In the event agreement proved less of a problem than it appeared. This was largely due to a changed attitude on the part of the Russians, brought about by a disastrous war with Japan. The Russian Far Eastern fleet was crippled at Port Arthur and the Baltic fleet sailed around the world to step into the breach, only to be unceremoniously sunk by the Japanese on 8 April 1905. This second naval catastrophe, following a land defeat a month earlier at Mukden, convinced the Russians of the need to make terms with Japan. The Anglo-Japanese Alliance, originally due to run for five years, was renewed ahead of schedule in August 1905 and was extended in scope to include mutual support in the event of war with even a single power. With this in mind, and in their weakened state, the Russians now proved far more amenable to the idea of reconciliation with Britain.

The agreement which was signed on 31 August 1907 resolved all the outstanding differences between Britain and Russia. Tibet was recognised as a neutral buffer-state and Russia renounced contact with Afghanistan. Persia was the crux of the agreement: Russia was to have a sphere of influence in the north while Britain had a comparable arrangement in the south, with a neutral zone in between where both countries had equal rights of access. The Persians were not consulted about any of this.

With this agreement British policy seemed to have achieved everything it could hope for on the diplomatic scene. All the existing areas of tension seemed to have been diffused and without need of recourse to any European alliance. Agreements had been struck with both Russia and France, without any commitment to aid either in the event of war. No agreements had been reached with Germany, for the simple reason that there seemed to be no outstanding disagreements to resolve.

B *Anglo-German rivalry 1900–14*

The growth of Anglo-German rivalry took both countries by surprise. So much so that for some time both sides seemed determined to ignore the growing tension as if hoping it would simply disappear. As was noted in the preceeding section, at the end of the nineteenth century Germany figured primarily in British minds as a possible partner in a 'natural' alliance. Even sceptics like Salisbury and Lansdowne were prepared to accept Chamberlain's attempts at negotiations if only to see what they might lead to. At the turn of the century, Anglo-German relations seemed set to improve still further. Some of the trade rivalry, which had marked the 1880s and 1890s, was receding as trade improved and Britain entered a new phase of economic prosperity in which German custom was an important element. Even the increase in German naval power did not appear unduly alarming when viewed against the Anglo-Japanese alliance, which had reduced the demands on the British Navy in the Far East, and the Anglo-French Entente which had eased the pressure in the Mediterranean. The Russian fleet had been eliminated and, over the period from 1898 to 1905, the balance of naval power moved decisively in Britain's favour. At that point Britain had massive superiority over France and Germany combined and German expansion, though vaguely disturbing in principle, scarcely mattered in practice. However, even in 1904 there were some prominent voices raised in warning against a possible anti-German interpretation of the Anglo-French Entente. Lloyd George recalled in his *War Memoirs* a conversation with Lord Rosebery (a former Prime Minister and Foreign Secretary):

> ... on the day when the Anglo-French Entente was announced, I arrived ... on a couple of days visit to the late Lord Rosebery. His first greeting to me was 'Well, I suppose you are just as pleased as the rest of them with this French agreement?' I assured him that I was delighted that our snarling and scratching relations with France had come to an end at last. He replied, 'You are all wrong. It means war with Germany in the end!' About a year after this prophetic utterance I became for the first time a Minister of the Crown. Had anyone then told me that before I ceased to hold office in the British Cabinet I should not only have witnessed a war between Britain and Germany, but have taken an active, and in fact leading part in its prosecution, I should have treated such a forecast as one of the many wild predictions of good or evil with which every public man is assailed by persons of unbalanced minds.

1 *Why should Rosebery, in the circumstances of 1904, have seen the Entente as meaning war with Germany?*

2 *Account for Lloyd George's view, at the time when he took office, that a war between Britain and Germany was unthinkable to anyone of sound mind?*

3 *How valuable is evidence of this kind to an understanding of subsequent events?*

The situation changed dramatically after 1905. In 1904 the British Government had commissioned the building of a new battleship, the *Dreadnought*. When launched in 1906, its immense firepower and the strength of its armour made all existing battleships obsolete. The British lead in naval power was thus seriously undermined by this single act, since German 'Dreadnoughts' would inevitably follow and would progressively eliminate Britain's superiority in conventional ships. The commissioning of *Dreadnought* in 1904 had been controversial for this very reason. Lloyd George was to argue in 1908 that Britain had not needed a new class of battleship and could easily have responded had another power built one. Against this was the fear that another power might contrive to build in secret and thus gain an initial and possibly decisive lead. From the British point of view there was no reason for Germany to engage in a naval race since, (again from the British point of view), there were no clashes of interest between them. This view, however, entirely overlooked the German desire for a great navy which would befit their status as a world power. The British viewpoint was underwritten by the assumption (correct as it turned out) that if a race did result it would be a race that Britain would win. As the years went by the tensions which arose between Britain and Germany over naval power proved intractable, not least because they were based on entirely different perspectives on each side. The Germans believed, or at least hoped, that their possession of a great navy would make Britain fear and respect Germany; this in turn would make Britain more amenable to German interests and sensitivities. In Britain the result of German expansion was not fear but resentment at the mounting expense of this naval race, which, from the British viewpoint was entirely pointless anyway. After all, as Balfour pointed out in an article written in 1912, 'Without a superior fleet, Britain would no longer count as a power. Without any fleet at all Germany would remain the greatest power in Europe.' This was unanswerable logic – unfortunately the German Naval Programme was based not on logic but on pride.

It proved impossible to break the deadlock. To the British there was only one possible solution – the Germans should reduce their building programme. The German response to this was that if Britain would make an alliance with Germany there would be no need for Britain to 'fear' the German fleet. As early as 1908 the estrangement between the two countries was clear enough for all to see. Nor was the tension solely due to the naval question. German resentment at the Anglo-French Entente and, in particular, at the way that Germany had not been consulted over the future of Morocco, led them to provoke a crisis over the issue in 1905. The Kaiser, visiting Morocco in March 1905, assured the Sultan of Morocco that Germany still recognised his independence. This repudiated the terms of the Anglo-French entente. Germany then demanded an international conference on Morocco. Germany hoped to expose what was assumed by her government to be Britain's lack of genuine commitment to France. Since Germany aimed to entice (or force) Britain into an alliance and isolate the French by detaching the

Russians from the Franco-Russian Alliance, the 1904 entente had been a major blow to German policy.

None of this made any sense from the British viewpoint. The entente was not intended to be anti-German, so far as Britain was concerned. Sir Edward Grey, who became Foreign Secretary in the new Liberal Government at the end of 1905, resented the crudity of Germany diplomacy and saw the danger of allowing the French to be left isolated in Europe, i.e. that they would fall under German domination. According to A J P Taylor, (in *The Struggle for Mastery in Europe*), Grey was 'concerned about the European Balance (of power) in a way that no British Foreign Secretary had been since Palmerston'. He feared a 'continental league' of powers under German hegemony. He therefore pursued a policy of constantly warning Germany against seeking greater influence, whilst at the same time seeking to encourage both the French and Russians to resist German pressure without actually making any British commitment to them. In attempting to bolster the French in the German-inspired Moroccan crisis Grey hit upon a new concept in British diplomacy. He authorised 'conversations' between the British and French military general staffs aimed at considering the means by which British forces could assist France on land in the event of war. This was all hypothetical of course, but it pointed to a consideration that had in a sense always been evident if never fully accepted – that Britain could not afford to allow France to be dominated by a greater power in Europe, any more than in the past she had been able to tolerate the domination of the rest of Europe by France. There was only one power capable of exercising such domination now and that was Germany. Thus, during the Algeçiras Conference on Morocco in 1906, called at the insistence of the Germans, Britain supported France unswervingly. When in 1911, the Germans provoked a second Moroccan crisis, fears that the French were about to do a deal with the Germans led to Lloyd George making his famous 'Mansion House' speech, which primarily warned the French against such a move. Nonetheless, the speech was widely interpreted as anti-German and war with Germany became a clear possibility for all to see. The British fleet was prepared for action and, for the first time, was ordered to give priority to the shipping of an expeditionary force to northern France. This was little short of a revolution in the state of European affairs and it revolved fundamentally around the deterioration in Anglo-German relations.

5 BRITAIN AND THE OUTBREAK OF WAR IN 1914

Specific rivalries or tensions between Britain and Germany played almost no part in the British decision to declare war on Germany on 4 August 1914. The assassination of the Austrian Archduke Franz

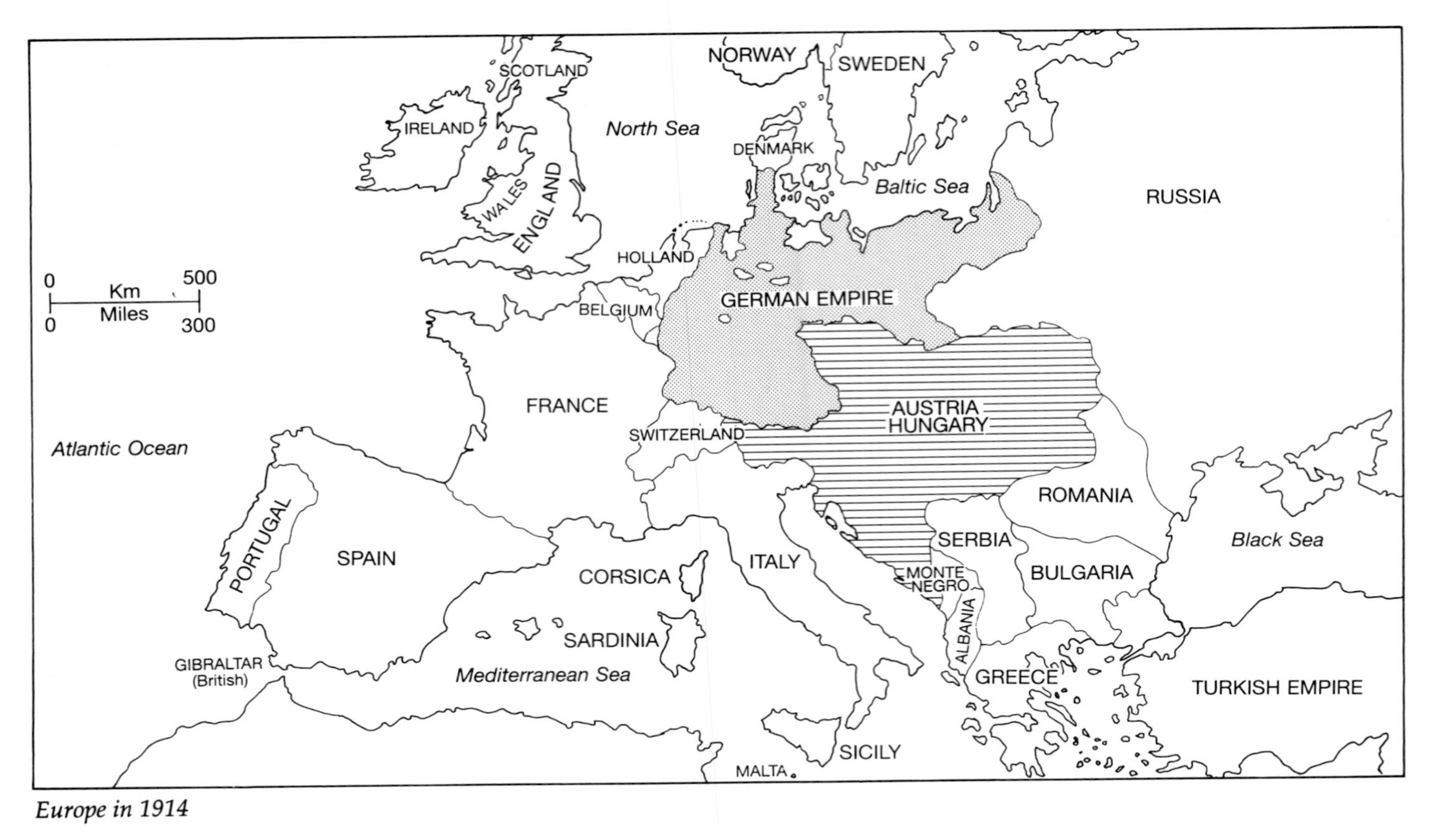

Europe in 1914

Ferdinand by a Bosnian Serb at Sarajevo on 28 June 1914, scarcely seemed to touch British interests at all. As late as 23 July, Lloyd George was telling the House of Commons that Anglo-German relations were better than they had been for many years. What decided the issue was the German declaration of war against France. Britain was already involved in an informal naval alliance with France, under which their fleets were arranged so that France would defend the Mediterranean and Britain the Channel and North Sea in the event of war. The fact that even the Cabinet knew little about the extent of Anglo-French preparations served to create confusion and hesitation at Cabinet level when matters drew to a head, but even this could not ultimately affect the outcome. The fact that the fate of Belgium lay bound up with German military plans helped to focus the minds of the doubters, like Lloyd George, who found it hard to countenance the horror of the impending conflict.

The issue of Belgium was significant because Belgian independence was a long-standing British commitment which even Gladstone had been willing to contemplate war to defend. That Belgium was a small power facing a mighty adversary was convenient for public opinion and in staking a claim to the moral high ground; it was not in itself decisive. Britain could turn a blind eye to the plight of small powers faced by aggression when it was expedient to do so, as the Danes had discovered to their cost in 1864. The Germans had long planned to attack France through Belgium if war came and the reaction of the British hardly weighed with them at all in this respect. Although the Germans hoped that by some means the British might be kept out of the war they never counted on this in their planning. On the contrary, they had always assumed that they must prepare for the contingency that Britain would assist France. Since they also assumed the war would be short they attached little importance to the British threat – the British Army being, in the words of the Kaiser, 'contemptible' in terms of its size.

Nothing that Sir Edward Grey could have done in his negotiations with the Germans could have averted the eventual outcome. He has been criticised for not making the British position clear enough to the Germans. On the contrary, he made the position entirely clear; Germany was not to count on British neutrality; France and Russia were not to count on British support. This sounds paradoxical but, in diplomatic terms, it was not. A war involving Russia alone might theoretically be possible without involving the intervention of Britain but a war involving France was not. In practice the Germans were not concerned to avoid a war with France, so the situation remained hypothetical. For Britain the issue was clear. To stand aside was to risk allowing the complete domination of the continent of Europe by Germany. This was inconceivable on strategic and economic grounds, to say nothing of the question of British prestige. Neutrality in 1870 had been argued to be beneficial to the balance of power; neutrality in 1914 would have destroyed the balance of power once and for all and, with it, the independence of Great Britain.

Grey himself put the issue squarely to the House of Commons on 3 August 1914 before the actual declaration of war by Germany against France. Russia and Germany had been at war since 1 August and Germany had invaded Luxembourg on 2 August, at the same time demanding freedom of passage through Belgium in return for a guarantee of Belgian territorial integrity:

> I ask the House from the point of view of British interests, to consider what may be at stake. If France is beaten in a struggle of life and death, beaten to her knees, loses her position as a great Power, becomes subordinate to the will and power of one greater than herself . . . if that were to happen, and if Belgium fell under the same dominating influence, and then Holland, and then Denmark, then would not Mr Gladstone's words come true, that just opposite to us there would be a common interest against the unmeasured aggrandizement of any Power? It may be said, I suppose, that we might stand aside, husband our strength, and that whatever happened in the course of this war at the end of it intervene with effect to put things right, and to adjust them to our own point of view. If, in a crisis like this, we run away from those obligations of honour and interest as regards the Belgian Treaty, I doubt whether, whatever material force we might have at the end, it would be of very much value in face of the respect we should have lost . . . I do not believe for a moment, that . . . we should be in a position . . . to undo what had happened in the course of the war, to prevent the whole of the rest of Europe opposite to us – if that has been the result of the war – falling under the domination of a single Power . . .

1 *How important is the role of Belgium according to Grey?*
2 *Why do you think Grey mentions Mr Gladstone?*
3 *How important is this extract in understanding Grey's approach to foreign policy and the reasons for the British declaration of war against Germany?*

6 Personalities, Principles and Policies 1870–1914

A *Gladstone and Disraeli*

Most historians take the view that, despite the animosity which existed between Gladstone and Disraeli over foreign policy, there were few genuine differences between them over essentials. This view rests upon the simple process of comparing what each of them said about each other's conduct of policy with what they actually did when in power – a case of actions speaking louder than words. It is certainly true that Gladstone and Disraeli disliked each other to a far greater extent than was usual in nineteenth-century political life and that this dislike caused an excessive polarisation of views between them. Gladstone, in particular, came to see Disraeli as the embodiment of all that was evil in politics. It is also true that, up until the 1870s, foreign policy had seemed to be the one area where the two men did share some common ground. Both had attacked Palmerston over the 'Don Pacifico affair' in 1850 and both condemned his China policy. Both drew attention to the cost of his policies to the Exchequer. Both rejected Palmerston's mistrust of the French and urged co-operation with other powers and particularly with France.

This picture is reinforced by considering what happened when the Liberals returned to power in 1880 after a campaign in which Gladstone had denounced Disraeli's foreign policy as 'dishonourable'. According to R Seton-Watson, writing in the 1930s, 'It was widely assumed that a complete reversion in foreign affairs would follow the Liberal victory'. In fact, nothing of the kind occurred. Not only did Gladstone's government pledge itself to the Treaty of Berlin; it also decided to keep the island of Cyprus, an arrangement which Gladstone had previously described as little short of theft. According to C Lowe, writing in the 1960s, the explanation is political: 'It is a basic error to take Gladsone's Midlothian pronouncements as Liberal foreign policy: this, after all, was an election campaign when he had to develop a line antagonistic to Disraeli, and his actions, once in office, were very different.'. K Bourne, in his book *The Foreign Policy of Victorian England*, pointed to the pragmatic reasons for Gladstone's policies: 'In spite of all the noise that Gladstone made over the Bulgarian horrors, he did not, it would seem, differ so very much even from Disraeli about the substance of British interests in the Near East ... he knew that the country still believed the strategic security of Constantinople to be a fundamental necessity ...'.

It would be wrong, however, to conclude that there were no serious differences between the two men in their attitudes and ideas. The apparent unity of views they shared in the Palmerstonian era can be misleading. Just as Gladstone can be said to have pursued a political line in his attacks on Disraeli in the late 1870s, so there was a strong political dimension to Disraeli's attacks on Palmerston. Disraeli was a man desperate for office in the 1850s and 1860s and he would waste no opportunity to bring a government down if there was a chance that he might hold office in its successor. Moreover, one of the areas where he genuinely did oppose Palmerston was in the matter of national movements in Europe: he condemned what he saw as Palmerston's 'sentimental' partiality to national causes. For Gladstone, Palmerston's support for the Italian national cause was the sole reason for the rapprochement between them which allowed Gladstone to serve under Palmerston in the period 1859–65.

In the final analysis it is clear that Disraeli placed virtually no emphasis in foreign policy, (or in any other sphere for that matter), on moral considerations. For Gladstone, this question of morality was the starting point of his approach. He might not always, by force of circumstances, have been able to adhere strictly to his principles and he may, on occasions, have allowed political necessities to guide his speeches, but he remained fundamentally moral in attitude. The rights of other nations and peoples mattered to Gladstone and it mattered also that Britain was seen to be acting fairly and with due regard to the feelings and needs of others. Disraeli was not interested in establishing Britain's moral superiority in Europe or elsewhere. To him the maintenance of British interests demanded that Britain be recognised as superior in prestige and that a kind of psychological supremacy be maintained which would allow Britain, if necessary, to intervene decisively to secure her interests. The interests of other nations were of no concern whatever to Disraeli, unless, in some way, they bore upon particular British interests. To him diplomacy, like politics, was a game and the point of the game was to win.

B *From Salisbury to Grey*

Lord Salisbury, who served Disraeli as Foreign Secretary from 1878 until 1880, and subsequently dominated both that office and that of Prime Minister for much of the remainder of the century was basically a fatalist. This is to say – he did not generally have much confidence in the ability of statesmen to divert the passage of events from their natural course. He once likened the conduct of foreign policy to drifting downstream in a boat, ocasionally putting out an oar to fend off the bank! He accepted that human intervention was at times necessary but he distrusted grand schemes, such as Chamberlain's projected German alliances. In this approach he was joined by his successor, Lord Lansdowne, who reached agreements with the USA, Japan and France in their turn without any attempt to involve Britain in a European alliance. Indeed, as AJP Taylor pointed out, in many ways the whole point of Lansdowne's policy was to make a European alliance unnecessary.

Although Salisbury and Lansdowne did not share Chamberlain's faith in the ultimate value of a German alliance, they did accept his view that Britain and Germany were natural allies in the informal sense. Both tended to take for granted the idea that Britain and Germany had no real differences which divided them and both persisted with the view that any tensions which surfaced between the two countries were somehow accidental aberrations. Lansdowne continued to hold to this view even during the First World War, advocating the benefits of a negotiated peace rather than complete victory, despite the unpopularity of such a policy.

Both Salisbury and Lansdowne were aristocrats who took their prominence in public affairs for granted and had immense faith in their own judgement. Salisbury, in particular, had little use for 'experts' and regarded the officials of the Foreign Office as sources of information rather than advice. Although he appeared to give some latitude to Chamberlain's attempts to involve himself in foreign affairs, in the last analysis Salisbury exercised absolute control of policy. Lansdowne was equally secure in his self-reliance, although more inclined to invite and consider the advice of officials and ambassadors than Salisbury. Unlike Salisbury, he had little parliamentary experience and, having succeeded to his peerage at the age of 21, no experience at all in the House of Commons. He had attended the House of Lords infrequently before becoming Secretary of State for War in 1895, having previously spent considerable periods out of the country as Governor-General of Canada and Viceroy of India. This background had nevertheless given him immense experience of high-level administration.

In comparison to his predecessors, Sir Edward Grey, who became Foreign Secretary in the new Liberal Government at the end of 1905, was a man of more modest claims. He had served as Under-Secretary at the Foreign Office under Lord Rosebery, who was Gladstone's last Foreign Secretary and who succeeded him as Prime Minister in 1894. Like most of the Liberals, however, he had been left short of administrative experience by the long years of Conservative dominance which had followed the break-up of Gladstone's second administration in 1885. Grey was certainly not controlled by his officials, as some of his contemporary critics claimed, but he consulted them to a far greater degree than either Salisbury or Lansdowne. In other respects, he was more like his predecessors. He too had a strong belief in his own judgement and, like them, he did not involve the Cabinet at large in his decisions.

In one crucial respect Grey did differ materially from Salisbury, Lansdowne, Chamberlain and even Rosebery. He was an advocate of the 'Liberal Alliance' theory which placed friendship with France ahead of the 'Natural Alliance' with Germany. Grey had approved wholeheartedly of Lansdowne's promotion of the 1904 entente and he made it the central pivot of his policy. He did not propose attempting to convert it into an alliance, but he was determined to extend the concept to include Russia and to resist any German attempts to undermine it. To quote MC Morgan in his book *Foreign Affairs 1886–1914* 'He wanted to pursue friendly relations with Germany provided Germany acquiesced in Britain's friendly relations with France and Russia,'. So Grey was not then anti-German, but he was far more aware than his predecessors of a growing problem of German power and influence in

Europe. For this reason, (as well as to reduce imperial tensions), Grey sought an understanding with Russia, which, he hoped, would help to re-establish Russia's presence in European diplomacy after her humiliation in the war with Japan. Russia and France together would provide counterpoises to Germany, with diplomatic support from Britain whenever required. Grey's policy was unpopular with some in his own party who disliked any connection with illiberal and autocratic Russia.

Finally, there are two points which need to be emphasised when considering the conduct of British foreign policy throughout this period. Firstly, all statesmen were increasingly aware of the importance of public opinion in a political system which, if not exactly democratic, was at least discernibly on the way to becoming so. Even the aristocratic Salisbury, for all his apparent detachment from mundane considerations, was aware of this factor. In 1901, in a memorandum setting out the reasons why it was impractical for Britain to consider joining the Triple Alliance, he wrote: 'The course of the English Government ... (in the event of war between Germany and France) must depend on the view taken by public opinion in this country ...'. This point was strongly felt by Grey in the last days of the crisis in 1914, as he strove to maintain peace without committing Britain to a policy which might not secure public approval when the time came to implement it. Secondly, throughout the whole period, the overall objective of all British statesmen, regardless of party, principles, personality or approach, was to maintain peace. This was as true of Disraeli as it was of Gladstone; it was the central purpose of Salisbury as it was of Grey. If it was an objective often left unspoken, this was only because it seemed so obvious to all that it scarcely needed to be articulated. In this sense, if in no other, the principles and conduct of British foreign policy remained consistent and unalterable until the disaster of war finally intervened.

7 Bibliography

Judith Ward *British Foreign Policy 1870–1914* (Blackie, 1978) is very useful. It consists of extracts from primary and secondary sources introduced and linked together by short explanatory comments. The extracts show contrasting views from both contemporary commentators and subsequent historians. The latter extracts provide a useful guide to further reading.

M C Morgan *Foreign Affairs 1886–1914* (Collins, 1973) gives an excellent, detailed coverage of the diplomacy of the period. In particular, it contains an very useful chapter on the origins of the First World War.

A J P Taylor *The Struggle for Mastery in Europe 1848–1918* (Oxford, 1954) is demanding, but excellent reading. Its great value is that it allows the reader to place British policy in a broad context. The main drawback

for some A level students is the awesome detail. Best used intially via the index or contents section to target specific topics.
K Bourne *The Foreign Policy of Victorian England* (Clarendon, 1970) is of particular value for its ideas on Britain's relationships with the European powers.

8 Discussion points and essay questions

A

1 Who was the more able in conducting British foreign policy – Disraeli or Gladstone?

2 Which was the more important factor in British imperial expansion after 1870 – economic advantage or national prestige?

3 Should Britain have tried harder to conclude an alliance with Germany before 1904?

4 Did Britain make a mistake in opting for the policy of 'ententes' with France and Russia from 1904?

5 Was Britain right to declare war on Germany in August 1914?

B *Essays questions*

1 Explain and account for the policy followed by Disraeli and Salisbury at the Congress of Berlin in 1878.

2 To what extent did British foreign policy undergo a 'diplomatic revolution' in the period 1900–7?

3 Assess the impact of British imperial expansion on British diplomacy between 1870 and 1914.

4 Why did Britain declare war on Germany in August 1914?

5 'A declining strategic position is the fundamental explanation for the developments in British foreign policy between 1895 and 1914'. Discuss.

9 Documentary exercise

Gladstone elaborated his principles for the conduct of foreign policy during his third Midlothian speech, November 1879.

> . . . I will tell what I think to be the right principles of foreign policy . . . The first thing is to foster the strength of the empire by just legislation and economy at home . . . and to reserve the strength of the empire, to reserve the expenditure of that strength, for great and worthy occasions abroad . . . My second

principle of foreign policy is this – that its aim ought to be to preserve to the nations of the world ... especially to the Christian nations of the world – the blessings of peace ... In my opinion the third sound principle is this – to strive to cultivate and maintain, ay, to the very uttermost, what is called the concert of Europe; to keep the powers of Europe in unison together ... by keeping all in union together you neutralise and fetter and bind up the selfish aims of each ... My fourth principle is – that you should avoid needless and entangling engagements ... if you increase engagements without increasing strength, you diminish strength, you abolish strength; you really reduce the empire ... you render it an inheritance less precious to hand on to future generations ... My fifth principle is this, gentlemen, to acknowledge the equal rights of all nations. You may sympathise with one nation more than another. Nay, you must sympathise in certain circumstances with one nation more than another ... But in point of right all are equal ... Let me give you a sixth (principle) and then I have done. And that sixth is, that in my opinion foreign policy, subject to all the limitations I have described, the foreign policy of England should always be inspired by the love of freedom ... in freedom you lay the firmest foundations both of loyalty and order ... the deepest and most profound love of order ... ought to be the very atmosphere in which a Foreign Secretary of England ought to live and move ...

1. *What evidence is there in this extract to suggest that Gladstone is aiming his remarks at the immediate issues of foreign policy as well as offering a general set of principles?*
2. *To judge from this extract, what was Gladstone's attitude towards the importance and role of the Empire?*
3. *To what extent did Gladstone live up to these principles during his periods in office? See also chapter IX.*
4. *How far did Prime Ministers and Foreign Secretaries, between 1870 and 1914, base their foreign policy decisions on the considerations which Gladstone is advocating here?*

XIII

TRADE UNIONS AND THE RISE OF LABOUR 1885–1914

1 INTRODUCTION: THE LATE NINETEENTH CENTURY CONTEXT

During the last two decades of the nineteenth century Britain's economic ascendancy was seriously challenged as Germany, France and the USA began to emerge as industrial powers in their own right. Although the British economy continued to grow, British firms were slow to innovate to meet this challenge, and as a result most industries at this time registered a decline in prices and a resultant fall in profit margins. The period 1873–96 is often called the 'Great Depression'. There has been considerable debate among historians over the appropriateness of this term, since this was not a depression in the accepted sense of a temporary decrease of production. Rather, it was a slowing down in the rate of growth in the economy, particularly in comparison with the developing economies of Britain's trading rivals. By 1885 it had become apparent that economic growth was decelerating.

This created a new context for the relationship between capital and labour. Increased international competition had the effect of putting social relations within the workplace under stress. As firms struggled to maintain profit levels, by increasing output or lowering wages, the industrial peace, which reached its zenith with the legalisation of trade unions in the 1870s, gave way to a renewed social conflict that recalled the old days of Chartism. In terms of working-class organisation the period saw two major developments. First, there was an unprecedented growth of trade unionism. In 1880 only 5 per cent of the total workforce were members of trade unions, but by 1914 the figure had grown to 25 per cent. The most dramatic manifestations of this development were major outbreaks of strikes in the years 1888–93 and 1910–14. Secondly, these years witnessed the emergence of a political party committed to the representation of working-class interests as its primary concern. In 1906 a group of 30 independent labour MPs were elected to Parliament and adopted as their name the 'Labour Party'. These two developments were clearly linked, in that the new Labour Party drew strength from its role as the political arm of the growing trade union movement.

The emergence of an independent working-class political party in these years was a reflection of the social changes of the period, in particular the opening up of the divisions between the classes. As we have seen, historians disagree on the extent to which a class society had existed in the first three-quarters of the nineteenth century. Yet, few historians would argue with the view that, as a result of increased urbanisation and industrialisation, 'class' had become the most important determinant of social behaviour by the eve of the First World War. For many this was the period that really saw the 'making' of the working class. The economic changes of the period meant that this class division was accompanied by aggravated social problems. Ironically, in a period dubbed the 'Great Depression', the *value* of wages, (the 'real wage'), was actually going up. Working people felt the benefit of international competition, particularly in the form of the cheaper foodstuffs now available from abroad as a result of the development of refrigerated transport. The rise in 'real wages' might have signalled a universal improvement in living standards were it not for the growth of the labour supply. The employable population grew by at least 10 per cent per decade between 1870 and 1910. Since this occurred during a slowing down of economic growth it resulted in intense competition for jobs. Significantly, the word 'unemployed' appeared in the Oxford English Dictionary for the first time in 1882. This entry was extended, for the 1888 edition, to include the term 'unemployment' which had, by then, been recognised as one of the major social problems of the day.

It was against this background that trade unionism grew in strength and a new political party emerged. The Labour Party would challenge and eventually supersede the Liberal Party as the nation's second major political party. Yet there was little real indication of this future development within the timescale under discussion here. Before 1914 Labour never secured more than 7.6 per cent of the national vote at a general election. On the eve of the First World War most working people retained their well-established loyalties to the Liberal and Conservative Parties. The new party challenged the complacent view that the free-market alone could provide all that working people needed and, in this respect, reflected the development of socialist thinking at the time. Yet it should be remembered that both the Liberal and the Conservative Parties were also advocating an increased role for the State in terms of welfare provision. In fact, Labour did not emerge with a programme that was fully socialist in its nature. (This continues to pain historians on the left, who tend to be very critical of the achievements of the early Labour Party.) Nevertheless, by 1914 the basis had been established from which Labour would go on to form its first national government in 1924. This had been achieved by means of a recognition, by leaders like Keir Hardie, of the real political context within which the new party had to operate. The policy of 'Labour Alliance', by which the Labour Party attempted to weld together a range of disparate working-class organisations and groups, grew from this realistic recognition. In this chapter we will explore the development of the policy of 'Labour Alliance' through the relationship between the new party and the growing trade union movement.

2 NEW UNIONISM 1888–93

In the three years from 1889 to 1891 the total membership of trade unions doubled. This 'explosion' of trade union activity was partly the result of the emergence of a number of new unions with a characteristically different approach to industrial relations. As we saw in chapter VII, the mid-Victorian 'model' unions, typified by the Amalgamated Society of Engineers, were exclusive bodies of skilled workers. Their high subscription rates restricted membership to the 'labour aristocracy' and, because they represented such a small proportion of the workforce they were, to some extent, accepted by employers.

The new unions of the 1880s were different in three important respects. First, they aimed at recruiting members among the less skilled sector of the workforce, many of whom had never previously been unionised. They were, therefore, less exclusive than the 'model' unions of the mid-Victorian period, and this was reflected in the fact that they levied lower subscriptions, (generally in the region of a penny a week). Secondly, they tended to be more militant than their craft-based counterparts. This was only partly because they were, in the main, led by active socialists. The commitment of the new unions to strike action was really a reflection of the position their members occupied in the workplace. Less skilled workers were more dispensible than skilled craftsmen. Employers were therefore less likely to make concessions to their organisations. In short, any industrial action by the less skilled was likely to be confrontational. Thirdly, many of the leaders of the new unions were members of the socialist clubs and associations that had grown in the 1880s.

In the late nineteenth century the growth of socialism was part of a Europe-wide phenomenon. The massacre of the Communards in Paris in 1871 had been widely deplored in Britain. Karl Marx's *Capital* appeared in its first English translation in 1887. The year 1884 saw the establishment of three socialist organisations in Britain, the Social Democratic Federation; the Socialist League; and the Fabian Society. In their different ways each contributed to the public debate on social and political reform by arguing that there was an alternative to market capitalism. There were marked differences in the strategy adopted by these organisations but each started from the assumption that a capitalist society was both unequal and exploitative in its nature. The Social Democratic Federation, under the leadership of the 'gentleman reformer' H M Hyndman, followed Marx closely and advocated a policy of 'class warfare' leading to a revolution and a subsequent reorganisation of society along fairer lines.

As the leading Socialist organisation of the 1880s, the SDF drew a number of significant recruits into its ranks. Among them was the poet and artist William Morris who swiftly broke with Hyndman to form the Socialist League. Like Hyndman, he came from a comfortable middle-class background and saw socialism as a way of reconstructing a divided society. Morris argued that industrialisation had separated the worker from the joy of creative work. Because, to use his words, 'useful work' had become 'useless toil', the worker in the factory had become distanced from the task being undertaken, employers became estranged from their employees and society became divided. Morris argued that society could be reconstructed as a 'Commonwealth', based on equality and a simple lifestyle. Like Hyndman, Morris accepted that it would require a revolution to bring about the desired changes.

The third socialist organisation formed in 1884 was the Fabian Society. This included in its ranks the Irish playwright George Bernard Shaw and a clerk from the Colonial Office called Sydney Webb. There is some debate among historians as to just how far the Fabians should now be seen as socialists at all. Unlike Hyndman and Morris, (who followed Marx in this respect), they did not accept that a revolution was necessary before a society based on socialist principles could be established. They were firmly committed to reformism and advocated working for change slowly from within society's existing institutions, a strategy they referred to as 'permeation'. For the Fabians the problem of capitalism lay in its inefficiency. They thought that by working away to influence the government at both a local and national level it would be possible to construct efficient institutions to work on behalf of the common good. Such was Fabianism's concentration on the 'nuts and bolts' details of 'efficient' administration that it was often disparagingly referred to at the time as 'gas and water socialism'. Above all, the Fabians differed from other socialist organisations in that they did not see the militant working class as the historic agent of social and economic change. Since they felt, in the words of Sydney Webb, that change would have to be 'peaceful and constitutional', in its nature, they concentrated their efforts on the rational persuasion of those already in authority.

It would be wrong to exaggerate the importance of these socialist groups at this time. Their membership was small and each of the societies drew heavily on support from middle-class intellectuals, or 'drawing room socialists'. The SDF, for example, had a membership of only 1000 in 1885 and when it put up two candidates in London constituencies in the election that year they polled a mere 59 votes between them. But both these organisations can claim some success in orchestrating a London-based protest movement at this time. The SDF in particular concentrated its efforts on the growing number of the unemployed in the capital. In 1886, during a particularly harsh winter an SDF open-air meeting of the unemployed turned into a riot, which *The Times* described as the greatest threat to private property since 1832. This was followed by two days of confrontations between demonstrators and police, greeted by Morris, ever the romantic, as 'the first skirmish of the Revolution'. In 1887, groups of the unemployed, organised by the SDF under the slogan 'Work not Charity', squatted in Trafalgar Square. On 13 November 1887, the Square was cleared by baton-wielding police, in an incident in which 200 demonstrators were injured and which was immediately christened 'Bloody Sunday'.

The real importance of these socialist organisations lay, not in the size of their membership, but rather in their propagation of alternative ideas at a time of increasing social crisis. Their influence in providing a political education for some of the most important union leaders of the period can be seen by examining the major industrial disputes of the day.

A *The matchworkers' strike 1888*

The first clear sign that trade unions would never again be the preserve of the male elite of the labour force came in July 1888 when the women match workers at Bryant and May's factory in the East End of London came out on strike against the horrific conditions in which they worked. They were encouraged in their action by Annie Besant, an influential middle-class socialist who was, rather unusually, a member of both the SDF and the Fabians. Besant, who was already well known as a campaigner for birth control, edited a socialist paper called *The Link*. In June 1888, in an article entitled 'White Slavery in London', she drew attention to the plight of one of the worst paid sectors of the workforce. Whilst Bryant and May paid shareholders a healthy dividend of 23 per cent their women workers received an average of 5 shillings (25p) for a 70-hour week in some of the unhealthiest conditions industry had to offer. Nearly 1400 women struck work for a fortnight in an action that brought significant concessions from the employers. Following the strike a union was established among the workers at the factory, with 800 members by 1889 and Besant as Secretary.

B *The great dock strike of 1889*

The summer of 1889 saw two more victories for groups of workers organising themselves virtually for the first time. In March the Gas Workers and General Labourers Union was formed in London by Will Thorne, a worker at the East Ham Gasworks. Thorne, an ex-navvy from Birmingham, was a member of the SDF and had been taught to read and write by Karl Marx's daughter, Eleanor. Within four months of its inception his union had 20 000 members throughout the country. In August 1889 Thorne brought his members out on strike demanding an eight-hour day. He was assisted in organising the strike by two other prominent members of the SDF, the engineering workers Tom Mann and John Burns. These three men epitomised the zeal of 'new unionism' and the way it was changing the face of trade unionism. Tom Mann started work in the mines of Warwickshire at the age of nine, having received less than three years schooling. He established the Eight Hours League in 1886 to agitate for a reduction of hours across industry. This in itself marked a significant change in the direction of trade unionism, with an attempt to establish aims common to all industries. In 'a similar way, in this period trade unionists began talking of the "living wage"', an issue that was of concern to all workers.

This attempt to address the general situation of all workers, rather than the sectional interests of one trade, was the key to the new unionism's style. 'Not since the high and palmy days of Chartism', noted the old Chartist leader George Julian Harney in 1889, 'have I witnessed a movement corresponding in importance and interest.' This comparison with Chartism is important for an understanding of the impact of new unionism. Mass support was being mobilised once more, utilising strategies from the Chartist tradition. John Burns, for example, was a platform orator with a style of delivery of which O'Connor might have been proud, but with one important difference. Burns was not a 'gentleman reformer'. Born into poverty as one of a family of ten children, he addressed working-class audiences on the issues of the day from personal experience.

Thorne's union was successful in its strike and this acted as an inspiration to other groups of workers. Burns, Thorne and Mann now turned their attention to London's docks. A small dispute had broken out at the South West India Dock over the method of piece-work payment. The men were led by Ben Tillett, an ex-sailor now a tea porter. The dispute swiftly snowballed. The dockers were employed on an entirely casual basis; they had to apply for work each day at the dock gates. Their work was punishing and their pay abysmally low. Tillett, assisted by Burns, Mann and Thorne now set about drawing all the 'dock rats', as they were scornfully called, into the dispute. They framed a demand for a minimum wage of sixpence an hour, the 'docker's tanner', and persuaded the Stevedores' Union, which represented the skilled dock workers, to come out in support.

As casual workers the dockers were very vulnerable to replacement by other workers. But the strike was solid. With 150 000 men on strike, for a month almost nothing was shipped through the Port of London, the heart of the nation's trade. Each day Burns led a huge procession through the City. The orderly nature of these demonstrations won the widespread support of public opinion, which had feared a repeat of the riots of 1887. The strike was hugely expensive for the union. At one point the meagre strike pay it was able to give its members amounted to fully £1250 per day. But the dockers were supported financially by workers both at home and abroad. Australian trade unionists contributed £30 000. The British public seemed to rally to the dock workers as a downtrodden group conducting themselves with quiet dignity. Even the Stock Exchange made a contribution to strike funds! Eventually an unlikely arbitrator between employers and employees appeared in the shape of the Roman Catholic Cardinal Manning. His intercession in this role was acceptable to the dockers since many of them were Irish Catholics. The strike ended, in an almost carnival atmosphere, with victory for the dockers.

Following the strike, the small Tea Operatives' Union that Tillett had formed in 1886 was re-modelled as the Dock, Wharf, Riverside and General Labourers' Union. Tom Mann became the union's first President, and it had 56 000 members by 1890. This was undoubtedly the most lasting effect of the dock strike. Tillett's union was to remain in existence until 1920, when it was again re-modelled, this time as the Transport and General Workers' Union. The age of mass general unionism seemed to have arrived. A Seamens' Union, established in 1889, for example, had a membership of 65 000 by 1891. In a similar way, the General Railway Workers' Union, formed in 1889, aimed at drawing in the unskilled grades of worker excluded by the more 'aristocratic' Amalgamated Society of Railway Servants, which had been established in 1871.

c *Changes in the 'craft unionism'*

The 'new unionists' attended the Trades Union Congress (TUC) for the first time in 1890. Their impact may be seen in the fact that in that year, not only did the Congress agree to back the demand for an eight-hour day, it also gave its name and support to the first May Day celebrations ever to have been held in Britain. This reflected changes that were taking place in some of the older craft unions. The relationship established between the skilled unions and the employers was deteriorating by 1875. In the conditions of intensified international competition that had become apparent by the late 1880s, employers could no longer afford to respect the demarcation of skills as defined by the craft unions.

Most unions took advantage of the temporary improvement in trade, and consequent demand for labour, between 1889 and 1891, to expand membership and to re-organise their structure. The mineworkers, for example, had a long history of industrial organisation, having established local associations in most areas in the 1860s. In 1889, following a series of successful wage demands throughout the pit areas, the Miners Federation of Great Britain was established. This included most of the local associations, and it supported the call of the 'new' unions for an eight-hour day. Most of the older unions, established in the mid-Victorian period, increased their membership in the last two decades of the nineteenth century, to such an extent that by 1900 the 'new' unionists still only accounted for less than one third of all trade unionists. Many of the older unions, recognising that the main threat to them lay in the use of less skilled workers to do their jobs, opened their ranks to lower grades of workers. The Amalgamated Society of Railway Servants, denied official recognition by the railway companies, dropped their entry prohibition for less skilled railway workers. The cotton textile workers of Lancashire began to open their unions to women, though in this respect they were still unusual.

3 THE EMPLOYERS' RESPONSE

If the logic of the changing social and economic context, in the late nineteenth century, suggested the need for greater organisation and solidarity within the workforce, the same was also increasingly true for the employers. Faced with the burgeoning of trade unions in the 1880s, and the need to meet the competition from abroad by introducing radical changes in workplace practices, employers drew together to defend their common interests. They did this in two ways; by forming associations for mutual support (this trend is explored below) and also by utilising the law. Where they took unions on in the 1890s they invariably won. But the legacy of bitterness that this counter attack engendered was to be long-lasting. Most importantly, it was to ensure trade union support for the establishment of the Labour Party in the early years of the twentieth century.

A *Employers' organisations*

The Shipping Federation was formed in 1890 and set to work to break the hold of the dockside and seamen's unions in the ports. It included in its ranks the owners of 7/8ths of British merchant vessels and in November 1890 it refused to recognise the settlement that had ended the Dock strike of the previous year. With the use of non-union labour it effectively drove Tillett's union from the London docks. Over the next three years there were strikes against the Federation at most British ports, culminating in a major defeat for the union at Hull in

1893. Here, the army and naval gunboats were used to protect strike-breakers. The impact of the employers' victory can be seen in the decline of dock-union membership. In 1890 Tillett's union claimed some 56 000 members. By the end of 1892 this had fallen to 23 000 and, by 1900, to just under 14 000.

In the cotton textile industry of Lancashire the employers formed the Federation of Master Cotton Spinners in 1891 and cut wages by 5 per cent in the following year. The ensuing lock-out of workers refusing to agree to the cuts lasted into early 1893. It was eventually resolved with the Brooklands Agreement which established the machinery of collective bargaining for the industry. A joint committee of employers and union representatives would, in future determine wage levels in relation to the price of cotton. In the mining areas employers responded in a similar way. A fall in the price of coal led the owners in the Yorkshire, Lancashire and Midlands coalfields to demand a 25 per cent reduction in wage levels. The newly-formed miners' union (the Miners' Federation of Great Britain) found itself confronted with unprecedented unity of action on the part of the owners. In the months following July 1893 every pit in these areas locked-out its workforce to force it to agree to the new terms. The dispute lasted until November, involving 300 000 miners and a series of clashes between troops and strikers which left two miners dead at a colliery near Featherstone in Yorkshire. It was finally ended by government intervention: Prime Minister Gladstone ordered the Foreign Secretary, Lord Rosebery, to bring the two sides together for a settlement. As a result a Conciliation Board was established, but the miners' demand for a minimum wage was not conceded.

This was the first strike to have been settled through the intervention of the government and for many this, as well as the Brooklands Agreement in the cotton industry, seemed to point the way forward. Because of the scale of organisation on both sides, strikes and lock-outs had come to have a crippling effect on the economy. The Conciliation Act of 1896 gave the Board of Trade the power to appoint conciliators to settle disputes. But this was to be a voluntary process and the Board would only act if its help was requested by one of the parties. There was no attempt to impose compulsory arbitration on parties in dispute. The Act did much to further the argument that disputes should be settled by the intervention of third parties, but it lacked the authority of legal compulsion and put its faith in the goodwill of the two sides involved. The great engineering lock-out of the following year suggested that this faith was misplaced.

The tensions in the engineering industry, caused by the introduction of new methods of work, came to a head in 1897. The Engineering Employers' Federation had been formed in 1896, with the avowed intent of reducing the control over production exercised by the Amalgamated Society of Engineers. When the ASE demanded an eight-hour day in July 1897 it found its members locked out by nation-wide action taken by the employers. The dispute lasted until January 1898, and ended in a humiliating defeat for the union. The employers imposed a settlement on the ASE which established that the union would not 'interfere' with 'the management of business'. Collective bargaining clauses in the agreement ensured against 'unofficial' strikes by local branches, by insisting that all decisions to cease work be approved by the ASE executive.

Thus, in the major industries, the employers came together to meet the threat of the new spirit of militancy in the unions. This was consolidated by the establishment, in 1898, of the Employers' Federation's Parliamentary Committee which was to lobby Parliament in the same way as the TUC's Parliamentary Committee. Historians have sometimes argued that by consolidating their own organisations the employers were clearly bent on the destruction of the trade unions. This is too simplistic a view of what was happening. In fact, the settlement of the disputes in coal, cotton and engineering gives a good insight into the aims of employers at this time. It was not that they wanted, in the main, to destroy trade unions as organisations. After all, it had been demonstrated earlier in the century that compliant unions, who were prepared to discipline their members, were useful to employers. It was in the employers' interests to have strong, centralised, unions with an acknowledged, but restricted, role in the workplace. Thus, most of these disputes, where unions were defeated, resulted not in the destruction of the unions but rather in the establishment of collective bargaining procedures for those industries. These procedures actually reaffirmed the existence of the unions as organisations but ensured that future disputes would be settled in a way that was favourable to the employers. In this way, the employers' counter attack created divisions within the unions between those officials who wished to continue with the militancy that had been re-born with 'new unionism', and those who felt that there was more to be gained by working within the constraints of collective bargaining, even if this was on the employers' terms. Sometimes the distinction was between a cautious union executive at head office and a militant 'rank and file' in the localities. Employers did all they could to limit the power of the militants within the unions, as a way of producing the kind of moderate trade unionism with which they were most comfortable.

B *Trade unions and the law*

The main source of power for militant trade unionism was, as always, the strike reinforced by well organised picketing. Such activity was given legal status by the legislation of the 1870s. In the 1890s, however, employers began to contest this legality by a series of court actions. In three cases in the 1890s, employers attempted successfully to restrict the actions a union could take in picketing during an industrial dispute. This was consolidated in 1901 by the celebrated Taff Vale decision.

Following a strike, in August 1900, by members of the Amalgamated Society of Railway Servants against the Taff Vale Railway Company in South Wales, the Company sued the union for damages caused to their business. The court upheld the Company's case, and although this was quashed on appeal, the House of Lords upheld the original decision in 1901. Damages in this case were set at £23 000 and the union was ordered to pay. This had enormous implications for all trade unions since it meant that they were considered in law to be corporate bodies who could be sued for actions committed on their behalf by their officials. In the case of Quinn v Leathem, heard by the Lords two weeks after their decision on Taff Vale, it was held that the threat of industrial action could be considered a conspiracy to injure. Given the earlier Taff Vale decision, a union could be sued for damages in such a case in its corporate capacity.

After Taff Vale a union could be sued for damages for organising a strike; after Quinn v Leathem it could be sued for planning a strike. All the achievements of the 1860s and the 1870s in establishing legal status for the unions had been reversed. The unions had re-entered the quasi-legal position they had occupied after the repeal of the Combination Acts in 1824: they were legal bodies but when they acted they were likely to break the law. Yet there were mixed reactions to Taff Vale within the unions. A few cautious union leaders hoped that, by discouraging strikes, the decision would help them discipline their militant 'rank and file'.

But most trade unionists do seem to have been alarmed at the implications of the Taff Vale decision. It demonstrated the vulnerability of the unions and the need for legislation that would verify their right to use industrial action on behalf of their members. Neither the Liberals nor the Conservatives were keen to introduce such a measure. Both parties tended to side with the employers when it came to industrial action. Since the late 1880s there had been socialist groups arguing that working people needed their own parliamentary party. Hitherto, the unions had not been persuaded of this need. Their position seemed secure and politically they could operate by lobbying the existing parties. Taff Vale changed this and the unions suddenly saw the potential benefits of independent labour representation in Parliament. Their support was to be decisive in the emergence of the Labour Party.

4 THE EMERGENCE OF THE LABOUR PARTY

Looking at the creation of the Labour Party in 1906, what seems to require explanation is not so much why it came about but rather why it took so long coming. There had been an articulate radical working-class presence in British politics, in one form or another, since 1815. The version of manhood suffrage introduced in 1884 was undoubtedly crippled by the cumbersome registration qualifications with which it had been deliberately hedged. But even when account is taken of this, little of substance seems to have been achieved, in terms of working-class representation in Parliament, by the end of the nineteenth century. The working-class voters chose either Liberals or Conservatives to represent their interests. The Liberals were the main beneficiaries of working-class support, though working-class Conservatism was strong in Lancashire, often as a form of opposition to Liberal employers.

Both parties recognised the need to placate the working-class voter, but neither was prepared to pass over much in the way of real political power. By the end of the nineteenth century it was becoming clear that neither popular Liberalism nor popular Conservatism could really 'deliver the goods'. The Liberal Party accepted working men as Parliamentary candidates in some areas. But there were a mere eight 'Lib-Lab' MPs in 1889, and this had only increased to 11 by 1900. Around half of these were from coal mining areas where the closeness of the community, and a well-developed trade union tradition, made it relatively easy to raise the funds to support working men in the unpaid role of MP. The idea of Lib-Lab representatives had seemed promising in the 1870s, but the result was a sparse and geographically very patchy representation of the working community. Even when the Lib-Lab MP Henry Broadhurst, an ex-stonemason and the Secretary of the TUC, had been made Under-Secretary at the Home Office in Gladstone's government of 1886, it seemed a token gesture. It was difficult to escape the conclusion that this was a very one-sided relationship between a middle-class leadership and a working-class 'rank and file'. Also, when in power, neither party's attempts at social reform seemed to address the issues of importance to the working class, particularly unemployment and the eight-hour day.

In fact, the working class-Liberal alliance was now being questioned by a number of working-class activists. It was the expansion of trade unions that caused this change. The new, and militant, trade unionism of the 1880s and the 1890s re-opened the debate on the distribution of wealth that had been pushed into the background since the demise of Chartism. It was difficult for the classes to stress their common values within a political alliance whilst confronting the issue that divided them most: the relationship between wages and profit. This shift, from Liberalism to a commitment to independent working-class representation, can perhaps best be seen in the personal development of James Keir Hardie.

5 KEIR HARDIE AND THE STRATEGY OF 'LABOUR ALLIANCE'

Hardie was undoubtedly the most influential of the early Labour leaders. He recognised that the working-class voter could not be drawn away from the existing pattern of political allegiances by the theoretical formulation of socialism as a body of ideas. Instead, he aimed to draw together the disparate working-class groups that were becoming increasingly disillusioned with the existing parties into a 'Labour Alliance', with clear and moderate objectives. Hardie was born the illegitimate son of a farm-servant, Mary Keir, in Lanarkshire, Scotland, in 1856. As an adult he became a skilled coal face-worker and a leading trade unionist among the Ayrshire coalminers. He was also a Nonconformist, a teetotaller and a Liberal, working hard to persuade the miners to vote Liberal when they were enfranchised in 1884. Yet he became disenchanted with the Liberal Party and convinced of the need for independent labour representation, as a result of two events: the breaking of a strike among the Lanarkshire miners in 1887, where police and the army had used a good deal of violence, and the failure of the Liberal opposition in Parliament to support the Scottish miners' call for an eight-hour day to be established by legislation.

Hardie was nominated as an independent candidate, sponsored by the miners, in the Mid-Lanarkshire by-election of 1888. This was the first time an independent labour candidate had stood against the two main parties. Although defeated he took heart from the 614 votes he received and two weeks after the by-election he established the Scottish Labour Party. This was the first time the term 'Labour Party' had been used in British politics. The party remained small, but it managed to field five candidates, albeit unsuccessfully, in the general election of 1892. London radicals and socialists, including Will Thorne, persuaded Hardie to stand as an independent Labour candidate for West Ham South in the general election of 1892. He was elected, as were two other independent labour candidates; John Burns for Battersea and the leader of the Seamens' Union, Joseph Havelock Wilson, for Middlesborough.

A *The Independent Labour Party*

The movement towards an independent representation for the working class was also gaining ground in the north of England. In 1891 the Manchester Labour Party was formed, on the lines of Hardie's Scottish example. By 1893 Labour Unions had been formed in a number of the northern textile towns. In the words of the Bradford Labour Union, the aim of these associations was to 'further the cause of direct Labour representation on local bodies and in Parliament.' In 1893 Hardie was asked to chair a conference in Bradford to bring these labour organisations together and unite them with those in other areas. From this meeting the Independent Labour Party was born.

Among the 120 delegates who met in Bradford there were few from those areas already represented by Lib-Lab MPs, such as the mining areas of Northumberland and Durham, and the Midlands. The Fabians and the SDF sent delegates, but the London socialist groups thought little could come of the move. More than a third of the delegates came from Yorkshire, and most of them from O'Connor's old stronghold, the West Riding. This area, and particularly Bradford, had by this time become the focus of the demand for Labour representation. On the face of it this was an unlikely location. It was dominated politically by families of large Liberal Nonconformist employers, supported by working men's Liberal Associations. In Bradford, as in so many other places, it was the experience of industrial conflict that had been the catalyst for change. The attempt by the owners of Manningham Mills, a large local woollen firm, to lower their employees' wages by 15–30 per cent in 1890 led to a protracted, and often violent, strike involving the Weavers' Association and thousands of workers. Although the owners, backed by the other textile employers in the area, were able to break the strike in 1891, the balance of class relations had been irrevocably destroyed in the process.

The ILP was a national organisation with a socialist programme. It committed itself to 'secure the collective ownership of the means of production, distribution and exchange.' It therefore argued that in its vision of the future 'the people', rather than individuals, would control and run the economy. But this was a version of socialism that was identifiably British in its nature. It drew on three important traditional roots – liberalism, trade unionism, and Nonconformity-and this made it very different from its more revolutionary socialist counterparts on the continent. Hardie, for example, led the Conference in its rejection of the 'class war' strategies of the SDF. Many of the ILP's leading lights in its early years were recent converts from the Liberal Party. James Ramsay MacDonald, a warehouse clerk turned journalist, spent four years as a private secretary to a radical Liberal MP. In 1894, disillusioned by the unwillingness of the Liberals to accept working men as Parliamentary candidates, he made the break and joined the ILP. He would, of course go on to become the first Labour Prime Minister, but his route from 'Liberalism' to 'Labourism' was typical of many who came to support independent labour representation. Inevitably, this influenced the nature of the new party. The programme and approach of the ILP bore the hallmarks of its progenitors' earlier commitment to liberalism. There was, for example, a total acceptance that the Parliamentary, rather than the revolutionary, path was the correct one to take. Progress would be made by persuasion and change would come gradually by a process of reforming existing institutions rather than overthrowing them. Historians sometimes refer to this as a policy of 'reformism'.

Along with a background in the Liberal Party, many of the ILP's supporters came to the new party through the experience of trade unionism and this could be seen in the pragmatism of its programme. Whilst this spoke of the the need for an 'Industrial Commonwealth founded upon the Socialisation of Land and Commerce', it was fairly vague on how this should be achieved. The ILP was always more comfortable with specific and concrete aims, like the call for Old Age Pensions and the eight-hour day, than with developing theories of class struggle. John Burns referred to the theory of socialism as 'the chattering of Continental magpies'. Within the ILP Hardie always played up this pragmatic approach. He felt that to broaden its appeal to trade unionists weaned on the approach of the Liberal Party, the ILP needed to stress its moderation. He even insisted that the term 'socialist' not appear in the name of the party, arguing 'labour' was of broader appeal.

The third major tradition from which the ILP drew its version of socialism was Nonconformist religion. Many of its leaders were more familiar with the Bible than with Marx. As Hardie was fond of explaining, 'the final goal of Socialism, is a form of Social Economy very closely akin to the principles set forth on the Sermon on the Mount.' One historian, examining those areas of the North and Scotland where the ILP expanded rapidly over the next few years, has referred to this phenomenon as the 'religion of socialism'. The enthusiasm generated in some areas certainly seems to have taken on aspects of a religious revival in terms of its energy and zest. By 1895 the ILP could boast 35 000 paid-up members.

Nevertheless, the ILP met with a good deal of working-class opposition, particularly from the trade unions. Worried that the formation of the ILP would eventually lead to the domination of the TUC by socialists from the new unions, the TUC's Parliamentary Committee introduced the 'block vote' in 1895. Previously, each delegate's vote counted equally; now they would be counted in proportion to the number of members in the union represented by the delegate. This served to strengthen the hand of the older unions, with their greater commitment to working with the existing political parties and developing the machinery of collective bargaining. As one Lib-Lab union leader put it, 'We saw that Congress was losing whatever influence it had, and we were determined to pull it back again into the old paths.' At the same time the TUC voted to exclude delegates from the Trades Councils which had, in many areas, been taken over by ILP supporters.

A further setback was suffered by the ILP when all 28 of its candidates in the general election of 1895 were defeated, including Hardie.

The party also found itself isolated with the outbreak of war against the Boers in South Africa in 1899. The ILP's anti-war stance ran counter to the jingoism engendered for what was widely expected to be a short and successful war against weak opponents. The ILP were labelled 'pro-Boer' and became the object of popular reaction. In these years it became clear to Hardie, and others within the party, that encouraging enthusiastic support at the 'grass roots' was an unpredictable process. The strategy of a 'Labour alliance' was a reluctant recognition that most working-class organisations were not socialist and thus the ILP would never vie with the major parties for power unless it subsumed its socialism within an alliance of wider working-class political opinion.

The opportunity to launch such an alliance came from the TUC conference of 1899. The Amalgamated Society of Railway Servants introduced a resolution calling on the Parliamentary Committee to convene a conference of all organisations committed to 'securing a better representation of the interests of labour in the House of Commons.' The resolution was passed by 546 000 votes to 434 000, an indication of the extent to which trade unionists were divided, at this stage, over the advisability of independent labour representation. Most of the votes against were exercised by the coal and cotton unions. Their satisfaction with the status quo was no longer typical. Trade unions generally were reeling under the concerted counter-attack of employers, and parliamentary representation was seen as a means of defence.

B *The Labour Representation Committee*

The 129 delegates who met in February 1900, in response to the TUC's resolution, came from the socialist societies (the SDF, Fabians and the ILP) and 67 trade unions representing about a quarter of total trade union membership at the time. The conference was a resounding success for the ILP. It was able to steer the delegates between the 'class war' advocated by the SDF, and the desire of some of the trade unionists to limit the Parliamentary actions of working-class MPs to particular issues. Hardie's resolution to create an organisation that would support a 'distinct Labour group in Parliament who shall have their own whips and agree upon their own policy', was accepted. He would have liked this to be called the 'United Labour Party' but the conference opted for the title Labour Representation Committee as being less contentious. With ILP man Ramsay MacDonald as Secretary, the Committee consisted of two ILP members, two SDF members, one Fabian and seven trade unionists.

The LRC depended on trade union support and, to retain this, Hardie accepted that compromises had to be made. A new word, 'socialistic', had crept into the debate, meaning generally sympathetic to the broad aims of socialism, but without a firm adherence to state ownership. The LRC was 'socialistic' and Hardie was prepared to accept this compromise as the price of union support. This was too much for the SDF who rapidly disaffiliated. Many of the activists had close links with the Liberal Party, and the LRC was open to any political alliance that would assist the election of their candidates, without compromising their independence. Thus, the LRC was drawn from groups with rather different objectives, who were aware of the political realities of the day and prepared to sink their differences to achieve a common goal. But whatever linked the men involved in this endeavour, there were inherent tensions built into the structure of the LRC, between socialists and moderate trade unionists, which would not go away.

Nevertheless, the new organisation got off to a good start when two of its candidates, Keir Hardie and Richard Bell, were elected for Merthyr and Derby respectively in the general election of 1900. Bell, who was the Secretary of the Amalgamated Society of Railway Servants, was no socialist. But the ASRS had been consistently refused recognition by the railway companies, and it saw Parliamentary action as the way to secure a legal status for all unions. This point was made emphatically by the drama that unfolded at Taff Vale later that same year, and which involved Bell's union. The Lords' judgement on the case in 1901, had the effect of converting previously sceptical unions to the cause of independent Labour representation, and it was this that really launched the LRC as a political force.

Both Liberal and Conservative Parties baulked at introducing legislation to protect the unions following Taff Vale and the LRC was on hand as the logical political alternative to which the unions could now turn. As a result of the Lords' ruling, 127 unions joined the LRC, including the Engineers and the Textile Workers, raising total membership from 353 000 before the ruling to 847 000 by 1903. The union affiliations continued over the next few years (though the Miners' Federation did not join until 1909) and affiliating unions levied their members to provide financial support for the LRC. The crucial link, sought by Hardie, between the parliamentary representation of working people and their most important organisations, the trade unions, had been secured as a result of the employers' campaign against the unions, culminating in Taff Vale. In 1904 Ramsay MacDonald explained in a speech to the TUC, that. 'The Labour Representation Committee is neither sister nor brother to the Congress, but its child'.

6 LABOUR AND LIBERALS IN PARLIAMENT

In most constituencies where the Labour Representation Committee hoped to be successful, their main rivals for the working-class vote were the Liberals. Having been defeated in the general elections of

1895 and 1900, the Liberals were very aware that the LRC could split the working-class vote in many constituencies. Soon after its inauguration the LRC won two by-elections, in 1902 and 1903. In neither of these elections were the successful LRC candidates opposed by Liberals, and this emphasised the advantages that might accrue to Labour from an electoral agreement between the two parties not to contest key seats. In 1903 an LRC candidate, Arthur Henderson of the Ironworkers, who had once worked as a Liberal election agent, beat both Conservatives and Liberals to win a by-election at Barnard Castle. This made the point rather forcefully that the Liberals might also stand to gain from an electoral arrangement with the LRC. In Parliament the five LRC members already acted closely with the Lib-Labs, and a working agreement between the parties to defeat the Conservatives seemed a logical extension of this, even if it was not popular with the socialist 'rank and file' of the ILP.

In 1903, Ramsay MacDonald negotiated an electoral agreement with the Liberal Chief Whip, Herbert Gladstone (the youngest son of WE Gladstone). By this, the Liberals agreed not to contest a number of seats at the next general election. In return, the successful LRC members of Parliament would support an elected Liberal government. The issue of an alliance with the Liberals was sufficiently sensitive for Hardie and MacDonald to keep the arrangement a secret from the rest of the LRC, even to the extent of denying its existence. This was to be only the first of a number of instances in the Labour Party's history when pragmatism and principle parted company. In the event the LRC gained greatly from the pact, and 29 of its candidates including Hardie, Philip Snowden and Ramsay Macdonald, were successful in the general election of 1906. This group in Parliament now adopted the name, Labour Party, and elected Hardie its Chairman.

Co-operation with the Liberals had been a vital element in establishing a Parliamentary presence for Labour in 1906. The Liberals (elected with a large majority) were confident that any political threat from the new party could be contained and were even prepared to make concessions to secure the co-operative relationship. For example, the parties worked together to ensure the passing of the Trades Disputes Act in 1906, which restored the unions' immunity to civil action and also the right to peaceful picketing, which Taff Vale had questioned. But the new party found it very difficult, in these early years, to establish itself as offering something different from the Liberals. This difficulty was exacerbated by the Liberals' new commitment to social reform (*see chapter XIV, section 4*). In fact, up to 1914, there was little to distinguish the policy of the Labour Party from that of the Liberals. This was hardly surprising since many of the Labour members had supported the Liberal Party until fairly recently. This, and the importance to the young party of retaining the support of moderate trade unionists, militated against the adoption of overtly socialist policies. Labour distinguished itself from the Liberals, not so much by its policies, but rather by its ability to see things from a distinctly working-class perspective. Despite their Lib-Labs, the Liberals remained a predominantly middle-class party with values and attitudes to match. This difference of perspective between the parties was demonstrated rather well in the response from Will Crooks, a cooper by trade and the Labour member for Woolwich, during the debate on Old Age Pensions in 1908. Conjuring up the orthodox belief that poverty was often self-inflicted by the poor, the Liberals proposed to exclude the 'drunken' from benefit. Crooks asked sarcastically, 'What particular degree of drunkenness was to disqualify for a pension? – half stewed, half drunk, steadily drunk, talkatively drunk, quarrelsome drunk, maudlin drunk, dead drunk?'. As he pointed out, drunkenness was not unknown at Westminister.

The real problem for the Labour Party, between 1906 and 1914, lay in translating this distinctively working-class viewpoint into a clear political programme. The issue became a source of intense debate within the Labour Party. In 1908 Ben Tillett, hero of the dock strike, and a member of the ILP, published a pamphlet entitled *Is the Parliamentary Labour Party a Failure?*, and it was widely read. Most of the pressure on the party to move to the left and to adopt a socialist programme came from the ILP, which continued to exist as a distinct organisation within the Labour Party. In 1910, frustrated by four years of living in the parliamentary shadow of the Liberals, a group in the ILP produced the so-called 'green manifesto', *Let us Reform the Labour Party*. This called for more overtly socialist policies and a shared platform with the SDF.

But the Labour Party resisted the calls to adopt a more clearly socialist stand. If anything, with the affiliation in 1909 of the Miners' Federation, with its Lib-Lab traditions, the party moved further away from socialism. For one thing, the alliance with the Liberals still paid concrete dividends. In the general election of January 1910 the Labour Party fielded 70 candidates, of which 40 were successful. None of these had been opposed by a Liberal, and the secret electoral arrangement was clearly still in place. In the second election of 1910, 42 Labour members were returned. Labour was still growing as a parliamentary force but the growth was painfully slow, and there was little sign, before 1914, that Labour was destined to replace the Liberals as the second major party by 1924. The table below clearly demonstrates Labour's role as a minority party before 1914.

Labour's percentage share of total vote in general elections was

1900	1.8	1910 (December)	7.1
1906	5.9	1918	22.2
1910(January)	7.6	1922	29.5

Labour's lack of electoral impact before 1918 was partly a reflection that not all working men were entitled to vote: some 40 per cent were still disenfranchised by the registration clauses attached to the legislation of 1884–5. The harsh reality for Labour in this period was that most working people who possessed the franchise still voted for the other two parties, and mostly for the Liberals. Labour's weakness in Westminster derived from this fact.

Much of this can be seen in Keir Hardie's own experience of elections. In the general election of 1900 Hardie stood successfully as a candidate for the two member constituency of Merthyr Tydfil in South Wales. In the same election he also stood, unsuccessfully, as a candidate in Preston. Merthyr had a long history of returning Liberal members and it was to Hardie's advantage that the two sitting Liberal members were at odds with one another over support for the Boer War. One of these, D A Thomas, was so opposed to the other Liberal's pro-war stance that he actually endorsed Hardie's candidature and supported his campaign. As historian Kenneth Morgan puts it: 'Hardie was returned as an unequivocal representative of the ILP and the LRC. Nevertheless, without this clear evidence of Liberal endorsement and the backing of Thomas's private machine, Hardie would have been as disappointed at Merthyr as he had been at Preston.' In Merthyr, Hardie's personal position was perhaps analogous to that of the young Labour Party at Westminister in the years before 1914. He was independent of the Liberals to the extent that he had defeated a Lib-Lab mineworkers' union leader to secure the LRC nomination to stand as a candidate. Nevertheless, he also benefited from a co-operative relationship with the local Liberals. Hardie stood for Merthyr in four general elections (those of 1900, 1906 and the two elections of 1910). On each of these occasions Hardie was elected in this two-member constituency but with substantially fewer votes than his Liberal opponent. It is also worth noting that in 1910 the population of Merthyr was 122 545 but the number of registered voters was only 23 219. The 1884 Reform Act had not delivered the kind of mass electorate which Labour needed to secure its position.

The vulnerability of the new party, with little funding outside that provided by the unions, was clearly demonstrated by the Osborne Judgement of 1909. A member of the Amalgamated Society of Railway Servants objected to paying the political levy, that part of a member's subscription with which affiliated unions supported the Labour Party. The courts, backed again by the House of Lords, ruled that it was illegal for unions to compel members to pay a political levy. This hit the funds of the Labour Party badly, whilst leaving the other parties virtually unscathed. Labour now found itself relying on the Liberals to legislate against the ruling. In 1911 the Liberals introduced an Act to provide a salary for MPs, for the first time. This went part of the way towards rectifying the problem, but Labour had to wait until 1913 and the Liberals' Trade Union Act of that year before the Osborne

Judgement was reversed. All of this reinforced Labour's Parliamentary dependence on the Liberals. As a leading member of the Parliamentary Labour Party put it in 1913:

> The present labour representation in Parliament is there mainly by the goodwill of the Liberals, and it will disappear when that goodwill is turned into active resentment.

Historians tend to take one of two views of Labour's performance in Parliament before the First World War. Those on the left invariably indict the party (as did some of its supporters at the time) for turning its back on a socialist programme. Ralph Miliband, in his book *Parliamentary Socialism*, relates this firmly to the origins of the party. The socialism of the ILP lacked the cutting edge of continental socialism, partly because many of its supporters were ex-Liberals. Yet even the socialism of the ILP was diluted on the formation of the LRC and the need to placate the trade unions. Labour's parliamentary impotence, Miliband believes, was a logical consequence of its failure to develop its distinctiveness through a socialist programme. Ramsay MacDonald seems to epitomise this failure, moving from the Liberals to the ILP in 1894, and on to become Secretary of the LRC in 1900 and leader of the Parliamentary party in 1911. MacDonald's view was that, 'Socialism is to come through a socialistic political party and not a socialist one.' Other historians have been less convinced of the potential appeal to the working-class voter of an explicitly socialist platform. In his biography of MacDonald, for example, David Marquand depicts a man, somewhere between an idealist and a political realist, attempting to nurture support for a new and growing party by demonstrating its fitness to govern. Since the mass appeal of socialism was at best unproven, the Labour Party's best hope initially was to attach itself to the Liberals, and push for reform as a gradual process.

The interpretations of historians to some extent reflect the strategic options open to Labour in Parliament at the time; to back the Liberals or to plough their own socialist furrow. After 1910 another strategic option appeared. The failure of the Liberals, despite their welfare reforms, to deal with contemporary social problems was reflected in another 'explosion' of trade union activity from 1910–14. This, and the growth of a militant women's movement claiming the right to vote (*see chapter XIV*), represented the re-birth of direct action. Its appearance was to some extent an indictment of Labour's parliamentary ineffectiveness and, inevitably, it challenged the parliamentary initiative as the way forward. For many activists in the labour movement it presented starkly the two alternative strategies available: the reformist approach of gradual change through constitutional processes or the path of direct action with its revolutionary implications. But if the Labour Party felt threatened by the growth of militant extra-parliamentary protest, it was the 'new Liberalism' that was the main casualty. By

1914 it had been shown to be inadequate to meet the problems of British society and the post-war Labour Party was to be the main beneficiary of the Liberals' difficulties.

7 Labour Unrest 1910–14

Membership of trade unions declined between the Taff Vale judgement of 1901 and the Trades Disputes Act of 1906. This decline led more unions to back the moves towards parliamentary representation for labour. But in the years after 1906 the unions grew, with a great increase in membership between 1910 and 1914. The Trades Disputes Act had secured the legal position of unions which had been so vigorously contested in the last decade of the nineteenth century. The overall picture was that trade union membership doubled from around two million members in 1900 to just over four million members in 1914. From 1910 until the outbreak of the war, union members demonstrated a willingness to return to the strike as the main weapon for achieving their objectives. 1912 was a crisis point with well over a million workers on strike.

The immediate cause of this period of unrest lay in a fall in real wages after 1900. This, in turn, was the result of declining productivity and comparatively low industrial investment as Britain's difficulties in the international market became increasingly apparent. In Britain's leading heavy industries costs increased and profits fell. The first sign of the malaise occurred in the cotton textile industry, the scene of relative industrial harmony since 1893 and of the establishment of the Brooklands collective bargaining machinery. In 1908 the industry suffered a seven-week strike when the employers lowered wages. This was an indication of things to come and in 1910 a strike wave broke on British industry. It focused initially on the coal mines of South Wales, particularly the Aberdare and Rhondda Valleys, where a dispute grew up over payment for miners working difficult or abnormal seams.

The miners were angry, not only at the owners' attempts to reduce their wages but also with the failure of their union leaders to protect them from such moves. The temperature of industrial conflict was clearly rising, with extensive clashes between the police and strikers, which left one striker dead and many injured at Tonypandy in 1911. In June 1911 the seamen went on strike and dock workers and railwaymen came out in sympathy. In August two strikers were shot dead by troops in Liverpool, as general rioting broke out. In the same week troops shot dead two men who were part of a crowd attacking a train at Llanelli. In 1912, the first ever national pit strike broke out, running from February to April. There were strikes in the London docks and among transport workers. In 1913 there were strikes in the metal-working industries of the Midlands and a major strike of transport workers in Dublin.

It is the sheer scale of the numbers involved in the industrial disputes of these years that is remarkable. This was really the culmination of the movement towards larger, confederated organisations that had been taking place on both sides of industry for nearly 30 years. It also indicated a growth of trade unionism among the unskilled. As we have seen, moves had been made in this direction during the last great 'explosion' of industrial conflict between 1889 and 1893. Yet, by 1910, still only 17 per cent of workers were members of unions. The years from 1910 to 1914 saw many previously unorganised groups drawn in so that, by 1914 25 per cent of the workforce were members of unions. Women were prominent among the new recruits. In 1904 there were 126 000 women in trade unions but by 1913 this had increased to 431 000, making up 10 per cent of all trade unionists.

This growth of trade unionism was essentially a movement of the rank and file, with strikes growing directly from the shop floor. Even where the established unions were involved, many of the strikes consisted of 'unofficial' action by rank-and-file trade unionists, acting without the constant of their central union leadership. Union leaders often complained that they were the last to know that a strike was taking place. Many observers noted that these strikes seemed qualitatively different to earlier disputes, in that grievances were often imprecisely spelled out, strikers frequently took action and decided afterwards what the dispute was actually about.

In this way the period represented a crisis for the unions, confronting them with the problem of how to control the actions of their members. It also created difficulties for the Labour Party since the focus of action now shifted from Westminster to the workplace, away from reformism and towards direct action.

Above all, the strike wave was an expression of discontent with the existing strategies for advancing labour's cause: collective bargaining in the industrial sphere and parliamentary support for moderate social reform in the political sphere. The promised benefits of these two strategies had not materialised; neither had been able to prevent the fall in real wages and the deterioration of working conditions. In the main, working people were unimpressed by the Liberal reforms; the decline of wages and the increase in job insecurity seemed to outweigh the benefits of any welfare legislation.

Troops and the police were used to combat strikes in this period to a far greater extent than ever before. The confrontations on the streets made it easy to see the strike movement in the revolutionary terms that many contemporary observers feared. The threat to the overall stability of society was emphasised by the role played by the ideas of Syndicalism. These were most popularly associated with the French left-wing political thinker Georges Sorel whose book, *Reflections on Violence*, was published in 1905, following the author's observation of French trade unions (*syndicats*) in action. The Syndicalists turned their backs on political action and argued that the trade union could be the basis of a society run by the workers. Instead of sectional unions, concerned with this or that detail of a particular trade, unions should amalgamate and act together. The ultimate aim was to stop society dead by a general strike that would paralyse the nation and precipitate a transfer of power to the unions. The syndicalists advocated class warfare and direct action, believing that every strike acted to increase the class awareness of the participants.

In Britain this approach was advocated by a journal called *The Syndicalist*, edited by Tom Mann, re-kindling the direct action of 'new unionism'. Mann was imprisoned in 1912 for inciting the troops, who confronted the strikers, to mutiny. Another familiar figure, Ben Tillett, fostered syndicalism among the dock workers. In South Wales the miners were led by men like A J Cook, who had been previously active in the local branches of the ILP, but was frustrated by its commitment to parliamentary reformism. In 1912 Cook and others published an influential pamphlet called *The Miner's Next Step*. In this they criticised the mining unions for their reliance on collective bargaining and advocated a fully integrated union of all coal miners that would take over and run the mines.

Certainly, Labour in Parliament saw the re-birth of industrial militancy as a weakening of its position. Ramsay MacDonald called syndicalism 'the impatient frenzied, thoughtless child of poverty, disappointment, (and) irresponsibility.' Similarly, George Barnes, a former general secretary of the ASE, and now a Labour member for Glasgow, poured scorn on the new approach:

> There are, however, some Labour leaders of anarchical proclivities who are leading newly organised labour into the ditch by strikes. They have become obsessed in favour of the strike policy, and in order to make it more attractive they present it in a fancy name imported from France ... That I say is fool's talk. I for one will be no party to a policy of that kind, because I know that nothing but disaster can come of it ... To talk of a general strike as a policy for organised Labour is sheer madness.

1 *Examine the language and the tone of this statement. How does Barnes make the case against Syndicalism?*

2 *Why should Barnes, a trade unionist himself, be opposed to a General Strike?*

In fact, it is easy to exaggerate the importance of the syndicalists. Their direct influence was less than they would have wished. The labour unrest of these years grew from the grass roots rather than being imported, in the form of new ideas, from the continent. The syndicalists simply tried to harness this movement. One of the government's arbitrators, appointed under the 1896 Conciliation Act, concluded that, 'it looks as if we are in the presence of one of those periodic upheavals in the labour world such as occurred in 1833–4, and from time to time since that date,'. There was much in this outburst of trade unionism that recalled the 'Plug disturbances' of 1842, or the advent of general unionism in 1889. Yet this particular 'periodic upheaval' was to have a lasting impact on trade unionism, both by extending union organisation among the unskilled and by the development of the 'sympathy' strike on behalf of other trades. Many of the disputes had taken this form, and this was reflected in the establishment of the Triple Alliance between the Miners, the Railwaymen and the Transport Workers in 1914. By this, the unions in three major industries agreed to take sympathetic action if any one of them was in dispute. Through the operation of this agreement the legacy of the pre-war period of unrest would be felt in the General Strike of 1926.

For the moment it was clear that, in the light of Labour's disappointing showing at Westminister, a large section of the working community had put its faith in extra-Parliamentary action. The re-birth of direct action also seemed to be, at least partly, a result of the exclusion of a large segment of the working population from participation in parliamentary politics. To counter this the Liberal government, under Asquith, now sought to underpin the role of the parliamentary parties as the more acceptable medium for expressing working-class aspirations. Thus in 1911, it brought in its measure introducing wages for MPs and, by the Trade Union Act of 1913, it reversed the Osborne judgement. This made it legal for unions to levy their members to support the Labour Party. Nevertheless, the growth of extra-Parliamentary action had been a forcible reminder that, even under the provisions of the 1884 Reform Act, around 40 per cent of men were still unenfranchised. The social conflict of 1910–14 pressed the case eloquently for a radical extension of the franchise. In 1917 the Russian Revolution would provide a chilling model of what happened when direct action was taken to its logical conclusion. The Representation of the People Act of 1918 extended the electorate from its pre-war figure of 8 million to a massive 21 million voters. For the first time the electoral system gave the effective right to vote to all men over 21. The registration clauses and mixed franchises of earlier Reform Acts were replaced by an altogether more accessible system that was less weighted against the interests of the working-class voter. Voters in receipt of poor relief were no longer barred from voting. The cautious inclusion of a limited female suffrage under this act may have been 'votes for ladies' rather than 'votes for women' but the principle of a female parliamentary franchise had now been conceded. Undoubtedly, it was the working-class voter who benefited from these changes to the franchise. The traditional fear of including the working class in the electoral system, a fear which had accompanied the earlier Reform Acts, had been replaced during the labour unrest of 1910–14 by a fear of the consequences of its continued exclusion.

In the inter-war period the Labour Party would consolidate the organisational basis and the electoral support that had been established since the days of the LRC. The Labour Party increasingly emerged as the political arm of the trade union movement and was able, by 1924, to present itself as the second major party. Yet, however 'inevitable' this may look with the benefit of hindsight, it is important to remember that little of this was evident on the eve of the First World War. In Parliament, the small number of Labour MPs relied heavily on Liberal Party support and had experienced difficulty in establishing a distinctive policy which set them apart from the Liberals. Also, the growth of trade union militancy highlighted some endemic strategic difficulties for the Labour Party which it would carry with it into the later years. It could legitimately speak out against the violence that was often used against the strikers, for example in South Wales. But it could not be seen to endorse militant trade unionism which stepped outside the law. This would infringe its role as a parliamentary party committed to the rule of law and directly bring into question its fitness to govern. Similarly, there was always a tension within the ranks of the Labour Party between socialists who wished to challenge the capitalist system directly and those who wished to work within it to bring about gradual change. As we have seen, the origins of the Labour Party in Liberalism, and its reliance upon the support of moderate trade unions, always pushed Labour towards reformism as its central strategy. Any judgement on what the Labour Party had achieved by 1914 must be balanced by an understanding of what could reasonably be expected given the nature of its support.

8 Bibliography

J Belchem *Class, Party and the Political System in Britain 1867–1914* (Blackwell, 1990) – A good overview of those years.

K D Brown (ed.) *The First Labour Party 1906–1914* (Croom Helm, 1985). A collection of useful essays on a range of important issues; in particular, see Pat Thane's essay on the Labour Party's approach to social reform before the First World War.

E Hobsbawm *Labouring Men* (Weidenfeld and Nicolson, 1964). A view from the left of the new unions and aspects of the rise of labour; particularly, see chapters 9–15. Hobsbawm has updated much of this work in his more recent collection of essays, *Worlds of Labour* (Weidenfeld and Nicolson, 1984).

K Leybourn and J Reynolds (eds) *Liberalism and the Rise of Labour 1890–1918* (Croom Helm, 1984). A collection of essays which explore the relationship between the two parties by examining one locality, West Yorkshire. Since the area became an important base for Labour this case study approach casts important light on a central theme.

D Marquand *Ramsay Macdonald* (Jonathan Cape, 1977). A biography which presents Macdonald as a pragmatist attempting to establish Labour's fitness to govern.
R McGibbon *The Evolution of the Labour Party 1910–1924* (Oxford University Press, 1974). This book is very detailed but contains a fine appreciation of the electoral and political difficulties faced by the young party.
R Miliband *Parliamentary Socialism. A Study in the Politics of Labour* (Allen and Unwin, 1961). A left-wing analysis which has little time for the pragmatism of the early party.
Kenneth O Morgan *Keir Hardie. Radical and Socialist* (Weidenfeld and Nicolson, 1975). A standard work, particularly useful for the early relationship with the Liberals.
G Phillips *The Rise of the Labour Party 1893–1931* (Routledge, 1992). A well-written general history of the party.
D Tanner *Political Change and the Labour Party 1900–1924* (Cambridge University Press, 1990), provides some good insights into Labour in Parliament.

9 DISCUSSION POINTS AND ESSAY QUESTIONS

A

1 Who supported Labour and why?
2 What were the problems for the Labour Party in establishing themselves as an alternative to the Liberals?
3 What were the political advantages and disadvantages of the Labour Party's link with the unions?
4 To what extent was the growth of extra-parliamentary unrest a comment on the Labour Party's performance?
5 How well placed were Labour to supersede the Liberals in 1914?
6 How far can Labour be seen as a socialist party in these years?

B *Essay questions*

Most essay questions on the Labour Party in this period concentrate on the mixed origins of the party and its relative weakness in the early years. They invariably involve examining the pressures towards disunity that were a consequence of drawing upon support from a range of organisations, as well as Labour's continuing reliance on the Liberals in Parliament before 1914. Below are some examples of the way these questions can be framed. There are three focal points in these questions:
(i) the relative importance of trade unionism in the emergence of Labour,

(ii) the parliamentary impact of Labour before the war,
(iii) the extent to which Labour should be seen as a socialist party in this period.

The emphasis on each of these issues varies from question to question and you will need to decide which should have priority. Yet all involve an appreciation of the support that Labour relied upon.

1 *How important a force was the Labour Party in British politics before 1914?*
2 *To what extent was the emergence of the Labour Party a result of the growing strength of the trade unions in the second half of the nineteenth century?*
3 *Assess the strengths and weaknesses of the Labour Party as an independent political force before 1914.*
4 *'Trade unionist rather than socialist'. Discuss this view of the Labour Party before 1914.*
5 *What movements combined to form the Labour Party, and how united and effective was that party in the period up to 1914?*
6 *'Socialist neither in its origins nor its policies.' Do you agree with this comment on the Labour Party before 1914?*
7 *'Keir Hardie, rather than the trade unions, deserves the credit for the emergence of the Labour Party.' How far do you agree with this view?*
8 *Discuss the reasons for the emergence of the Labour Party in the years up to 1906.*
9 *How did the position and aspirations of the trade unions change between 1885 and 1914?*

10 Documentary Exercise – Politics and Strikes in South Wales 1910

Read carefully the following documents. The first is a first-hand account of a miners' strike in the Aberdare Valley, taken from the autobiography of a miner, William J Edwards, *From the Valley I Came*. The second is a poster, issued in November 1910, as part of Keir Hardie's campaign in the second general election of that year.

> To this day the strike of 1910 is known as the Block Strike and for a reason that may seem trivial. It had been the custom for miners to bring out from the pit odd and useless blocks of wood, which they took to their cottages to cut up into kindling. In those days there were no modern conveniences like gas or electric heating units, and, in consequence, there was no other method of boiling a kettle or cooking a breakfast than by

kindling a fire and, of necessity, getting it going quickly. Thus this well-dried wood from the pits was of immense service as it quickly responded to the old-fashioned bellows which hung at the side of all fireplaces.

When orders got through to the miners that the taking of this useless wood had been forbidden from then on, the miners went on strike. But this petty prohibition, irritating and annoying as it was, was not the reason for the strike: it was the last straw, and merely symbolic of a thousand grievances which had accumulated throughout the years, grievances which, in effect, made it impossible for even the best and most skilful miners to make more than a bare living when, as happened at intervals, coal-seams deteriorated, and no matter how hard a man worked, he could only contemplate a seriously reduced pay-packet.

The coal-owners could have restored the kindling wood privilege; but that would not have ended the strike. In a sense the miners were like those accused persons who, before being sentenced, ask for a large number of other offences to be considered: the miners insisted that all their grievances should be discussed before they would return to work. Nearly a third of the South Wales coal-field was soon affected; and within three weeks of the strike's beginning that third was on the Parish.

In the end, driven by debt and near-hunger, we returned to work as we had come out; but we had learnt much and this experience, we knew, would serve us well in the next strike, which we believed to be inevitable . . .

. . . That the national authorities were taking a serious view of this strike became plain when, after it had been going for some time, they sent extra police into the strike area. At first these came from the neighbourhood, but later they came from all over the country, including London . . .

. . . As we marched down the tow-path following the canal, the men began singing popular choruses, while the boys, less sophisticated, fell back on the simple hymns they had learnt in Sunday school.

When the tow-path reached a point near the power station, the column wheeled to the right and began approaching the place where the blacklegs were working. But we had not gone far before there suddenly rose before us a barrage of water rising and glistening quite beautifully in the brilliant afternoon sunshine before falling at our feet. There was something quite fascinating about this water display; but less fascinating was the charge made by the police, armed with batons, through the gleaming curtain of water. We fell back in a confused mass of bodies as the police came on, using their batons freely. Every now and again my face was slightly splashed with blood, not my own, fortunately.

Eventually, we were beaten back into the canal, whose bed at this point was full of soft mud. As I stood there shouting orders to the crowd, I got a beauty from a baton on the side of the head which sent me down into the canal, where I lay as if knocked out, although I was still conscious. It seemed judicious not to move, because I knew that if I got up the two policemen on the bank would knock me down again ...

... Somewhat later, our area was invaded by soldiers. We did not believe that the demonstration at the power house was the cause of their appearance: we believed that the soldiers had been sent to intimidate the people and, in consequence, to break the strike. However, there they were in our valley and in the Rhondda, and what with them and the police, the area was like an armed camp. The soldiers and their horses were billetted on the colliery owners' properties, and, from these centres, they embarked on regular patrols to look for trouble, and to make it, if they could not find it.

Winston Churchill's name was on everybody's lips: to us, he was the arch criminal who had sent the soldiers to frighten us with an arrogant display of force. This has never been forgotten in the valley, and even to this day, when he appears on a cinema screen, his reception is not good.

It seemed to us that the tactics shown by the military during their occupation of our valley was based on a cool, calculated strategy of intimidation.

Answer the following questions.

1 *What was the cause of the strike?*

2 *What indications are there, in this description, of the scale and nature of the strike?*

3 *Why is Churchill held responsible by the author? (You may need to consult Chapter XIV in order to answer this question.)*

4 *How useful might such an account be to the historian of industrial relations in this period?*

5 *What difficulties did trade union action of this kind pose for the Parliamentary Labour Party?*

MERTHYR TYDFIL BOROUGHS

GENERAL ELECTION, 1910.

"TO THE MERTHYR LABOUR REPRESENTATION ASSOCIATION

COMRADES,

In response to your invitation I am willing to again become your Candidate. This is the fourth time you have so honoured me, and, if again elected, I shall continue to do what I can to REPRESENT and SAFEGUARD YOUR INTERESTS.

The events of the past few weeks in the Aberdare and Rhondda Valleys must have shown you anew that a Liberal Government is first and foremost a CAPITALIST GOVERNMENT. If the Bloodshed and Riotous Conduct of which the Police have been guilty had taken place under a Conservative Government every Liberal Platform would have rung with denunciation of the wicked Tories; but, because it is the LIBERALS who are RESPONSIBLE there is a

CONSPIRACY OF SILENCE IN THE PRESS, AND EVERY LIBERAL SPEAKER IS DUMB.

The HOME SECRETARY not only DEFENDS THE ACTIONS OF THE POLICE and REFUSES an ENQUIRY into the charges against them but also EULOGISES the HOOLIGANS in UNIFORM, whilst LIBERAL M.P.'s, with few exceptions, back him up by their Votes in the Division Lobby.

As a consequence of this the MEN ON STRIKE are BELIEVED by Millions of People who KNOW NOTHING OF THE FACTS to be WILD, RIOTOUS, DRUNKEN, WORTHLESS SCAMPS, whereas the very OPPOSITE IS THE TRUTH. THE MILITARY and POLICE have been sent to HELP the MASTERS to CRUSH THE MEN.

THE TRICK WON'T SUCCEED.

During the Contest I shall be a good deal in other Constituencies where Labour Men are being opposed. Both Parties fear the presence in Parliament of Labour Men whom they can neither SILENCE nor CONTROL. I want to see the NUMBER of SUCH MEN INCREASED, so that POLITICAL HYPOCRITES of the CHURCHILL TYPE may be UNMASKED, and the Health, Comfort, Safety, and General Well-being of the Working Class promoted. I know you will HOLD THE FORT for LABOUR in my absence

Fraternally Yours,

J. KEIR HARDIE."

MERTHYR TYDFIL, Nov. 8th, 1910.

Printed and Published by The LABOUR PIONEER PRESS, Ltd., Williams' Square, Glebeland, Merthyr Tydfil.

1 *What is meant by the statement 'The Home Secretary ... EULOGISES THE HOOLIGANS IN UNIFORM ...'?*

2 *How is Hardie able to establish common cause with the miners in this poster?*

3 *What light does the poster cast on the relationship between the Labour Party and the trade unions?*

4 *In what ways does the poster establish that the Labour Party is different from the Liberal Party?*

XIV

LIBERALS AND UNIONISTS 1902–14

1 INTRODUCTION

THE period 1902–14 was one of the most turbulent periods of British political history. During that time both of the main political parties, the Liberals and the Conservatives, suffered fluctuating fortunes and underwent traumatic changes. A completely new political force, the Labour Party, came into being and secured a foothold within the House of Commons. The issue of female suffrage was transformed from a relatively obscure issue into a national crusade which defied the political system to respond to its demand and ultimately challenged the rule of law. The House of Lords, which had regarded itself for so long as the guardian of the Constitution, was reduced to a shadow of its former power and prestige. Welfare legislation raised government intervention to new and unprecedented heights. Irish affairs (*see pages 317–20*) plunged political life into turmoil and threatened to create the first civil war within the British Isles for over 250 years. Disputes between Labour and Capital (*see chapter XIII*), often with the government sandwiched uncomfortably between them, brought class antagonisms to a pitch which, at times, seemed to threaten the fabric of society with disintegration.

In 1902 the political world was dominated by the alliance between the Conservative Party and those Liberal Unionists who had split from Gladstone over the issue of Irish Home Rule in 1886 (*see pages 284–8*). This alliance had formally crystallised in June 1895, when the Liberal Prime Minister, Lord Rosebery resigned and Lord Salisbury formed a coalition with the Liberal Unionist leaders Joseph Chamberlain and the Duke of Devonshire (formerly Lord Hartington). This coalition immediately fought a hugely successful general election which crushed the Liberals and cemented the relationship into a permanent alliance. Then the 'Khaki' election of 1900 (so-called because it was held during the Boer War) resulted in a slightly reduced majority for the coalition, but clearly perpetuated its political ascendancy as a 'Unionist' administration. So all-pervading did this theme of 'Unionism' become that, for a time, the term 'Conservative' almost seemed to lapse from the political vocabulary. Even the leaders of the Conservative Party began to refer to the 'great Unionist Party' and for a while it seemed as though the expression 'Conservative Party' was destined to become no more than an outdated piece of historical terminology.

Liberalism, too, underwent a dramatic change. The Liberal Party which came to power in 1905 was a very different one from that which had been led by Gladstone little more than a decade previously. Many active Liberal supporters had defected to the Unionist side, including, in particular, many from the world of industry and commerce who abandoned their traditional liberalism for the apparent safety of the Conservatives or Liberal Unionists. Their defections were partly the result of increasing signs of radicalism within the Liberal Party: Gladstone's emphasis on Irish Home Rule seemed either irrelevant or dangerous; the 'Newcastle Programme' of 1891 (*see page 290*), though not seriously translated into policies, alarmed them; the Liberal Government's budget of 1894, with its restructuring of death duties into a consolidated and graduated scale, appeared to be the thin edge of a socialist wedge. The Liberal Party was gradually taking on that more collectivist approach to social issues, once advocated by its 'leader-lost', Joseph Chamberlain. This 'New Liberalism', epitomised most dramatically in the new generation of Liberal MPs by the Welsh Radical, David Lloyd George, was far removed from the non-interventionist and individualist traditions of Gladstonian Liberalism. The huge scale of the Liberal Party's victory in the 1906 general election, guaranteed many new faces among the ranks of Liberal MPs. This New Liberalism element among them ensured that traditional Liberal emphasis on the importance of individual liberties and 'self-help' would increasingly give way to the collectivist values of social welfare.

The political rivalry between Liberalism and Unionism took shape within a context of increasing concern about the whole question of Britain's future as a nation, a great power and an empire. The future of the nation was most seriously and immediately compromised by the Irish Question. Unionism as a political force was based primarily on the assumption that Irish Home Rule would prove to be merely the precursor to complete separation of Ireland from Great Britain. This, in turn, raised the question of the status of Wales and Scotland and whether Home Rule could or should be applied to them. Some politicians saw 'Home Rule all round' as a viable vehicle for the preservation of the British Isles as a single unit – Joseph Chamberlain had suggested just such a solution to the Irish crisis in 1886. However, others believed that such a development would compromise the whole concept of the British Empire and lead to its disintegration. If that happened, it was argued, Britain would ultimately be condemned to a decline towards the second rank of nations. Such concerns about the future of the Home Countries and the Empire inevitably raised the question – just how secure was Britain's long-term status as a 'Great Power'?

2 A GREAT POWER IN DECLINE?

The concern about Britain's future as a Great Power gathered momentum in the 1890s. It was based, broadly, on three considerations. First, there was the question of Britain's diplomatic 'isolation' and the increasing hostility with which she was regarded by other nations. This question is discussed in chapter XII. Second, there was the question of Britain's economic performance and the extent to which other nations were catching up with, or even overtaking, Britain as the leading manufacturing and commercial power. Third, there was the question of the condition of the working classes in Britain and the extent to which this was undermining Britain both economically and socially.

A *The economy*

Concern about the performance of the British economy stemmed from the 1870s when, after nearly three decades of relatively consistent and pronounced growth, the economy was suddenly beset by a series of slumps interspersed by temporary revivals. The last of these slumps ended in 1896 and was followed by a steady, if slow, period of economic expansion up to 1914, with only one relative downturn in the period 1907–10. However, despite this 'recovery', the cycle of slumps over a 25-year period up to 1896 had been enough to undermine the confidence in British economic strength which had been taken for granted in the middle years of the century – a period which has been characterised as 'The Great Victorian Boom'. Economic historians are not agreed about the significance of this period after 1870. At one time it was customary to refer to the last quarter of the nineteenth century as 'The Great Depression'. More recently however, most economic historians have rejected this view, preferring to present the period as one involving a 'retardation of growth', that is to say, a slowing down of the earlier, rapid expansion of the economy, until a lower, more sustainable pattern of growth was reached in the 1890s.

In retrospect it is easy to see that fears about the strength of the British economy in this period were exaggerated. In fact, the economy was performing in rather a mixed way. For example, the period after 1870 was precisely when Britain was emerging as the world's leading shipbuilding nation – a status she was to maintain through many trials and tribulations until the Second World War. Output of iron and steel continued to increase, despite competition from Germany and the USA and even the inefficient coal industry continued to remain profitable in the years up to 1914, buoyed up by consistently increasing world demand for coal. However, it is also true that Britain did not expand as rapidly in the newer industrial sectors, such as electrical engineering and chemical production, as did Germany or the USA.

The agricultural sector faced a more intractable problem, in that cheap imports of cereals from the 1870s put pressure on British arable farmers and forced them to reduce their corn production. Even livestock farmers faced some competition as steamships with refridgerated cargo holds allowed the importation of cheap meat from abroad. In short, British farmers faced the kind of situation which the previous generation had feared would arise at the time of the repeal of the corn laws, but which had then failed to materialise. The case for a 'Great Depression' in the agricultural sector is thus more convincing than that for industry, but even so the picture was not one of unrelieved gloom. Cheaper imports of cereals meant cheaper foodstuffs for livestock farmers and in some parts of the country, such as Lancashire, farm rents actually rose in this period as profits soared. Moreover, the availability of cheaper food meant that, across the nation as a whole, the value of real wages was consistently rising, despite the effects of the periodic slumps.

The most obvious, and most discussed aspect of economic performance, was the question of international trade. More specifically, there was the question of German imports and the size of the 'trade-gap' on visible earnings which began to increase after 1870. The 'trade-gap' meant that the value of those items imported into the country exceeded the value of exports in some years. Such gaps had, however, existed even in the 1850s and were always more than covered by the value of so-called 'invisible' earnings from insurance, shipping charges and banking services which brought increasingly vast profits into the British economy. London remained the commercial centre of the world and its dominance was unchallenged. Nevertheless, having noted that much of the concern about British economic performance was exaggerated, it is important to realise that what people at the time believed to be the case is often more important to understanding that period, than what subsequent historical research and deliberation reveals to have been the case.

B *The condition of the working classes*

Concern about the condition of the working classes arose out of the publication of evidence resulting from more 'scientific' investigations of poverty which began to appear in the 1880s. Charles Booth, a shipping magnate, published details of his investigation into the London district of Tower Hamlets in 1887. He claimed that one-third of the population was living below the poverty line. Booth went on to conduct a series of investigations between 1891 and 1903. His work was paralleled by the study of poverty in York undertaken by Seebohm Rowntree and published in 1901. These investigations and other less well-known ones like them, were prompted partly by genuine humanitarian concerns and partly by violent demonstrations by unemployed men in the mid-1880s coinciding with one of the periodic economic slumps. They were also intended to provide factual evidence about poverty, in contrast to the rather emotional and sensational accounts which were becoming rather common in the 1880s. Booth, for example, was a Conservative politically and a firm believer in individual enterprise. Their chief value was to demonstrate that unemployment and poverty could not be viewed solely as the result of vice or indolence. Indeed, one result of Booth's findings was to show clearly that the chief factor in poverty was family size and that the number of children in a family was a more significant element in determining living standards than unemployment.

The poor physical condition of many of the would-be recruits for the Boer War of 1899–1902 added fuel to the fires of publicity which scientific investigation had stoked. The idea that poverty and degradation were turning the British lower classes into some kind of sub-species had already provoked prognostications of doom from the Social Darwinists who foresaw the decline of the British race. Booth had written that the 'lives of the poor lay hidden from view behind curtains on which were painted terrible pictures; starving children, suffering women, overworked men...'. His (unrelated) namesake, William Booth, the founder of the Salvation Army, published a pamphlet in 1890 entitled *'In Darkest England and the Way Out'*, in which he portrayed the working-class districts as more remote than darkest Africa in terms of their remoteness from the experience of the upper and middle classes. This idea that the condition of the working classes posed some kind of nameless threat to civilised standards was to prove a potent force in promoting the acceptability of interventionist social reform.

C *National efficiency and the reform of education*

It was perhaps inevitable that people concerned with both the apparent economic decline of Britain and the supposed 'physical deterioration' of the working classes, should seek to establish some link between the two. The more extreme responses to the 'problem' envisaged selective breeding programmes and sterilisation and called for bans on foreign immigration which was allegedly polluting the 'bloodstock' of the British race, contributing to unemployment and spreading diseases. The idea that national efficiency was being undermined and that something needed to be done about it was embraced by a wide range of writers, from socialists such as the Webbs, to imperialists such as Lord Rosebery. Social reform was an obvious objective for those who argued that poverty was the main cause of the social degradation which was threatening national efficiency and the future the British Empire. One particularly relevant social issue was that of popular education and the effectiveness of the system which had been put into place during Gladstone's first administration in 1870. The idea that Britain's education system was inferior in specific respects to that of other countries had long been taking shape. Most attention was usually focused on the deficiencies of British technical and scientific education compared to that offered to the general population in Germany or France.

The belief that national efficiency could be promoted, or, to put it another way, that national decline could be halted by a reform of the education system was one of the reasons for the passing of a controversial Education Act by the Unionist Government in 1902. The Duke of Devonshire, who was the Cabinet Minister responsible for education and Arthur Balfour, Salisbury's nephew and the Leader of the House of Commons, both favoured a fundamental reform of the education system. Both were impressed by the argument that an efficient and properly funded education system was a prerequisite for a modern state aiming to maintain its place in the world. In 1902, these two took charge of the drafting of an education bill designed to bring about a substantial measure of reform. Lord Salisbury was dubious about it, but since he intended to retire from the premiership in the near future he did not oppose the idea. Joseph Chamberlain was also unenthusiastic, not because he undervalued education, but because, as a Nonconformist, he could anticipate the storm which would result from any attempt at government interference in the role played by the churches in the provision of education, or from any attempt to fund Anglican schools from local rates. However, Chamberlain could not overrule Balfour who was the clear successor to Salisbury as Prime Minister.

The purpose of the 1902 Education Act was to provide a new structure for both elementary and secondary education under local authority control. The School Boards which had been set up under the 1870 Act had legal powers only in respect of elementary provision. Over the years many Boards had gone well beyond their authority by providing secondary education as well. This meant that they were using ratepayers' money without any legal basis. The situation came to a head in 1901, when a court case was brought against the London School Board for the recovery of expenses which they had incurred in providing secondary education courses. The judge ruled against the Board on the grounds that the 1870 Act implied that rates could only be spent on children taking basic subjects. This judgment led to severe restrictions on school board spending on technical, evening and adult classes, all of which had been expanding in recent years and all of which could be argued to be contributing to the formation of a better-educated population. At central level, responsibility for both elementary and secondary education had been assumed by the Board of Education, which had been created in 1899 on the advice of a Royal Commission. Balfour and Devonshire therefore proposed to extend this principle to the local level.

The Education Act of 1902 was passed, as Salisbury and Chamberlain had foreseen, amidst great controversy. The Act swept away the old school boards and created Local Education Authorities under the County and County Borough Councils. These 'LEAs' had responsibility for both elementary and secondary education and were also required to support the voluntary (church) schools out of the rates. This latter provision caused the political controversy. Nonconformists were outraged by the idea of ratepayers' money being used to support the Anglican schools. The Liberals, conscious of their traditional political support among the Nonconformists, fought the proposal every inch of the way in the House of Commons and a great national campaign of opposition began, in which the Welsh radical, David Lloyd George, himself a Nonconformist, took a leading role. Attempts at compromise failed completely. Joseph Chamberlain suggested avoiding using the rates altogether by increasing government grants, but the cost of the Boer War ruled out that idea. Another possibility was a clause introducing an 'adoptive principle', under which it would have been left to local authorities to decide whether or not to use the rates in this way. Balfour was against this on the grounds that it would politicise the whole question permanently and lead to endless arguments at local level as well as leaving some Anglican schools at the mercy of hostile local councils. A good many Tories sympathised with Balfour's position and the clause was removed.

The passing of the 1902 Education Act cost the Unionist government dearly in political terms. There were over 70 000 prosecutions for non-payment of rates in the following year and in Wales, where Nonconformity was strong, the opposition was bitter. The Liberals reaped the benefit of a great revival in the political significance of Nonconformity which had been markedly on the decline. It was also an issue which enabled Liberals to re-unite after the split which had occurred in their ranks over the Boer War. Within the Government itself the Education Act had a divisive effect. One of the fundamental realities of the Unionist Coalition was its bringing together of Anglican and Nonconformist opinion – the latter being most obviously represented by the prominent position of Chamberlain. The maintenance of a kind of status quo had been central to this understanding. Chamberlain was deeply embarrassed with his own Nonconformist supporters by the controversy and it undermined his own feelings of obligation, towards his Conservative partners, not to rock the political boat with his own developing ideas.

3 Tariff Reform and the Decline of the Unionists

In September 1902 Lord Salisbury retired from the premiership and was succeeded by Arthur Balfour. The death of the Queen in January 1901 had released him from any long-term continuation in an office which he had come to regard as an intolerable burden. A sense of duty compelled him to remain in office whilst the war in South Africa continued and until the new King had been crowned, but once the coronation had been held he gratefully relinquished office. There was no question of a struggle for the succession. The only conceivable alternative to Balfour was Chamberlain and the latter knew perfectly well that he was not acceptable, as leader, to most of the Conservatives. Chamberlain accepted this situation realistically and never made any attempt to intervene, despite some press efforts to stir up a campaign on his behalf. His acceptance of Balfour, however, did not mean that he was satisfied with the state of affairs within the Unionist Government.

Chamberlain's dissatisfaction stemmed from a variety of frustrations in his political life. He wanted to be Prime Minister but he knew that there was almost no prospect of this happening; increasingly he felt that the Government's lack of achievements in social policy was undermining his credibility and playing into the hands of the socialists; he was worried at the lack of progress, as he saw it, in ending British isolation in foreign policy; most of all, he was frustrated at the lack of progress which his plans for imperial integration and development were making. Since 1897 Chamberlain had made repeated efforts to advance the idea of an imperial federation based initially on economic union. So far, however, all his efforts to interest the Prime Ministers of the various Dominions and Colonies of the Empire, had failed. To Chamberlain this spelled disaster for the future of both the Empire and the United Kingdom. He firmly believed that the future lay with large countries, possessed of large populations and access to vast natural resources. For Britain to compete with the likes of the USA, Germany and, eventually, Russia there was, according to Chamberlain's analysis, no alternative but the unification of the Empire or a decline to minor international status.

By 1902 Chamberlain was little short of desperate for a political initiative. The 'triumph' of the Boer War – 'Joe's War' as it was often called – had turned sour; the Education Bill was an acute embarrassment; Chamberlain became determined to embark upon a major scheme that would seize the public's imagination, rescue Unionism from the doldrums and, ultimately, capture opinion throughout the Empire for a great imperial cause. For many years he had been privately dubious about the wisdom of the United Kingdom continuing with a policy of free trade in a world that was increasingly turning to economic protection. It was not, it should be emphasised, that he was personally a protectionist in outlook. On the contrary, he hoped that international free trade could be restored. For the time being, however, he had come to the conclusion that British interests demanded the restoration of protection in order to give British industry a breathing space against cheap imports from government-subsidised producers abroad. The money raised from import tariffs, he believed, could be used to fund social reforms, as well as to assist the regeneration of Britain's industrial base.

Such a policy was politically dangerous. Taxing imports meant a certain rise in food prices; it would be difficult to sell the idea to the working classes; it would unite the Liberals in ferocious opposition; it risked dividing the Unionists. On the other hand, the scheme offered almost the last chance to inject some life into the concept of imperial unification: a protective tariff could be introduced, within a scheme of 'imperial preference' under which imperial trade could be exempted from taxation or subjected to reduced rates. Whatever the risks, Chamberlain was not the man to shirk a challenge when such a prize was at stake. As early as May 1902 he hinted at the idea of an imperial trading system in a speech in his political stronghold, Birmingham. The Government had just been forced to introduce a small tariff on imported corn to help pay for the costs of the Boer War and had suffered criticism for doing so. In defending the tariff, Chamberlain hoped to undermine the inviolability of what he termed 'old shibboleths' – an oblique reference to free trade.

This speech occurred just before a Colonial Conference at which Chamberlain yet again failed to convince the visiting Prime Ministers of the case for greater imperial integration. In the autumn of 1902 he left on a tour of South Africa which, contrary to some expectations, turned out to be a considerable success. Returning in early 1903 Chamberlain prepared himself for the launching of his great crusade. In May 1903, once more in Birmingham, he made a momentous speech which unquestionably changed the course of politics in the years up to the First World War. He declared himself in favour of an imperial preference tariff system designed to bring about an economic integration of the Empire. This speech initiated a debate which split the Unionists as a whole, with both Conservatives and Liberal Unionists divided over their response. Balfour attempted to preserve unity by adopting a fence-sitting strategy: he did not wish to break with Chamberlain and his supporters (who now, after all, included mainstream Conservatives), but on the other hand he was personally unconvinced of the case for 'tariff reform'. In any case, his main priority was party unity. While Balfour was using all his political skills (which were not inconsiderable) to keep the Unionists together, the opposing groups were formalising their positions. Chamberlain headed a Tariff Reform

League; the free trade Unionists formed the Unionist Free Food League. Some Unionists, including the young Winston Churchill, decided to defect to the Liberals. The cartoon reflects the nature of the opposition to the idea of abandoning the principle of free trade.

THROUGH THE BIRMINGHAM LOOKING-GLASS.

OFF TO GLASGOW. *(With Apologies to Sir John Tenniel.)*

'Through the Birmingham Looking Glass', *Westminster Gazette*, 6 October 1903

1 *In what ways does the cartoon present an unsympathetic view of the tariff reform campaign?*

2 *How would a supporter of tariff reform have countered the charges made in the cartoon?*

3 *How fully does the cartoon contribute to an understanding of the issues raised in the tariff reform campaign?*

In September 1903, Chamberlain resigned from the Government in order to carry on a full-time campaign in the country at large. Leading free-traders in the Cabinet also resigned, including the Duke of

Devonshire. Balfour's weakened administration limped on unconvincingly until the end of 1905, when, following an unexpectedly good showing in a by-election, Balfour decided to resign without asking for a dissolution and a general election. Balfour's decision was the result of a complex series of calculations based on the confused political situation. Chamberlain's campaign had gained considerable ground within the ranks of the Unionists, but it had stalled badly in the country. The Trade Unions were hostile and there was no evidence to suggest that Chamberlain was converting the nation as a whole to his grand vision. Thus the Unionists remained divided, with no real prospect of resolving their debate, whilst the Liberals had a clear and united opposition to tariff reform which seemed to be in tune with public opinion. In these circumstances Balfour realised that to continue in office much longer, with a general election due no later than the summer of 1907, would be fatal. In November 1905, two of the the Liberal leaders, Campbell-Bannerman and Lord Rosebery, crossed swords publically over the issue of Irish Home Rule, which Rosebery wished to renounce. Balfour hoped that, by forcing the Liberals to take office, he would expose their internal divisions, (not the least of these being over who would actually lead a Liberal administration), and reap the benefit of diverting attention from the Unionists' own difficulties.

The strategy was too subtle for its own good. The Liberals were by no means as divided as they appeared. Rosebery had little or no personal support in the party and Campbell-Bannerman had no real difficulty in forming a government. He was then able to call a general election for January 1906 from a position of unity and strength: he cited the moribund nature of Unionist government since the tariff reform issue had been raised and revived the lingering hostility to the 1902 Education Act. A new scandal in South Africa, concerning the terrible conditions suffered by Chinese immigrant workers, helped to complete the Liberal campaign. 'Chinese Slavery', as the press dubbed it, had little to do with Balfour's administration, but it helped reawaken the scandal of the 'concentration camps', into which Boer civilians had been herded in the recent war, and enabled the Liberals to portray the Unionists as exploiters of the workers. The result was an election triumph for the Liberals on a totally unexpected scale. They won 400 seats; the Unionists were reduced to a mere 157, some two-thirds of whom were Chamberlainite tariff reformers. Balfour himself lost his seat and suffered the indignity of having to fight a further contest at a by-election to get back into the House of Commons. The overall result meant that the Liberals had a clear majority of 130. With the support of the Irish and Labour contingents this would generally rise to over 350. The Unionist catastrophe was complete and could scarcely have been more humiliating.

4 THE LIBERALS IN GOVERNMENT 1905–14

A *The creation of a welfare society*

The Liberals took office in 1905 with a general commitment to the principle of social reform, but with little in the way of specific proposals. In part this was due to the suddenness of the general election, but it also stemmed from the divisions which they had endured in recent years and the potentially controversial nature of new social reform legislation. Advocates of 'New Liberalism', such as David Lloyd George, who entered the Cabinet as President of the Board of Trade in 1905, wished to see a far more interventionist (or collectivist) approach to improving life for the lower classes. More traditional Liberals still clung to the notion of individual effort and enterprise as the means to self-improvement. Although the leading Liberals mostly leaned towards intervention, they were only too aware of the need to move cautiously in the interests of maintaining unity within the parliamentary party.

The debate about the condition of the working classes in 1905 revolved around three basic issues: the condition of children; the condition of the elderly; and the problems associated with poverty resulting from sickness and unemployment. The least controversial of these, by far, was the question of the situation of working-class children. This group was not only the most directly vulnerable in society, it was also the only group which could not be held in any way accountable for its problems. Sickness could be characterised as malingering; unemployment as the result of sheer idleness; even the elderly could be seen as poverty-stricken in old-age because of a lack of thrift during their working lives; none of these accusations could be levelled at children. Even so, some Liberals still instinctively felt that children were solely the responsibility of their parents and that any supportive intervention on their behalf would undermine the basic parental role. Despite such views however, there was a general feeling (in which many Unionists joined) that the pitiful conditions of the poorest working-class children was nothing short of a national disgrace.

The first direct move to alleviate the plight of deprived children came in 1906 with the passing of the Education (Provision of Meals) Act. The issue of malnourished children had increasingly surfaced since the extension of rate aid to all schools and the creation of LEAs in 1902, so that the problem of children too hungry and generally debilitated to benefit from education was well-documented by 1906. However, the 1906 Act was not the result of any preconceived Liberal policy. It resulted from a Private Member's Bill introduced by a Labour MP, which the Government, lacking any concrete proposals of its own, took over and adopted as Government policy. The Act enabled local education authorities to provide school meals for destitute children by levying an additional rate of a halfpenny in the pound, but it was not compulsory and local authorities did not rush to take up this new power which they now enjoyed. By 1911 less than a third of all education authorities were using rates to support school meals provision and by 1914 the Board of Education had taken additional powers to make such provision compulsory.

Meanwhile, in 1907, the Education (Administrative Provisions) Act made medical inspections for children compulsory. Under this Act the Board of Education was able to specify that at least three inspections must take place during a child's school years and that these were to be conducted on school premises and during school hours, with the first inspection coming as soon as possible after the child had started school. The more compulsory nature of this legislation was the result of two factors: first, the established nature of compulsory legislation on public health issues; and, secondly, the sense of urgency engendered by the recruitment of volunteers for the Boer War, which had revealed the appalling health suffered by large numbers of the working-class population. Finally, in 1908, the Children's Act introduced a consolidation of measures to deal with child neglect and abuse and set up juvenile courts and remand homes to remove child offenders from the adult courts and prisons.

These attempts to improve the welfare of children constituted the principal achievements of the Liberals in terms of social legislation during their first two years in office. The Liberals failed in their attempt to introduce an eight-hour day for the mining industry and, although Workmen's Compensation was extended in its scope to cover some six million workers, overall it was not a very impressive record. Certainly some of the more radical Liberals, such as Lloyd George, were less than satisfied. In April 1908, Campbell-Bannerman was forced to resign through ill-health. Asquith was his natural successor and his elevation to the premiership occasioned a general reshuffle of the Cabinet. Lloyd George, who in a short time had built a formidable reputation for administration at the Board of Trade, was promoted to replace Asquith at the Exchequer. In turn, Lloyd George was succeeded at the Board of Trade by Winston Churchill who, since his recent conversion, had established himself as a radical reformer. Lloyd George and Churchill had become close political friends and they were determined to use their new seniority to push for a much more ambitious programme of social reform. Quite apart from the fact that a more progressive policy was what they genuinely wanted, they both also believed that it was a political necessity for the Liberals, in the longer term, to show themselves capable of developing a dynamic policy.

During the last phase of his time as Chancellor of the Exchequer, Asquith had been working on proposals to introduce Old Age Pensions. The budget proposals for 1908 contained provision for financing the introduction of a scheme and it was Lloyd George's good fortune to inherit the responsibility for finalising and presenting the budget details. He then piloted the Old Age Pensions Bill (which was essentially Asquith's Bill), through the Commons. The provision which this legislation made for the poorest of the elderly was limited, especially when set against the length of time it had taken to get any form of assistance provided, outside of the hated Poor Law. The Act provided for pensions of 5s (25p) per week to be paid to those aged 70 or over who had annual incomes of £21 or less. For incomes over £21 a sliding scale of descending, graduated payments would be made up to a ceiling of a £31 annual income, at which point the payments ceased. There were a number of exclusions: those who had claimed poor relief in the previous year or had been in prison in the previous ten years had no entitlement. Also excluded were those who had failed to work regularly. In practice these barriers did not result in much curtailment of the number of claimants. The qualifying period for ex-convicts was subsequently reduced to two years and, by 1914, there were 970 000 claimants, costing the Exchequer £12 million a year.

Once the issue of Old Age Pensions had at last been addressed, however limitedly, Lloyd George was determined to confront the problem of loss of earning due to unemployment and sickness. By the middle of 1908 this was a pressing issue because the general economic situation was becoming difficult for the lower-income groups. Unemployment was rising and wages were static or falling. At the same time, inflation was reducing the real value of wages. At the Board of Trade, Churchill initiated work on the setting up of labour exchanges which eventually resulted in legislation in 1909. Meanwhile, in 1908, Lloyd George went to Germany to study the German system of social insurance at first hand. By the autumn of 1908 civil servants were working on the principles of a scheme to introduce unemployment and sickness insurance. Prominent among them was the young William Beveridge, later the author of the famous 'Beveridge Report' of 1942 which was the blueprint for the introduction of the Welfare State after 1945.

Although work on the schemes was well advanced by 1909 their eventual implementation was delayed until the National Insurance Act of 1911 while the first payments were not made until the summer of 1912 (for unemployment) and the beginning of 1913 (for health). The delay was primarily due to the wish of the leading politicians associated with the legislation (Lloyd George and Churchill) to deal with both sickness and unemployment at the same time. Unemployment insurance was relatively uncontroversial and, standing alone, could probably have been introduced without difficulty in 1909. Sickness benefits, however, were an entirely different matter. There were some powerful vested interests already entrenched in this field. The Friendly Societies, industrial insurance companies and doctors would all be affected by the intrusion of the state into this kind of benefit provision. The insurance companies and friendly societies collected millions of pounds a year in premiums from working-class families and it took months of difficult negotiations for Lloyd George to work out and agree suitable safeguards and compromises with the various companies, who were often as suspicious of each other as they were of the Government. Opposition from the doctors' organisation, the British Medical Association, came mainly at the instigation of the wealthier medical practitioners who feared that the status of their profession might be compromised. However the adoption of the panel system, which allowed insured patients to choose their own doctor from a panel of practitioners under the control of a local health committee, proved popular with the less well-off doctors, especially those in the inner cities, who quickly saw that their incomes must rise from this new source of patients. Thus the BMA, for neither the first time nor the last, were appeased where it counted most – in their members' pockets!

The National Insurance Act was in two distinct parts. Part I dealt with Health Insurance and was the responsibility of the Treasury. Part II dealt with Unemployment Insurance and was the responsibility of the Board of Trade. For health purposes all workers earning less than £160 per year and aged between 16 and 60 were included – around 15 million in all. Weekly contributions were raised from the worker (4d), the employer (3d) and the government (2d). This encouraged Lloyd George to coin the slogan '9d, for 4d,' in his attempts to popularise the concept. The resulting entitlement was: – sickness benefit of 10s (50p) per week for 13 weeks (7s 6d for women); 5s (25p) per week for a further 13 weeks thereafter; a 30s maternity grant; 5s a week disability benefit; and free medical treatment under a panel doctor. Wives and children were not covered by the scheme, nor was hospital treatment, except for admission to a sanatorium which was intended to benefit tuberculosis sufferers. Subsequently, the reduced benefit for the second 13-week period was abolished in favour of full benefit throughout the term of 26 weeks. Unemployment Insurance covered far less workers: a total of some 2¼ million, mainly in construction and engineering trades which were susceptible to fluctuating employment levels. Weekly contributions were 2½d each from workers, employers and the Government, which entitled the insured workers to a payment of 7s per week benefit for up to a maximum of 15 weeks.

The impact of the introduction of these schemes of insurance, plus the provision of labour exchanges, old age pensions and child welfare provision, though in many ways modest in relation to the scale of need they were intended to address, were significant in terms of their implication for government intervention. The State had now assumed an unprecedented degree of responsibility in its relationship to individuals in society. A great expansion in the Civil Service was required to oversee the administration of the new machinery. The sums expended on benefits exceeded all estimates. This welfare legislation entirely circumvented the operations of the Poor Law and, to a considerable degree, appeared to render the question of its reform irrelevant. The

Unionist Government had set up a Royal Commission to examine the Poor Laws in 1905. By the time it reported in 1909 there was little political will in any quarter to consider a major overhauling of the system.

B *The constitutional crisis 1909–11*

The origins of the constitutional crisis, which was triggered by Lloyd George's budget proposals of 1909, did not lie in reactionary opposition to 'New Liberalism' as exemplified by the government's welfare reforms. On the contrary, the Unionist leadership generally welcomed the welfare reforms and even promised to improve upon them if returned to office. The real roots of the crisis lay in the political impotence to which the Unionists were reduced in the House of Commons after the 1906 general election. With only 157 MPs the Unionists were virtually an irrelevance in the Lower House and it was not surprising that they considered how they might use their continued predominance in the Lords to try to redress this imbalance. Balfour's imprudent comment in the heat of the electoral campaign, that 'the great Unionist Party should still control, whether in power or opposition, the destinies of this great Empire', was not intended as a commitment to blanket opposition to a future Liberal Government. Rather it was aimed at the specific issue of Irish Home Rule. Balfour was only too aware that the power of the Lords needed to be used selectively and with caution, if it was to be effective. From 1906 to 1909, therefore, the targets chosen for obstruction by the Unionist peers were identified carefully, in the hope of extracting the maximum embarrassment for the Liberals whilst steering away from issues where the government might secure popular support.

The first confrontation came in 1906 over the government's proposed Education Bill. This amounted to a political pay-off to the Nonconformists for their support following the Education Act of 1902. The government felt indebted to its Nonconformist supporters and was committed to addressing their grievances, despite the fact that some members of the Cabinet privately accepted the value of the 1902 Act. The 1906 Education Bill proposed that all denominational schools should be taken over by the local authorities, who would appoint teachers without applying sectarian tests. No denominational teaching would be allowed, except in limited areas where four-fifths of parents requested it, and even then only where there was sufficient non-denominational provision. This limited latitude to provide denominational religious teaching was designed not to help the Anglican schools, which were most unlikely to be able to benefit from it, but rather to appease the Roman Catholics whose existing schools were already operating over and above the normal local requirement for places.

The provisions of the Education Bill angered the Anglicans as bitterly as the 1902 Act had the Nonconformists. A compromise was sought, with both the Archbishop of Canterbury and the King eventually becoming involved. Balfour had planned that controversial legislation should be opposed initially in the Commons and then amended to reach a compromise in the Lords. In this first test, however, the strategy failed since it proved impossible to hammer out a compromise which both sides could accept. Consequently, the government was forced to withdraw the Bill, which they had seen as forming the centrepiece of their programme for the session. Two other major bills were rejected by the Lords in the period 1906 to 1908: a bill to end plural voting (i.e. the right to vote in more than one constituency) and a licensing bill aimed at further restrictions on the sale and consumption of alchohol. This hardly amounted to a wholesale wrecking of the government's legislative programme. Nor was it arbitrary action, in so far as the targets were carefully selected. Trade Union reform in 1906 (*see page 438*) was allowed to pass, as were the social reforms.

The objective of the Unionists was to try to confuse and demoralise the Liberals and in this they were to some extent successful. By 1907 the government was trying to decide whether or not to confront the peers. One major problem was the lack of a really popular cause with which to appeal to the electorate. The Education Bill was important to certain sections of the Liberal Party, but it was hardly a matter of great moment to the public at large. In 1907, therefore, Campbell-Bannerman did no more than introduce resolutions into the Commons calling for limitations on the power of the Lords to delay, amend or veto legislation. These resolutions were naturally passed by a huge majority, but they remained no more than a warning shot at the Upper House. When the 1908 session of Parliament opened, reform of the House of Lords remained a conspicuous absentee from the government's proposals.

It was not surprising that the government failed to address the issue of the powers of the Lords in 1908, since the Cabinet was entirely undecided as what exactly to do. Some, like Campbell-Bannerman, simply wished to curb the power of the peers over legislation but others, including Sir Edward Grey, preferred to make reform of the composition of the Lords the priority. Some moderate Unionist peers themselves were in favour of the latter course and there had even been a proposal from them to end automatic hereditary entry to the Lords during 1907. This proposition had been opposed by both the government and the more right-wing Unionist peers, though obviously for differing reasons. The right-wing peers opposed any interference with the Lords' powers or composition. The government feared that reform of the composition of the Lords would make it harder in the end to justify a curtailment of their legislative powers.

The political climate in 1907 and 1908 was hardly encouraging for the Liberals. Overall, the trend in by-election results was against them and most commentators expected a considerable Unionist revival when the next general election came, unless the government could do something to turn the tide. Despite the introduction of Old Age Pensions and Child Welfare reform there was little improvement in the political fortunes of the Liberals by the beginning of 1909. The problem was that however worthy these two groups might be as recipients of the government's attention, neither actually amounted to much in electoral terms. The government therefore urgently needed something compelling with which to regain the political initiative. Fortunately for them there was a very obvious issue upon which to make a stand.

The budget for 1909 was going to have to be a major reforming piece of legislation. There was no alternative to this because increasing expenditure on defence, along with increased actual and projected spending on social welfare, meant that taxation had to be increased. The government could not afford politically to cut back in either sector but nor could it fund both (at least not for long) with the existing taxation arrangements. There was also the obvious point that, since budgets were not, by convention, subject to the powers of the Lords, some reforms might be incorporated into it to avoid obstruction in the Upper House. All these issues were already being widely debated in political circles by the end of 1908, including the possibility that the peers might break with convention and reject the budget or at least amend parts of it.

Some of the proposals which eventually found their way into Lloyd George's famous budget of 1909, were projected by Asquith during the final phase of his tenure of the Exchequer. As Lloyd George became increasingly aware of the extent of the future budget deficits which might be looming, so the pressure which he and Asquith exerted on the rest of the Cabinet to agree to an extensive measure grew. Many of their colleagues were less than enthusiastic about some of the proposals and there was a row within the Cabinet (which became public) over naval spending, which Lloyd George wanted to limit as far as possible. It was hardly the best background against which to launch a revival of the government's fortunes and there is little doubt that, far from hoping to invite a confrontation, Lloyd George and Asquith hoped that the budget would strike enough of a balance to pass without attracting the active hostility of the peers.

This, however, was a forlorn hope. Lloyd George proposed to:

(i) raise income tax on incomes over £3000 p.a. to 1s.2d. (6p) from the standard rate of 9d. (4p) whilst additionally bringing in a surtax of 6d. (2½p) in the £ on incomes over £5000 p.a.;

(ii) increase duties on spirits, tobacco, liquor licenses and stamp duties;

(iii) increase death duties on estates valued between £5000 and £1 million;

(iv) introduce land taxes on (a) the increased value of land when it changed hands (20 per cent), (b) the annual value of land (1½d in £), and (c) the annual value of land leased to mining companies (1s in £).

(v) set up a Road Fund by putting taxes on petrol and introducing licenses for motor vehicles.

Lloyd George closed his presentation of the budget with the following comments:-

> The money thus raised is to be expended, first of all, in insuring the inviolability of our shores. It has also been raised in order not merely to relieve but to prevent unmerited distress within those shores. It is essential that we should make every necessary provision for the defence of our country. But surely it is equally imperative that we should make it a country even better worth defending for all and by all ... I am told that no Chancellor of the Exchequer has ever been called on to impose such heavy taxes in a time of peace. This is a War Budget. It is for raising money to wage implacable warfare against poverty and squalidness. I cannot help hoping and believing that before this generation has passed away we shall have advanced a great step towards that good time when poverty and wretchedness and human degradation ... will be as remote to the people of this country as the wolves which once infested its forests.

1 *In what ways does the tone and use of language in this extract suggest that Lloyd George is both conciliatory towards, and yet challenging, any potential opposition?*

2 *What evidence is there that it is aimed at a wider audience than simply the House of Commons?*

Concern about the budget and even opposition to it was more widespread than is generally appreciated in the traditional 'Peers versus the People' version of the constitutional crisis. Many Liberals (including some in the Cabinet) had their doubts; the Irish Nationalist MPs opposed the duty on spirits; the brewers were outraged; the motorists (not as large an aggrieved lobby then, of course, as they have since become) were similarly unimpressed. Most of all it was the landowners who felt that they were being subjected to unfair treatment and they were particularly incensed by Lloyd George's intention to set up a Development Commission, one of whose tasks would be to carry out a comprehensive land valuation survey to provide the basis for calculating the new taxation on land. This seemed to be the thin end of a socialist wedge, which in future years could be used to attack wealth and force a redistribution of property on a significant scale.

Initially Balfour and Lansdowne did not intend that the Lords should go so far as to actually reject the budget. They thought in terms of extracting concessions which would undermine the budget and keep up the mounting pressure on the government. This, however, was a miscalculation. Neither Balfour nor Lansdowne appreciated at first the limited room for manoeuvre which each side had. Lansdowne, in particular, underestimated the intensity of the emotions which had been raised amongst the rank-and-file Unionist peers. A major reason for this was the fact that the Unionist leaders did not view the budget in quite the same way as their supporters. To the latter the budget proposals were an offence against the sanctity of property; the former were much more concerned about the future political implications which the proposals raised for Unionist policies.

The crux of the problem was that by 1909 Unionism had effectively been won over to tariff reform. One of the key arguments in the armoury of the tariff reformers was the idea that larger-scale social reform could only be funded effectively through the revenue which would accrue to government through tariffs. The Liberals' budget, by proposing a method of funding social reform whilst preserving free trade, therefore cut right to the heart of the popular appeal of tariff reform. The government knew this only too well of course and saw that this was a golden opportunity to underpin free trade once and for all and land the Unionists with a dead weight of political irrelevance around their necks. Thus the budget crisis of 1909 was in essence an extension of the Free Trade versus Protection debate and both sides believed that their political fortunes were at stake in its outcome.

It was the Unionists who were in the most difficult position. Their case was difficult to put in a popular campaign since it involved some fairly complex arguments over the relationship between tariff reform, taxation, and spending on both social welfare and defence. The government had the much easier task of presenting the issue as simply one of the selfishness of a privileged class. By-elections in the summer of 1909 showed a swing to the Liberals and underlined the fact that the government was winning the argument in the country. Balfour and Lansdowne were increasingly driven into a corner. Surrender would split the party because of the expectations of resistance which had been raised. Resistance could only lead to a constitutional crisis. In the event the matter was taken out of their hands since Lansdowne effectively lost control of the Unionist peers. In November 1909 the Lords rejected the budget and Asquith immediately asked for a dissolution of Parliament.

The general election of January 1910 produced results which were unsatisfactory for almost everybody. The Liberals won 275 seats; the Unionists 273, Labour won 40; only the Irish could take much encouragement since, with 82 seats, they now held the balance of power. The Liberals could continue in office but only as a minority government. Worse still, Asquith had failed to get the King to agree to a mass creation of peers if the Lords refused to accept constitutional changes limiting their powers, a measure which the government now had no choice but to introduce. This meant that if the peers refused to accept any limitation to their role, another general election would be needed before mass-creation could be threatened. In view of the result of the election the Lords had no choice but to pass the budget, but the battle had now moved on to the question of their powers and the rank and file showed no inclination to moderate their new liking for confrontation.

The Parliament Bill which the government introduced in 1910 contained no surprises. It was based on the Campbell-Bannerman resolutions of 1907 and provided for the statutory exclusion of the Lords from voting on financial legislation and a limit of two rejections or amendments on other legislation in successive sessions within the life of a Parliament. The maximum duration of a parliament was reduced from seven to five years. In essence this meant that the Lords could expect to delay legislation for a minimum period of two years, assuming that the proposals were immediately passed again by the Commons after each rejection as long as there was no general election in the interim. The Lords resisted this to the bitter end but to no avail. The death of King Edward VII in May 1910 gave them a temporary respite since Asquith was anxious not to appear to be pressing the new King, George V, too soon on the question of creating new peers. However, the delay was brief and by the end of 1910 Asquith was ready to call a second election, this time armed with the mandate to create as many new peers as might be necessary to see the Parliament Bill through.

The result of the general election of December 1910 produced no real change in the political balance. The Irish and Labour both advanced marginally to 84 and 42 seats respectively; The Liberals and Unionists tied on 272 seats each. This left the government in position to force through the bill. In August 1911, after Asquith had publically threatened a mass creation of peers, the Parliament Bill was finally passed. Even then some of the moderate (or more responsible) Unionist peers had to be drafted in to vote for the government in order to ensure that the bill was not voted down by the 'last-ditchers', some of whom by now had so lost their grip on reality that they preferred to bring the Lords to Armageddon rather than relent.

The constitutional crisis was a classic case of political miscalculations which led to political passions running out of control. This was most obviously the case on the Unionist side, but the government had also miscalculated, at the start, the impact which the budget would have and Asquith was eventually forced into threatening a mass-creation of peers which was very much against his inclination. Lloyd George raised passions to fever pitch during the summer of 1909 with highly provocative speeches designed to whip up support for the budget and put pressure on the Lords. However, despite his revolutionary utterances, Lloyd George was not really intent on destroying the wealthy classes. On the contrary, during the same period, he was employing his considerable abilities to the task of becoming wealthy himself! During 1910 the political leaders on both sides had tried, behind the scenes, to get a grip on the situation and restore some order to the political chaos.

Between June and November 1910 a series of meetings was held between the Liberal and Unionist leadership aimed at finding a compromise. This process, known as the 'Constitutional Conference', failed in the end to find a solution but it was indicative of the realisation on both sides that things were getting out of hand. In August, Lloyd George proposed a coalition government be set up, with an agenda covering all the major issues of the day – economic, social and constitutional – so as to seek consensus solutions for them all. Balfour was much attracted to this idea in theory but doubted whether it was practical given the political climate. Asquith was also interested, but both leaders found a hostile response within their parties and the scheme came to nothing.

The outcome of the constitutional crisis was scarcely revolutionary. Its most immediate effect, as was seen in chapter X, was on the Irish Question. It did not result in a flood of legislation needing to be forced through the Lords, indeed the main reforming zeal of the Liberals had exhausted itself by 1911. Its chief victim was Balfour, who paid the penalty for a failed campaign which he had never wanted in the first place! Late in 1911, faced with mounting criticism of his leadership, he decided upon a dignified stepping down rather than awaiting the inevitable and distasteful coup. He was succeeded by the relatively unknown Andrew Bonar Law, who had only entered Parliament in 1900, and whose chief qualification at that point was that he was a compromise between the two leading figures Walter Long and Austen Chamberlain (eldest son of the great Joe), who had fairly even support among the rank and file. Neither would agree to withdraw in favour of the other, so in the end, on Chamberlain's suggestion, they both withdrew leaving the field to Bonar Law, whom few had initially supposed had any chance. The crisis cost the Liberals their overall majority and exposed them to the demands of the Irish Nationalists. The reputations of their leaders, particularly Asquith and Lloyd George, were enhanced, but the necessity for dealing immediately with the question of Irish Home Rule ruled out any chance there might have been of further measures of domestic reform.

c *The women's suffrage campaign*

One issue which the Liberals totally failed to come to grips with was the difficult matter of the claim of women to the parliamentary franchise. On the surface it appeared to be a fairly straightforward matter of basic logic and individual rights. During the second half of the nineteenth century women had made steady, if unspectacular, progress in legal and educational emancipation. The employment of women in clerical posts had expanded enormously and they had even made some inroads in the professions. Political rights were an obvious target for similar progress. The question of granting the parliamentary franchise to women on the same terms as men in borough seats was raised during the passage of the 1867 Reform Act and, though rejected, the illogicality of a system which granted votes to men, who might in their turn be employed by women, was obvious enough. In 1869 women gained the vote in town council elections in the municipal boroughs and they then gained the right of election to School Boards (1870) and as Poor Law Guardians (1875). They were included in the local government franchise in 1889, although they did not have the right to take office on the new County and County Borough Councils.

There were two main schools of thought amongst those who wished to see the political emancipation of women. One argued for the immediate inclusion of women in the franchise on the same terms as men. The other wished to press for complete adult suffrage which would bring in the remaining excluded men at the same time. The danger of this second option, from the women's point of view, was that it opened up the risk that the end result would be complete adult male suffrage, with the claim of women still ignored. This divergence of view led to a split within the ranks of female suffragists. Emmeline Pankhurst, the widow of a long-time radical campaigner for women's rights, formed a new movement called the Womens' Social and Political Union in 1903. Mrs Pankhurst had already broken an earlier connection with the Liberals, in favour of the Independent Labour Party (*see page* 433), which she saw as a better vehicle for her aims of economic and social equality for women. Assisted by her daughters Christabel and Sylvia, she mobilised the WSPU to press the issue of the female suffrage within the Independent Labour Party.

The problem for the Pankhursts was that the ILP was itself divided, and even ambivalent, about the issue. Most of the leaders were genuinely in favour of the basic concept; some, however, like Keir Hardie, were sympathetic to the Pankhurst demand for immediate female suffrage on terms of equality with men, while others, such as Philip Snowden, later to be a Labour Chancellor of the Exchequer, preferred to wait for complete adult suffrage. Whichever view they took, the ILP leaders were also uncomfortably aware of the extent of hostility to female equality amongst working-class males, particularly within the trades unions, where female industrial equality was seen as unthinkable! In 1905 Keir Hardie introduced a private member's bill to extend the vote to women on the existing franchise. This was the highpoint of WSPU/ILP collaboration as Mrs Pankhurst worked with Keir Hardie to promote the bill. Its loss was a foregone conclusion, of course, and the lack of real enthusiasm for it within the ILP at large soured relations. The WSPU helped Labour candidates in the 1906 campaign but Mrs Pankhurst was now convinced that women must seize the initiative themselves and secure their own political destiny.

When the Liberals came to power in 1905, they were also divided over female suffrage. Some, still following Gladstone's views, were opposed to it altogether whilst others, although sympathetic, were uncertain how best to proceed. For the Liberals the dilemma was that any piecemeal or gradual enfranchisement of women based on property qualifications of any kind seemed most likely to benefit the Unionists. The results of granting full adult suffrage were incalculable, especially with the Labour Party's ultimate political appeal still an unknown quantity. In the 1906 election many Liberal candidates expressed their support for female suffrage, fuelling hopes among women campaigners that legislation might soon materialise. This was a false hope. In reality the Liberal Government had no intention, in 1906, of raising a political controversy over female suffrage any more than over Ireland (*see page 315*). The most they would do was to remove the obvious anomaly of the exclusion of women from the local councils, by passing the Qualification of Women Act of 1907. This was naturally welcomed by the WSPU, but it hardly constituted a great leap forward in itself, nor was it an acceptable commitment for the future.

Frustrated by the lack of progress the WSPU became more militant. Harassment of politicians at meetings, already employed during the 1906 campaign, was intensified. From such traditional tactics the WSPU graduated on to attacks on property: window-smashing, arson and destruction of mail. Pepper-filled letters were despatched to politicians to provide a literally irritating reminder, to the recipients, of the women's displeasure with the lack of progress. The more aggressive the WSPU became however, the harder any kind of concession became or, at least, the easier it became to justify inaction. The more entrenched the government became the more intense the anger of the women became. Criminal proceedings resulted in imprisonments which led to hunger strikes, which in turn led the prison authorities to resort to force-feeding. It was an unpalatable state of affairs for any government, least of all one calling itself 'Liberal', but, as with the constitutional crisis, neither side had a great deal of room for manouevre.

Again, following the pattern of the constitutional crisis, both sides tried to extricate themselves from the mess. After the campaign leading up to the 1910 general election, during which Liberal ministers had come in for some rough treatment at the hands of women activists, the WSPU called for a truce in the hope that the gesture would ease the deadlock. Parliament, rather than the government, responded with a 'Conciliation' Bill drafted by an all-party committee. It proposed the enfranchisement of women, on the basis of either a householder or occupation franchise, and would have meant in practice nearly 8 per cent of women getting the vote. On its second reading this proposal had a majority of 110. The WSPU welcomed the Bill and had high hopes that it was the long-awaited breakthrough. However, the Bill was doomed to failure because some leading Cabinet ministers opposed it from the start. Asquith was against it: he was not a supporter of female suffrage anyway and had been deeply angered by the militancy of the recent campaigns. To him, concessions now smacked of giving in to fanatics. Other leading Liberals, like Lloyd George, were against it because they saw it as enfranchising the most conservative-minded sections of women and in the long-run detrimental to the Liberals' electoral well-being. It is only fair to point out that Sylvia Pankhurst, the most socialist-minded of the Pankhurst clan, who was by now emersed in her work among the poor of East London and less involved with the suffrage campaign as such, also doubted the wisdom of the bill for this same reason. Asquith's opposition ended the hopes for a Conciliation Bill in 1910. He made vague promises of a government bill to replace it but would not commit himself to a timetable.

The loss of the Conciliation Bill ended the truce which had been declared by the WSPU. There was a mass demonstration and some violent episodes at the end of 1910, after which the truce was resumed in the hope of a fresh initiative. Asquith's next move, however, was to announce, at the end of 1911, the introduction of a Franchise Bill in the next session of Parliament. This was to be aimed at full adult male suffrage. The WSPU was incensed and, from this point onwards, the bitter confrontation between them and the government continued unabated until the outbreak of the First World War, when the Pankhursts changed tack and, adopting a suitably patriotic line, pressed for the fuller participation of women in the war effort. In the meantime, the government withdrew the Franchise Bill and opted for the abolition of plural voting instead.

The failure to make progress on female suffrage, the deterioration of the campaign into terrorism and the dubious morality of force-feeding made this a grim and discreditable episode in political life before the First World War. The government was reduced to 'illiberal' expedients such as the 'Cat and Mouse' Act of 1913, under which women on hunger-strike were released and then rearrested, to try to control the situation. The WSPU leaders became hunted refugees and Christabel Pankhurst fled to Paris to continue her direction of operations. The main blame for the situation, as it existed by 1914, must lie with Asquith, as Prime Minister, because he had passed over the chance to engineer some kind of compromise out of the Conciliation Bill in 1910. That crucial opportunity was missed largely on his insistence. A lesser responsibility lies with the leadership of the WSPU for allowing their campaign to get so far out of hand that their actions began to blur the essential justice of their demands.

5 British Politics on the Eve of the First World War

A *Confrontation and consensus*

Much of this chapter has been concerned with confrontation. It deals with a period in which issues were raised that are discussed in other chapters (e.g. Ireland in chapter X and Labour and the Trades Unions in chapter XIII) and there is also a very strong flavour of confrontation to be found in that coverage. In particular, the relationship between Liberalism and Unionism seems to have been one of unremitting hostility over a period of years. The raising of the issue of tariff reform by Joseph Chamberlain and its eventual adoption, albeit cautiously and rather non-committally by the Unionist Party, seemed to polarise party principles into the apparently irreconcilable corners of free trade and protection. The constitutional crisis formalised that division and led into the bitter period of confrontation surrounding the Ulster crisis of 1912–14. On the eve of the First World War, therefore, it would seem at first sight that the principal political parties had never been further apart in their policies and rarely more mutually hostile in their attitude to each other.

The bitter climate of party politics was real enough. It worried many contemporaries who saw in it the seeds of the disintegration of the political system. Few could have predicted, in the middle of 1914, that a war would soon engulf Europe and render irrelevant, temporarily at least, the issues over which these divisions had emerged. Lloyd George's proposal for a coalition government, dismissed as impractical in 1910, became a reality in 1915 under the pressure of war, and coalitions, in one guise or another, were to rule the country for 21 out of the next 30 years. Of course, the circumstances which brought these coalitions about and then kept them together were exceptional, but the ease with which politicians of all parties slipped into coalitions reveals something deeper about the nature of politics in the period before the First World War.

The reality was that, underneath the veneer of hostility, there was a greater degree of consensus than the confrontational atmosphere would suggest. This was particularly true of the leadership of the parties. Their clashes in public seem to be the very epitome of the highly-charged political atmosphere. Yet all the time, behind the scenes, these very leaders were to be found seeking compromises and conciliations which were often wrecked, not by their own divisions or hostilities, but by the nature of the problems they were seeking to resolve. For example, during the constitutional crisis the failure to reach a compromise was largely due to the fact that neither side could afford, politically, to be seen to be giving in, rather than to the existence of a genuinely unbridgeable gulf. During the Ulster crisis it was the entrenched positions of the Irish Nationalists and the Ulster Unionists which made progress in the 1914 negotiations impossible.

On a broad range of issues there was a remarkable degree of consensus amongst the major politicians on both sides. The Unionists were more willing to consider social reform than is often supposed and, after 1903, free traders and tariff reformers within the Unionist Party sought to outbid each other with promises of social reform. Once the economy went into a slump between 1907 and 1910 the Unionists, by now committed to some kind of new deal on tariffs, linked their policy to social reform and tried to outbid the Liberals on the issue. In fact, the desire to preserve *laissez-faire* values in social policy was stronger amongst the more traditional Liberals than it was amongst the Unionists. The demand for female suffrage found both supporters and opponents amongst the Liberals and Unionists and both sides were ultimately more concerned about the practical political problems that the issue posed than they were about the moral principle.

Even the division between Liberalism and Unionism over protection and free trade was not so clear-cut as it appeared. The adherence of the Liberal leadership to free trade was a political necessity. Privately, leaders such as Asquith and Lloyd George knew that there was a case to be made for the reform of fiscal policy: specifically, the methods by which government revenue was obtained. The budget of 1909 was barely sufficient to meet the projected spending requirements of immediate policies. Even with Lloyd George's 'unprecedented' tax increases, the government still required a £3 million transfer from the Sinking Fund (the money set aside for paying off the National Debt) in order to balance the books. It was perfectly obvious that some other method of raising revenue would be needed in the longer term if further social reform was to be contemplated. The Unionist answer was tariff reform. The socialist solution was never an option for the Liberals, (even the Labour Party leaders could not bring themselves to face that fully!), therefore they had to be prepared to think about that which was officially 'unthinkable'. Lloyd George once remarked to a close colleague that he did not regard free trade as 'sacred' and his inclusion of the question of tariffs as part of his agenda for a coalition government in 1910 was a tacit recognition of this reality.

The picture that emerges of political life in the period before the First World War is one in which the two main parties were both as divided internally as they were from each other. This is especially true of the relationships between the party leaders and their respective followers. Both Liberal and Unionist leaders had to face the problem of trying to reconcile conflicting attitudes within their parliamentary parties and in the constituencies at large. Frequently it was not simply a case of trying to accommodate differing opinions, but also of trying to force party members to abandon their intransigence and face up to political realities. It is hardly surprising in these circumstances that the party leaders frequently found it easier to deal with each other, than to satisfy the demands of their own supporters

B *Was the Liberal Party doomed in 1914?*

This question has caused controversy amongst historians ever since the appearance of Trevor Wilson's book, *The Downfall of the Liberal Party, 1914–35.* Wilson argued that the decline of the Liberal Party was the result of the political damage caused by divisions within the party (principally between Lloyd George and Asquith) which were themselves brought about by the impact of the First World War. This interpretation directly contradicted the conventional view, originally put forward by GR Dangerfield in his famous book *The Strange Death of Liberal England,* which had first appeared in 1936. According to Dangerfield, the crucial period in the Liberal decline was 1911–14, following the constitutional crisis, during which the basic inadequacies of liberal philosophy had rendered the Government incapable of governing effectively. Until the publication of Wilson's book, the decline of the Liberal Party had received little attention from Labour historians since it had been assumed that the fall of the party could be satisfactorily explained by the Dangerfield thesis and as the natural result of the rise of the Labour Party. It had been further assumed, by some, that the decline had begun much earlier than Dangerfield had supposed, and that the impact of the First World War had been to act as the accelerator of a natural process of political evolution, or natural selection, in which the Labour Party, as the fittest instrument for advancing social reform and representing working-class aspirations, had simply inherited the role of opposition to the forces of conservatism.

Following the publication of the 'Wilson thesis' a number of historians began to develop the theme that the Liberal Party had still had a viable future in British politics on the eve of the War. These historians, for the most part, concentrated on the invigorating impact of 'New Liberalism' in order to argue that the party had freed itself, by the Edwardian era, of the limitations which had been imposed on it by Gladstonian principles, and had instead become a party with a particularly relevant message and undoubted electoral appeal in an increasingly democratic and class-based political climate. The clear implication of this view was that the Labour Party was destined either to remain a minor third force on the political fringe or to be absorbed through coalition or fusion into the greater body of the Liberal Party. Such a concept naturally incensed those Labour historians for whom the destiny of the Labour Party was an unquestionable inevitability. A series of studies, intended to counter Wilson's 'heresy', culminated, in 1974, in the publication of Ross McKibbin's *The Evolution of the Labour Party 1910–1924.*

The central thrust of this counter-attack was to emphasise the extent to which the Labour Party was a competitor, rather than a collaborator, with the Liberals and to insist that Labour was making genuine inroads into Liberal support. This argument rests upon analyses of Labour progress in local elections and by-elections during the period 1911 to 1914, and on studies of local politics which show that rivalry between the Liberals and Labour at local level was often intense. Meanwhile, less ideologically committed historians have also contributed to the debate about the long-term survival of the Liberal Party by questioning the strength of enthusiasm for the principles of New Liberalism amongst traditional Liberal supporters and party activists.

Supporters of Liberal Party survivalism have tried, in their turn, to counter the attacks on the Wilson thesis by arguing that, but for the outbreak of war in 1914, the Liberals would have sustained or even increased their electoral appeal. Certainly there is no doubt that the Liberal Government intended to embark upon a major political offensive in the period before the First World War. It was Lloyd George, inevitably, who supplied the strategy. In 1912 he began to revive the idea of land reform. The intention was to offer a comprehensive package of reforms, including a guaranteed minimum wage for agricultural workers with rent tribunals to ensure fair rents and, possibly, even arrange for deductions to be made directly from rental income to fund the minimum wage. Lloyd George also intended to include urban land in the reforms, though he had no specific ideas for this more complex area. Initially he merely indicated that he hoped that rural land reform would help to halt the flow of migrants from the land to the towns and thus help to raise urban wages. Lloyd George intended the land campaign to be the centrepiece of the Liberal revival which would carry them through the next general election, due by the end of 1915 at the latest. He set up a Land Enquiry Committee to provide detailed information and proposals. The committee, however, was not an independent group. It was a political body appointed and directed by Lloyd George and even financed privately by some of his wealthy political associates.

The land campaign was specifically intended to damage the Unionists electorally. It aimed to shore up Liberal support in the rural constituencies as well as play on the sympathies of the urban working class. It was also intended to exacerbate divisions amongst the Unionists, who found it difficult to respond with land reform initiatives of their own, without risking the alienation of at least some of their supporters. However, the need for some kind of initiative of this kind was pressing. By 1912 it was apparent that land taxation as envisaged in the 1909 budget was never going to raise the amount of revenue needed to fund even the existing provision of social welfare, let alone any extension of it. The National Insurance scheme was far from popular with many sections of the working classes, especially the lower paid such as agricultural labourers, who found the contributions a burden. Liberalism desperately needed a new electoral appeal and, by 1914, the evidence of by-elections seemed to suggest that the land campaign was having the desired effect. Moreover, the Unionists were openly divided between those supporting the Unionist Social Reform Committee, who wished to respond to Lloyd George's campaign with their own radical proposals, and members of the reactionary 'Land Union' who were still hoping to commit the party to the repeal of the 1909 land taxes.

Ultimately the question of the electoral strength and viability of the Liberal Party, in 1914, remains a matter of historical judgement upon which historians are bound to disagree. Because of the First World War, the effect of the land campaign must remain a matter of speculation since its impact in a general election was never put to the test. Similarly, we cannot be certain that the progress made by the Labour Party before 1914, at local level and in by-elections, provides a genuine guide to its likely fortunes in a general election. All we can say is that success in local and by-elections is not a sure indicator that similar success would be sustained in a general election. On balance there would appear to be no clear evidence to suggest that the Liberals were already in irreversible decline in 1914. Even leading members of the Labour Party, such as Ramsay MacDonald, did not rule out an ultimate alliance with the Liberals at that stage. Similarly, the land campaign, though not conclusive in outcome, clearly shows that the Liberals were capable of launching and sustaining a significant new programme to seize the initiative in matters of social and economic policy.

6 BIBLIOGRAPHY

E J Feuchtwanger *Democracy and Empire: Britain 1865–1914* (Edward Arnold, 1985). The last three chapters relate to this period and are stimulating and challenging reading.
Robert Blake *The Conservative Party from Peel to Thatcher* (Fontana Press, 1985). Chapters 5 and 6 provide excellent coverage of the Unionist years.
Judith Loades (ed.) *The Life and Times of David Lloyd George* (Headstart History, 1990). A collection of short studies published to coincide with the centenary of Lloyd George's first election to the House of Commons. Ian Packer's contribution on the period 1912–14 is particularly valuable.
John Grigg, *Lloyd George – The People's Champion 1902–12* (Methuen, 1978). The second volume (of three so far) provides not only a detailed biographical study but a useful analysis of the political context in which Lloyd George operated.
G R Searle *The Liberal Party – Triumph and Disintegration, 1886–1929*

(Macmillan) chapters 5 and 6 examine the ministries of Campbell-Bannerman and Asquith and the problems facing them.

7 DISCUSSION POINTS AND ESSAY QUESTIONS

A

1 What advantages did Tariff Reform and Imperial Preference have over Free Trade for Britain in this period?
2 Was the result of the 1906 general election a genuine triumph for Liberalism?
3 Were the Liberals the champions of the lower classes or merely shoring-up the existing system against the threat of socialism?
4 Does the budget of 1909 deserve the title 'the Peoples' Budget'?
5 Was the outcome of the constitutional crisis more damaging to the Liberals or the Unionists?
6 Why were both the Liberals and the Unionists so interested in social reform issues during this period?
7 Was the WSPU a negative or positive factor in the cause of female political emancipation?
8 Was the Liberal Party a 'Party in decline' by 1914?
9 Was Britain in danger of social disintegration at any point during this period?

B *Essay questions*

1 'Joseph Chamberlain's role in British politics, during the period 1895 to 1906, was essentially destructive'. Discuss
2 Why did the Unionists suffer such a devastating defeat in the general election of 1906?
3 How significant was the influence of 'New Liberalism' between 1906 and 1911?
4 To what extent was the constitutional crisis of 1909–11 the result of social class antagonisms?
5 Why did women fail to achieve the right to the parliamentary franchise before the First World War?

8 DOCUMENTARY EXERCISE – LLOYD GEORGE AND A PRE-WAR COALITION?

In his war memoirs, written and published in the early 1930s, Lloyd George looked back on the period before the First World War and reflected on his plan for a party truce and a coalition based on conciliation and consensus:

In the year 1910 we were beset by an accumulation of grave issues – rapidly becoming graver ... It was becoming evident to discerning eyes that the Party and Parliamentary system was unequal to coping with them ... the shadow of unemployment was rising ... Our international rivals were forging ahead at a great rate and jeopardising our hold on the markets of the world. ... Our working population ... were becoming sullen with discontent ... we were growing more dependent on overseas supplies for our food ... A great Constitutional struggle over the House of Lords threatened revolution at home, another threatened civil war at our doors in Ireland. Great nations were arming feverishly ... Were we prepared for all the terrifying contingencies?

Moved by this prospect I submitted to Mr Asquith a Memorandum urging that a truce should be declared between the Parties for the purpose of securing the co-operation of the leading party statesmen in a settlement of our national problems – Second Chamber, Home Rule, the development of our agricultural resources, National Training for Defence, the remedying of social evils, and a fair and judicial enquiry into the working of our financial system. [i.e. tariff reform.] Mr Asquith regarded the proposal with considerable favour ... the only Cabinet Ministers who were called into consultation were Lord Crewe, Sir Edward Grey, Lord Haldane and Mr. Winston Churchill ... They all approved of the idea in principle, and it was agreed that the proposal should be submitted to Mr Balfour ... Mr Balfour was by no means hostile; in fact he went a long way towards indicating that, personally, he regarded the proposal with a considerable measure of approval ... he consulted some of his leading colleagues ... Lord Lansdowne, Lord Cawdor, Lord Curzon, Mr Walter Long and Mr Austen Chamberlain favoured the plan ... But when Mr Balfour proceeded later to sound the opinion of less capable and therefore more narrowly partisan members of his party, he encountered difficulties which proved insurmountable ... and there was an end to it. It very nearly came off. It was not rejected by the real leaders ... There is much to be said for the Party system ... But there are times when it stands seriously in the way of the highest national interests.

1 *In what ways does the evidence in this source counter the view that a vast gulf separated the Liberals and Unionists before the First World War?*

2 *How reliable is this evidence?*

3 *What light does the evidence shed on the workings of the political system in the period before the First World War?*

TIME LINE

	Domestic (including Irish) Policy
1812	
1815	Corn Laws introduced: import of foreign corn banned until domestic price exceeds 80s. per quarter.
1817	Upsurge of Radicalism (Blanketeers; Pentrich Rising) leads to harsh Government reaction.
1818	
1819	August – Peterloo 'Massacre'; November – 'Six Acts' passed.
1820	Death of George III: George IV succeeds; Queen Caroline affair; Cato Street Conspiracy.
1822	Castlereagh commits suicide.
1823	O'Connell founds Irish Catholic Association; 'Master and Servant' Act.
1824	Repeal of Combination Acts.
1827	Liverpool suffers stroke and resigns.
1828	January – Goderich resigns; repeal of Test and Corporation Acts; O'Connell wins County Clare election.
1829	Catholic Emancipation granted; Metropolitan Police founded.
1830	Death of George IV; William IV succeeds; Wellington forced to resign after extreme anti-reform speech; 'Swing' riots in southern agricultural counties.
1831	First Reform Bill introduced; sweeping Whig victory in general election (May); Lords' rejection of the Bill (October) leads to riots.
1832	Commons pass Reform Bill but Lords obstructive; Grey resigns, and 'Days of May' follow; Grey returns and Lords pass the bill; general election leads to large Whig majority.
1833	Factory Act; abolition of slavery.
1834	Poor Law Amendment Act; Tolpuddle Martyrs deported; Grey resigns, Melbourne succeeds him but is dismissed by the King in November; Tamworth Manifesto.
1835	General election sees Conservative gains but the Lichfield House compact forces Peel to resign; Municipal Corporations Act.
1837	William IV succeeded by Queen Victoria; New Poor Law applied in the North; Feargus O'Connor starts *Northern Star*.
1838	Anti-Corn Law League founded; Peoples Charter published.
1839	Chartist National Convention opens but Parliament rejects Petition (July); Bull Ring riots in Birmingham; Newport Rising crushed; hundreds of Chartists arrested.
1840	National Charter Association established.
1841	Conservatives win general election.

Foreign Policy	
Treaty of Chaumont agrees terms of peace settlement following French defeat.	1812
Wellington defeats Napoleon at Waterloo; Congress of Vienna; Second Treaty of Paris.	1815
	1817
Congress of Aix-la-Chappelle.	1818
	1819
Revolutions in Spain and Italy; Troppau Congress.	1820
Congress of Verona.	1822
	1823
	1824
Treaty of London to protect Greeks against Turks.	1827
Battle of Navarino.	1828
	1829
Revolution in France.	1830
	1831
Palmerston fails to get Cabinet support for helping Turkey against Mehemet Ali.	1832
Treaty of Unkiar Skelessi.	1833
	1834
	1835
	1837
	1838
Opium War with China; second Mehemet Ali crisis begins.	1839
	1840
Straits Convention signed.	1841

	Domestic (including Irish) Policy
1842	Second Chartist petition rejected; strike wave in the North; Complete Suffrage Union formed; Peel's 'great budget' introduces income tax.
1843	Agitation for Repeal of The Union in Ireland; O'Connell arrested.
1844	
1845	Peel increases grant to Maynooth College; Irish Famine begins; Chartist Land Company formed.
1846	Repeal of Corn Laws splits Conservative Party and Peel resigns (June).
1847	Ten Hours Act; Feargus O'Connor elected MP for Nottingham.
1848	Chartist meeting on Kennington Common; Third Petition rejected; Public Health Act.
1850	Death of Sir Robert Peel.
1851	Great Exhibition; formation of Amalgamated Society of Engineers.
1852	Palmerston undermines Russell's government; Derby's government defeated after rejection of Disraeli's budget.
1853	Gladstone's first budget enhances his reputation.
1854	
1855	Aberdeen's coalition government resigns under criticism for its handling of Crimean War.
1856	
1858	Whig–Liberal rifts bring Palmerston down.
1859	Disraeli's Reform Bill defeated; Whigs, Peelites and Liberals join to form Liberal Party; Derby's government defeated in June.
1860	
1861	Repeal of Paper Duties.
1863	
1864	Gladstone's speech in favour of Parliamentary reform.
1865	Palmerston dies.
1866	Fenian unrest in Ireland; Liberals defeated in Parliament.
1867	Second Reform Act passed; Fenian attacks in England; first Trades Union Congress (TUC) held in Manchester.
1868	Liberals, led by Gladstone, win general election.
1869	Disestablishment of the (Anglican) Church of Ireland.
1870	First Irish Land Act; Elementary Education Act; Civil Service Reforms.
1871	Trade Union Act and Criminal Law Amendment Act; University Tests Act; abolition of purchase in the Army.
1872	Secret ballot introduced; Licensing Act.

Foreign Policy	
Opium War ends.	1842
	1843
Visit of Tsar to London.	1844
	1845
	1846
	1847
Revolts in Europe disrupt the diplomatic system.	1848
Don Pacifico debate in Parliament.	1850
Palmerston dismissed from Foreign Office.	1851
	1852
	1853
Start of Crimean War.	1854
Sebastopol captured by Allies.	1855
Treaty of Paris ends Crimean War; Anglo-Chinese War.	1856
	1858
British support for Italian unification.	1859
Anglo-French Trade Treaty.	1860
	1861
Palmerston tries to deter Prussia from intervention in Schleswig-Holstein.	1863
Prussia resolves Schleswig-Holstein problem by force.	1864
	1865
	1866
	1867
	1868
	1869
Outbreak of Franco-Prussian War.	1870
France defeated by Prussia; Gladstone opts for policy of non-intervention.	1871
Settlement of Anglo-US dispute over the *Alabama* affair.	1872

	Domestic (including Irish) Policy
1873	Gladstone resigns after defeat of Irish University Act but Disraeli refuses to form a minority government.
1874	General election leads to Conservative victory; two 'Lib-Labs', both trade unionists, elected to Parliament; emergence of Irish National Party as dominant force among Irish MPs in Parliament.
1875	Public Health Act; Artisans' Dwellings Act; Sale of Food and Drugs Act; Merchant Shipping Act; Conspiracy and Protection of Property Act; Employers and Workmen Act replaces Master and Servant Legislation.
1876	Disraeli created Earl of Beaconsfield.
1877	National Liberal Federation founded by Joseph Chamberlain.
1878	Derby resigns as foreign secretary and is succeeded by Salisbury.
1879	Irish Land League formed.
1880	Liberals win general election.
1881	Second Irish Land Act; suspension of *Habeas Corpus* in Ireland; Parnell imprisoned; death of Beaconsfield (Disraeli).
1882	'Kilmainham Treaty'; Phoenix Park murders.
1883	Corrupt and Illegal Practices Act.
1884	Third Reform Act; Formation of Social Democratic Federation, The Socialist League and The Fabian Society.
1885	Parliamentary reform completed by Redistribution Act; Gladstone resigns; his commitment to Home Rule is revealed. General election (Nov.) indecisive.
1886	Liberals and Irish Nationalists unite to defeat Conservatives; Gladstone's Home Rule splits Liberals and government is defeated (June); general election – Conservatives and Liberal Unionists have 100+ seat majority over Liberals and Irish Nationalists.
1887	Queen Victoria's Golden Jubilee.
1888	Local Government Act; women matchworkers strike in London.
1889	London Dock Strike.
1890	Divorce scandal wrecks Parnell's career.
1891	Liberals adopt the 'Newcastle Programme'; Parnell dies; introduction of free elementary education.
1892	General election – Liberals and Irish Nationalists have majority over Conservatives and Liberal Unionists; Keir Hardie elected as Independent Labour MP.
1893	Second Home Rule Bill rejected by House of Lords; first meeting of the Independent Labour Party.

Foreign Policy	
	1873
	1874
Purchase of Suez Canal shares by Disraeli; start of new 'Eastern crisis'.	1875
Gladstone publishes his pamphlet on *The Bulgarian Horrors*; Queen Victoria made Empress of India.	1876
Russia declares war on Turkey.	1877
March – Treaty of San Stefano. June – Congress of Berlin revises terms of San Stefano; Britain takes control of Cyprus; Afghan War begins.	1878
British defeat by Zulus at Isandhlwana; Gladstone, in Midlothian campaign, denounces Disraeli's foreign policy.	1879
	1880
Britain defeated in S. Africa; Pretoria Convention.	1881
British Navy bombards Alexandria.	1882
Rebellion in the Sudan.	1883
London Convention on the Transvaal; General Gordon sent to Sudan.	1884
Gordon and his troops massacred at Khartoum; Anglo-Russian tension, then compromise, over Afghanistan.	1885
	1886
'Mediterranean' Treaties with Italy and Austria.	1887
	1888
	1889
	1890
	1891
	1892
	1893

	Domestic (including Irish) Policy
1894	Gladstone resigns.
1895	Lord Rosebery resigns; Salisbury forms coalition with Liberal Unionists; general election results in huge Unionist majority.
1896	Conciliation Act.
1897	Queen Victoria's Diamond Jubilee; Workmen's Compensation Act; lock-out of engineering workers.
1898	
1899	Campbell-Bannerman becomes Liberal Leader.
1900	Formation of Labour Representation Committee; general election results in crushing Unionist victory.
1901	Queen Victoria dies; Edward VII succeeds; Taff Vale judgement.
1902	Salisbury retires; Education Act.
1903	Joseph Chamberlain begins campaign for Tariff Reform; electoral pact between Liberals and Labour Representation Committee; Emmeline Pankhurst forms WSPU.
1904	
1905	Suffragette agitation begins; Balfour resigns.
1906	Crushing victory for Liberals in general election; Trade Disputes Act; Workmen's Compensation Act.
1907	
1908	Campbell-Bannerman resigns; Old Age Pensions Act.
1909	Lloyd George's budget rejected by Lords; Osborne judgement.
1910	January and December elections leave Liberals dependent on Irish Nationalist support for a majority; King Edward VII dies; succeeded by George V.
1911	Parliament Act reduces power of House of Lords; National Insurance Act; strike wave; riots in South Wales and Liverpool; Parliament agrees to pay wages to MPs; Trade Union Act reverses Osborne judgement.
1912	Third Irish Home Rule Bill introduced; industrial disputes worsen; Suffragette militancy increases; Ulster Covenant signed; first national coal strike; *Daily Herald* commences publication.
1913	Lords twice reject Irish Home Rule Bill.
1914	Triple Alliance of miners, railwaymen and transport workers

Foreign Policy	
	1894
Jameson Raid.	1895
	1896
Colonial Conference.	1897
Fashoda Crisis.	1898
Boer War begins.	1899
Relief of Mafeking and annexation of Orange Free State.	1900
	1901
Alliance with Japan; Treaty of Vereeniging ends Boer War.	1902
	1903
Anglo-French Entente.	1904
First Moroccan Crisis.	1905
Dreadnought launched; Algeciras Conference rejects German position over Morocco.	1906
Anglo-Russian Entente; Creation of British Expeditionary Force.	1907
	1908
	1909
	1910
Second Moroccan Crisis.	1911
	1912
	1913
Britain declares war on Germany.	1914

MINISTRIES

Date formed	Prime Minister	Foreign Secretary	Chancellor of Exchequer
June 1812	Lord Liverpool (T)	Lord Castlereagh (From September 1822, George Canning)	
April 1827	George Canning (T)	Lord Dudley	George Canning
September 1827	Lord Goderich (T)		
January 1828	Duke of Wellington (T)	(From June 1828, Lord Aberdeen)	
November 1830	Lord Grey (W)	Lord Palmerston	Lord Althorp
July 1834	Lord Melbourne (W)	Lord Palmerston	Lord Althorp
December 1834	Sir Robert Peel (C)	Duke of Wellington	Sir Robert Peel
April 1835	Lord Melbourne (W)	Lord Palmerston	
September 1841	Sir Robert Peel (C)	Lord Aberdeen	
July 1846	Lord Russell (W)	Lord Palmerston	
February 1852	Lord Derby (C)	Lord Malmesbury	B Disraeli
December 1852	Lord Aberdeen (Coalition)	Lord Russell	W E Gladstone
February 1855	Lord Palmerston (W)	Lord Clarendon	W E Gladstone
February 1858	Lord Derby (C)	Lord Malmesbury	B Disraeli
June 1859	Lord Palmerston (W-L)	Lord Russell	W E Gladstone
October 1865	Lord Russell (W-L)	Lord Clarendon	W E Gladstone
June 1866	Lord Derby (C)	Lord Stanley	B Disraeli
February 1868	B Disraeli (C)	Lord Stanley	
December 1868	W E Gladstone (L)	Lord Clarendon (From June 1870, Lord Granville)	R Lowe
February 1874	B Disraeli (C)	Lord Derby (From April 1878, Lord Salisbury)	
April 1880	W E Gladstone (L)	Lord Granville	W E Gladstone
June 1885	Lord Salisbury (C)	Lord Salisbury	M Hicks Beach
February 1886	W E Gladstone (L)	Lord Rosebery	M V Harcourt
August 1886	Lord Salisbury (C)	Lord Salisbury	Lord Randolph Churchill (From January, 1887 G J Goschen)
August 1892	W E Gladstone (L)	Lord Rosebery	W V Harcourt
March 1894	Lord Rosebery (L)	Lord Kimberley	W V Harcourt
June 1895	Lord Salisbury (C)	Lord Salisbury (From October 1900, Lord Lansdowne)	M Hicks Beach
July 1902	A J Balfour (C)	Lord Lansdowne	C T Ritchie (From May 1903, Austen Chamberlain)
December 1905	H Campbell-Bannerman (L)	Sir Edward Grey	H H Asquith
April 1908	H H Asquith (L)	Sir Edward Grey	D Lloyd George

T = Tory; W = Whig; C = Conservative; L = Liberal

INDEX